D1356875

BREAD

BREAD

CHRISTINE INGRAM and JENNIE SHAPTER

LORENZ BOOKS

This edition is published by Lorenz Books, an imprint of Anness Publishing Ltd,
Hermes House, 88–89 Blackfriars Road, London SE1 8HA
tel. 020 7401 2077; fax 020 7633 9499
www.lorenzbooks.com; www.annesspublishing.com

If you like the images in this book and would like to investigate using them for publishing, promotions or advertising,
please visit our website www.practicalpictures.com for more information.

UK agent: The Manning Partnership Ltd; tel. 01225 478444; fax 01225 478440; sales@manning-partnership.co.uk
UK distributor: Book Trade Services; tel. 0116 2759086; fax 0116 2759090; uksales@booktradeservices.com; exportsales@booktradeservices.com
North American agent/distributor: National Book Network; tel. 301 459 3366; fax 301 429 5746; www.nbnbooks.com
Australian agent/distributor: Pan Macmillan Australia; tel. 1300 135 113; fax 1300 135 103; customer.service@macmillan.com.au
New Zealand agent/distributor: David Bateman Ltd; tel. (09) 415 7664; fax (09) 415 8892

PUBLISHER Joanna Lorenz
MANAGING EDITOR: Judith Simons
EDITOR: Mariano Kalfors
DESIGNER: Nigel Partridge
PHOTOGRAPHERS: Nicki Dowey and Amanda Heywood
HOME ECONOMISTS: Jennie Shapter (all recipes plus the bread machines section) and Jill Jones (traditional bread-making and breads of the world sections)

ETHICAL TRADING POLICY
Because of our ongoing ecological investment programme, you, as our customer, can have the pleasure and reassurance of knowing
that a tree is being cultivated on your behalf to naturally replace the materials used to make the book you are holding.
For further information about this scheme, go to www.annesspublishing.com/trees

Previously published in two separate volumes, *The World Encyclopedia of Bread and Bread Making* and
The Ultimate Bread Machine Cookbook

NOTES
Bracketed terms are intended for American readers.
The bread machine recipes in this book have all been tested and written for use in a variety of
machines available from leading manufacturers. For best results, always refer to your manufacturer's
handbook and instructions if you are unsure, and to confirm the proportion of flour to liquids.
You may need to adjust the recipes to suit your machine.
For all recipes, quantities are given in both metric and imperial measures and, where appropriate,
measures are also given in standard cups and spoons. Follow one set, but not a mixture, because
they are not interchangeable.
Standard spoon and cup measures are level.
1 tsp = 5ml, 1 tbsp = 15ml, 1 cup = 250ml/8fl oz
Australian standard tablespoons are 20ml. Australian readers should use 3 tsp in place of 1 tbsp for
measuring small quantities of gelatine, flour, salt, etc.
Medium (US large) eggs are used unless otherwise stated.

CONTENTS

—

Introduction   6
Making Bread by Hand   8
Making Bread in a Bread Machine   10
History   12
Grains and Milling   16

Breads of the World   **18**
British Breads   20
French Breads   38
Italian Breads   46
Spanish Breads   52
Portuguese Breads   54
German Breads   56
Dutch Breads   61
Swiss Breads   62
Nordic Breads   65
Eastern European and Russian Breads   70
The Breads of Greece, Cyprus and Turkey   74
The Breads of the Middle East and North Africa   78
Jewish Breads   80
Breads of the Americas   84
Caribbean and Mexican Breads   96
Indian Breads   98
Australian Breads   100
Chinese Breads   103
Japanese Breads   104

Traditional Bread Making   **106**
Ingredients for Bread Making   108
Techniques   116
Bread-making Equipment   125

Bread Recipes of the World   **130**
British Breads   132
French Breads   156
Mediterranean Breads   172
North European and Scandinavian Breads   200
Breads of the Americas   224
Breads of India and the Middle East   240

Using a Bread Machine   **254**
Introducing the Bread Machine   256
A Bakery in Your Kitchen   258
Getting Down to Basics   260
How to Use Your Bread Machine   262
Baking, Cooling and Storing   266
Hand-shaped Loaves   268
Glazes   272
Toppings   274
Using Sourdoughs and Starters   278
Getting the Best from Your Machine   282
Adapting Recipes for Use in a Bread Machine   284
Troubleshooting   286
Flour   288
Leavens and Salt   292
Liquids   294
Fats and Sweeteners   296
Additional Ingredients   298
Equipment   306

Recipes Using a Bread Machine   **310**
Basic Breads   312
Speciality Grains   330
Flatbreads and Pizzas   348
Sourdoughs and Starter Dough Breads   364
Savoury Breads   378
Vegetable Breads   400
Rolls, Buns and Pastries   420
Sweet Breads and Yeast Cakes   454
Teabreads and Cakes   482

Suppliers   502
Index   504
Acknowledgements   512

INTRODUCTION

There is something undeniably special about bread. The flavour of a good loaf, the texture of the soft crumb contrasting with the crispness of the crust, is almost a sensual experience. Who can walk home with a fresh baguette without slowly, almost absent-mindedly breaking off pieces to eat en route? Or resist the promise of a slice of a soft white farmhouse loaf, spread simply with butter? Most people have their own favourite: ciabatta, rich with olive oil; dark, malty rye; honeyed *challah* or a Middle Eastern bread, freshly baked and redolent of herbs and spices. Whatever the shape or texture, bread has a special place in our affections.

Even today, at the start of the 21st century, when bread is taken largely for granted, seen as an accompaniment or a "carrier" for other foods, we still have a sense of its supreme significance. In some languages the word "bread" means "food", and in certain of the more rural parts of Spain and Italy, for example, you may find that bread is blessed or kissed before being broken or eaten. There are numerous rituals and traditions attached to bread. Slashing the dough with a cross or making a sign of the Cross over the loaf before baking was believed to let the devil out. Cutting the bread at both ends was also recommended to rid the house of the devil. One extraordinary custom was

BELOW: Cutting a cross in an unbaked loaf was believed to let the devil out.

ABOVE: Just a few of the many shapes and types of bread.

sin-eating, a practice at funerals, whereby someone would eat a loaf of bread and by so doing would take on the sins of the dead person.

The obvious explanation for bread's importance is that until quite recently, it was for many, quite literally the "staff of life" – the single essential food. Today, most people have more varied diets. Potatoes, pasta and rice are all enjoyed in the West and are important staple foods, but in some countries, for example France and Italy, bread is easily the most popular of the carbohydrates, eaten with every meal and in many cases with every course.

Like wine tasters, true aficionados taste bread *au naturel* in order to savour its unique taste and texture, unadulterated by other flavours. Good as this can be, the best thing about bread is that it goes so well with other foods. Throughout Europe bread is most frequently cut or broken into pieces to be eaten with a meal – to mop up soups and sauces or to eat with hams, pâtés and cheese. Dark rye breads, spread with strongly flavoured cheese or topped with smoked fish, are popular in northern Europe, and in the Middle East breads are split and stuffed with meats and salads – a tradition that has been warmly embraced in the West too. In

Britain and the USA, the European custom of serving bread with a meal, with or instead of potatoes or rice, is catching on, but sandwiches are probably still the favourite way of enjoying bread. Sandwiches have been going strong for a couple of hundred years – invented, it is said, by John Montagu, 4th Earl of Sandwich, so that he could eat a meal without having to leave the gaming table. Although baguettes and bagels are naturally ideally suited for linking bread with meat, the sandwich, clearly an English concept, is unique and continues to be the perfect vehicle for fillings that become more and more adventurous.

BREADS OF TODAY

Figures show that throughout Europe bread consumption declined after World War II. Until then it was the single most important food in the diet, but due to increased prosperity, which meant a wider choice of other foods, and mass production, which led to bread becoming increasingly insipid and tasteless, people moved away from their "daily bread". The situation was more noticeable in some countries than others. In France, Italy and Spain, where people continued to demand the best, eating of bread did not decline so sharply, although even in those countries, the quality did deteriorate for a time.

BELOW: In northern Europe, dark rye bread is served sliced with colourful, rich-tasting toppings.

In Britain, however, most bread was notoriously bland – the ubiquitous white sliced loaf being little more than a convenient shape for the toaster. In supermarkets, certainly, there was a time, not so long ago, when apart from the standard pre-wrapped white loaf, the only baked goods on sale were croissants and a selection of fruited teabreads, vaguely labelled as "Continental". Yet within the last ten years, things have improved by leaps and bounds. Perhaps supermarkets, finding that the smell of freshly baked bread enticed shoppers into their stores, installed more in-store bakeries. Or perhaps shoppers who travelled abroad and sampled the breads of other countries created a demand for better breads made with better flours, using more imaginative recipes and untreated with additives.

Nowadays there is a huge choice of breads both from independent bakeries and from the large supermarkets. Italian ciabatta and focaccia are now a regular sight, even in the smallest food stores, as are the various Spanish, Indian and Middle Eastern breads. There is an increasingly interesting choice of German, Danish, Scandinavian and eastern European breads and, among the French breads, there is now a truly good range on offer. If the supermarket has an in-store bakery, baguettes are likely to be freshly baked and some are now as good as the real thing. The availability of *pain de campagnes*, *levains* and other rustic breads means that you can choose breads to suit the style of meal you are serving, while sweet breads, such as brioches and croissants from France, *pane al cioccolato* from Italy and numerous offerings from Germany mean that there is much more to choose from than simply toast at breakfast and malt loaf at tea time.

Local bakers, although competing with the supermarkets, have paradoxically benefited from the range on offer from supermarkets. The more breads there are available, the more people feel inclined to try other baked goods. Small bakers, who could easily have lost customers to the big stores, have risen to the challenge by producing their own range of country-style and fine breads. Craft bakers are

ABOVE: A huge range of traditionally baked French breads are offered for sale in this specialist bakery.

producing traditional breads, at the same time experimenting with recipes they have devised themselves. Bread making has never been a tradition that stood still. The best craft bakers have ensured that bread making has continued to evolve, resulting in the emergence of all sorts of corn and barley breads, mixed grain loaves and a range of new sourdoughs.

Added to this are the many European-style bakeries. Set up and run by émigrés from all parts of Europe and beyond, these bakeries are the best source of many of the most authentic European breads. In supermarkets you will invari-

BELOW: Traditional country-style breads are enjoying a renaissance.

ably find ciabatta or focaccia, but for *paesano*, *pagnotta* or *pane sciocco* you are likely to need an Italian baker, who will be only too happy to provide you with the loaves and tell you all about them while they are being wrapped.

Once you have found a bakery you like, there are no particular tips for buying bread; the baker will be pleased to explain the different styles of loaves and advise on their keeping qualities. Crusty breads, such as baguettes, round cobs or Italian country loaves, are known as "oven bottom" or "oven bottom-baked", which means they have been baked, without tins (pans) or containers, on the sole of the oven or on flat sheet trays. They are evenly crusty, although the type of dough, the humidity during proving, the steam in the oven and the heat itself determines whether the crust is fragile or chewy. Loaves, such as the English farmhouse, baked in metal tins, characteristically have a golden top, but with thinner crusts on the sides. Rolls or breads baked up against each other have even softer sides and are described as "batch-baked". Sourdough breads are made without yeast – using a natural leaven instead – and are often labelled as "yeast-free" breads or "naturally leavened". There are many varieties, some made entirely from wheat, some from rye, others from a blend of both of these or other cereals. They are normally heavier than an average loaf, with a dense texture and pleasantly tart flavour.

MAKING BREAD BY HAND

Making bread requires little more than a pair of hands, some time, an oven and a few basic ingredients – just flour and water in its simplest form. Add yeast and a sprinkling of salt to control the yeast, mix with the flour and water to a dough, shape and leave to rise, and on baking it will transform into a crusty loaf permeating the air with a mouthwateringly delicious aroma. Many people enjoy the artistry of a homemade hand-shaped loaf, as well as the satisfaction that comes from kneading the dough by hand. The ritual of kneading, proving and shaping bread dough is a very personal activity, which is why, even today with the option of electric food mixers with dough hooks or food processors to do the job, many people still get great pleasure from kneading by hand.

TYPES OF BREAD

The first part of this book begins with an insight into the history of bread and how it has developed through the generations of bakers in Europe, America, the Middle East and Asia. It continues with a fascinating look at the huge array of breads available from around the world explaining the wide variety of texture, tastes and shapes that exist.

Many breads are made from wheat flour which contains protein. When kneaded it develops into gluten, an elastic substance which lets the dough stretch trapping the carbon-dioxide generated by the leavening agent and so allowing it to

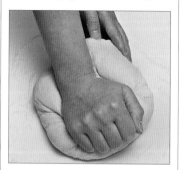

ABOVE: Part of the allure of making bread is the satisfaction of kneading.

ABOVE: Classic Italian white bread, Focaccia, made using olive oil.

rise. However, many other flours such as barley, millet, corn meal, rice, rye and buckwheat, containing little or no gluten, are also used to make bread, so these are usually combined with wheat flours to achieve the lightness desired in bread. In the recipe section, these flours are often mixed with other ingredients apart from water, such as milk, eggs, fat and sugar to make a variety of doughs that are proved and shaped differently to produce various textures and tastes.

WHITE BREADS

White breads are perhaps the largest and most popular group of breads. Some of the most famous include the long thin shaped Baguette, a crackly, crusted loaf with a light chewy interior achieved by adding some lighter French flour into this white flour and water dough along with a triple fermentation and baking in a very hot oven with steam.

One ingredient probably defines many Italian breads: olive oil. It softens and enriches the crumb and produces a smooth shiny finish such as the elaborately shaped rolls known as Panini all'Olio or the classic round shaped, dimple topped Italian flat bread – Focaccia, sometimes further flavoured with any number of ingredients such as aromatic herbs,

sun-dried tomatoes, olives or garlic. Another distinctive Italian bread is the irregular shaped Ciabatta. The light holey texture is achieved by using a slowly ripened wet dough, which just holds its shape. It is poured on to floured baking sheets and roughly shaped using floured hands. Crispy Breadsticks from north-west Italy are hand-crafted into thin pencil sticks before brushing with olive oil to give a crispy crust. In Sicily semolina is incorporated into the white bread dough and is then formed into a broad "S" shape.

Breads like Indian Naan, Turkish Pitta Bread and Lavash, originally from Lebanon but eaten throughout the Middle East, are all types of flat bread typical of these regions. These easy to make breads are shaped into ovals or rounds before baking in a hot oven to form a puffed flat bread with a hollow pocket. Naan breads are brushed with melted ghee to soften and enrich the cooked dough.

British loaves include Split Tins, Bloomers, Cottage Loaves, Irish Soda Bread, soft Scottish rolls and intricately shaped Dinner Rolls to name but a few. The variety found in hand-shaped British breads is increased still further by the cooking methods. A number of regional breads such as Crumpets, Scottish Oatcakes and English Muffins are cooked on the hob on a heavy griddle or girdle. Crumpets are made with an aerated batter that is poured into rings; the rings being removed once the batter has risen and set.

ABOVE: French Baguette doughs all ready to go in the oven.

WHOLEMEAL, BROWN AND GRANARY BREADS

Breads made with wholemeal (whole-wheat) or brown flours are continually gaining in popularity due to their texture and flavour as well as the dietary benefits. Wholemeal flour contains 100% of the bran and wheat germ of the original grain while brown flour contains around 85%. These breads are a closer textured nutty flavoured loaf, often classically shaped like a Granary Cob, or shaped into a rectangle and baked in a bread tin. The free-form round and oval breads are often slashed, this being very evident in many of the sourdough breads that incorporate whole-meal flour, such as San Francisco Sour Dough bread; the slashes are an impor-tant factor in the production of these breads as they encourage more even rising and therefore help to retain the shape. The Russians make a light whole-meal bread using mashed potatoes, which adds moisture and substance to the bread. Again this loaf is slashed.

SWEET BREADS

Many sweetened breads originate from the ancient customs of baking breads to celebrate the various seasons and religious holidays. These breads usually include more expensive and therefore special ingredients such as aromatic flavourings and spices, dried and candied fruits. They are also some of the most artistically hand-shaped breads. The classic shapes of the ceremonial breads have special symbolic meanings. The Jewish Challah is traditionally shaped into a braid to denote a ladder to heaven. Tsoureki is a sweet-ened, spiced Greek Easter bread, embellished with whole eggs, which nes-tle in the plaited shape, to ensure the fertility of earth and renewal of life. Another Greek bread, Christopsomo is baked for Christmas, and is shaped into a round plump loaf, finished with dough shaped into a Byzantine cross studded with walnuts for luck. Other Christmas breads include Stollen, which is symboli-cally folded to represent the baby Jesus in swaddling clothes and Twelfth Night bread or Bolo-Rei, an ornamental bread ring or crown to represent the crowns of

ABOVE: A selection of British breads: white, wholemeal and granary.

the three wise men. Panettone is the Italian bread traditionally associated with Christmas. This very tall dome-topped bread from Milan is said to resemble the cupola domes of the churches.

UNLEAVENED BREADS

Most of the breads eaten in India are unleavened, that is made without any raising agent. These are always shaped by hand into small balls and then flattened or rolled into discs. Chapatis and Parathas are made with a similar dough using a finely ground wholemeal flour called atta. Chapatis are cooked as discs while Parathas are brushed with melted ghee and folded into triangular shapes to make a layered bread. Both varieties are cooked on a very hot griddle and the intense heat makes them puff up.

Pooris are shaped into discs and then deep-fried. The hot oil makes the poori dough puff up into a crispy soft light bread, which remains puffy. Missi Rotis are made with gram flour or milled dhal; both of which are gluten free. These breads are also shaped into discs that are fried on a griddle, but because there is no gluten the bread remains flat and soft. The West Indians make

a Roti more akin to the layered Paratha, using atta, but include a small amount of baking powder (bicarbonate of soda) for increased puffiness.

BREADS MADE WITH NON-WHEAT FLOURS

A number of traditional country breads in Europe and the USA incorporate other grains with wheat. Crusty topped Portuguese bread or Broa is made with corn meal while the Spanish country bread Pan de Cebada combines barley flour with corn meal and wholemeal flour. Both are traditionally shaped into plump round loaves. Corn meal is often found in breads made in America. In the south, corn bread is made from a soft batter-like mixture and baked more like a cake and served cut into wedges, or as a "Spoon Bread" in Virginia where it is often flavoured with cheese and corn kernels and resembles a soufflé.

Rye is a common staple in German, Northern European and Scandinavian breads. The textures and shapes vary from lighter Polish style oval split loaves and caraway flavoured German sour-doughs, often shaped into rounds and proved in a basket to a give a charac-teristic patterned crust to dense German Pumpernickel breads or traditional flat round Knackerbröd or crisp bread.

BELOW: A selection of flours, the largest single ingredient used in bread.

MAKING BREAD IN A BREAD MACHINE

Few people have the time to enjoy kneading, proving, shaping and baking bread on a daily basis. A bread machine is the perfect addition to home baking. It still allows you to create your own bread with the ingredients you wish to use, but with the minimum of effort and time. The bread machine also seems to evoke interest from all members of the family. Whereas bread made by hand is often only actually produced by the person who prepares the majority of the food, all the family enjoy the ease with which they can transform a few ingredients into a loaf of crusty brown bread and insist on joining in.

THE BENEFITS OF
A BREAD MACHINE

In common with many kitchen appliances the bread machine is a labour-saving device. It will mix together the ingredients for a loaf of bread, then knead it, leave it to rise and finally bake it, all within a self-contained unit. Bread machines are made in a variety of sizes so you can select a machine that is perfect for your needs. A machine that makes a larger loaf will not necessarily be more expensive than one that bakes only small loaves. In fact some machines will bake more than one size of loaf, while another will bake two loaves at the same time. By selecting a size to complement your requirements you can eliminate waste.

If you have little or no experience in making bread by hand the machine is pre-programmed, so it will automatically knead and prove the dough, so you do not need to know how to recognise these stages of bread making. The temperature within the bread machine is controlled throughout the kneading and proving periods to ensure the optimum results.

All machines have a choice of programmes, offering options to bake a wide variety of breads from basic white breads, wholemeal (whole-wheat), through to various whole grain, sweet and crusty French-style breads. This is achieved by varying the kneading, rising and baking periods. The baking time is increased to give a crusty French loaf while the baking temperature is reduced to minimize over-browning of the dough with higher sugar contents. The machine is programmed to operate these variations for you. All you have to do is select the programme. Many machines also include a rapid programme for when the speed of making a loaf is the most critical factor; some machines will make a loaf of bread from start to finish in just one hour. A number of machines will mix and bake a variety of cakes and teabreads. Even machines without this programme, but with a bake only facility, mean that you can make the cake mixture first, place it in the bread machine pan and use the bread machine as an oven, to cook it, which is a perfect cost-effective alternative to heating an full-sized conventional oven for one item.

One very useful benefit of a bread machine is the delay timer. This lets you pre-programme the machine, usually up to 12–13 hours in advance, so the machine can be filled with ingredients before you go to bed and set to finish baking just before breakfast, or set it to prepare bread for your return from work. If for any reason you are delayed and are not able to remove the bread from the machine as soon as it is cooked, the bread machine automatically changes to a keep warm setting and will keep the bread warm for

ABOVE: Machines will beep to alert you as to when to add extra ingredients.

up to one hour. This warming facility helps prevent the loaf from becoming soggy with the condensation of the steam within the unit and obviously ensures it does not over-cook, unlike if it had remained in a conventional oven without any attention.

Once you have mastered using a bread machine to automatically prepare loaves of bread, you can use it to help you make hand-shaped breads. Most machines have a dough only cycle. This will mix and knead the dough, removing the physical work required with hand prepared doughs. It also proves the dough in a perfect temperature-controlled environment to ensure a well-risen dough ready for shaping into rolls, pizzas, different free-form loaves such as cottage loaves, plaits, braids, bloomers or pastries. This is a really convenient, effortless way of getting to the point for creating a culinary delight.

The bread machine requires minimal cleaning after use. You do not have to wash bowls, clean down floured working surfaces and baking trays etc. All you need to do after baking is rinse the removable bread pan and kneading blade. Most bread pans are finished with a non-stick coating that helps the baked loaf slide out of the pan easily, eliminating any tedious cleaning.

ABOVE: This Farmhouse Loaf has been mixed and baked in a machine.

VERSATILITY OF YOUR BREAD MACHINE

The variety of breads that can be created with the help of your bread machine is almost infinite. The bread machine recipes in this book just begin to show you the various possibilities. Start with some basic white breads such a Farmhouse or a Buttermilk or Egg-enriched loaf, then maybe try Malted Fruit bread or a classic Granary or speciality grain such as Buckwheat and Walnut, Bran and Yogurt or Polenta and Wholemeal. Savoury breads such as Cottage Cheese and Pepperoni, Grainy Mustard and Beer or Carrot and Fennel provide some interesting flavour alternatives and bake wonderfully in the bread machine. For a couple of loaves with a kick, try the Chickpea and Peppercorn or the Chilli Bread. Don't think that the bread machine only makes savoury breads; there are recipes which include sweet flavourings and ingredients such as blueberries, bananas, mangoes, dried fruits and chocolate. There is information on the various glaze finishes and toppings you can add to your machine-baked loaves to add flavour and texture and also individuality to your baking.

After you have made breads baked in the machine progress to using it to mix and rise the dough before shaping it yourself. Try a traditional cottage loaf with a twist, such as the Mixed Herb Cottage Loaf or make a Partybrot, a bread made from small rolls. The machine also makes perfect pizza dough for a traditional Pizza or variations such as Calzone, French Pissaladière, Sicilian Sfincione or a Leek and Pancetta tray bake.

Use machine-prepared dough to make an enticing array of coffee-time treats such as Peach Streuselkuchen, Lemon and Pistachio Strudel, Apricot and Vanilla Slices or English tea-time specialities like Devonshire Splits, Yorkshire Teacakes, Doughnuts and Pikelets.

ESSENTIAL GUIDELINES FOR SUCCESSFUL BREAD MACHINE BAKING

Like any new kitchen appliance it takes a few attempts to achieve the best results; also some of the considerations for optimum result may differ from bread made by hand. Each programme has been designed to knead, prove and bake for different times to reflect the differences in the ingredients of the loaf.

Always add the ingredients in the order recommended by the machine manufacturer and keep the yeast separate from any liquid or moist ingredients.

Always stay within the recommended amount of ingredients for your machine, to prevent over-loading it. In any case too large a quantity will spill over the top of the bread pan during rising or baking.

ABOVE: Care should be taken when removing as the loaf will be quite hot.

ABOVE: Part of your machine's versatility includes cake-making.

The finished breads will turn out best when the ingredients are added at room temperature, especially the liquids. If your machine does not have a pre-warming facility, a quick 30–60 second burst on HIGH in the microwave will take the chill off cold water or milk and bring it up to room temperature.

If any ingredients, such as vegetables and nuts, are roasted or fried to develop the flavour or cooked to soften, leave them to cool back to room temperature before adding to the rest of the ingredients in the bread pan.

Always use accurate measurements of the chosen ingredients. If you omit or incorrectly measure an ingredient, then leave the machine to get on with making the bread, it may not be until the end of the programme that you realize your error.

Heavier breads containing high percentages of whole-wheat grains or added ingredients such as nuts, seeds, dried fruits and cheese, will make the dough slower to rise, so do not expect the loaf to rise quite as high as a typical white loaf.

Loaves with a high egg, cheese, sugar or fat content are best cooked on a light crust setting where this is available or on a sweet bread setting to avoid an over-browned crust.

HISTORY

Bread seems to be a recurring theme in history. Most people could be forgiven for thinking that history was driven by great scientists and ambitious men. But look closer and you will find that the incentive behind many of our greatest inventions was the availability, production and delivery of food – our "daily bread" in the widest terms. The wheel, the plough and the windmill right through to steam and motorization all plot a course that was concerned specifically with agriculture and producing food. Similarly, the aspirations of any king or queen were intimately connected with the feeding of their people. The poorer and hungrier the population, the more insecure was their ruler's position. "Give them bread and circuses!" said Juvenal in the 1st century AD, referring to the Roman mob, in a constant state of unrest because of poverty and starvation; and Queen Marie Antoinette famously said "Let them eat cake", on being told that the peasants were rioting because they had no bread. Almost all revolutions came about because of famine, and bread was the single food that might alone have averted such an event.

THE FIRST BREAD

Archaeology and history show that bread has been eaten since the earliest times. Remains of stone querns indicate that cereal was ground in prehistoric Britain to make a branny-type grain. It is likely that this would have been fashioned into

BELOW: By the 1st century AD, Roman bakers had perfected their craft, as this mural shows.

ABOVE: Distributing bread to the poor in Paris after the famine in 1662.

cakes and cooked over an open fire to make a coarse flat cake. At the same time in Egypt, where civilization was considerably more advanced, bread was a regular part of daily life and indeed the Egyptians are credited with being the first people to make bread. Paintings on the walls of tombs depict bread being offered to the gods and the flat oval-shaped breads look uncannily like *aiysh*, the Egyptian bread still eaten today. Other pictures show round or cone-shaped breads and it is likely that they were all leavened, since the water from the Nile contains the same strain of yeast that is used in baking today. The Greeks initially made unleavened breads, but during the last millennium BC leavens were introduced to raise their breads and the loaves were baked in bread ovens. Once wheat flour replaced barley meal, the Greeks became very partial to bread, their bakers producing a huge range of different breads made with honey or milk or sprinkled with sesame or poppy seed, according to one account written in the 1st century AD.

Elsewhere, the leavening of bread became commonplace, even if at first it might have come about by accident. Natural yeasts exist in the air around us and a warm paste of flour and water will

ABOVE: Throughout Europe, windmills were built to make milling easier.

spontaneously start to ferment if left for a couple of hours, so leavened bread is probably almost as ancient as the unleavened cakes baked over hot stones. Sourdoughs made by this natural method became popular in many parts of Europe, and the traditions continue to this day with sourdough ryes from eastern Europe and Germany, wheaten *levains* such as *pain de campagne* and Italian country loaves from more southerly regions.

In ancient Britain, about the time of the Roman invasion, beer barm – the yeasty froth on fermenting liquor – began to be used as a leaven. Barley was by far the most important crop at that time and ale was widely brewed. Once the use of natural leavens had become widespread, it would have been but a small step to realize that beer barm, with the same sweet/sour smell, could be used as well.

In Biblical times, leavened bread was common. In the Book of Genesis, Lot, the son of Abraham, welcomes two angels to his house and "baked for them unleavened bread", which suggests that leavened

bread was the more usual food for non-angels. Today, Jews bake unleavened bread – *matzos* – for Passover, in remembrance of the Hebrews' escape from Egypt, and unleavened bread is frequently the bread for ritual or sacred occasions.

Bread also plays a central role in Christianity. Jesus fed the five thousand

BELOW: The original bread ovens were often made of fireproof stone or bricks.

with bread, and at the last supper he broke unleavened bread (it being Passover), giving thanks to the Lord and literally identifying with it, with the words "this is my body", the act of which is recalled in every Christian Mass.

BREAD IN BRITAIN AND EUROPE DURING THE MIDDLE AGES

The Romans brought wheat, oats and rye to Britain along with many of their bread-making techniques. However, while for a time bread making became more sophisticated, it suffered a setback once the Romans had left. During the Dark Ages, the growing and harvesting of cereal and then the making and baking of bread would have been a hit-or-miss affair. Families would have gathered cereals from their local fields and threshed the grain either in their own home or by using a quern stone belonging to the village.

By the Middle Ages, however, horses had begun to be used for ploughing and cultivation began to be more organized. The watermill and then the windmill were invented, probably first in England and then elsewhere in Europe. Perhaps this was something of a mixed blessing, for while the mill certainly took the backache out of the task, the lord of the manor retained rights over the mill and would oblige the serfs who worked his land to pay a tithe for the use of the mill. To add insult to injury, the bakehouse, often adjoining the mill, also made a charge to the families who used it and in a period when cottages were flimsy constructions without ovens or even chimneys, families often had little option but to take their bread to the communal oven.

The loaves themselves were normally huge, weighing more than 4.5kg/10lb, and would be expected to feed the family for several days. Made of a mixture of grain – wheat, barley, millet and rye – they would have been coarse mealy loaves. If the winters were not too harsh, the summers warm and the rainfall neither too great nor too little, harvests would be good and people could survive on a diet of bread, ale and pottage (a stew made of pulses and meat). However, after a poor harvest, cereal became scarce and people would have to use almost anything that could be ground to a meal. Acorns and roots were often the stand-bys in times of famine in Europe, while in England the poor would have to resort to horse bread, a type of mealy cake made of ground beans, so-called as it was normally fed to animals.

BELOW: In 15th-century France a flattish bread was cooked over an open fire.

ABOVE: This 16th-century bake-house in Scandinavia was built next door to a public bath – perhaps the oven also warmed the water.

In 1266 laws were introduced in England, known as the Assizes of Bread, which regulated that the weight of bread should be fixed to a certain price. For the price of one penny it was set down that three types of bread should be available: white loaves made from bolted (sifted) flour, which were the lightest breads, wheaten loaves made of more coarsely sifted meal and weighing half as much again, and finally the household loaf, the heaviest of all three and made of unrefined meal. The Assize system was deeply unpopular with bakers, but it nevertheless continued for some 450 years, which testifies to the importance the government attached to bread being available and affordable for the whole population.

BRITAIN IN TUDOR TIMES

Bread and pottage continued to be the staple foods for most people of England

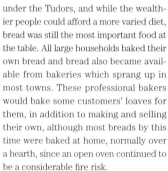

under the Tudors, and while the wealthier people could afford a more varied diet, bread was still the most important food at the table. All large households baked their own bread and bread also became available from bakeries which sprang up in most towns. These professional bakers would bake some customers' loaves for them, in addition to making and selling their own, although most breads by this time were baked at home, normally over a hearth, since an open oven continued to be a considerable fire risk.

For the poor, most bread was made of a mixture of grains, which would vary depending on the part of the country: rye in Norfolk; barley in north-west England and the lowlands of Scotland, Wales and Cornwall; and oats in the uplands of Wales and the Scottish Highlands. For the poorest, a mixed grain called maslin was often used, while peasant bread made from peas and beans continued to be made during severe hardship.

Although the more affluent people did eat plain brown bread, they also began to acquire a liking for white bread. White bread was considered superior for several reasons: it was more expensive, owing to the time and effort required to sift out the bran, and it implied prestige; added to which the Church used a white bread called Pandemain, by definition more refined, as the sacramental bread. People took this to mean better, and white bread acquired a cachet which has only really been dented in the last 20 years.

Known by various names, this white bread eventually came to be known as manchet. Manchets were made from the finest wheat flour and were relatively small, sometimes not much bigger than a large roll; compared with the large plain breads, they were not considered sufficient for one person at a meal.

Another common practice, dating from the Middle Ages and surviving until the end of the 16th century, was the use of trenchers. These were thick slices of bread from large four-day-old wholemeal (wholewheat) loaves, which served as plates for both the less affluent and the wealthy, hard-baked for the purpose and cut into squares or oblongs. The custom was also practised in France, and trencher breads were made in Corbeil and sold in the markets of Paris. Meat and fish would be placed on top of each slice, the bread soaking up any gravy. Those who were still hungry would then eat their trencher – from where we get the expression "trencherman", someone renowned for the amount he eats. In wealthy families it would have been unseemly to eat the trencher, not to say unnecessary, as there would have been sufficient food offered at table. Instead, the servants would take the pieces of bread and give them to the almshouses.

LATER CENTURIES

Within the British Isles and across Europe, the lot of the peasant farmer contrasted sharply with that of the wealthy. During the 18th century the price of wheat rose steeply. In Britain, the Corn Laws, which were largely responsible for the price increases, were finally repealed in 1846. In France, the State's failure to respond to the crisis resulted in revolution. Around this time, the potato – introduced to Europe at the beginning of the 17th century – finally gained acceptance. In France and the south of England, wheat continued to be the favoured staple, but potatoes were used increasingly and by the middle of the 19th century, potatoes were as much a staple as bread. For the poor, bread and potatoes together formed the basis of a meagre diet. In Ireland, however, potatoes were often the only food, resulting in the catastrophic famine of the 1840s when potato blight struck.

BELOW: Most affluent homes had a built-in oven, fired by wood or peat.

ABOVE: In Victorian times all large households baked their own bread.

BAKING METHODS

The first means of baking or cooking a bread was simply by placing the dough on a heated stone over the dying embers of a fire. This technique is not dissimilar to that used today by the Australian bushmen when making their damper bread. The first English settlers in Virginia also used the same principle for their maize breads, baking the dough over hot ashes or in hot sand. The advantage is that no hardware or utensils are required; the disadvantage is that the bread, even if leavened, is mainly flat. At some point someone came up with the idea of placing a pot over the bread. The steamy heat caused the bread to rise and variations on this theme continued for hundreds of years among poorer people.

At the same time, most villages had a bakehouse, either attached to the mill or owned by the baker. Farmers and larger households often had their own bread ovens, fired with wood and furze (gorse). Although these fuels were cheap to collect, lighting and heating the oven would have been a time-consuming process and for most households it would be lit only once a week. After the week's bread had been baked, biscuits (cookies) and cakes, which required lower temperatures, would be placed in the cooling oven.

Originally, ovens were heated using wood that was burnt on the oven floor. Once the oven was hot, the embers were removed using a long-handled tool, called a peel. These ancient ovens were built of fire-proof stone, and later replaced by bricks. The stone or bricks would become white hot and then very gradually the heat would decrease as the bread was baked. Flat breads, such as the Italian *focaccia*, would have been the first breads to go into these immensely hot ovens, where they would be baked quickly and crisply. Larger loaves would then be baked, the slowly decreasing heat ensuring that the bread had a good thick crust, which meant that it kept well for the days ahead.

In the USA, Australia, Britain, France and other parts of Europe, enthusiasts have restored these wood-burning ovens and their bread, which is made to traditional recipes, is quite delicious.

In Ireland, bread was cooked in a type of Dutch oven, which was set in peat with burning embers piled around it. A similar type of oven is still used by the people of Dutch ancestry in South Africa, who make their pot bread by baking it in a cast-iron pot piled high with smouldering embers.

GRAINS AND MILLING

Wheat is by far the most popular cereal for bread making. First grown in Asia Minor, it has been cultivated for some ten thousand years. For most of that time, the sowing and cultivating, threshing and milling were laborious jobs that required toil and effort for both farmer and miller. Today, mechanization makes the task of getting bread to our table far less arduous, and the skills acquired from our ancestors, although refined, are still very much with us today.

Wheat is a member of the grass family, and flour is produced from the grains in the ear. It is a tolerant cereal and grows in a wide range of climates, although it prefers cooler temperatures. There are two basic species of wheat: bread wheat used in baking, and durum used for pasta. Of the bread wheats, the so-called hard ones, which contain a higher proportion of protein, are best for bread flour.

THE WHEAT GRAIN

The wheat grain is one of nature's perfect foods. Crammed with energy and low in fat, it contains fibre, carbohydrates, protein and important vitamins and minerals.

The wheat grain is 5mm/¼in long and golden when ripe. The ripeness of wheat is determined by its colour; a farmer may also chew a few grains to check that the wheat is dry and crunchy.

WHOLEMEAL (WHOLE-WHEAT) GRAIN

This is the whole grain from which wholemeal flour is made. Wheat grains are cleaned to remove grit and debris before milling, but nothing else is removed.

BRAN

The bran is the thin, papery skin covering the wheat grain. Some or all of it is removed for brown and white flour respectively. Bran cannot be digested, but it does provide valuable fibre in the diet and can be bought separately for use in bran loaves and for other baking purposes.

WHEAT KERNEL

This is the inner part of the wheat grain, revealed when the bran has been peeled away. It is made up of starch bound together by gluten, the protein needed for bread making to give dough its elasticity. Strong wheats tend to contain a greater proportion of gluten and are therefore the preferred wheats for bread making.

WHEAT GERM

This tiny wheat seed is rich in vitamins B and E, salts, proteins and fatty acids. It is present in wholemeal flour but partly removed in brown flour. Wheat germ can

BELOW: Nowadays, most of the barley grown in Europe is used for brewing.

ABOVE: The ripeness of wheat grain is determined by its golden colour.

be bought separately for adding to loaves or sprinkling over the sides of the baking tins prior to cooking bread. Since its natural oil eventually becomes rancid, wheat germ will keep for only a short period. Store in the refrigerator and check the "use-by" date on the packet.

OTHER GRAINS

BARLEY

Barley has been grown across Europe for centuries, and was used for bread making when wheat was expensive and rye was unavailable. Today the grain is mostly grown for brewing.

BUCKWHEAT

Buckwheat is a member of the same family as rhubarb and dock and is therefore not strictly a cereal. It is now mostly grown in north-east Europe.

CORN (MAIZE)

The term "corn" has given rise to considerable confusion. In Britain it was historically used to describe the predominant cereal crop of a region (for instance, wheat in England and oats in Scotland). An English field of corn, therefore, meant a field of wheat, not the tall annual grass with yellow edible grains, which was also known by its 16th-century Spanish name – maize (*maiz*).

Sailors from Spain and Portugal, who accompanied the early explorers, were responsible for introducing corn into

ABOVE: At Crowdy Mill in North Devon, England, flour is still milled in the traditional way.

Europe. Until then it was unknown in the Old World, although a staple crop in the southern parts of America. It needs higher temperatures and more sunshine than wheat and is therefore grown mainly in the more southerly parts of Europe. It is still widely grown in Mexico and the southern states of America.

MILLET

Mostly grown for animal feeds, millet thrives in both tropical and arid countries.

OATS

Oats have been cultivated in northern Europe for centuries, but although among the most nutritious of all the cereals, they were mostly grown for animal feed. Thanks, however, to the Scots' love of porridge this grain continues to be cultivated for human consumption.

RICE

Widely grown in China and other parts of Asia, as well as the USA and parts of Spain and Italy, rice is an important cereal crop. Rice flour contains no gluten, but can be used in the same way as cornflour (cornstarch).

RYE

Rye prefers colder, dry climates and acid soils and is therefore ideally suited to the cooler parts of Europe, such as Germany, Scandinavia, northern Russia and Poland.

SPELT

This is one of the oldest cultivated species of wheat. It continues to be grown, but only in small areas in Germany and other parts of northern Europe.

MILLING

Flour is milled by passing the grain through a series of grinders. Traditionally, these were huge stones that were placed closer and closer together and turned by water or wind power. Nowadays the stones have been replaced by steel rollers, driven by machine. The ribbed cylinders separate the bran and wheat germ from the white kernel and the flour is sifted through a series of increasingly fine meshes. The advantage of roller mills, apart from the obvious one of not being dependent upon the weather for power, is that the rollers themselves wear far better than grindstones, which needed replacing regularly. The disadvantages are that the rollers automatically expel the bran and wheat germ and the faster process means that the flour loses some of its flavour and character.

GRIST

The grist is the blend of different wheats a miller selects to make flour. Most flours are made from a mixture of wheats.

WINDMILLS

The stone towers of old windmills are still dotted across Europe. Although they are a reminder of a simpler age, windmills were complex machines that required a great deal of skill. The miller was consequently an important and respected member of the community. Farmers who had spent much of a year growing and harvesting their crop relied on the miller to turn their efforts into flour so that they could feed their families.

The principle of the windmill is very simple. Huge grindstones, turned by the action of the wind on the sails, slowly milled the grain into flour. The miller's task was to make sure the stones turned at a steady speed: too slowly and the grain would pile up, too quickly and it would overheat and spoil. It was most important to ensure that the hopper remained topped up with grain, for if there was no grist on the mill, the stones would spark and the whole mill could catch alight.

Nowadays only a small amount of flour is milled using windmills. Compared with modern methods, the process is very slow. Nevertheless a few smaller flour producers use windmills for their stoneground flours and thus keep this tradition alive.

BELOW: This 17th-century windmill is a reminder of a simpler age.

BREADS OF THE WORLD

Bread is a particularly fundamental aspect of a country's cuisine – it reflects the climate and geography, as well as the customs, culture and religious beliefs of the people. This comprehensive guide includes the world's best-loved breads and many less well-known loaves, too. It will help you recognize the different breads that are sold in supermarkets and bakeries, act as a guide if you are travelling abroad, and encourage you to sample local breads, whether you've travelled halfway across the world, or simply moved to a new area.

BRITISH BREADS

British bread is now considered as good as any bread from Europe, something that could not have been said 20, or even 10 years ago. In the 1970s and 80s British holiday-makers discovered the delights of French baguettes, Italian ciabatta and all the other wonderful breads of Europe, and began asking why their own bread was so uninteresting. Many small bakers, of course, had been producing excellent bread for years, a delight for their customers but unknown to all those who shopped mostly in supermarkets. Things changed when supermarkets introduced their own in-store bakeries. Suddenly fresh bread was easily and readily available. The equation was simple. Fresh bread tasted great; people started eating more of it, and thus more bread, and in greater diversity, was made and sold. It's an equation where everyone gains. Bread is relatively cheap; it's an excellent food; it can be eaten with almost any meal and there is now a huge choice for the consumer. Small bakers have risen to the challenge of the supermarkets by producing their own speciality breads. All sorts of sourdoughs, ryes and corn breads are now available, along with a vast range of the more traditional British breads. The following breads are among the better known shapes, and are the breads you are

RIGHT: A bloomer can be distinguished by the diagonal slashes across the top.

likely to find in almost any good bakery and in most supermarkets, too. White breads are defined by their shape rather than the dough, and the majority of loaves are made using the same dough. However, once you start tasting and comparing breads, you will discover that the shape, the method of cooking and even the amount of slashing on the loaf will alter the flavour.

BATCHED BREAD
These loaves are baked together without tins (pans) so that there are no crusts along the sides, the individual loaves being broken apart when baked. The top crust is normally soft. Brick or sister brick loaves are two loaves baked together in large square or rectangular tins and then broken apart to give a half-batched effect.

BLOOMER
This is a popular oven bottom-baked loaf, i.e. one that is baked without a tin, either on a tray or on the sole of the oven. It has a plump, oval shape and is distinguished by five or six diagonal slashes across the upper crust. A bloomer from a good baker's has a soft crumb and a fragile and sharp crust. However, store-bought bloomers that have been pre-wrapped in plastic often have a disappointingly flabby crust. Bloomers can be made using brown wheat flour,

ABOVE: Batched loaves are not necessarily uniform in shape, but always have soft sides. White and brown loaves are available.

ABOVE: Corn meal loaf (top) and brown and white cobs. The even texture of the crumb on the cob loaves means that they make excellent toast.

rye or multigrain; however, the most popular type is white.

COB

The cob is perhaps the oldest and most basic of British loaves. The loaf is round and completely plain without slashes or decoration, and is oven-baked and crusty. The word "cob" is an old English word for a head, and plain round loaves made with coarse, brown meal would have been the basic loaf for many families for genera-tions. Cobs today can be white, but are usually brown, wholemeal (whole-wheat) or Granary.

COBURG

This white, round, oven bottom-baked loaf has a cross slash on the upper crust, dis-tinguishing it from the cob. Some bakers slash the loaf before the final rising to produce a wide-spread loaf with four clover-leaf corners. Others slash more conservatively for a loaf that retains its basic round shape.

PAN COBURG

This loaf is baked in a shallow round tin (pan), the diagonally slashed crust rising up and over the sides of the tin to look a bit like a cauliflower, a name by which it is also known. Specialist craft bakers some-times make this loaf, either on order or because they have an appreciative clientele, but it is a popular bread to make at home.

CHEQUERBOARD

Also known as a porcupine or rumpy loaf, this bread is cross-hatched to give a "che-querboard" crust. The loaf is usually floured before being cut, and the deeper the cuts, the more the crust will spread.

CORN MEAL

This is not a traditional British loaf, but is becoming increasingly popular, especially among some of the small craft bakers who have developed their own recipes, blending corn meal with a strong white or wholemeal (whole-wheat) flour. Sometimes whole corn kernels are also added to give a delicious loaf with good texture.

DANISH

A traditional – or proper – Danish loaf is a round loaf with one central lengthways cut. Originally oven bottom-baked to give a good crust,

RIGHT: A good Danish loaf should have a floury, but firm crust and a fairly dense crumb.

BELOW: Hovis loaves come in various sizes but all have the familiar tin shape with "Hovis" on the sides.

it was always made using white flour – unlike the cobs and coburgs which would have used the cheaper and more widely available brown meal. Danish loaves today, however, are as likely to be more oval in shape. A good Danish from a bakery still has the firm crust and is cut with frequent and deep diagonal slashes on top. A common supermarket version of a Danish is a pre-wrapped, cylindrical sliced loaf that is distinguished mainly by the lightness of the crumb. Although this is advertised as virtue, there is very little that can be said in its favour, since it is bland to the extent of being quite tasteless. So, whenever possible, buy from your baker instead.

RIGHT: Plaits (braids) can be elaborate. Most are enriched with eggs and butter.

FARMHOUSE LOAF

Farmhouse tins are shallow and somewhat squat, producing the characteristic plump tin loaves. At one time special bread tins (pans) were used, which impressed the word "Farmhouse" along the side of the loaf. This was a fashion introduced towards the end of the 19th century when there was a move away from the "whiter-than-white" breads that had become immensely popular, to a more healthy bread. The original farmhouse loaves were made using a brown flour to satisfy the more health conscious, although ironically today most farmhouse loaves are white. Today some craft bakers make their own farmhouse breads using a dough that has been fermented for longer than usual, but the majority of farmhouse loaves are made using exactly the same dough as other white breads. The difference, as is often the case, is in the shape.

HOVIS

No sooner had the poor in Britain been converted to the values and merits of white bread, than a movement began to persuade people that breads containing wheat germ, the bits discarded by the roller mills, were highly valuable nutritionally. A flour was developed that put the wheat germ back into the flour, after first stabilizing it to prevent rancidity. The flour was called Hovis (from the Latin *hominis vis*, meaning "the life of man") and one of the most enduring proprietary breads was born. All Hovis loaves, whether baked at home or bought from a bakery, are made using Hovis flour, although there are a variety of different mixes, some containing more of the wholemeal (whole-wheat) along with other grains. Hovis loaves have their name impressed along the side.

INNES

Innes Original is one of the few sourdough loaves widely available in Britain today, although individual bakers may well make their own favourite sourdough.

PLAIT

Specialist bakers often produce their own plaited (braided) loaves, which can be made from anything between three and eight strands of dough. Plaits emulate the popular European and Jewish breads. They are normally white and can be crusty, made using plain dough, or they can be enriched with butter, eggs and milk and are therefore soft.

SPIRAL

Several of the European breads are shaped by rolling the dough into a sausage shape and then twisting it around to make a spiral or snail shape. Specialist bakers may produce their own particular favourite, which may be white and crusty or enriched and sprinkled with poppy seeds or glazed with egg.

ABOVE: A spiral loaf

RIGHT: Ground nuts give this walnut bread a slightly beige colour.

WALNUT BREAD

There are two styles of British walnut loaf, though the French *pain aux noix* is more commonly available. The white bloomer-shaped walnut loaf contains coarsely ground walnuts while the walnut Granary (whole-wheat) is made using larger chunks of walnut. Both are fairly soft loaves with an airy texture.

OPPOSITE: The white farmhouse loaf produced today (top) is somewhat squat in shape with a characteristic central slash. Wholemeal and Granary loaves (left and right) can be tin-baked or oven bottom-baked.

TIN/SPLIT TIN LOAVES

These loaves are baked in tins (pans), the crust either forming a domed shape (tin), or being slashed along the centre before baking (split tin), so that there is a larger crust area. The crust is normally fairly soft, particularly on loaves that have been pre-packed. A sandwich loaf, which is baked in a completely enclosed tin, is – as the name suggests – popular for making sandwiches since all the slices are conveniently square.

VITBE

Like Hovis, this is another loaf made from a proprietary brand of flour, which also returns the stabilized wheat germ to the white flour. There are several VitBe loaves: the original wheat germ bread and a Hi-Bran loaf.

BELOW: The obvious choice for making sandwiches is the eponymous sandwich loaf, but any tin or split tin loaf works well, despite the more irregular shape.

VIENNA BATONS

A Vienna baton is a slashed long loaf which was, until very recently, the British approximation of the French baguette. The crumb is light and airy, the crust crisp and flaky.

The French baguette was developed partly from a process that originated in Vienna where steam was injected into the oven. Known as the "Vienna" technique, the process was adopted by British bakers in the forlorn hope of reproducing the increasingly popular baguette. The experiment wasn't entirely successful. Vienna batons resemble baguettes only in shape. Their light airy crumb and crisp flaky crust nevertheless have a character of their own and they are surprisingly good, sliced, topped with grated cheese, then toasted and added to French onion soup.

ENGLISH BREADS

ENGLISH OATMEAL BREAD

Oats have always been an important crop in England and other parts of the British Isles, although mainly for animal feed. Oatmeal contains no gluten, so breads made entirely using oats were inevitably flat, baked on stones or on a griddle. Many parts of England, as well as Wales and Scotland, have their own traditional oatmeal cakes, but the meal can be used for baking loaves if it is mixed with wheat flour.

CORNISH SAFFRON CAKE

This Cornish sweet bread is yeast-leavened, enriched with fruit and spiced with nutmeg, cinnamon and saffron. Saffron was an important crop in England in the 16th century and although it gradually declined, it continued to survive in the West Country, where numerous traditional breads and cakes include the tiny threads of saffron, adding a delicate flavour and pretty colouring.

BELOW: Cornish saffron cake is one of the best known of the English currant breads.

LEFT: An English favourite – cottage loaf

COTTAGE LOAF

The cottage loaf must be among the oldest shapes of English breads. The distinctive arrangement of a smallish round loaf baked on top of a larger round loaf seems to be a peculiarity to England and Elizabeth David in her *English Bread and Yeast Cookery* suggests that it might have originated as an improvised way of economizing on baking space in a small oven. The two loaves are wedded together by pushing a wooden spoon handle or fingers down the centre of the two rounds and sometimes the sides are snipped to give an extra crusty finish. Traditionally, cottage loaves would have been baked on the floor of the oven and the best cottage loaves today have a thick, dark bottom crust. Sadly, few high-street bakers have the time or oven space for these celebrated loaves and they are not widely available. For special occasions or on request, some of the smaller specialist bakers will bake a cottage loaf and, no doubt, take great pleasure in doing so.

ABOVE: A harvest loaf gives bakers an opportunity to practise their skill and can be quite spectacular.

GUERNSEY GÂCHE

From this small British island off the coast of Normandy come two breads that are both known as "gâche". The French, brioche-style gâche is highly spiced with cloves and made in proper Normandy style with apples. The British version is heavier, enriched with candied peel and sultanas, and made with eggs and rich Guernsey butter and milk.

HARVEST LOAF

Harvest loaves are not really intended for eating but are made by bakers in the autumn to coincide with harvest festivals in churches and schools. It is a tradition that has happily endured in many of the smaller villages of England and bakers clearly enjoy the opportunity to demonstrate their skill and expertise.

HOT CROSS BUNS

Small yeasted buns have been popular in England since medieval times. Small breads, enriched with eggs, currants and raisins and spiced with nutmeg and cinnamon, were served to accompany wine at the end of a feast. They became a particular Lent favourite among the Elizabethans, who enjoyed displaying their wealth and sophistication by using

CRUMPETS

Crumpets are another traditional bread, and are similar to pikelets and muffins. Recipes for crumpets date from the 18th century and then, just as now, they were always toasted and eaten with lashings of butter. Today, crumpets are made using yeast and baking powder (or bicarbonate of soda and cream of tartar), which accounts for their characteristic holey surface. Crumpets are widely available pre-packed from supermarkets but the superior crumpets from specialist bakers are harder to find and it might be simpler in the long run to make your own.

ABOVE: Crumpets are traditionally served warm with butter.

the expensive and much sought-after spices from the Far East. During the Middle Ages it was common practice to mark loaves with a deep cross before baking to ward off evil spirits and, although the custom was abandoned after the Reformation as being popish, the buns made for Good Friday continued the custom for this most significant of religious days. Hot cross buns are now available almost all year round. They normally make an appearance shortly after Christmas so the significance of Easter and the pleasure of enjoying food according to the season, like so many things, is but a distant memory. Small bakers, however, continue to bake their own hot cross buns only during Lent and most have the attraction of not being so horribly over-spiced.

LEFT: Hot cross buns are the traditional Easter treat.

LARDY CAKE

There are many different versions of this unequivocally English bread, but all go by the same name and all are very rich. Originally, lardy cakes were made for celebrations, notably harvest festivals, but as sugar and fruit became more affordable they became popular all year round. Various English counties lay claim to lardy cake. You can certainly eat delicious lardy cake in Lancashire and Yorkshire, and Northumberland, too, has its own speciality. The Midlands and Derbyshire are partial to a very sweet variety, while further south, in Surrey and Hampshire, there are versions of fruitless lardy cakes. The round, flattish breads are made using a basic white dough, which is layered with fat, sugar and fruit. Lardy cake, almost by definition, is very calorific (so be warned) and it contains pork lard (shortening) and is therefore a prohibited food for vegetarians. The cake is still often sold by weight or by the piece.

ABOVE: A sticky, rich and tasty lardy cake

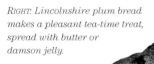

RIGHT: Lincolnshire plum bread makes a pleasant tea-time treat, spread with butter or damson jelly.

LINCOLNSHIRE PLUM BREAD

Just as with plum pudding or plum cake, plum means dried fruit in this context, namely currants, raisins and sultanas (golden raisins). There are several of these plum breads – fruited breads – sold in supermarkets, distributed by a variety of producers. However, the Lincolnshire plum bread seems to be the best known. This, too, is widely available but visitors to Lincolnshire should try if possible to sample the non-commercial version, as baked by smaller specialist bakers.

MUFFINS

English muffins – to give them their correct name and to differentiate them from American muffins, which resemble English fairy cakes – belong to the same tradition as crumpets, although there are several differences, as enthusiasts would be only too keen to point out. Like crumpets, they are a part of an English folk memory that includes the muffin man, winter afternoons in front of the fire, toasting forks and tea time. Although muffins and crumpets are made from the same, or similar, basic recipes, muffins use a stiffer mixture and are consequently thicker with a thin skin or crust on each side and without the characteristic holes of crumpets. Like crumpets, muffins are delicious toasted, either split and then toasted or toasted and then split (it makes a difference!) and served with butter. Pre-packed muffins are available in any supermarket. Bakers also occasionally make their own. (Look out for those made by small craft bakeries, which are likely to have a better flavour and a crisper crust.)

BELOW: Once mostly white, brown muffins are now almost as popular.

LEFT: Pikelets are a speciality of northern England.

to the townspeople. The story goes that Sally Lunn, a Huguenot, brought her recipe from France and adapted it to the English oven. Alternatively, although less romantically, the word is thought to be a corruption of the French *soleil lune* or "sun and moon" cake. Either way, Sally Lunn is a distinctive-looking bread with tall sides and a billowing top like the *kugelhopf* of Alsace. Although there is no one authorized version, Sally Lunn is always made using white flour and yeast, enriched with butter and cream. It can be lightly spiced and slightly citrusy, but should not be over-flavoured. It is often sold in cake shops, split and spread with butter or clotted cream.

SOURDOUGH

There is no tradition of making sourdoughs in England but many of the more adventurous bakers are now producing loaves using a sourdough leaven. There are all sorts of breads using various blends of wheat and rye flours, and some are made using a potato starter. Most loaves of this type are, however, flattish and fairly dense with a definite sour/acid flavour.

PIKELETS

Some people say pikelet is just another name for crumpet and in some parts of the country the words are synonymous. However, while both pikelets and crumpets have the distinctive holey tops, pikelets are not cooked in rings but are free form in shape, being cooked straight on the griddle like Scotch pancakes or the Welsh crumpets *bara pyglyd* (pronounced piglet, and from which pikelets may well get their name). The mixture for pikelets is very much the same as crumpets, but perhaps a bit thinner for pikelets. Bakers in the counties of Leicestershire, Derbyshire, Yorkshire and Lancashire may produce them on a regular basis, and they are sometimes available from larger supermarkets. Otherwise you will need to find a baker who specializes in regional breads and cakes.

SALLY LUNN

This brioche-style cake is a speciality of the West Country, or more particularly Bath, where supposedly a lass called Sally Lunn once sold her cakes

ABOVE: Sally Lunn, with its delicate citrus flavour, is often sliced into three layers and filled with clotted cream.

BELOW: Sourdough

STOTTIE

This flattish bread is native to the north-east of England, where it is widely available, although almost unheard of anywhere else. Almost always white, it is flat with a soft, floury crust, often (but not always) scored with a single slash or cross. Local bakers explain that stotties were traditionally the last things to be baked in the oven at the end of the day, the name itself coming from the local word "stott", meaning to throw to the ground. The bread apparently was ready for eating if it rebounded from the floor! Stottie bread (perhaps as a result of such bad treatment) is rather dry with an open crumb and fairly chewy texture. It is, however, delicious with another regional dish, ham and pease pudding (based on split peas).

STAFFORDSHIRE OATCAKES

Unlike the small, crumbly Scottish oatcake, Staffordshire oatcakes are soft and floppy and are the size of small pancakes. They are known locally as "turnstall tortillas" and they are indeed similar to a tortilla, although unlike the Mexican bread, these are eaten in true English fashion with eggs and bacon for breakfast or butter and honey for tea.

The oatcakes are made from a mixture of oatmeal and flour, yeast and milk or water. It is likely that they have been made in Staffordshire for centuries, as all sorts of oatcakes and griddle cakes were common in the North of England from Tudor times. With the Industrial Revolution though, they became associated with the Staffordshire potteries and while available from many supermarkets, the best are those that are baked on the premises of local bakers in places such as Stoke-on-Trent.

YORKSHIRE FARL

This is a round soda bread, similar to the Irish soda breads, that is cross-slashed into quarters (farls) before being baked.

BELOW: Stotties are a favourite in the north of England.

WELSH BREADS

BARA BRITH

Bara brith is one of the best-known fruit breads of the British Isles. "Bara" is the Welsh word for bread, while "brith", meaning spotted, describes the currants that are an essential ingredient. Although there are brown or "wholemeal" versions, bara brith is normally made using white flour. A good bara brith is yeast-leavened, lightly spiced and fairly dense in texture. Today, raisins and mixed peel are often added, but currants are the essential ingredient and bakers in Wales will commonly plump these first in cold tea, perhaps to emulate the juicy blackcurrants thought to have been the original fruit in bara brith. The bread is sold in most large supermarkets and some delicatessens, but for a really traditional bara brith you may need to travel to Wales, where there are many different versions from which you can choose your own particular favourite.

RIGHT: Bara brith was considered a luxury loaf when dried fruit was expensive. It is still one of the most delicious teabreads.

WELSH COB

Unlike the round English cob, a Welsh cob is something like a cross between an English farmhouse and a stottie. It is baked oven crusty and is normally made from white flour. Usually dusted with flour before baking, these loaves may also have a cut along the centre.

ABOVE: Welsh cob

WELSH COTTAGE

The Welsh cottage loaf, like its English equivalent, is not often made by bakers as it is time-consuming and takes up a lot of oven space. However, specialist bakers and some restaurants may produce these loaves for their customers. The bottom half of the loaf is sometimes slashed vertically before the final rising.

WELSH POT BREAD

In the days before families had ovens for baking, people improvised in the most ingenious ways. Dough, which would normally have been a fairly coarse, brown meal, would be moulded in an iron pot and then turned upside-down on to a flat stone lying over a wood-burning fire. Alternatively, the dough was baked in a three-legged pot, which also would be placed over an open fire, and smouldering peat would then have been piled on top. Pot breads like these are not made these days, but occasionally some restaurants will make their own version, using earthenware pots to create interesting and crusty loaves.

LEFT: Welsh cottage

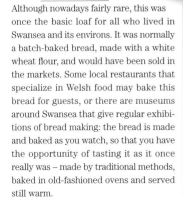

WELSH TINS

Welsh tins have a crusty appearance with a pleasant soft crumb. The white loaves are sometimes cross-hatched but are often, like the wholemeal (whole-wheat) and Granary versions, left plain. Like most tin (pan) loaves, this bread makes great toast and is often served buttered with delicious, slightly salty Welsh butter.

LEFT: Swansea loaf, now made only rarely, was a popular bread in the 18th century.

BELOW: Left to right: white, wholemeal (whole-wheat) and Granary Welsh tin loaves

SWANSEA LOAF

Although nowadays fairly rare, this was once the basic loaf for all who lived in Swansea and its environs. It was normally a batch-baked bread, made with a white wheat flour, and would have been sold in the markets. Some local restaurants that specialize in Welsh food may bake this bread for guests, or there are museums around Swansea that give regular exhibitions of bread making: the bread is made and baked as you watch, so that you have the opportunity of tasting it as it once really was – made by traditional methods, baked in old-fashioned ovens and served still warm.

SCOTTISH BREADS

ABERDEEN BUTTERY ROWIES

Scottish bakers, especially when explaining their wares to the uninitiated, may well describe these delicious little rolls as Scottish croissants. There are certainly similarities. Although the shape differs, rowies being round or oval, they are both made in a similar way: layered with butter so they have a delicious texture that resembles pastry. Rowies, however, are lighter and more savoury than croissants, using less butter but more salt. They are widely available in Scotland, less so as you move further south.

LEFT: Despite the name, soft rolls are slightly crusty.

SELKIRK BANNOCK

This fruited loaf is popular throughout Britain and is available from most large supermarkets, although there was once a time when these breads were only made in the town of Selkirk. It is a round loaf (normally white) and, unlike barm brack and bara brith to which it is often compared, should be completely unspiced. It, too, contains fruit, some versions using only sultanas (golden raisins), others containing currants and candied peel as well. Traditionally it would have been made with lard (shortening), making it similar to lardy cake, but most bought versions today use butter or vegetable fat instead, although some older recipes may still suggest a mixture of butter and lard.

BARLEY BANNOCK

"Bannock" is an Old English word of Celtic origin and was probably the first word used to describe bread, as long ago as the 5th century AD. The word still has a rather antiquated ring to it. It generally describes a type of flat, scone-like bread and in Scotland the two words "bannock" and "scone" are used interchangeably. Bannocks were originally unleavened, made with barley or oatmeal and cooked on a griddle. Such flat, dense breads are unheard of these days. Most of today's bannocks are made using baking powder or bicarbonate of soda (baking soda) as a raising agent, which gives them a light, airy texture. Some craft bakeries produce bannocks using a natural leaven. The sour flavour is something of an acquired taste, especially when coupled with that of the barley. The breads are still cooked on a griddle and have the characteristic earthy flavour of barley.

MELROSE LOAF

This is Scotland's best-known soda bread. It is a proprietary bread, made by a bakery in the south of Scotland. It is a wholemeal (wholewheat), malted loaf with a dense texture and is a popular bread for breakfast, often being spread with butter and marmalade.

LEFT: Aberdeen buttery rowies

SCOTCH BREAD

Scottish bakers are renowned for their bread and these fine loaves are the most popular bread in Scotland, used for sandwiches and toast. Often simply called a "plain" loaf, the bread has the characteristic soft sides of a batch-baked loaf and the top is baked to a dark brown. It has a particularly good flavour, thanks to the longer than usual fermentation period.

MORNING ROLLS

These soft and flattish, floury rolls are found in every bakery and supermarket in Scotland. They are called "baps" in some parts of Scotland; in other parts such a word is completely unheard of and the rolls are called "morning rolls" or just "rolls". The product, however, is clearly the same: made with plain, rather than strong flour, the rolls can be wholemeal (whole-wheat) or brown, but are more commonly white. They are made with lard (shortening), which is rubbed into the flour. This is mixed to a dough with milk and water and, of course, yeast, creating the characteristic soft texture. The rolls are normally batched together on large baking trays and are pulled apart after cooking so, like batched bread, they have little or no side crust and are often almost square in shape. A little dimple in the centre of the roll, pressed into the dough just before baking to stop the tops blistering, is a sign of a traditional morning roll but these

ABOVE: Scotch bread is mostly used for sandwiches.

marks frequently disappear in the oven and their absence should not deter you from buying the rolls if they look and smell fresh. They are best eaten very fresh, and are noticeably salty, like most Scottish bread. They are popular almost any time of the day, but are a favourite at breakfast, for bacon "butties" and with various fillings. A variation of Scottish "baps" or morning rolls are soft rolls. Rather confusingly, these rolls are often not as soft as morning rolls. They have a golden glaze, produced by brushing the rolls with cream both before and after baking.

RIGHT: Morning rolls may be known by different names in Scotland but are all similar, being white, flattish and soft.

IRISH BREADS

WHITE SODA BREAD

Soda bread is the traditional bread of Ireland, which has quite different bread-baking traditions from mainland Britain. The old Irish hearth had no built-in oven, and bread was cooked either on a griddle set over the fire, or in a *bastable*, a type of Dutch oven or oven-pot that would have been set in the smouldering peat. These methods continued to be popular even when iron cooking ranges were introduced to Ireland, and even today specialist Irish bakers will make their traditional breads in cast-iron casseroles with the lid on. Another significant difference in bread making in Ireland was the popularity of bicarbonate of soda (baking soda), as opposed to yeast, as a raising agent. Buttermilk provides the necessary acid to the alkaline bicarbonate of soda and the best soda breads are made using this, although cream of tartar is often used as an alternative to the buttermilk.

There is a vast range of different soda breads, and almost every bakery in Ireland, as well as most restaurants, has its own favourite recipe. Outside Ireland there is still a reasonable selection of white, brown and wholemeal (whole-wheat) soda breads available in most supermarkets. Better still are those breads made on the premises by craft bakers. If the baker is Irish, so much the better.

RIGHT: Soda bread can be baked whole and then broken into farls.

Irish round soda bread is normally marked with a cross. Cut the bread into quarters before cooking, and you have soda farls. These are either baked in the oven or cooked on a covered griddle and have a pale, crusty, floury appearance.

OATMEAL SODA BREAD

In a country with a history of more than its fair share of poverty, almost any edible material that could be ground to a meal would have been used for making bread. Oatmeal is high in protein and would have made a nourishing if flattish bread.

BARM BRACK

This is the Irish version of the Welsh bara brith, the words also translating as "speckled bread". It is linked with several Irish festivals, notably St Brighid's Day – 1 February and the first day of spring – and the festival of Luanasa, which celebrated the start of harvest on 1 August. Barm brack is associated with Hallowe'en and there is also a tradition of baking a wedding ring into the bread, the finder being thus assured of becoming engaged before the year is out. The traditional barm brack, normally made with white flour, is one of the few yeasted Irish breads. Made with sugar, sultanas (golden raisins), mixed (candied) peel and currants, it is enriched with butter and eggs. Barm brack is widely available in Britain and is well worth looking out for.

RIGHT: Barm brack is one of Ireland's most delicious teabreads. Toast and eat with butter or just cut into chunks or serve with jam.

POTATO BREAD

Potatoes, since their introduction in the 17th century, have been an essential food in Ireland. At various times, up to and including the early parts of the 20th century, wheat was scarce and expensive. Potatoes were regularly used to help "stretch" the flour, producing a nourishing and, if lard (shortening) was available, a well-flavoured griddle bread. Today, potato breads made by blending mashed potatoes with some proportion of white flour are baked by Irish bakers and some restaurants. The dough is then normally marked or cut into farls and either cooked over a griddle or baked in the oven.

RIGHT: Soda farls are wedges of soda bread, cut from a loaf either before baking or after.

RIGHT: This potato bread was formed into a star shape before being baked.

SODA FARLS

As already mentioned in the entry on white soda bread, the term "farl" describes a wedge-shaped soda bread (usually a quarter of a loaf). The word derives from "fardel", which meant "fourth part", and in Ireland, soda bread is often marked into quarters, or "farls", before baking, as indeed is the Yorkshire farl. In addition, some are actually cut into farls (either into quarters or thirds) before baking, to give a thick wedge-shaped bread with a good crust. Most of these soda farls are made using a white flour, although some are wholemeal (whole-wheat) breads, made with Irish-milled flour and creamy buttermilk. Properly made, soda farls, like soda bread, are delicious. Their main problem is that they stale quickly, so if possible, consume on the day of purchase.

WHEATEN LOAF

This wheaten loaf is a soda bread that is baked in a tin (pan), so that it is "loaf" shaped, rather than the usual rough round. In Ireland, round soda breads are often called "cakes" or "cakes of bread"; whereas a tin-baked soda bread is called a loaf. Wheaten loaves are normally made with soft Irish wholemeal flour.

BELOW: An Irish wheaten loaf, which is a type of soda bread.

FRENCH BREADS

The French are passionate about their bread. A baguette is one of France's most potent symbols and, whether carried in a basket, strapped to a bicycle or simply tucked under a schoolboy's arm on the way to school, it is as much a sign that you are in France as are the streets of Paris or the vineyards of Provence.

Bread is eaten with every meal and with every course apart from dessert. Although, as in most countries, pre-packaged bread is available, the French seem to attach much importance to their bread, and consequently most families eat fresh bread bought daily – if not from their local *boulangerie*, then at least from the fresh bread counter of the supermarket.

By far the majority of loaves consumed in France are baguettes but there are nevertheless many other types of French bread. The *pain de campagne* and the *levains* are popular throughout the country but there are also countless regional breads of all shapes and sizes. Home-made bread is relatively unusual in France, which surely must be because excellent fresh bread is so easily and readily available. Every village has at least one *boulangerie* where bread is made three or four times a day. French people shop daily – sometimes twice daily – for their bread. Baguettes have to be eaten as fresh as possible, and walking or cycling to the bakery is a small price to pay for the treat.

BAGUETTE

The baguette was developed in Paris in the 1930s and came about due to a combination of factors. White bread was becoming increasingly popular, being synonymous, so it was believed at the time, with quality and excellence. The new baker's yeasts that had been developed meant bakers could experiment with other ways of adding yeast to flour, and mechanized kneading and steam ovens led to substantial improvements in techniques and baking. There are many explanations today for why the best baguettes (and they are not all excellent, even in France) are such a delight, yet so difficult to recreate. The soft French flours certainly play a significant part, producing a soft, light crumb with a wonderful wheaty flavour. The small amounts of yeast used, together with a long kneading and rising period and finally, but not least, the skill of the baker, all contribute to the flavour and texture of a baguette, with its sharp, thin crust and delicious, soft crumb.

The baguette was first known as *pain de fantaisie* ("fancy bread") but the word baguette, meaning "stick", was soon adopted, being obviously the more descriptive nomenclature. *Flutes, bâtards, ficelles, pains* and *petits pains* all belong to the same family, made using the same dough and method. *Pain* is a rounder French bread, normally found only in rural areas. The *bâtard* ("bastard") is a cross between the baguette and the *pain*. It is shorter and slightly fatter than a baguette but weighs about the same. The *flute* is a slim 200g/7oz baguette, while the little *ficelle* ("string") is slimmer still, weighing half as much as a baguette. The baguette itself measures some 68cm/27in in length and weighs 250g/9oz. *Petits pains* are individual sized breads and are often eaten for breakfast.

The baguette has been available outside France for some 20 years and thankfully continues to get better and better.

ABOVE: French baguettes: there are many different varieties, but they should all have a crisp crust and a soft crumb.

Other baguette-style breads are *baguette à l'ancienne* or *baguette de tradition*, *baguette rustique* and *baguette campagne*, often dark, slightly floury and with small paper labels. These breads are an effort by some traditional bakers to re-create the original baguette, as opposed to the modern version, which has, particularly since the 1970s, been subject to ever-faster production methods. These "traditional" baguettes may be made by a sourdough method, can contain rye or other grains or may be a wholemeal (whole-wheat) or bran version. You will need to ask to find out.

Although breads sold as French sticks are worth avoiding, more and more baguettes, sold either by French-style bakeries or by discerning supermarkets, can be very good. They are likely to contain the essential soft wheat and may have been imported from France part-baked.

VIENNA ROLLS

These little milk breads and their cousins, *petits pains au lait*, are enriched with milk and egg and are normally served for breakfast. Do not confuse French Vienna rolls with British rolls of the same name, which are a crusty torpedo-shape and made with a plain dough. French

LEFT: Vienna rolls are soft and slightly sweet, making a good choice for breakfast.

Vienna rolls are similar to bridge rolls and are fairly small and soft. They may be slashed three or four times across the top, while *petits pains au lait* are rounded, often with a cross cut on top, or long and tapered at either end. They sometimes have a sprinkling of sugar on top.

BRIOCHE

Brioche is one of France's favourite breakfast breads, made with white flour and yeast, enriched with butter, milk and eggs and sweetened with just a little sugar. It is similar to many of the British enriched breads, such as Sally Lunns, although generally richer, using a half to three-quarters butter to flour ratio, which is as rich as or richer than most pastries. Although not as popular as croissants outside France, brioche makes a perfect bread for breakfast, with its soft texture and rich flavour. It tastes wonderful served with marmalade or a fruit conserve.

Brioche is made in a variety of shapes and sizes. The most

ABOVE: A loaf-shaped brioche and small individual brioche buns.

RIGHT: The unmistakable crescent-shaped croissant is popular at breakfast almost everywhere.

famous is undoubtedly the *brioche à tête*, with its fluted sides and little brioche cap perched on top, and which in turn comes in various sizes – from individual buns to large loaves. The *brioche Nanterre* is made by arranging six or eight balls of brioche dough in a zigzag pattern along the bottom of a loaf pan, while the *brioche Parisienne* is made in a similar way, but with nine or ten balls of dough placed in a circle. Both rise to fill out the pan but the divisions still exist so that small chunks can be broken off.

Savoury brioche, made using cheese in place of some of the butter, is becoming more widely available outside France. This is likely to be loaf-shaped, rather than the traditional round, and can be used for savoury dishes (as indeed can the sweeter versions). One of the most delicious ways of using savoury brioche is to hollow out the centre and stuff with wild mushrooms or grilled (broiled) sweet (bell) peppers.

CROISSANTS

Another essentially French creation, these popular pastries are available almost everywhere, served not only for breakfast but stuffed with savoury fillings and sold wherever there is a demand for food that can be eaten on the hoof. In France, a distinction is drawn between the *croissant au beurre*, which is small and straight and is made using butter, and the *croissant ordinaire*, which is the more familiar crescent shape made with vegetable fat. The distinction is by no means clear cut, however, as some producers who use only butter in their croissants favour the crescent shape. If the croissants are pre-packed, you can check the packet; otherwise you will need to ask your baker. Ideally, buy croissants fresh in the morning from a local baker, when they will be soft inside, with a slightly crackly crust.

EPI

This translates as "wheat ear" and is the traditional bread at harvest festivals, the French equivalent of a harvest loaf. The little ears of bread are made separately and fashioned into sticks or into a large round called a *couronne* ("crown"). The breads can then be broken off, piece by piece, for eating. *Epis* are normally made using a baguette-style dough and are light and crusty.

FOUGASSE

These large, flat breads are quite unmistakable with their deep cuts representing branches of a tree, cogwheels or even the grate of a fire. They are a speciality of Languedoc and Provence although they originally came from Italy and are closely akin to the Italian focaccia. Sometimes known as *fouacés*, or "hearth bread", they were traditionally baked on the floor of the oven after the embers had been

ABOVE: Epi is an unusual bread.

scraped out, but while it was still too hot to bake a normal loaf. There are several varieties of *fougasse* – most use a sourdough-style leaven and all are flat, deeply cut and baked in a very hot oven.

PAIN DE CAMPAGNE

Next to baguettes, this is the best-known of French breads. In spite of its name, the loaf was the invention of a Parisian baker and is as much enjoyed in towns and cities as it is in the country. Made using a *chef* starter, it has a thick, slightly grey and floury crust and a discernibly sour smell and taste. No rules exist for its shape, although, like almost all French bread, it is oven bottom-baked (i.e. without using tins (pans)) and is therefore a convenient round (or a rather misshapen) baton. Outside France and in French cities, the breads are normally of manageable size, weighing about 450g/1lb, but visit a rural *boulangerie* in France and you will find huge cartwheel-size breads or sturdy, long loaves, which will keep a large family going for several days. These are sometimes called *pain ménage* ("household bread") and may be sold by weight.

LEFT: Fougasse is the equivalent of Italy's focaccia but has characteristic slashes.

Since it is very much a local product, you will find the bread changes from region to region, even from village to village. Although most use white wheat flour, rye meal and wholemeal (whole-wheat) grain is occasionally added, especially for *pain de campagne rustique*, and the flavour and shape will vary enormously. Being a sourdough bread, it keeps well for 4–5 days and indeed is better the day after baking – quite the opposite of the refined baguette.

Pain de campagne is widely available in supermarkets. Shop around for the variety you prefer.

RIGHT: Pain de Campagne comes in many shapes and sizes.

PAIN AUX NOIX

This favourite French bread, although it translates as "nut bread", is understood to be walnut bread. The walnuts give it a teabread feel, but it is very much a savoury bread, best served with soft cheese, such as Brie or Camembert or, if you prefer, strong-flavoured Cheddar or Stilton. It is made using a wholemeal (whole-wheat) bread flour, which contrasts and complements the nutty and savoury walnuts.

PAIN DE MIE

This is the French version of a British sandwich loaf. It is cooked in an enclosed tin (pan), so that the bread has square sides and a soft crust, making it the ideal shape for sandwiches. Unlike the British loaf, however, it is normally enriched with milk and butter so that, in flavour, it is more like brioche than a plain white loaf.

PAIN DE SEIGLE/PAIN AU SEIGLE

Pain de seigle is French rye and the choice bread for eating with oysters. Regulations insist that it must contain at least two-thirds rye, the remaining proportion made up with wheat flour, which gives it a lighter flavour and colour than German and Scandinavian rye breads. *Pain au seigle* ("bread with rye") needs to contain only some 10 per cent rye and is a lighter bread again.

PAIN POILÂNE

This proprietary loaf is produced and distributed by the famous Poilâne bakers in Paris, not just throughout France, but all

ABOVE: Pain au seigle (left) contains a small amount of rye and has a mild flavour. A brown pain de mie (centre) stands alongside pain aux noix (right), a savoury walnut loaf which is excellent with a strong cheese.

over the world. Based on the traditional and long-forgotten country loaves of France's past, the bakery prides itself on the methods used for making and baking the bread – a natural sourdough leaven is kneaded briefly but long fermented, then hand-moulded and finally baked in wood-fired ovens. Because the sourdough method, by definition, produces a different loaf each time, breads in the shop can vary to a surprising degree, some being wonderful, others disappointing.

PAIN POLKA

A speciality bread of the Loire region, this is an oval or round loaf, somewhat flat and criss-crossed with deep slashes. It is baked using the *levain* method of keeping back part of the previous day's dough and using this as the starter for the bread.

PAIN BATTU AU FROMAGE

This is a cheese batter bread, which uses Parmesan cheese, a fact that suggests that the bread originally came from Italy or the Alpes-Maritimes region of France. The cheese is stirred into the batter and also sprinkled over the top before baking, to give a golden crust. The bread can be loaf-shaped or baked in brioche-style individual tins (pans).

PAIN ALLEMAND AUX FRUITS

This translates as German fruit bread, but is nevertheless a French bread from Strasbourg, a city on the border with Germany. Strasbourg is in the heart of Alsace, a region famous for its rich breads, notably *kugelhopf*. *Pain Allemand* is a rich fruit bread

ABOVE: Pain polka can be plain or may contain chopped olives.

LEFT: Pain poilâne is easily recognized by the four slashes making a rough square on its top.

ABOVE: There are many variations on pain au levain (back) but all will be made using the sourdough method. The boule de meule is a very substantial loaf best eaten with hearty soups and stews.

that is spiced with cinnamon, cloves and aniseed and rich with raisins, prunes, apricots and figs. It is, needless to say, a festive bread.

PAIN AU LEVAIN

A white or sometimes wholemeal (whole-wheat) bread that has become almost as popular in the United Kingdom as it is in France. A *levain* is a bread made by the natural sourdough method, *levain* being the French expression for a sourdough. The breads come in a variety of shapes, often resembling a rather short and flat baguette, or can be moulded into rough squares. *Pain rustique* is made using the same sourdough method, but using a proportion of wholemeal flour or a blend of grains.

BOULE DE MEULE

The word *boulangerie* comes from the French word for a round of dough, *une boule*, which also accounts for the name of this bread. *Boule de meule* translates literally as a round of stoneground dough, which pretty well sums up this bread, except that it is baked, ideally on the sole of the oven, until it is crusty. *Boules de meule* are normally quite large, with an excellent flavour.

GÂTEAU DE GANNAT

This rich festive bread is popular in the Gannatois region of France. Its principal distinguishing feature is the fromage blanc which is stirred into the batter-like dough with eggs and butter to make a soft crumbly loaf with a sweet/sour flavour. This taste is particularly noticeable if brandy has been added.

PAIN DE PROVENCE

Provence is so rich in all sorts of wonderful foods that it would be nonsense to

RIGHT: Cereale is normally a torpedo-shaped loaf.

ascribe a single bread to this region. If you visit Provence you are likely to find a range of *pains de Provence*, either fashioned roughly into small loaves or made into slender baguettes. Along with the herbs of Provence – savory, thyme and basil – the dough is made with lavender flowers and fennel. It has a heady flavour and is superb served with cheese or to accompany a soup.

CEREALE

This is a well-flavoured light brown loaf with a good crust and a tender crumb. It is made from eight cereals and seeds and typically includes wheat, corn, rye, millet, malted wheat and oats, with sunflower and sesame seeds. The shape is quite distinctive. *Cereale* is usually formed into a broad torpedo shape and is lightly dusted with flour.

BELGIAN BREADS

PISTOLET

Pistolets are the Belgian equivalent to the croissants of France. They are small, butter-enriched round rolls, easily distinguished by their central indentation, which is made using a stick dipped in oil before baking. They have a soft texture under a thin, glossy crust and can be found in many parts of northern France, too, where they are just as popular as they are in their native Belgium. *Pistolets* are normally enjoyed for breakfast or for tea, split and spread with preserve or, alternatively, are broken into chunks and eaten French-style dipped in café au lait.

CRAMIQUE

A popular Belgian teabread, this is stuffed with raisins and enriched with butter and milk. It is rather squat in shape and can be made using a wholemeal (whole-wheat) or a white flour, or a blend of the two. Whiter versions have a soft crumb with the texture and flavour of brioche, while the wholemeal *cramique* has a more malted flavour. Bought fresh, *cramique* is wonderful simply buttered or spread with a preserve. Breads that are two or three days old taste good toasted, buttered and spread with jam, or served with a soft cheese, such as Brie or Camembert.

ABOVE: Fruity cramique

ITALIAN BREADS

Italian bread has had something of a renaissance in the past few years and rightly so. Italian breads are a delight, delicious served with pasta, fish, meats and poultry, as well as cheese. Any Italian baker will tell you that there are thousands of different Italian breads. This could actually be true should anyone ever try to count! Italy was once made up of a number of independent states, and each developed its own favourite cuisine, including, of course, breads. Geography and climate played a part, as did prosperity. Some of the best-known loaves, such as ciabatta and *pagnotta* are "national" breads, available everywhere. Other breads – the more peasant-style loaves – from rural areas would have been coarse, mealy loaves, made with whatever grain could be gathered together. Olive oil was frequently added, not only for flavour, but to add extra nourishment and to help the keeping qualities of the loaf. Nowadays these rustic loaves are still made using olive oil. They are normally white, although wholemeal (whole-wheat) and mixed grain loaves are not unheard of. They can be yeast-leavened but originally would have been made using a natural leaven. Small bakeries, especially those in the south of Italy, a region only mildly influenced by tourism and fashion, still produce these loaves for their loyal customers, made in the traditional way from time-honoured recipes. If you visit these parts, be sure to buy and sample some of these regional breads; you cannot fail to be delighted. Outside Italy, various country-style breads, such as *pagnotta* and *pugliese*, are available from Italian-style bakers, although these loaves are likely to be standardized. Nevertheless, many first-generation Italian bakers in Britain and North America, who learnt their baking skills from their parents and grandparents, bake their own favourite regional bread and these are likely to be as good and authentic as the breads of their homeland.

The distinguishing feature of most Italian breads, especially those bought from an Italian-style baker, is the shape rather than the dough. By and large, bakers do not make up different doughs for different breads – they would not have the time, the space or the labour. The difference lies in the shaping, the slashing and the baking – a small distinction you may think, but wait until you try the bread and you will be surprised.

BIOVA

This regional bread comes from the north of Italy, around Piedmont. It is cylindrical in shape with little pointed horns. Made with lard, it has a thick crust and soft crumb and has an excellent flavour.

CARTA DA MUSICA

This extraordinary harvest sheaf loaf from Sardinia, also sometimes called *carasaù*, is made with paper thin leaves of dough, piled up to make a tower that looks like a stack of unevenly shaped pancakes. The leaves of bread are brittle but can be eaten as a snack with an aperitif or with salads. Alternatively, the leaves of bread can be softened in a light dressing or even just water and olive oil, then wrapped around a filling.

CIABATTA

This ubiquitous loaf has surprisingly not suffered for all that it is produced on a massive scale so as to be available from almost every supermarket in the country.

LEFT: Carta da musica means sheets of music and does look not unlike sheets of parchment piled on top of each other.

LEFT: *Plain ciabatta served with olive and sun-dried tomato versions.*

It is an oval, slightly flattish loaf, and looks rather like a squashed slipper, which is what the word, rather unromantically, means. It is made with generous quantities of olive oil and has a thin, friable crust. The crumb is light, holey and slightly chewy. Ciabatta is delicious served as an accompaniment to soups or tomato salads, as it will mop up the juices beautifully.

Like the French baguette, ciabatta is a relatively new shape of bread. It is normally a white loaf, made using a sponge dough method – flour, yeast and water are fermented for up to 24 hours before being incorporated into the rest of the dough. Another particular feature of ciabatta, making it a tricky bread to bake at home, is the soft consistency of the dough. It has a minimum of 75 per cent water and oil and is thus quite unlike any other kind of bread. A long kneading process also contributes to ciabatta's unique flavour, which should be sweet/sour, as well as its texture: a crisp crust and an open crumb. Numerous flavourings can be added to ciabatta – from olives and sun-dried tomatoes to cheese and walnuts. Many supermarket loaves are sold part-baked and should be finished off in a hot oven before being served. The final baking enhances both the flavour and texture of what is undeniably one of the world's favourite breads.

FOCACCIA AND FOCACCETTE

Focaccia is another Italian bread that has captured the imagination of the rest of the world. Known variously as "Italian country flat bread", *pizza rustica* or *pizza genovese*, it is a large, flat bread, slightly puffy when fresh and dimpled all over the surface with little indentations. It can be round, square or a rather misshapen rectangle; shape is not particularly important. This is the original Italian hearth bread, made from surplus pieces of dough and baked at a very high heat before the oven cooled slightly for the massive family loaves. It is easy to imagine the children waiting impatiently for their share of the warm bread as it came out of the oven. Today, most store-bought focaccia, particularly those from supermarkets, are round and can be rather bland in flavour. However, Italian bakers who know and love this bread will produce far more tasty loaves, baking them in a very hot oven so that, like pizzas, they are floury and flecked with black.

Focaccia is a wonderfully versatile bread. Apart from the olive oil that is kneaded into the basic dough, the flattish bread can be sprinkled with sea salt, herbs,

BELOW: *Focaccia is often sprinkled with crushed rosemary.*

onions, prosciutto or cheese. Smaller versions of focaccia, *focaccette,* are small rolls sprinkled with salt and onions.

GRISSINI

These long, thin breadsticks, mainly popular as an aperitif, are made from wheat flour and have been cooked until completely dry, so that they are basically all crust and no crumb. The better grissini are made using olive oil; best of all are those that are hand-made by craft bakers, having considerably more character than the bland, smooth breadsticks available in most supermarkets.

Grissini come from the north-west of Italy, around Turin and Piedmont. Here they also make a more substantial type of breadstick, called *francescine*. These are thicker breadsticks with a softer centre and they not only have a better flavour, but have a decidedly good crunch, too. Grissini are mostly made using white flour, although wholemeal (whole-wheat) ones are sometimes available, especially if

ABOVE: The best grissini are bought from Italian bakers or delicatessens.

made on the premises by smaller bakers. Grissini are commonly rolled in poppy seeds or sesame seeds or coarsely ground sea salt before baking to add extra flavour.

MICHETTA

This is a round white roll with a well-flavoured crust, which is called *rosetta* in Rome.

MEZZA LUNA

This simple crusty loaf is shaped like a half moon. It is made with the standard white dough used for *pagnotta* and other country breads.

PAESANA

This round, simple white loaf that is cross-cut to divide into farls, tastes rather like focaccia or ciabatta. *Paesana* is generally less rich in olive oil

BELOW: Paesana

and, without the addition of herbs, sun-dried tomatoes or olives, tends to be a far plainer loaf than its cousins. It is nevertheless very good with soups and stews.

PAGNOTTA

This large, round farmhouse loaf is probably the most common and popular bread in Italy, sold all over the country. Loaves can be small and round, but in Italy some may be huge, cut in portions, each still big enough to feed a large family. The bread is traditionally made using the sourdough method. Outside the country, some Italian delicatessens sell this bread, either imported from Italy or made to an original recipe. Italian-style bakers, however, do not always use the classic but lengthy process for their breads. They argue that for most, *pagnotta* means a standard wheat loaf, so they use the same dough as for other Italian breads. In Italy *pagnotta* can be white, wholemeal (whole-wheat) or a mixture, depending on the region, and all types are available outside Italy, with white being the most common.

PANE AL CIOCCOLATO

A yeasted bread made with olive oil and studded with dark (bittersweet) chocolate which is kneaded into the dough, it can be wholemeal, but is more commonly coloured a rich brown with cocoa powder. In Italy, chocolate bread is served with mascarpone or Gorgonzola cheese as a snack.

PANE CON NOCI

There are several different Italian breads

ABOVE: Pagnotta is Italian country bread; loaves can be huge.

LEFT: Pane al cioccolato, made as rolls.

RIGHT: Pane con noci is a savoury nut bread.

that go under the title of "bread with nuts". The oval-shaped bread is similar to the British and French walnut breads, while a slim, flat loaf with sultanas (golden raisins) and walnuts is a sweet version of ciabatta.

PANETTONE

Panettone is a Milanese speciality, sold around Christmas as a traditional festive cake. In Italy and in delicatessens outside the country, it is sold wrapped in cellophane and tied with coloured ribbons. For all its richness – made with liberal amounts of butter, eggs and milk, together with sultanas, candied peel and sometimes chocolate – *panettone* is surprisingly light in texture. This may have something to do with the traditional *panettone* shape, which is like a squat cylinder or dome, slightly wider at the top where the bread has billowed out into a deep golden crust.

PANE DI MAIS

Made using polenta, a coarse ground cornmeal, *pane di*

RIGHT: Pugliese is one of the best-known and loved Italian breads.

RIGHT: Panettone is the classic Christmas bread.

mais is one of the few Italian corn breads. It normally also contains some olive oil. It is flatter than most Italian breads, owing to the high proportion of corn, but pieces are perfect for mopping up sauces and salad dressings.

PANE TOSCANO (TUSCAN SALTLESS BREAD)

Alternatively called *pane sciocco* or *pane sciapo Toscano*, this bread is a favourite among Tuscans, who love it for the flavour of the wheat, which is more pronounced in the absence of salt. The bread was made at a time when salt was heavily taxed. Unlike many Italian breads, *pane sciocco* does not contain olive oil either. If you try eating it by itself, a common reaction is "something's wrong", or "something's missing from this bread". However, eaten with goat's cheese, anchovies, olives or salami, the bread comes into its own.

PUGLIESE

This much-loved Italian bread was once the regional bread from Puglia, in the southern region of Apulia. Perhaps it is the extra virgin olive oil from this region or the excellence of the wheat, but *pugliese*

RIGHT: Sfilatino look like small baguettes.

is considered to be among the jewels of Italian breads, popular all over the country and beyond as well. The bread is normally white, with a pale, floury crust and a soft crumb, quite dense by Italian standards, compared with the holey ciabatta and the open-textured *pagnotta*.

SFILATINO

Looking something like a French baguette that has perhaps been crossed with a baby ciabatta, these little Italian breads are a wonderful addition to the bread counter at the supermarket and are excellent served with an Italian meal. Although similar in shape to the baguette, any comparison ends there. *Sfilatino* loaves are noticeably smaller than the baguette, without the slashes on top and with a darker, more floury crust. Made using lots of virgin olive oil,

the crust is crisper and less flaky than the baguette, while the crumb is softer.

ITALIAN OLIVE BREAD

Olives are grown throughout Italy and it's not surprising to find all sorts of olive bread. The more commercially produced loaves are enriched with eggs and butter and normally contain pitted green olives and sometimes whole olives stuffed, Spanish-style,

with red pimiento. Smaller bakers often also produce their own olive breads. These are plainer doughs, which usually contain black olives, sometimes pitted, but sometimes not – so take care when biting into a slice.

TORTINO

Tortino is similar to an olive bread, but is much larger and more rustic, with a dense crumb. It can be stuffed with olives, spinach or tomatoes or a mixture of all these.

SICILIAN SCROLL

Sicily has a strong tradition of bread making. Over the centuries, monks and nuns of the island's many monasteries perfected their baking skills as a sign of devotion to God. Sicilian scroll is unusual in that it contains a high proportion of semolina. Shaped into a broad "S", it has a soft, pale yellow crumb and a crisp crust that is traditionally topped with sesame seeds.

ABOVE: Pane Toscano goes by several names, including "sciocco" and "Tuscan saltless bread". It has a dense crumb, which to palates unused to its salt-free nature is very bland. However, it has its devotees and is good with cheese.

SPANISH BREADS

Bread is the symbol of all food in Spain. In villages, where bread is still often made at home, the housewife will kiss and make the sign of the Cross over the loaf before baking, and children are taught never to snatch bread as this is seen as a sign of disrespect, not only to their parents but also to God.

If you visit Spain, you are likely to find that the first breads of the day are the morning rolls, such as *bollo* or *chica* (meaning "little girl"). Later in the morning the *panadería* (bakery) will start producing larger breads. These are of almost every conceivable shape and size, but will mostly be yeast-fermented, white, wheat breads. Spain is famous for its simple white breads, with their smooth crust and soft white crumb. Bread is eaten with every meal and with every course. More simple still, and a tradition much loved by the Spanish, is the custom of pouring virgin olive oil over fresh bread to eat as a snack at any time of the day.

While wheat is the principal crop, oats, barley and other cereals are sometimes blended with wheat flour for more rustic loaves. In the north-west corner of the country, in Santiago and La Coruña, wholemeal (whole-wheat) and rye breads can be found. Here, near the north of Portugal, corn meal is blended with wheat flour to make rich yellow loaves. Corn was brought back to Spain from the New World by sailors returning home, but is not as popular today in Spain as it is in Portugal.

PAN CATETO

This is the traditional Spanish country bread, made from a starter called the *levadura de masa*.

BELOW: The pan gallego often looks like a squashy cottage loaf with a top knot.

HORNAZO

This is a Castilian flat bread customarily made at Easter. The dough is filled with chunks of *chorizo* (spicy sausage), cheese and hard-boiled eggs so that when it is baked and cut, everybody receives a different piece of bread. *Horno* is the Spanish word for an oven, from which the bread probably gets its name. At one time in Spain, people would take loaves of bread, as well as large joints of meat, turkeys or even whole lambs, to the local baker's for cooking in the stone *horno*.

PAN GALLEGO

This country-style bread is made using olive oil and has a pleasant, unassuming flavour. It can be a rather misshapen round, and a whole loaf can be huge. Much of the *pan gallego* sold outside Spain are quarters of a large loaf. The crust is soft and floury, the crumb light with an open texture. Seed *gallego* is a similar loaf but is studded with pumpkin and sesame seeds, which give it a delicious flavour and texture.

BELOW: *Pan aceite*

PAN QUEMADO

This is one of the best-known of Spanish sweet breads. It has a rather squashed, sunken look, a bit like an enlarged English lardy cake with its glossy brown top, but in spite of appearances, this is a delicious sweet loaf, a little like a French brioche in texture, although it is made with olive oil rather than butter.

GOFIO

This unusual bread is classified as Spanish, coming as it does from the Canary Islands, but has a fascinating and ancient history that suggests it might more rightly belong with the Arabian or Moroccan breads. Although the Canaries have belonged to Spain for hundreds of years, they were once the home of a group of Berbers called the Guanches. Now extinct, little knowledge of these original people remains apart from a few artefacts. *Gofio*, however, is thought to survive from these North African people. The bread is the shape of a large ball and is made from a variety of flours – wheat, barley, corn and gram (dried chickpeas), which are sometimes blended and always toasted before milling. The dough is mixed with water or milk and, although yeast is used today, originally the dough would have been fermented using a natural leaven. Once risen, the bread is baked, either conventionally in an oven or, even today in some parts of the Canaries, in a Dutch oven, a pot-like construction where the embers of the fire are piled around the outside of the pot. The result is a crusty round loaf with a fairly dense crumb, quite unlike the light and airy Spanish breads, and indeed unlike most traditional Moroccan breads as well, which are mostly flat and baked very quickly in unusually hot ovens. Perhaps the scarcity of wheat meant these ancient people needed to be more inventive, or perhaps their settled life on the islands, as opposed to the nomadic life of the Berbers, meant they had more time for the task of baking.

ENSAIMADAS

A speciality of Majorca (Mallorca), these small yeasted pastry buns are the Spanish answer to the croissant, except that instead of being crescent-shaped they look more like little Moorish turbans. Normally a little sweeter than croissants, they have the same soft texture and are served at breakfast with jam or honey in the island's many hotels. Consignments of these little rolls are regularly sent to Barcelona, where they are much appreciated by both tourists and local city dwellers.

A much larger version of the *ensaimada* can also be found in Majorca. This is often topped with cream or a sweet custard-like topping made with pumpkin pulp, sugar, lemon juice and spices. This dessert is particularly popular at fiestas, when the *ensaimada* is decorated with small pieces of marrow and thin slices of *sobrasada*, a type of Majorcan sausage.

MAJORCAN POTATO BUNS

Although a relatively small group of islands, the Balearic Islands have a surprisingly rich and varied cuisine. Along with their own local fish and meat dishes, they have a variety of delicious breads, including these Majorcan potato buns. These small buns are made using either sweet or ordinary potatoes. They have a very sweet taste and are normally eaten at breakfast, during mid-morning or for tea, and are usually served with either jam or honey.

PAN ACEITE (OLIVE OIL BREAD)

This is similar to the French *fougasse* and the Italian *focaccia* breads. *Pan Aceite* is commonly a rather misshapen-looking bread. It is baked on the sole of the oven, after being brushed liberally with olive oil (hence the name olive oil bread).

TWELFTH NIGHT BREAD

In Spain and Portugal children receive their presents not on Christmas Day but on Twelfth Night (5 January). Appropriately for the Epiphany, the gifts are delivered by a figure representing the Magi, the three wise men who made their journey from the East to bring gifts to the infant Jesus. It is customary for a special bread called *roscon de reyes* in Spain and *bolo-rei* in Portugal to be baked for this day. The rich teabread is stuffed with fruits and candied peel and traditionally contains a coin or figurine, bringing luck to the person who is given the piece of bread in which it is discovered.

PORTUGUESE BREADS

Portuguese bakers, like their counter-parts in other countries, frequently use the same basic dough for making loaves and rolls. It is the shape and manner of baking that gives each bread its own idiosyncratic flavour and texture. Many Portuguese breads are made using a yeasted white flour dough.

ALENTEJANO
This is a white bread with a fairly thick crust and a well-flavoured crumb, which has a distinctive, salty/sour flavour. Like almost all Portuguese and Spanish breads, the bread is oven bottom-baked and has an even, golden crust.

BROA DE MILO
This simple loaf from Minho in northern Portugal, the name of which translates as "corn bread", is normally referred to simply as *broa* and is eaten by everyone. Corn is a popular grain for making bread in Portugal and Spain. The conquistadors and sailors brought home not only potatoes, tomatoes and (bell) peppers, but

RIGHT: Alentejano has a good flavour.

BELOW: Papo secos are soft yet crusty.

ABOVE: Rosquilha is an attractive round bread.

corn as well, together with the skills needed to grind it into meal. Corn proved to be a successful crop in the north of Portugal where wheat does not flourish, and it would have been quickly selected as the preferred crop. It is likely that even from the beginning, bakers would have blended corn meal with wheat in order to provide some gluten, but when this was scarce barley and alfalfa flour was used and, even today, loaves are made from a mixed grain. *Broa de milo* is a robust, well-flavoured loaf, which goes well with Portuguese soups and *cozidos* – stewed meat, vegetables and beans.

ROSQUILHA
This is a ring-shaped white bread with a pleasant crust and a slightly chewy texture and salty flavour. It will normally be made using the same dough as *alentejano* but the shape means *rosquilha* is crustier, although it does not stay fresh as long. *Rosquilha* can be bought and eaten at any time of day but is very popular for breakfast or during the mid-morning, and is served with coffee.

CANTELO

This wedding bread is a traditional bread from the northern region of Portugal. The loaf is baked in a ring, and custom dictates that the bride and groom break the bread into pieces to give to their wedding guests with a glass of wine.

PAPO SECOS

These small white rolls are a popular breakfast bread all over Portugal. They have a soft white crumb and a delicious crust that is crisp without being hard. Like

RIGHT: Bolo do caco is a hearth bread like focaccia and fougasse.

many breads from Portugal, they are baked with lots of steam which accounts for their good crust yet ensures that the crumb is light and airy.

CARACAS

Caracas are similar in size and shape to *papo secos* but are more akin to an English or Scottish bap, batch-baked and cooked with less steam so they are softer and less crusty.

BOLO DO CACO

This flattish loaf is similar to the Spanish olive oil bread. It is another type of hearth bread, cooked on

ABOVE: If you live near a Portuguese baker, try caracas as an alternative to regular hamburger buns.

the sole of a very hot oven. It is best eaten very fresh with dressed salads or with other foods that have plenty of liquids that need mopping up.

MAIA BREAD

This is a long white loaf, normally made using a plain white dough. It is popular all over Portugal and is one of the better-known everyday breads, eaten with fish soups and salads, and Portuguese cheese.

BELOW: Maia bread is almost always a white loaf and has a good, slightly chewy crust.

GERMAN BREADS

There is an enormous range of German breads. Outside Germany – in Britain for instance – you could be forgiven for thinking that all German breads come in neat packages wrapped in cellophane. These are in fact the *kastenbrots* (box breads) and include the well-known pumpernickel. In Germany, however, and increasingly available throughout Europe and North America, there are also the German *krustenbrots* (crusty breads). These are the freshly baked breads, bought from a bakery or from the fresh bread counters at supermarkets, and they are as varied and delicious as the loaves to be found in the rest of continental Europe. The German word *brot* means either wheat or rye bread, with other breads named for the type of grain used in their making: oats, corn or barley.

KASTENBROTS

In the customary way that German words very often describe exactly what they mean, *kastenbrots* translates as "box bread". The bread is steam-baked for some 20 hours in an enclosed tin (pan),

BELOW: Pumpernickel is the best-known of the German kastenbrots.

which results in a dense and heavy loaf which is both moist and crumbly with a chewy texture. It has a sour flavour but with a certain sweet, malty overtone and, unlike most breads, has a distinctive but not unpleasant after-taste. *Kastenbrots* are not breads to be eaten with wine, but are best enjoyed with a jug of cool German beer.

These breads almost invariably use rye flour (normally a wholemeal grain that can be coarsely or more finely ground according to the type of bread). The dough uses a natural, sourdough leaven, which adds to the sour taste of the bread and complements the flavour of the rye, with its own earthy taste. The darkest *kastenbrots* contain only rye but wheat flour is added in varying proportions to give a loaf that is lighter in appearance, texture and flavour. Other grains, such as oats or barley, as well as sunflower and sesame seeds, are added to certain loaves, and there are therefore numerous variations on the basic theme. The bread always comes thinly sliced, wrapped in cellophane and clearly labelled. While moist in texture, the bread, with its sweet/sour yet dry flavour tastes best buttered or spread with a soft cheese. Savoury foods, such as smoked salmon, soused herring or German sausage, are most commonly served with the darker breads, but the lighter breads are excellent with marmalade or other sharply flavoured conserves.

PUMPERNICKEL

The best known of all the *kastenbrots*, pumpernickel is also the darkest of these breads. It is usually made with 100 per cent coarsely ground rye grain, and has an unmistakable sour, earthy flavour, but some are made with slightly less rye flour

LEFT: Vollkornbrot (left) is a 100 per cent rye bread, while roggenbrot (back) is slightly lighter, containing some wheat flour. Sonnenblumenbrot (right) is made with sunflower seeds, which give a lighter flavour and a good texture.

and a small amount of wheat flour. Like many German breads, pumpernickel is sometimes flavoured with caraway seeds.

VOLLKORNBROT OR SCHWARZBROT

This is another strongly flavoured bread, the names of which translate as "whole corn" or "black" bread. The whole "corn" in this instance is rye, which again is coarsely ground. The bread also contains molasses, adding to the dark colour and the malty flavour of the bread – which is probably one for devotees only.

ROGGENBROT

Roggen is German for rye, but this bread in fact often contains a small proportion of wheat flour, too. *Roggenbrot* is a dark oblong tin (pan) loaf with a hard crust that is sometimes encrusted with whole grains. In spite of the added wheat flour, this is still an intensely flavoured bread, best eaten with strong-tasting foods.

SONNENBLUMENBROT

Sunflower seeds give this bread a pleasant crunchy texture. *Sonnenblumenbrot* is made mainly using rye flour, but a small proportion of wheat flour together with the sunflower seeds makes this a more palatable loaf for those sampling *kastenbrot* for the first time.

WEISENKEIMBROT

This means "wheat germ bread" and it is made using the wheat germ, along with rye grain and flour. *Grahamsbrot* uses a higher

proportion of wholemeal (whole-wheat) flour, specifically the American-style Graham wholewheat flour.

MUESLIBROT

This is a multigrain *kastenbrot*, made using a muesli-style (granola-style) mix of cereals, chopped nuts and whole grains. It is a popular choice in Germany for those who want a healthy teabread that has plenty of texture and is not overly sweet.

ABOVE: Three krustenbrots: Black Forest (left), Bavarian rye (right) and roggenbrot.

KRUSTENBROTS

These crusty breads are the day-to-day breads of Germany, and are also popular in parts of Canada and in the American states around the Great Lakes, where German emigrés settled in the 1840s. In other European countries, German-style bakers import the flours from Germany or bake them using locally bought flours and meals, but sometimes import the sourdough culture from their native home. Many, although not all, German breads contain rye flour.

LEFT: Weisenkeimbrot (back) is made with both rye and wheat flours, while mueslibrot contains a mixture of cereals, nuts and whole grains.

ABOVE: Landbrot

BELOW: German square rye

Rye was once the main cereal in northern Europe. It tolerates the cooler drier climatic conditions, and for centuries, while the more affluent enjoyed white bread made with imported wheat, the poor continued to eat bread made with the grain that was cheap and readily available. When wheat became relatively inexpensive in Germany white wheat flour was used by all but the very poorest, either by itself or with rye flour. There is consequently a great variety of German breads. Some are baked in tins (pans), but the majority are baked on the floor of the oven and are evenly crusty.

RIGHT: German rye

GERMAN SQUARE RYE

This is an easily recognized bread: it is a large square loaf that is cross-hatched on top. It is often just known as German rye, but unlike other ryes of that name it has a pleasant, gentle flavour, due partly to the blend of rye and wheat flours,

and also partly to the long fermentation process. Like most German ryes, it too uses the sourdough principle and consequently has a noticeable yet mild, sour flavour. It is good with German meats and sausages or with creamy cheeses.

LANDBROT

This is a traditional country bread, made using a large proportion of wheat flour but with enough rye to give a pale, beige-coloured crumb. It has an excellent sweet/sour flavour, partly from the rye and partly from the buttermilk, which is used instead of milk or water. It comes in all sorts of shapes and sizes, sometimes with a floury crust and sometimes without. Inside, the bread is always open-textured and slightly chewy, and is good with soups and stews.

ROGGENBROT

Unlike the *kastenbrot* of the same name, this crusty bread contains only rye grain and rye flour. It is a robust, sourdough loaf with a thick, chewy crust.

GERMAN RYE BREAD

There are many varieties of this sturdy loaf, including the well-known Bavarian rye. Rye breads come in various shapes and sizes, but are most often tin or bloomer-shaped. The loaf typically has more rye than usual, but wheat flour is

there too, for a lighter texture. Like many German breads, it is made by the sour-dough method. The culture is made by mixing rye flour with water to produce just the right balance of acids to work the dough. Although these cultures can last for many years if fed and reinvigorated correctly, most bakers will start a new culture every week, mainly so that they – and you – know what you are getting.

A 100 per cent rye bread contains, as you might expect, only rye flour and is therefore suitable for anyone with an allergy to wheat. This, too, uses the sour-dough method and has a dense texture and strong, sour flavour.

GEBILDBROTE (PICTURE BREAD)

Now something of a rarity, these breads can still be found in villages on festive occasions. The bread is moulded into complex shapes and patterns, normally with symbolic meanings. Loaves may be embossed with horses, deer, serpents, flowers and sheaves of wheat or they may be fashioned into shapes of men and women. The origin of this custom most likely dates from pagan times when bread would have been offered to appease the gods. Christianity also used breads in many rituals and many of the *gebildbrote* bear Christian symbols, such as crucifixes, loaves and fishes.

PRETZELS

Although extremely popular as snacks in America, and well known among the Jewish breads, pretzels are nevertheless German in origin. Like *gebildbrote,* pretzels have a symbolic meaning, which may have had its origins in pagan times. The distinctive knot shape is believed by some to have been a symbol for the solar cycle; others believe the crossed arms symbol-ize the Cross and that pretzels were originally made as a Lenten bread. Whatever the explanation, pretzels clearly have important significance in Germany and beyond – the same symbol of inter-locking rings is the sign of a baker's store throughout northern Europe.

Pretzels are almost always made using white flour and, according to a decree of 1256 in Landshut, it was a punishable

ABOVE: Stollen is a popular Christmas treat in many European countries. It is rich with fruit and often has a sweet marzipan centre.

offence for a baker to bake pretzels from anything but the finest white flour. Unlike the more familiar salted biscuit (crackers), German pretzels in many ways resemble a bagel. Along with the white flour, they contain yeast and milk and are poached, sprinkled liberally with sea salt and then baked until the crust is hard and golden. This salty, crunchy crust contrasts with the soft, sweet-flavoured crumb.

ROLLS

There is an enormous variety of German-style rolls. Most are made from white flour and may be sprinkled with caraway or poppy seeds. *Semmel,* with their star-shaped design on top, and *Eiweckerl* are mainly served at breakfast.

STOLLEN

There are many German sweet breads but perhaps the best-known and -loved is stollen, sold almost everywhere as a treat around Christmas. It is an oval-shaped loaf, which tapers at each end. The shape is said to represent the infant Jesus wrapped in swaddling clothes. The bread is packed with sultanas (golden raisins), currants and mixed (candied) peel, and is usually spiced and enriched with eggs, butter and milk. Almonds may be finely chopped and added to the dough with the fruit, or they may be ground and made into a paste that is then rolled into the bread, giving it a sweet, moist centre. Stollen is unfailingly delicious, although it is predictably on the calorific side.

FOUR CEREAL BREAD

This dark, solid loaf is made using a blend of cereals but always including both rye and wheat.

BELOW: Four cereal bread.

GOLDGRAIN

Sometimes called a *multigrained* loaf, this baguette-shaped loaf is made using wheat, rye, barley, oats, soya, linseed, sunflower seeds, wheat bran, semolina and millet. For all this vast array of ingredients it is not unduly heavy and it has a texture not dissimilar to a Granary (wholewheat) bread, with a wholesome, nutty flavour. Goldgrain sometimes is made with the addition of chopped walnuts. Both varieties are popular in health-conscious Germany and are becoming more easily available elsewhere. They are distributed by several producers.

BELOW: Mehrkorn is available as both a crusty bread and as a thinly sliced box bread.

GERMAN BREAD WITH CARAWAY SEEDS

Caraway is a favourite ingredient in German rye breads, adding its unmistakable aniseed flavour. Although often called "German rye with caraway" or "light rye with caraway", the bread does contain a large proportion of wheat flour, giving it a light texture and flavour.

KUGELHOPF

This bread belongs equally to the Alsace region of France and to Vienna in Austria. There are various ways of spelling *kugelhopf* and even more ways for making and baking it. In Alsace it is a savoury bread made with bacon, lard (shortening) and/or fromage blanc and cream cheese. The German and Austrian *kugelhopf,* by contrast, is a yeasted brioche-style bread, made using sultanas (golden raisins) and raisins and enriched with butter and eggs. A good *kugelhopf* has a delicious citrus flavour, provided by lemon rind and juice.

The *kugelhopf* is baked in a fluted mould with a central funnel, and the top billows out like a "kugel", or ball.

MEHRKORN

Mehrkorn means "more grain" and this bread is a multigrain loaf. The mixture of grains means that the bread is noticeably lighter than many of the principally rye breads.

AUSTRIAN BREADS

As you would expect, a large number of the most popular Austrian breads are similar, if not identical, to those of neighbouring Switzerland, Italy, and Germany. However, Austria may well have been responsible for many of the more elaborate continental breads. It was the Austrians who developed the *poolisch* or sponge method of leavening dough, also used in France. This was particularly popular for white breads or those using finer flours, and breads made by this method were noted for their excellent flavour. Not surprisingly, Vienna became the home of fine baking. Croissants are just one among many delicacies that may originally have come from the master bakers of Austria, although any French person will certainly disagree!

BAURNBROT

While Austria is paradise for all those who love rich breads and pastries, there are still country-style loaves to be found. Not least of these is *baurnbrot*, made using buckwheat and wheat flour and molasses, flavoured with caraway seeds and leavened using a rye sourdough starter. This makes for a robust and strongly flavoured loaf, which tastes best with simple foods, such as country cheeses, sausages and meats, or simply dunked in soup.

DUTCH BREADS

KORNKRACKER

Kornkracker can refer to either loaves or rolls. The bread is popular throughout Germany and Holland. The word means "cracked corn" and the bread is made with cracked whole grain wheat, together with malted wheat and seeds.

RIGHT: Kornkracker

DUTCH FRUIT LOAF

This lightly malted Granary (whole-wheat) loaf rich with fruit and sprinkled with sugar is popular with coffee at any time of the day. It is also a favourite treat for children and is sometimes served with a mild cheese, such as Edam or Gouda.

DUTCH CRISPBREADS

The Dutch enjoy crispbreads almost as much as the Scandinavians. They are usu-ally served at breakfast, eaten with cheese or smoked hams, or spread with jam or marmalade. The round breads that are commonly available outside The Netherlands are baked until completely crisp. They have a unique, vaguely sweet flavour, which is surprisingly good with savoury foods. Dutch crispbreads come in cylindrical packets and are generally avail-able everywhere.

FRISIAN SUGAR LOAF

This unusual sweet bread is made using whole sugar lumps that melt as the bread is baked to give delicious pockets of sweetness, which contrast with the cinnamon in the soft white crumb.

ABOVE: Dutch fruit bread

RIGHT: Dutch crispbreads – popular everywhere.

DUTCH ROGGEBROOD

Holland also has its own varieties of *kas-tenbrots* and *krustenbrots*. This box-style bread is similar to the German *roggen-brot*, made with rye flour and leavened using the sourdough method. It often con-tains molasses and is consequently very dark with a strong malty taste.

Holland even has its own pumpernickel which, like the German variety, contains 100 per cent rye flour. The Dutch pumper-nickel is a little sweeter than the German version, but with the same strong flavour. It is not for the faint-hearted!

SWISS BREADS

One of the least accessible and smallest countries of Western Europe, Switzerland has an extraordinary wealth of unusual and tasty breads. There are probably two explanations for this. First, the mountains that cover 70 per cent of Switzerland mean that, until quite recently, villages have existed in relative isolation, and rural traditions, such as baking and bread making, have endured, undiluted by commercialization and mass markets. The other significant factor is that four of Switzerland's five neighbours (the fifth is tiny Liechtenstein) – France, Germany, Italy and Austria – are home to most of the best breads in the world.

As well as producing many loaves that will be familiar to its neighbours, Switzerland has borrowed some of the best breads to develop its own specialities. These, too, reflect the influence of near neighbours and, in common with the pattern elsewhere, rye breads are baked in the north; soft white loaves in the south and east.

BELOW: Crusty bauerruch

APFELNUSSBROT

The name denotes the Germanic origins of this unusual bread, but it seems to be a distillation of a variety of traditions from France as well as Germany. The round, crusty loaf is made from a blend of grains including wheat, rye, barley and spelt, which points to a German influence, yet the apples and walnuts seem typically French and the bread is not unlike the *pain aux pommes* from France. The best loaves are said to be found in Valais, in the south of the country.

BANGELI

This crusty loaf is a cross between the French baguette and the long white loaves of Germany. It comes from Basel, a Swiss town on the border of France and Germany, which perhaps explains its hybrid appearance. It is a long loaf that looks rather rustic, with seven or eight horizontal slashes and a thick, floury crust. The bread is often cut into chunks to serve with fondue.

BAUERRUCH

Swiss bakers take an enormous pride in their work and some of the Swiss breads are beautifully crafted, for example the *bauerruch*, which is a rounded crusty loaf shaped in a swirl like a turban or a seashell. It is a fairly dense white or brown bread with a thick, golden crust.

PANIS LUNATIS

This means moon bread. In Switzerland, some believe it was the precursor to the croissant. Indeed moon bread was baked as long ago as the 8th century. Today Swiss bakers sell croissants only, but they always claim to have invented them.

SAKO

Although some wheat is grown in Switzerland, neither the soil nor the climate favour agriculture and the little wheat that was coaxed from the land was frequently blended with other grains to make tasty and healthy loaves. The *sako* is a round multigrain loaf made with eight different cereals. It is usually risen in a floured basket, then turned out for baking. *Sako* is often slashed off-centre across the top and is generally sprinkled with cracked wheat

or rolled oats. It is a somewhat dense loaf, excellent for mopping up soups.

ABOVE: The attractive and simple Swiss peasant loaf.

SWISS PEASANT LOAF

There are many variations on the theme of a Swiss rustic loaf, but most are round, free-form loaves, made with a blend of wheat and rye flours but with cracked rye and chopped walnuts giving the loaves a pleasant texture.

RIGHT: Healthy Vogel loaf

VOGEL LOAF

This is a proprietary Swiss loaf that is renowned for its healthy properties. It was developed over 30 years ago by a Swiss nutritionist, Dr Alfred Vogel. A multi-grain bread, it contains kibbled wheat, rye grain and bran, giving it a high fibre

Right: Zupfe is also known as Swiss braid.

where the tradition of plaiting bread came is not known, only that it is extremely old. It may have symbolized the braid of hair offered by the wife or widow of a warrior to ensure his safe return from battle. Shaped into a round, it could have represented the course of the sun, while the crescent may have signified the moon. The Swiss plaited breads are almost always yeast-leavened, made using white wheat flour, and may be plaited with three or more strands of dough. There is really no limit to the baker's art and the Swiss have a reputation for their skill with shaping bread.

GIPFELTEIG

These are essentially tiny croissants and are quite the best thing to eat for breakfast if you are visiting

Switzerland. They are so small – three or four will fit comfortably in your hand – and so delicious, that it is easy to consume far too many before you decide you have probably had enough! They resemble, and may be identical to, the tiny croissants you will be served in the Alsace area and other parts of western France and, like them, the bakers use lard (shortening) as well as butter in the dough to give a texture that is very soft. *Gipfelteig* are best eaten fresh and warm as they are, or spread with a little apricot jam or some tangy orange marmalade.

WEGGLITAG

These little rolls are often served for breakfast along with *gipfelteig*. The small, oval white rolls are always glazed with beaten egg and notched across the top with scissors to give a crenellated effect and a crunchy crust.

content, which is one of its main selling points. The whole and cracked grain gives the loaf plenty of texture, yet the flavour is not too strong, making it a popular choice for those who like their fibre to be subtle rather than overpowering.

ZUPFE (ZOPF)

Known variously as *zupfe*, *zopf* or Swiss braid, this is a plaited loaf made from a rich dough, which typically contains soured cream or milk, egg and butter. It has a glossy crust and beautifully light crumb. Like its neighbours, Austria and Germany, Switzerland has a great affection for these rich doughs, which are shaped, plaited (braided) or twisted into spectacular loaves. This is where the tradition of the Jewish *challah* – another plaited loaf – is believed to have evolved. Exactly from

Above and Below: Wegglitag and gipfelteig are a great way to start the day.

NORDIC BREADS

R ye, oats and barley were once the only crops that would grow in the cooler climate and acidic soils of northern Europe. While wheat was imported for the prosperous, for the majority of people bread was inevitably made using one type or a blend of these cereals. Rye, which contains gluten, was favoured for leavened bread since it would rise and produce a lighter loaf. In Norway, however, where there was a fondness for unleavened bread, oats and barley and sometimes pea-flour were for many centuries the favoured ingredients for making their popular *flatbrød*.

Nowadays, wheat can be grown in the more temperate parts of Denmark and Sweden, and of course, being widely imported, white breads are commonly available. Traditionally, the festive breads have always been made from the finest white flours. Scandinavians set great store by their festivals and each year buy or make their Christmas and Easter breads, along with a host of other breads made for celebrations in between.

White breads are particularly popular in the cities, but the Scandinavians continue to love their dark rye breads and visitors will find that there is a wide choice of breads – from the weird and

wonderful breads of Lapland to the *flatbrøds* of Norway, and the rich pumpernickel breads baked in Denmark.

RIGHT: Danish rye bread is lighter in texture and colour than German ryes.

DANISH BREADS

RYE BREAD

There are numerous types of Danish rye breads and you will need to sample a few to discover the ones you like best. Danish ryes tend to be lighter and sweeter than most German ryes. Molasses and malt extract are popular ingredients, adding to the dark colour, but this is tempered by the greater proportion of white wheat flour. Danish ryes also tend to contain a proportion of fat, either buttermilk or butter or both. This helps to

RIGHT: Rye breads are popular throughout Scandinavia.

RIGHT: The plaited tresse

preserve the loaf and gives a richer and more open-textured bread. Danish ryes are the popular breads for *smørrebrød* (the equivalent to the Swedish *smörgåsbord*), the buffet-style open sandwiches topped with meats and cheese.

KERNEBROD

A seeded loaf, normally made with a Granary meal, sprinkled liberally with sunflower seeds and linseeds.

TRESSE

This is a plaited (braided) white loaf, enriched with milk, eggs and butter. It may be sprinkled freely with poppy or sesame seeds and is popular throughout the year, although at one time this loaf was probably made for special occasions.

DANISH FESTIVE FRUIT LOAF (JULEKAGE)

This is one of the most famous of all the Danish Christmas loaves. Christmas is a hugely important festival in all parts of Scandinavia, not only for its Christian significance, but also because it heralds the halfway point of the long Nordic winter. Similar breads, filled with fruit, nuts and spices, and enriched with butter and eggs, are made all over Scandinavia. *Julekage* is traditionally spiced with vanilla and cardamom. Crushed sugar is then sprinkled over the top before baking and, finally, icing (confectioners') sugar is drizzled over the bread when it is cooked.

CARNIVAL BUNS (FASTERLAVNSBOILLER)

Any Dane will be able to tell you about these treats, which they will remember from their childhood and probably now make for their own children. They are traditionally made on the Monday before Shrove Tuesday, which is celebrated not only with breads and cakes but also with some games, including "beating a cat off the barrel", which involves children chasing each other and which thankfully has nothing to do with cats, in spite of its name. The little square or round buns are something like a cross between a bread and an English Yorkshire pudding, made with white flour and yeast and enriched with egg, butter and milk. Carnival buns are flavoured with cardamom and filled with almond paste and sometimes with chopped peel, and are normally liberally dusted with icing sugar.

SMØRREBRØD

The word simply means "buttered bread" but the famous Danish open sandwiches are so much more than that. Delicious toppings – their ingredients limited only by the imagination of the cook – are laid on thin slices of bread. The aim of the exercise is to produce a snack that is as appealing to the eye as it is to the stomach, and the results are as colourful as they are good to eat. Danish sour rye bread is the preferred base, although for some more delicate toppings, such as smoked salmon, baby shrimps, prawns or lobster, a crusty white bread is sometimes used. Fish and shellfish are favourite toppings, one of the most popular choices being pickled herring with marinated onion rings. Liver paste, salami, cheeses (including the famous blue cheese of Denmark), roast pork, hard-boiled eggs – the list of potential toppings is apparently limitless, as is the Danes' capacity for enjoying their favourite lunchtime snack.

NORWEGIAN AND SWEDISH BREADS

NORWEGIAN FLAT BREAD

Flatbrød is the oldest of all the Norwegian breads and was, until fairly recently, the bread most commonly eaten by the people of Norway. A long time ago these wafer-thin crispbreads would have been made with any cereal that was to hand – mostly oats, rye, barley or pea-flour, or a mixture of all these. The unleavened dough would have been rolled into very thin, large circles and baked on a griddle or on a stone over an open fire. The breads were known to last for months, even up to a year, and would be stored on the beams over the kitchen. These days the breads are factory-baked and sold ready-cut into convenient rectangles. Some bakers, however, continue to make their own, and in parts of Norway the large breads are served at harvest meals, dampened with a little water so they become pliable and can be wrapped around Norwegian sweet cheese or other suitable pieces of food.

NORWEGIAN WHOLEMEAL BREAD

This fine bread is made with whole wheat kernels, skimmed milk, yeast, cottage cheese and wholemeal (whole-wheat) flour, and is topped with crushed wheat.

RIGHT: Lomper is a soft flat bread cooked on a griddle.

LEFT: Flatbrød

LIMPA

Limpa is a Swedish favourite – a leavened rye loaf, sweetened with molasses or honey, flavoured with orange and lightly spiced with cardamom, cumin, fennel and anise. Since wheat flour makes up the greater proportion of flour, the loaf is not as heavy as some rye loaves, although it has the typical dense yet crumbly texture of rye breads. *Vortlimpa* is a far darker loaf than *limpa*, containing a greater proportion of rye flour together with the dark molasses. It, too, contains orange rind, either grated or finely chopped, and can also be made with ground or whole fennel seeds. In spite of the sweet molasses, this dark, savoury loaf is intended to be eaten with soft cheese or salted herring.

ROGBROD

Røgbröd is the traditional rye bread of Sweden, made in large flat loaves and often containing molasses, which has been valued by Sweden and the other Baltic states since it was first imported. Unlike the flat Norwegian ryes, *røgbröd* is a leavened bread, traditionally made using a sourdough method, but also using normal yeast. Buttermilk is often used instead of ordinary milk, adding to the acidic flavour of the bread, which is also flavoured with fennel or caraway seeds.

Ragbröd is much the same as *røgbröd* – made of rye and often containing molasses – but is shaped into a ring by being rolled out into a flat round and then having a hole cut in the middle. Traditionally, *ragbröd* would have been looped across the kitchen with string, and even today you may see them displayed in such a way in some bakeries.

LEFT: *Swedish krisprolls*

SWEDISH CARDAMOM BRAID
This is a delicious sweet fruit bread, made with white flour, enriched with milk, eggs and butter and spiced with the distinctive flavour of cardamom.

SWEDISH CARAWAY BREAD
This is a half-sweet, half-savoury white bread, made with a little sugar and butter, yet given a subtle savoury flavour by the caraway seeds.

ST LUCIA ROLLS
Throughout Scandinavia, the days leading up to Christmas are as much a time of festivity as Christmas Day itself. St Lucia Day (13 December) is celebrated widely in Sweden. Children dress up in white and visit each other's homes. They wear crowns of glowing candles, symbolizing the light that will come once winter is over. The favourite food for the children are the little St Lucia rolls, traditionally made with saffron and enriched with eggs, butter and milk. Each bread is shaped in the letter "S" and topped with a raisin.

KNACKERBROD
Sweeter than the Finnish *knackebrod,* these Swedish flat breads are made with rolled oats and taste a little like sweet Scottish oatcakes. Unlike Scottish oatcakes, however, they are leavened using bicarbonate of soda (baking soda) and buttermilk, and are baked in the oven.

SCANDINAVIAN STAR
This unusual and pretty bread is a modern adaptation of some of the best Scandinavian baking traditions. It is made using a blend of white and Granary (wholewheat) flours but its fine flavour is due mainly to the sponge method of making the dough, which allows the flavours to develop, and the longer-than-usual rising. Sunflower seeds and linseeds are added for flavour and the bread is liberally sprinkled with sesame seeds before being stamped into its distinctive star shape. The bread has a good crisp crust, while the crumb is soft with a rich nutty flavour. It makes an excellent breaking bread, which is appropriate since pulling off pieces of bread is preferred in Scandinavia to slicing bread conventionally.

SCANDINAVIAN CRISPBREADS
There are many Scandinavian crispbreads, ranging from crisp rusks to wafer-thin biscuits. Norwegian crispbreads are made mainly with whole rye, although there are also many made with a blend of wheat flours. *Krisprolls* are popular in Sweden, eaten at almost any time of the day, but particularly at breakfast. They are baked until entirely crisp and have a noticeably sweet flavour.

LEFT: *The Scandinavian star bread, with its liberal sprinkling of sesame seeds, looks attractive and has an excellent flavour.*

FINNISH AND ARCTIC BREADS

FINNISH KNACKEBROD

This thin, cracker-like bread with its characteristic central hole is made using a blend of rye and corn. Freshly made *knackebrod* are crisp and are delicious with a fresh goat's cheese or smoked salmon. *Wiborgs kringla* are also from Finland and are similar in many ways to Germany's pretzels: the entwined strands, like a lover's knot, appear in bakers' shop signs in Finland. The enriched yeast bread was traditionally baked on straw, and even today the bread is cooked in a similar way, and it is a feature of the bread that bits of straw need to be pulled off the bottom before it is eaten.

FINNISH EASTER BREAD

For most of Scandinavia, and certainly for those who were better off, most of the original festive breads were made from what was considered the best flour, namely white wheat flour. In the poorer villages and towns, however, most people had to make do with what they could find – usually rye, barley and oatmeal. For festivals special breads were made to

LEFT: Icelandic bread

celebrate using only these three cereals. Easter bread was a particular favourite, moulded in a traditional round, and made with yogurt and honey or molasses and packed with raisins, sultanas (golden raisins) and nuts. Easter bread is unlikely to be widely available in the cities, but should you travel through villages at the right time of year, you may find these dark specialities with their shiny tops.

HALKAKA

This heavy black rye bread was once the only food for a number of Finnish peasants during the winter. Extremely large loaves were baked and then gradually eaten over the next few months until the bread was finished and it was time to bake once more.

RIESKA

Further north in Finland, the leavened breads give way to hard flat loaves. *Rieska* is a Finnish word and comes from Lapland, a region that extends across the northern parts of Norway, Sweden and Finland, and most of which is within the Arctic Circle. *Rieska* are round breads, mostly fairly small and rather flattish. They are normally made with oats or barley, but can also be made with potatoes or any starchy food. Although there is no wheat or rye to raise the dough, they do use a little yeast or baking powder, which makes them slightly less dense.

ICELANDIC BREAD

Most Icelandic breads are based on rye. Various loaves are made, from the crusty loaf with open crumb pictured above to the pancake-like *flatbrauð*, which are enjoyed with *skyr*, a fresh curd cheese that resembles yogurt.

POLAR FLAT BREAD

Called "polar rounds" or "polar thins", these small breads are easily available, sold in many large supermarkets or in delicatessens as a style of crispbread. They contain a mixture of rye and wheat flours and have a pleasant, slightly nutty flavour. They go well with strong-flavoured cheese, such as goat's cheese.

ABOVE: Polar flat breads are now made commercially.

EASTERN EUROPEAN AND RUSSIAN BREADS

In the cool latitudes of northern Europe, rye, buckwheat and barley were the principal cereals for centuries. Large dark breads made from these flours were not only the staple food, but during severe famine were often the only food for all but the most wealthy. "If we have bread and *kvas* (beer) what more do we need?" goes a Russian saying. Links with southern Europe meant that wheat flour gradually became popular, at first only among the aristocracy but later filtering through to the general population, where the flour was especially used for festive bread and cakes. Today, thanks to genetic manipulation, wheat is widely grown in Russia, Poland and other parts of eastern Europe, but the fondness for breads made from rye and buckwheat continues to this day and these traditional breads are still the mainstay for rural communities.

BLINIS

Although not strictly breads, these little buckwheat pancakes were the equivalent of festive sweet breads in a country where buckwheat rather than wheat was the principal crop. Buckwheat was widely cultivated in Russia in the past. At *Maslenitsa*, the week before Lent, large numbers of blinis were consumed. They are just as popular now, eaten at any time of the year, most famously with *smetana* (a sour cream) and caviare, although also delicious with crème fraîche and smoked salmon. Blinis resemble in shape and size a Scotch pancake, but are normally far darker in colour with a savoury, slightly bitter flavour from the buckwheat flour. The most authentic blinis are made entirely of buckwheat but many are now a compromise with a blend of buckwheat and plain flour. The best blinis are yeast-risen, made using buttermilk or yogurt. Store-bought blinis may have used baking powder instead and some contain so little buckwheat flour that they hardly merit the name "blini".

LEFT: Polish wholemeal rye uses wholemeal flour with a proportion of rye.

RIGHT: Polish rye bread

Pre-wrapped bought pancakes are best heated slightly in the microwave or wrapped in a cloth in the oven, so that they warm up without drying out.

BARLEY BREAD

Barley bread has long been baked in regions stretching from Finland to the shores of the Black Sea in the Ukraine. Barley made a change from the dark rye breads although, since it contains no gluten, loaves were consequently dense and heavy. Even today, many of the barley breads from the countries around the Baltic Sea are sturdy loaves, made with a blend of barley and wholemeal (whole-wheat) flour. The bread is generally moist and chewy. Cabbage leaves are sometimes used to line the baking tins (pans), a time-honoured trick which keeps the crust moist.

POLISH RYE

As the name implies, this is made from rye, although some wheat flour is generally added. This bread, however, is made from refined rye meal, unlike Polish black rye which uses a coarser rye and wheat meal. Although they might sound not particularly appetizing, both breads are pleasantly flavoured.

ABOVE: Once the basic loaf for all poor families, Polish sourdough is now baked by craft bakers and is enjoyed by all bread enthusiasts.

RIGHT: Caraway seeds give Polish caraway a noticeable aniseed flavour.

POLISH BLACK BREAD

This is a large flattish and round bread, eaten in Poland, Lithuania and Latvia. Wheat flour is added to give some volume to the loaf, but it is principally made with buckwheat and has a distinctive, rather bitter flavour.

POLISH SOURDOUGH

This is a classic northern peasant-style rye bread. Originally, oats and barley may well have been added to the rye to make a loaf that would feed the family for as long as possible. Each household would take its grain to be milled and the bread would then be set to rise in proving troughs. The blend of grain plus the use of troughs gave a noticeably different flavour and texture to each loaf, from family to family and even from loaf to loaf.

POLISH CARAWAY BREAD

A traditional Polish medium rye bread, this is made with rye and wheat flour flavoured with caraway seeds.

ESTONIAN RYE

This is a sourdough bread made entirely with rye. It is a tin-shaped bread with a distinctive flavour arising from both the rye and the natural leaven.

SWEET PUMPERNICKEL

There are many styles of pumpernickel breads, all made entirely or principally from rye.

RUSSIAN BRAIDED BREAD

Braided yeasted loaves made using white flour are among the most familiar breads of eastern Europe. They are similar, and sometimes identical, to the Jewish *challah* since this part of Europe was home to many Jewish people. Many of these spectacular breads are enriched with milk, eggs and butter and are made as festive breads for special occasions. Others are plainer, sometimes using milk to obtain a softer crust, and are frequently sprinkled with poppy seeds.

RUSSIAN BLACK BREAD

Bread was by far the most important food in Russia until this century. In the 19th century, the Russian peasant ate on average 1.5kg/3–3½ lb of bread a day and even more at harvest time. White breads are now popular in Moscow and other large cities but it is the ryes that are the best-known and -loved of Russian breads. There are numerous types of black breads, varying in colour, density and sour/sweet flavour. Molasses, favoured throughout the Baltic States, is frequently added and originally the breads would have been made on the sourdough principle, although some today are yeast-leavened. Many are similar to German rye breads, since techniques and styles cross borders as easily as weather. A classic Russian black bread, however, is usually made with an equal blend of rye and wheat flour, using a sourdough starter. It

ABOVE: Estonian rye is one of the few tin breads baked in this region.

RIGHT: Russian black bread owes its dark colour to molasses and rye.

is spiced and oven bottom-baked. A round loaf, it has an attractive, coarse top. It is normally roughly broken rather than cut and is often eaten with soups and stews. In the Ukraine a version of a black rye bread is known as *chenyi khilb,* which is another large round loaf.

ROSSISKY

This is among the better-known Russian rye breads and is now made and sold out-side Russia in some supermarkets, delicatessens and health food stores. It is 100 per cent rye bread, made using a sourdough starter, and has a distinctive yet pleasant flavour.

BORODINSKY

This small but compact loaf, traditionally flavoured with crushed coriander seeds, is becoming increasingly available outside Russia. Consequently, it represents, for many, the essence of Russian bread.

The story goes that the wife of a Russian general, Marshal Mikhail Kutuzov, made this sweet, aromatic bread for the army, which was defending Borodino, outside Moscow, from the onslaught of Napoleon's army. Although Napoleon then entered Moscow, the French were shortly forced to withdraw, which led to Napoleon's downfall. The Battle of Borodino thus became enshrined in Russian history and the bread was named

to remember both the eventual victory and the 42,000 men who lost their lives.

The Borodinsky loaf is baked, like the German box breads, in a sealed container; but unlike them it is cooked for only some 2½ hours, and uncovered for the final 15–30 minutes so that the bread is slightly risen with a firm crust. It is made either entirely with dark rye or with a blend of rye and wheatmeal. Barleymeal is also often used, giving an earthy flavour, while buttermilk or yogurt is also occasionally added and enhances the natural sour-dough flavour. Molasses, however, is traditionally used and malt is frequently added so that the bread acquires a sweet flavour, albeit with distinct sour/savoury overtones. Borodinsky is the most expen-sive and most popular of the Russian rye breads, and is served thinly sliced with strongly flavoured fish, such as pickled herring or smoked salmon.

RUSSIAN POTATO BREAD WITH CARAWAY SEEDS

Potatoes were another mainstay for the Russian peasant; breads were often made by using a mixture of a grain and potatoes that had been cooked and mashed. If the mixture included wheat, a flattish but loaf-shaped bread could be made. Caraway seeds were a popular flavouring.

HUNGARIAN CHRISTMAS BREAD

Called *makos es dios kalacs* in Hungarian, this is a popular festive enriched white bread, with the dough rolled around poppy seeds and raisins.

BALABUSKY

These little rolls speckled with caraway seeds are a speciality of the Ukraine, a region known for the variety of its breads. The rolls combine rye and wheat flours in varying proportions, but are made with sour cream, which gives a pleasant acidic flavour. Sour cream and curd cheese are an inheritance from the Tartars who invaded Russia and the Ukraine from Asia in the 13th century. The liking for sour cream, used in bread making and served with bread, is a feature of much eastern European cooking.

KOLACH (KALACH)

Kolach (kalach) is a sweet yeasted white bread, popular at Christmas in Bulgaria and Russia and especially in St Petersburg where it was said it should only be made from the water transported to the city from the Moskva river. It is normally plaited, although in the Ukraine and Moldova it is often formed into a round, like the sun – a reminder of warmer days to come.

KULICH

Kulich is the traditional Russian Easter cake. Apparently, in Tsarist Russia

RIGHT: Rossisky (back) and Borodinsky (front) are the cream of Russian breads.

labourers were not permitted to walk through the kitchen in case their heavy steps caused the dough to fall or the bread to collapse in the oven. The bread is similar to a brioche, made with white flour, eggs, butter and milk and rich with raisins, candied peel, angelica and chopped almonds. The tall, round bread is either glazed or iced and then decorated with glacé (candied) cherries, angelica or crystallized fruit. It is served, unusually, by slicing off the top and then slicing horizontally again for eating. The top is then replaced to keep the cake fresh for as long as possible.

The cake was also baked for Remembrance Monday, which is the Russian equivalent to All Souls' Day (2 November), when traditionally it would have been taken to the church in order to be blessed by the priest.

KRENDEL

Krendel or *kolindet* is a popular Russian sweet bread. With its intertwining loops, its shape is reminiscent of a pretzel and, similarly, has a significance that has been lost over the years. These breads were popular for birthdays and to celebrate name-days. They were also given to children on Christmas Eve so they may have been connected with the winter solstice. They are yeast-leavened, made with white flour and enriched with eggs, butter and cream. The breads have a deliciously soft, cake-like consistency and are sometimes served for tea in restaurants or at a *chaikhana* (tea house).

CZECHOSLOVAKIAN HOSKA

Another festive bread, this braided loaf is often decorated with whole almonds and then glazed with egg before and during cooking, so that it bakes to a beautiful golden hue. The bread is quite spectacular and no mean feat for the baker. The three tiers of braids are made successively smaller so that the braids balance on top of each other.

UKRAINIAN RYE

The Ukraine is renowned for its huge variety of breads. It is the second largest country in Europe, after Russia, and almost the entire country is one vast plain of extremely fertile black soils. Once known as the bread basket of the USSR, the Ukraine has a rich tradition of bread making. Emigré bakers in Britain and America, as well as European bread specialists, produce some excellent breads. A popular Ukrainian loaf is a sourdough bread made with a half rye, half wheat flour blend. It is baked on the sole of the oven and has a good chewy crust and a noticeably sour flavour.

RIGHT: Ukrainian rye is hugely popular wherever these Slav people have settled.

THE BREADS OF GREECE, CYPRUS AND TURKEY

Greece has a wonderful array of breads, arising from historical and geographical influences. Here, not only are there the Arabian-style breads of the Ottoman Empire, but also indigenous breads with a long history, which are still baked, particularly on the islands, by people who keep these traditions alive. On some of the Aegean Islands, up until very recently, the wheat and barley harvested by smallholders would be carried to the windmill for milling into flour. The dough would then be made and shaped, before being taken to the village oven for baking. Such traditions have now almost entirely died out, and in the cities the bakeries are as sophisticated as those anywhere else in Europe. But in many small villages, on the islands or in the mountains, people still buy the simple but large white crusty bread, which is frequently still baked in an old brick oven, the brushwood being collected by the baker or his family each evening ready for the next day's baking.

Throughout Greece, local bakers produce their own particular bread, which necessarily becomes a favourite with their customers. In the cities, the more enterprising bakeries produce a wide range of breads flavoured with raisins, olives and herbs, but among the islands and in the mountains, most loaves continue to be of the plain, farmhouse variety – large and crusty and sometimes sprinkled with sesame seeds. The bread has a slightly coarse texture to it, which makes it excellent for mopping up sauces and dressings.

Travelling eastwards from Greece, the leavened breads of Europe give way to the characteristic flat breads of the Middle East. However, inevitably there are breads that are common to Greece and Turkey, partly because of the crossover of ideas and partly because some breads, such as pitta, are so versatile that their popularity endures.

BREADSTICKS

Although similar to Italian *grissini*, Greek and Turkish breadsticks are somewhat chunkier, although just as crunchy. They are mostly sprinkled with sesame or poppy seeds, or may be made using fennel, which gives them a noticeable aniseed flavour. *Koulouria* are similar but the bread has been formed into rings, like pretzels. Sold by itinerant street vendors from their large wicker baskets, these too are often liberally sprinkled with sesame seeds, in which case they are referred to as *thessalonikis*.

PAN BREAD

You are only likely to come across this bread, called *tiganópsoma* in Greek, if you visit the delightful Greek island of Santorini, believed by some to be the site of the lost world of Atlantis. It is a simple unleavened bread, mixed to a thick batter and combined with onions and tomatoes before being fried.

GREEK CELEBRATION BREADS

Bread has religious significance all over the world, but nowhere more so than in Greece. Almost all of the important days in the religious calendar have their own speciality bread – some rich with fruit, eggs and butter, others completely plain, depending on the holy day that is being celebrated.

Prosforo (holy bread) is the bread of the Greek Mass, prepared by bakers every Saturday and taken to the church on Sunday by a member of the congregation. The large, round white loaf is stamped with the church seal and is the Host of the Communion, shared out by the priest to the faithful during the Mass.

LEFT: Breadsticks

RIGHT: Daktyla is a popular Greek bread.

On Clean Monday, which is the first day of Lent in the Greek Orthodox Church, the *lagana* is the centrepiece of a traditional meal of seafood and salads. Clean Monday is so-called since on this day Greek house-wives are expected to scrub the kitchens and all utensils, to make sure nothing remains of Celebration – the three-week long festival that precedes the fasting of Lent. Appropriately, the *lagana* is a completely plain unleavened bread, made by local bakers solely for this one day of the year. The dough is formed into a large oval and then sprinkled with sesame seeds before baking.

Tsoureki is the famous Greek Easter bread. The yeasted bread is made from an enriched dough flavoured with orange and spices. It can be coiled into a round, but is more frequently made into a long plait (braid) and then sprinkled with almonds and sesame or caraway seeds and deco-rated with the characteristic red hard-boiled eggs. If you visit Greece just before Easter, you will find packets of red-dyed eggs sold everywhere. They sym-bolize the Resurrection and are knocked together after the Midnight Mass on Easter Saturday evening with the words, "Christ is Risen". On many of the Greek islands, where old customs still continue, *tsoureki* is the traditional Easter gift from children to their godpar-ents. Another festive and enriched bread is the *christopsomo*, the Greek Christmas bread. The top is decorated with a large cross, fashioned from the dough, the ends of which encircle cherries or walnuts.

OLIVE BREAD (ELIOTI)

Originally this bread was a Lenten food for the priests of the Eastern Orthodox Church, although now *elioti* is produced all over the country and can be enjoyed at any time of the year. It is gen-erally a white bread, enriched with a little olive oil, flavoured with marjoram or oregano and studded with black olives.

DAKTYLA

This unmistakable loaf is a style of bread that belongs equally to Greece, Cyprus and Turkey. Its defining characteristic is the liberal addition of nigella seeds in the bread itself, and the white sesame and black nigella seeds sprinkled over

LEFT: There is a rich variety of white breads in Greece, often sprinkled with sesame seeds.

BELOW:
Ekmek

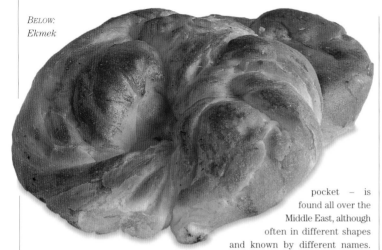

the top. The bread is oval and is normally large. It has deep slashes along the crust and looks like a large bloomer. It has a slightly peppery flavour thanks to the nigella seeds, and an open, coarse texture.

CILICIAN BREAD

Available now in many countries, these small flat breads sprinkled with cheese and spices are like miniature pizzas.

PITTA (PIDE)

Pitta breads, or *pide* to give them their Turkish name, are probably the best-known Greek and Turkish breads. This style of bread – flat and baked so that it contains a pocket – is found all over the Middle East, although often in different shapes and known by different names. Although pitta is a flat bread, it is not an unleavened bread. There is little crumb but the crust is soft and it is leavened with yeast; the flatness and characteristic pocket, called the *mutbag*, are due to the method of baking – ideally in an extremely hot clay oven. Pitta breads are widely eaten outside of Greece and Turkey, used as they are intended for stuffing with meats and vegetables. In restaurants in Istanbul, *pide* are served straight from the oven, stuffed with chunks of lamb that has been cooked over hot embers on a nearby spit, and with yogurt and mint. There is a huge range of different pitta breads available, for example wholemeal (whole-wheat) pittas, round mini pittas, pittas flavoured with herbs or sprinkled with sesame seeds. They are best eaten warm and, when store-bought, should be sprinkled with a little water and then placed in a hot oven or under the grill (broiler) until they begin to puff up.

EKMEK

This is a large round or oval leavened bread, often dimpled like an Italian focaccia and made simply with a plain white dough. Like pitta bread, the crust is soft and is used either for stuffing for sandwiches, or using as a scoop for picking up food. *Ekmek* can also refer to other breads – the word *ekmek* simply means "bread". In Turkey you will find numerous longish loaves, sometimes made using wholemeal, but normally white flour. More elaborate *ekmeks*, baked in rounds or sprinkled with sesame seeds, can be found in bakeries in the large cities.

BELOW: Sutlu ekmek

RIGHT: Pitta bread is served almost everywhere in Greece and Turkey.

TURKESTAN BREAD

This is a proprietary loaf sold in Britain but said to be based on the bread made by Turkoman tribes who lived in the Turkestan region around the Caspian Sea.

SIMITS

These little crusty golden bread rings are sold in almost every town in Turkey, and generally first thing

ABOVE: Many Turkish bakers still use wood-burning ovens. Breads, such as pide (right) and tuzsuz (left), cook quickly with a beautifully flavoured crust and soft crumb. Hashas (centre) is a large loaf that is cooked as the oven begins to cool.

in the morning when the *simit* seller takes his wares down to the harbour and into the market to entice workers and tourists alike. *Simits* are closely related to bagels, indeed they clearly look like them, and in fact an authentic *simit* is made in the same way as a bagel, being first poached in boiling water before being sprinkled with

LEFT: Simits coated with sesame seeds.

ABOVE: Turkestan bread

sesame seeds and baked. Until quite recently, the *simit* seller would carry the rings piled high on a tray on his head or looped on to long sticks, but nowadays, food regulations mean that *simits* are more likely to be found wheeled around under glass.

THE BREADS OF THE MIDDLE EAST AND NORTH AFRICA

—

Apart from in Morocco, which bestrides Arabia and western Europe, almost all the breads of this enormous region are versions of flat breads. Tradition and culture play a part here. In many of these regions people have always led a nomadic existence, living in tents and moving frequently from place to place. There was never any time nor inclination for plates or cutlery and when it came to eating, bread was used both as a food in its own right and as a means of conveying other food to the mouth. In addition, fuel was scarce and bread had to be cooked quickly while the fire was hot. Flat breads that cooked in minutes were a far better option than large, sturdy loaves. Even today, clay ovens almost identical to those depicted on walls of ancient tombs can still be found in some of the smaller villages of Egypt, Iran and Turkey. The ovens are fuelled with wood, corn kernels or even camel dung and, when they are hot, the flattened dough is baked against the sides of the walls.

Although the bread is flat, Middle Eastern bread is generally not unleavened, apart from rare exceptions, such as the

BELOW: The flat breads of the Middle East can be indistinguishable from each other. These khoubiz are very similar to the Egyptian aiysh.

Arabian crisp bread *ragayig*. The ancient Egyptians mastered the art of leavening bread and by the 12th century BC, 40 kinds of breads and pastries were available to upper-class Egyptians from their bakeries. Wheat has always been the preferred grain. It is indigenous to Turkey and the Middle East, and the first wheat to be cultivated came from this region.

AIYSH

Aiysh is the Egyptian word for "life" and these flat round loaves must be one of the oldest breads known to mankind. We know that as long ago as 1500 BC, *aiysh* was made and sold by Egyptian bakers and the same baking methods are still used today in some parts of the country. The bread is similar to pitta bread, but smaller and thicker. It should be made with wholemeal (whole-wheat) flour. This same bread is found throughout the Middle East. The shape varies and the size ranges from 15cm/6in to 30cm/12in rounds, or ovals of up to 38cm/15in. In Yemen the bread is known as *saluf*; in Jordan and Palestine as *shrak;* and as *aiysh shami* in Syria. The bread is delicious when freshly cooked, puffing up to leave a hollow centre and a soft crust.

KHOUBIZ (KHOBZ)

This bread from the Levant and Arabian peninsula, means simply "bread" in Arabian and is virtually identical to Egyptian *aiysh*. Flat and slightly leavened, it is made in rounds varying between 15cm/6in and 30cm/12in in diameter. Originally made with a finely ground wholemeal flour similar to chapati flour, it is now more often made using white flour.

BARBARI

These white breads from Iran can be oval, rectangular or round in shape, varying from small breads, about 10cm/4in long, to much larger breads measuring up to 30cm/12in. All are flattish breads and the loaves are often slashed four or five times like the French *fougasse* to give a fretwork effect. They may be brushed with oil before baking, and spiced versions with cumin or caraway seeds scattered on top are sometimes to be found.

MANKOUSH (MANNAEESH)

Spelt in many different ways, this is the typical Lebanese version of *khoubiz*. Here the bread is rolled into 13cm/5in rounds and indented slightly in the middle so that it is concave. It is then brushed with olive oil and *za'atar*, a blend of sesame seeds,

RIGHT: Barbari are sometimes called Persian flat breads.

unleavened. Like *lavash*, this is a large flat bread, which is quite crisp and brittle when cooked. Almost certainly the most ancient of all breads, predating even *aiysh* and *khoubiz*, *ragayig* is nevertheless still eaten today, cooked in the same way as *lavash* until it is crisp and sometimes further dried in the sun. *Nane lavash* is oval-shaped with a softer texture and is a cross between *lavash* and an Indian naan.

thyme, marjoram and *sumac*, a spice made from the dried red berries of a bush native to Sicily and western Asia. This herb and spice blend has an unusual sour flavour, thanks mainly to the *sumac*.

LAVASH

Lavash is one of the largest of the Middle Eastern flat breads. It can be round or oval, is extremely thin and can be up to 60cm/2ft in diameter. The bread came originally from Armenia and Iran, although its popularity has spread and it is widely eaten all over the Middle East. The dough is often taken by villagers to the local bakery to be slowly baked in clay ovens called *furunji*. Alternatively, it is baked in a *sorj*, a dome-covered oven like an inverted

BELOW: Flat breads, such as this mankoush from the Lebanon, cook quickly and are ideal in lands where fuel is scarce.

wok. Cooked in this way, the bread becomes brittle and crisp and is generally eaten straight away, torn in large pieces. *Lavash* can be unleavened or leavened, but its close relative, *ragayig*, is always

PIDEH

This is an Armenian version of the Turkish *pide*; it is always made using wholemeal (whole-wheat) flour. The rolled-out breads are sprinkled with sesame seeds before being baked in the oven.

MOROCCAN AND TUNISIAN BREADS

There are several types of Moroccan bread, mostly variations on the same theme. The wheat flour dough can be white, wholemeal or a blend of both, and may be enriched with olive or peanut oil. It may be leavened naturally, although yeasts are more commonly used these days. Either way, the loaf is almost always round and flattish and equally invariably, is made by wives and daughters at home. In the past, and even now among some families, the unbaked loaves are carried to the local bakery to be cooked.

MOROCCAN HOLIDAY BREAD

Cornmeal, together with pumpkin and sunflower seeds, makes this a tasty bread. It is baked for special occasions.

TUNISIAN KESRET

This version of the Arabian bread, *khoubiz*, is mainly distinguished by the fact that it is cooked in a tagine, a North African earthenware cooking pot.

MELLA

This round flat bread, made by Tunisian nomads and sometimes containing caraway seeds, is covered with sand before being placed on the embers of a fire.

MARRAKESH SPICED BREAD

Moroccan cuisine reveals a number of cultural influences. France's short but significant domination with its invasion in the middle of the 19th century is noticeable in a number of spheres. French is still an important language in Morocco and many dishes clearly owe their inspiration to French cuisine, albeit with spicy flavours that are entirely local. Marrakesh spiced bread owes much to the French brioche – made with a yeasted white dough and enriched with butter and sometimes eggs – yet it is very much a product of Morocco. Flower water, either orange or rose, gives it a strongly perfumed taste and it is also sugary sweet, especially when served with honey or jam.

JEWISH BREADS

You do not have to travel far to enjoy this rich selection of breads. Wherever there is a Jewish community, a huge range of their particular breads will be produced, both for daily eating and for festivals and celebrations. The other singular aspect of Jewish breads, in contrast to English or French breads, for example, is that by definition, they do not belong to one country or region. Jewish cuisine embraces an enormous spectrum of culinary traditions, ranging across eastern and central Europe, through the Mediterranean, the Middle East, north-east Africa and India.

Visit a Jewish delicatessen and you will find a surprising number of loaves bearing a close resemblance to the breads of Germany, Russia or eastern Europe. The harmonization of ideas that occurs when people become neighbours is particularly apparent with age-old traditions such as bread making, and cultures are decidedly richer for it.

ABOVE: Rich challah spirals

CHALLAH

There are many variations on this spectacular festive bread with its deep brown crust and soft white crumb. Challah is traditionally made for the Sabbath or for other Jewish holidays and while it is most often seen plaited (braided), it can be shaped into spirals or wreaths, or baked in a tin (pan). The dough is made using eggs and vegetable oil, which gives it a soft texture somewhere between that of a brioche and a soft white loaf. It is normally slightly sweetened, with either sugar or honey; the sweeter loaves also being stuffed with raisins. The most popular *challahs*, however, are simply liberally sprinkled with poppy seeds, which is one of their most characteristic features.

In Orthodox Jewish families two loaves of *challah* are placed on the traditional embroidered tablecloth. A blessing is said over the bread, before it is broken and handed to members of the family. The Hebrew word for "blessing" is *brachah*, which derives from the Ashkenazi (eastern European) word for plaited bread. The two loaves represent the manna sent down by God to the Israelites after leaving Egypt.

Challah can be plaited with three, six or twelve strands of dough. At Rosh Hashanah, it is customary to have round *challahs*, often sweetened with honey and sometimes enriched with raisins or sultanas (golden raisins). On the eve of Yom Kippur, *challah* is baked in the shape of wings, a ladder or raised arms, symbolizing prayers being made to heaven.

ABOVE: A plaited challah

BOULKAS

These are small roll-sized *challahs*, shaped into rounds, plaits (braids) or spirals and made especially for weddings. However, they are often baked and sold by large bakeries for any occasion.

BAGELS

The bagel – "the roll with a hole" – is the customary bread at Bar Mitzvahs although nowadays they can be bought almost anywhere and enjoyed literally at any time of the year. Their unique feature, apart from the central hole, is that they are briefly poached in boiling water, or steamed for a minute, before being finally baked. The process means that the dough puffs up in the water but

BELOW: Boulkas

does not rise any more during baking, producing the characteristic dense texture. Even savoury-style bagels contain some sugar or malt extract, and a little is also added to the water during boiling. The bagel is then glazed with egg or egg white before being baked to give it a glossy crust and the result is a noticeably sweet-flavoured bread with a compact crumb and a chewy crust.

Bagels are almost always yeast-leavened, but beyond that there are countless variations. They can be made with egg, may contain cheese and/or butter, or may be made with just

BELOW: Mixed bagels

RIGHT: Shabbat bread

Jewish culture. The small, rather solid roll is basically a small dimpled bun, stuffed with fried onions. The *baily* earns its name from the city of Bailystok in Poland, which was home to many Jews before they were forced to flee due to persecution.

SUMSUMS

Sumsums are the traditional breads of the Syrian Jews and look similar to bagels, although these little rolls with a hole are not boiled before baking, but go straight into the oven after shaping. *Sumsums* are usually sprinkled with sesame seeds.

SHABBAT BREAKFAST BREAD

Known as *kubaneh*, this unique bread is always cooked overnight so it is ready for the Sabbath breakfast. The bread is from the Yemen, which has its own Jewish cuisine, and is a yeasted white dough, enriched with butter and sweetened with sugar or honey. The rolled-out dough is spread with more butter and then rolled

water and margarine. Like so many Jewish breads, the bagel seems to have originated in Europe – created, it is said, by a Polish Jew in the Middle Ages to celebrate winning a war. Centuries later, such culinary techniques were taken to New York where many Jewish immigrants settled at the turn of the 20th century. The best bagels in the world are considered to be found in New York bakeries.

Bagels are mostly eaten sliced into two flat rings. They can be plain or toasted, and are commonly spread with cream cheese, topped with lox (smoked salmon) and then eaten as a sandwich. There is, of course, no end of other fillings, kosher or not, and similarly there are countless variations. In a Jewish bakery, you are likely to find wholemeal (whole-wheat), rye and Granary versions, along with bagels sprinkled with poppy, sesame, caraway and sunflower seeds, sea salt or chopped onion. Among the many sweet bagels, which are widely available prepacked in supermarkets as well as bakeries, are cinnamon and raisin-flavoured treats.

BAILYS

These are almost as popular in North America as the bagel, and both come from the same Ashkenazi

LEFT: Plain bagels

RIGHT: Matzos

JEWISH RYE BREAD

There are many varieties of Jewish rye bread, most of which originated in Eastern Europe, where rye is such a popular grain. The sourdough starter for this well-known rye is made using the crusts of previous rye breads. It is then combined with white and rye flour and caraway seeds.

MANDEL BREAD (MANDELBROT)

This is a strange kind of hybrid – part loaf, part teabread and part biscuit. The word *mandelbrot* is Yiddish for "almond bread", and the dough is fashioned into a rough loaf shape before being baked. It is not a yeasted bread but is risen using self-raising (self-rising) flour or baking powder and, being enriched with eggs, flavoured with lemon and vanilla and studded with almonds, it is more like a biscuit than an ordinary bread. After baking it is cut into thick diagonal slices and baked again, which transforms the loaf/teabread into chunky biscuits. Mandel breads were once extremely popular among many Jewish people throughout the world, served with wine or other drinks. However, their popularity has declined over the years and, while still baked by some Jewish bakers, they are difficult to find nowadays outside Israel and North America.

up in a spiral and then steamed in a covered baking dish in a very low oven for up to 12 hours. It can be served with sugar but is also popular Yemeni-style with spicy or garlic chutneys.

MATZO

Matzo is a piece of unleavened bread that is served in Jewish households during Passover, Feast of the Unleavened Bread. The flat, brittle bread is made and baked with great speed and under strict dietary regulations by Jewish bakers to ensure that the flour and water mixture does not start to ferment, even by accident.

Passover is the most important holiday in the Jewish calendar and celebrates the Hebrews' deliverance from slavery in Egypt. *Matzo* is a reminder of how, in their escape from the Egyptians, the Hebrews had no time to let their bread rise. Leavened bread therefore became a prohibited food during the eight days of Passover although, paradoxically, the holiday is otherwise a time of celebration and good food.

Matzo is sometimes served at the table but more commonly the bread is ground into meal and used for cakes, biscuits (cookies) and dumplings during Passover (see next entry).

PASSOVER ROLLS

Since leavened bread is forbidden during Passover, Ashkenazi Jews found intriguing ways of making breads without normal flour, which even without yeast will start a natural fermentation. The trick was to use *matzos*, flat and brittle breads, that have been ground to a fine meal.

Passover rolls, which are popular among Jewish communities in Paris and other parts of Europe, are almost identical to little choux buns, made with water, butter, *matzo* meal and eggs, and baked in the oven until golden. They are normally split and filled with cream cheese or cream.

LATKES

These small potato pancakes are thought to have originated in the Ukraine, where *kartoflani placke* were a popular dish at Christmas, served with goose. The dish was apparently adopted by the large Jewish population of the area, and is now traditionally served on the feast of Chanukkah.

RIGHT: Jewish or seeded rye

BREADS OF THE AMERICAS

The United States of America yields a fabulous potpourri of breads. The thousands of people from Ireland, Italy, Germany and Scandinavia who emigrated to America at the turn of the century had little to take with them save the customs and traditions they held most dear. Baking bread would have been one of the very first tasks for the wife once a home had been established and, understandably, the breads she baked were the breads of her own country – a reminder of home and perhaps a promise of a better future.

Thriving communities were gradually established. Norwegians and other Scandinavians settled in many of the North Central states, such as Wisconsin, Minnesota and Iowa; German immigrants also settled around the Great Lakes, while in New York and in other large cities along the Eastern Seaboard, Italians and Jews made their home.

Grain, of course, was no problem in this "Land of Plenty". The United States were already world producers of grain, particularly wheat, but also rye, barley and oats. German and Eastern-European rye breads, country breads from Italy and a vast range of Jewish loaves were produced by the many

RIGHT: Hamburger buns can normally be distinguished by their sesame seed topping.

bakeries that sprang up to serve their own communities. Added to this, of course, were the established American loaves, themselves versions of breads brought to the New World by the early settlers, while in the South people moving north from Mexico continued to make their customary corn breads and tortillas. If indigenous breads can be said to exist in the United States, they are the breads made by Native Americans – whose bread-making traditions were kept alive by people of American Indian descent in North and South Dakota and other central states.

ALL-AMERICAN BREADS

While some breads are mainly popular in, for example, north-eastern, southern or south-western states, certain loaves are extremely well known throughout the whole of the United States. Some of these, such as anadama bread, are best known by reputation. These loaves are sold occasionally by small bakeries as a curiosity, but they are more widely known from recipe books as the breads handed down

by generations. Other breads, however, are the standard loaves, sold in various shapes and sizes in every supermarket and convenience store. The best are, as ever, those made by craft bakeries.

As a general rule, you will find that standard American loaves – as opposed to those made by local Italian or French bakers, for example – have a more tender and softer crumb. This is because most American loaves contain fat in the form of milk and/or melted butter.

BURGER BUN

Burgers are almost an American way of life, which makes it all the more surprising that store-bought burger buns can be sadly disappointing. While good burger buns do exist, many of the store-bought burger buns are not dissimilar to those found outside America – white, squashy and with a smattering of sesame seeds on top. Perhaps their very blandness is considered a necessity to contrast with the beef and relishes inside, but any American burger aficionado will tell you that, on the contrary, the bun is an integral part of the eating experience. The best burger buns are made with a simple dough but, unlike the commercial supermarket variety, do not contain the emulsifiers that give the impression you are eating soft foam. The answer, as with so many breads, is to find a good baker. Italian, French and Jewish bakers are all likely to make their own versions, using the same dough as for their standard country breads and thus producing a bun with a pleasant texture and fine flavour.

GRAHAM BREAD

There is a wide variety of American wholemeal (wholewheat) loaves, among which Graham bread is probably king – the name being synonymous with healthy eating. The bread is named after a 19th-century doctor, Rev

RIGHT: Graham bread

Sylvester Graham, who was a keen advocate of using the whole grain for milling flour, recognizing the benefits of bran in the diet. Graham flour, Graham bread and Graham crackers are all named after him, the best and most authentic flour being stoneground and coarsely milled wholemeal flour.

BASIC WHITE BREAD

This is a simple, well-flavoured tin loaf with a slightly chewy crust and a close but soft texture.

CORNELL BREAD

This light-textured wheat germ bread is mainly of historic interest since, although it is a nutritious loaf, it has less than happy antecedents and is rarely made these days. In the 1930s Cornell University pioneered a high-protein loaf, made with wheat germ, white and soya flours, sugar and milk for patients who lived in mental hospitals. Gradually, other public institutions, such as schools and hospitals, started producing the loaf. When, in the early 1940s, during World War II, meat was either rationed or extremely expensive, people looked for a high-protein alternative and the Cornell loaf became recommended eating. The bread clearly never recovered from such damning acclaim – even the most wonderful bread is, for most, a poor substitute to meat – and for that war generation, the scarcity and poor food that the Cornell loaf represented, meant that it became deeply unfashionable. A pity really, as recipes suggest that it is not at all bad.

BROWN AND WHOLEMEAL BREAD

There are many variations of wholemeal (whole-wheat) bread. Whole-wheat bread is widely available, normally in a loaf shape. There are also variations of brown bread, containing a blend of wholemeal and white flour. Wheat germ may also be added – you will need to ask or read the side of the packet to be sure. Cracked wheat bread has a delicious nutty flavour and crunchy texture, and is a good, nutritious loaf. It is usually round, although short batons and loaves are also available. It is made using milk or buttermilk, together with honey, molasses or brown sugar. The most nutritious breads are made with stoneground wholemeal flour, although white flour with added wheat germ and/or cracked wheat is still a healthy alternative with a good texture

ABOVE: Basic white bread has a soft, close texture.

ABOVE: American seven-grain (top), wholewheat (round) and cracked wheat loaves

and flavour. Seven-grain bread is another healthy loaf. It contains seven grains: normally wheat, rye and corn; and then four of the following – brown rice, buckwheat, soya, oats, barley, millet, sunflower seeds, sesame seeds or flaxseed. As you might expect, it is a dense, sturdy loaf and is popular with health-food enthusiasts.

PULLMAN LOAF

This white loaf is named after the Pullman railway coach, the box shape of which is exactly that of the bread. The bread is similar to *pain de mie*, the French sandwich loaf. It is made in a rectangular tin (pan), longer than a standard loaf tin, sometimes with a sliding lid so that the crust is soft on all sides. Like *pain de mie*, it is used for sandwiches and toasting and is normally white, made American-style with butter or other fat.

SWIRL BREAD

This very attractive loaf is widely available throughout the United States. It is made by using two doughs: one of white flour, the other using a wholemeal (whole-wheat) flour mixed with molasses. The doughs are rolled out after their first rising and the wholemeal rectangle is placed on top of the white one. The two are then rolled up together. When cut, each slice of bread has a swirl pattern.

BEER BREAD

Beer and butter are the ingredients that make this a most unusual bread. It comes from Georgia and is raised by

LEFT: The Pullman loaf is used for sandwiches.

RIGHT: Swirl bread: molasses gives the dough an intense colour.

cheese and has a distinctive and pleasant sour flavour. As the name suggests, it is baked in a casserole. Another dill loaf, but quite unlike the dilly casserole loaf, is the sour dill rye, which is made from a blend of wheat and rye flours, and is strongly flavoured with dillweed, caraway seeds and dill pickle brine.

CHOCOLATE BREAD

Chocolate breads are well known in the USA; bakers across the land all make their own favourite. One such

using self-raising (self-rising) flour or baking powder. A whole can of beer is poured into the flour mixture to make a thick batter, which is then poured into a round or rectangular loaf tin (pan) in which 50g/2oz/¼ cup butter has been melted. Once the loaf is cooked, it is turned upside down and the butter trickles through the bread. The result is a moist and beautifully flavoured loaf.

DILL BREAD

Dill is a popular ingredient in American breads and there are several well-known dill loaves. The dilly casserole bread is a favourite among home bakers but it can sometimes be found in delicatessens and specialist stores. As well as dill, it contains cottage

ABOVE: Dill bread

LEFT: Rustic, Italian-style sun-dried tomato bread

TOMATO BREAD

With bakers from so many nationalities, it is not surprising to find loaves in the United States that are reminiscent of other breads of the world. Tomato bread may remind you of Italian or even some Greek breads, yet here the bread has been thoroughly naturalized, the pretty, pale pink colouring coming from tomato juice, which gives the bread a definite but not overpowering taste of tomato.

SUN-DRIED TOMATO BREAD

Sun-dried tomato bread is similar to tomato bread but contains pieces of sun-dried tomatoes. It has a rustic appearance. The shape is usually a free-form round, which may be slashed across the top and dusted with flour before baking. Sun-dried tomato bread is popular served with pasta or soup.

BELOW: Triticale bread

OATMEAL BREAD

For the early settlers in America, oats were one of the easier cereals to grow and oatmeal would have been used for oatcakes, cooked over a griddle, or, if wheat was available, added in varying proportions to flour to make loaves. Since oatmeal contains no gluten, only small quantities can be used if attempting to make anything that resembles a loaf. Wheat flour and occasionally rye flour form the basis of the dough, but oatmeal adds a pleasant flavour and texture.

chocolate loaf is called *babka*. This is a Russian-style bread that has many variations and comes in all sorts of extraordinary shapes. The dough, which is enriched with eggs and butter, can be plain or rich with bittersweet chocolate, and it is also sometimes filled with almond paste, raisins, nuts and more roughly chopped chocolate so that the centre is moist and soft and deliciously rich.

modern gene manipulation techniques and is a hybrid of rye, durum and red winterwheat. This probably sounds more alarming than it is – farmers and agriculturists have been cross-breeding wheat and other cereals for hundreds of years in order to improve both yields and resistance to disease. The triticale grain is particularly high in protein, but low in gluten. When making dough the flour is blended with at least an equal amount of wheat flour, either white or wholemeal (whole-wheat). The bread has a sweet and nutty flavour, that is reminiscent of rye yet without its characteristic density.

BANANA BREAD

Teabreads are immensely popular throughout the USA and all sorts of fruits and vegetables are used for flavouring them. The breads are mostly made using baking powder and the mixture has more the consistency of a cake than a dough. Consequently most American teabreads are baked in tins (pans), after which they

TRITICALE BREAD

Triticale (pronounced so as to rhyme with "daily") is a grain that has been developed using

OPPOSITE: Babka, a Russian-style chocolate loaf, comes in all shapes and sizes.

ABOVE: Oatmeal bread has a good texture and flavour.

are turned out and thickly sliced to serve with tea or with morning coffee. Bananas are a favourite teabread ingredient.

LEMON BREAD

Lemon bread is as popular as all the other teabreads. It is a finer flavoured and more textured loaf than most teabreads. Lemon in the form of rind or extract is often added to other teabreads, but is wonderful when given a starring role.

RIGHT: Plaited Cheddar cheese bread that is flavoured with beer.

ABOVE: Lemon bread and banana bread

CHEDDAR CHEESE BREAD

There are all sorts of flavoured breads in the United States and cheese is a favourite ingredient. Grated cheese can be kneaded into the dough to give it a rich, soft flavour, or else sprinkled on top to melt into the crust. Cheddar cheese bread is a simple but tasty yeast-leavened loaf that is almost always made with white flour. It is excellent with soups and barbecues, and is delicious toasted. A plaited (braided) cheese loaf is sometimes made using beer rather than milk or water.

NORTH-EAST AMERICAN BREADS

This is the area of the original 13 colonies, founded by the Pilgrim Fathers. The Dutch came, too, as well as other pilgrims seeking religious freedom. Among these people were the Amish, whose communities can today be found in Ohio and Indiana but most famously in Pennsylvania. New York is the epicentre of this region and here can be found a breathtaking range of breads from countries all over the world. But the most famous of all New York's bread, notwithstanding the Italian ciabattas, Irish soda breads, and baguettes and *pain de campagne* from France, are the Jewish breads. New York has the biggest community of Jews outside Israel and the city is distinguished for having the best bagels in the world. National breads can be found under their own separate heading, but the following are a selection of breads that have evolved from the recipes settlers adapted to the cereals and climate they found in the New World.

ANADAMA BREAD

The anecdote behind this bread is so good that few bread books can resist it, although it is not generally a bread found in most bakers or supermarkets. The bread dates back to colonial times and is unusual since it is one of the rare corn-meal breads made with yeast. The story goes that an irritable New England woodsman had a wife by the name of Anna, who fed him nothing but a corn meal and molasses mush for supper. One evening, having had more than he could take, he grabbed some flour and yeast off the shelf, mixed it into the mush and put it in the oven to bake, muttering "Anna, damn her" over and over again. Thus the name, "anadama" came about. The loaf is made with yellow corn meal and wheat flour in varying proportions and is normally baked in a round cake tin (pan).

BOSTON BROWN BREAD

The Pilgrims who arrived in Massachusetts and other New England states must have quickly found that rye, rather than wheat, flourished better in the cold snowy winters and cool summers of their new home. This bread is one of the best known of the old breads – made with rye blended with corn meal and white flour, which was a common practice in poorer families where corn was easily available but wheat was not. The bread is steamed – these days normally in large coffee cans, but presumably originally in ceramic pudding moulds. The advantage was that the bread could be made without the need for an oven, another sign that this was a bread of poor people, who strove to make do with the resources they had. The bread is often sweetened with molasses and/or buttermilk, which gives it a distinctive sour/sweet flavour, and is a favourite to eat with Boston baked beans.

BAKED BROWN BREAD/DUTCH OVEN BREAD

This is similar in many ways to Boston brown bread: it is made using rye flour, corn meal and wheat flour, with molasses and buttermilk. The difference is in the baking. Unlike Boston brown bread, which is steamed, this loaf is baked in the oven. It was originally baked in a Dutch oven, a round type of pot set over a fire. Today, it is normally cooked in a covered casserole. The bread is placed in a cold oven and then baked until firm.

NEW ENGLAND BUTTERMILK ROLLS

These small, yeast and soda-risen breads are light and flaky with a delightful soft crumb, thanks to the buttermilk from which they are made.

EGG HARBOUR BREAD

The bread is made by the Amish, a Mennonite people of Swiss and Dutch origin, who fled their own countries in the 18th century due to religious persecution in Europe. They migrated first to Pennsylvania, where their descendants are called Pennsylvania Dutch, and then moved to Ohio and other Midwest states. Everything about their life and lifestyle is plain and simple. This white bread from a village on the shores of Lake Michigan is typical – a plain white yeasted dough that is allowed six risings before being baked, which gives a beautifully textured loaf with a soft crumb. Old-order Amish bread is made by the families in northern Indiana. The bread is

RIGHT: New England buttermilk rolls are light and flaky.

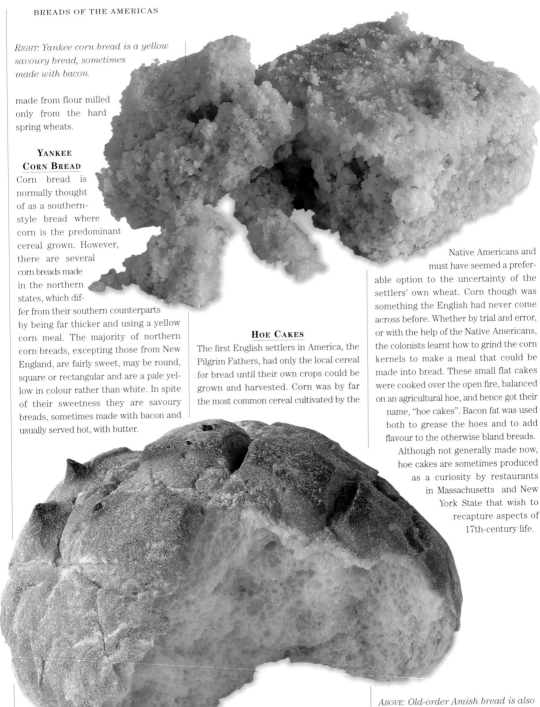

RIGHT: Yankee corn bread is a yellow savoury bread, sometimes made with bacon.

made from flour milled only from the hard spring wheats.

YANKEE CORN BREAD

Corn bread is normally thought of as a southern-style bread where corn is the predominant cereal grown. However, there are several corn breads made in the northern states, which differ from their southern counterparts by being far thicker and using a yellow corn meal. The majority of northern corn breads, excepting those from New England, are fairly sweet, may be round, square or rectangular and are a pale yellow in colour rather than white. In spite of their sweetness they are savoury breads, sometimes made with bacon and usually served hot, with butter.

HOE CAKES

The first English settlers in America, the Pilgrim Fathers, had only the local cereal for bread until their own crops could be grown and harvested. Corn was by far the most common cereal cultivated by the Native Americans and must have seemed a preferable option to the uncertainty of the settlers' own wheat. Corn though was something the English had never come across before. Whether by trial and error, or with the help of the Native Americans, the colonists learnt how to grind the corn kernels to make a meal that could be made into bread. These small flat cakes were cooked over the open fire, balanced on an agricultural hoe, and hence got their name, "hoe cakes". Bacon fat was used both to grease the hoes and to add flavour to the otherwise bland breads.

Although not generally made now, hoe cakes are sometimes produced as a curiosity by restaurants in Massachusetts and New York State that wish to recapture aspects of 17th-century life.

ABOVE: Old-order Amish bread is also known as North American spring loaf. The long fermentation period means it has an excellent flavour.

MIDWEST AND NORTH CENTRAL AMERICAN BREADS

These are the heartlands of America, stretching from the dairy farms of Wisconsin to the prairies of Wyoming. Here in middle America, great store is set by family life with family meals being a central part. These states were settled mainly by Scandinavians, Germans and Slavs who brought with them the traditions of their homeland. Sourdough ryes and mixed-grain loaves are therefore among the most common breads available.

SALT-RISING BREAD

There are several recipes in American cookbooks for salt-rising breads, but it is thought that the bread was originally made by pioneers crossing the Midwest and western prairies. The starter dough would have been carried in crocks, as the horse- or oxen-drawn wagons made their way across the plains. "Salt-rising" refers to the practice of keeping the active starter in a bowl nestling in a bed of salt, which is easy to warm and retains its heat for a long time. The starter would provide the leaven for fresh bread, which would have been made and baked in makeshift ovens each time the wagon train stopped.

BELOW: Seeded rye (left) and old Milwaukee rye

Although an authentic bread of the prairies, nowadays this bread is a speciality of some of the East Coast bakers. The 19th-century sourdough loaf is known for its delicious and delicate crumb, yet also renowned for the difficulty in actually getting it to work. Several bakeries have succeeded with the bread, but the starter, made from scalded milk, sugar and corn meal, is a notoriously tricky one to prepare. Once the starter begins to ferment, milk, white flour, fat, sugar and salt are added to make a sponge. This adds another potential complication as salt is never usually added to a starter or sponge because it tends to inhibit the yeast. Given the right conditions of warmth and humidity, however, the sponge should rise and fall, after which the remaining flour is added and the dough made into bread in the usual fashion.

LEFT: Heavy sour rye bread

RYE BREAD

There are many rye breads in the Midwest states of Wisconsin, Ohio, Minnesota, Iowa and Nebraska. Pumpernickel is commonly sold, as is a crusty rye bread made using rye and wheat flour but often with butter added, which is a feature of many American breads. Like most traditional ryes, Old Milwaukee rye is a sourdough loaf, made with molasses and flavoured in typical Germanic-style with caraway seeds. The bread may be shaped into round loaves or fashioned into long, slender ones.

SEEDED RYE

Seeded rye bread is often known as Jewish rye and is popular not only in the Midwest, but as far east as New York.

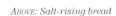
ABOVE: Salt-rising bread

HEAVY SOUR RYE BREAD

This is known as "corn bread" from the corn meal that is sprinkled on the baking sheet, but is otherwise a rye sourdough made with a proportion of wheat flour. It is normally liberally sprinkled with caraway seeds. The bread is frequently sold by weight and can be recognized by its sides, which are liberally sprinkled with corn meal, and its top, which is sprinkled with caraway seeds.

WEST COAST AMERICAN BREADS

In California, fashions come and go so quickly that it is surprising to find that some of the most traditional American breads are not only still being produced but are ever more popular – in the delicatessens, the restaurants and on the dinner party circuit. Many influences have come to play a part. The Pacific Coast was the end of the journey for pioneers hoping to find opportunity and freedom: Hispanics, from the south, gravitated towards the cities of Los Angeles and San Francisco, while Europeans settled all over the region, each culture establishing its own favourite styles of cooking and enthusiastically sampling others.

SAN FRANCISCAN SOURDOUGH

San Franciscan sourdough is probably the best-known American bread outside the United States, and is one that can be truly said to be all-American. It is a round, wheat, oven-baked loaf, with a star slash or a cross-hatched pattern on top. These breads, like the salt-rising breads, were brought to the West Coast by pioneers who crossed the prairies and plains of middle America in search of gold. The trip took the early pioneers five or six months and was extremely hazardous. The Forty-Niners – the men who took part in the 1849 Gold Rush – gave their camps names like Hell's Half Acre and Hangtown, which gives an idea of what life must have been like. Provisions for the journey included sacks of flour, together with a small piece of leavening kept back from the last batch of dough, so that bread could be baked en route. The leavening was stored in a crock inside a sack of flour.

The word "sourdough" refers quite simply to the bread's flavour. The bread has the same sharp/sour taste of yogurt or buttermilk.

It is said that it is impossible to make San Franciscan sourdough outside the city itself. The climate of San Francisco, with

its warmth and humidity, is particularly conducive to sourdough breads, and the bacterium, which feeds on the flour and water mixture, is unique to that area. However, home bakers often attempt

approximations, while professional bakeries all over California produce their own versions, including the *Berkeley sourdough*, which is a baguette-shaped loaf.

MONKEY BREAD

This bread goes under a variety of names, including bubble loaf or poppy seed bubble loaf. The bread normally comprises seven or eight small dough balls baked in a ring mould so that when it is baked the bread does look like lots of bubbles. The little balls are dipped into melted butter and then sprinkled with poppy seeds or currants, raisins, nuts and/or sugar and cinnamon before being baked.

SOUTH-WEST AMERICAN BREADS

Texas, New Mexico and Arizona all border Mexico and their cuisine, including the bread, shows all the influences of its southern neighbour. Food can be spicy and very hot, and tortillas and other corn breads are as common as breads made with wheat.

JALAPEÑO CORN BREAD

This is a typical Tex-Mex-style bread, made with a blend of corn meal and white flour. Hot jalapeño chillies are kneaded into the dough, and some loaves may contain whole corn kernels and cheese, too. The bread can be baked in loaf tins (pans) or shaped into rounds and oven bottom-baked and it has a unique, snappy flavour.

SOPAIPILLAS

These small, puffy breads are a speciality of New Mexico. They are made by mixing together flour, baking powder and salt, adding water to make a

dough and then incorporating some vegetable fat, as when making puff pastry. The dough is then rolled out extremely thinly and cut into small squares, which are deep-fried until puffy. If made professionally in a restaurant or by a baker, the corners can then be snipped off and filled with honey. Otherwise honey or syrup can simply be poured over the breads. A savoury alternative uses refried beans.

HOBO BREAD

Hobo bread is so-called, not because it is a favourite among tramps and vagrants, but because it is traditionally eaten outdoors. It is a sweet bread, rich with sultanas (golden raisins) and nuts, that has been baked in a coffee can so that it is shaped like a long cylinder. Its popularity as an outdoor bread is probably due to the fact that the bread keeps well for several months. It is normally stored in the can in which it is cooked.

BREADS OF THE SOUTHERN STATES

This region includes Mississippi, Alabama and Georgia among others. Corn is cultivated in many of these states and the popularity of corn breads is well known, many people preferring the flat and rather mealy flavour of the corn to the wheat breads popular in the north.

NEW ORLEANS BREAD

New Orléans has many visible French influences – including its name, after Orléans in France – and not least its excellent breads. *Pain perdu* (French toast) is a favourite breakfast for many New Orléans citizens. New Orléans' French bread is softer than the real French version. It is sometimes known as feather bread and is very light. It has the same open texture as the French baguette, but has added fat and sugar, which makes it slightly richer and sweeter.

SPOON BREAD

This corn confection is part bread, part dessert, known as spoon bread for the simple reason that it has to be eaten with a spoon. It is the consistency of custard and is puffy and creamy when cooked. It is then liberally doused in corn syrup or honey and is very sweet. The bread is made with corn meal, a little white flour, eggs, milk and baking powder. One story suggests that the bread was created when too much liquid was added to a corn bread batter and the baked bread had to be spooned out of the tin (pan). Be that as it may, the Virginians insist that this event happened in one of their kitchens and thus claim spoon bread as their own. In Virginia, you will find this served both as a dessert and as a savoury course, made with bacon, cheese and garlic.

SOUTHERN CORN BREAD

There are numerous corn breads in the southern states. Convenience stores and supermarkets sell the more standard-type loaves, but in the home people still make their own breads, and since corn bread is best eaten as soon as possible, these are going to be the most tasty. Corn breads only rarely use yeast, and are relatively quick and easy to make. Southerners like white corn meal for their breads, rather than the yellow meal preferred in the north and the breads are generally much thinner. Wheat flour is added to these breads in varying proportions, but in southern corn bread neither wheat flour nor fat is added, so that the corn flavour is predominant.

Other breads, such as rich corn bread, are made using cream, milk, butter and eggs. Corn pone is thought to be directly inspired by the Native Americans. It is a small, moist loaf, which is made from finely ground corn meal along with buttermilk and lard (shortening).

NATIVE AMERICAN FRY-BREAD

People have lived in America for thousands of years, developing into various local populations of Native Americans who made bread from both wheat and corn for special occasions and for everyday eating. Hoe cakes made by early English settlers may well be adaptations or even pure copies of the breads made by the local people. Nowadays, there are reservations for Native Americans in various American states such as Oklahoma, and several of the more northern states. Their breads vary a little in size but are surprisingly similar across the continent, being small flat breads made from a flour and water dough that is rolled thinly and cut into diamonds, circles or squares. In North and South Dakota on the Sioux reservation, the breads are called "fry-breads" and are made for powwows – ceremonies or intertribal gatherings featuring much feasting and dancing.

SALLY LUNN

This famous bread from Bath in England is said to have been brought to America by the English settlers. It is well known all over the United States but has become a popular speciality bread in the South, where it is served for lunch or tea. The American version was originally made in a Turk's-head mould, but is now less elaborate, baked in a tube tin. There are also miniature versions baked in *petit four* tins, and muffin-size versions made in muffin tins.

CRANBERRY NUT BREAD

This loaf is a bread enriched with eggs and butter, and is famous for the bright red berries that speckle the loaf. Cranberries are in season during November which is why the bread is often associated with Thanksgiving and Christmas. Cranberry nut bread is commonly given as a gift at this time and is popular for its tart taste, which is often accentuated with the flavour of orange.

ZUCCHINI BREAD

Courgettes, or zucchini as they are known in the USA, are hugely popular, not only as a side vegetable, but for use in cakes, muffins and bread. The sweet bread, made with coarsely grated courgettes, sweet spices and sugar, and enriched with eggs and oil, can be iced or served as a dessert cake.

ABOVE: Southern corn bread is made from white corn meal.

CARIBBEAN AND MEXICAN BREADS

HARD-DOUGH BREAD

This fairly heavy tin or plaited (braided) white loaf is almost the standard Caribbean bread. It is the most popular bread for the islanders and is becoming increasingly popular in those parts of Britain or the United States with a sizeable Afro-Caribbean population. It has a dense, chewy texture and, like many West Indian breads, has a distinctly sweet flavour.

JOHNNY CAKES

Johnny cakes do not seem to have a single origin. There are recipes for them in a number of cookbooks from the USA as well as those from the Caribbean. Most agree however that the word is a corruption of "journey cake" – a bread that can be packed up and given to travellers for their day's journey. In Jamaica, in corroboration of this, johnny cakes can be bought freshly made from roadside stalls all over the island. Just as there is apparently no definitive ancestry, there is equally no single recipe for johnny cakes. Recipes suggest they can be made from corn meal, wheat flour or a mixture of both. Some contain eggs and milk, while the Jamaican

ABOVE: Johnny cakes are a famous Jamaican bread.

johnny cake is made with butter or lard (shortening) and coconut oil. Here the dough is shaped into balls and fried in oil. Other johnny cakes have a batter-like consistency. Cooked on a griddle or in a pan, they are served as a flat bread.

BULLA BUNS

These are spicy, round discs. They resemble English muffins in appearance but are dense, dark and spicy, flavoured with allspice and rich with raisins and molasses.

CARIBBEAN BUN

A spicy teabread, this is liberally flavoured with allspice and is packed with fruit. The round buns are dark in colour and look sticky, thanks to the molasses which gives them an intense bitter/sweet flavour. Beyond the Caribbean, the buns are often available from ethnic markets and shops in larger cities and come either in small bun sizes or as a larger loaf.

TORTILLAS

Although other wheat loaves are available, tortillas are rightly known as the bread of Mexico. Freshly made and still warm, these flat breads are an essential part of every Mexican meal. Tortillas are

ABOVE: Hard-dough bread

also used in an enormous number of Mexican dishes, wrapped round meat, fish, vegetables or cheese and eaten for street food as well as snacks, suppers and elegant dinners.

There are basically two types of tortilla. Maize tortillas are made using a type of corn meal called *masa harina,* literally meaning dough flour. These are the older of the two, having been made and eaten by native people for literally thousands of years. Until the arrival of the Spanish in the 16th century, there was no wheat in Mexico, but in northern parts of the country, where wheat flourished, wheat flour (called just flour) became the preferred choice for tortillas.

HAWAIIAN BREADS

In this delightful tropical paradise, there is a fabulous amalgamation of cultures and cuisines: along with the indigenous Hawaiians, there are Chinese, Japanese, Portuguese and people of Filipino origin.

HAWAIIAN BREAD

This is a perfect tropical bread, made with fresh coconut and macadamia nuts, which give it a delicious crunchy texture. The yeast-leavened white dough is enriched with eggs, butter and milk.

PORTUGUESE SWEET BREAD

Towards the end of the last century, Portuguese immigrants came to Hawaii to work in the sugar fields. Over the years their bread has acquired a character that is part Portuguese and part Hawaiian. The dough is usually yeast-leavened and enriched with eggs and butter. It is also made with condensed rather than fresh milk since the latter was once a scarce commodity on an island given over entirely to fields of sugar cane. Currants and raisins also go into the doughs, as well as being used for decoration. It may be baked in a round in a coil, but is more usually plaited (braided) and sprinkled with coarse granulated sugar.

BELOW: Bulla buns

BREAD OF THE DEAD

Should you visit Mexico around 2 November, All Souls' Day, you may find this famous and traditional bread, called *Pan de Muerto.* It is made as part of the celebrations in memory of the deceased but, paradoxically, it is not a sad day but a fiesta. Everyone visits their relatives' graves, bringing a picnic, wearing bright colourful clothes and carrying candies and flowers along with the special bread. The bread itself comes in various forms but most often seems to be a white, yeast-risen dough, flavoured with orange and sometimes with spices. It can be a simple round or a plaited loaf coiled into a circle. The bread is then decorated with pieces of dough formed into teardrops, bones or bunches of flowers.

ABOVE: Tortillas

WEST INDIAN ROTIS

West Indian *rotis* are huge and used, as they would be in India, for mopping up stews and curries, such as curried goat. Like Indian *rotis,* they are made with chapati flour, a very fine wholemeal (wholewheat) flour, and are cooked on a griddle.

Rotis are best eaten warm and if you do find them in Caribbean shops, they should be sprinkled with a little water, then heated in a hot oven.

ABOVE: Spicy Caribbean bun

INDIAN BREADS

There are principally two types of Indian bread, although all share the characteristic of being flat and oval or round. In Punjab and Kashmir in the north-west and in Pakistan, Afghanistan and Bangladesh there are the naan-style breads. Their defining feature is that naans, unlike the *chapatis* and *parathas* of the south, are leavened and when cooked become light and puffy, unlike the southern breads that are unleavened and much flatter.

The north Indian breads have much in common with many of the Middle Eastern breads – they are large and flat and used as a vehicle for other foods. Recipes for naans and many breads from Syria, Egypt, Iraq and Iran are almost interchangeable. The main difference is the way in which the breads are baked.

BHAKRIS

Bhakris are flat unleavened breads made from *jowar* flour, and sometimes known as *jowar rotis*. *Jowar* is widely grown in central and southern India. The tiny green seeds from the plant can be roasted and eaten as they are, or can be milled into flour. The dough is moulded and patted flat by hand and then baked on a griddle. *Bhakris* can be plain or baked with sesame seeds, and are served with butter as a snack.

CHAPATIS

Also unleavened, chapatis are now widely known throughout Britain thanks to the popularity of Indian food. While once a more exotic request from a restaurant menu, chapatis are now almost commonplace, although the commercially available product is a rather poor imitation of the real thing. In India the chapati is popular in central and southern parts of the country, served with meals and used with the fingers to scoop up food and sauces. These authentic chapatis are made with *atta* (chapati flour), which is a very fine wholemeal (whole-wheat) flour.

ROTLAS

There are many variations of chapatis, called *rotlas, rotis,* and *dana rotis* to name but a few. They are all unleavened breads, made using wholemeal flour, to which ghee, oil, celery seeds and/or fresh coriander (cilantro) might be added. They are rolled out until thin and cooked like chapatis.

PARATHAS

Parathas are a richer and flakier version of chapatis. The chapati dough is spread with ghee, folded and then cooked over a *tava* (griddle) until puffy.

POORIS (PURIS)

These are puffier still and are available (and worth eating) only from a restaurant or by making them yourself, since they need to be eaten as soon as possible after cooking. They are normally made using a chapati dough. Small balls of dough are rolled out into 2.5cm/1in rounds and deep-fried on both sides.

NAAN

The naan, unlike the chapatis of the south, is a leavened bread. The leaven varies from region to region and probably from home to home, according to the cook's preferred method. Yeast or a sourdough method can be used; others prefer using a chemical raising agent, such as bicarbonate of soda (baking soda) or self-raising (self-rising) flour. Yogurt, however, is the main ingredient that differentiates naans from its many Middle Eastern counterparts. It plays a part in fermenting the dough and some naan are made entirely using a yogurt fermentation. It is this fermentation that gives the bread its characteristic light and puffy texture and soft crust. The

BELOW: Parathas are cooked with ghee and therefore have a golden appearance. Chapatis are cooked without any fat or oil and are thus flatter. They do not have the golden crust.

LEFT: Poppadoms are popular everywhere with Indian food.

produces the teardrop shape. As the dough bakes, it scorches and puffs up to give a bread that is both crisp and soft in parts.

GOAN BATCH BREAD

In Goa, until recently part of Portuguese India, there is a white loaf called *pio*, possibly a corruption of *pao*, the Portuguese word for bread.

POPPADOMS

These thin crisp discs are widely available outside India, either ready-cooked or ready-to-cook. In India they are commonly served with vegetarian meals. Poppadoms are sold in markets and by street vendors: plain or flavoured with spices or seasoned with black or red pepper. The dough is generally made from dried lentils, but can also be made from potatoes or sago. It is then rolled thinly and left to dry in the sun. Poppadoms can be cooked by either deep-frying or placing under a hot grill (broiler). Either way they brown in seconds and need close attention while cooking.

flavour comes partly from the soured yogurt and partly, without doubt, from the *tandoor*, in which breads are traditionally cooked. A *tandoor* is a clay oven sunk into the ground and the flattened dough is baked against the blisteringly hot walls of the oven. The pull of gravity

*RIGHT:
Naans can be
plain or stuffed.*

AUSTRALIAN BREADS

Australia, like other countries with large immigrant communities, has a wealth of wonderful breads whose origins lie in far-off lands, plus one bread which is indigenous to the country, the famous damper. Once baked in the bush, in the embers of campfires, damper is today a favourite "barbie" food, and is almost as popular outside Australia as it originally was in the Outback.

In recent years there has been something of a revolution in Australian cooking, with some of the world's most innovative chefs producing delicious dishes based on the fine fresh ingredients for which the country is famous. Part of this revolution has been a back-to-basics approach, with more cooks seeking to get away from bland, mass-produced meals in favour of "real" food.

This is certainly true of baked goods. There has been a move away from the handy yet often horrid "cotton wool" breads, which once stacked every supermarket bakery shelf, and a return to real bread, with texture and taste.

Australian versions of Italian breads, such as focaccia, ciabatta, olive Toscano, *casalinga* and *bassotto*, and flat, Turkish

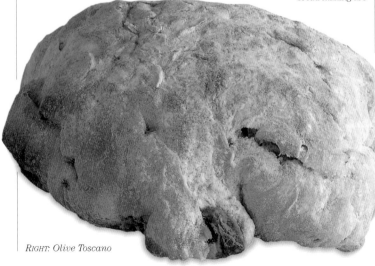

Above: The colourful and unusual vegetable il gianfornaio

bread are becoming increasingly popular, as is the brightly coloured *il gianfornaio*, which is a mosaic of red, green, yellow and orange doughs, each flavoured with a different coloured vegetable.

Leading the revolution in Australian bread making are small wood-burning bakeries, such as New Norcia in Western Australia. New Norcia is a monastic town, some 83 miles (133km) north-east of Perth. The wood-fired oven that had produced bread for the Benedictine Monks for over a century was shut down in 1989. Four years later it was fired again, and now produces – and sells – a wide range of breads, from a simple old-fashioned white loaf to their popular courgette (zucchini) bread. The monks also bake their own focaccia, an olive bread and an olive, rosemary and sun-dried tomato bread.

The breads proved so popular that a second wood-fired bakery was opened, this time in the city of Perth. Here the range is even more extensive, and includes several sourdoughs such as raisin and walnut sourdough, San Franciscan sourdough and both a light rye and a dark rye sourdough. Their unusual fig and fennel sourdough is very popular.

Supermarkets, too, have become much more adventurous, and the range of what are loosely termed "Continental breads" includes mixed grain and rye loaves with flavourings as diverse as

RIGHT: Olive Toscano

ABOVE: Ciabatta

sunflower seed and pineapple, walnut and fruit, and herb and tomato.

Many Australians bake their own bread, whether in ovens or in bread-making machines, and the range of bread mixes available is almost as interesting as the variety of breads on sale in bakeries.

AUSTRALIAN SOURDOUGH

There are a number of sourdoughs made by craft bakers. Some are made to French recipes, using a similar recipe to that used

LEFT: Potato sourdough

for the French *pain de campagne*. Potato sourdoughs, made with a potato starter, are similar to San Franciscan sourdoughs.

OLIVE TOSCANO

Like the Italian *pane Toscano*, this is a crusty, close-textured, and slightly chewy bread, made without any salt. Olive Toscano has green olives added to the dough, which add flavour and contrast well with the salt-free crumb.

DAMPER BREAD

Damper bread is the most famous and probably the only traditional bread of Australia. Like the United States' Native

ABOVE: Bassotto

American bread, it is designed to be made in the open country – in this case, in the bush. The dough, made from wheat flour and water, and sometimes flavoured with spices, is patted into cakes and baked either on hot stones or under a pot. The name "damper" comes from the fact that the fire was damped down so that the embers were just the right heat for

RIGHT: Flat Turkish bread has become one of Australia's favourite breads.

DR ALLINSON
This bread is based on the original recipe that Dr Allinson developed in the 19th century. It is a yeast-leavened bread made of organic stoneground wholemeal (whole-wheat) flour and canola (a type of cereal) and is rolled in sesame seeds before being baked in a deep-sided loaf tin (pan).

cooking the bread. Damper bread was also sometimes made by wrapping the dough around sticks and baking it over the fire – the same method as was used for a traditional South African bread called stick bread. The sticks are removed after cooking and the holes in the bread filled with either cheese or butter.

RIGHT: Densely textured rye bread (left) and farmer rye are generally available from bakeries in the larger Australian cities.

TURKISH BREAD
Turkish bread is one of the most popular breads in Australia, particularly in Sydney. The same as Turkish *ekmek*, it too can come in varying sizes, from small rounds to large ovals. The best breads are made according to traditional Turkish methods, and are baked in wood-burning stoves.

RYE BREAD
There are various rye breads available in the cities; farmer rye is a small dense loaf, while a lite rye has a much lighter flavour and texture with a hint of malt. *Black rye* is strictly for rye lovers, and is made to an old European recipe, using a rye sourdough starter, blended with stoneground rye and wheat flour.

LEFT: Dr Allinson bread is made from organic flour and is rolled in sesame seeds before being baked in a loaf tin.

CHINESE BREADS

While for the people of southern China rice is the staple food, in the wheat-growing region of the north, bread is eaten in lieu of rice.

French-style baked loaves and rolls are becoming increasingly popular throughout the country (especially in the cities), but the traditional breads are almost always steamed. Some *dim sum* breads are fried or baked on a griddle.

MAN TO

Man to are widely eaten throughout the north of China. The small, steaming hot buns are sold everywhere – in restaurants and teahouses, on street stalls and by itinerant sellers. They are eaten sometimes as snacks, but more commonly as the traditional accompaniment to a meal, in the same way as those in the southwest of the country eat rice. They are made from white flour, yeast and sugar and then formed into small balls and steamed in wicker baskets for about 20 minutes. *Man to* have the consistency of many of the steamed *dim sum* dumplings. They can also be added to soups and other dishes.

CHICKEN BUNS (GEE BAO)

These are little steamed buns filled with a mixture of chicken and oyster sauce, and served as *dim sum.*

SPRING ONION BREAD (CHUNG YAU BENG)

From Hong Kong comes this extraordinary pan-fried bread, made uniquely using a hot roux (a cooked flour and butter paste) that is worked into a similar dough made with cold water. The complicated process involves spreading each piece of dough with a hot oil and flour roux, and then finally rolling it up with spring onions (scallions). This is not a recipe for the faint-hearted, but if you are lucky you may be offered these treats at a restaurant. The ring-shaped breads are fried in oil and have a delicious crisp outside while inside you bite into layers of soft dough around the spring onions.

SWEET BUNS (HWA JWEN)

These sweet steamed buns are a popular snack food.

PEONY BUNS

These pretty buns are often served as a sweetmeat in Hong Kong. Like *chung yau beng* they are made from two types of dough, the first made by mixing three parts wheat flour with one part root flour, and adding lard (shortening), sugar and water. A second dough, made simply from cornflour (cornstarch) and lard, is then prepared. Both doughs are divided into 12 balls and the more elaborate dough is wrapped around the simpler one. Each ball is then rolled to a round and spread with lotus seed paste before being shaped once more into a ball. A star-shape is cut in the top of each bun and they are then deep-fried until they are crisp. The points of the star on each bun open out to create the peony shape for which the buns are named.

LEFT: Pineapple (left) and cocktail pork man to (steamed buns)

JAPANESE BREADS

There is no tradition of bread-making in Japan. Rice was, and still is, the staple food and, until relatively recently, bread was completely unknown to all but the most travelled of the Japanese. Japan, unlike other countries in Asia, was virtually untouched by European influences until around the middle of the last century when a new philosophy was adopted and the country began to court positively the governments of Europe. Many Japanese were sent to France, Britain, Holland and Germany to see what could be learnt from the West in terms of seafaring, technology and government. Foodstuffs were probably not high on the agenda, but inevitably these Japanese visitors would have been struck by the concept of baking a food made from the flour of a grain. Recipes were taken back to Japan and very gradually more and more people acquired a liking for bread so that by the middle of this century, a few Japanese bakeries sprang up, making

RIGHT: Melon (left) and melon and milk chocolate rolls have a soft crumb.

breads often in the image of favourite breads from Britain and France but with their own special character.

DOUBLE SOFT WHITE
This is a typical and extremely popular Japanese loaf, which is simply the Japanese version of an English white loaf. Indeed it is often known as "English bread" and in shape is like a tin loaf. However, the flour used by Japanese bakers is particularly soft and dense and the bread has more the texture of a soft milk bread, with a similar soft smooth

LEFT: Double soft white is about the most popular Japanese bread.

crust. The bread is normally cut into thick slices and then lightly toasted and eaten with butter or, more conventionally in Japan, with a spread or fruit conserve.

JAPANESE FRENCH BREAD
This is simply a French baguette, but again made with the very soft Japanese flour, so that the crumb is slightly denser and the crust less fragile than that on an authentic baguette. It can be used for sandwiches or eaten by itself with butter or a spread.

MELON BREAD
A flavoured bread, this one is popular in Britain among Japanese expatriots. The breads can be loaf-shaped but are more commonly made as rolls. Melon and milk chocolate rolls contain chunks of chocolate and are a popular tea-time bread.

JAPANESE CREAM BREAD
These small soft rolls contain cream and are consequently very soft, not unlike an English bridge roll. Like the soft white bread, these rolls are eaten at tea time with a conserve or even with butter.

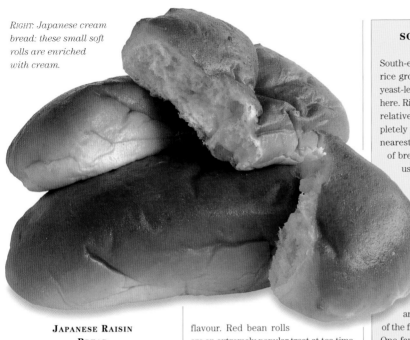

RIGHT: Japanese cream bread: these small soft rolls are enriched with cream.

SOUTH-EAST ASIAN BREADS

South-east Asia is part of the largest rice growing area of the world and yeast-leavened breads are not typical here. Rice is the staple food and until relatively recently bread was completely unknown. Rice cakes are the nearest thing to the Western idea of bread. Flat and sticky, they are usually sweetened and eaten as delicacies and sweets.

However, bread is not unheard of in South-east Asia. Western influences mean that there is now an established appetite for American and European foods and bread is becoming more popular. In Indonesia, flour mills are now springing up and much of the flour is used for bread making. One favourite white bread is called *roti tawar*. Another bread, *panada*, shows a more adventurous spirit, combining wheat flour with coconut milk. These light, sweet rolls sometimes have vegetable or meat fillings.

JAPANESE RAISIN BREAD

A simple white fruit bread, this may be tin-baked or baked in the oven so that it is evenly crusty.

JAPANESE CREAM FAIRY-TALE ROLLS

These popular tea-time rolls are filled with cream and sometimes with a mixture of chocolate and cream.

RED BEAN ROLLS

Red bean rolls are a delicious combination of ideas and flavours from countries with very different culinary backgrounds. From the outside these little bread rolls look similar to large English muffins – soft white breads with a thin, chewy crust. Inside though, these little rolls have a delicious sweet filling that is typically Japanese – red bean paste with its distinctive sweet and sour flavour. Red bean rolls are an extremely popular treat at tea time.

JAPANESE CURRY BREAD

Like red bean rolls, these are a delicious "East meets West" dish. The breads are deep-fried and have a curry-flavoured filling of potatoes, with a hint of meat.

LEFT: Japanese curry bread

TRADITIONAL BREAD MAKING

There is something undeniably special about freshly baked bread. Why does it smell so good? What makes it so hard to resist? This section contains all the practical information you need about flours, yeasts and other ingredients. It also illustrates in detail all the techniques involved, from mixing, kneading and shaping the dough to baking and finishing the loaf. A round-up of useful bread-making equipment, from measures to moulds and from baking sheets to bannetons, completes the section.

INGREDIENTS FOR BREAD MAKING

—

WHEAT FLOURS

The simplest breads are a mixture of flour and water and some type of leavening agent. Beyond that narrow definition, however, lies an infinite number of possibilities. The flour is most likely to come from wheat, but may be derived from another type of grain or even, in the case of buckwheat, from another source entirely. The liquid may be water, but could just as easily be milk, or a mixture. Yeast is the obvious raising agent, but there are other options. Salt is normally essential, fats are often added, and other ingredients range from sweeteners like sugar or molasses to dried fruit, spices and savoury flavourings.

WHITE FLOUR

This flour contains about 75 per cent of the wheat grain with most of the bran and the wheat germ extracted. Plain flour is used for pastry, sauces and biscuits (cookies); while self-raising (self-rising) flour, which contains a raising agent, is used for cakes, scones (US biscuits) and puddings. It can also be used for soda bread. American all-purpose flour is a medium-strength flour, somewhere between the British plain and strong white flour. Soft flour, sometimes known as American cake flour, has been milled very finely for sponge cake and similar bakes.

UNBLEACHED WHITE FLOUR

Unbleached flour is more creamy in colour than other white flours, which have been whitened artificially. Bleaching, which involves treating the flour with chlorine, is becoming increasingly rare and the majority of white flours are unbleached, although check the packet to be sure. In Britain, flour producers are required by law to add, or fortify their white flours with, certain nutrients such as vitamin B1, nictinic acid, iron and calcium. These are often added in the form of white soya flour, which has a natural bleaching effect.

RIGHT: Organic flours are being used increasingly for bread making.

STRONG WHITE/WHITE BREAD FLOUR

For almost all bread making, the best type of flour to use is one which is largely derived from wheat that is high in protein. This type of flour is described as "strong" and is often labelled "bread flour", which underlines its suitability for the task. Proteins in the flour, when mixed with water, combine to make gluten and it is this that gives dough its elasticity when kneaded, and allows it to trap the bubbles of carbon dioxide given off by the yeast. A soft flour produces flat loaves that stale quickly; conversely, if the flour is too hard, the bread will have a coarse texture. A balance is required and most millers blend hard and soft wheats to make a flour that produces a well-flavoured loaf with good volume. Most strong white flours have a lower protein content than their wholemeal equivalent and a baker would probably use a flour with a protein level of 12 per cent. The protein value of a flour can be found listed on the side of the packet under "Nutritional Value".

FINE FRENCH PLAIN FLOUR

French bakers use a mixture of white bread flour and fine plain flour to make baguettes and other specialities. Fine French plain flour is called *farine fluide* in its country of origin because it is so light and free-flowing. Such is the popularity of French-style baked goods that this type of flour is now available in supermarkets.

WHOLEMEAL (WHOLE-WHEAT) FLOUR

This flour is made using the whole of the wheat grain and is sometimes called 100 per cent extraction flour: nothing is added and nothing is taken away. The bran and wheat germ, which are automatically separated from the white inner portion if milled between rollers, are returned to the white flour at the end of the process. *Atta* is a fine wholemeal flour used for Indian breads (see Other Flours).

STONEGROUND WHOLEMEAL FLOUR

This wholemeal flour has been ground in the traditional way between two stones. The bran and wheat germ are milled with the rest of the wheat grain, so there is no separation of the flour at any stage. Stoneground flour is also considered to have a better flavour, owing to the slow grinding of the stones. However, because the oily wheat germ is squashed into the flour, rather than churned in later, stoneground flour has a higher fat content and may become rancid if stored for too long.

ORGANIC WHOLEMEAL FLOUR

This flour has been milled from organic wheat, which is wheat produced without the use of artificial fertilizers or pesticides. There are organic versions of all varieties of wholemeal and white flours available from most large supermarkets and health-food stores.

STRONG WHOLEMEAL/ WHOLEMEAL BREAD FLOUR

A higher proportion of high gluten wheat is necessary in wholemeal flours to counteract the heaviness of the bran. If the flour is not strong enough, the dough may rise unevenly and is likely to collapse in the oven. The miller selects his grist (the blend) of hard and soft wheat grains, according to the type of flour required. Bakers would probably look for a protein content of about 13.5 per cent; the strong flours available in supermarkets are normally between 11.5 and 13 per cent.

ABOVE: Clockwise from top right: strong white flour, stoneground wholemeal, wholemeal, wheat germ, organic wholemeal, plain white flour, organic plain flour, semolina, organic stoneground wholemeal and Granary flour. The three flours in the centre are (clockwise from top) brown, spelt and self-raising flour.

GRANARY FLOUR

Granary (whole-wheat) is the proprietary name of a blend of brown and rye flours and malted wheat grain. The malted grain gives this bread its characteristic sweet and slightly sticky flavour and texture. It is available from health food stores and supermarkets.

MALTHOUSE FLOUR

A speciality flour available from some large supermarkets and health food stores, this is a combination of stone-ground brown flour, rye flour and malted wheat flour with malted wheat flakes. It resembles Granary flour.

GRAHAM FLOUR

This popular American flour is slightly coarser than ordinary wholemeal. It is named after a 19th-century Connecticut cleric, Rev. Sylvestor Graham, who developed the flour and advocated using the whole grain for bread making because of the beneficial effects of the bran.

BROWN FLOUR

This flour contains about 85 per cent of the original grain, with some of the bran and wheat germ extracted. It produces a lighter loaf than 100 per cent wholemeal flour, while still retaining a high percentage of wheat germ, which gives bread so much of its flavour.

WHEAT GERM FLOUR

A wheat germ flour can be brown or white but must contain at least 10 per cent added wheat germ. Wheat germ is highly nutritious and this bread is considered particularly healthy. Wheat germ bread has a pleasant nutty flavour.

SEMOLINA

This is the wheat kernel or endosperm, once the bran and wheat germ have been removed from the grain by milling, but before it is fully milled into flour. Semolina can be ground either coarsely or finely and is used for certain Indian breads, including *bhatura*.

SPELT

Although spelt, a variety of wheat, is no longer widely grown, one or two smaller flour mills still produce a spelt flour, which is available in some health food stores.

OTHER FLOURS

Alternative grains, such as barley, corn-meal and oatmeal, are full of flavour but contain little or no gluten. Breads made solely from them would rise poorly and would be extremely dense. The milled grains are therefore often mixed with strong wheat flour. Rye is rich in gluten, but pure rye doughs are difficult to handle; once again the addition of strong wheat flour can provide a solution.

BARLEY MEAL

Barley is low in gluten and is seldom used for bread making in Britain and western Europe. In Russia and other eastern European countries, however, barley loaves continue to be produced, the flour mostly blended with some proportion of wheat or rye flour to give the loaf volume. These loaves are definitely on the robust side. They tend to be rather grey and flat and have an earthy, rather mealy flavour. Similar loaves must have been baked in parts of the British Isles in the past, when times were hard or the wheat harvest had failed. There are several old Welsh recipes for barley bread, which was rolled out flat before being baked on a baking stone. Finnish barley bread is made in much the same way.

Barley meal is the ground whole grain of the barley, while barley flour is ground pearl barley, with the outer skin removed.

BELOW: Finnish barley bread

Either can be added in small quantities to wholemeal or to white flour to produce a bread with a slightly rustic flavour.

BUCKWHEAT FLOUR

This grain is blackish in colour, hence its French name, *blé noir*. It is not strictly a cereal but is the fruit of a plant belonging to the dock family. The three-cornered grains are milled to a flour and used for pancakes, blinis and, in France, for crêpes or galettes. It can also be added to wheat flour and is popular mixed with other grains in multigrained loaves. It has a distinctive, earthy flavour and is best used in small quantities.

CORN MEAL (MAIZEMEAL)

This meal is ground from white or yellow corn and is normally available in coarse, medium or fine grinds. Coarse-ground corn meal is used for the Italian dish of polenta; for bread making choose one of the finer grinds, available from most health food stores. There are numerous corn breads from the southern states of America, including the famous double corn bread. Corn was brought back to Europe by the Spanish and Portuguese and corn breads are still popular in these countries today, particularly in Portugal. Corn contains no gluten so will not make a loaf unless it is blended with wheat flour, in which case the corn adds a pleasant flavour and colour.

MILLET FLOUR

Although high in protein, millet flour is low in gluten and is not commonly used by itself in bread making. It is pale yellow in colour, with a gritty texture. The addition of wheat flour produces an interesting, slightly nutty flavour.

OATMEAL

Oatmeal does not contain gluten and is only very rarely used by itself for bread making. The exception is in Scotland where flat crisply baked oatmeal biscuits have been popular for centuries. These are baked on a griddle and served with butter or marmalade. Oatmeal can also be used in wheat or multigrained loaves. Choose finely ground oatmeal for making oatcakes or for using in loaves. Rolled oats are not a flour but are the steamed and flattened whole oats. They look good scattered over the crust of leaves and rolls, and add a pleasant flavour.

RICE FLOUR

Polished rice, if ground very finely, becomes rice flour. It can be used as a thickening agent and is useful for people with wheat allergies. It is also occasionally used for some Indian breads.

> ### STORAGE
>
> Although most flours keep well, they do not last indefinitely and it is important to pay attention to the "use-by" date on the packet. Old flour will begin to taste stale and will make a disappointing loaf. Always store flour on a cool dry shelf. Ideally, the flour should be kept in its bag and placed in a tin or storage jar with a tight-fitting lid. Wash and dry the jar thoroughly whenever replacing with new flour and avoid adding new flour to old. Wholemeal (whole-wheat) flour, because it contains the oils in wheatgerm, keeps less well than white flours. Consequently, do not buy large quantities at a time and keep it in a very cool place or in the salad drawer of the refrigerator.

ABOVE: A selection of non-wheat grains and specialist flours. Clockwise from top centre: rye flour, buckwheat flour, corn meal, bajra flour, organic rye flour, millet grain, jowar flour, gram flour and atta or chapati flour. In the centre are (clockwise from top) barley meal, fine oatmeal and rice flour.

RYE FLOUR

Rye is the only other cereal, apart from wheat, that is widely used to make bread. It has a good gluten content, although the gluten in rye is different from wheat gluten, and rye doughs are notoriously sticky and difficult to handle. For this reason, rye meal is often blended with other flours to create a dough that is more manageable. There are as many different rye meals as there are wheat flours, ranging in colour and in type of grind. Pumpernickel and other dense and steamed box-shaped rye breads use a coarsely ground wholemeal rye, while finer flour, which contains neither the bran nor the germ, is used for the popular crusty black breads.

INDIAN FLOURS
ATTA/CHAPATI FLOUR

This is a very fine wholemeal (whole-wheat) flour, which is normally found only in Indian grocers where it is sometimes labelled *ata*. As well as being used to make chapatis, it is also the type of flour used for making rotis and other Indian flat breads.

BAJRA FLOUR

This plant grows along the west coast of India. The grains are a mixture of yellow and grey but when ground, the flour is a more uniform grey. It has a strong nutty aroma and a distinct flavour. *Bajra* bread or *rotla* is cooked, like all unleavened breads, on a griddle.

JOWAR FLOUR

Jowar grows over most of central and southern India. The flour, ground from the pretty pale yellow grains, is a creamy-white colour. The flat breads usually made from this flour, called *bhakris*, are roasted on a griddle and are traditionally served with a rich-flavoured, spicy, coconut, garlic and red chilli chutney.

GRAM FLOUR

This is a flour made from ground chick-peas. It is also known as *besan*. The Indian missi rotis – spicy, unleavened breads from northern India – are made using gram flour or a mixture of whole-wheat and gram flours.

YEAST AND OTHER LEAVENS

Almost all breads today are leavened in some way, which means that a substance has been added to the dough to initiate fermentation and make the dough rise.

Without yeast or another leavening agent, the mixture of flour and water, once cooked, would be merely a flat, unappetizing cake. At some point in our history, our ancestors discovered how dough, if left to ferment in the warmth, produced a lighter and airier bread when cooked.

The transformation of dough into bread is caused by yeast or another leavening ingredient producing carbon dioxide. The carbon dioxide expands, the dough stretches and tiny pockets of air are introduced into the dough. When the bread is cooked the process is set and the air becomes locked in.

LEAVENING AGENTS

The most popular and most widely known leavening ingredient in bread making is yeast. However, raising agents such as

BELOW: Clockwise from top left: fresh yeast, dried yeast, fast-action dried yeast and easy-blend dried yeast.

bicarbonate of soda (baking soda) and baking powder are also used for making certain breads.

YEAST

Yeast is the most popular leavening agent for bread making. It is simple to use, more reliable than a natural leaven and considerably quicker to activate. Conventional dried yeast, easy-blend (rapid-rise) and fast-action yeast are all types of dried yeast, produced for the convenience of those making bread at home. Almost all bakers prefer fresh yeast, since it is considered to have a superior flavour and to be more reliable. However, when fresh yeast is not available or convenient, dried yeast is a handy substitute.

There are several ways of adding yeast to flour. Fresh yeast is usually blended with lukewarm water before being mixed into the flour; conventional dried yeast is first reconstituted in warm water and then left until frothy; easy-blend and fast-action dried yeasts are added directly to the flour.

THE SPONGE METHOD

Some yeasted breads are made by the sponge method, whereby the yeast is dissolved in more lukewarm water than usual, and then mixed with

some of the flour to make a batter. This can be done in a bowl, or the batter can be made in a well in the centre of the flour, with only some surrounding flour included at the start, as in the recipe for split tin loaf. The batter is left for at least 20 minutes – often much longer – until bubbles appear on the surface, a process known as sponging. It is then mixed with the remaining flour, and any other ingredients are added. The advantage of this method is that it enables the yeast to start working without being inhibited by ingredients like eggs, fat and sugar, which slow down its action.

Many French breads are also sponged. A slightly different technique is used and the batter is left to ferment for a lot longer – for 2–12 hours. The slow fermentation creates what is described as a *poolish* sponge, and makes for a wonderfully flavoured bread, with very little acidity, yet with a fragile and crunchy crust. *Pain polka* is made by this method, as are the best baguettes. Two factors affect the rise: the temperature of the room and the wetness of the mixture. A wet sponge will rise more quickly than a firmer one. Italian bakers employ a similar process called a *biga*. This uses less liquid and the sponge takes about 12–15 hours to mature. For an example of the use of a *biga* starter, see the recipe for ciabatta.

BAKING POWDER

This is made up of a mixture of acid and alkaline chemicals. When these come into contact with moisture, as in a dough or a batter, the reaction of the chemicals produces tiny bubbles of air so the dough rises and becomes spongy, just as it does with yeast. Unlike when making yeast-leavened breads, however, it is important to work fast as the carbon dioxide will quickly escape and the loaf will collapse.

BICARBONATE OF SODA

Bicarbonate of soda (baking soda), sometimes just called soda, is the leavening ingredient in Irish soda bread. It is an alkaline chemical which, when mixed with an acid in a moisture-rich environment, reacts to produce carbon dioxide. Cream of tartar, an acid that is made from fermented grapes, is commonly used in conjunction with bicarbonate of soda for soda breads, or else the soda is combined with soured milk, which is naturally acidic. Buttermilk may also be used.

LEFT: Pain de campagne is one of the many French sourdough breads.

can be made and kept in the refrigerator until it is ready for use. Each time part of the starter is used, the remaining starter is refreshed with equal amounts of flour and water. Looked after in this way, some starters have been known to survive for many years.

Starters for sourdoughs, as well as the breads themselves, vary hugely – not only from country to country but from village to village. Many recipes, and indeed many bakers, recommend using a little yeast to get started since a true starter is likely to be rather a hit-or-miss affair. Wild yeasts may be all around us, but for some reason they seem to vanish as soon as you decide to make a sourdough. Starters also improve with age, so do not be discouraged if your first sourdoughs are rather bland. After a few attempts, you should find your breads developing their own tangy personality.

BREWER'S YEAST

Old cookbooks sometimes call for brewer's yeast or ale or beer barm. Until the last century, this was the common and only leavening ingredient. Since then brewer's yeast has acquired something of a cult status, and during the 1950s in the USA and Britain it was considered a wonder food owing to its nutritional value. It is not however, suitable for bread making, being too bitter, and should only be used for making beer.

NATURAL LEAVENS

Natural leavens, made using a medium of flour, or grown from potatoes, yogurt, treacle or buttermilk, were once very popular and are enjoying a renaissance.

SOURDOUGHS

Sourdoughs are breads based on a natural leaven. An authentic sourdough relies entirely on the wild yeasts that exist in the air. Given the right conditions, any dough of flour and water or batter of vegetable origin will start to ferment spontaneously and will continue to do so if starch or sugar is added to feed it. Recipes for some of the traditional American and German breads use a variety of rather surprising starters for their sourdoughs, from potatoes to treacle. With the renewed interest in rustic breads, there are all sorts of sourdough breads in supermarkets and specialist bakers, and numerous books explaining how to make them at home.

There are many, many types of sourdough. In France the sourdough method is known as the *chef* or *levain*, and is used

for *pain de campagne* as well as for sourdough baguettes.

Despite their many variations, sourdoughs do have some elements in common. Each begins with a "starter", which can take anything up to a week to ferment and become established. This "starter" or leaven is used, daily by bakers or less frequently by home bread makers, for the day's bread. A small amount of the dough is then kept back and used for the next batch of bread. Alternatively, a slightly more liquid starter

YEAST KNOW-HOW

◆ Yeast needs warmth to activate it, but must not be subjected to too hot a temperature or it will die. Whether dissolving yeast in water or adding liquid to the yeast and flour, make sure the liquid is not too warm. The optimum heat is 38°C/100°F. If you do not have a thermometer, experts recommend mixing 300ml/½ pint/1¼ cups boiling water with 600ml/1pint/2½ cups cold water, and measuring the required water from the mixture.

◆ If you are using easy-blend or fast-action dried yeast you can afford to have the water slightly hotter, since the yeast is mixed with the flour, and the heat of the water will rapidly dissipate.

◆ Check "use-by" dates on dried and fast-action yeasts. If a product is past its "use-by" date, replace it. If it is marginal and you cannot immediately replace it, take a measuring jug (cup)

and pour in 120ml/4fl oz/½ cup warm water (43–46°C/110–115°F). Add 5ml/1 tsp sugar, stir to dissolve and then sprinkle over 10ml/2 tsp dried yeast. Stir and leave for 10 minutes. The yeast should begin to rise to the surface after the first 5 minutes, and by 10 minutes there should have developed a rounded crown of foam that reaches to the 250ml/8fl oz/1 cup level of the measuring jug. If this happens the yeast is active; if not, the yeast has lost its potency and should be discarded.

◆ The amount of yeast you require should not increase proportionally as the amount of flour increases, so take care if you decide to double the quantities in a recipe. You will not need to double the amount of yeast. Similarly, if you halve a recipe, you are likely to need proportionally more yeast or be prepared to wait longer for the bread to rise.

ADDITIONAL INGREDIENTS

Although flour and yeast are the most obvious ingredients used in bread making, there are a number of other ingredients that are just as important.

WATER OR MILK

As a general rule, savoury loaves are made using water; teabreads and sweeter breads use milk. Whatever the liquid, it is always heated slightly. Breads made with milk are softer in both the crumb and the crust than those using water.

ABOVE: Welsh bara brith is packed with dried fruits.

SALT

Almost all bread recipes add salt at the beginning, stirring or sifting it right into the flour.

Salt is one of the few essential ingredients in bread making. It is important for both flavour and the effect it has on the yeast and dough. Essentially, it slows down the yeast's action – which is why it should not be added directly to the yeast. This means that the dough rises in a controlled and even way, giving a well-risen even loaf. Too little salt means the loaf will stale more quickly; too much and the crust will harden, so do take care when measuring salt.

LEFT: The French petit pains au lait, made with milk rather than water, have a lovely soft crumb and crust.

SUGAR

Sugar, once invariably added to all breads (usually with the yeast), is now no longer necessary for savoury breads since modern yeasts can be activated without it. However, some bakers still prefer to add a little sugar, even when making savoury baked goods, contending that results with sugar are better than when it is omitted.

White and brown sugar, honey, treacle (molasses) and golden (light corn) syrup can be used to sweeten teabreads and fruit breads. Sugars are normally added with the flour, while syrups are more often stirred into the lukewarm liquid so that they are gently warmed as well.

BUTTER AND EGGS

Enriched breads are made with the addition of both butter and eggs and normally use milk rather than water. These breads, such as Sally Lunn, barm brack and many of the festive European breads, have a delicious cake-like texture and soft crust. The butter is either melted or diced and the eggs beaten before being worked into other ingredients to make a fairly sticky batter. This is then beaten by hand or in an electric mixer. In some instances, the butter is kneaded into the dough after the initial rising, since large quantities of butter can inhibit the action of the yeast.

BELOW: Sally Lunn, one of the richest breads of all, is traditionally served sandwiched with clotted cream.

FRUIT

Almost any dried fruit can be added to bread. Raisins, sultanas (golden raisins), currants and mixed (candied) peel have always been popular for fruit loaves. Chopped dates, apricots and prunes can all be kneaded in, as can more exotic fruits, such as dried mango or papaya. Fruit can be added to a dough during mixing or left until the second kneading. If adding at the second kneading, warm the fruit first, so that it does not inhibit the action of the yeast. If you are using an electric mixer or food processor for kneading, note that the blades will chop the fruit. This spoils both the appearance and the flavour of the loaf, so only knead by machine to begin with, then knead the fruit in by hand after the initial rising.

FATS

Fats, in the form of butter, oil, lard (shortening) or vegetable fat, are sometimes added to savoury loaves. They add flavour and help to preserve the freshness of the loaf. The Italians particularly love adding olive oil to their breads, which they do in generous quantities. Although oils and melted butter can be poured into the flour with the yeast and liquid, solid butter or fats are normally kneaded into the flour before the liquid is added.

NUTS, HERBS AND OTHER SAVOURY INGREDIENTS

Some of our favourite breads today are flavoured with herbs, nuts and other

BELOW: Ciabatta, like many Italian breads, is made with olive oil.

such savoury ingredients. *Manoucher*, "Mediterranean nights" bread, is a rainbow of colours. Based on the Italian *focaccia*, it contains rosemary, red, green and yellow (bell) peppers along with goat's cheese. The Italians add olives or sun-dried tomatoes to their ciabatta, while walnut bread (*pain aux noix* in France, *pane con noci* in Italy) is one of the best-known and best-loved savoury loaves.

Nuts, herbs, pitted olives and sun-dried tomatoes should be roughly chopped before being kneaded into the dough after the first rising.

SPICES

The sweet spices are cinnamon, nutmeg, cloves and ginger, and for savoury breads cumin, fennel, caraway and anise impart a delicious flavour. Mace, pepper and coriander seeds can be used for both sweet and savoury breads. Spices can be added with the flour or kneaded in with fruit or nuts, or other ingredients.

TECHNIQUES
—

USING YEAST

There are several different forms of yeast, some easier to use than others, but none of them particularly tricky if you follow a few simple rules. Whichever yeast you use, it must be in good condition – neither old nor stale – and must not be subjected to too much heat.

USING FRESH YEAST

Fresh yeast is available from baker's stores, health food stores and most super-markets with an in-store bakery. It is pale beige, has a sweet, fruity smell and should crumble easily. It can be stored in the refrigerator, wrapped in clear film (plastic wrap), for up to 2 weeks or can be frozen for up to 3 months. A quantity of 15g/1/2oz fresh yeast should be sufficient for 675–900g/ 11/2–2lb/6–8 cups flour, although this will depend on the recipe.

1 Put the yeast in a small bowl. Using a spoon, mash or "cream" it with a little of the measured water until smooth.

2 Pour in the remaining measured liquid, which may be water, milk or a mixture of the two. Mix well. Use as directed in the recipe.

USING DRIED YEAST

Dried yeast is simply the dehydrated equivalent of fresh yeast, but it needs to be blended with lukewarm liquid before use. Store dried yeast in a cool dry place and check the "use-by" date on the can or packet. You will need about 15g/1/2oz (7.5ml/11/2 tsp) dried yeast for 675g/ 11/2lb/6 cups flour. Some bakers add sugar or honey to the liquid to which the yeast is added, but this is not necessary, as the granules contain enough nourishment to enable the yeast to work.

1 Pour the measured lukewarm liquid into a small bowl and sprinkle the dried yeast evenly over the surface.

2 Cover with clear film and leave in a warm room for 10–15 minutes until frothy. Stir well and use as directed.

WATER TEMPERATURE
For fresh and regular dried yeast, use lukewarm water; for easy-blend and fast-action yeast the water can be a little hotter, as the yeast is mixed with flour before the liquid is added.

USING EASY-BLEND (RAPID-RISE) AND FAST-ACTION DRIED YEASTS

These are the most convenient of the dried yeasts as they can be stirred directly into the flour. Fast-action yeasts and some easy-blends contain a bread improver, which eliminates the need for two kneadings and risings – check the instructions on the packet to make sure. Most of these yeasts come in 7g/1/4oz sachets, which are sufficient for 675g/ 11/2lb/6 cups flour. Do not store opened sachets as the yeast will deteriorate quickly.

Sift together the flour and salt into a medium bowl and rub in the fat, if using. Stir in the easy-blend or fast-action dried yeast, then add warm water or milk, plus any other ingredients, as directed in the recipe.

BELOW: Small, shaped rolls are very quick to make using easy-blend yeast.

MAKING A YEAST DOUGH BY THE SPONGE METHOD

This method produces bread with an excellent flavour and soft texture. The quantities listed are merely an example and can be increased proportionately. See individual recipes.

1 Mix 7g/¼oz fresh yeast with 250ml/8fl oz/1 cup lukewarm water in a large bowl. Stir in 115g/4oz/1 cup unbleached plain (all-purpose) flour, using a wooden spoon, then use your fingers to draw the mixture together until you have a smooth liquid with the consistency of a thick batter. (Do not add salt to the sponge as this would inhibit the yeast.)

2 Cover with a damp dishtowel and leave in a warm place. The sponge will double or triple in bulk and then fall back, which indicates it is ready to use (after about 5–6 hours).

3 The sponge starter is now ready to be mixed to a dough with the remaining flour and any other ingredients, such as butter as directed in the recipe.

MAKING AN ITALIAN STARTER (BIGA)

If you wish to make an Italian *biga* for Pugliese or a similar Italian country bread, use 175g/6oz/1½ cups unbleached plain flour. Cream the yeast with 90ml/6 tbsp lukewarm water, then pour it into a well in the centre of the flour. Gradually mix in the surrounding flour to form a firm dough. The dough should be kneaded for a few minutes and then left, covered with lightly oiled clear film (plastic wrap) for 12–15 hours.

MAKING A FRENCH SOURDOUGH STARTER (CHEF)

It is not difficult to make a sourdough starter. The starter can be kept in the refrigerator for up to 10 days, but for longer than that it should be frozen. Bring the starter to room temperature before adding to the next batch of bread.

1 Place 115g/4oz/1 cup flour in a large bowl and add 75ml/5 tbsp water. Mix together, then knead for 3–4 minutes to form a dough. Cover the bowl with clear film and set aside at room temperature for 2–3 days. The flour that you choose will depend on the bread you wish to make; it can be wholemeal (whole-wheat), white or rye, or a combination of two or three.

2 After 2–3 days, the mixture will rise and aerate slightly and turn a greyish colour. A soft crust may form on top of the starter and it should develop a slightly sweet-sour smell.

3 Remove any crust that has formed on top of the starter and discard. Stir in 120ml/4fl oz/½ cup lukewarm water to make a paste and then add 175g/6oz/1½ cups flour. The flour can be wholemeal or a mixture of wholemeal and white. Mix together to make a dough, then transfer to a work surface and knead lightly until firm.

SOURDOUGH

The actual word "sourdough" is thought to have come from America as this style of bread was commonly made by pioneers and the word was sometimes used to describe old "Forty-Niners". However bread made by the sourdough method dates back long before the 19th century. Many traditional European rye breads are based on this method, particularly in Germany and Scandinavia where the sour flavour of the leaven complements the flavour of the rye.

In Britain sourdoughs are sometimes called acids or acid breads. Some restaurants and home bread makers have their own favourite acid breads, but generally there is not much of a tradition of sourdoughs in the British Isles. Except in Ireland, where soda was popular, ale barm (the fermentation liquor from beer) was the most commonly used leaven for bread making until it was replaced by baker's yeast around the middle of the last century.

4 Place the ball of dough in a bowl, cover again with clear film and leave for 1–2 days at room temperature.

5 Remove and discard any crust that forms. What remains – the *chef* – can now be used to make a sourdough bread, such as *pain de campagne rustique*. To keep the *chef* going, save about 225g/8oz of the dough each time.

6 Place the dough starter in a crock or bowl, cover and keep in the refrigerator for up to 10 days or freeze.

MIXING, KNEADING AND RISING

The sequence and method of adding ingredients to make your dough are vital. For some breads, fresh or dried yeast is dissolved in lukewarm water and then stirred into the flour; if easy-blend (rapid-rise) dried yeast or fast-action dried yeast is used, this is added directly to the flour with warm water or milk added after-wards. Read your recipe carefully before starting and warm your bowls if they are in the least bit chilly, so that the yeast gets off to a good start.

MIXING

The easiest way to mix the dough is with your hand but, if you prefer, start mixing with a spoon until the mixture is too stiff to stir, then mix by hand.

1 If using fresh or regular dried yeast, mix it with lukewarm water or milk as described in the recipe. Sift the flour, salt and any other dry ingredients (including easy-blend or fast-action dried yeast, if using) into a large, warm mixing bowl.

2 If using butter or lard (shortening), rub it in. Make a well in the centre of the flour mixture and pour in the yeast mixture with the remaining lukewarm water. If oil is being used, add it now.

3 Mix the liquid into the flour using your hand, stirring in a smooth, wide motion so that all the dry ingredients are evenly incorporated and the mixture forms a dough. Knead lightly in the bowl.

KNEADING

Kneading is something you just cannot skip in bread making. If you do not have strong wrists, or simply do not enjoy it, you will have to resort to using the food processor, which takes all the effort – and much of the time – out of kneading. Better still though, learn to love it.

Kneading dough, whether by hand or machine, is the only way of warming and stretching the gluten in the flour. As the strands of gluten warm and become more elastic, so the dough becomes more springy. It is the elasticity of the dough, combined with the action of the yeast, that gives bread its light, springy texture. Insufficient kneading means that the dough cannot hold the little pockets of air, and the bread will collapse in the oven to leave a heavy and dense loaf.

HOW TO KNEAD BY HAND

1 Place the mixed dough on a floured surface and flour your hands generously.

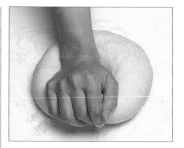

2 Press the heel of your hand firmly into the centre of the dough, then curl your fingers around the edge of the dough.

3 Pull and stretch the dough towards you and press down again, giving the dough a quarter turn as you do so.

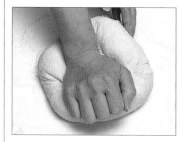

4 Continue pressing and stretching the dough, making quarter turns so that it is evenly kneaded. After about 10 minutes the dough should be supple and elastic; however, some breads need more kneading, so do check the recipe.

ADDING EXTRA INGREDIENTS

Ingredients, such as olives, can be added after kneading, or they can be kneaded in after the first rising.

KNEADING IN A FOOD PROCESSOR

Unless you have an industrial-size machine, it is likely that your food processor will only be able to knead moderate amounts of dough. Don't attempt to knead more dough than recommended by the manufacturer as it may damage the motor. If necessary, knead in small batches and then knead the dough balls together by hand afterwards.

Fit the dough blade into the processor and then blend together all the dry ingredients. Add the yeast mixture, and extra lukewarm liquid and butter or oil, if required; process until the mixture comes together. Knead for 60 seconds, or according to the manufacturer's instructions, then knead by hand on a floured board for 1–2 minutes.

KNEADING IN A FOOD MIXER

Check the manufacturer's instructions to make sure bread dough can be kneaded in your machine.

Mix the dry ingredients together. Add the yeast, liquid and oil or butter, if using, and mix slowly, using the dough hook. The dough will tumble and fall to begin with, and then it will slowly come together. Continue kneading the dough for 3–4 minutes or according to the manufacturer's instructions.

RISING

This is the easy part of bread making – all you need now is to give the dough the right conditions, and nature and chemistry will do the rest. While kneading works and conditions the gluten in the flour, during rising the yeast does the work. The fermentation process creates carbon dioxide, which is trapped within the dough by the elastic gluten. This process also has the effect of conditioning the flour, improving the flavour and texture of the eventual loaf.

The number of times you leave your bread to rise will depend on the yeast you are using and the recipe. An easy-blend or a fast-action yeast needs no first rising, but dough using fresh yeast and other dried yeasts normally requires two risings, with some recipes calling for even more.

TEMPERATURE AND TIME

For most recipes, dough is left to rise at a temperature of about 24–27°C/75–80°F, the equivalent of an airing cupboard or near a warm oven. At a cooler temperature the bread rises more slowly and some of the best-flavoured breads, including baguettes, use a slower rising, giving the enzymes and starches in the flour more time to mature. The quantity of yeast used will also determine the time required for rising. More yeast means quicker rising.

1 Place the kneaded dough in a bowl that has been lightly greased. This will prevent the dough from sticking. Cover the bowl with a damp dishtowel or a piece of oiled clear film (plastic wrap), to prevent a skin from forming on top.

2 Leave to rise until the dough has doubled in bulk. At room temperature, this should take 1½–2 hours – less if the temperature is warmer; more if the room is cool. It can even be left to rise in the refrigerator for about 8 hours.

A FEW SIMPLE RULES

◆ Warm bowls and other equipment.

◆ Use the correct amount of yeast: too much will speed up the rising process but will spoil the flavour and will mean the loaf stales more quickly.

◆ If you have a thermometer, check the temperature of the lukewarm liquid, at least until you can gauge it accurately yourself. It should be between 37–43°C/98–108°F. Mixing two parts cold water with one part boiling water gives you water at roughly the right temperature.

◆ The amount of liquid required for a dough depends on several factors – type of flour, other ingredients, even the room temperature. Recipes therefore often give approximate quantities of liquid. You will soon learn to judge the ideal consistency of a dough.

◆ Do not skimp on kneading. Kneading is essential for stretching the gluten to give a well-risen, light-textured loaf.

◆ Avoid leaving dough to rise in a draught and make sure the ambient temperature is not too high, or the dough will begin to cook.

◆ Always cover the bowl during rising as a crust will form on top of the dough if the air gets to it. Clear film can be pressed on to the dough itself or can be stretched over the bowl. Either way, oil the film first or the dough will stick to it as it rises.

◆ Remember: the slower the rising, the better the taste of the bread.

KNOCKING BACK, SHAPING AND FINAL RISING

KNOCKING BACK

After all the effort by the yeast to create a risen dough, it seems a shame to knock it back. However, this process not only redistributes the gases in the dough that were created by fermentation, it also reinvigorates the yeast, making sure that it is evenly distributed, and ensures the bread has an even texture. It should take only a few minutes and the bread is then ready for shaping. The dough is fully risen when it has doubled in bulk. If you are not sure that it is ready, test by gently inserting a finger into the centre of the dough. The dough should not immediately spring back. If it does, leave for a little longer.

1 Knock back the risen dough using your knuckles. Americans call this "punching down the dough", which is an accurate description of the process. Having knocked back the dough, place it on a floured work surface and knead lightly for 1–2 minutes.

SHAPING

There are several ways of shaping the dough to fit a loaf tin (pan).

1 The easiest way is to shape the dough roughly into an oval and place it in the tin, with the smooth side on top.

2 Alternatively, roll out the dough into a rectangle, a little longer than the tin. Roll it up like a Swiss roll, tuck in the ends and place the roll in the tin, with the seam side down.

3 Another method for shaping the dough is to roll it out into a rectangle and fold it in half lengthways, pinching the edges together on the sides and flattening the dough out slightly with the heel of your hand. Fold the dough over once more to make a double thickness and pinch the edges together again. Now gently roll the dough backwards and forwards until it has a well-rounded shape.

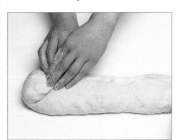

4 Fold in the two short ends and place the dough in the prepared tin with the seam along the bottom.

SHAPING A COB LOAF

1 Shape the dough into a round and then press along the centre with your hand. Turn the dough over, so that the smooth side is uppermost.

2 Shape the dough into a round or oval and place it on a baking sheet.

TIPS

◆ Always knock back the dough after the first rising and knead lightly to redistribute the yeast and the gases formed by fermentation, otherwise you may end up with large holes in the loaf or the crust may lift up and become detached from the crumb.

◆ Rising the dough in a warm place is not always necessary – it is simply a method of speeding up the process. Dough will rise (albeit very slowly) even in the refrigerator. However, wherever you decide to rise your dough the temperature must be constant. Avoid draughts or hot spots, as both will spoil the bread and may cause it to bake unevenly.

◆ Some breads may need slashing either before final rising or during this period (see next section).

SHAPING A BAGUETTE

1 Divide the dough into equal pieces. Shape each piece into a ball and then into a rectangle measuring 15 × 7.5cm/ 6 × 3in. Fold the bottom third up and the top third down lengthways. Press the edges together to seal them. Repeat twice, then stretch each piece to a 33–35cm/13–14in loaf.

2 Place within the folds of a pleated, floured dishtowel or in *bannetons*.

SHAPING A PLAIT

1 Divide the dough into three equal pieces. Roll each piece into a 25cm/10in sausage about 4cm/1½in thick.

2 Place the three "sausages" on a greased baking sheet. Either start the plait (braid) in the centre, plaiting to each end in turn, or pinch the pieces firmly together at one end then plait.

3 When you have finished, pinch the ends together, and turn them under.

FINAL RISING

After shaping the dough and placing it on the baking sheet or in the tin (pan), there is usually a final rising before baking. Depending on the warmth of the room, this can take ¾–1½ hours and in a very cool room up to 4 hours. Cover the dough so that the surface does not crust over. Oiled clear film (plastic wrap) placed over the tin or directly on the bread is best. The timing is important as over-rising means the loaf may collapse in the oven, while too little proving will mean the loaf will be heavy and flat.

BELOW: A loaf ready for the final rising.

BELOW: After rising the dough should be double in size – no more.

COOK'S TIP

When stretching dough for baguettes or plaits, work with care so that you don't overstretch it. If the dough feels as if it is going to tear, leave that strand to rest for a minute or two and work on one of the other pieces of dough. When you go back to the first piece, you will find that the gluten has allowed the dough to stretch and you can work it some more.

PROVING BASKETS

Professional bakers use proving baskets called *bannetons* for baguettes, and circular *couronnes* for round loaves. Some are lined with linen. Proving baskets are available from good kitchenware shops but, depending on the shape you require, you can improvise with baskets and/or earthenware dishes. Simply dust a linen dishtowel liberally with flour and use to line the container.

BELOW: A proving basket will give your loaves a professional finish.

CHOOSING TINS

Choosing the right size of loaf tin (pan) can be tricky. If it is too small the dough will spill over the top. If it is too large, the final loaf will be uneven. As a rule the tin should be about twice the size of the dough. Professional bakers use black tins, which are considered to be better than shiny metal ones as they absorb the heat better, giving a crisper crust. Always warm a tin before using and then grease it with melted lard (shortening), vegetable oil or unsalted (sweet) butter. Experiment to see what you find most successful. Baking sheets should also be greased to prevent sticking.

TOPPING AND BAKING

The actual baking is perhaps the simplest part of the bread-making process, yet even here the yeast still has a part to play and it is important that you play your part too, by making sure conditions are as ideal as possible. When the loaf goes into the oven the heat kills the yeast, but for the first few minutes, there is a final burst of life and the bread will rise even further before the entire process is set and the air is finally locked in.

PREPARING TO BAKE

While the shaped dough is having its final rise, you will need to preheat the oven to the required temperature. It is important that the oven is at the right temperature when the bread goes in – almost always a hot oven, between 220–230°C/425–450°F/ Gas 7–8, although check the recipe since sweet loaves or those containing a lot of butter cook at a lower temperature. Many recipes suggest that the oven temperature is reduced either immediately after putting the bread in the oven or some time during cooking. This means the bread gets a good blast of heat to start with, and then cooks more gradually. This mimics the original bread ovens, which would have cooled down slowly once the embers had been removed.

SLASHING

Once the loaf is ready for baking, all that is needed is to slash and glaze the loaf. This is done not only for appearance, but also to improve the baking of the loaf. When the loaf goes into the oven, the yeast will continue to produce carbon dioxide for a short time and the loaf will rise. This is called the "spring". Slashing provides escape routes for the gas and gives direction to the spring, so that the loaf will open out around the slashes and retain an even shape. Loaves that have not been allowed enough time to rise will tend to have more spring, and it is therefore important to slash these fairly deeply. If you think your loaf may have over-risen, only slash it gently.

You will also find that some recipes suggest slashing either before the final rising

or some time during it. This will depend on how much you want your loaf to "open up". The earlier it is slashed the more the split will develop. However, unless the recipe specifies otherwise, the general rule is to slash the loaf just before you put it in the oven.

ABOVE: Cob or coburg – just before baking, slash a deep cross across the top of the loaf.

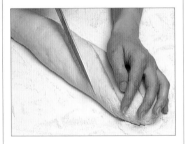

ABOVE: Baguette – slash four or five times on the diagonal just before the baking process.

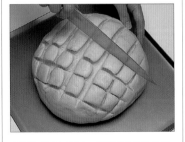

ABOVE: Porcupine – slashing not only looks attractive, but gives a wonderful crunchy crust to this bread. Make five or six cuts across the bread in one direction, then cut again at right angles, chequerboard fashion.

ABOVE: Tin loaf – part-way through rising, make one deep slash along the length of the loaf.

GLAZING

Glazing has two important functions. It gives an attractive finish to the loaf and it introduces moisture during cooking. This moisture produces steam which also helps to expand the gases in the loaf and ensures it cooks through completely. Glazes also change the consistency and taste of the crust. Bread can be glazed before, during or just after baking: sometimes recipes will suggest all three. If you glaze before and during baking, take care not to brush sticky glazes up to the sides of a tin (pan) or let the glaze drip on to the baking sheet, thereby gluing the bread to its container. This will cause the loaf to crack and rise unevenly.

All sorts of glazes can be used – egg yolk, egg white, milk, butter, sugar solutions, salt solutions and olive oil are regularly used. They also help the toppings to stick to the surface of the loaf.

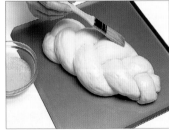

ABOVE: Brushing a plait (braid) with beaten egg yolk and milk before baking gives it a golden glaze and a professional-looking finish.

TOPPINGS

There are as many toppings as there are glazes, all of which add to the appearance, taste and texture of your bread. The dough can be rolled in a topping before the second rising, or it can be glazed and sprinkled with the topping just before baking. Good toppings to try include seeds, grated cheese, cracked wheat, oats, sea salt, herbs, corn meal or wheat flakes.

For basic breads and rolls, toppings are simply a matter of preference – for dinner parties offer guests a selection of white and wholemeal (whole-wheat) rolls, each sprinkled with a different topping. Some breads traditionally have their own topping. *Challah*, for instance, is usually sprinkled with poppy seeds. Many British and American breads have no toppings as such, but a dusting of flour gives an attractive finish to the loaf.

Grated cheese and fried onion rings make more substantial as well as tasty and attractive toppings and many of the Italian breads excel themselves in their rich

ABOVE: A split tin loaf can be dusted with flour before baking.

ABOVE: Roll the dough for a Granary (whole-wheat) loaf in sunflower seeds.

BELOW: For a dinner party or a buffet meal, bake a batch of rolls with assorted toppings. From left to right: top row: wheat flakes, poppy seeds, sunflower seeds, sesame seeds; middle row: caraway seeds, sea salt, cracked wheat, corn meal; bottom row: wheat flakes, chopped fresh herbs, grated cheese, chopped black olives.

variety of toppings – olives, sun-dried tomatoes and roasted (bell) peppers are frequently added.

Toppings can also be added during and sometimes after cooking. Small breads, such as Vienna rolls, are baked until just golden, brushed with milk and then strewn with sea salt, cumin or caraway seeds. They are then returned to the oven for a few more moments until cooked.

BAKING TIMES

This will depend on the recipe, the size of the loaf and the heat of the oven. As a general rule, rolls take about 20 minutes, round country breads 40–50 minutes and tin loaves a little longer, 45–60 minutes. To check if bread is ready, remove it from the oven and tap firmly on the base of the loaf with your knuckles. It should have a hollow sound. If it seems soft or does not sound hollow, bake for a little longer.

ABOVE: Check rolls are ready by gently turning one over in a clean dishtowel. The underside should be firm and golden.

ABOVE: To check that a loaf is cooked, tap the base with your knuckles. It should be firm and sound hollow.

ADDING MOISTURE TO THE OVEN

A baker's oven is completely sealed and therefore produces the necessary steam for an evenly risen loaf. At home, glazing helps to produce steam, as does a can of boiling water placed in the bottom of the oven, or you can spray water into the oven two or three times during cooking.

WHAT WENT WRONG

DOUGH WON'T RISE

You may have forgotten the yeast or the yeast may be past its "use-by" date and is dead. To save the dough, make up another batch, making certain the yeast is active. This dough can then be kneaded into the original dough. Alternatively, dissolve the new yeast in warm water and work it into the dough. Another time, always check that yeast is active before adding to flour.

SIDES AND BOTTOM OF BREAD ARE TOO PALE

The oven temperature was too low, or the tin (pan) did not allow heat to penetrate the crust. To remedy this, turn the loaf out of its tin and return it to the oven, placing it upside down on a shelf, for 5–10 minutes.

CRUST TOO SOFT

There was insufficient steam in the oven. You could glaze the crusts before baking next time and spray the inside of the oven with water. Alternatively, place a little hot water in an ovenproof dish in the bottom of the oven during baking. This problem particularly besets French breads and other crusty loaves, which require a certain amount of steam in the oven.

CRUST TOO HARD

Using too much glaze or having too much steam in the oven can harden the crust, so use less glaze next time. To soften a crusty loaf, leave it overnight in a plastic bag.

CRUST SEPARATES FROM THE BREAD

This is caused either by the dough drying out during rising, or by the oven temperature being too low and the dough expanding unevenly. Next time, cover the dough with clear film (plastic wrap) or waxed paper to prevent any moisture loss while rising, and ensure that the oven is preheated to the correct temperature, so that heat penetrates uniformly.

SOFT PALE CRUST

This could be because the bread was not baked for long enough or perhaps the oven temperature was too low. When you think the bread is ready, tap it firmly underneath; it should sound hollow. If it does not, return the bread to the oven, only this time placing it directly on the oven shelf.

LOAF IS CRUMBLY AND DRY

Either the bread was baked for too long or you used too much flour. Next time check the quantities in the recipe. It is also possible that the oven was too hot. Next time reduce the temperature and check the loaf when the crust looks golden brown.

LARGE HOLES IN LOAF

Either the dough was not knocked back (punched down) properly before shaping or it was not kneaded enough originally.

BREAD HAS A YEASTY FLAVOUR

Too much yeast was used. If doubling recipe quantities, do not double the amount of yeast but use one and a half times the amount. In addition, do not overcompensate for a cool room by adding extra yeast unless you don't mind a yeasty flavour. Wait a little longer instead – the bread will rise in the end.

LOAF COLLAPSES IN THE OVEN

Either the wrong flour was used for a particular recipe or the dough was left too long for the second rising and has over-risen. As a rule, the dough should only double in bulk.

LOAF IS DENSE AND FLAT

Too much liquid was used and the dough has become too soft, or was not kneaded enough. Always check the recipe for quantities of liquid needed until you are confident about judging the consistency of the dough. The dough should be kneaded firmly for at least 10 minutes.

BREAD-MAKING EQUIPMENT

Bread making is not an exact science and you do not need a fully equipped kitchen with state-of-the-art utensils if you decide to have a go. In the long run, though, you may decide that some things are essential and others could be useful.

SCALES/WEIGHTS

Balance scales are more accurate but spring balance scales are easier to use and more convenient (especially if you have a tendency to lose the weights). Bear in mind, if buying scales for bread making, that you will probably be using large quantities of flours and will therefore need large-size scales with a deep basin.

MEASURING JUGS (CUPS)

Heatproof glass jugs are most convenient as liquids can safely be heated in them in

BELOW: Be sure to get scales with a large measuring bowl.

LEFT: Sieves for flour or spices

the microwave and they are dishwasher safe. Measurements should be clearly marked on the outside; be sure to buy jugs with both imperial and metric measurements so that you can follow any recipe with ease.

MEASURING SPOONS

These are always useful in the kitchen for adding small quantities of spices etc. A set of spoons measures from 1.5ml/ ¼ tsp to 15ml/1 tbsp.

FOOD PROCESSOR

Most food processors can mix and knead dough extremely efficiently and in a fraction of the time it would take by hand. Always check the instruction book about bread making since only the larger machines can handle large amounts of dough, and you may find that it is necessary to knead the dough in batches.

FOOD MIXER

An electric mixer fitted with a dough hook will knead dough in a time similar to that taken to knead by hand but with much less effort. Small machines can cope with only small amounts of dough and if you are considering buying a machine for bread-making purposes, make sure that the equipment is suitable for the quantities of bread you are likely to want to make.

SIEVES

Some finer breads may require the flour to be sifted so it is worth having at least one large sieve for flours and a smaller sieve for adding ground spices or dusting the loaves with flour or icing (confectioners') sugar after baking them.

ABOVE: A selection of glass bowls

BOWLS

If you have not got a selection already, it is worth buying some now since it is not possible to make bread (at least in the kitchen) without at least two good-sized bowls. Choose a bowl with a wide mouth, which is still deep enough to contain the batter or dough. A smaller bowl is also useful (although you can use the measuring jug or cup) for making up dried yeast.

ROLLING PIN

Some doughs need to be rolled out and you will need a large rolling pin for this job. A wooden rolling pin that is long and smooth and has no separate handles is ideal for bread making.

DOUGH KNIFE OR SCRAPER

This is extremely handy when kneading dough by hand. The rectangular piece of steel on a wooden handle is particularly useful in the early part of kneading, for lifting and working sticky or difficult doughs. The blades normally measure about 10 × 13cm/4 × 5in and should ideally be slightly flexible rather than rigid.

COOK'S KNIFE

You will need a sharp knife for slashing the dough – either during rising or just before baking. Some recipe books suggest using a razor for this job but the blade does need to be very sharp indeed. Since a good cook's knife can be kept in razor-sharp condition, this is the preferable option and adds a professional touch to your loaves.

ABOVE: Bread knife and cook's knife

LEFT: Dough knife/scraper

ABOVE: Rolling pin

ABOVE: Pastry brushes

BREAD KNIFE

A dull knife can wreak havoc on a fresh loaf of bread, so make sure you use a good bread knife. Bread should be cut in a sawing motion, which is why bread knives have long serrated blades. A plain cook's knife, although it will cut through the bread, will spoil the texture of the crumb.

PASTRY BRUSH

This is essential for glazing loaves and rolls. Choose a good, wide brush. It is worth spending extra for a brush that will not lose its bristles. Use a brush made from natural fibres; nylon will melt if used for brushing hot loaves during cooking.

BREAD TINS

Bread tins (pans) come in all sizes and it is worth having a selection. Include a 450g/1lb and preferably two 1kg/2¼ lb tins so that you can make loaves in a variety of shapes and sizes. If the tins are labelled with their dimensions, rather than their

BELOW: Shallow loaf and cake tins

capacity, look out for 18 × 7.5cm/7 × 3in (equivalent to 450g/1lb) and 23 × 13cm/9 × 5in (equivalent to 1kg/2¼ lb). Other useful sizes are 30 × 10cm/12 × 4in and 25 × 10cm/10 × 4in. Professional bakers prefer matt black tins, which absorb the heat better than the shiny ones and therefore make the crust crisper. The wider

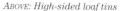

ABOVE: High-sided loaf tins

shallow tins are mostly used for fruit breads. Tin loaves are baked in plain, high-sided tins; farmhouse loaves are slightly shallower and tins may be stamped with the word "Farmhouse". Cake tins (pans) are sometimes used for bread making. Monkey bread, for instance, is baked in a 23cm/9in springform ring cake tin, while buchty – breakfast rolls that are batch-baked – require a square, loose-bottomed cake tin with straight sides that will support the rolls as they rise.

Several speciality breads are baked in a deep 15cm/6in cake tin. These breads include *panettone* and Sally Lunn.

If you are fond of baking focaccia, you will find a 25cm/10in pizza pan or shallow round cake tin invaluable.

MOULDS

There are various sizes of brioche mould for the traditional fluted brioche, including individual bun size. A *kugelhopf* mould is a fluted ring mould essential for making the Alsace or German *kugel-hopf* or the Viennese *gugelhupf*. A savarin mould is a straight-sided ring mould for

savarins and other ring-shaped breads. If you don't have the correct mould, it is sometimes possible to improvise. Boston brown bread, for instance, can be baked in a special mould, but the heatproof glass jar from a cafetière coffee jug (carafe) can be used instead, or even two 450g/1lb coffee cans, without the lids, work perfectly well once washed and dried.

BAKING SHEETS

When buying baking sheets, look for ones that are either completely flat, or have a lip only on one long edge. This makes it easier to slide bread or rolls on to a wire rack. Strong, heavy baking sheets distribute the heat evenly.

MUFFIN TINS AND PATTY TINS

Muffin tins (pans) with 7.5cm/3in cups are very useful for making elaborately shaped rolls like the aptly named New England Fantans, while the larger patty tins and

Yorkshire pudding tins come into their own for specialities like Georgian Khachapuri. The tins support the dough while it is filled with cheese and then tied into a topknot.

FLOWER POTS

Earthenware flower pots can also be used for baking. These need to be tempered before being used for bread. Brush the

new, perfectly clean pots liberally inside and out with oil and place in a hot oven (about 200°C/400°F/Gas 6) for about 30 minutes. (This can conveniently be done while you are cooking something else.) Do this several times until the pots are impregnated with oil. They can then be used for baking bread and will need very little greasing.

BELOW: Earthenware flower pots make unusual moulds for loaves.

LEFT: A French fluted brioche mould and a savarin or ring mould

LONGUETS

Longuets are moulded pieces of steel, like corrugated iron, used for baking baguettes. They are designed with the professional baker in mind and are unlikely to be suitable for an average size oven.

BAKING STONE

Baking stones are now widely available, sold principally for pizzas but also useful for making thick crusted loaves. They are the nearest thing to replicating an authentic brick-floored oven. The stones are heated in the oven and then the bread is placed on top.

BANNETONS AND COURONNES

These are the canvas-lined proving baskets used by French bakers for their bread: *bannetons* are used for baguettes, *couronnes* for round loaves. In Germany, sourdough bread is sometimes proved in a floured basket, which has the effect of creating a crust that looks like wicker.

GRIDDLE

This is a heavy cast-iron pan used on top of the stove for griddle cakes, soda farls, bannocks and even Indian breads like missi rotis and chapatis. Weight is the important feature with griddles, so that heat can be evenly dispersed.

Griddles can have handles or have the more old-fashioned design of a hooped handle over the entire pan, often with a small hoop in the centre which would have been used to hang the griddle over a peat fire. In Scotland, where they are still widely used, griddles are also known as girdles.

Square-shaped griddles that come with metal hoops for muffins and crumpets are also available in good kitchen stores. The hoops have a diameter of about 10cm/4in and are about 2.5cm/1in deep.

BELOW: This short, deep banneton is ideal for shorter French loaves.

ABOVE: Very long bannetons are designed for supporting baguettes during the final rising.

BELOW: A griddle for pikelets and other free form breads, such as griddle-baked soda bread and oatcakes.

BREAD RECIPES OF THE WORLD

There are few things more pleasurable than the aroma and taste of freshly cooked home-made bread. This collection of recipes includes savoury and sweet classics from around the world, as well as a good selection of lesser-known specialities. A wide variety of flours, all of which are readily available, has been used to create distinctive breads which reflect the different flavours of the regions. These recipes aim to take the mystery out of bread making and inspire you to try baking many different and delicious breads.

BRITISH BREADS

The range of British breads is extensive and includes a variety of shapes with picturesque names, including the bloomer, cob, split tin, cottage loaf and ornamental harvest loaf. The textures and tastes are influenced by different ingredients and cooking methods. Irish soda bread, as its name suggests, is leavened with bicarbonate of soda instead of yeast, while in Scotland, where bannocks and oatcakes are cooked on a girdle or griddle, grains such as barley and oatmeal contribute to the country-fresh flavours. Doughs enriched with dried fruits, such as Welsh bara brith and Cornish saffron bread, are delicious regional specialities.

GRANARY COB

450g/1lb/4 cups Granary (whole-wheat) or malthouse flour
10ml/2 tsp salt
15g/½ oz fresh yeast
300ml/½ pint/1¼ cups lukewarm water or milk and water mixed

FOR THE TOPPING
30ml/2 tbsp water
2.5ml/½ tsp salt
wheat flakes or cracked wheat, to sprinkle

MAKES 1 ROUND LOAF

Cob is an old word meaning "head". If you make a slash across the top of the dough, the finished loaf, known as a Danish cob, will look like a large roll. A Coburg cob has a cross cut in the top before baking.

1 Lightly flour a baking sheet. Sift the flour and salt together in a large bowl and make a well in the centre. Place in a very low oven for 5 minutes to warm.

2 Mix the yeast with a little of the water or milk mixture then blend in the rest. Add the yeast mixture to the centre of the flour and mix to a dough.

3 Turn out on to a floured surface. Knead for 10 minutes until smooth and elastic. Place in a lightly oiled bowl, cover with oiled clear film (plastic wrap) and leave to rise, in a warm place, for 1¼ hours, or until doubled in bulk.

4 Turn the dough out on to a lightly floured surface and knock back (punch down). Knead for 2–3 minutes, then roll into a ball, making sure the dough looks like a plump round cushion, otherwise it will become too flat. Place in the centre of the prepared baking sheet. Cover with an inverted bowl and leave to rise, in a warm place, for 30–45 minutes.

5 Mix the water and salt and brush over the bread. Sprinkle with wheat flakes or cracked wheat.

6 Meanwhile, preheat the oven to 230°C/ 450°F/Gas 8. Bake for 15 minutes, then reduce the oven temperature to 200°C/ 400°F/Gas 6 and bake for a further 20 minutes, or until the loaf is firm to the touch and sounds hollow when tapped on the base. Cool on a wire rack.

GRANT LOAVES

This quick and easy recipe was created by Doris Grant and was included in her cookbook, published in the 1940s – the dough requires no kneading and takes only a minute to mix. The loaves should keep moist for several days.

1 Grease three loaf tins (pans), each about 21 × 11 × 6cm/8½ × 4½ × 2½ in and set aside in a warm place. Sift the flour and salt together in a large bowl and warm slightly to take off the chill.

2 Sprinkle the dried yeast over 150ml/¼ pint/⅔ cup of the water. After a couple of minutes stir in the sugar. Leave for 10 minutes.

3 Make a well in the centre of the flour and stir in the yeast mixture and remaining water. The dough should be slippery. Mix for about 1 minute, working the sides into the middle.

4 Divide among the tins, cover with oiled clear film (plastic wrap) and leave in a warm place, for 30 minutes, or until the dough has risen by about a third to within 1cm/½ in of the top of the tins.

1.4kg/3lb/12 cups wholemeal (whole-wheat) bread flour
15ml/1 tbsp salt
15ml/1 tbsp easy-blend (rapid-rise) dried yeast
1.2 litres/2 pints/5 cups lukewarm water
15ml/1 tbsp muscovado (molasses) sugar

MAKES 3 LOAVES

COOK'S TIP
Muscovado sugar gives this bread a rich flavour. An unrefined cane sugar, it is dark and moist.

5 Meanwhile, preheat the oven to 200°C/400°F/Gas 6. Bake for 40 minutes, or until the loaves are crisp and sound hollow when tapped on the base. Turn out on to a wire rack to cool.

POPPY-SEEDED BLOOMER

675g/1½ lb/6 cups unbleached white
bread flour
10ml/2 tsp salt
15g/½ oz fresh yeast
430ml/15fl oz/1⅞ cups water

FOR THE TOPPING
2.5ml/½ tsp salt
30ml/2 tbsp water
poppy seeds, for sprinkling

MAKES 1 LARGE LOAF

This satisfying white bread, which is the British version of the chunky baton
loaf found throughout Europe, is made by a slower rising method and with
less yeast than usual. It produces a longer-keeping loaf with a fuller flavour.
The dough takes about 8 hours to rise, so you'll need to start this bread
early in the morning.

1 Lightly grease a baking sheet. Sift the flour and salt together into a large bowl and make a well in the centre.

2 Mix the yeast and 150ml/¼ pint/⅔ cup of the water in a jug (pitcher) or bowl. Mix in the remaining water. Add to the centre of the flour. Mix, gradually incorporating the surrounding flour, until the mixture forms a firm dough.

COOK'S TIP
The traditional cracked, crusty appearance of this loaf is difficult to achieve in a domestic oven. However, you can get a similar result by spraying the oven with water before baking. If the underneath of the loaf is not very crusty at the end of baking, turn the loaf over on the baking sheet, switch off the heat and leave in the oven for a further 5–10 minutes.

VARIATION
For a more rustic loaf, replace up to half the flour with wholemeal (whole-wheat) bread flour.

3 Turn out on to a lightly floured surface and knead the dough very well, for at least 10 minutes, until smooth and elastic. Place in a lightly oiled bowl, cover with lightly oiled clear film (plastic wrap) and leave at cool room temperature, about 15–18°C/60–65°F, for 5–6 hours, or until doubled in bulk.

4 Knock back (punch down) the dough, turn out on to a lightly floured surface and knead it thoroughly and quite hard for about 5 minutes. Return the dough to the bowl, and re-cover. Leave to rise, at cool room temperature, for a further 2 hours or slightly longer.

5 Knock back again and repeat the thorough kneading. Leave the dough to rest for 5 minutes, then roll out on a lightly floured surface into a rectangle 2.5cm/1in thick. Roll the dough up from one long side and shape it into a square-ended thick baton shape about 33 × 13cm/13 × 5in.

6 Place it seam side up on a lightly floured baking sheet, cover and leave to rest for 15 minutes. Turn the loaf over and place on the greased baking sheet. Plump up by tucking the dough under the sides and ends. Using a sharp knife, cut 6 diagonal slashes on the top.

7 Leave to rest, covered, in a warm place, for 10 minutes. Meanwhile preheat the oven to 230°C/450°F/Gas 8.

8 Mix the salt and water together and brush this glaze over the bread. Sprinkle with poppy seeds.

9 Spray the oven with water, bake the bread immediately for 20 minutes, then reduce the oven temperature to 200°C/400°F/Gas 6; bake for 25 minutes more, or until golden. Transfer to a wire rack to cool.

COTTAGE LOAF

675g/1½lb/6 cups unbleached white
bread flour
10ml/2 tsp salt
20g/¾ oz fresh yeast
400ml/14fl oz/1⅔ cups lukewarm
water

MAKES 1 LARGE ROUND LOAF

COOK'S TIPS
• To ensure a good-shaped cottage loaf
the dough needs to be firm enough to
support the weight of the top ball.
• Do not over-prove the dough on
the second rising or the loaf may
topple over – but even if it does it will
still taste good.

*Snipping the top and bottom sections of the dough at 5cm/2in intervals not
only looks good but also helps the loaf to expand in the oven.*

1 Lightly grease two baking sheets. Sift
the flour and salt together into a large
bowl and make a well in the centre.

2 Mix the yeast in 150ml/¼ pint/⅔ cup
of the water until dissolved. Pour into
the centre of the flour with the
remaining water and mix to a firm dough.

3 Knead on a lightly floured surface for
10 minutes until smooth and elastic.
Place in a lightly oiled bowl, cover with
lightly oiled clear film (plastic wrap) and
leave to rise, in a warm place, for about
1 hour, or until doubled in bulk.

4 Turn out on to a lightly floured surface
and knock back (punch down). Knead
for 2–3 minutes then divide into two-
thirds and one-third; shape each to a ball.

5 Place the balls of dough on the prepared
baking sheets. Cover with inverted bowls
and leave to rise, in a warm place, for
about 30 minutes (see Cook's Tips).

6 Gently flatten the top of the larger
round of dough and, with a sharp knife,
cut a cross in the centre, about 4cm/
1½in across. Brush with a little water
and place the smaller round on top.

7 Carefully press a hole through the
middle of the top ball, down into the
lower part, using your thumb and first
two fingers of one hand. Cover with
lightly oiled clear film and leave to rest
in a warm place for about 10 minutes.
Preheat the oven to 220°C/ 425°F/Gas 7
and place the bread on the lower shelf.
It will finish expanding as the oven heats
up. Bake for 35–40 minutes, or until
golden brown and sounding hollow
when tapped. Cool on a wire rack.

CHEESE AND ONION LOAF

Almost a meal in itself, this hearty bread tastes delicious as an accompaniment to salads and cold meats, or with soup.

1 Lightly grease a 25 × 10cm/10 × 4in loaf tin (pan). Melt 25g/1oz/2 tbsp of the butter in a heavy frying pan and sauté the onion until it is soft and light golden. Set aside to cool.

2 Sift the flour into a large bowl and stir in the yeast, mustard, salt and pepper. Stir in three-quarters of the grated cheese and the onion. Make a well in the centre. Add the milk and water; blend to a soft dough. Turn out on to a lightly floured surface and knead for 10 minutes until smooth and elastic.

3 Place the dough in a lightly oiled bowl, cover with oiled clear film (plastic wrap) and leave in a warm place, for about 45–60 minutes, until doubled in bulk.

4 Turn the dough out on to a lightly floured surface, knock back (punch down), and knead gently. Divide into 20 equal pieces and shape into small rounds. Place half in the prepared tin and brush with some melted butter. Top with the remaining rounds of dough and brush with the remaining butter.

5 Cover with oiled clear film and leave to rise for 45 minutes, until the dough reaches the top of the tin. Meanwhile, preheat the oven to 190°C/375°F/Gas 5.

6 Sprinkle the remaining cheese over the top. Bake for 40–45 minutes or until risen and golden brown. Cool on a wire rack.

1 onion, finely chopped
45g/1¾oz/3½ tbsp butter
450g/1lb/4 cups unbleached white bread flour
6g/¼oz sachet easy-blend (rapid-rise) dried yeast
5ml/1 tsp mustard powder
175g/6oz/1½ cups grated mature (sharp) Cheddar cheese
150ml/¼ pint/⅔ cup lukewarm milk
150ml/¼ pint/⅔ cup lukewarm water
salt and ground black pepper

MAKES 1 LARGE LOAF

COOK'S TIP

If you prefer, use 20g/¾ oz fresh yeast instead of the easy-blend yeast. Mix the fresh yeast with the milk until dissolved, then add to the flour.

SPLIT TIN

500g/1¼lb/5 cups unbleached white
bread flour, plus extra for dusting
10ml/2 tsp salt
15g/½oz fresh yeast
300ml/½ pint/1¼ cups lukewarm
water
60ml/4 tbsp lukewarm milk

MAKES 1 LOAF

As its name suggests, this homely loaf is so called because of the centre split.
Some bakers mould the dough in two loaves – they join together whilst
proving but retain the characteristic crack after baking.

1 Lightly grease a 900g/2lb loaf tin (pan) (18.5 × 11.5cm/7¼ × 4½in). Sift the flour and salt together into a large bowl and make a well in the centre. Mix the yeast with half the lukewarm water in a jug (pitcher), then stir in the remaining water.

2 Pour the yeast mixture into the centre of the flour and using your fingers, mix in a little flour. Gradually mix in more of the flour from around the edge of the bowl to form a thick, smooth batter.

3 Sprinkle a little more flour from around the edge over the batter and leave in a warm place to "sponge". Bubbles will appear in the batter after about 20 minutes. Add the milk and remaining flour; mix to a firm dough.

4 Place on a lightly floured surface and knead for about 10 minutes until smooth and elastic. Place in a lightly oiled bowl, cover with oiled clear film (plastic wrap) and leave in a warm place, for 1–1¼ hours, or until nearly doubled in bulk.

5 Knock back (punch down) the dough and turn out on to a lightly floured surface. Shape it into a rectangle, the length of the tin. Roll up lengthways, tuck the ends under and place seam side down in the prepared tin. Cover and leave to rise, in a warm place, for about 20–30 minutes, or until nearly doubled in bulk.

6 Using a sharp knife, make one deep central slash the length of the bread; dust with flour. Leave for 10–15 minutes.

7 Meanwhile, preheat the oven to 230°C/450°F/Gas 8. Bake for 15 minutes, then reduce the oven temperature to 200°C/400°F/Gas 6. Bake for 20–25 minutes more, or until the bread is golden and sounds hollow when tapped on the base. Turn out on to a wire rack to cool.

WELSH CLAY POT LOAVES

These breads are flavoured with chives, sage, parsley and garlic. You can use any selection of your favourite herbs. For even more flavour, try adding a little grated raw onion and grated cheese to the dough.

115g/4oz/1 cup wholemeal
(whole-wheat) bread flour
350g/12oz/3 cups unbleached white
bread flour
7.5ml/1½ tsp salt
15g/½ oz fresh yeast
150ml/¼ pint/⅔ cup lukewarm milk
120ml/4fl oz/½ cup lukewarm water
50g/2oz/4 tbsp butter, melted
15ml/1 tbsp chopped fresh chives
15ml/1 tbsp chopped fresh parsley
5ml/1 tsp chopped fresh sage
1 garlic clove, crushed
beaten egg, for glazing
fennel seeds, for sprinkling (optional)

MAKES 2 LOAVES

COOK'S TIP

To prepare and seal new clay flower pots, clean them thoroughly, oil them inside and outside and bake them three or four times. Preheat the oven to about 200°C/400°F/Gas 6 and bake for 30–40 minutes. Try to do this while you are baking other foods.

4 Turn the dough out on to a lightly floured surface and knock back (punch down). Divide in two. Shape and fit into the prepared flower pots. They should about half fill the pots. Cover with oiled clear film and leave to rise for 30–45 minutes, in a warm place, or until the dough is 2.5cm/1in from the top of the pots.

5 Meanwhile, preheat the oven to 200°C/400°F/Gas 6. Brush the tops with beaten egg and sprinkle with fennel seeds, if using. Bake for 35–40 minutes or until golden. Turn out on to a wire rack to cool.

1 Lightly grease 2 clean 14cm/5½ in diameter, 11cm/4½ in high clay flower pots. Sift the flours and salt together into a large bowl and make a well in the centre. Blend the yeast with a little of the milk until smooth, then stir in the remaining milk. Pour the yeast liquid into the centre of the flour and sprinkle over a little of the flour from around the edge. Cover the bowl and leave in a warm place for 15 minutes.

2 Add the water, melted butter, herbs and garlic to the flour mixture and blend together to form a dough. Turn out on to a lightly floured surface and knead for about 10 minutes until the dough is smooth and elastic.

3 Place in a lightly oiled bowl, cover with lightly oiled clear film (plastic wrap) and leave in a warm place, for 1¼–1½ hours, or until doubled in bulk.

HARVEST FESTIVAL SHEAF

This is one of the most visually stunning breads. Celebratory loaves can be seen in various forms in churches and at some bakers throughout Britain around the September harvest.

900g/2lb/8 cups unbleached white bread flour
15ml/1 tbsp salt
15g/½oz fresh yeast
75ml/5 tbsp lukewarm milk
400ml/14fl oz/1⅔ cups cold water

FOR THE TOPPING
1 egg
15ml/1 tbsp milk

MAKES 1 LARGE LOAF

1 Lightly grease a large baking sheet, at least 38 × 33cm/15 × 13in. Sift the flour and salt together into a large bowl and make a well in the centre.

2 Cream the yeast with the milk in a jug (pitcher). Add to the centre of the flour with the water and mix to a stiff dough. Turn out on to a lightly floured surface and knead for about 10–15 minutes until smooth and elastic.

3 Place in a lightly oiled bowl, cover with lightly oiled clear film (plastic wrap) and leave at room temperature, for about 2 hours, or until doubled in bulk.

4 Turn the dough out on to a lightly floured surface, knock back (punch down) and knead for about 1 minute. Cover and leave to rest for 10 minutes.

5 Divide the dough in two. Roll out one piece to a 35 × 24cm/14 × 10in oblong. Fold loosely in half lengthways. Using a sharp knife, cut out a half mushroom shape for the sheaf (leave the folded edge uncut). Make the stalk "base" about 18cm/7in long.

6 Place the dough on the prepared baking sheet and open out. Prick all over with a fork and brush with water to prevent a skin from forming. Reserve 75g/3oz of the trimmings for the tie. Cover and set aside. Divide the remaining dough in two pieces and mix the rest of the trimmings with one half. Cover and set aside. Beat together the egg and milk for the glaze.

7 Roll out the remaining dough on a lightly floured surface to a rectangle, 28 × 18cm/11 × 7in, and cut into 30–35 thin strips 18cm/7in long. Place side by side lengthways on the base, as close as possible, to represent wheat stalks. Brush with some glaze.

8 Take the larger piece of reserved dough and divide into four. Divide each piece into about 25 and shape into oblong rolls to make about 100 wheat ears. Make each roll pointed at one end.

9 Holding one roll at a time, snip along each side towards the centre, using scissors, to make wheat ear shapes.

10 Preheat the oven to 220°C/425°F/ Gas 7. Arrange the ears around the outer edge of the top of the mushroom shape, overlapping on to the baking sheet. Repeat a second row lower down, placing the row between the first ears. Repeat until they are all used. Brush with some glaze as you proceed to prevent the dough from drying out.

11 Divide the smaller piece of reserved dough into six pieces and roll each to a 43cm/17in strip. Make two braids each with three strips. Place across the wheat stalks to make a tied bow. Brush with some glaze. Prick between the wheat ears and stalks using a sharp knife and bake for 15 minutes.

12 Reduce the oven temperature to 180°C/350°F/Gas 4. Brush the bread with the remaining glaze and bake for a further 30–35 minutes, or until golden and firm. Leave to cool on the baking sheet.

COOK'S TIPS
• Check the bread occasionally while baking, and cover the ends with foil after the first 15 minutes if they start to over-brown.
• Harvest loaves are often baked for display, rather than for eating. If you'd like to do this, then leave the baked loaf in the oven, reduce the temperature to very low, 120°C/250°F/Gas ½, for several hours until the dough dries out.

Scottish Morning Rolls

These rolls are best served warm, as soon as they are baked. In Scotland they are a firm favourite for breakfast with a fried egg and bacon.

450g/1lb/4 cups unbleached plain (all-purpose) white flour, plus extra
10ml/2 tsp salt
20g/¾ oz fresh yeast
150ml/¼ pint/⅔ cup lukewarm milk
150ml/¼ pint/⅔ cup lukewarm water
30ml/2 tbsp milk, for glazing

MAKES 10 ROLLS

1 Grease two baking sheets. Sift the flour and salt together into a large bowl and make a well in the centre. Mix the yeast with the milk, then mix in the water. Add to the centre of the flour and mix together to form a soft dough.

2 Knead the dough lightly in the bowl, then cover with lightly oiled clear film (plastic wrap) and leave in a warm place, for 1 hour, or until doubled in bulk. Turn the dough out on to a lightly floured surface and knock back (punch down).

3 Divide the dough into 10 equal pieces. Knead lightly and, using a rolling pin, shape each piece to a flat oval 10 × 7.5cm/4 × 3in or a flat round 9cm/3½ in.

4 Transfer to the prepared baking sheets, spaced well apart, and cover with oiled clear film. Leave to rise, in a warm place, for about 30 minutes.

5 Meanwhile, preheat the oven to 200°C/400°F/Gas 6. Press each roll in the centre with the three middle fingers to equalise the air bubbles and to help prevent blistering. Brush with milk and dust with flour. Bake for 15–20 minutes or until lightly browned. Dust with more flour and cool slightly on a wire rack. Serve warm.

SHAPED DINNER ROLLS

These professional-looking rolls are perfect for entertaining. You can always make double the amount of dough and freeze half, tightly wrapped. Just thaw, glaze and bake as required.

450g/1lb/4 cups unbleached white
bread flour
10ml/2 tsp salt
2.5ml/½ tsp caster (superfine) sugar
6g/¼oz sachet easy-blend (rapid-rise)
dried yeast
50g/2oz/¼ cup butter or margarine
250ml/8fl oz/1 cup lukewarm milk
1 egg

FOR THE TOPPING
1 egg yolk
15ml/1 tbsp water
poppy seeds and sesame seeds

MAKES 12 ROLLS

1 Lightly grease two baking sheets. Sift the flour and salt into a large bowl and stir in the sugar and yeast. Add the butter or margarine and rub in until the mixture resembles fine breadcrumbs.

3 Turn the dough out on to a lightly floured surface, knock back (punch down) and knead for 2–3 minutes. Divide the dough into 12 equal pieces and shape into rolls as described in steps 4–8.

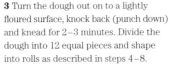

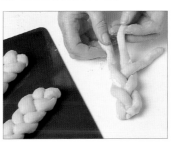

2 Make a well in the centre. Add the milk and egg to the well and mix to a dough. Knead on a floured surface for 10 minutes until smooth and elastic. Place in a lightly oiled bowl, cover with lightly oiled clear film (plastic wrap) and leave to rise, in a warm place, for 1 hour, or until doubled in bulk.

4 *To make braids:* divide each piece of dough into three equal pieces. Working on a lightly floured surface, roll each piece to a sausage, keeping the lengths and widths even. Pinch three strips together at one end, then braid them neatly but not too tightly. Pinch the ends together and tuck under the braid.

5 *To make trefoils:* divide each piece of dough into three and roll into balls. Place the three balls together in a triangular shape.

6 *To make batons:* shape each piece of dough into an oblong and slash the surface of each with diagonal cuts just before baking.

7 *To make cottage rolls:* divide each piece of dough into two-thirds and one-third and shape into rounds. Place the small one on top of the large one and make a hole through the centre with the handle of a wooden spoon.

8 *To make knots:* shape each piece of dough into a long roll and tie a single knot, pulling the ends through.

9 Place the dinner rolls on the prepared baking sheets, spacing them well apart, cover the rolls with oiled clear film and leave to rise, in a warm place, for about 30 minutes, or until doubled in bulk.

10 Meanwhile, preheat the oven to 220°C/425°F/Gas 7. Mix the egg yolk and water together for the glaze and brush over the rolls. Sprinkle some with poppy seeds and some with sesame seeds. Bake for 15–18 minutes or until golden. Lift the rolls off the sheet using a metal spatula and transfer to a wire rack to cool.

IRISH SODA BREAD

*225g/8oz/2 cups unbleached
plain (all-purpose) flour
225g/8oz/2 cups wholemeal (whole-
wheat) flour, plus extra for dusting
5ml/1 tsp salt
10ml/2 tsp bicarbonate of soda (baking soda)
10ml/2 tsp cream of tartar
40g/1½ oz/3 tbsp butter or lard (shortening)
5ml/1 tsp caster (superfine) sugar
350–375ml/12–13fl oz/1½–1⅔ cups
buttermilk*

Makes 1 Round Loaf

VARIATION
Shape into two small loaves and bake
for 25–30 minutes.

*Soda bread can be prepared in minutes and is excellent served warm, fresh
from the oven. You can use all plain white flour, if preferred, to create a bread
with a finer texture.*

1 Preheat the oven to 190°C/375°F/Gas 5.
Lightly grease a baking sheet. Sift the
flour and salt into a large bowl.

2 Add the bicarbonate of soda and
cream of tartar, then rub in the butter or
lard. Stir in the sugar.

3 Pour in sufficient buttermilk to mix to
a soft dough. Do not over-mix or the
bread will be heavy and tough. Shape
into a round on a lightly floured surface.

4 Place on the prepared baking sheet
and mark a cross using a sharp knife,
cutting deep into the dough.

5 Dust lightly with wholemeal flour and
bake for 35–45 minutes or until well
risen and the bread sounds hollow when
tapped on the base. Serve warm.

CORNISH SAFFRON BREADS

Often called saffron cake, this light, delicately spiced bread contains threads of saffron and is made in a loaf tin. Whatever the name, the flavour and texture are superb.

300ml/½ pint/1¼ cups milk
2.5ml/½ tsp saffron threads
400g/14oz/3½ cups unbleached white
bread flour
25g/1oz fresh yeast
50g/2oz/½ cup ground almonds
2.5ml/½ tsp grated nutmeg
2.5ml/½ tsp ground cinnamon
50g/2oz/¼ cup caster (superfine) sugar
2.5ml/½ tsp salt
75g/3oz/6 tbsp butter, softened
50g/2oz/⅓ cup sultanas (golden raisins)
50g/2oz/¼ cup currants

FOR THE GLAZE
30ml/2 tbsp milk
15ml/1 tbsp caster (superfine) sugar

MAKES 2 LOAVES

1 Grease two 900g/2lb loaf tins (pans). Heat half the milk until almost boiling.

2 Place the saffron threads in a small heatproof bowl and pour over the milk. Stir gently, then leave to infuse (steep) for 30 minutes.

3 Heat the remaining milk in the same pan until it is just lukewarm.

4 Place 50g/2oz/½ cup flour in a small bowl, crumble in the yeast and stir in the lukewarm milk. Mix well, then leave for about 15 minutes until the yeast starts to ferment.

5 Mix the remaining flour, ground almonds, spices, sugar and salt together in a large bowl and make a well in the centre. Add the saffron infusion, yeast mixture and softened butter to the centre of the flour and mix to a very soft dough.

6 Turn out on to a lightly floured surface and knead for 5 minutes until smooth and elastic. Place in a lightly oiled bowl, cover with lightly oiled clear (plastic wrap) film and leave in a warm place, for 1½–2 hours, or until doubled in bulk.

7 Turn the dough out on to a lightly floured surface, knock back (punch down), and knead in the sultanas and currants. Divide in two and shape into two loaves. Place in the prepared tins. Cover with oiled clear film and leave to rise, in a warm place, for 1½ hours, or until the dough reaches the top of the tins.

8 Meanwhile, preheat the oven to 220°C/425°F/Gas 7. Bake the loaves for 10 minutes, then reduce the oven temperature to 190°C/375°F/Gas 5 and bake for 15–20 minutes or until golden.

9 While the loaves are baking, make the glaze. Heat the milk and sugar in a small pan, stirring until the sugar has dissolved. As soon as the loaves come out of the oven, brush them with the glaze, leave in the tins for 5 minutes, then turn out on to a wire rack to cool.

CRUMPETS

*225g/8oz/2 cups unbleached plain
(all-purpose) flour
225g/8oz/2 cups unbleached white
bread flour
10ml/2 tsp salt
600ml/1 pint/2½ cups milk and
water mixed
30ml/2 tbsp sunflower oil
15ml/1 tbsp caster (superfine) sugar
15g/½oz fresh yeast
2.5ml/½ tsp bicarbonate of soda
(baking soda)
120ml/4fl oz/½ cup lukewarm water*

MAKES ABOUT 20 CRUMPETS

COOK'S TIP
If the batter does not produce the
characteristic bubbles, add a little
more water before cooking the next
batch of crumpets.

---

*Home-made crumpets are less doughy and not as heavy as most supermarket
versions. Serve them lightly toasted, oozing with butter.*

1 Lightly grease a griddle or heavy frying
pan and 4 × 8cm/3¼in plain pastry
(cookie) cutters or crumpet rings.

2 Sift the flours and salt together into a
large bowl and make a well in the
centre. Heat the milk and water
mixture, oil and sugar until lukewarm.
Mix the yeast with 150ml/¼ pint/⅔ cup
of this liquid.

3 Add the yeast mixture and remaining
liquid to the centre of the flour and beat
vigorously for about 5 minutes until
smooth and elastic. Cover with oiled
clear film (plastic wrap) and leave in a
warm place, for about 1½ hours, or until
the mixture is bubbly and about to fall.

4 Dissolve the soda in the lukewarm
water and stir into the batter. Re-cover
and leave to rise for 30 minutes.

5 Place the cutters or crumpet rings on
the griddle and warm over a medium
heat. Fill the cutters or rings a generous
1cm/½in deep. Cook over a gentle heat
for 6–7 minutes. The tops should be
dry, with a mass of tiny holes.

6 Carefully remove the cutters or rings
and turn the crumpets over. Cook for
1–2 minutes or until pale golden. Repeat
with remaining batter. Serve warm.

ENGLISH MUFFINS

*450g/1lb/4 cups unbleached white
bread flour
7.5ml/1½ tsp salt
350–375ml/12–13fl oz/1½–1⅔ cups
lukewarm milk
2.5ml/½ tsp caster (superfine) sugar
15g/½oz fresh yeast
15ml/1 tbsp melted butter or olive oil
rice flour or semolina, for dusting*

MAKES 9 MUFFINS

COOK'S TIPS
• Muffins should be cut around the
outer edge only using a sharp knife
and then torn apart. If toasting, toast
the whole muffins first and then split
them in half.
• If you'd like to serve the muffins
warm, transfer them to a wire rack to
cool slightly before serving.

---

*Perfect served warm, split open and buttered for afternoon tea; or try these
favourites toasted, split and topped with ham and eggs for brunch.*

1 Generously flour a non-stick baking
sheet. Very lightly grease a griddle. Sift
the flour and salt together into a large
bowl and make a well in the centre.
Blend 150ml/¼ pint/⅔ cup of the milk,
sugar and yeast together. Stir in the
remaining milk and butter or oil.

2 Add the yeast mixture to the centre of
the flour and beat for 4–5 minutes until
smooth and elastic. The dough will be
soft but just hold its shape. Cover with
lightly oiled clear film (plastic wrap) and
leave to rise, in a warm place, for 45–60
minutes, or until doubled in bulk.

3 Turn out on a floured surface and
knock back (punch down). Roll out to
1cm/½in thick. Using a floured 7.5cm/3in
plain cutter, cut out nine rounds.

4 Dust with rice flour or semolina and
place on the prepared baking sheet.
Cover and leave to rise, in a warm place,
for about 20–30 minutes.

5 Warm the griddle over a medium heat.
Carefully transfer the muffins in batches
to the griddle. Cook slowly for about
7 minutes on each side or until golden
brown. Transfer to a wire rack to cool.

LARDY CAKE

450g/1lb/4 cups unbleached white
bread flour
5ml/1 tsp salt
15g/½ oz/1 tbsp lard (shortening)
25g/1oz/2 tbsp caster (superfine) sugar
20g/¾ oz fresh yeast
300ml/½ pint/1¼ cups lukewarm water

FOR THE FILLING
75g/3oz/6 tbsp lard (shortening)
75g/3oz/6 tbsp soft light brown sugar
115g/4oz/½ cup currants,
slightly warmed
75g/3oz/½ cup sultanas (golden
raisins), slightly warmed
25g/1oz/3 tbsp mixed chopped
(candied) peel
5ml/1 tsp mixed (apple pie) spice

FOR THE GLAZE
10ml/2 tsp sunflower oil
15–30ml/1–2 tbsp caster
(superfine) sugar

MAKES 1 LARGE LOAF

*This special rich fruit bread was originally made throughout many counties
of England for celebrating the harvest. Using lard rather than butter or
margarine makes an authentic lardy cake.*

1 Grease a 25 × 20cm/10 × 8in shallow roasting pan. Sift the flour and salt into a large bowl and rub in the lard. Stir in the sugar and make a well in the centre.

2 In a bowl, cream the yeast with half of the water, then blend in the remainder. Add to the centre of the flour and mix to a smooth dough.

3 Turn out on to a lightly floured surface and knead for 10 minutes until smooth and elastic. Place in a lightly oiled bowl, cover with oiled clear film (plastic wrap) and leave in a warm place, for 1 hour, or until doubled in bulk.

4 Turn the dough out on to a lightly floured surface and knock back (punch down). Knead for 2–3 minutes. Roll into a rectangle about 5mm/¼ in thick.

5 Using half the lard for the filling, cover the top two-thirds of the dough with flakes of lard. Sprinkle over half the sugar, half the dried fruits and peel and half the mixed spice. Fold the bottom third up and the top third down, sealing the edges with the rolling pin.

6 Turn the dough by 90 degrees. Repeat the rolling and cover with the remaining lard, fruit and peel and mixed spice. Fold, seal and turn as before. Roll out the dough to fit the prepared pan. Cover with lightly oiled clear film and leave to rise, in a warm place, for 30–45 minutes, or until doubled in size.

7 Meanwhile, preheat the oven to 200°C/400°F/Gas 6. Brush the top of the lardy cake with sunflower oil and sprinkle with caster sugar.

8 Score a criss-cross pattern on top using a sharp knife, then bake for 30–40 minutes until golden. Turn out on to a wire rack to cool slightly. Serve warm, cut into slices or squares.

MALTED CURRANT BREAD

*This spiced currant bread makes a good tea or breakfast bread, sliced and
spread with a generous amount of butter. It also makes superb toast.*

*50g/2oz/3 tbsp malt extract
30ml/2 tbsp golden (light corn) syrup
50g/2oz/¼ cup butter
450g/1lb/4 cups unbleached white
bread flour
5ml/1 tsp mixed (apple pie) spice
20g/¾ oz fresh yeast
175ml/6fl oz/¾ cup lukewarm milk
175g/6oz/¾ cup currants,
slightly warmed*

*FOR THE GLAZE
30ml/2 tbsp milk
30ml/2 tbsp caster (superfine) sugar*

MAKES 2 LOAVES

COOK'S TIP
When you are making more than one
loaf, the easiest way to prove them is
to place the tins in a lightly oiled large
plastic bag.

4 Turn the dough out on to a lightly
floured surface, knock back (punch
down), then knead in the currants. Divide
the dough in two and shape into two
loaves. Place in the prepared tins. Cover
with oiled clear film and leave to rise, in
a warm place, for 2–3 hours, or until the
dough reaches the top of the tins.

5 Meanwhile, preheat the oven to 200°C/
400°F/Gas 6. Bake for 35–40 minutes or
until golden. While the loaves are baking
heat the milk and sugar for the glaze in
a small pan. Turn out the loaves on to a
wire rack, then invert them, so that they
are the right way up. Immediately brush
the glaze evenly over the loaves and
leave to cool.

2 Sift the flour and mixed spice together
into a large bowl and make a well in the
centre. Cream the yeast with a little of
the milk, then blend in the remaining
milk. Add the yeast mixture and cooled
malt mixture to the centre of the flour
and blend together to form a dough.

3 Turn out the dough on to a lightly
floured surface and knead for about
10 minutes until smooth and elastic.
Place in a lightly oiled bowl, cover with
lightly oiled clear film (plastic wrap) and
leave to rise, in a warm place, for 1½–2
hours, or until doubled in bulk.

1 Lightly grease two 450g/1lb loaf tins
(pans). Place the malt extract, golden
syrup and butter in a pan and heat
gently until the butter has melted. Set
aside to cool completely.

BARLEY BANNOCK

*115g/4oz/1 cup barley flour
50g/2oz/½ cup unbleached plain
(all-purpose) flour or wholemeal
(whole-wheat) flour
2.5ml/½ tsp salt
2.5ml/½ tsp cream of tartar
25g/1oz/2 tbsp butter or margarine
175ml/6fl oz/¾ cup buttermilk
2.5ml/½ tsp bicarbonate of soda
(baking soda)*

MAKES 1 ROUND LOAF

COOK'S TIPS

• If you cannot locate buttermilk,
then use soured milk instead. Stir
5ml/1 tsp lemon juice into
175ml/6 fl oz/¾ cup milk and set aside
for an hour to sour.
• If you find the earthy flavour of
barley flour too strong, reduce it to
50g/2oz/½ cup and increase the plain
white flour to 115g/4oz/1 cup.
Alternatively, replace half the barley
flour with fine oatmeal.

*Bannocks are flat loaves about the size of a dinner plate. They are
traditionally baked on a griddle or girdle (which is the preferred name in
Scotland). Barley flour adds a wonderfully earthy flavour to the bread.*

1 Wipe the surface of a griddle with a
little vegetable oil. Sift the flours, salt
and cream of tartar together into a large
bowl. Add the butter or margarine and
rub into the flour until it resembles
fine breadcrumbs.

2 Mix the buttermilk and bicarbonate of
soda together. When the mixture starts
to bubble add to the flour. Mix together
to form a soft dough. Do not over-mix
the dough or it will toughen.

3 On a floured surface pat the dough out
to form a round about 2cm/¾in thick.
Mark the dough into four wedges, using
a sharp knife, if you prefer.

4 Heat the griddle until hot. Cook the
bannock on the griddle for about 8–10
minutes per side over a gentle heat. Do
not cook too quickly or the outside will
burn before the centre is cooked. Cool
the bannock slightly on a wire rack and
eat while still warm.

SCOTTISH OATCAKES

*115g/4oz/1 cup medium or
fine oatmeal
1.5ml/¼ tsp salt
pinch of bicarbonate of soda
(baking soda)
15ml/1 tbsp melted butter
or lard (shortening)
45–60ml/3–4 tbsp hot water*

MAKES 8 OATCAKES

VARIATIONS

• Oatcakes are traditionally cooked
on the griddle, but they can also
be cooked in the oven at 180°C/
350°F/Gas 4 for about 20 minutes, or
until pale golden in colour.
• Small round oatcakes can be
stamped out using a 7.5cm/3in plain
cutter, if preferred.

*The crunchy texture of these tempting oatcakes makes them difficult to resist.
Serve with butter and slices of a good cheese.*

1 Very lightly oil a griddle or heavy
frying pan. Mix the oatmeal, salt and
soda together in a bowl.

2 Add the melted butter or lard and
sufficient hot water to make a dough.
Lightly knead on a surface dusted with
oatmeal until it is smooth. Cut the
dough in half.

3 On an oatmeal-dusted surface roll
each piece of dough out as thinly as
possible into a round about 15cm/6in
across and 5mm/¼in thick.

4 Cut each round into four quarters or
farls. Heat the griddle over a medium
heat until warm. Transfer four farls,
using a spatula or fish slice, to the
griddle and cook over a low heat for 4–5
minutes. The edges may start to curl.

5 Using the spatula or slice, carefully
turn the farls over and cook for about
1–2 minutes. If preferred the second
side can be cooked under a preheated
grill (broiler) until crisp, but not brown.
Transfer to a wire rack to cool. Repeat
with the remaining farls.

WELSH BARA BRITH

This rich, fruity bread – the name literally means "speckled bread" – is a speciality from North Wales. The honey glaze makes a delicious topping.

20g/¾ oz fresh yeast
210ml/7fl oz/scant 1 cup lukewarm milk
450g/1lb/4 cups unbleached white bread flour
75g/3oz/6 tbsp butter or lard (shortening)
5ml/1 tsp mixed (apple pie) spice
2.5ml/½ tsp salt
50g/2oz/⅓ cup light brown sugar
1 egg, lightly beaten
115g/4oz/⅔ cup seedless raisins, slightly warmed
75g/3oz/scant ½ cup currants, slightly warmed
40g/1½ oz/¼ cup mixed chopped (candied) peel
15–30ml/1–2 tbsp clear honey, for glazing

MAKES 1 LARGE ROUND LOAF

1 Grease a baking sheet. Blend the yeast with a little of the milk, then stir in the remainder. Set aside for 10 minutes.

2 Sift the flour into a large bowl and rub in the butter or lard until the mixture resembles breadcrumbs. Stir in the mixed spice, salt and sugar and make a well in the centre.

3 Add the yeast mixture and beaten egg to the centre of the flour and mix to a rough dough.

4 Turn out the dough on to a lightly floured surface and knead for about 10 minutes until smooth and elastic. Place in a lightly oiled bowl, cover with lightly oiled clear film (plastic wrap) and leave to rise, in a warm place, for 1½ hours, or until doubled in bulk.

5 Turn out on to a lightly floured surface, knock back (punch down), and knead in the dried fruits and peel. Shape into a round and place on the baking sheet. Cover with oiled clear film and leave to rise, in a warm place, for 1 hour, or until the dough doubles in size.

6 Meanwhile, preheat the oven to 200°C/ 400°F/Gas 6. Bake for 30 minutes or until the bread sounds hollow when tapped on the base. If the bread starts to over-brown, cover it loosely with foil for the last 10 minutes. Transfer the bread to a wire rack, brush with honey and leave to cool.

VARIATIONS
• The bara brith can be baked in a 1.5–1.75 litre/2½–3 pint/6¼–7½ cup loaf tin (pan) or deep round or square cake tin (pan), if you prefer.
• For a more wholesome loaf, replace half the white flour with wholemeal (whole-wheat) bread flour.

SALLY LUNN

Sally Lunn is traditionally served warm sliced into three layers horizontally, spread with clotted cream or butter and re-assembled. It looks fantastic.

1 Lightly butter a 15cm/6in round cake tin (pan), 7.5cm/3in deep. Dust lightly with flour, if the tin lacks a non-stick finish. Melt the butter in a small pan and then stir in the milk or cream and sugar. The mixture should be tepid. Remove from the heat, add the yeast and blend thoroughly until the yeast has dissolved. Leave for 10 minutes, or until the yeast starts to work.

2 Sift the flour and salt together into a large bowl. Stir in the lemon rind and make a well in the centre. Add the yeast mixture to the centre of the flour and mix together to make a soft dough just stiff enough to form a shape.

3 Turn out the dough on to a lightly floured surface and knead for about 10 minutes until smooth and elastic. Shape into a ball and place in the prepared tin. Cover with lightly oiled clear film (plastic wrap) and leave in a warm place, for 1¼–1½ hours.

4 When the dough has risen almost to the top of the tin, remove the clear film.

5 Meanwhile, preheat the oven to 220°C/425°F/Gas 7. Bake for 15–20 minutes or until light golden. While the loaf is baking, heat the milk and sugar for the glaze in a small pan until the sugar has dissolved, then bring to the boil. Brush the glaze over the bread.

6 Leave to cool in the tin for 10 minutes, or until the bread comes away from the side easily, then cool slightly on a wire rack before slicing and filling.

25g/1oz/2 tbsp butter
150ml/¼ pint/⅔ cup milk or
double (heavy) cream
15ml/1 tbsp caster (superfine) sugar
15g/½ oz fresh yeast
275g/10oz/2½ cups unbleached white
bread flour
2.5ml/½ tsp salt
finely grated rind of ½ lemon

For the Glaze
15ml/1 tbsp milk
15ml/1 tbsp caster (superfine) sugar

Makes 1 Round Loaf

FRENCH BREADS

*Although best known for the baguette, France has many more breads to offer, from
specialities like fougasse or pain aux noix – which introduce cheese and walnuts – to rustic
crusty breads like pain de campagne rustique, pain polka and that old-fashioned rye bread,
pain bouillie. Enriched doughs are popular with the French and include the rich, buttery yet
light classic breakfast treats of croissants and brioche. Perfect with a cup of coffee!*

FRENCH BAGUETTES

500g/1¼ lb/5 cups unbleached white
bread flour
115g/4oz/1 cup fine French plain
(all-purpose) flour
10ml/2 tsp salt
15g/½ oz fresh yeast
525ml/18fl oz/2¼ cups lukewarm
water

MAKES 3 LOAVES

VARIATION

If you make baguettes regularly you
may want to purchase baguette
frames to hold and bake the breads in,
or long *bannetons* in which to prove
this wonderful bread.

*Baguettes are difficult to reproduce at home as they require a very hot oven
and steam. However, by using less yeast and a triple fermentation you can
produce a bread with a superior taste and far better texture than mass-
produced baguettes. These are best eaten on the day of baking.*

1 Sift the flours and salt into a large bowl. Add the yeast to the water in another bowl and stir to dissolve. Gradually beat in half the flour mixture to form a batter. Cover with clear film (plastic wrap) and leave at room temperature for about 3 hours, or until nearly trebled in size and starting to collapse.

2 Add the remaining flour a little at a time, beating with your hand. Turn out on to a lightly floured surface and knead for 8–10 minutes to form a moist dough. Place in a lightly oiled bowl, cover with lightly oiled clear film and leave to rise, in a warm place, for about 1 hour.

3 When the dough has almost doubled in bulk, knock it back (punch it down), turn out on to a lightly floured surface and divide into three equal pieces. Shape each into a ball and then into a rectangle measuring about 15 × 7.5cm/6 × 3in.

4 Fold the bottom third up lengthways and the top third down and press down to make sure the pieces of dough are in contact. Seal the edges. Repeat two or three more times until each loaf is an oblong. Leave to rest in between folding for a few minutes, if necessary, to avoid tearing the dough.

5 Gently stretch each piece of dough lengthways into a 33–35cm/13–14in long loaf. Pleat a floured dishtowel on a baking sheet to make three moulds for the loaves. Place the breads between the pleats of the towel, to help hold their shape while rising. Cover with lightly oiled clear film and leave to rise, in a warm place, for 45–60 minutes.

6 Meanwhile, preheat the oven to maximum, at least 230°C/450°F/Gas 8. Roll the loaves on to a baking sheet, spaced well apart. Using a sharp knife, slash the top of each loaf several times with long diagonal slits. Place at the top of the oven, spray the inside of the oven with water and bake for 20–25 minutes, or until golden. Spray the oven twice more during the first 5 minutes of baking. Transfer to a wire rack to cool.

PAIN POLKA

This attractive, deeply cut, crusty bread is made by using a little of the previous day's dough as a starter. However, if you do not have any you can make a starter dough, the details for which are given.

FOR THE STARTER
225g/8oz/1 cup 6–15-hours-old French baguette dough
or 7g/¼ oz fresh yeast
120ml/4fl oz/½ cup lukewarm water
115g/4oz/1 cup unbleached plain (all-purpose) flour

FOR THE DOUGH
7g/¼ oz fresh yeast
280ml/scant ½ pint/scant 1¼ cups lukewarm water
450g/1lb/4 cups unbleached white bread flour, plus extra for dusting
15ml/1 tbsp salt

MAKES 1 LOAF

COOK'S TIP
The piece of previously made dough can be kept covered in the refrigerator for up to 2 days, or frozen for up to one month. Just let it come back to room temperature and allow it to rise for an hour before using.

1 Lightly flour a baking sheet. If you have leftover bread dough, proceed to step 3. Make the starter. Mix the yeast with the water, then gradually stir in sufficient flour to form a batter. Beat vigorously, then gradually add the remaining flour and mix to a soft dough.

2 Knead for 5 minutes. Place in a bowl; cover with oiled clear film. Leave at room temperature for 4–5 hours, or until risen and starting to collapse.

3 In a bowl, mix the yeast for the dough with half of the water, then stir in the remainder. Add the previously made dough or starter (*left*) and knead to dissolve the dough. Gradually add the flour and salt and mix to a dough. Turn out on to a lightly floured surface and knead for 8–10 minutes until the dough is smooth and elastic.

4 Place the dough in a lightly oiled bowl, cover with lightly oiled clear film and leave to rise, in a warm place, for about 1½ hours, or until doubled in bulk.

5 Turn out on to a lightly floured surface, knock back (punch down) and shape into a round ball. Flatten slightly and place on the baking sheet.

6 Cover with lightly oiled clear film and leave to rise, in a warm place, for 1 hour, or until almost doubled in size.

7 Dust the top of the loaf with flour and, using a sharp knife, cut the top fairly deeply in a criss-cross pattern. Leave to rest for 10 minutes. Meanwhile, preheat the oven to 230°C/450°F/Gas 8.

8 Bake for 25–30 minutes, or until browned. Spray the inside of the oven with water as soon as the bread goes into the oven, and three times during the first 10 minutes of baking. Transfer to a wire rack to cool.

CROISSANTS

Golden layers of flaky pastry, puffy, light and flavoured with butter is how the best croissants should be. Serve warm on the day of baking.

350g/12oz/3 cups unbleached white bread flour
115g/4oz/1 cup fine French plain (all purpose) flour
5ml/1 tsp salt
25g/1oz/2 tbsp caster (superfine) sugar
15g/¹/₂ oz fresh yeast
225ml/scant 8fl oz/scant 1 cup lukewarm milk
1 egg, lightly beaten
225g/8oz/1 cup butter

For the Glaze
1 egg yolk
15ml/1 tbsp milk

Makes 14 Croissants

COOK'S TIP
Make sure that the block of butter and the dough are about the same temperature when combining, to ensure the best results.

1 Sift the flours and salt together into a large bowl. Stir in the sugar. Make a well in the centre. Cream the yeast with 45ml/3 tbsp of the milk, then stir in the remainder. Add the yeast mixture to the centre of the flour, then add the egg and gradually beat in the flour until it forms a dough.

2 Turn out on to a lightly floured surface and knead for 3–4 minutes. Place in a large lightly oiled bowl, cover with lightly oiled clear (plastic wrap) film and leave in a warm place, for about 45-60 minutes, or until doubled in bulk.

3 Knock back (punch down), re-cover and chill for 1 hour. Meanwhile, flatten the butter into a block about 2cm/¾in thick. Knock back the dough and turn out on to a lightly floured surface. Roll out into a rough 25cm/10in square, rolling the edges thinner than the centre.

4 Place the block of butter diagonally in the centre and fold the corners of the dough over the butter like an envelope, tucking in the edges to completely enclose the butter.

5 Roll the dough into a rectangle about 2cm/¾in thick, approximately twice as long as it is wide. Fold the bottom third up and the top third down and seal the edges with a rolling pin. Wrap in clear film and chill for 20 minutes.

6 Repeat the rolling, folding and chilling twice more, turning the dough by 90 degrees each time. Roll out on a floured surface into a 63 × 33cm/25 × 13in rectangle; trim the edges to leave a 60 × 30cm/24 × 12in rectangle. Cut in half lengthways. Cut crossways into 14 equal triangles with 15cm/6in bases.

7 Place the dough triangles on two baking sheets, cover with clear film and chill for 10 minutes.

8 To shape the croissants, place each one with the wide end at the top, hold each side and pull gently to stretch the top of the triangle a little, then roll towards the point, finishing with the pointed end tucked underneath. Curve the ends towards the pointed end to make a crescent. Place on two baking sheets, spaced well apart.

9 Mix together the egg yolk and milk for the glaze. Lightly brush a little glaze over the croissants, avoiding the cut edges of the dough. Cover the croissants loosely with lightly oiled clear film and leave to rise, in a warm place, for about 30 minutes, or until they are nearly doubled in size.

10 Meanwhile, preheat the oven to 220°C/425°F/Gas 7. Brush the croissants with the remaining glaze and bake for 15–20 minutes, or until crisp and golden. Transfer to a wire rack to cool slightly before serving warm.

VARIATION
To make chocolate-filled croissants, place a small square of milk or plain (semisweet) chocolate or 15ml/1 tbsp coarsely chopped chocolate at the wide end of each triangle before rolling up as in step 8.

PAIN BOUILLIE

This is an old-fashioned style of rye bread, made before sourdough starters were used. Rye flour is mixed with boiling water like a porridge and left overnight to ferment. The finished bread has a rich earthy flavour, with just a hint of caraway.

FOR THE PORRIDGE
225g/8oz/2 cups rye flour
450ml/³/4 pint/1³/4 cups boiling water
5ml/1 tsp clear honey

FOR THE DOUGH
7g/¹/4 oz fresh yeast
30ml/2 tbsp lukewarm water
5ml/1 tsp caraway seeds, crushed
10ml/2 tsp salt
350g/12oz/3 cups unbleached white bread flour
olive oil, for brushing

MAKES 2 LOAVES

1 Lightly grease a 23.5 × 13cm/9¼ × 5in loaf tin (pan). Place the rye flour for the porridge in a large bowl. Pour over the boiling water and leave to stand for 5 minutes. Stir in the honey. Cover with clear film (plastic wrap) and leave in a warm place for about 12 hours.

2 Make the dough. Put the yeast in a measuring jug (cup) and blend in the water. Stir the mixture into the porridge with the crushed caraway seeds and salt. Add the white flour a little at a time, mixing first with a wooden spoon and then with your hands, until the mixture forms a firm dough.

3 Turn out on to a lightly floured surface and knead for 6–8 minutes until smooth and elastic. Return to the bowl, cover with lightly oiled clear film (plastic wrap) and leave to rise, in a warm place, for 1½ hours, or until doubled in bulk.

4 Turn out on to a lightly floured surface and knock back (punch down). Cut into two equal pieces and roll each piece into a rectangle 38 × 12cm/15 × 4½in. Fold the bottom third up and the top third down and seal the edges. Turn over.

5 Brush one side of each piece of folded dough with olive oil and place side by side in the prepared tin, oiled edges next to each other. Cover with lightly oiled clear film and leave to rise, in a warm place, for 1 hour, or until the dough reaches the top of the tin.

6 Meanwhile, preheat the oven to 220°C/425°F/Gas 7. Brush the tops of the loaves with olive oil, and using a sharp knife, slash with one or two cuts. Bake for 30 minutes, then reduce the oven temperature to 190°C/375°F/Gas 5 and bake for a further 25–30 minutes. Turn out on to a wire rack to cool.

COOK'S TIP
Serve very thinly sliced, with a little butter, or as an accompaniment to cold meats and cheeses.

EPI

This pretty, wheat-ear shaped crusty loaf makes a good presentation bread. The recipe uses a piece of fermented French baguette dough as a starter, which improves the flavour and texture of the finished bread.

*7g/¹/₄ oz fresh yeast
275ml/9fl oz/generous 1 cup
lukewarm water
115g/4oz/¹/₂ cup 6–10-hours-old
French baguette dough
225g/8oz/2 cups unbleached white
bread flour
75g/3oz/³/₄ cup fine French plain
(all-purpose) flour
5ml/1 tsp salt*

MAKES 2 LOAVES

COOK'S TIP
You can use any amount up to 10 per cent of previously made French baguette dough for this recipe. The épi can also be shaped into a circle to make an attractive crown.

5 Let the dough rest between rolling for a few minutes if necessary to avoid tearing. Pleat a floured dishtowel on a baking sheet to make two moulds for the loaves. Place them between the pleats of the towel, cover with lightly oiled clear film and leave to rise, in a warm place, for 30 minutes.

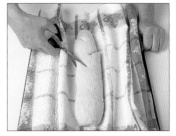

6 Meanwhile, preheat the oven to 230°C/450°F/Gas 8. Using scissors, make diagonal cuts halfway through the dough about 5cm/2in apart, alternating the cuts along the loaf. Gently pull the dough in the opposite direction.

7 Place on the prepared baking sheet and bake for 20 minutes, or until golden. Spray the inside of the oven with water 2–3 times during the first 5 minutes of baking. Transfer to a wire rack to cool.

1 Sprinkle a baking sheet with flour. Mix the yeast with the water in a jug (pitcher). Place the French bread dough in a large bowl and break up. Add a little of the yeast water to soften the dough. Mix in a little of the bread flour, then alternate the additions of yeast water and both flours until incorporated. Sprinkle the salt over the dough and knead in. Turn out the dough on to a lightly floured surface and knead for about 5 minutes until smooth and elastic.

2 Place in a lightly oiled bowl, cover with lightly oiled clear film (plastic wrap) and leave in a warm place, for about 1 hour, or until doubled in bulk.

3 Knock back the dough with your fist, then cover the bowl again with the oiled clear film and leave to rise, in a warm place, for about 1 hour.

4 Divide the dough into two equal pieces, place on a lightly floured surface and stretch each piece into a baguette.

For the Chef
50g/2oz/¹/2 cup wholemeal
(whole-wheat) bread flour
45ml/3 tbsp warm water

For the 1st Refreshment
60ml/4 tbsp warm water
75g/3oz/³/4 cup wholemeal bread flour

For the 2nd Refreshment
120ml/4fl oz/¹/2 cup lukewarm water
115g/4oz/1 cup unbleached white bread flour
25g/1oz/¹/4 cup wholemeal bread flour

For the Dough
150–175ml/5–6fl oz/²/3–³/4 cup lukewarm water
350g/12oz/3 cups unbleached white bread flour
10ml/2 tsp salt

Makes 1 Loaf

COOK'S TIPS
• You will need to start making this bread about four days before you'd like to eat it.
• To make another loaf, keep the piece of starter dough (see step 6) in the refrigerator for up to three days. Use the reserved piece of starter dough for the 2nd refreshment in place of the *levain* in step 3, gradually mix in the water, then the flours and leave to rise as described.

1 To make the *chef*, place the flour in a small bowl, add the water and knead for 3–4 minutes to form a dough. Cover with clear film (plastic wrap) and leave the *chef* in a warm place for 2 days.

Pain de Campagne Rustique

This superb country bread is made using a natural French chef starter to produce a rustic flavour and texture. In France, breads like this are often made three or four times the size of this loaf.

2 Pull off the hardened crust and discard, then remove 30ml/2 tbsp of the moist centre. Place in a large bowl and gradually mix in the water for the 1st refreshment. Gradually mix in the flour and knead for 3–4 minutes to form a dough or *levain*, then cover with clear film and leave in a warm place for 1 day.

3 Discard the crust from the *levain* and gradually mix in the water for the 2nd refreshment. Mix in the flours a little at a time, mixing well after each addition to form a firm dough. Cover with lightly oiled clear film and leave to rise, in a warm place, for about 10 hours, or until doubled in bulk.

4 Lightly flour a baking sheet. For the final stage in the preparation of the dough, gradually mix the water into the *levain* in the bowl, then gradually mix in the flour, then the salt. Turn out the dough on to a lightly floured surface and knead for about 5 minutes until smooth and elastic.

5 Place the dough in a large lightly oiled bowl, cover with lightly oiled clear film and leave to rise, in a warm place, for 1¹/2–2 hours, or until the dough has almost doubled in bulk.

6 Knock back (punch down) the dough and cut off 115g/4oz/¹/2 cup. Set aside for making the next loaf. Shape the remaining dough into a ball – you should have about 350g/12oz/1¹/2 cups.

7 Line a 10cm/4in high, 23cm/9in round basket or large bowl with a dishtowel and dust with flour.

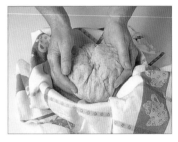

8 Place the dough ball seam side up in the prepared basket or bowl. Cover with lightly oiled clear film and leave to rise, in a warm place, for 2–3 hours, or until almost doubled in bulk.

9 Preheat the oven to 230°C/450°F/Gas 8. Invert the loaf on to the prepared baking sheet and sprinkle with flour.

10 Slash the top of the loaf, using a sharp knife, four times at right angles to each other, to form a square pattern.

11 Sprinkle with a little more flour, if you like, then bake for 30–35 minutes, or until the loaf has browned and sounds hollow when tapped on the base. Transfer to a wire rack to cool.

FOUGASSE

450g/1lb/4 cups unbleached white
bread flour
5ml/1 tsp salt
20g/³/4 oz fresh yeast
280ml/9fl oz/generous 1 cup
lukewarm water
15ml/1 tbsp extra virgin olive oil

FOR THE FILLING
50g/2oz/¹/3 cup Roquefort
cheese, crumbled
40g/1¹/2oz/¹/3 cup walnut
pieces, chopped
25g/1oz/2 tbsp drained, canned
anchovy fillets, soaked in milk
and drained again, chopped
olive oil, for brushing

MAKES 2 LOAVES

VARIATIONS
• Replace the cheese with 15ml/1 tbsp
chopped fresh sage or thyme or
40g/1½oz/⅓ cup chopped pitted olives.
• To make a sweet fougasse, replace
15ml/1 tbsp of the water with orange
flower water. Include 50g/2oz/⅓ cup
chopped candied orange peel and
25g/1oz/2 tbsp sugar.

A fougasse is a lattice-shaped, flattish loaf from the South of France. It can be cooked as a plain bread or flavoured with cheese, anchovies, herbs, nuts or olives. On Christmas Eve in Provence a fougasse flavoured with orange flower water is part of a table centrepiece of thirteen desserts, used to symbolize Christ and the Twelve Apostles.

2 Place the dough in a lightly oiled bowl, cover with lightly oiled clear film (plastic wrap) and leave in a warm place, for about 1 hour, or until doubled in bulk.

3 Turn out on to a lightly floured surface and knock back (punch down). Divide into two equal pieces and flatten one piece. Sprinkle over the cheese and walnuts and fold the dough over on itself two or three times to incorporate. Repeat with the remaining piece of dough using the anchovies. Shape each piece of flavoured dough into a ball.

4 Flatten each ball of dough and fold the bottom third up and the top third down, to make an oblong. Roll the cheese dough into a rectangle measuring about 28 × 15cm/11 × 6in. Using a sharp knife, make four diagonal cuts almost to the edge. Pull and stretch the dough evenly, so that it resembles a ladder.

5 Shape the anchovy dough into an oval with a flat base, about 25cm/10in long. Using a sharp knife, make three diagonal slits on each side towards the flat base, and pull to open the cuts. Transfer to the prepared baking sheets, cover with lightly oiled clear film and leave to rise, in a warm place, for about 30–45 minutes, or until nearly doubled in bulk.

6 Meanwhile, preheat the oven to 220°C/425°F/Gas 7. Brush both loaves with a little olive oil and bake for 25 minutes, or until golden. Transfer to a wire rack to cool.

1 Lightly grease two baking sheets. Sift the flour and salt together into a large bowl and make a well in the centre. In a measuring jug (cup), cream the yeast with 60ml/4 tbsp of the water. Pour the yeast mixture into the centre of the flour with the remaining water and the olive oil and mix to a soft dough. Turn out on to a lightly floured surface and knead the dough for 8–10 minutes until smooth and elastic.

PAIN AUX NOIX

This delicious butter- and milk-enriched wholemeal bread is filled with walnuts. It is the perfect companion for cheese.

50g/2oz/¹/₄ cup butter
350g/12oz/3 cups wholemeal (whole-wheat) bread flour
115g/4oz/1 cup unbleached white bread flour
15ml/1 tbsp light muscovado (brown) sugar
7.5ml/1¹/₂ tsp salt
20g/³/₄ oz fresh yeast
275ml/9fl oz/generous 1 cup lukewarm milk
175g/6oz/1¹/₂ cups walnut pieces

MAKES 2 LOAVES

3 Knead on a lightly floured surface for 6–8 minutes. Place in a lightly oiled bowl, cover with lightly oiled clear film (plastic wrap) and leave in a warm place, for 1 hour, or until doubled in bulk.

4 Turn out the dough on to a lightly floured surface and gently knock back (punch down). Press or roll out to flatten and then sprinkle over the nuts. Gently press the nuts into the dough, then roll it up. Return to the oiled bowl, re-cover and leave, in a warm place, for 30 minutes.

5 Turn out on to a lightly floured surface, divide in half and shape each piece into a ball. Place on the baking sheets, cover with lightly oiled clear film and leave to rise, in a warm place, for 45 minutes, or until doubled in bulk.

6 Meanwhile, preheat the oven to 220°C/425°F/Gas 7. Using a sharp knife, slash the top of each loaf three times. Bake for about 35 minutes, or until the loaves sound hollow when tapped on the base. Transfer to a wire rack to cool.

1 Lightly grease two baking sheets. Place the butter in a small pan and heat until melted and starting to turn brown, then set aside to cool. Mix the flours, sugar and salt in a large bowl and make a well in the centre. Cream the yeast with half the milk. Add to the centre of the flour with the remaining milk.

2 Pour the cool melted butter through a fine strainer into the centre of the flour so that it joins the liquids already there. Using your hand, mix the liquids together in the bowl and gradually mix in small quantities of the flour to make a batter. Continue until the mixture forms a moist dough.

PETITS PAINS AU LAIT

These classic French round milk rolls have a soft crust and a light, slightly sweet crumb. They won't last long!

450g/1lb/4 cups unbleached white bread flour
10ml/2 tsp salt
15ml/1 tbsp caster (superfine) sugar
50g/2oz/¼ cup butter, softened
15g/½ oz fresh yeast
280ml/9fl oz/generous 1 cup lukewarm milk, plus 15ml/1 tbsp extra milk, for glazing

MAKES 12 ROLLS

1 Lightly grease two baking sheets. Sift the flour and salt together into a large bowl. Stir in the sugar. Rub the softened butter into the flour.

2 Cream the yeast with 60ml/4 tbsp of the milk. Stir in the remaining milk. Pour into the flour mixture and mix to a soft dough.

3 Turn out on to a lightly floured surface and knead for 8–10 minutes until smooth and elastic. Place in a lightly oiled bowl, cover with lightly oiled clear film (plastic wrap) and leave in a warm place, for 1 hour, or until doubled in bulk.

4 Turn out the dough on to a lightly floured surface and gently knock back (punch down). Divide into 12 equal pieces. Shape into balls and space on the baking sheets.

5 Using a sharp knife, cut a cross in the top of each roll. Cover with lightly oiled clear film and leave to rise, in a warm place, for about 20 minutes, or until doubled in size.

6 Preheat the oven to 200°C/400°F/Gas 6. Brush the rolls with milk and bake for 20–25 minutes, or until golden. Transfer to a wire rack to cool.

VARIATION

These can also be made into long rolls. To shape, flatten each ball of dough and fold in half. Roll back and forth, using your hand to form a 13cm/5in long roll, tapered at either end. Just before baking, slash the tops horizontally several times.

FRENCH DIMPLED ROLLS

A French and Belgian speciality, these attractive rolls are distinguished by the split down the centre. They have a crusty finish while remaining soft and light inside – they taste lovely, too.

400g/14oz/3½ cups unbleached white bread flour
7.5ml/1½ tsp salt
5ml/1 tsp caster (superfine) sugar
15g/½ oz fresh yeast
120ml/4fl oz/½ cup lukewarm milk
175ml/6fl oz/¾ cup lukewarm water

MAKES 10 ROLLS

1 Grease two baking sheets. Sift the flour and salt into a large bowl. Stir in the sugar and make a well in the centre.

2 Cream the yeast with the milk until dissolved, then pour into the centre of the flour mixture. Sprinkle over a little of the flour from around the edge. Leave at room temperature for 15–20 minutes, or until the mixture starts to bubble.

3 Add the water and gradually mix in the flour to form a fairly moist, soft dough. Turn out on to a lightly floured surface and knead for 8–10 minutes until smooth and elastic. Place in a lightly oiled bowl, cover with lightly oiled clear film (plastic wrap) and leave to rise, at room temperature, for about 1½ hours, or until doubled in bulk.

4 Turn out on to a lightly floured surface and knock back (punch down). Re-cover and leave to rest for 5 minutes. Divide into 10 pieces. Shape into balls by rolling the dough under a cupped hand, then roll until oval. Lightly flour the tops. Space well apart on the baking sheets, cover with lightly oiled clear film and leave at room temperature, for about 30 minutes, or until almost doubled in size.

5 Lightly oil the side of your hand and press the centre of each roll to make a deep split. Re-cover and leave to rest for 15 minutes. Meanwhile, place a roasting pan in the bottom of the oven and preheat the oven to 230°C/450°F/Gas 8. Pour 250ml/8fl oz/1 cup water into the tin and bake the rolls for 15 minutes, or until golden. Cool on a wire rack.

KUGELHOPF

150g/5oz/⅔ cup unsalted (sweet)
butter, softened
12 walnut halves
675g/1½lb/6 cups unbleached white
bread flour
7.5ml/1½ tsp salt
20g/¾oz fresh yeast
300ml/10fl oz/1¼ cups milk
115g/4oz smoked bacon, diced
1 onion, finely chopped
15ml/1 tbsp vegetable oil
5 eggs, beaten
freshly ground black pepper

MAKES 1 LOAF

This inviting, fluted ring-shaped bread originates from Alsace, although Germany, Hungary and Austria all have their own variations of this popular recipe. Kugelhopf can be sweet or savoury; this version is richly flavoured with nuts, onion and bacon.

VARIATION
To make a sweet kugelhopf replace the walnuts with whole almonds and the bacon and onion with 115g/4oz/1 cup raisins and 50g/2oz/⅓ cup mixed chopped (candied) peel. Add 50g/2oz/¼ cup caster (superfine) sugar in step 2 and omit the black pepper.

1 Use 25g/1oz/2 tbsp of the butter to grease a 23cm/9in kugelhopf mould. Place eight walnut halves around the base and chop the remainder.

2 Sift the flour and salt together into a large bowl and season with pepper. Make a well in the centre. Cream the yeast with 45ml/3 tbsp of the milk. Pour into the centre of the flour with the remaining milk. Mix in a little flour to make a thick batter. Sprinkle a little of the remaining flour over the top of the batter, cover with clear film (plastic wrap) and leave in a warm place for 20–30 minutes until the yeast mixture bubbles.

3 Meanwhile, fry the bacon and onion in the oil until the onion is pale golden.

4 Add the eggs to the flour mixture and gradually beat in the flour, using your hand. Gradually beat in the remaining softened butter to form a soft dough. Cover with lightly oiled clear film and leave to rise, in a warm place, for 45–60 minutes, or until almost doubled in bulk. Preheat the oven to 200°C/400°F/Gas 6.

5 Knock back (punch down) the dough and gently knead in the bacon, onion and nuts. Place in the mould, cover with lightly oiled clear film and leave to rise, in a warm place, for about 1 hour, or until it has risen to the top of the mould.

6 Bake for 40–45 minutes, or until the loaf has browned and sounds hollow when tapped on the base. Cool in the mould for 5 minutes, then on a wire rack.

BRIOCHE

—

Rich and buttery yet light and airy, this wonderful loaf captures the essence of the classic French bread.

1 Sift the flour and salt together into a large bowl and make a well in the centre. Put the yeast in a measuring jug (cup) and stir in the milk.

2 Add the yeast mixture to the centre of the flour with the eggs and mix together to form a soft dough.

3 Using your hand, beat the dough for 4–5 minutes until smooth and elastic. Cream the butter and sugar together. Gradually add the butter mixture to the dough in small amounts, making sure it is incorporated before adding more. Beat until smooth, shiny and elastic.

350g/12oz/3 cups unbleached white bread flour
2.5ml/¹/₂ tsp salt
15g/¹/₂ oz fresh yeast
60ml/4 tbsp lukewarm milk
3 eggs, lightly beaten
175g/6oz/³/₄ cup butter, softened
25g/1oz/2 tbsp caster (superfine) sugar

FOR THE GLAZE
1 egg yolk
15ml/1 tbsp milk

MAKES 1 LOAF

4 Cover the bowl with lightly oiled clear film (plastic wrap) and leave the dough to rise, in a warm place, for 1–2 hours or until doubled in bulk.

5 Lightly knock back (punch down) the dough, then re-cover and place in the refrigerator for 8–10 hours or overnight.

6 Lightly grease a 1.6 litre/2³/₄ pint/ scant 7 cup brioche mould. Turn the dough out on to a lightly floured surface. Cut off almost a quarter and set aside. Shape the rest into a ball and place in the prepared mould. Shape the reserved dough into an elongated egg shape. Using two or three fingers, make a hole in the centre of the large ball of dough. Gently press the narrow end of the egg-shaped dough into the hole.

7 Mix together the egg yolk and milk for the glaze, and brush a little over the brioche. Cover with lightly oiled clear film and leave to rise, in a warm place, for 1¹/₂–2 hours, or until the dough nearly reaches the top of the mould.

8 Meanwhile, preheat the oven to 230°C/ 450°F/Gas 8. Brush the brioche with the remaining glaze and bake for 10 minutes. Reduce the oven temperature to 190°C/ 375°F/Gas 5 and bake for a further 20–25 minutes, or until golden. Turn out on to a wire rack to cool.

MEDITERRANEAN BREADS

*The warm, rich flavours of the Mediterranean find their way into the breads. Olive oil,
sun-dried tomatoes, olives, garlic and fresh herbs all feature in breads that are so delicious
that they are now widely enjoyed all over the world. Ciabatta, panini all'olio rolls, focaccia
and schiacciata are just a few examples. Spanish, Moroccan and Portuguese breads include
local grains like corn and barley, together with seeds such as sesame, sunflower and
pumpkin. Elaborate speciality breads are baked for religious festivals, the Greek
Easter bread – tsoureki – and the Christmas breads – christopsomo and
Twelfth Night bread – being some of the most spectacular.*

PUGLIESE

This classic Italian open-textured, soft-crumbed bread is moistened and flavoured with fruity olive oil. Its floured top gives it a true country feel.

For the Biga Starter
175g/6oz/1½ cups unbleached white bread flour
7g/¼ oz fresh yeast
90ml/6 tbsp lukewarm water

For the Dough
225g/8oz/2 cups unbleached white bread flour, plus extra for dusting
225g/8oz/2 cups unbleached wholemeal (whole-wheat) bread flour
5ml/1 tsp caster (superfine) sugar
10ml/2 tsp salt
15g/½ oz fresh yeast
275ml/9fl oz/generous 1 cup lukewarm water
75ml/5 tbsp extra virgin olive oil

MAKES 1 LARGE LOAF

VARIATION
Incorporate 150g/5oz/1 cup chopped black olives into the dough at the end of step 5 for extra olive flavour.

1 Sift the flour for the *biga* starter into a large bowl. Make a well in the centre. In a small bowl, cream the yeast with the water. Pour the liquid into the centre of the flour and gradually mix in the surrounding flour to form a firm dough.

2 Turn the dough out on to a lightly floured surface and knead for 5 minutes until smooth and elastic. Return to the bowl, cover with lightly oiled clear film (plastic wrap) and leave to rise, in a warm place, for 8–10 hours, or until the dough has risen well and is starting to collapse.

3 Lightly flour a baking sheet. Mix the flours, sugar and salt for the dough in a large bowl. Cream the yeast and the water in another large bowl, then stir in the *biga* and mix together.

4 Stir in the flour mixture a little at a time, then add the olive oil in the same way, and mix to a soft dough. Turn out on to a lightly floured surface and knead the dough for 8–10 minutes until smooth and elastic.

5 Place in a lightly oiled bowl, cover with lightly oiled clear film and leave to rise, in a warm place, for 1–1½ hours, or until doubled in bulk.

6 Turn out on to a lightly floured surface and knock back (punch down). Gently pull out the edges and fold under to make a round. Transfer to the prepared baking sheet, cover with lightly oiled clear film and leave to rise, in a warm place, for 1–1½ hours, or until almost doubled in size.

7 Meanwhile, preheat the oven to 230°C/450°F/Gas 8. Lightly dust the loaf with flour and bake for 15 minutes. Reduce the oven temperature to 200°C/400°F/Gas 6 and bake for a further 20 minutes, or until the loaf sounds hollow when tapped on the base. Transfer to a wire rack to cool.

CIABATTA

This irregular-shaped Italian bread is so called because it looks like an old shoe or slipper. It is made with a very wet dough flavoured with olive oil; cooking produces a bread with holes and a wonderfully chewy crust.

1 Cream the yeast for the *biga* starter with a little of the water. Sift the flour into a large bowl. Gradually mix in the yeast mixture and sufficient of the remaining water to form a firm dough.

2 Turn out the *biga* starter dough on to a lightly floured surface and knead for about 5 minutes until smooth and elastic. Return the dough to the bowl, cover with lightly oiled clear film (plastic wrap) and leave in a warm place for 12–15 hours, or until the dough has risen and is starting to collapse.

3 Sprinkle three baking sheets with flour. Mix the yeast for the dough with a little of the water until creamy, then mix in the remainder. Add the yeast mixture to the *biga* and gradually mix in.

4 Mix in the milk, beating thoroughly with a wooden spoon. Using your hand, gradually beat in the flour, lifting the dough as you mix. Mixing the dough will take 15 minutes or more and form a very wet mix, impossible to knead on a work surface.

5 Beat in the salt and olive oil. Cover with lightly oiled clear film and leave to rise, in a warm place, for 1½–2 hours, or until doubled in bulk.

6 With a spoon, carefully tip one-third of the dough at a time on to the baking sheets without knocking back (punching down) the dough in the process.

7 Using floured hands, shape into rough oblong loaf shapes, about 2.5cm/1in thick. Flatten slightly with splayed fingers. Sprinkle with flour and leave to rise in a warm place for 30 minutes.

8 Meanwhile, preheat the oven to 220°C/425°F/Gas 7. Bake for 25–30 minutes, or until golden brown and sounding hollow when tapped on the base. Transfer to a wire rack to cool.

For the Biga Starter
7g/¼ oz fresh yeast
175–200ml/6–7fl oz/¾–scant 1 cup lukewarm water
350g/12oz/3 cups unbleached plain (all-purpose) flour, plus extra for dusting

For the Dough
15g/½ oz fresh yeast
400ml/14fl oz/1⅔ cups lukewarm water
60ml/4 tbsp lukewarm milk
500g/1¼ lb/5 cups unbleached white bread flour
10ml/2 tsp salt
45ml/3 tbsp extra virgin olive oil

MAKES 3 LOAVES

VARIATION

To make tomato-flavoured ciabatta, add 115g/4oz/1 cup chopped, drained sun-dried tomatoes in olive oil. Add with the olive oil in step 5.

PANINI ALL'OLIO

The Italians adore interesting and elaborately shaped rolls. This distinctively flavoured bread dough, enriched with olive oil, can be used for making rolls or shaped as one large loaf.

450g/1lb/4 cups unbleached white bread flour
10ml/2 tsp salt
15g/¹/₂ oz fresh yeast
250ml/8fl oz/1 cup lukewarm water
60ml/4 tbsp extra virgin olive oil, plus extra for brushing

MAKES 16 ROLLS

1 Lightly oil three baking sheets. Sift the flour and salt together in a large bowl and make a well in the centre.

2 In a jug (pitcher), cream the yeast with half of the water, then stir in the remainder. Add to the centre of the flour with the oil and mix to a dough.

3 Turn the dough out on to a lightly floured surface and knead for 8–10 minutes until smooth and elastic. Place in a lightly oiled bowl, cover with lightly oiled clear film (plastic wrap) and leave in a warm place, for about 1 hour, or until nearly doubled in bulk.

4 Turn on to a lightly floured surface and knock back (punch down). Divide into 12 equal pieces of dough and shape into rolls as described in steps 5, 6, 7 and 8.

5 For *tavalli* (twisted spiral rolls): roll each piece of dough into a strip about 30cm/12in long and 4cm/1½ in wide. Twist each strip into a loose spiral and join the ends of dough together to make a circle. Place on the prepared baking sheets, spaced well apart. Brush the *tavalli* lightly with olive oil, cover with lightly oiled clear film and leave to rise, in a warm place, for 20–30 minutes.

6 For *filoncini* (finger-shaped rolls): flatten each piece of dough into an oval and roll to about 23cm/9in in length without changing the basic shape. Make it 5cm/2in wide at one end and 10cm/4in wide at the other. Roll up, starting from the wider end. Using your fingers, gently stretch the dough roll to 20–23cm/8–9in long. Cut in half. Place on the prepared baking sheets, spaced well apart. Brush the finger shapes with olive oil, cover with lightly oiled clear film and leave to rise, in a warm place, for 20–30 minutes.

7 For *carciofi* (artichoke-shaped rolls): shape each piece of dough into a ball and space well apart on the prepared baking sheets. Brush with olive oil, cover with lightly oiled clear film and leave to rise, in a warm place, for 20–30 minutes. Meanwhile, preheat the oven to 200°C/400°F/Gas 6. Using scissors, snip four or five 5mm/¼ in deep cuts in a circle on the top of each *carciofo*, then make five larger horizontal cuts around the sides. Bake the rolls for 15 minutes. Transfer to a wire rack to cool.

OLIVE BREAD

Black and green olives and good-quality fruity olive oil combine to make this strongly flavoured and irresistible Italian bread.

1 Lightly grease a baking sheet. Mix the flours, yeast and salt together in a large bowl and make a well in the centre.

2 Add the water and oil to the centre of the flour and mix to a soft dough. Knead the dough on a lightly floured surface for 8–10 minutes until smooth and elastic. Place in a lightly oiled bowl, cover with lightly oiled clear film (plastic wrap) and leave in a warm place, for 1 hour, or until doubled in bulk.

3 Turn out on to a lightly floured surface and knock back (punch down). Flatten out and sprinkle over the olives. Fold up and knead to distribute the olives. Leave to rest for 5 minutes, then shape into an oval loaf. Place on the baking sheet.

4 Make six deep cuts in the top of the loaf, and gently push the sections over. Cover with lightly oiled clear film and leave to rise, in a warm place, for 30–45 minutes, or until doubled in size.

275g/10oz/2¹/₂ cups unbleached white bread flour
50g/2oz/¹/₂ cup wholemeal (whole-wheat) bread flour
6g/¹/₄ oz sachet easy-blend (rapid-rise) dried yeast
2.5ml/¹/₂ tsp salt
210ml/7¹/₂ fl oz/ 1 cup lukewarm water
15ml/1 tbsp extra virgin olive oil, plus extra, for brushing
115g/4oz/1 cup pitted black and green olives, coarsely chopped

MAKES 1 LOAF

VARIATIONS
• Increase the proportion of wholemeal flour to make the loaf more rustic.
• Add some hazelnuts or pine nuts.

5 Meanwhile, preheat the oven to 200°C/400°F/Gas 6. Brush the bread with olive oil and bake for 35 minutes. Transfer to a wire rack to cool.

FOCACCIA

20g/³/₄ oz fresh yeast
325–350ml/11–12fl oz/1¹/₃–1¹/₂ cups
lukewarm water
45ml/3 tbsp extra virgin olive oil
500g/1¹/₄ lb/5 cups unbleached white
bread flour
10ml/2 tsp salt
15ml/1 tbsp chopped fresh sage

For the Topping
60ml/4 tbsp extra virgin olive oil
4 garlic cloves, chopped
12 fresh sage leaves

Makes 2 Round Loaves

This simple dimple-topped Italian flat bread is punctuated with olive oil and the aromatic flavours of sage and garlic to produce a truly succulent loaf.

VARIATION
Flavour the bread with other herbs, such as oregano, basil or rosemary and top with chopped black olives.

1 Lightly oil 2 × 25cm/10in shallow round cake tins (pans) or pizza pans. Cream the yeast with 60ml/4 tbsp of the water, then stir in the remaining water. Stir in the oil.

2 Sift the flour and salt together into a large bowl and make a well in the centre. Pour the yeast mixture into the well in the centre of the flour and mix to a soft dough.

3 Turn out the dough on to a lightly floured surface and knead for 8–10 minutes until smooth and elastic. Place in a lightly oiled bowl, cover with lightly oiled clear film (plastic wrap) or a large, lightly oiled plastic bag, and leave to rise, in a warm place, for about 1–1¹/₂ hours, or until doubled in bulk.

4 Knock back (punch down) and turn out on to a lightly floured surface. Gently knead in the chopped sage. Divide the dough into two equal pieces. Shape each into a ball, roll out into 25cm/10in circles and place in the prepared tins.

5 Cover with lightly oiled clear film and leave to rise in a warm place for about 30 minutes. Uncover, and using your fingertips, poke the dough to make deep dimples over the entire surface. Replace the clear film cover and leave to rise until doubled in bulk.

6 Meanwhile, preheat the oven to 200°C/400°F/Gas 6. Drizzle over the olive oil for the topping and sprinkle each focaccia evenly with chopped garlic. Dot the sage leaves over the surface. Bake for 25–30 minutes, or until both loaves are golden. Immediately remove the focaccia from the tins and transfer them to a wire rack to cool slightly. These loaves are best served warm.

POLENTA BREAD

Polenta is widely used in Italian cooking. Here it is combined with pine nuts to make a truly Italian bread with a fantastic flavour.

50g/2oz/1/2 cup polenta
300ml/1/2 pint/11/4 cups lukewarm water
15g/1/2 oz fresh yeast
2.5ml/1/2 tsp clear honey
225g/8oz/2 cups unbleached white bread flour
25g/1oz/2 tbsp butter
45ml/3 tbsp pine nuts
7.5ml/11/2 tsp salt

FOR THE TOPPING
1 egg yolk
15ml/1 tbsp water
pine nuts, for sprinkling

MAKES 1 LOAF

1 Lightly grease a baking sheet. Mix the polenta and 250ml/8fl oz/1 cup of the water together in a pan and slowly bring to the boil, stirring continuously with a large wooden spoon. Reduce the heat and simmer for 2–3 minutes, stirring occasionally. Set aside to cool for 10 minutes, or until just warm.

2 In a small bowl, mix the yeast with the remaining water and honey until creamy. Sift 115g/4oz/1 cup of the flour into a large bowl. Gradually beat in the yeast mixture, then gradually stir in the polenta mixture to combine. Turn out on to a lightly floured surface and knead for 5 minutes until smooth and elastic.

3 Cover the bowl with lightly oiled clear film (plastic wrap) or a lightly oiled plastic bag. Leave the dough to rise, in a warm place, for about 2 hours, or until it has doubled in bulk.

4 Meanwhile, melt the butter in a small pan, add the pine nuts and cook over a medium heat, stirring, until pale golden. Set aside to cool.

5 Add the remaining flour and the salt to the polenta dough and mix to a soft dough. Knead in the pine nuts. Turn out on to a lightly floured surface and knead for 5 minutes until smooth and elastic.

6 Place in a lightly oiled bowl, cover with lightly oiled clear film and leave to rise, in a warm place, for 1 hour, or until doubled in bulk.

7 Knock back (punch down) and turn it out on to a lightly floured surface. Cut the dough into two equal pieces and roll each piece into a fat sausage about 38cm/15in long. Plait (braid) together and place on the baking sheet. Cover with lightly oiled clear film and leave in a warm place, for 45 minutes. Preheat the oven to 200°C/400°F/Gas 6.

8 Mix the egg yolk and water and brush over the loaf. Sprinkle with pine nuts and bake for 30 minutes, or until golden and sounding hollow when tapped on the base. Cool on a wire rack.

PANE TOSCANO

This bread from Tuscany is made without salt and probably originates from the days when salt was heavily taxed. To compensate for the lack of salt, this bread is usually served with salty foods, such as anchovies and olives.

550g/1¼ lb/5 cups unbleached white
bread flour
350ml/12fl oz/1½ cups boiling water
15g/½ oz fresh yeast
60ml/4 tbsp lukewarm water

MAKES 1 LOAF

COOK'S TIP
Salt controls the action of yeast in bread so the leavening action is more noticeable. Don't let this unsalted bread over-rise or it may collapse.

6 Fold the sides of the round into the centre and seal. Place seam side up on the prepared baking sheet. Cover with lightly oiled clear film and leave to rise, in a warm place, for 30–45 minutes, or until doubled in size.

1 First make the starter. Sift 175g/6oz/1½ cups of the flour into a large bowl. Pour over the boiling water, leave for a couple of minutes, then mix well. Cover the bowl with a damp dishtowel and leave for 10 hours.

2 Lightly flour a baking sheet. Cream the yeast with the lukewarm water. Stir into the starter.

3 Gradually add the remaining flour and mix to form a dough. Turn out on to a lightly floured surface and knead for 5–8 minutes until smooth and elastic.

4 Place in a lightly oiled bowl, cover with lightly oiled clear film (plastic wrap) and leave in a warm place, for 1–1½ hours, or until doubled in bulk.

5 Turn out the dough on to a lightly floured surface, knock back (punch down), and shape into a round.

7 Flatten the loaf to about half its risen height and flip over. Cover with a large upturned bowl and leave to rise, in a warm place, for 30 minutes.

8 Meanwhile, preheat the oven to 220°C/425°F/Gas 7. Slash the top of the loaf, using a sharp knife, if wished. Bake for 30–35 minutes, or until golden. Transfer to a wire rack to cool.

SICILIAN SCROLL

A wonderful pale yellow, crusty-topped loaf, enhanced with a nutty flavour from the sesame seeds. It's perfect for serving with cheese.

450g/1lb/4 cups finely ground semolina
115g/4oz/1 cup unbleached white bread flour
10ml/2 tsp salt
20g/³/₄ oz fresh yeast
360ml/12¹/₂ fl oz/generous 1¹/₂ cups lukewarm water
30ml/2 tbsp extra virgin olive oil
sesame seeds, for sprinkling

MAKES 1 LOAF

4 Turn out on to a lightly floured surface and knock back (punch down). Knead gently, then shape into a fat roll about 50cm/20in long. Form into an "S" shape.

5 Carefully transfer the dough to the prepared baking sheet, cover with lightly oiled clear film and leave to rise, in a warm place, for 30–45 minutes, or until doubled in size.

6 Meanwhile, preheat the oven to 220°C/425°F/Gas 7. Brush the top of the scroll with water and sprinkle with sesame seeds. Bake for 10 minutes. Spray the inside of the oven with water twice during this time. Reduce the oven temperature to 200°C/400°F/Gas 6 and bake for a further 25–30 minutes, or until golden. Transfer to a wire rack to cool.

1 Lightly grease a baking sheet. Mix the semolina, white bread flour and salt together in a large bowl and make a well in the centre.

2 In a jug (pitcher), cream the yeast with half the water, then stir in the remainder. Add the creamed yeast to the centre of the semolina mixture with the olive oil and gradually incorporate the semolina and flour to form a firm dough.

3 Turn out the dough on to a lightly floured surface and knead for 8–10 minutes until smooth and elastic. Place in a lightly oiled bowl, cover with lightly oiled clear film (plastic wrap) and leave to rise, in a warm place, for 1–1¹/₂ hours, or until the dough has doubled in bulk.

VARIATION
Although sesame seeds are the traditional topping on this delectable Italian bread, poppy seeds, or even crystals of sea salt, could be used instead.

PROSCIUTTO LOAF

This savoury Italian bread from Parma is spiked with the local dried ham.
Just a small amount fills the loaf with marvellous flavour.

1 Lightly grease a baking sheet. Sift the flour and salt together into a large bowl and make a well in the centre. Cream the yeast with 30ml/2 tbsp of the water, then gradually mix in the rest. Pour into the centre of the flour.

2 Gradually beat in most of the flour with a wooden spoon to make a batter. Beat gently to begin with and then more vigorously as the batter thickens. After most of the flour has been incorporated, beat in the remainder with your hand to form a moist dough.

3 Turn out on to a lightly floured surface and knead for 5 minutes until smooth and elastic. Place in a lightly oiled bowl, cover with oiled clear film (plastic wrap) and leave in a warm place, for 1½ hours, or until doubled in bulk.

4 Turn out the dough on to a lightly floured surface, knock back (punch down) and then knead for 1 minute. Flatten to a round, then sprinkle with half the prosciutto and pepper. Fold the dough in half and repeat with the remaining ham and pepper. Roll up, tucking in the sides.

350g/12oz/3 cups unbleached white bread flour
7.5ml/1½ tsp salt
15g/½ oz fresh yeast
250ml/8fl oz/1 cup lukewarm water
40g/1½ oz prosciutto, torn into small pieces
5ml/1 tsp freshly ground black pepper

MAKES 1 LOAF

VARIATIONS
• To make pesto bread, spread 45ml/ 3 tbsp pesto over the flattened dough in step 6, then continue as above.
• For sweet pepper bread, add 45ml/3 tbsp finely chopped roasted yellow and red (bell) peppers instead of the ham in step 4.

5 Place on the prepared baking sheet, cover with lightly oiled clear film and leave to rise, in a warm place, for about 30 minutes. On a lightly floured surface, roll into an oval, fold in half and seal the edges. Flatten and fold again. Seal and fold again to make a long loaf.

6 Roll into a stubby long loaf. Draw out the edges by rolling the dough under the palms of your hands. Place on the baking sheet, cover with lightly oiled clear film and leave to rise, in a warm place, for 45 minutes, or until the loaf has doubled in size. Meanwhile, preheat the oven to 200°C/400°F/Gas 6.

7 Slash the top of the loaf diagonally three or four times, using a sharp knife, and bake for 30 minutes, or until golden. Cool on a wire rack.

SESAME-STUDDED GRISSINI

*225g/8oz/2 cups unbleached white
bread flour
7.5ml/1½ tsp salt
15g/½ oz fresh yeast
135ml/4½ fl oz/scant ⅔ cup lukewarm
water
30ml/2 tbsp extra virgin olive oil,
plus extra for brushing
sesame seeds, for coating*

Makes 20 Grissini

*These crisp, pencil-like breadsticks are easy to make and far more delicious
than the commercially manufactured grissini. Once you start to nibble one, it
will be difficult to stop.*

1 Lightly oil two baking sheets. Sift the flour and salt together into a large bowl and make a well in the centre.

2 In a jug (pitcher), cream the yeast with the water. Pour into the centre of the flour, add the olive oil and mix to a soft dough. Turn out on to a lightly floured surface and knead for 8–10 minutes until smooth and elastic.

3 Roll the dough into a rectangle about 15 × 20cm/6 × 8in. Brush with olive oil, cover with lightly oiled clear film (plastic wrap) and leave in a warm place, for about 1 hour, or until doubled in bulk.

4 Preheat the oven to 200°C/400°F/ Gas 6. Spread out the sesame seeds. Cut the dough in two 7.5 x 10cm/3 x 4in rectangles. Cut each piece into ten 7.5cm/3in strips. Stretch each strip gently until it is about 30cm/12in long.

5 Roll each grissini, as it is made, in the sesame seeds. Place the grissini on the prepared baking sheets, spaced well apart. Lightly brush with olive oil. Leave to rise, in a warm place, for 10 minutes, then bake for 15–20 minutes. Transfer to a wire rack to cool.

COOK'S TIP
When baking the grissini turn them over and change the position of the baking sheets halfway through the cooking time, so they brown evenly.

PIADINE

*175g/6oz/1½ cups unbleached
white flour
5ml/1 tsp salt
15ml/1 tbsp olive oil
105ml/7 tbsp lukewarm water*

Makes 4 Piadine

*These soft unleavened Italian breads, cooked directly on the hob, were
originally cooked on a hot stone over an open fire. They are best eaten while
still warm. Try them as an accompaniment to soups and dips.*

1 Sift the flour and salt together into a large bowl; make a well in the centre.

2 Add the oil and water to the centre of the flour and gradually mix in to form a dough. Knead on a lightly floured surface for 4–5 minutes until smooth and elastic. Place in a lightly oiled bowl, cover with oiled clear film (plastic wrap) and leave to rest for 20 minutes.

3 Heat a griddle over a medium heat. Divide the dough into four equal pieces and roll each into an 18cm/7in round. Cover until ready to cook.

4 Lightly oil the hot griddle, add one or two piadine and cook for about 2 minutes, or until they are starting to brown. Turn the piadine over and cook for a further 1–1½ minutes. Serve warm.

COOK'S TIPS
• If you don't have a griddle, a large heavy frying pan will work just as well. Keep the cooked piadine warm while cooking successive batches.
• Although not traditional in Italy, these flat breads can also be flavoured with herbs. Add 15ml/1 tbsp of dried oregano. They also taste delicious made with garlic- or chilli-flavoured olive oil.

PANETTONE

*400g/14oz/3½ cups unbleached white
bread flour
2.5ml/½ tsp salt
15g/½ oz fresh yeast
120ml/4fl oz/½ cup lukewarm milk
2 eggs plus 2 egg yolks
75g/3oz/6 tbsp caster (superfine) sugar
150g/5oz/⅔ cup butter, softened
115g/4oz/⅔ cup mixed chopped
(candied) peel
75g/3oz/½ cup raisins
melted butter, for brushing*

MAKES 1 LOAF

COOK'S TIP
Once the dough has been enriched
with butter, do not prove in too warm
a place or the loaf will become greasy.

1 Using a double layer of baking parchment, line and butter a 15cm/6in deep cake tin (pan) or soufflé dish. Finish the paper 7.5cm/3in above the top of the tin.

*This classic Italian bread can be found throughout Italy around Christmas.
It is a surprisingly light bread even though it is rich with butter
and dried fruit.*

2 Sift the flour and salt together into a large bowl. Make a well in the centre. Cream the yeast with 60ml/4 tbsp of the milk, then mix in the remainder.

3 Pour the yeast mixture into the centre of the flour, add the whole eggs and mix in sufficient flour to make a thick batter. Sprinkle a little of the remaining flour over the top and leave to "sponge", in a warm place, for 30 minutes.

4 Add the egg yolks and sugar and mix to a soft dough. Work in the softened butter, then turn out on to a lightly floured surface and knead for 5 minutes until smooth and elastic. Place in a lightly oiled bowl, cover with lightly oiled clear film (plastic wrap) and leave to rise, in a slightly warm place, for 1½–2 hours, or until doubled in bulk.

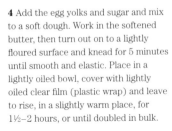

5 Knock back (punch down) the dough and turn out on to a lightly floured surface. Gently knead in the peel and raisins. Shape into a ball and place in the prepared tin. Cover with lightly oiled clear film and leave to rise, in a slightly warm place, for about 1 hour, or until doubled.

6 Meanwhile, preheat the oven to 190°C/ 375°F/Gas 5. Brush the surface with melted butter and cut a cross in the top using a sharp knife. Bake for 20 minutes, then reduce the oven temperature to 180°C/350°F/Gas 4. Brush the top with butter again and bake for a further 25–30 minutes, or until golden. Cool in the tin for 5–10 minutes, then turn out on to a wire rack to cool.

PANE AL CIOCCOLATO

This slightly sweet chocolate bread from Italy is often served with creamy mascarpone cheese as a dessert or snack. The dark chocolate pieces add texture to this light loaf.

350g/12oz/3 cups unbleached white bread flour
25ml/1½ tbsp cocoa powder (unsweetened)
2.5ml/½ tsp salt
25g/1oz/2 tbsp caster (superfine) sugar
15g/½ oz fresh yeast
250ml/8fl oz/1 cup lukewarm water
25g/1oz/2 tbsp butter, softened
75g/3oz plain continental chocolate, coarsely chopped
melted butter, for brushing

MAKES 1 LOAF

1 Lightly grease a 15cm/6in round deep cake tin (pan). Sift the flour, cocoa powder and salt together into a large bowl. Stir in the sugar. Make a well in the centre.

2 Cream the yeast with 60ml/4 tbsp of the water, then stir in the rest. Add to the centre of the flour mixture and gradually mix to a dough.

3 Knead in the softened butter, then knead on a floured surface until smooth and elastic. Place in a lightly oiled bowl, cover with lightly oiled clear film (plastic wrap) and leave in a warm place, for about 1 hour, or until doubled in bulk.

4 Turn out on to a lightly floured surface and knock back (punch down). Gently knead in the chocolate, then cover with oiled clear film; rest for 5 minutes.

5 Shape the dough into a round and place in the tin. Cover with lightly oiled clear film and leave to rise, in a warm place, for 45 minutes, or until doubled; the dough should reach the top of the tin.

6 Preheat the oven to 220°C/425°F/Gas 7. Bake for 10 minutes, then reduce the oven temperature to 190°C/375°F/Gas 5 and bake for a further 25–30 minutes. Brush the top with melted butter and leave to cool on a wire rack.

VARIATION
You can also shape this bread into one large, or two small rounds and bake on a lightly greased baking sheet. Reduce the baking time by about 10 minutes.

SCHIACCIATA

350g/12oz/3 cups unbleached white
bread flour
2.5ml/½ tsp salt
15g/½ oz fresh yeast
200ml/7fl oz/scant 1 cup lukewarm
water
60ml/4 tbsp extra virgin olive oil

FOR THE TOPPING
30ml/2 tbsp extra virgin olive oil,
for brushing
30ml/2 tbsp fresh rosemary leaves
coarse sea salt, for sprinkling

MAKES 1 LARGE LOAF

This Tuscan version of Italian pizza-style flat bread can be rolled to varying
thicknesses to give either a crisp or soft, bread-like finish.

1 Lightly oil a baking sheet. Sift the flour and salt into a large bowl and make a well in the centre. Cream the yeast with half the water. Add to the centre of the flour with the remaining water and olive oil and mix to a soft dough. Turn out the dough on to a lightly floured surface and knead for 10 minutes until smooth and elastic.

2 Place in a lightly oiled bowl, cover with lightly oiled clear film (plastic wrap) and leave to rise, in a warm place, for about 1 hour, or until doubled in bulk.

3 Knock back (punch down) the dough, turn out on to a lightly floured surface and knead gently. Roll to a 30 × 20cm/ 12 × 8in rectangle and place on the prepared baking sheet. Brush with some of the olive oil for the topping and cover with lightly oiled clear film.

4 Leave to rise, in a warm place, for about 20 minutes, then brush with the remaining oil, prick all over with a fork and sprinkle with rosemary and sea salt. Leave to rise again in a warm place for 15 minutes.

5 Meanwhile, preheat the oven to 200°C/ 400°F/Gas 6. Bake for 30 minutes, or until light golden. Transfer to a wire rack to cool slightly. Serve warm.

PORTUGUESE CORN BREAD

While the Spanish make a corn bread with barley flour, the Portuguese use white bread flour and corn meal. This tempting version has a hard crust with a moist, mouthwatering crumb. It slices beautifully and tastes wonderful served simply with butter or olive oil, or with cheese.

20g/¾ oz fresh yeast
250ml/8fl oz/1 cup lukewarm water
225g/8oz/2 cups corn meal
450g/1lb/4 cups unbleached white bread flour
150ml/¼ pint/⅔ cup lukewarm milk
30ml/2 tbsp olive oil
7.5ml/1½ tsp salt
polenta, for dusting

MAKES 1 LARGE LOAF

VARIATION
Replace 50 per cent of the corn meal with polenta for a rougher textured, slightly crunchier loaf.

1 Dust a baking sheet with a little corn meal. Put the yeast in a large bowl and gradually mix in the lukewarm water until smooth. Stir in half the corn meal and 50g/2oz/½ cup of the flour and mix to a batter, with a wooden spoon.

6 Turn out the dough on to a lightly floured surface and knock back (punch down). Shape into a round ball, flatten slightly and place on the prepared baking sheet. Dust with polenta, cover with a large upturned bowl and leave to rise, in a warm place, for about 1 hour, or until doubled in size. Meanwhile, preheat the oven to 230°C/450°F/Gas 8.

7 Bake for 10 minutes, spraying the inside of the oven with water two or three times. Reduce the temperature to 190°C/375°F/Gas 5 and bake for a further 20–25 minutes, or until golden and hollow sounding when tapped on the base. Transfer to a wire rack to cool.

2 Cover the bowl with lightly oiled clear film (plastic wrap) and leave the batter undisturbed in a warm place for about 30 minutes, or until bubbles start to appear on the surface. Remove the film.

3 Stir the milk into the batter, then stir in the olive oil. Gradually mix in the remaining corn meal, flour and salt to form a pliable dough.

4 Turn out the dough on to a lightly floured surface and knead for about 10 minutes until smooth and elastic.

5 Place in a lightly oiled bowl, cover with lightly oiled clear film and leave to rise, in a warm place, for 1½–2 hours, or until doubled in bulk.

PAN GALLEGO

Here, a typical round bread with a twisted top from Galicia. The olive oil gives a soft crumb and the millet, pumpkin and sunflower seeds sprinkled through the loaf provide an interesting mix of textures.

350g/12oz/3 cups unbleached white bread flour
115g/4oz/1 cup wholemeal (whole-wheat) bread flour
10ml/2 tsp salt
20g/¾ oz fresh yeast
275ml/9fl oz/generous 1 cup lukewarm water
30ml/2 tbsp olive oil
30ml/2 tbsp pumpkin seeds
30ml/2 tbsp sunflower seeds
15ml/1 tbsp millet
corn meal, for dusting

Makes 1 Large Loaf

COOK'S TIP
If you like, replace fresh yeast with a 6g/¼ oz sachet of easy-blend (rapid-rise) dried yeast. Stir into the flours in step 1. Continue as in the recipe.

1 Sprinkle a baking sheet with corn meal. Mix the flours and salt together in a large bowl.

2 In a bowl, mix the yeast with the water. Add to the centre of the flours with the olive oil and mix to a firm dough. Turn out on to a lightly floured surface and knead for about 10 minutes until smooth and elastic. Place in a lightly oiled bowl, then cover with lightly oiled clear film (plastic wrap) and leave to rise, in a warm place, for about 1½–2 hours, or until doubled in bulk.

3 Knock back (punch down) the dough and turn out on to a lightly floured surface. Gently knead in the pumpkin seeds, sunflower seeds and millet. Re-cover and leave to rest for 5 minutes.

4 Shape into a round ball; twist the centre to make a cap. Transfer to the prepared baking sheet and dust with corn meal. Cover with a large upturned bowl and leave to rise, in a warm place, for 45 minutes, or until doubled in bulk.

5 Meanwhile, place an empty roasting pan in the bottom of the oven. Preheat the oven to 220°C/425°F/Gas 7. Pour about 300ml/½ pint/1¼ cups cold water into the roasting pan. Lift the bowl off the risen loaf and immediately place the baking sheet in the oven, above the roasting pan. Bake the bread for 10 minutes.

6 Remove the tin of water and bake the bread for a further 25–30 minutes, or until well browned and sounding hollow when tapped on the base. Transfer to a wire rack to cool.

PAN DE CEBADA

This Spanish country bread has a close, heavy texture and is quite satisfying. It is richly flavoured, incorporating barley and maize flours.

FOR THE SOURDOUGH STARTER
175g/6oz/1½ cups corn meal
560ml/scant 1 pint/scant 2½ cups water
225g/8oz/2 cups wholemeal (whole-wheat) bread flour
75g/3oz/¾ cup barley flour

FOR THE DOUGH
20g/¾ oz fresh yeast
45ml/3 tbsp lukewarm water
225g/8oz/2 cups wholemeal bread flour
15ml/1 tbsp salt
corn meal, for dusting

MAKES 1 LARGE LOAF

1 In a pan, mix the corn meal for the sourdough starter with half the water, then blend in the remainder. Cook over a gentle heat, stirring continuously, until thickened. Transfer to a large bowl and set aside to cool.

2 Mix in the wholemeal flour and barley flour. Turn out on to a lightly floured surface and knead for 5 minutes. Return to the bowl, cover with lightly oiled clear film (plastic wrap) and leave the starter in a warm place for 36 hours.

5 Knock back (punch down) the dough and turn out on to a lightly floured surface. Shape into a plump round. Sprinkle with a little corn meal.

6 Place the shaped bread on the prepared baking sheet. Cover with a large upturned bowl. Leave to rise, in a warm place, for about 1 hour, or until nearly doubled in bulk. Place an empty roasting pan in the bottom of the oven. Preheat the oven to 220°C/425°F/Gas 7.

7 Pour 300ml/½ pint/1¼ cups cold water into the roasting pan. Lift the bowl off the risen loaf and immediately place the baking sheet in the oven. Bake the bread for 10 minutes. Remove the pan of water, reduce the oven temperature to 190°C/375°F/Gas 5 and bake for about 20 minutes. Cool on a wire rack.

3 Dust a baking sheet with corn meal. In a small bowl, cream the yeast with the water for the dough. Mix the yeast mixture into the starter with the wholemeal flour and salt and work to a dough. Turn out on to a lightly floured surface and knead for 4–5 minutes until smooth and elastic.

4 Transfer the dough to a lightly oiled bowl, cover with lightly oiled clear film or an oiled plastic bag and leave, in a warm place, for 1½–2 hours to rise, or until nearly doubled in bulk.

TWELFTH NIGHT BREAD

450g/1lb/4 cups unbleached white
bread flour
2.5ml/½ tsp salt
25g/1oz yeast
140ml/scant ¼ pint/scant ⅔ cup
mixed lukewarm milk and water
75g/3oz/6 tbsp butter
75g/3oz/6 tbsp caster
(superfine) sugar
10ml/2 tsp finely grated
lemon rind
10ml/2 tsp finely grated
orange rind
2 eggs
15ml/1 tbsp brandy
15ml/1 tbsp orange flower water
silver coin or dried bean
(optional)
1 egg white, lightly beaten,
for glazing

FOR THE DECORATION
a mixture of candied and glacé
fruit slices
flaked (sliced) almonds

MAKES 1 LARGE LOAF

COOK'S TIP
If you like, this bread can be baked
in a lightly greased 24cm/9½ in
ring-shaped cake tin (pan) or savarin
mould. Place the dough seam side
down into the tin or mould and seal
the ends together.

1 Lightly grease a large baking sheet.
Sift the flour and salt together into a
large bowl. Make a well in the centre.

January 6th, Epiphany or the Day of the Three Kings, is celebrated in
Spain as a time to exchange Christmas presents. Historically this date was
when the Three Wise Men arrived bearing gifts. An ornamental bread ring is
specially baked for the occasion. The traditional version contains a silver
coin, china figure or dried bean hidden inside – the lucky recipient is
declared King of the festival!

2 In a bowl, mix the yeast with the milk
and water until the yeast has dissolved.
Pour the yeast mixture into the centre
of the flour and stir in enough of the
flour from around the sides of the bowl
to make a thick batter.

3 Sprinkle a little of the remaining flour
over the top of the batter and leave to
"sponge", in a warm place, for about
15 minutes or until frothy.

4 Using an electric whisk or a wooden
spoon, beat the butter and sugar
together in a bowl until soft and creamy,
then set aside.

5 Add the citrus rinds, eggs, brandy and
orange flower water to the flour mixture
and use a wooden spoon to mix to a
sticky dough.

6 Using one hand, beat the mixture until
it forms a fairly smooth dough.
Gradually beat in the reserved butter
mixture and beat for a few minutes until
the dough is smooth and elastic. Cover
with lightly oiled clear film (plastic
wrap) and leave in a warm place, for
about 1½ hours, or until doubled in bulk.

7 Knock back (punch down) the dough
and turn out on to a lightly floured
surface. Gently knead for 2–3 minutes,
incorporating the coin or bean, if using.

8 Using a rolling pin, roll out the dough
into a long strip measuring about 66 ×
13cm/26 × 5in.

9 Roll up the dough from one long side
like a Swiss roll to make a long sausage
shape. Place seam side down on the
prepared baking sheet and seal the ends
together. Cover with lightly oiled clear
film and leave to rise, in a warm place,
for 1–1½ hours, or until doubled in size.

10 Meanwhile, preheat the oven to
180°C/350°F/Gas 4. Brush the dough
ring with lightly beaten egg white and
decorate with candied and glacé fruit
slices, pushing them slightly into the
dough. Sprinkle with almond flakes
and bake for 30–35 minutes, or until
risen and golden. Turn out on to a wire
rack to cool.

MALLORCAN ENSAIMADAS

These spiral- or snail-shaped rolls are a popular Spanish breakfast treat. Traditionally lard or saim was used to brush over the strips of sweetened dough, but nowadays mainly butter is used to add a delicious richness.

225g/8oz/2 cups unbleached white bread flour
2.5ml/½ tsp salt
50g/2oz/¼ cup caster (superfine) sugar
15g/½ oz fresh yeast
75ml/5 tbsp lukewarm milk
1 egg
30ml/2 tbsp sunflower oil
50g/2oz/¼ cup butter, melted
icing (confectioners') sugar, for dusting

MAKES 16 ROLLS

1 Lightly grease two baking sheets. Sift the flour and salt together into a large mixing bowl. Stir in the sugar and make a well in the centre.

2 Cream the yeast with the milk, pour into the centre of the flour mixture, then sprinkle a little of the flour mixture evenly over the top of the liquid. Leave in a warm place for about 15 minutes, or until frothy.

3 In a small bowl, beat the egg and sunflower oil together. Add to the flour mixture and mix to a smooth dough.

4 Turn out on to a lightly floured surface and knead for 8–10 minutes until smooth and elastic. Place in a lightly oiled bowl, cover with lightly oiled clear film (plastic wrap) and leave in a warm place, for 1 hour, or until doubled in bulk.

5 Turn out the dough on to a lightly floured surface. Knock back (punch down) and divide the dough into 16 equal pieces. Shape each piece into a thin rope about 38cm/15in long. Pour the melted butter on to a plate and dip the ropes into the butter to coat.

6 On the baking sheets, curl each rope into a loose spiral, spacing well apart. Tuck the ends under to seal. Cover with lightly oiled clear film and leave to rise, in a warm place, for about 45 minutes, or until doubled in size.

7 Meanwhile, preheat the oven to 190°C/375°F/Gas 5. Brush the rolls with water and dust with icing sugar. Bake for 10 minutes, or until light golden brown. Cool on a wire rack. Dust again with icing sugar and serve warm.

PITTA BREAD

These Turkish breads are a firm favourite in both the eastern Mediterranean and the Middle East, and have crossed to England and the USA. This versatile soft, flat bread forms a pocket as it cooks, which is perfect for filling with vegetables, salads or meats.

225g/8oz/2 cups unbleached white bread flour
5ml/1 tsp salt
15g/1/2 oz fresh yeast
140ml/scant 1/4 pint/scant 2/3 cup lukewarm water
10ml/2 tsp extra virgin olive oil

MAKES 6 PITTA BREADS

VARIATIONS

To make wholemeal (whole-wheat) pitta breads, replace half the white bread flour with wholemeal bread flour. You can also make smaller round pitta breads about 10cm/4in in diameter to serve as snack breads.

5 Roll out each ball of dough in turn to an oval about 5mm/1/4in thick and 15cm/6in long. Place on a floured dishtowel and cover with lightly oiled clear film. Leave to rise at room temperature for about 20–30 minutes.

1 Sift the flour and salt together into a bowl. Mix the yeast with the water until dissolved, then stir in the olive oil and pour into a large bowl.

2 Gradually beat the flour into the yeast mixture, then knead the mixture to make a soft dough.

3 Turn out on to a lightly floured surface and knead for 5 minutes until smooth and elastic. Place in a large bowl, cover with lightly oiled clear film (plastic wrap) and leave to rise, in a warm place, for 1 hour, or until doubled in bulk.

4 Knock back (punch down) the dough. On a floured surface, divide into six equal pieces and shape into balls. Cover with oiled clear film; rest for 5 minutes.

6 Meanwhile, preheat the oven to 230°C/ 450°F/Gas 8. Place three baking sheets in the oven to heat at the same time.

7 Place two pitta breads on each baking sheet and bake for 4–6 minutes, or until puffed up; they do not need to brown. If preferred, cook the pitta bread in batches. It is important that the oven has reached the recommended temperature before the pitta breads are baked. This ensures that they puff up.

8 Transfer the pittas to a wire rack to cool until warm, then cover with a dishtowel to keep them soft.

CHRISTOPSOMO

A Byzantine cross flavoured with aniseed tops this Greek Christmas bread, which is also decorated with walnuts for good fortune. The fluffy, light, butter-enriched bread contains orange rind, cinnamon and cloves – all the lovely warm tastes associated with Christmas.

15g/¹⁄₂ oz fresh yeast
140ml/scant ¹⁄₄ pint/scant ²⁄₃ cup lukewarm milk
450g/1lb/4 cups unbleached white bread flour
2 eggs
75g/3oz/6 tbsp caster (superfine) sugar
2.5ml/¹⁄₂ tsp salt
75g/3oz/6 tbsp butter, softened
grated rind of ¹⁄₂ orange
5ml/1 tsp ground cinnamon
1.5ml/¹⁄₄ tsp ground cloves
pinch of crushed aniseed
8 walnut halves
beaten egg white, for glazing

MAKES 1 LOAF

COOK'S TIP
If you do not have any aniseed, flavour the dough with 5ml/1 tsp pastis, anisette or ouzo.

1 Lightly grease a large baking sheet. In a large bowl, mix the yeast with the milk until the yeast is dissolved, then stir in 115g/4oz/1 cup of the flour to make a thin batter. Cover with lightly oiled clear film (plastic wrap) and leave to "sponge" in a warm place for 30 minutes.

2 Beat the eggs and sugar until light and fluffy. Beat into the yeast mixture. Gradually mix in the remaining flour and salt. Beat in the softened butter and knead to a soft but not sticky dough. Knead on a lightly floured surface for 8–10 minutes until smooth and elastic. Place in a lightly oiled bowl, cover with lightly oiled clear film and leave to rise, in a warm place, for 1¹⁄₂ hours, or until doubled in bulk.

3 Turn out on to a lightly floured surface and gently knock back (punch down). Cut off about 50g/2oz of dough; cover and set aside. Gently knead the orange rind, ground cinnamon and cloves into the large piece of dough and shape into a round loaf. Place on the baking sheet.

4 Knead the aniseed into the remaining dough. Cut the dough in half and shape each piece into a 30cm/12in long rope. Cut through each rope at either end by one-third of its length. Place the two ropes in a cross on top of the loaf, then curl each cut end into a circle, in opposite directions.

5 Preheat the oven to 190°C/375°F/ Gas 5. Place a walnut half inside each circle. Cover the loaf with lightly oiled clear film (plastic wrap) and leave to rise for 45 minutes, or until doubled in size. Brush the bread with the egg white and bake for 40–45 minutes, or until golden. Cool on a wire rack.

TSOUREKI

Topped with brightly coloured eggs, this braided bread is an important part of the Greek Easter celebrations.

FOR THE EGGS
3 eggs
1.5ml/¼ tsp bright red food
colouring paste
15ml/1 tbsp white wine vinegar
5ml/1 tsp water
5ml/1 tsp olive oil

FOR THE DOUGH
450g/1lb/4 cups unbleached white
bread flour
2.5ml/½ tsp salt
5ml/1 tsp ground allspice
2.5ml/½ tsp ground cinnamon
2.5ml/½ tsp caraway seeds
20g/¾ oz fresh yeast
175ml/6fl oz/¾ cup lukewarm milk
50g/2oz/¼ cup butter
40g/1½oz/3 tbsp caster
(superfine) sugar
2 eggs

FOR THE GLAZE
1 egg yolk
5ml/1 tsp clear honey
5ml/1 tsp water

FOR THE DECORATION
50g/2oz/½ cup split almonds, slivered
edible gold leaf, optional

MAKES 1 LOAF

1 Lightly grease a baking sheet. Place the eggs in a pan of water and bring to the boil. Boil gently for 10 minutes. Meanwhile, mix the red food colouring, vinegar and water together in a shallow bowl. Remove the eggs from the boiling water, place on a wire rack for a few seconds to dry then roll in the colouring mixture. Return to the rack to cool and completely dry.

2 When cold, drizzle the olive oil on to absorbent kitchen paper, lift up each egg in turn and rub all over with the oiled paper.

3 To make the dough, sift the flour, salt, allspice and cinnamon into a large bowl. Stir in the caraway seeds.

4 In a jug (pitcher), mix the yeast with the milk. In a bowl, cream the butter and sugar together, then beat in the eggs. Add the creamed mixture to the flour with the yeast mixture and gradually mix to a dough. Turn out the dough on to a lightly floured surface and knead until smooth and elastic.

5 Place in a lightly oiled bowl, cover with lightly oiled clear film (plastic wrap) and leave in a warm place, for about 2 hours, or until doubled in bulk.

6 Knock back (punch down) the dough and knead for 2–3 minutes. Return to the bowl, re-cover and leave to rise again, in a warm place, for about 1 hour, or until doubled in bulk.

7 Knock back and turn out on to a lightly floured surface. Divide the dough into three equal pieces and roll each into a 38–50cm/15–20in long rope. Braid these together from the centre to the ends.

8 Place on the prepared baking sheet and push the dyed eggs into the loaf. Cover and leave to rise, in a warm place, for about 1 hour.

9 Meanwhile, preheat the oven to 190°C/375°F/Gas 5. Mix the egg yolk, honey and water together for the glaze, and brush over the loaf. Sprinkle with almonds and edible gold leaf, if using. Bake for 40–45 minutes, or until golden and sounding hollow when tapped on the base. Transfer to a wire rack to cool.

GREEK OLIVE BREAD

The flavours of the Mediterranean simply ooze from this decorative bread, speckled with black olives, red onions and herbs.

675g/1½ lb/6 cups unbleached white bread flour, plus extra for dusting
10ml/2 tsp salt
25g/1oz fresh yeast
350ml/12fl oz/1½ cups lukewarm water
75ml/5 tbsp olive oil
175g/6oz/1½ cups pitted black olives, roughly chopped
1 red onion, finely chopped
30ml/2 tbsp chopped fresh coriander (cilantro) or mint

MAKES 2 LOAVES

VARIATION
Make one large loaf and increase the baking time by about 15 minutes.

1 Lightly grease two baking sheets. Sift the flour and salt together into a large bowl and make a well in the centre.

2 In a jug (pitcher), blend the yeast with half of the water. Add to the centre of the flour with the remaining water and the olive oil; mix to a soft dough.

3 Turn out the dough on to a lightly floured surface and knead for 8–10 minutes until smooth. Place in a lightly oiled bowl, cover with lightly oiled clear film (plastic wrap) and leave to rise, in a warm place, for 1 hour, or until doubled in bulk.

4 Turn out on to a lightly floured surface and knock back (punch down). Cut off a quarter of the dough, cover with lightly oiled clear film and set aside.

5 Roll out the remaining, large piece of dough to a round. Sprinkle the olives, onion and herbs evenly over the surface, then bring up the sides of the circle and gently knead together. Cut the dough in half and shape each piece into a plump oval loaf, about 20cm/8in long. Place on the prepared baking sheets.

6 Divide the reserved dough into four equal pieces and roll each to a long strand 60cm/24in long. Twist together and cut in half. Brush the centre of each loaf with water and place two pieces of twisted dough on top of each, tucking the ends underneath the loaves.

7 Cover with lightly oiled clear film and leave to rise, in a warm place, for about 45 minutes, or until the loaves are plump and nearly doubled in size.

8 Meanwhile, preheat the oven to 220°C/425°F/Gas 7. Dust the loaves lightly with flour and bake for 35–40 minutes, or until golden and sounding hollow when tapped on the base. Transfer to a wire rack to cool.

MOROCCAN HOLIDAY BREAD

The addition of corn meal and a cornucopia of seeds gives this superb loaf an interesting flavour and texture.

275g/10oz/2½ cups unbleached white bread flour
50g/2oz/½ cup corn meal
5ml/1 tsp salt
20g/¾ oz fresh yeast
120ml/4fl oz/½ cup lukewarm water
120ml/4fl oz/½ cup lukewarm milk
15ml/1 tbsp pumpkin seeds
15ml/1 tbsp sesame seeds
30ml/2 tbsp sunflower seeds

MAKES 1 LOAF

5 Turn out the dough on to a lightly floured surface and knock back (punch down). Gently knead the pumpkin and sesame seeds into the dough. Shape into a round ball and flatten slightly.

6 Place on the prepared baking sheet, cover with lightly oiled clear film or slide into a large, lightly oiled plastic bag and leave to rise, in a warm place, for 45 minutes, or until doubled in bulk.

1 Lightly grease a baking sheet. Sift the flours and salt into a large bowl.

3 Turn out the dough on to a lightly floured surface and knead for about 5 minutes until smooth and elastic.

4 Place in a lightly oiled bowl, cover with lightly oiled clear film (plastic wrap) and leave in a warm place, for about 1 hour, or until doubled in bulk.

VARIATIONS
Incorporate all the seeds in the dough in step 5 and leave the top of the loaf plain. Alternatively, use sesame seeds instead of sunflower seeds for the topping and either incorporate the sunflower seeds in the loaf or leave them out.

2 Cream the yeast with a little of the water in a jug (pitcher). Stir in the remainder of the water and the milk. Pour into the centre of the flour and mix to a fairly soft dough.

7 Meanwhile, preheat the oven to 200°C/400°F/Gas 6. Brush the top of the loaf with water and sprinkle evenly with the sunflower seeds. Bake the loaf for 30–35 minutes, or until it is golden and sounds hollow when tapped on the base. Transfer the loaf to a wire rack to cool.

NORTH EUROPEAN AND SCANDINAVIAN BREADS

The northern Europeans and Scandinavians make many different loaves, from the dense, dark German pumpernickel to a light Polish rye bread. Also from these northern climes come the famous Swedish crispbreads, Russian potato bread and blinis, a variety of sweet breads, lightly scented saffron buns and port-flavoured rye bread. Christmas breads are enriched with fruit, while Bulgaria has its own poppy-seeded circular bread for religious festivals.

SWISS BRAID

*350g/12oz/3 cups unbleached white
bread flour
5ml/1 tsp salt
20g/¾ oz fresh yeast
30ml/2 tbsp lukewarm water
150ml/¼ pint/⅔ cup sour cream
1 egg, lightly beaten
50g/2oz/¼ cup butter, softened*

*FOR THE GLAZE
1 egg yolk
15ml/1 tbsp water*

MAKES 1 LOAF

COOK'S TIP
If you prefer, use a 7g/¼ oz sachet of
easy-blend (rapid-rise) dried yeast.
Add directly to the flour with the salt,
then add the warmed sour cream and
water and mix together.

This braided, attractively tapered loaf is known as zupfe *in Switzerland. Often
eaten at the weekend, it is has a glossy crust and a wonderfully light crumb.*

1 Lightly grease a baking sheet. Sift the
flour and salt together into a large bowl
and make a well in the centre. Mix the
yeast with the water in a jug (pitcher).

2 Gently warm the sour cream in a
small pan until it reaches blood heat
(35–38°C). Add to the yeast mixture
and mix together.

3 Add the yeast mixture and egg to the
centre of the flour and gradually mix to
a dough. Beat in the softened butter.

4 Turn out on to a lightly floured surface
and knead for 5 minutes until smooth
and elastic. Place in a lightly oiled bowl,
cover with oiled clear film (plastic wrap)
and leave in a warm place, for about 1½
hours, or until doubled in size.

5 Turn out on to a lightly floured surface
and knock back (punch down). Cut in
half and shape each piece of dough into
a long rope about 35cm/14in in length.

6 To make the braid, place the two
pieces of dough on top of each other to
form a cross. Starting with the bottom
rope, fold the top end over and place
between the two bottom ropes. Fold
the remaining top rope over so that all
four ropes are pointing downwards.
Starting from the left, braid the first
rope over the second, and the third rope
over the fourth.

7 Continue braiding in this way to form
a tapered bread. Tuck the ends
underneath and place on the prepared
baking sheet. Cover with lightly oiled
clear film and leave to rise, in a warm
place, for about 40 minutes.

8 Meanwhile, preheat the oven to 190°C/
375°F/Gas 5. Mix the egg yolk and water
for the glaze, and brush over the loaf.
Bake the bread for 30–35 minutes, or
until golden. Cool on a wire rack.

PRETZELS

*Pretzels or brezeln, as they are known in Germany, are said to be derived
from the Latin* bracellae *or arms, referring to the crossed "arms" of dough
inside the oval shape. This shape is also used for biscuits in Germany and
Austria, and in Alsace the pretzel shape is part of the wrought iron emblem of
quality that bakers display outside their shops.*

For the Yeast Sponge
7g/¼ oz fresh yeast
75ml/5 tbsp water
15ml/1 tbsp unbleached plain
(all purpose) flour

For the Dough
7g/¼ oz fresh yeast
150ml/¼ pint/⅔ cup lukewarm water
75ml/5 tbsp lukewarm milk
400g/14oz/3½ cups unbleached white
bread flour
7.5ml/1½ tsp salt
25g/1oz/2 tbsp butter, melted

For the Topping
1 egg yolk
15ml/1 tbsp milk
sea salt or caraway seeds

MAKES 12 PRETZELS

4 Turn out the dough on to a lightly
floured surface. Divide the dough into
12 equal pieces and form into balls.
Take one ball of dough and cover the
remainder with a dishtowel. Roll into a
thin stick 46cm/18in long and about
1cm/½in thick in the middle and thinner
at the ends. Bend each end of the dough
stick into a horseshoe. Cross over and
place the ends on top of the thick part of
the pretzel. Repeat with the remaining
dough balls.

5 Place on the floured baking sheet to
rest for 10 minutes. Meanwhile, preheat
the oven to 190°C/375°F/Gas 5. Bring a
large pan of water to the boil, then
reduce to a simmer. Add the pretzels to
the simmering water in batches, about
2–3 at a time and poach for about
1 minute. Drain the pretzels on a
dishtowel and place on the greased
baking sheets, spaced well apart.

1 Lightly flour a baking sheet. Also
grease two baking sheets. Cream the
yeast for the yeast sponge with the
water, then mix in the flour, cover with
clear film (plastic wrap) and leave to
stand at room temperature for 2 hours.

2 Mix the yeast for the dough with the
water until dissolved, then stir in the
milk. Sift 350g/12oz/3 cups of the flour
and the salt into a large bowl. Add the
yeast sponge mixture and the butter;
mix for 3–4 minutes. Turn out on to a
lightly floured surface and knead in the
remaining flour to make a medium firm
dough. Place in a lightly oiled bowl, cover
with lightly oiled clear film and leave to
rise, in a warm place, for 30 minutes, or
until almost doubled in bulk.

3 Turn out on to a lightly floured surface
and knock back (punch down) the dough.
Knead into a ball, return to the bowl,
re-cover and leave to rise for 30 minutes.

6 Mix the egg yolk and milk together
and brush this glaze over the pretzels.
Sprinkle with sea salt or caraway seeds
and bake the pretzels for 25 minutes, or
until they are deep golden. Transfer to a
wire rack to cool.

PUMPERNICKEL

This famous German bread is extremely dense and dark, with an intense flavour. It is baked very slowly and although cooked in the oven, it is more like a steamed bread than a baked one.

450g/1lb/4 cups rye flour
225g/8oz/2 cups wholemeal (whole-wheat) flour
115g/4oz/⅔ cup bulgur wheat
10ml/2 tsp salt
30ml/2 tbsp molasses
850ml/1 pint 8fl oz/3½ cups warm water
15ml/1 tbsp vegetable oil

MAKES 2 LOAVES

COOK'S TIP
This bread improves on keeping. Keep for at least 24 hours double-wrapped inside a plastic bag or greaseproof (waxed) paper and foil before slicing.

1 Lightly grease two 18 × 9cm/7 × 3½in loaf tins (pans). Mix the rye flour, wholemeal flour, bulgur wheat and salt together in a large bowl.

2 Mix the molasses with the warm water and add to the flours with the vegetable oil. Mix together to form a dense mass.

3 Place in the prepared tins, pressing well into the corners. Cover with lightly oiled clear film (plastic wrap) and leave in a warm place for 18–24 hours.

4 Preheat the oven to 110°C/225°F/ Gas ¼. Cover the tins tightly with foil. Fill a roasting pan with boiling water and place a rack on top.

5 Place the tins on top of the rack and transfer very carefully to the oven. Bake the loaves for 4 hours. Increase the oven temperature to 160°C/325°F/Gas 3. Top up the water in the roasting pan if necessary, uncover the loaves and bake for a further 30–45 minutes, or until the loaves feel firm and the tops are crusty.

6 Leave to cool in the tins for 5 minutes, then turn out on to a wire rack to cool completely. Serve cold, very thinly sliced, with cold meats.

GERMAN SOURDOUGH BREAD

This bread includes rye, wholemeal and plain flours for a superb depth of flavour. Serve it cut in thick slices, with creamy butter or a sharp cheese.

1 Mix the rye flour, warm water and caraway for the starter together in a large bowl with your fingertips, to make a soft paste. Cover with a damp dishtowel and leave in a warm place for about 36 hours. Stir after 24 hours.

2 Lightly grease a baking sheet. In a measuring jug (cup), blend the yeast for the dough with the lukewarm water. Add to the starter and mix thoroughly.

3 Mix the rye flour, wholemeal bread flour and unbleached white bread flour for the dough with the salt in a large bowl; make a well in the centre. Pour in the yeast liquid and gradually incorporate the surrounding flour to make a smooth dough.

4 Turn out the dough on to a lightly floured surface and knead for 8–10 minutes until smooth and elastic. Place in a lightly oiled bowl, cover with lightly oiled clear film (plastic wrap) and leave to rise, in a warm place, for 1½ hours, or until nearly doubled in bulk.

5 Turn out on to a lightly floured surface, knock back (punch down) and knead gently. Shape into a round and place in a floured basket or *couronne*, with the seam up. Cover with lightly oiled clear film and leave to rise, in a warm place, for 2–3 hours.

6 Meanwhile, preheat the oven to 200°C/400°F/Gas 6. Turn out the loaf on to the prepared baking sheet and bake for 35–40 minutes. Cool on a wire rack.

For the Sourdough Starter
75g/3oz/¾ cup rye flour
80ml/3fl oz/⅓ cup warm water
pinch caraway seeds

For the Dough
15g/½ oz fresh yeast
315ml/11fl oz/1⅓ cups lukewarm water
275g/10oz/2½ cups rye flour
150g/5oz/1¼ cups wholemeal (whole-wheat) bread flour
150g/5oz/1¼ cups unbleached white bread flour
10ml/2 tsp salt

MAKES 1 LOAF

COOK'S TIP
Proving the dough in a floured basket or *couronne* gives it its characteristic patterned crust, but is not essential. Make sure that you flour the basket well, otherwise the dough may stick.

STOLLEN

75g/3oz/¹/2 cup sultanas (golden raisins)
50g/2oz/¹/4 cup currants
45ml/3 tbsp rum
375g/13oz/3¹/4 cups unbleached white
bread flour
2.5ml/¹/2 tsp salt
50g/2oz/¹/4 cup caster (superfine)
sugar
1.5ml/¹/4 tsp ground cardamom
2.5ml/¹/2 tsp ground cinnamon
40g/1¹/2 oz fresh yeast
120ml/4fl oz/¹/2 cup lukewarm milk
50g/2oz/¹/4 cup butter, melted
1 egg, lightly beaten
50g/2oz/¹/3 cup mixed (candied) peel
50g/2oz/¹/3 cup blanched whole
almonds, chopped
melted butter, for brushing
icing (confectioners') sugar to dust

FOR THE ALMOND FILLING
115g/4oz/1 cup ground almonds
50g/2oz/¹/4 cup caster sugar
50g/2oz/¹/2 cup icing sugar
2.5ml/¹/2 tsp lemon juice
¹/2 egg, lightly beaten

MAKES 1 LARGE LOAF

COOK'S TIP
You can dust the cooled stollen with
icing sugar and cinnamon, or drizzle
over a thin glacé icing.

*This German speciality bread, made for the Christmas season, is rich with
rum-soaked fruits and is wrapped around a moist almond filling. The folded
shape of the dough over the filling represents the baby Jesus wrapped in
swaddling clothes.*

3 Mix the yeast with the milk until
creamy. Pour into the flour and mix a
little of the flour from around the edge
into the milk mixture to make a thick
batter. Sprinkle some of the remaining
flour over the top of the batter, then
cover with clear film (plastic wrap) and
leave in a warm place for 30 minutes.

4 Add the melted butter and egg and
mix to a soft dough. Turn out the dough
on to a lightly floured surface and knead
for 8–10 minutes until smooth and
elastic. Place in a lightly oiled bowl,
cover with lightly oiled clear film and
leave to rise, in a warm place, for
2–3 hours, or until doubled in bulk.

7 Pat out the dough into a rectangle
about 2.5cm/1in thick and sprinkle over
the sultanas, currants, mixed peel and
almonds. Fold and knead the dough to
incorporate the fruit and nuts.

8 Roll out the dough into an oval about
30 × 23cm/12 × 9in. Roll the centre
slightly thinner than the edges. Place
the almond paste filling along the centre
and fold over the dough to enclose it,
making sure that the top of the dough
doesn't completely cover the base. The
top edge should be slightly in from
the bottom edge. Press down to seal.

9 Place the loaf on the prepared baking
sheet, cover with lightly oiled clear film
and leave to rise, in a warm place, for
45–60 minutes, or until doubled in size.

10 Meanwhile, preheat the oven to
200°C/400°F/Gas 6. Bake the loaf for
about 30 minutes, or until it sounds
hollow when tapped on the base. Brush
the top with melted butter and transfer
to a wire rack to cool. Dust with icing
sugar just before serving.

1 Lightly grease a baking sheet. Preheat
the oven to 180°C/350°F/Gas 4. Put the
sultanas and currants in a heatproof
bowl and warm for 3–4 minutes. Pour
over the rum and set aside.

2 Sift the flour and salt together into a
large bowl. Stir in the sugar and spices.

5 Mix the ground almonds and sugars
together for the filling. Add the lemon
juice and sufficient egg to knead to a
smooth paste. Shape into a 20cm/8in
long sausage, cover and set aside.

6 Turn out the dough on to a lightly floured
surface and knock back (punch down).

BUCHTY

*450g/1lb/4 cups unbleached white
bread flour
5ml/1 tsp salt
50g/2oz/¼ cup caster (superfine) sugar
90g/3½oz/scant ½ cup butter
120ml/4fl oz/½ cup milk
20g/¾ oz fresh yeast
3 eggs, lightly beaten
40g/1½ oz/3 tbsp butter, melted
icing (confectioners') sugar, for dusting*

MAKES 16 ROLLS

*Popular in both Poland and Germany as breakfast treats, these are also
excellent split and toasted, and served with cured meats.*

COOK'S TIP
If you do not have a square tin use a
round one. Place two rolls in the
centre and the rest around the edge.

1 Grease a 20cm/8in square loose-
bottomed cake tin (pan). Sift the flour and
salt together into a large bowl and stir in
the sugar. Make a well in the centre.

2 Melt 50g/2oz/¼ cup of the butter in a
small pan, then remove from the heat
and stir in the milk. Leave to cool until
lukewarm. Stir the yeast into the milk
mixture until it has dissolved.

3 Pour into the centre of the flour and
stir in sufficient flour to form a thick
batter. Sprinkle with a little of the
surrounding flour, cover and leave in a
warm place for 30 minutes.

4 Gradually beat in the eggs and
remaining flour to form a soft, smooth
dough. This will take about 10 minutes.
Cover with oiled clear film (plastic
wrap) and leave in a warm place, for
about 1½ hours, or until doubled in bulk.

5 Turn out the dough on to a lightly floured
surface and knock back (punch down).
Divide into 16 equal pieces and shape
into rounds. Melt the remaining butter,
roll the rounds in it to coat, then place,
slightly apart, in the tin. Cover with lightly
oiled clear film and leave to rise, in a warm
place, for about 1 hour, or until doubled.

6 Meanwhile, preheat the oven to 190°C/
375°F/Gas 5. Spoon any remaining
melted butter evenly over the rolls and
bake for 25 minutes, or until golden
brown. Turn out on to a wire rack to
cool. If serving buchty as a breakfast
bread, dust the loaf with icing sugar
before separating it into rolls.

POLISH RYE BREAD

This rye bread is made with half white flour which gives it a lighter, more open texture than a traditional rye loaf. Served thinly sliced, it is the perfect accompaniment for cold meats and fish.

225g/8oz/2 cups rye flour
225g/8oz/2 cups unbleached white
bread flour
10ml/2 tsp caraway seeds
10ml/2 tsp salt
20g/¾ oz fresh yeast
140ml/scant ¼ pint/scant ⅔ cup
lukewarm milk
5ml/1 tsp clear honey
140ml/scant ¼ pint/scant ⅔ cup
lukewarm water
wholemeal (whole-wheat) flour, to dust

MAKES 1 LOAF

1 Lightly grease a baking sheet. Mix the flours, caraway seeds and salt in a large bowl and make a well in the centre.

2 In a bowl or measuring jug (cup), cream the yeast with the milk and honey. Pour into the centre of the flour, add the water and gradually incorporate the surrounding flour and caraway mixture until a dough forms.

3 Turn out the dough on to a lightly floured surface and knead for 8–10 minutes until smooth, elastic and firm. Place in a large, lightly oiled bowl, cover with lightly oiled clear film (plastic wrap) and leave in a warm place, for about 3 hours, or until doubled in bulk.

4 Turn out the dough on to a lightly floured surface and knock back (punch down). Shape into an oval loaf and place on the prepared baking sheet.

5 Dust with wholemeal flour, cover with lightly oiled clear film and leave to rise, in a warm place, for 1–1½ hours, or until doubled in size. Meanwhile, preheat the oven to 220°C/425°F/Gas 7.

6 Using a sharp knife, slash the loaf with two long cuts about 2.5cm/1in apart. Bake for 30–35 minutes, or until the loaf sounds hollow when tapped on the base. Transfer the loaf to a wire rack and set aside to cool.

HUNGARIAN SPLIT FARMHOUSE LOAF

*450g/1lb/4 cups unbleached white
bread flour
10ml/2 tsp salt
2.5ml/½ tsp fennel seeds, crushed
15ml/1 tbsp caster (superfine) sugar
20g/¾ oz fresh yeast
275ml/9fl oz/1⅛ cups lukewarm water
25g/1oz/2 tbsp butter, melted*

*FOR THE TOPPING
1 egg white
pinch of salt
10ml/2 tsp fennel seeds, for sprinkling*

MAKES 1 LOAF

*A golden, fennel seed-encrusted loaf with a moist white crumb. It is equally
delicious made into rolls – just reduce the baking time to 15–20 minutes.*

1 Lightly grease a baking sheet. Sift the white bread flour and salt together into a large bowl and stir in the crushed fennel seeds and caster sugar. Make a well in the centre.

2 Cream the yeast with a little water, stir in the rest, then pour into the centre of the flour. Stir in sufficient flour to make a runny batter. Sprinkle more of the flour on top, cover and leave in a warm place for 30 minutes, or until the sponge starts to bubble and rise.

3 Add the melted butter and gradually mix in with the remaining flour to form a dough. Turn out on to a lightly floured surface and knead for 8–10 minutes until smooth and elastic. Place in a lightly oiled bowl, cover with lightly oiled clear film (plastic wrap) and leave to rise, in a warm place, for 45–60 minutes, or until doubled in bulk.

4 Turn out on to a lightly floured surface and knock back (punch down). Shape into an oval and place on the prepared baking sheet. Cover with lightly oiled clear film and leave to rise, in a warm place, for 30–40 minutes, or until doubled in size.

5 Meanwhile, preheat the oven to 220°C/425°F/Gas 7. Mix the egg white and salt together, and brush this glaze over the loaf. Sprinkle with fennel seeds and then, using a sharp knife, slash along its length. Bake for 20 minutes, then reduce the oven temperature to 180°C/350°F/Gas 4 and bake for 10 minutes more, or until sounding hollow when tapped on the base. Transfer to a wire rack to cool.

GEORGIAN KHACHAPURI

*These savoury buns are sold from street stalls as warm snacks. The sealed
bread parcels envelop a meltingly delicious cheese filling;
goat's cheese is typically used in Georgia.*

225g/8oz/2 cups unbleached white
bread flour
5ml/1 tsp salt
15g/½ oz fresh yeast
150ml/¼ pint/⅔ cup lukewarm milk
25g/1oz/2 tbsp butter, softened

FOR THE FILLING
225g/8oz/2 cups grated mature
(sharp) Cheddar cheese
225g/8oz Munster or Taleggio cheese,
cut into small cubes
1 egg, lightly beaten
15ml/1 tbsp butter, softened
salt and freshly ground black pepper

FOR THE GLAZE
1 egg yolk
15ml/1 tbsp water

MAKES 4 BUNS

3 Turn the dough out on to a lightly
floured surface and knead for 2–3
minutes. Divide into four equal pieces
and roll each out into a 20cm/8in circle.

4 Place one dough circle in one hole of
the Yorkshire pudding tin and fill with a
quarter of the cheese filling. Gather the
overhanging dough into the centre and
twist to form a topknot. Repeat with the
remaining dough and filling. Cover with
lightly oiled clear film and leave to rise,
in a warm place, for 20–30 minutes.

1 Lightly grease a Yorkshire pudding tin
(muffin pan) with four 10cm/4in holes.
Sift the flour and salt into a large bowl.
Cream the yeast with the milk, add to
the flour and mix to a dough. Knead in
the butter, then knead on a lightly
floured surface until smooth and elastic.
Place in a lightly oiled bowl, cover with
lightly oiled clear film (plastic wrap) and
leave to rise, in a warm place, for 1–1½
hours, or until doubled in bulk.

2 Meanwhile, put the cheeses in a bowl
and stir in the egg and softened butter
for the filling. Season with plenty of salt
and pepper.

VARIATIONS
• Use Red Leicester or Parmesan in
place of the Cheddar.
• Make one large bread instead of the
buns. Bake for 50–55 minutes.

5 Meanwhile, preheat the oven to 180°C/
350°F/Gas 4. Mix the egg yolk and water,
and brush over the dough. Bake for
25–30 minutes, or until light golden.
Cool for 2–3 minutes in the tin, then
turn out on to a wire rack. Serve warm.

POPPY SEED ROLL

A favourite sweet yeast bread in both Poland and Hungary, this has an unusual filling of poppy seeds, almonds, raisins and citrus peel spiralling through the dough.

*350g/12oz/3 cups unbleached white
bread flour
2.5ml/½ tsp salt
25g/1oz/2 tbsp caster (superfine) sugar
20g/¾ oz fresh yeast
120ml/4fl oz/½ cup lukewarm milk
1 egg, lightly beaten
50g/2oz/¼ cup butter, melted
115g/4oz/1 cup icing
(confectioners') sugar
15ml/1 tbsp lemon juice
10–15ml/2–3 tsp water
15ml/1 tbsp toasted flaked
(sliced) almonds*

*For the Filling
115g/4oz/⅔ cup poppy seeds
50g/2oz/¼ cup butter
75g/3oz/6 tbsp caster (superfine) sugar
75g/3oz/½ cup raisins
50g/2oz/½ cup ground almonds
50g/2oz/⅓ cup mixed (candied) peel,
finely chopped
2.5ml/½ tsp ground cinnamon*

Makes 1 Large Loaf

1 Lightly grease a baking sheet. Sift the flour and salt together into a large bowl. Stir in the sugar. Cream the yeast with the milk. Add to the flour with the egg and melted butter and mix to a dough.

2 Turn out on to a lightly floured surface and knead for 8–10 minutes until smooth and elastic. Place in a lightly oiled bowl, cover with lightly oiled clear film (plastic wrap) and leave to rise, in a warm place, for 1–1½ hours, or until doubled in size.

3 Meanwhile, pour boiling water over the poppy seeds for the filling, then leave to cool. Drain thoroughly in a fine sieve. Melt the butter in a small pan, add the poppy seeds and cook, stirring, for 1–2 minutes. Remove from the heat and stir in the sugar, raisins, ground almonds, peel and cinnamon. Leave to cool.

4 Turn the dough out on to a lightly floured surface, knock back (punch down) and knead lightly. Roll out into a rectangle 35 × 25cm/14 × 10in. Spread the filling to within 2cm/¾in of the edges.

5 Roll up the dough, starting from one long edge, like a Swiss (jelly) roll, tucking in the edges to seal. Place seam side down on the prepared baking sheet. Cover with lightly oiled clear film and leave to rise, in a warm place, for 30 minutes, or until doubled in size.

6 Meanwhile, preheat the oven to 190°C/ 375°F/Gas 5. Bake for 30 minutes, or until golden brown. Transfer to a wire rack to cool until just warm.

7 Mix the icing sugar, lemon juice and sufficient water together in a small pan to make an icing stiff enough to coat the back of a spoon. Heat gently, stirring, until warm. Drizzle the icing over the loaf and sprinkle the flaked almonds over the top. Leave to cool completely, then serve sliced.

RUSSIAN POTATO BREAD

In Russia, potatoes are often used to replace some of the flour in bread recipes. They endow the bread with excellent keeping qualities.

225g/8oz potatoes, peeled
and diced
7g/¼ oz sachet easy-blend
(rapid-rise) dried yeast
350g/12oz/3 cups unbleached white
bread flour
115g/4oz/1 cup wholemeal
(whole-wheat) bread flour,
plus extra for sprinkling
2.5ml/½ tsp caraway
seeds, crushed
10ml/2 tsp salt
25g/1oz/2 tbsp butter

MAKES 1 LOAF

1 Lightly grease a baking sheet. Add the potatoes to a pan of boiling water and cook until tender. Drain and reserve 150ml/¼ pint/⅔ cup of the cooking water. Mash and sieve the potatoes and leave to cool.

2 Mix the yeast, bread flours, caraway seeds and salt together in a large bowl. Add the butter and rub in. Mix the reserved potato water and sieved potatoes together. Gradually work this mixture into the flour mixture to form a soft dough.

3 Turn out on to a lightly floured surface and knead for 8–10 minutes until smooth and elastic. Place in a lightly oiled bowl, cover with oiled clear film (plastic wrap) and leave in a warm place, for 1 hour, or until doubled in bulk.

4 Turn out on to a lightly floured surface, knock back (punch down) and knead gently. Shape into a plump oval loaf, about 18cm/7in long. Place on the prepared baking sheet and sprinkle with a little wholemeal bread flour.

5 Cover the dough with lightly oiled clear film and leave to rise, in a warm place, for 30 minutes, or until doubled in size. Meanwhile, preheat the oven to 200°C/400°F/Gas 6.

6 Using a sharp knife, slash the top with 3–4 diagonal cuts to make a criss-cross effect. Bake for 30–35 minutes, or until golden and sounding hollow when tapped on the base. Transfer to a wire rack to cool.

VARIATION

To make a cheese-flavoured potato bread, omit the caraway seeds and knead 115g/4oz/1 cup grated Cheddar, Red Leicester or a crumbled blue cheese, such as Stilton, into the dough before shaping.

KOLACH

675g/1½ lb/6 cups unbleached white
bread flour
10ml/2 tsp salt
25g/1oz fresh yeast
120ml/4fl oz/½ cup lukewarm milk
5ml/1 tsp clear honey
2 eggs
150ml/¼ pint/⅔ cup natural
(plain) yogurt
50g/2oz/¼ cup butter, melted
beaten egg, for glazing
poppy seeds, for sprinkling

MAKES 1 LARGE LOAF

Often prepared for religious celebrations and family feasts, this Bulgarian
bread gets its name from its circular shape – kolo, which means circle. It has
a golden crust sprinkled with poppy seeds and a moist crumb, which makes
this loaf a very good keeper.

1 Grease a large baking sheet. Sift the flour and salt together into a large bowl and make a well in the centre.

2 Cream the yeast with the milk and honey. Add to the centre of the flour with the eggs, yogurt and melted butter. Gradually mix into the flour to form a firm dough.

3 Turn out on to a lightly floured surface and knead for 8–10 minutes until smooth and elastic. Place in a lightly oiled bowl, cover with lightly oiled clear film (plastic wrap) or slip into an oiled plastic bag. Leave in a warm place, for 1½ hours, or until doubled in bulk.

5 Gradually enlarge the cavity, turning the dough to make a 25cm/10in circle. Transfer to the baking sheet, cover with lightly oiled clear film (plastic wrap) and leave to rise, in a warm place, for 30–45 minutes, or until doubled in size.

6 Meanwhile, preheat the oven to 200°C/400°F/Gas 6. Brush the loaf with beaten egg and sprinkle with poppy seeds. Bake for 35 minutes, or until golden. Cool on a wire rack.

VARIATION
For a special finish, divide the dough into three equal pieces, roll into long thin strips and braid together, starting with the centre of the strips. Once plaited, shape into a circle and seal the ends together. Make sure the hole in the centre is quite large, otherwise the hole will fill in as the bread rises.

4 Knock back (punch down) the dough and turn out on to a lightly floured surface. Knead lightly and shape into a ball. Place seam side down and make a hole in the centre with your fingers.

BLINIS

50g/2oz/½ cup buckwheat flour
50g/2oz/½ cup unbleached plain
(all-purpose) flour
2.5ml/½ tsp freshly ground
black pepper
5ml/1 tsp salt
15g/½ oz fresh yeast
200ml/7fl oz/scant 1 cup lukewarm
milk
1 egg, separated

MAKES ABOUT 10 BLINIS

Blinis are the celebrated leavened Russian pancakes. Traditionally served
with sour cream and caviar, they have a very distinctive flavour and
a fluffy, light texture.

1 Mix the buckwheat flour, plain flour, pepper and salt together in a large bowl.

2 In a small bowl, cream the yeast with 60ml/4 tbsp of the milk, then mix in the remaining milk.

3 Add the egg yolk to the flour mixture and gradually whisk in the yeast mixture to form a smooth batter. Cover with clear film (plastic wrap) and leave to stand in a warm place for 1 hour.

4 Whisk the egg white until it forms soft peaks and fold into the batter. Lightly oil a heavy frying pan and heat it.

5 Add about 45ml/3 tbsp of the batter to make a 10cm/4in round pancake. Cook until the surface begins to dry out, then turn the pancake over using a metal spatula and cook for 1–2 minutes. Repeat with the remaining batter. Serve warm.

VARIATION
You can use all buckwheat flour, which will give the blinis a stronger flavour.

SUNSHINE LOAF

For the Starter
60ml/4 tbsp lukewarm milk
60ml/4 tbsp lukewarm water
7g/¹/₄ oz fresh yeast
100g/3¾oz/scant 1 cup unbleached
white bread flour

For the Dough
15g/¹/₂ oz fresh yeast
500ml/17fl oz/generous 2 cups
lukewarm water
450g/1lb/4 cups rye flour
225g/8oz/2 cups unbleached white
bread flour
15ml/1 tbsp salt
milk, for glazing
caraway seeds, for sprinkling

Makes 1 Large Loaf

VARIATION
This bread can be shaped into one
large round or oval loaf, if preferred.

Scandinavia, Land of the Midnight Sun, has numerous breads based on rye.
This splendid table centrepiece is made with a blend of rye and white flours,
the latter helping to lighten the bread.

1 Combine the milk and water for the
starter in a large bowl. Mix in the yeast
until dissolved. Gradually add the bread
flour, stirring it with a metal spoon.

2 Cover the bowl with clear film (plastic
wrap) and leave the mixture in a warm
place for 3–4 hours, or until well risen,
bubbly and starting to collapse.

3 Mix the yeast for the dough with
60ml/4 tbsp of the water until creamy,
then stir in the remaining water.
Gradually mix into the starter to dilute
it. Gradually mix in the rye flour to form
a smooth batter. Cover with lightly oiled
clear film and leave in a warm place, for
3–4 hours, or until well risen.

4 Stir the bread flour and salt into the
batter to form a dough. Turn on to a
lightly floured surface and knead for
5 minutes until smooth and elastic.
Place in a lightly oiled bowl, cover with
lightly oiled clear film and leave to rise,
in a warm place, for about 1 hour, or
until doubled in bulk.

5 Knock back (punch down) on a lightly
floured surface. Cut the dough into five
pieces. Roll one piece into a 50cm/20in
"sausage" and roll up into a spiral shape.

6 Cut the remaining pieces of dough in
half and shape each one into a 20cm/8in
rope. Place in a circle on a large baking
sheet, spaced equally apart, like rays of
the sun, and curl the ends round,
leaving a small gap in the centre. Place
the spiral shape on top. Cover with
lightly oiled clear film and leave to rise,
in a warm place, for 30 minutes.

7 Meanwhile, preheat the oven to 230°C/
450°F/Gas 8. Brush the bread with milk,
sprinkle with caraway seeds and bake
for 30 minutes, or until lightly browned.
Transfer to a wire rack to cool.

SAVOURY DANISH CROWN

Filled with golden onions and cheese, this butter-rich bread ring is quite
irresistible and needs no accompaniment.

1 Lightly grease a baking sheet. Sift the flour and salt together into a large bowl. Rub in 40g/1½ oz/3 tbsp of the butter. Mix the yeast with the milk and water. Add to the flour with the egg and mix to a soft dough.

2 Turn out on to a lightly floured surface and knead for 10 minutes until smooth and elastic. Place in a lightly oiled bowl, cover with lightly oiled clear film (plastic wrap) and leave to rise, in a warm place, for about 1 hour, or until doubled in bulk.

3 Knock back (punch down) and turn out on to a lightly floured surface. Roll out into an oblong about 1cm/½ in thick.

4 Dot half the remaining butter over the top two-thirds of the dough. Fold the bottom third up and the top third down and seal the edges. Turn by 90 degrees and repeat with the remaining butter. Fold and seal as before. Cover the dough with lightly oiled clear film and leave to rest for about 15 minutes.

5 Turn by a further 90 degrees. Roll and fold again without any butter. Repeat once more. Wrap in lightly oiled clear film and leave to rest in the refrigerator for 30 minutes.

6 Meanwhile, heat the oil for the filling. Add the onions and cook for 10 minutes until soft and golden. Remove from the heat and stir in the breadcrumbs, almonds, Parmesan and seasoning.

7 Add half the beaten egg to the breadcrumb mixture and bind together.

8 Roll out the dough on a lightly floured surface into a rectangle measuring 56 × 23cm/22 × 9in. Spread with the filling to within 2cm/¾ in of the edges, then roll up like a Swiss (jelly) roll from one long side. Using a very sharp knife, cut in half lengthways. Braid together with the cut sides up and shape into a ring. Place on the prepared baking sheet, cover with lightly oiled clear film and leave to rise, in a warm place, for 30 minutes.

9 Meanwhile, preheat the oven to 200°C/400°F/Gas 6. Brush the remaining beaten egg over the dough. Sprinkle with sesame seeds and Parmesan cheese and bake for 40–50 minutes, or until golden. Transfer to a wire rack to cool slightly if serving warm, or cool completely to serve cold, cut into slices.

350g/12oz/3 cups unbleached white
bread flour
5ml/1 tsp salt
185g/6½ oz/generous ¾ cup butter,
softened
20g/¾ oz fresh yeast
200ml/7fl oz/scant 1 cup mixed
lukewarm milk and water
1 egg, lightly beaten

FOR THE FILLING
30ml/2 tbsp sunflower oil
2 onions, finely chopped
40g/1½ oz/¾ cup fresh breadcrumbs
25g/1oz/¼ cup ground almonds
50g/2oz/½ cup freshly grated
Parmesan cheese
1 egg, lightly beaten
salt and freshly ground black pepper

FOR THE TOPPING
15ml/1 tbsp sesame seeds
15ml/1 tbsp freshly grated
Parmesan cheese

MAKES 1 LARGE LOAF

DANISH JULEKAGE

25g/1oz fresh yeast
75ml/5 tbsp lukewarm milk
*450g/1lb/4 cups unbleached white
bread flour*
10ml/2 tsp salt
75g/3oz/6 tbsp butter
15 cardamom pods
2.5ml/½ tsp vanilla essence (extract)
50g/2oz/⅓ cup soft light brown sugar
grated rind of ½ lemon
2 eggs, lightly beaten
*50g/2oz/¼ cup ready-to-eat dried
apricots, chopped*
*50g/2oz/¼ cup glacé (candied)
pineapple pieces, chopped*
*50g/2oz/¼ cup red and green glacé
(candied) cherries, chopped*
25g/1oz/3 tbsp dried dates, chopped
*25g/1oz/2 tbsp crystallized stem
ginger, chopped*

For the Glaze
1 egg white
10ml/2 tsp water

For the Decoration
15ml/1 tbsp caster (superfine) sugar
2.5ml/½ tsp ground cinnamon
*8 pecan nuts or whole
blanched almonds*

Makes 1 Loaf

In Scandinavia special slightly sweet holiday breads containing fragrant cardamom seeds are common. This exotic bread, enriched with butter and a selection of glacé and dried fruits or "jewels", is traditionally served over the Christmas period with hot spiced punch.

1 Lightly grease a 23 × 13cm/9 × 5in loaf tin (pan). In a measuring jug (cup), cream the yeast with the milk.

2 Sift the flour and salt together into a large bowl. Add the butter and rub in. Make a well in the centre. Add the yeast mixture to the centre of the flour and butter mixture and stir in sufficient flour to form a thick batter. Sprinkle over a little of the remaining flour and set aside in a warm place for 15 minutes.

3 Remove the seeds from the cardamom pods. Put them in a mortar or strong bowl and crush with a pestle or the end of a rolling pin. Add the crushed seeds to the flour with the vanilla essence, sugar, lemon rind and eggs, then mix to a soft dough.

4 Turn out on to a lightly floured surface and knead for 8–10 minutes until smooth and elastic. Place in a lightly oiled bowl, cover with oiled clear film (plastic wrap) and leave in a warm place, for 1–1½ hours, or until doubled in bulk.

5 Knock back (punch down) the dough and turn it out on to a lightly floured surface. Flatten into a rectangle and sprinkle over half of the apricots, pineapple, cherries, dates and ginger. Fold the sides into the centre and then fold in half to contain the fruit. Flatten into a rectangle again and sprinkle over the remaining fruit. Fold and knead gently to distribute the fruit. Cover the fruited dough with lightly oiled clear film and leave to rest for 10 minutes.

6 Roll the fruited dough into a rectangle 38 × 25cm/15 × 10in. With a short side facing you, fold the bottom third up lengthways and the top third down, tucking in the sides, to form a 23 × 13cm/9 × 5in loaf. Place in the prepared tin, seam side down. Cover with lightly oiled clear film and leave to rise, in a warm place, for 1 hour, or until the dough has reached the top of the tin.

7 Meanwhile, preheat the oven to 180°C/350°F/Gas 4. Using a sharp knife, slash the top of the loaf lengthways and then make diagonal slits on either side.

8 Mix together the egg white and water for the glaze, and brush over the top. Mix the sugar and cinnamon in a bowl, then sprinkle over the top. Decorate with pecan nuts or almonds. Bake for 45–50 minutes, or until risen and browned. Transfer to a wire rack to cool.

VARIATIONS
• You can vary the fruits for this loaf. Try glacé peaches, yellow glacé cherries, sultanas (golden raisins), raisins, candied angelica, dried mango or dried pears and use in place of some or all of the fruits in the recipe. Use a mixture of colours and make sure that the total weight is the same as above.
• Use walnuts in place of the pecan nuts or almonds.

COOK'S TIP
Keep a close watch on the bread, especially during the final 15 minutes of cooking. If the top of the loaf starts to brown too quickly, cover loosely with foil or greaseproof (waxed) paper.

450g/1lb/4 cups rye flour
5ml/1 tsp salt
50g/2oz/¼ cup butter
20g/¾ oz fresh yeast
275ml/9fl oz/generous 1 cup
lukewarm water
75g/3oz/2 cups wheat bran

MAKES 8 CRISPBREADS

COOK'S TIP
The hole in the centre of these
crispbreads is a reminder of the days
when breads were strung on a pole,
which was hung across the rafters to
dry. Make smaller crispbreads, if you
like, and tie them together with
bright red ribbon for an unusual
Christmas gift.

KNACKERBRÖD

A very traditional Swedish crispbread with a lovely rye flavour.

1 Lightly grease two baking sheets.
Preheat the oven to 230°C/450°F/Gas 8.
Mix the rye flour and salt in a large
bowl. Rub in the butter, then make a
well in the centre.

2 Cream the yeast with a little water,
then stir in the remainder. Pour into the
centre of the flour, mix to a dough, then
mix in the bran. Knead on a lightly
floured surface for 5 minutes until
smooth and elastic.

3 Divide the dough into eight equal
pieces and roll each one out on a lightly
floured surface, to a 20cm/8in round.

4 Place two rounds on the prepared
baking sheets and prick all over with a
fork. Cut a hole in the centre of each
round, using a 4cm/1½ in cutter.

5 Bake for 15–20 minutes, or until the
crispbreads are golden and crisp.
Transfer to a wire rack to cool. Repeat
with the remaining crispbreads.

FINNISH BARLEY BREAD

225g/8oz/2 cups barley flour
5ml/1 tsp salt
10ml/2 tsp baking powder
25g/1oz/2 tbsp butter, melted
120ml/4fl oz/½ cup single
(light) cream
60ml/4 tbsp milk

MAKES 1 SMALL LOAF

COOK'S TIPS
• This flat bread tastes very good with
cottage cheese, especially cottage
cheese with chives.
• For a citrusy tang, add 10–15ml/
2–3 tsp finely grated lemon, lime or
orange rind to the flour mixture
in step 1.

*In Northern Europe breads are often made using cereals such as barley and
rye, which produce very satisfying, tasty breads. This quick-to-prepare flat
bread is best served warm with lashings of butter.*

1 Lightly grease a baking sheet. Preheat
the oven to 200°C/400°F/Gas 6. Sift the
dry ingredients into a bowl. Add the
butter, cream and milk. Mix to a dough.

2 Turn out the dough on to a lightly
floured surface and shape into a flat
round about 1cm/½ in thick.

3 Transfer to the prepared baking sheet
and using a sharp knife, lightly mark the
top into six sections.

4 Prick the surface of the round evenly
with a fork. Bake for 15–18 minutes, or
until pale golden. Cut into wedges and
serve warm.

LUSSE BRÖD

120ml/4fl oz/½ cup milk
pinch of saffron threads
400g/14oz/3½ cups unbleached white
bread flour
50g/2oz/½ cup ground almonds
2.5ml/½ tsp salt
75g/3oz/6 tbsp caster (superfine) sugar
25g/1oz fresh yeast
120ml/4fl oz/½ cup lukewarm water
few drops of almond essence (extract)
50g/2oz/¼ cup butter, softened

FOR THE GLAZE
1 egg
15ml/1 tbsp water

MAKES 12 BUNS

VARIATION
Gently knead in 40g/1½ oz/3 tbsp
currants after knocking back the
dough in step 4.

*Saint Lucia Day, the 12th of December, marks the beginning of Christmas in
Sweden. As part of the celebrations, young girls dressed in white robes wear
headbands topped with lighted candles and walk through the village
streets offering saffron buns to the townspeople.*

1 Lightly grease two baking sheets.
Place the milk in a small pan and bring
to the boil. Add the saffron, remove
from the heat and leave to infuse
(steep) for about 15 minutes.
Meanwhile mix the flour, ground almonds,
salt and sugar together in a large bowl.

2 Cream the yeast with the water. Add
the saffron liquid, yeast mixture and
almond essence to the flour mixture and
mix to a dough. Gradually beat in the
softened butter.

3 Turn out on to a lightly floured surface
and knead for 5 minutes until smooth
and elastic. Place in a lightly oiled bowl,
cover with lightly oiled clear film
(plastic wrap) and leave in a warm place,
for about 1 hour, or until doubled in bulk.

4 Turn out on to a lightly floured surface
and knock back (punch down). Divide
into 12 equal pieces and make into
different shapes: roll into a long rope and
shape into an "S" shape; to make a star,
cut a dough piece in half and roll into
two ropes, cross one over the other and
coil the ends; make an upturned "U"
shape and coil the ends to represent
curled hair; divide a dough piece in half,
roll into two thin ropes and twist together.

5 Place on the prepared baking sheets,
spaced well apart, cover with lightly
oiled clear film and leave to rise, in a
warm place, for about 30 minutes.

6 Meanwhile, preheat the oven to 200°C/
400°F/Gas 6. Beat the egg with the
water for the glaze, and brush over the
rolls. Bake for 15 minutes, or until
golden. Transfer to a wire rack to cool
slightly to serve warm, or cool
completely to serve cold.

VÖRT LIMPA

*This festive Swedish bread is flavoured with warm spices and fresh orange.
The beer and port work nicely to soften the rye taste. The added sugars also
give the yeast a little extra to feed on and so help aerate and lighten the
bread. It is traditionally served with cheese.*

350g/12oz/3 cups rye flour
350g/12oz/3 cups unbleached white
bread flour
2.5ml/½ tsp salt
25g/1oz/2 tbsp caster (superfine) sugar
5ml/1 tsp grated nutmeg
5ml/1 tsp ground cloves
5ml/1 tsp ground ginger
40g/1½ oz fresh yeast
300ml/½ pint/1¼ cups light ale
120ml/4fl oz/½ cup port
15ml/1 tbsp molasses
25g/1oz/2 tbsp butter, melted
15ml/1 tbsp grated orange rind
75g/3oz/½ cup raisins
15ml/1 tbsp malt extract, for glazing

MAKES 1 LARGE LOAF

VARIATION
This bread can be shaped into a
round or oval and baked on a baking
sheet if you prefer.

5 Turn out the dough on to a lightly
floured surface and knock back (punch
down). Gently knead in the orange rind
and raisins. Roll into a 30cm/12in square.

1 Lightly grease a 30 × 10cm/12 × 4in
loaf tin (pan). Mix together the rye and
white flours, salt, sugar, nutmeg, cloves
and ginger in a large bowl.

2 In another large bowl, using a wooden
spoon, blend the yeast into the ale until
dissolved, then stir in the port, molasses
and melted butter.

3 Gradually add the flour mixture to the
yeast liquid, beating to make a smooth
batter. Continue adding the flour a little
at a time and mixing until the mixture
forms a soft dough.

4 Turn out on to a lightly floured surface
and knead for 8–10 minutes until
smooth and elastic. Place in a lightly
oiled bowl, cover with oiled clear film
(plastic wrap) and leave in a warm place,
for 1 hour, or until doubled in size.

6 Fold the bottom third of the dough
up and the top third down, sealing the
edges. Place in the prepared tin, cover
with lightly oiled clear film and leave to
rise, in a warm place, for 1 hour, or until
the dough reaches the top of the tin.

7 Meanwhile, preheat the oven to 190°C/
375°F/Gas 5. Bake for 35–40 minutes, or
until browned. Turn out on to a wire
rack, brush with malt extract and leave
to cool.

BREADS OF THE AMERICAS

Yeast breads, quick breads based on baking powder, Mexican flat breads and sweet breads are all part of the diverse range found in the Americas. Traditional American ingredients such as corn meal, molasses, sweetcorn and pumpkin provide the distinctive flavours associated with Boston brown bread, Anadama bread, corn bread, Virginia spoon bread and pumpkin and walnut bread. There's a strong Jewish influence in specialities like challah, which is traditionally baked to celebrate religious holidays, and the ubiquitous bagel.

SAN FRANCISCO SOURDOUGH BREAD

In San Francisco this bread is leavened using a flour and water paste, which is left to ferment with the aid of airborne yeast. The finished loaves have a moist crumb and crispy crust, and will keep for several days.

FOR THE STARTER
50g/2oz/¹/₂ cup wholemeal
(whole-wheat) flour
pinch of ground cumin
15ml/1 tbsp milk
15–30ml/1–2 tbsp water
1ST REFRESHMENT
30ml/2 tbsp water
115g/4oz/1 cup wholemeal flour
2ND REFRESHMENT
60ml/4 tbsp water
115g/4oz/1 cup white bread flour

FOR THE BREAD: 1ST REFRESHMENT
75ml/5 tbsp very warm water
75g/3oz/³/₄ cup unbleached plain
(all-purpose) flour
2ND REFRESHMENT
175ml/6fl oz/³/₄ cup lukewarm water
200–225g/7–8oz/1³/₄–2 cups
unbleached plain flour

FOR THE SOURDOUGH
280ml/9fl oz/1¹/₄ cups warm water
500g/1¹/₄lb/5 cups unbleached white
bread flour
15ml/1 tbsp salt
flour, for dusting
ice cubes, for baking

MAKES 2 ROUND LOAVES

1 Sift the flour and cumin for the starter into a bowl. Add the milk and sufficient water to make a firm but moist dough. Knead for 6–8 minutes to form a firm dough. Return the dough to the bowl, cover with a damp dishtowel and leave in a warm place, 24–26°C/75–80°F, for about 2 days. When it is ready the starter will appear moist and wrinkled and will have developed a crust.

2 Pull off the hardened crust and discard. Scoop out the moist centre (about the size of a hazelnut), which will be aerated and sweet smelling, and place in a clean bowl. Mix in the water for the 1st refreshment. Gradually add the wholemeal flour and mix to a dough.

3 Cover with clear film (plastic wrap) and return to a warm place for 1–2 days. Discard the crust and gradually mix in the water for the 2nd refreshment to the starter, which by now will have a slightly sharper smell. Gradually mix in the white flour, cover and leave in a warm place for 8–10 hours.

4 For the bread, mix the sourdough starter with the water for the 1st refreshment. Gradually mix in the flour to form a firm dough. Knead for 6–8 minutes until firm. Cover with a damp dishtowel and leave in a warm place for 8–12 hours, or until doubled in bulk.

5 Gradually mix in the water for the 2nd refreshment, then gradually mix in enough flour to form a soft, smooth elastic dough. Re-cover and leave in a warm place for 8–12 hours. Gradually stir in the water for the sourdough, then gradually work in the flour and salt. This will take 10–15 minutes. Turn out on to a lightly floured surface and knead until smooth and very elastic. Place in a large lightly oiled bowl, cover with lightly oiled clear film and leave to rise, in a warm place, for 8–12 hours.

6 Divide the dough in half and shape into two round loaves by folding the sides over to the centre and sealing.

7 Place seam side up in flour-dusted *couronnes*, bowls or baskets lined with flour-dusted dish towels. Re-cover and leave to rise in a warm place for 4 hours.

8 Preheat the oven to 220°C/425°F/Gas 7. Place an empty roasting pan in the bottom of the oven. Dust two baking sheets with flour. Turn out the loaves seam side down on the prepared baking sheets. Using a sharp knife, cut a criss-cross pattern by slashing the top of the loaves four or five times in each direction.

9 Place the baking sheets in the oven and immediately drop the ice cubes into the hot roasting pan to create steam. Bake the bread for 25 minutes, then reduce the oven temperature to 200°C/400°F/Gas 6 and bake for a further 15–20 minutes, or until sounding hollow when tapped on the base. Transfer to wire racks to cool.

COOK'S TIP
If you'd like to make sourdough bread regularly, keep a small amount of the starter covered in the refrigerator. It will keep for several days. Use the starter for the 2nd refreshment, then continue as directed.

MONKEY BREAD

This American favourite is also called bubble bread – because of the "bubbles"
of dough. The pieces of dough are tossed in a heavenly coating of butter, nuts,
cinnamon and rum-soaked fruit.

7g/¹/4 oz sachet easy-blend
(rapid-rise) dried yeast
450g/1lb/4 cups unbleached white
bread flour
2.5ml/¹/2 tsp salt
15ml/1 tbsp caster (superfine) sugar
120ml/4fl oz/¹/2 cup lukewarm milk
120ml/4fl oz/¹/2 cup lukewarm water
1 egg, lightly beaten

FOR THE COATING
75g/3oz/¹/2 cup sultanas
(golden raisins)
45ml/3 tbsp rum or brandy
115g/4oz/1 cup walnuts, finely chopped
10ml/2 tsp ground cinnamon
115g/4oz/²/3 cup soft light brown sugar
50g/2oz/¹/4 cup butter, melted

MAKES 1 LOAF

1 Lightly grease a 23cm/9in springform
ring cake tin (pan). Mix the dried yeast,
flour, salt and caster sugar together in a
large bowl and make a well in the centre.

2 Add the milk, water and egg to the
centre of the flour and mix together to
a soft dough. Turn out on to a lightly
floured surface and knead for about
10 minutes until smooth and elastic.
Place in a lightly oiled bowl, cover with
lightly oiled clear film (plastic wrap) and
leave to rise, in a warm place, for 45–60
minutes, or until doubled in bulk.

3 Place the sultanas in a small pan, pour
over the rum or brandy and heat for
1–2 minutes, or until warm. Take care
not to overheat. Remove from the heat
and set aside. Mix the walnuts,
cinnamon and sugar in a small bowl.

4 Turn out the dough on to a lightly
floured surface and knead gently. Divide
into 30 equal pieces and shape into
small balls. Dip the balls, one at a time
into the melted butter, then roll them in
the walnut mixture. Place half in the
prepared tin, spaced slightly apart.
Sprinkle over all the soaked sultanas.

VARIATION
Replace the easy-blend dried yeast
with 20g/³/4 oz fresh yeast. Mix with
the liquid until creamy before
adding to the flour.

5 Top with the remaining dough balls,
dipping and coating as before. Sprinkle
over any remaining walnut mixture
and melted butter. Cover with lightly
oiled clear film or slide the tin into a
lightly oiled large plastic bag and leave
to rise, in a warm place, for about
45 minutes, or until the dough reaches
the top of the tin.

6 Meanwhile, preheat the oven to 190°C/
375°F/Gas 5. Bake for 35–40 minutes, or
until well risen and golden. Turn out on
to a wire rack to cool.

Pumpkin and Walnut Bread

—

Pumpkin, nutmeg and walnuts combine to yield a moist, tangy and slightly sweet bread with an indescribably good flavour. Serve partnered with meats or cheese, or simply lightly buttered.

1 Grease and neatly base line a loaf tin (pan) measuring 21.5 × 11cm/8½ × 4½in. Preheat the oven to 180°C/350°F/Gas 4.

2 Place the pumpkin in a pan, add water to cover by about 5cm/2in, then bring to the boil. Cover, lower the heat and simmer for 20 minutes, or until the pumpkin is very tender. Drain well, then purée in a food processor or blender. Leave to cool.

3 Place 275g/10oz/1¼ cups of the purée in a large bowl. Add the sugar, nutmeg, melted butter and eggs to the purée and mix together. Sift the flour, baking powder and salt together into a large bowl and make a well in the centre.

4 Add the pumpkin mixture to the centre of the flour and stir until smooth. Mix in the walnuts.

500g/1¼ lb pumpkin, peeled, seeded and cut into chunks
75g/3oz/6 tbsp caster (superfine) sugar
5ml/1 tsp grated nutmeg
50g/2oz/¼ cup butter, melted
3 eggs, lightly beaten
350g/12oz/3 cups unbleached white bread flour
10ml/2 tsp baking powder
2.5ml/½ tsp salt
75g/3oz/¾ cup walnuts, chopped

Makes 1 Loaf

COOK'S TIP
You may have slightly more pumpkin purée than you actually need – use the remainder in soup.

5 Transfer to the prepared tin and bake for 1 hour, or until golden and starting to shrink from the sides of the tin. Turn out on to a wire rack to cool.

BOSTON BROWN BREAD

90g/3¹/2 oz/scant 1 cup corn meal
90g/3¹/2 oz/scant 1 cup unbleached
plain (all-purpose) white flour or
wholemeal (whole-wheat) flour
90g/3¹/2 oz/scant 1 cup rye flour
2.5ml/¹/2 tsp salt
5ml/1 tsp bicarbonate of soda
(baking soda)
90g/3¹/2 oz/generous ¹/2 cup raisins
120ml/4fl oz/¹/2 cup milk
120ml/4fl oz/¹/2 cup water
120ml/4fl oz/¹/2 cup molasses

MAKES 1 OR 2 LOAVES

Rich, moist and dark, this bread is flavoured with molasses and can include raisins. In Boston it is often served with savoury baked beans.

4 Fill the jug or cans with the dough; they should be about two-thirds full. Cover neatly with foil or greased greaseproof paper and tie securely.

5 Bring water to a depth of 5cm/2in to the boil in a deep, heavy pan large enough to accommodate the jug or cans. Place a trivet in the pan, stand the jug or cans on top, cover the pan and steam for 1¹/2 hours, adding more boiling water to maintain the required level as necessary.

6 Cool the loaves for a few minutes in the jug or cans, then turn them on their sides and the loaves should slip out. Serve warm, as a teabread or with savoury dishes.

COOK'S TIP
If you do not have empty coffee jugs, cans or similar moulds, cook the bread in one or two heatproof bowls of equivalent capacity.

1 Line the base of one 1.2 litre/2 pint/ 5 cup cylindrical metal or glass container, such as a heatproof glass coffee jug (carafe), with greased greaseproof (waxed) paper. Alternatively, remove the lids from two 450g/1lb coffee cans, wash and dry them thoroughly, then line with greased greaseproof paper.

2 Mix together the corn meal, plain or wholemeal flour, rye flour, salt, bicarbonate of soda and raisins in a large bowl. Warm the milk and water in a small pan and stir in the molasses.

3 Add the molasses mixture to the dry ingredients and mix together using a spoon until it just forms a moist dough. Do not overmix.

ANADAMA BREAD

A traditional bread from Massachusetts, made with molasses, corn meal, wholemeal and unbleached white flour. According to legend, it was created by the husband of a woman called Anna, who had left a corn meal mush and some molasses in the kitchen. On finding only these ingredients for supper her husband mixed them with some flour, water and yeast to make this bread, while muttering "Anna, damn her"!

1 Grease two 1.5 litre/2½ pint/6 cup loaf tins (pans). Heat the butter, molasses and measured water in a pan until the butter has melted. Stir in the corn meal and salt and stir over a low heat until boiling. Cool until lukewarm.

2 In a small bowl, cream the yeast with the lukewarm water, then set aside for 5 minutes.

3 Mix the corn meal mixture and yeast mixture together in a large bowl. Fold in the wholemeal flour and then the unbleached white bread flour to form a sticky dough. Turn out on to a lightly floured surface and knead for 10–15 minutes until the dough is smooth and elastic. Add a little more flour if needed.

4 Place in a lightly oiled bowl, cover with lightly oiled clear film (plastic wrap) and leave in a warm place, for about 1 hour, or until doubled in bulk.

40g/1½ oz/3 tbsp butter
120ml/4fl oz/½ cup molasses
560ml/scant 1 pint/scant 2½ cups water
50g/2oz/½ cup corn meal
10ml/2 tsp salt
25g/1oz fresh yeast
30ml/2 tbsp lukewarm water
275g/10oz/2½ cups wholemeal (whole-wheat) flour
450g/1lb/4 cups unbleached white bread flour

MAKES 2 LOAVES

VARIATION
Use a 7g/¼ oz sachet easy-blend (rapid-rise) dried yeast instead of fresh. Mix it with the wholemeal flour. Add to the corn meal mixture, then add the lukewarm water, which would conventionally be blended with the fresh yeast.

5 Knead the dough lightly on a well floured surface, shape into two loaves and place in the prepared tins. Cover with lightly oiled clear film and leave to rise, in a warm place, for about 35–45 minutes, or until doubled in size and the dough reaches the top of the tins.

6 Meanwhile, preheat the oven to 200°C/400°F/Gas 6. Using a sharp knife, slash the tops of the loaves three or four times. Bake for 15 minutes, then reduce the oven temperature to 180°C/350°F/Gas 4 and bake for a further 35–40 minutes, or until sounding hollow when tapped on the base. Turn out on to a wire rack to cool slightly. Serve warm.

CHALLAH

500g/1¼ lb/5 cups unbleached white bread flour
10ml/2 tsp salt
20g/¾ oz fresh yeast
200ml/7fl oz/scant 1 cup lukewarm water
30ml/2 tbsp caster (superfine) sugar
2 eggs
75g/3oz/6 tbsp butter or margarine, melted

FOR THE GLAZE
1 egg yolk
15ml/1 tbsp water
10ml/2 tsp poppy seeds, for sprinkling

MAKES 1 LARGE LOAF

COOK'S TIP
If wished, divide the dough in half and make two small challah, keeping the plaits quite simple. Decorate with the poppy seeds or leave plain. Reduce the baking time by about 10 minutes.

Challah is an egg-rich, light-textured bread baked for the Jewish Sabbath and to celebrate religious holidays. It is usually braided with three or four strands of dough, but eight strands or more may be used to create especially festive loaves.

3 Knock back (punch down), re-cover and leave to rise again in a warm place for about 1 hour. Knock back, turn out on to a lightly floured surface and knead gently. Divide into four equal pieces. Roll each piece into a rope about 45cm/18in long. Line up next to each other. Pinch the ends together at one end.

4 Starting from the right, lift the first rope over the second and the third rope over the fourth. Take the fourth rope and place it between the first and second ropes. Repeat, starting from the right, and continue until braided.

5 Tuck the ends under and place the loaf on the prepared baking sheet. Cover with lightly oiled clear film and leave to rise in a warm place, for about 30–45 minutes, or until doubled in size. Meanwhile, preheat the oven to 200°C/400°F/Gas 6. Beat the egg yolk and water for the glaze together.

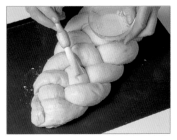

6 Brush the egg glaze gently over the loaf. Sprinkle evenly with the poppy seeds and bake for 35–40 minutes, or until the challah is a deep golden brown. Transfer to a wire rack and leave to cool before slicing.

1 Lightly grease a baking sheet. Sift the flour and salt together into a large bowl and make a well in the centre. Mix the yeast with the water and sugar, add to the centre of the flour with the eggs and melted butter or margarine and gradually mix in the surrounding flour to form a soft dough.

2 Turn out on to a lightly floured surface and knead for 10 minutes until smooth and elastic. Place in a lightly oiled bowl, cover with lightly oiled clear film (plastic wrap) and leave in a warm place, for 1 hour, or until doubled in bulk.

BAGELS

Bagels are eaten in many countries, especially where there is a Jewish community, and are very popular in the USA. They can be made from white, wholemeal or rye flour and finished with a variety of toppings, including caraway, poppy seeds, sesame seeds and onion.

350g/12oz/3 cups unbleached white
bread flour
10ml/2 tsp salt
6g/¼ oz sachet easy-blend
(rapid-rise) dried yeast
5ml/1 tsp malt extract
210ml/7½ fl oz/scant 1 cup
lukewarm water

FOR POACHING
2.5 litres/4 pints/2½ quarts water
15ml/1 tbsp malt extract

FOR THE TOPPING
1 egg white
10ml/2 tsp cold water
30ml/2 tbsp poppy, sesame or
caraway seeds

MAKES 10 BAGELS

5 Meanwhile, preheat the oven to 220°C/425°F/Gas 7. Place the water and malt extract for poaching in a large pan, bring to the boil, then reduce to a simmer. Place the bagels in the water two or three at a time and poach for about 1 minute. They will sink and then rise again when first added to the pan. Using a spatula or large slotted spoon, turn over and cook for 30 seconds. Remove and drain on a dishtowel. Repeat with the rest.

6 Place five bagels on each prepared baking sheet, spacing them well apart. Beat the egg white with the water for the topping, brush the mixture over the top of each bagel and sprinkle with poppy, sesame or caraway seeds. Bake for 20–25 minutes, or until golden brown. Transfer the bagels to a wire rack to cool.

3 Turn out on to a lightly floured surface and knock back (punch down). Knead for 1 minute, then divide into 10 equal pieces. Shape into balls, cover with clear film and leave to rest for 5 minutes.

4 Gently flatten each ball and make a hole through the centre with your thumb. Enlarge the hole slightly by turning your thumb around. Place on a floured tray; re-cover and leave in a warm place, for 10–20 minutes, or until they begin to rise.

1 Grease two baking sheets. Sift the flour and salt together into a large bowl. Stir in the dried yeast. Make a well in the centre. Mix the malt extract and water, add to the centre of the flour and mix to a dough. Knead on a floured surface until elastic.

2 Place in a lightly oiled bowl, cover with lightly oiled clear film (plastic wrap) and leave in a warm place, for about 1 hour, or until doubled in bulk.

WHEAT TORTILLAS

*225g/8oz/2 cups unbleached plain
(all-purpose) flour
5ml/1 tsp salt
4ml/³⁄4 tsp baking powder
40g/1¹⁄2 oz/3 tbsp lard (shortening)
or vegetable fat
150ml/¹⁄4 pint/²⁄3 cup warm water*

MAKES 12 TORTILLAS

Tortillas are the staple flat bread in Mexico, where they are often made from masa harina, a flour milled from corn. These soft wheat tortillas are also popular in the South-western states of the USA.

1 Mix the flour, salt and baking powder in a bowl. Rub in the fat, stir in the water and knead lightly to a soft dough. Cover with clear film (plastic wrap) and leave to rest for 15 minutes. Divide into 12 pieces and shape into balls. Roll out on a floured surface into 15–18cm/ 6–7in rounds. Re-cover to keep moist.

2 Heat a heavy frying pan or griddle, add one tortilla and cook for 1¹⁄2–2 minutes, turning over as soon as the surface starts to bubble. It should stay flexible. Remove from the pan and wrap in a dishtowel to keep warm while cooking the remaining tortillas in the same way.

COOK'S TIPS
• Tortillas are delicious either as an accompaniment or filled with roast chicken or cooked minced (ground) meat, refried beans and/or salad to serve as a snack or light lunch.
• To reheat tortillas, wrap in foil and warm in a moderate oven, 180°C/350°F/Gas 4, for about 5 minutes.

DOUBLE CORN BREAD

*75g/3oz/³⁄4 cup unbleached white
bread flour
150g/6oz/1¹⁄2 cups yellow corn meal
5ml/1 tsp salt
25ml/1¹⁄2 tbsp baking powder
15ml/1 tbsp caster (superfine) sugar
50g/2oz/4 tbsp butter, melted
250ml/8fl oz/1 cup milk
3 eggs
200g/7oz/scant 1¹⁄4 cups canned corn,
drained*

MAKES 1 LARGE LOAF

In the American South, corn bread is made with white corn meal and is fairly flat, while in the North it is thicker and made with yellow corn meal. Whatever the version it's delicious – this recipe combines yellow corn meal with sweetcorn. It is marvellous served warm, cut into wedges and buttered.

1 Preheat the oven to 200°C/400°F/ Gas 6. Grease and base line a 22cm/ 8¹⁄2 in round cake tin (pan). Sift the flour, corn meal, salt and baking powder together into a large bowl. Stir in the sugar and make a well in the centre.

3 Using a wooden spoon, stir the canned corn quickly into the mixture. Pour into the prepared tin and bake for 20–25 minutes, or until a metal skewer inserted into the centre comes out clean.

VARIATIONS
• Bake this corn bread in a 20cm/8in square cake tin (pan) instead of a round one if you wish to cut it into squares or rectangles.
• If you would prefer a more rustic corn bread, replace some or all of the white bread flour with wholemeal (whole-wheat) bread flour.

2 Mix the melted butter, milk and eggs together. Add to the centre of the flour mixture and beat until just combined.

4 Invert the bread on to a wire rack and lift off the lining paper. Cool slightly. Serve warm, cut into wedges.

VIRGINIA SPOON BREAD

450ml/¾ pint/1¾ cups milk
75g/3oz/⅔ cup corn meal
15g/½ oz/1 tbsp butter
75g/3oz/¾ cup grated mature
(sharp) Cheddar cheese
1 garlic clove
3 eggs, separated
75g/3oz/½ cup corn
kernels (optional)
salt and freshly ground black pepper

MAKES 1 LARGE LOAF

VARIATIONS
Add 115g/4oz fried chopped bacon
or 5–10ml/1–2 tsp finely chopped
green chilli for different flavoured
spoon breads.

*Spoon bread is a traditional dish from the southern states of America, which,
according to legend, originated when too much water was added to a corn
bread batter and the baked bread had to be spooned out of the tin. Served hot
from the oven, this ethereally light offering – enhanced with Cheddar cheese
and a hint of garlic – is delicious.*

1 Preheat the oven to 180°C/350°F/
Gas 4. Grease a 1.5 litre/2½ pint/6 cup
soufflé dish.

2 Place the milk in a large heavy pan.
Heat gently, then gradually add the corn
meal, stirring. Add salt and slowly bring
to the boil, stirring all the time. Cook for
5–10 minutes, stirring frequently, until
thick and smooth.

3 Remove from the heat and stir in the
butter, Cheddar cheese, garlic and egg
yolks. Season to taste.

4 In a bowl, whisk the egg whites until
they form soft peaks. Stir one-quarter
into the corn meal mixture and then
gently fold in the remainder. Fold in the
well-drained corn, if using.

5 Spoon the mixture into the prepared
soufflé dish and bake for 45–50
minutes, or until puffed and beginning
to brown. Serve at once.

COOK'S TIPS
• Use a perfectly clean bowl and
whisk for whisking the egg whites and
make sure it is free of grease by
washing and drying thoroughly, then
wiping out with a little lemon juice.
• If any shell drops in with the egg,
scoop it out with another, larger
piece of shell.

NEW ENGLAND FANTANS

*These fantail rolls look stylish and are so versatile that they are equally
suitable for a simple snack, or a gourmet dinner party!*

1 Grease a muffin sheet with 9 × 7.5cm/
3in cups or foil cases. Mix the yeast with
the buttermilk and sugar and then leave
to stand for 15 minutes.

2 In a pan, heat the milk with 40g/1½oz/
3 tbsp of the butter until the butter has
melted. Cool until lukewarm.

3 Sift the flour and salt together into a
large bowl. Add the yeast mixture, milk
mixture and egg and mix to a soft
dough. Turn out on to a lightly floured
surface and knead for 5–8 minutes until
smooth and elastic. Place in a lightly
oiled bowl, cover with oiled clear film
(plastic wrap) and leave in a warm place,
for about 1 hour, until doubled in size.

4 Turn out on to a lightly floured surface,
knock back (punch down) and knead until
smooth and elastic. Roll into an oblong
measuring 45 × 30cm/18 × 12in and about
5mm/¼ in thick. Melt the remaining
butter, brush over the dough and cut it
lengthways into five equal strips. Stack on
top of each other and cut across into nine
equal 5cm/2in strips.

5 Pinch one side of each layered strip
together, then place pinched side down
into a prepared muffin cup or foil case.
Cover with lightly oiled clear film and
leave to rise, in a warm place, for
30–40 minutes, or until the fantans have
almost doubled in size. Meanwhile,
preheat the oven to 200°C/400°F/Gas 6.
Bake for 20 minutes, or until golden.
Turn out on to a wire rack to cool.

15g/½ oz fresh yeast
75ml/5 tbsp buttermilk, at room
temperature
10ml/2 tsp caster (superfine) sugar
75ml/5 tbsp milk
65g/2½ oz/5 tbsp butter
375g/13oz/3¼ cups unbleached white
bread flour
5ml/1 tsp salt
1 egg, lightly beaten

MAKES 9 ROLLS

VARIATION

To make Cinnamon-spiced Fantans,
add 5ml/1 tsp ground cinnamon to the
remaining butter in step 4 before
brushing over the dough strips.
Sprinkle the rolls with a little icing
(confectioners') sugar as soon as they
come out of the oven, then leave to
cool before serving.

MEXICAN "BREAD OF THE DEAD"

3 star anise
90ml/6 tbsp cold water
675g/1½ lb/6 cups unbleached white
bread flour
5ml/1 tsp salt
115g/4oz/½ cup caster (superfine) sugar
25g/1oz fresh yeast
175ml/6fl oz/¾ cup lukewarm water
3 eggs
60ml/4 tbsp orange liqueur
115g/4oz/½ cup butter, melted
grated rind of 1 orange
icing (confectioners') sugar, for dusting

MAKES 1 LARGE LOAF

VARIATION
Top the baked bread with orange icing. Blend 60g/2oz/½ cup icing sugar and 15–30ml/1–2 tbsp orange liqueur. Pour the icing over the bread and let it dribble down the sides.

A celebratory loaf made for All Souls' Day. Even though the name of this bread suggests otherwise, it is actually a very happy day when both Mexicans and Spanish people pay their respects to the souls of their dead. Traditionally the bread is decorated with a dough skull, bones and tears.

1 Grease a 26cm/10½ in fluted round cake tin (pan). Place the star anise in a small pan and add the cold water. Bring to the boil and boil for 3–4 minutes, or until the liquid has reduced to 45ml/3 tbsp. Discard the star anise and leave the liquid to cool.

2 Sift the flour and salt together into a large bowl. Stir in the sugar and make a well in the centre.

3 In a jug (pitcher), dissolve the yeast in the lukewarm water. Pour into the centre of the flour and mix in a little flour, using your fingers, until a smooth, thick batter forms. Sprinkle over a little of the remaining flour, cover with clear film(plastic wrap) and leave the batter in a warm place for 30 minutes, or until the mixture starts to bubble.

4 Beat the eggs, the reserved liquid flavoured with star anise, orange liqueur and melted butter together. Gradually incorporate into the flour mixture to form a smooth dough.

5 Turn out the dough on to a lightly floured surface and gently knead in the orange rind. Knead for 5–6 minutes until smooth and elastic. Shape into a 26cm/10½ in round and place in the prepared tin. Cover with lightly oiled clear film and leave to rise, in a warm place, for 2–3 hours, or until almost at the top of the tin and doubled in bulk.

6 Meanwhile, preheat the oven to 190°C/375°F/Gas 5. Bake the loaf for 45–50 minutes, or until golden. Turn out on to a wire rack to cool. Dust with icing sugar to serve.

WEST INDIAN ROTIS

Caribbean food is based on cuisines from many areas of the world, influenced by a wide range of cultures. It is the Anglo-Indian connection that brought the Indian flatbread called roti to Trinidad in the West Indies.

450g/1lb/4 cups atta or fine wholemeal (whole-wheat) flour
5ml/1 tsp baking powder
5ml/1 tsp salt
300ml/½ pint/1¼ cups water
115–150g/4–5oz/8–10 tbsp clarified butter or ghee

MAKES 8 ROTIS

1 Mix the flour, baking powder and salt together in a large bowl, and make a well in the centre. Gradually mix in the water to make a firm dough.

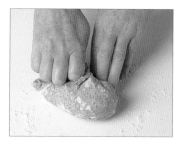

2 Knead on a lightly floured surface until smooth. Place in a lightly oiled bowl; cover with oiled clear film (plastic wrap). Leave to stand for 20 minutes.

3 Divide the dough into eight equal pieces and roll each one on a lightly floured surface into an 18cm/7in round. Brush the surface of each round with a little of the clarified butter or ghee, fold in half and half again. Cover the folded rounds with lightly oiled clear film and leave for 10 minutes.

4 Take one roti and roll out on a lightly floured surface into a round about 20–23cm/8–9in in diameter. Brush both sides with some clarified butter or ghee.

5 Heat a griddle or heavy frying pan, add the roti and cook for about 1 minute. Turn over and cook for 2 minutes, then turn over again and cook for 1 minute. Wrap in a dishtowel to keep warm while cooking the remaining rotis. Serve warm.

BREADS OF INDIA AND THE MIDDLE EAST

Chapatis, rotis and pooris are typical unleavened Indian flatbreads. Chillies, herbs and spices are popular additions. The tradition of baking flatbreads continues into the Middle East, although their specialities – crisp lavash, onion breads and barbari – include yeast. All these breads are perfect for serving with soups or dips. In southern India flour is replaced with rice and lentils or beans, which are fermented to make a pancake-style flatbread.

BHATURAS

*These light, fluffy leavened breads, made with semolina and flour and
flavoured with butter and yogurt, taste delicious served warm.*

15g/¹/₂ oz fresh yeast
5ml/1 tsp sugar
120ml/4fl oz/¹/₂ cup lukewarm water
200g/7oz/1³/₄ cups plain
(all-purpose) flour
50g/2oz/¹/₂ cup semolina
2.5ml/¹/₂ tsp salt
15g/¹/₂ oz/1 tbsp butter or ghee
30ml/2 tbsp natural (plain) yogurt
oil, for frying

MAKES 10 BHATURAS

COOK'S TIP
Ghee can be found in Asian and
Indian supermarkets, but it is easy to
make at home. Melt unsalted (sweet)
butter in a heavy pan over a low heat.
Simmer very gently until the residue
changes to a light golden colour, then
leave to cool. Strain through muslin
(cheesecloth) before using.

1 Mix the yeast with the sugar and
water in a jug (pitcher). Sift the flour
into a large bowl and stir in the semolina
and salt. Rub in the butter or ghee.

2 Add the yeast mixture and yogurt and
mix to a dough. Turn out on to a lightly
floured surface and knead for
10 minutes until smooth and elastic.

3 Place in a lightly oiled bowl, cover
with lightly oiled clear film (plastic
wrap) and leave in a warm place, for
about 1 hour, or until doubled in bulk.

4 Turn out on to a lightly floured surface
and knock back (punch down). Divide
into 10 equal pieces and shape each
one into a ball. Flatten into discs with the
palm of your hand. Roll out on a lightly
floured surface into 13cm/5in rounds.

5 Heat oil to a depth of 1cm/¹/₂ in in a
deep frying pan and slide one bhatura
into the oil. Fry for about 1 minute,
turning over after 30 seconds, then
drain on kitchen paper. Keep warm in a
low oven while frying the remaining
bhaturas. Serve warm.

TANDOORI ROTIS

There are numerous varieties of breads in India, most of them unleavened.
This one, as its name suggests, would normally be baked in a tandoor – a clay
oven which is heated with charcoal or wood. The oven becomes extremely hot,
cooking the bread in minutes.

350g/12oz/3 cups atta *or fine*
wholemeal (whole-wheat) flour
5ml/1 tsp salt
250ml/8fl oz/1 cup water
30–45ml/2–3 tbsp melted ghee or
butter, for brushing

MAKES 6 ROTIS

COOK'S TIP
The rotis are ready when light brown
bubbles appear on the surface.

1 Sift the flour and salt into a bowl. Add the water and mix to a soft dough. Knead on a lightly floured surface for 3–4 minutes until smooth. Place in a lightly oiled bowl, cover with oiled clear film (plastic wrap); leave for 1 hour.

2 Turn out on to a lightly floured surface. Divide the dough into six pieces and shape each into a ball. Press out into a larger round with the palm of your hand, cover with lightly oiled clear film and leave to rest for 10 minutes.

3 Meanwhile, preheat the oven to 230°C/ 450°F/Gas 8. Place three baking sheets in the oven to heat. Roll the rotis into 15cm/6in rounds, place two on each sheet and bake for 8–10 minutes. Brush with ghee or butter and serve warm.

225g/8oz/2 cups unbleached white
bread flour
2.5ml/¹/₂ tsp salt
15g/¹/₂ oz fresh yeast
60ml/4 tbsp lukewarm milk
15ml/1 tbsp vegetable oil
30ml/2 tbsp natural (plain) yogurt
1 egg
30–45ml/2–3 tbsp melted ghee or
butter, for brushing

MAKES 3 NAAN

NAAN

*From the Caucasus through the Punjab region of northwest India and
beyond, all serve these leavened breads. Traditionally cooked in a very hot
clay oven known as a tandoor, naan are usually eaten with dry meat or
vegetable dishes, such as tandoori.*

1 Sift the flour and salt together into a
large bowl. In a smaller bowl, cream the
yeast with the milk. Set aside for
15 minutes.

VARIATIONS

You can flavour naan in numerous
different ways:
• To make spicy naan, add 5ml/1 tsp
each ground coriander and ground
cumin to the flour in step 1. If you
would like the naan to be extra
fiery, add 2.5–5ml/¹/₂–1 tsp hot
chilli powder.
• To make cardamom-flavoured naan,
lightly crush the seeds from
4–5 green cardamom pods and add to
the flour in step 1.
• To make poppy seed naan, brush
the rolled-out naan with a little ghee
and sprinkle with poppy seeds. Press
lightly to make sure that they stick.
• To make peppered naan, brush the
rolled-out naan with a little ghee and
dust generously with coarsely ground
black pepper.
• To make onion-flavoured naan, add
114g/4oz/¹/₂ cup finely chopped or
coarsely grated onion to the dough in
step 2. You may need to reduce the
amount of egg if the onion is very
moist to prevent making the
dough too soft.
• To make wholemeal naan, substitute
wholemeal (whole-wheat) bread flour
for some or all of the white flour.

2 Add the yeast mixture, oil, yogurt and
egg to the flour and mix to a soft dough.

3 Turn out the dough on to a lightly
floured surface and knead for about
10 minutes until smooth and elastic.
Place in a lightly oiled bowl, cover with
lightly oiled clear film (plastic wrap) and
leave to rise, in a warm place, for 45
minutes, or until doubled in bulk.

4 Preheat the oven to its highest setting,
at least 230°C/450°F/Gas 8. Place three
heavy baking sheets in the oven to heat.

5 Turn the dough out on to a lightly floured
surface and knock back (punch down).
Divide into three and shape into balls.

6 Cover two of the balls of dough with
oiled clear film and roll out the third into
a teardrop shape about 25cm/10in long,
13cm/5in wide and with a thickness of
about 5mm–8mm/¹/₄–¹/₃in.

7 Preheat the grill (broiler) to its
highest setting. Meanwhile, place the
naan on the hot baking sheets and bake
for 3–4 minutes, or until puffed up.

8 Remove the naan from the oven
and place under the hot grill for a few
seconds, or until the top of the naan
browns slightly. Wrap the cooked naan
in a dishtowel to keep warm while
rolling out and cooking the remaining
naan. Brush with melted ghee or butter
and serve warm.

COOK'S TIP

To help the naan dough to puff up
and brown, place the baking sheets in
an oven preheated to the maximum
temperature for at least 10 minutes
before baking to ensure that they are
hot. Preheat the grill while the naan
are baking.

RED LENTIL DOSAS

150g/5oz/³/4 cup long grain rice
50g/2oz/¹/4 cup red lentils
250ml/8fl oz/1 cup warm water
5ml/1 tsp salt
2.5ml/¹/2 tsp ground turmeric
2.5ml/¹/2 tsp freshly ground
black pepper
30ml/2 tbsp chopped fresh
coriander (cilantro)
oil, for frying and drizzling

MAKES 6 DOSAS

VARIATION
Add 60ml/4 tbsp grated coconut,
15ml/1 tbsp grated fresh root ginger
and 1 finely chopped chilli to the
batter just before cooking.

Dosas and idlis are the breads of southern India. They are very different from traditional north Indian breads as they are made from lentils or beans and rice rather than flour. Dosas are more like pancakes; they are eaten freshly cooked, often at breakfast time, with chutney.

1 Place the rice and lentils in a bowl, cover with the water and leave to soak for 8 hours.

2 Drain off the water and reserve. Place the rice and lentils in a food processor and blend until smooth. Blend in the reserved water.

3 Scrape into a bowl, cover with clear film (plastic wrap) and leave in a warm place to ferment for about 24 hours.

4 Stir in the salt, turmeric, pepper and coriander. Heat a heavy frying pan over a medium heat for a few minutes until hot. Smear with oil and add about 30–45ml/2–3 tbsp batter.

5 Using the rounded bottom of a soup spoon, gently spread the batter out, using a circular motion, to make a 15cm/6in diameter dosa.

6 Cook for 1¹/2–2 minutes, or until set. Drizzle a little oil over the dosa and around the edges. Turn over and cook for about 1 minute, or until golden. Keep warm in a low oven over simmering water while cooking the remaining dosas. Serve warm.

PARATHAS

These triangular-shaped breads, made from a similar dough to that used for chapatis, are enriched with layers of ghee or butter to create a wonderfully rich, flaky bread.

1 Sift the flours and salt together into a large bowl. Add the oil with sufficient water to mix to a soft dough. Turn out the dough on to a lightly floured surface and knead vigorously for 8–10 minutes until smooth.

2 Place in a lightly oiled bowl and cover with a damp dishtowel. Leave to rest for 30 minutes.

3 Turn out on to a lightly floured surface. Divide the dough into nine equal pieces. Cover eight pieces of dough with oiled clear film (plastic wrap). Shape the remaining piece into a ball and then flatten it. Roll into a 15cm/6in round.

4 Brush with a little of the melted ghee or clarified butter and fold in half. Brush and fold again to form a triangular shape. Repeat with the remaining dough. Stack, layered between clear film, to keep moist. Heat a griddle or heavy frying pan.

115g/4oz/1¼ cups unbleached plain (all-purpose) flour
115g/4oz/1 cup wholemeal (whole-wheat) flour
2.5ml/½ tsp salt
15ml/1 tbsp vegetable oil
120–150ml/4–5fl oz/½–⅔ cup water
90–120ml/3–4fl oz/scant ½ cup melted ghee or clarified butter

MAKES 9 PARATHAS

5 Keeping the shape, roll each piece of dough to a larger triangle, each side measuring 15–18cm/6–7in. Brush with ghee or butter and place on the griddle or in the pan, brushed side down. Cook for about 1 minute, brush again and turn over. Cook for about 1 minute, or until crisp and dotted with brown speckles. Keep warm in a low oven while cooking the remaining parathas. Serve warm.

POORIS

*115g/4oz/1 cup unbleached plain
(all-purpose) flour
115g/4oz/1 cup wholemeal (whole-
wheat) flour
2.5ml/1/2 tsp salt
2.5ml/1/2 tsp chilli powder (optional)
30ml/2 tbsp vegetable oil
100–120ml/31/2–4fl oz/
scant 1/2 cup water
oil, for frying*

MAKES 12 POORIS

*Pooris are small discs of dough that, when fried, puff up into light airy
breads. They will melt in your mouth!*

1 Sift the flours, salt and chilli powder, if using, into a large bowl. Add the vegetable oil then add sufficient water to mix to a dough. Turn out on to a lightly floured surface and knead for 8–10 minutes until smooth.

2 Place in a lightly oiled bowl and cover with lightly oiled clear film (plastic wrap). Leave to rest for 30 minutes.

3 Turn out on to a lightly floured surface. Divide the dough into 12 equal pieces. Keeping the rest of the dough covered, roll one piece into a 13cm/5in round. Repeat with the remaining dough. Stack the pooris, layered between clear film, to keep moist.

4 Heat oil to a depth of 2.5cm/1in in a deep frying pan to 180°C/350°F. Using a fish slice (metal spatula), lift one poori and gently slide it into the oil; it will sink but return to the surface and begin to sizzle. Gently press the poori into the oil. It will puff up. Turn over after a few seconds and cook for 20–30 seconds.

5 Remove the poori from the pan and drain on kitchen paper. Keep warm in a low oven while cooking the remaining pooris. Serve warm.

VARIATION
To make spinach-flavoured pooris, thaw 50g/2oz frozen chopped spinach, drain it well and add it to the dough with a little grated fresh root ginger and 2.5ml/1/2 tsp ground cumin.

CHAPATIS

*175g/6oz/11/2 cups atta or wholemeal
(whole-wheat) flour
2.5ml/1/2 tsp salt
100–120ml/scant 4fl oz/
scant 1/2 cup water
5ml/1 tsp vegetable oil
melted ghee or butter, for brushing
(optional)*

MAKES 6 CHAPATIS

*These chewy, unleavened breads are eaten throughout Northern India. They
are usually served as an accompaniment to spicy dishes.*

2 Knead for 5–6 minutes until smooth. Place in a lightly oiled bowl, cover with a damp dishtowel and leave to rest for 30 minutes. Turn out on to a floured surface. Divide the dough into six equal pieces. Shape each piece into a ball.

4 Heat a griddle or heavy frying pan over a medium heat for a few minutes until hot. Take one chapati, brush off any excess flour, and place on the griddle. Cook for 30–60 seconds, or until the top begins to bubble and white specks appear on the underside.

5 Turn the chapati over using a metal spatula and cook for a further 30 seconds. Remove from the pan and keep warm, layered between a folded dishtowel, while cooking the remaining chapatis. If you like, the chapatis can be brushed lightly with melted ghee or butter immediately after cooking. Serve warm.

COOK'S TIP
Atta or *ata* is a very fine wholemeal flour, which is only found in Indian stores and supermarkets. It is sometimes simply labelled chapati flour. *Atta* can also be used for making rotis and other Indian flatbreads.

1 Sift the flour and salt into a bowl. Add the water and mix to a soft dough. Knead in the oil, then turn out on to a lightly floured surface.

3 Press the dough into a larger round with your palm, then roll into a 13cm/5in round. Stack, layered between clear film (plastic wrap), to keep moist.

MISSI ROTIS

These unleavened breads are a speciality from Punjab in India.
Gram flour, known as besan, is made from chickpeas and is combined here
with the more traditional wheat flour.

115g/4oz/1 cup gram flour
115g/4oz/1 cup wholemeal
(whole-wheat) flour
1 green chilli, seeded and chopped
1/2 onion, finely chopped
15ml/1 tbsp fresh
coriander (cilantro)
2.5ml/1/2 tsp ground turmeric
2.5ml/1/2 tsp salt
15ml/1 tbsp oil or melted butter
120–150ml/4–5fl oz/1/2–2/3 cup
lukewarm water
30–45ml/2–3 tbsp ghee

MAKES 4 ROTIS

VARIATION
Use 1.25–2.5ml/1/4–1/2 tsp chilli
powder in place of the fresh chilli.

1 Chop the coriander and mix with the flours, chilli, onion, turmeric and salt together in a large bowl. Stir in the 15ml/1 tbsp oil or melted butter.

2 Mix in sufficient water to make a pliable soft dough. Turn out the dough on to a lightly floured surface and knead until smooth.

3 Place in a lightly oiled bowl, cover with lightly oiled clear film (plastic wrap) and leave to rest for 1 hour.

4 Turn the dough out on to a lightly floured surface. Divide into four equal pieces and shape into balls. Roll out each ball into a thick round 15–18cm/6–7in in diameter.

5 Heat a griddle or heavy frying pan over a medium heat for a few minutes until hot.

6 Brush both sides of one roti with the ghee. Add it to the griddle or frying pan and cook for about 2 minutes, turning after 1 minute. Brush the cooked roti lightly with melted butter or ghee again, slide it on to a plate and keep warm in a low oven while cooking the remaining rotis in the same way. Serve the rotis while still warm.

LAVASH

*Thin and crispy, this flatbread is universally eaten throughout the Middle
East. It's ideal for serving with soups and appetizers, and can be made in any
size and broken into pieces as desired.*

1 Sift the white and wholemeal flours
and salt together into a large bowl and
make a well in the centre. Mix the yeast
with half the lukewarm water until
creamy, then stir in the remaining water.

2 Add the yeast mixture and yogurt or
milk to the centre of the flour and mix
to a soft dough. Turn out on to a lightly
floured surface and knead for 8–10
minutes until smooth and elastic. Place
in a lightly oiled bowl, cover with lightly
oiled clear film (plastic wrap) and leave in
a warm place, for about 1 hour, or until
doubled in bulk. Knock back (punch
down), re-cover with lightly oiled clear
film and leave to rise for 30 minutes.

3 Turn the dough back out on to a
lightly floured surface. Knock back
gently and divide into 10 equal pieces.
Shape into balls, then flatten into discs
with the palm of your hand. Cover and
leave to rest for 5 minutes. Meanwhile,
preheat the oven to the maximum
temperature – at least 230°C/450°F/
Gas 8. Place three or four baking sheets
in the oven to heat.

4 Roll the dough as thinly as possible,
then lift it over the backs of your hands
and gently stretch and turn the dough.
Let rest in between rolling for a few
minutes if necessary to avoid tearing.

*275g/10oz/2½ cups unbleached white
bread flour
175g/6oz/1½ cups wholemeal
(whole-wheat) flour
5ml/1 tsp salt
15g/½ oz fresh yeast
250ml/8fl oz/1 cup lukewarm water
60ml/4 tbsp natural (plain) yogurt
or milk*

MAKES 10 LAVASH

5 As soon as they are ready, place
four lavash on the baking sheets and
bake for 6–8 minutes, or until starting
to brown. Stack the remaining uncooked
lavash, layered between clear film or
baking parchment, and cover, to keep
moist. Transfer to a wire rack to cool
and cook the remaining lavash.

SYRIAN ONION BREAD

The basic Arab breads of the Levant and Gulf have traditionally been made with a finely ground wholemeal flour similar to chapati flour, but now are being made with white flour as well. This Syrian version has a tasty, aromatic topping.

450g/1lb/4 cups unbleached white bread flour
5ml/1 tsp salt
20g/³⁄₄oz fresh yeast
280ml/9fl oz/scant 1¹⁄₄ cups lukewarm water

FOR THE TOPPING
60ml/4 tbsp finely chopped onion
5ml/1 tsp ground cumin
10ml/2 tsp ground coriander
10ml/2 tsp chopped fresh mint
30ml/2 tbsp olive oil

MAKES 8 BREADS

COOK'S TIP
If you haven't any fresh mint to hand, then add 15ml/1 tbsp dried mint. Use the freeze-dried variety if you can as it has much more flavour.

1 Lightly flour two baking sheets. Sift the flour and salt together into a large bowl and make a well in the centre. Cream the yeast with a little of the water, then mix in the remainder.

2 Add the yeast mixture to the centre of the flour and mix to a firm dough. Turn out on to a lightly floured surface and knead for 8–10 minutes until smooth and elastic.

3 Place in a lightly oiled bowl, cover with lightly oiled clear film (plastic wrap) and leave in a warm place, for about 1 hour, or until doubled in size.

4 Knock back (punch down) the dough and turn out on to a lightly floured surface. Divide into eight equal pieces and roll into 13–15cm/5–6in rounds. Make them slightly concave. Prick all over and space well apart on the baking sheets. Cover with lightly oiled clear film and leave to rise for 15–20 minutes.

5 Meanwhile, preheat the oven to 200°C/400°F/Gas 6. Mix the chopped onion, ground cumin, ground coriander and chopped mint in a bowl. Brush the breads with the olive oil for the topping, sprinkle them evenly with the spicy onion mixture and bake for 15–20 minutes. Serve the onion breads warm.

BARBARI

*These small Iranian flatbreads can be made in a variety of sizes. For a
change, make two large breads and break off pieces to scoop up dips.*

1 Lightly dust two baking sheets with
flour. Sift the flour and salt together into
a bowl and make a well in the centre.

2 Mix the yeast with the water. Pour
into the centre of the flour, sprinkle a
little flour over and leave in a warm
place for 15 minutes. Mix to a dough,
then turn out on to a lightly floured
surface and knead for 8–10 minutes
until smooth and elastic.

3 Place in a lightly oiled bowl, cover
with oiled clear film (plastic wrap) and
leave for 45–60 minutes, or until doubled.

4 Knock back (punch down) the dough
and turn out on to a lightly floured
surface. Divide into six equal pieces and
shape into rectangles. Roll each one out
to about 10 × 5cm/4 × 2in and about 1cm/
½in thick. Space well apart on the baking
sheets, and make four slashes in the tops.

*225g/8oz/2 cups unbleached white
bread flour
5ml/1 tsp salt
15g/½oz fresh yeast
140ml/scant ¼ pint/scant ⅔ cup
lukewarm water
oil, for brushing*

MAKES 6 BARBARI

VARIATION
Sprinkle with sesame or caraway
seeds before baking.

5 Cover the breads with lightly oiled
clear film and leave to rise, in a warm
place, for 20 minutes. Meanwhile,
preheat the oven to 200°C/400°F/Gas 6.
Brush the breads with oil and bake for
12–15 minutes, or until pale golden.
Serve warm.

USING A BREAD MACHINE

Bread machines can help you to create sensational baked goods with minimal effort.

This detailed techniques section explains the bread machine's features and settings.

It also shows you how to utilize traditional bread-making techniques, such as hand-shaping

and glazing, to make more unusual breads. The section concludes with a look at the basic

ingredients used in all loaves, other ingredients that you can add for a special touch,

and the kitchen equipment that you may find useful.

Introducing the Bread Machine

In recent years there has been a huge upsurge in the popularity of home-baked bread. Men and women are coming home from work to the comforting aroma of freshly baked bread once only associated with an idyllic childhood. But making and eating home-baked bread is not only the stuff of dreams. No. The bread that stands cooling in many of our kitchens is real. It has a beautiful golden crust, an even crumb and a delicious flavour. It

BELOW: To many people, a Farmhouse Loaf is the traditional bread they associate with their childhood.

looks and tastes as if aching effort went into its making, but nothing could be further from the truth. Much of today's tastiest bread is made at home with the aid of an easy-to-operate machine, which takes the hard work out of bread making while retaining all the pleasure.

The first automatic domestic bread-maker appeared on the market in Japan in the late 1980s, and since then bread machines have gained popularity all over the world. These excellent appliances have helped to rekindle the pleasure of making home-made bread, by streamlining the process and making it incredibly

simple. All the "home baker" needs to do is to measure a few ingredients accurately, put them into the bread machine pan and push a button or two.

At first it is easy to feel overwhelmed by all the settings on a bread machine. These are there to help you bake a wide range of breads, both sweet and savoury, using different grains and flavourings. In time you'll get to grips with them all, but there's no need to rush. Start by making a simple white loaf and watch while your machine transforms a few ingredients first into a silky, smooth dough and finally into a golden loaf of bread.

No matter what make of machine you have, it is important to focus on the bread, not the machine. Even the best type of machine is only a kitchen aid. The machine will mix, knead and bake beautifully, but only after you have added the necessary ingredients and programmed it. The machine cannot think for itself; it can only carry out your instructions, so it is essential that you add the correct ingredients in the right proportions, in the order specified in the instructions for your particular breadmaking machine, and that you choose the requisite settings. Do not become frustrated if your first attempts do not look one hundred per cent perfect; they will probably still taste wonderful. Get to know your bread machine and be willing to experiment to find the correct ratio of dry ingredients to liquids. There are a number of variables, including the type of ingredients used, the climate and the weather, which can affect the moisture level, regardless of the type of machine you are using.

When you make bread by hand you can feel whether it is too wet or dry, simply by kneading it. However, when you use a bread machine, you need to adopt a different strategy to determine if your bread has the right moistness and, if not, how you may adjust it to produce a perfect loaf.

After the machine has been mixing for a few minutes, take a quick look at the dough – it should be pliable and soft. When the machine stops kneading, the

dough should start to relax back into the shape of the bread machine pan. Once you have made a few loaves of bread you will soon recognize what is an acceptable dough, and you will rapidly progress to making breads with different grains, such as rye, buckwheat or barley, or breads flavoured with vegetables such as potatoes or courgettes. The range of both savoury and sweet breads you ultimately will be able to produce will only be limited by your imagination. Creative thinking can produce some magical results.

The breads in this book are either made entirely by machine or the dough is made in the machine, then shaped by hand and baked in a conventional oven. Teabreads are mixed by hand and baked in the bread machine. Where the loaves are made automatically you will usually find three separate lists of ingredients, each relating to a different size of machine. The small size is recommended for bread machines that are designed for loaves using 350–375g/12–13oz/3–3¼ cups of flour, the medium size for machines that make loaves using 450–500g/1lb– 1lb 2oz/4–4½ cups of flour and the large size for bread machines that are capable of making loaves using up to 675g/1½lb/

BELOW: Mix the dough for Pistolets in the machine and shape by hand.

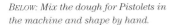

ABOVE: Babka is a traditional Polish Easter cake.

6 cups of flour. Refer to your manufacturer's handbook if you are not sure of the capacity of your machine. If only one set of ingredients is given for a loaf that is to be baked automatically, relate these to the size of your machine to make sure it is suitable for the job.

Where a bread machine is used solely for preparing the dough, which is then shaped by hand and baked conventionally, quantities are not so crucial, and only one set of ingredients is given.

It is very pleasurable to shape your own loaves of bread, and setting the machine to the "dough only" cycle takes all the hard work out of the initial mixing and kneading. The machine provides an ideal climate for the initial rising period, leaving you to bring all your artistry to bear on transforming the dough into rolls, shaped breads or yeast cakes. Once you master the technique, you can make breads from all around the world, including Middle Eastern flatbreads, American Doughnuts, French Brioches, and Jewish Challah – to name but a few. Sourdoughs and breads made from starters are becoming increasingly popular, and there is a whole chapter illustrating how the bread machine can be used to help you make them. It is also possible to make gluten-free breads, but as this is a specialist area, it is best to follow the instructions given by your manufacturer, or contact their helpline, if you wish to do this.

A BAKERY IN YOUR KITCHEN

Bread making is a tremendously satisfying activity. With the help of your machine, delectable breads you will not find at the bakery or supermarket can be made with very little effort. From basic breads containing little more than flour, yeast and water to more elaborate loaves based on stoneground flours milled from a variety of grains – the possibilities are endless. What's more, you know precisely what goes into the bread, and can tailor loaves to your family's own tastes, adding sweet or savoury ingredients.

For everyday use, basic white loaves, possibly enriched with milk or egg, or flavoursome Granary and Light Wholemeal Breads are perfect for breakfast, whether freshly baked or toasted, and these can also be used for sandwiches and quick snacks. These types of bread are the easiest to make in your machine and are the ones you are likely to make over and over again. In time, however, you will probably progress to baking loaves with added ingredients such as potato, to provide, for example, an enhanced lightness to the dough. Leftover rice makes a tasty bread; and another delicious treat is the New England Anadama Bread, made with white, wholemeal (whole-wheat) and corn meal flours flavoured with molasses.

BELOW: Strawberry Teabread

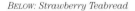

ABOVE: Hazelnut Twist Cake

With the addition of other grains, you can make more complex, hearty loaves. Breads containing oats, rye, wheatgerm and wild rice, perhaps with added whole seeds and grains, can all be baked in the bread machine. These provide extra fibre and are a good source of complex carbohydrates, and are thus a wonderfully healthy option as well as being simply scrumptious. Try Multigrain Bread, a flavour-packed healthy loaf made from Granary (whole-wheat), rye and wholemeal flours with whole oats. Alternatively, experiment with a mixed-seed bread such as Four Seed Bread. The added seeds not only contribute crunchiness and flavour, but are also very nutritious.

The bread machine will happily incorporate such ingredients as caramelized onions, sun-dried tomatoes, chargrilled (bell) peppers, crispy bacon, slivers of ham and other cured meats, fresh chopped herbs and grated or crumbled cheese, to produce mouthwatering vegetable and other savoury breads. Spices and nuts, and dried, semi-dried and fresh fruits can also be added to make classic malted fruit loaves. Try succulent Cranberry and Orange Bread or Mango and Banana Bread. Other sweet breads include crunchy Buckwheat and Walnut Bread and – every chocolate lover's dream – Three Chocolate Bread.

You can also cook succulent teabreads, Honey Cake, Gingerbread, Madeira Cake and Passion Cake, to name but a few, which provides an alternative to using your traditional oven for one cake. Fresh fruits such as strawberries and raspberries plus more exotic offerings can also be used as flavourings for these tea-time treats, as can traditional dried fruits, such as apricots, dates, prunes and raisins.

These breads, mixed, proved and baked automatically, illustrate just a part of the bread machine's capabilities. You

BELOW: A flavoured bread, such as Grainy Mustard and Beer Loaf, is delicious served with cheese and pickle as a simple lunch.

can also use the "dough only" setting to make an endless variety of doughs for hand-shaping. Classic French breads, such as Fougasse, Couronne and baguettes, or rustic breads, such as Pain de Campagne and Pain de Seigle are all possible, as are Italian breads, such as Ciabatta, Pan all'Olio and Breadsticks (grissini). You will be able to experiment in making flat-breads such as Indian Naan, Middle Eastern Lavash and Pitta Breads, or Italian Focaccia, Stromboli, Sfincione or pizzas.

Sweet yeast doughs also work well in a bread machine. Try making Strawberry Chocolate Savarin, Peach Brandy Babas

or Austrian Coffee Cake, as well as strudels and classic festive breads such as Polish Babka (Easter bread) or a Finnish Festive Wreath. You can even impress your friends by baking the traditional Italian Christmas bread, Mocha panettone.

There are endless shaped rolls, buns and pastries to try out, from American Breakfast Pancakes to English Chelsea Buns, and the Chinese-style Chicken Buns, topped with sesame seeds. These breads can be easily shaped by hand after the machine has mixed and proved the dough, and then baked to golden perfection in a conventional oven.

GETTING DOWN TO BASICS

A bread machine is designed to take the hard work out of making bread. Like most kitchen appliances, it is a labour-saving device. It will mix the ingredients and knead the dough for you, and allows the bread to rise and bake at the correct time and temperature.

For most breads, all you will need to do is to measure the ingredients for your chosen bread, put them into the pan in the correct order, close the lid, select a suitable baking programme and opt for light, medium or dark crust. You may also choose to delay the starting time, so that you have freshly baked bread for breakfast or when you return from work. Press the Start button and in a few hours you will have a beautifully baked loaf, the machine having performed the kneading, rising and baking cycles for you.

Bread machines offer a selection of programmes to suit different types of flour and varying levels of sugar and fat. You can explore making a whole variety of raw

BELOW: The three different sizes of bread machine pans that are available. From left to right: large, small and medium.

ABOVE: The shape of the kneading blade varies among different models of bread machine.

doughs for shaping sweet and savoury breads, sourdough breads, mixed-grains, Continental-style breads and many more.

All bread machines work on the same basic principle. Each contains a removable non-stick bread pan, with a handle, into which a kneading blade is fitted. When inserted in the machine, the pan fits on to a central shaft, which rotates the blade. A lid closes over the bread pan so that the ingredients are contained within a controlled environment. The lid includes an air vent and may have a window, which can be useful for checking the progress of your bread. The machine is programmed by using the control panel.

The size and shape of the bread is determined by the shape of the bread pan. There are two shapes currently available; one rectangular and the other square. The rectangular pan produces the more traditional shape, the actual size varying from one manufacturer to another. The square shape is mostly to be found in smaller machines and produces a tall loaf, which is similar to a traditional rectangular loaf that has been stood on its end. The vertical square loaf can be turned on its side for slicing, if preferred, in order to give smaller slices of bread.

The size of the loaf ranges from about 500g/1lb 2oz to 1.4kg/3lb, depending on the machine, with most large machines offering the option of baking smaller loaves as well. One machine will make small, medium and large loaves.

BUYING A BREAD MACHINE

There is plenty of choice when it comes to selecting a bread machine to buy. Give some thought to which features would prove most useful to you, then shop around for the best buy available in your price range. First of all, consider the size

of loaf you would like to bake, which will largely be governed by the number in your family. Remember that a large bread machine will often make smaller loaves but not vice versa.

You will need to consider whether the shape of the bread is important to you, and choose a machine with a square or rectangular bread pan accordingly.

Are you likely to want to make breads with added ingredients? If so, a raisin beep is useful. Does the machine have special-ity flour cycles for whole-wheat loaves? Would this matter to you? Another fea-ture, the dough cycle, adds a great deal of flexibility, as it allows you to make hand-shaped breads. Extra features, such as jam-making and rice-cooking facilities, are very specialized and only you know whether you would find them worth having.

One important consideration is whether the manufacturer offers a well-written manual and an after-sales support system

or help line. If these are available, any problems or queries you might have can be answered quickly, which is particularly useful if this is your first machine.

A bread machine takes up a fair amount of room, so think about where you will store it, and buy one that fits the available space. If the bread machine is to be left on the work surface and aesthetics are important to you, you'll need to buy a machine that will be in keeping with your existing appli-ances. Most bread machines are available in white or black, or in stainless steel.

Jot down the features important to you, listing them in order of your preference. Use a simple

process of elimination to narrow your choice down to two or three machines, which will make the decision easier.

BELOW: A typical bread machine. Although each machine will have a control panel with a different layout, most of the basic features are similar. More specialist cycles vary from machine to machine.

BUILT-IN SAFETY DEVICES

Most machines include a power fail-ure override mode which can prove to be extremely useful. If the machine is inadvertently unplugged or there is a brief power cut the programme will continue as soon as the power is restored. The maximum time allowed for loss of power varies from 10 to 30 minutes. Check the bread when the power comes back on; depending on what stage the programme had reached at the time of the power cut, the rising or baking time of the loaf may have been affected.

An over-load protection is fitted to some models. This will cut in if the kneading blade is restricted by hard dough and will stop the motor to pro-tect it. It will automatically re-start after about 30 minutes, but it is important to rectify the problem dough first. Either start again or cut the dough into small pieces and return it to the bread pan with a little more liquid to soften the dough.

HOW TO USE YOUR BREAD MACHINE

The instructions that follow will help you to achieve a perfect loaf the first time you use your bread machine. The guidelines are general, that is they are applicable to any bread machine, and should be read in conjunction with the handbook provided for your specific machine. Make sure you use fresh, top quality ingredients; you can't expect good results with out-of-date flour or yeast.

1 Stand the bread machine on a firm, level, heat-resistant surface. Place away from any heat source, such as a stove or direct sunlight, and also in a draught-free area, as these factors can affect the temperature inside the machine. Do not plug the bread machine into the power socket at this stage. Open the lid. Remove the bread pan by holding both sides of the handle and pulling upwards or twisting slightly, depending on the design of your particular model.

2 Make sure the kneading blade and shaft are free of any breadcrumbs left behind when the machine was last used. Fit the kneading blade on the shaft in the base of the bread pan. The blade will only fit in one position, as the hole in the blade and the outside of the shaft are D-shaped.

3 Pour the water, milk and/or other liquids into the bread pan, unless the instructions for your particular machine require you to add the dry ingredients first. If so, reverse the order in which you add the liquid and dry ingredients, putting the yeast in the bread pan first.

4 Sprinkle over the flour, ensuring that it covers the liquid completely. Add any other dry ingredients specified in the recipe, such as dried milk powder. Add the salt, sugar or honey and butter or oil, placing them in separate corners so they do not come into contact with each other.

SPECIAL FEATURES

Extra programmes can be found on more expensive machines. These include cooking jam or rice and making pasta dough. While these facilities would not be the main reason for buying a bread machine they can be useful extras. For instance, jam-making couldn't be easier: you simply add equal quantities of fresh fruit and sugar to the bread machine pan, set the jam programme and, when the cycle ends, you will have jam ready to pour into clean sterilized jars.

EASY MEASURING

If you have a set of electronic scales with an add and weigh facility, then accurate measuring of ingredients is very easy. Stand the bread pan on the scale, pour in the liquid, then set the display to zero. Add the dry ingredients directly to the pan, each time zeroing the display. Finally, add the fat, salt, sweetener and yeast and place the bread pan in your machine.

5 Make a small indent in the centre of the flour (but not down as far as the liquid) with the tip of your finger and add the yeast. If your indent reached the liquid below the dry ingredients, then the yeast would become wet and would be activated too quickly. Wipe away any spillages from the outside of the bread pan.

6 Place the pan inside the machine, fitting it firmly in place. Depending on the model of your machine, the pan may have a designated front and back, or clips on the outer edge which need to engage in the machine to hold the bread pan in position. Fold the handle down and close the lid. Plug into the socket and switch on the power.

7 Select the programme you require, including crust colour and loaf size, if available. Press Start. The kneading process will begin, unless your machine has a "rest" period to settle the temperature first.

8 Towards the end of the kneading process the machine will beep to alert you to add any additional ingredients, such as dried fruit, if wished. Open the lid, add the extra ingredients, and close the lid again.

9 At the end of the cycle, the machine will beep once more to let you know that the dough is ready or the bread is cooked. Press Stop. Open the lid of the machine. If you are removing baked bread, remember to use oven gloves to lift out the bread pan, as it will be extremely hot. Avoid leaning over and looking into the machine when you open the lid as the hot air escaping from the machine could cause you discomfort.

BELOW: A basic white bread is an excellent choice for the novice bread maker. If you follow these instructions and weigh the ingredients carefully, you are sure to achieve a delicious loaf of bread. Once you have gained confidence, experiment with the recipe, by adding other ingredients or changing the crust colour.

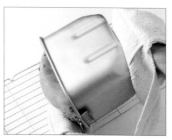

10 Still using oven gloves, turn the pan upside down and shake it several times to release the bread. If necessary, tap the base of the pan on a heatproof board.

11 If the kneading blade for your bread machine is not of the fixed type, and comes out inside the bread, use a heat-resistant utensil to remove it, such as a wooden spatula. It will come out easily.

12 Place the bread on a wire rack to cool. Unplug the bread machine and leave to cool before using it again. A machine which is too hot will not make a successful loaf, and many will not operate if they are too hot for this reason. Refer to the manufacturer's manual for guidance. Wash the pan and kneading blade and wipe down the machine. All parts of the machine must be cool and dry before you store it.

BASIC CONTROLS

It will take you a little while and some practice to become familiar with and confident about using your new bread machine. Most manufacturers now produce excellent manuals, which are supplied with their machines. The manual is a good place to start, and should also be able to help you if you come up against a problem. Programmes obviously differ slightly from machine to machine, but an overview will give you a general idea of what is involved.

It is important to understand the function of each control on your bread machine before starting to make a loaf of bread. Each feature may vary slightly between different machines, but they all work in a basically similar manner.

START AND STOP BUTTONS

The Start button initiates the whole process. Press it after you have placed all the ingredients required for the bread-making procedure in the bread pan and after you have selected all the required settings, such as loaf type, size, crust colour and delay timer.

The Stop button may actually be the same control or a separate one. Press it to stop the programme, either during the programme, if you need to override it, or at the end to turn off the machine. This cancels the "keep warm" cycle at the end of baking.

TIME DISPLAY AND STATUS INDICATOR

A window displays the time remaining until the end of the programme selected. In some machines the selected programme is also shown. Some models use this same window or a separate set of lights to indicate what is happening inside the machine. It gives information on whether the machine is on time delay, kneading, resting, rising, baking or warming.

PROGRAMME INDICATORS OR MENU

Each bread machine has a number of programmes for different types of bread. Some models have more than others. This function allows you to choose the appropriate programme for your recipe and indicates which one you have selected. These programmes are discussed in more detail later.

PRE-HEAT CYCLE

Some machines start all programmes with a warming phase, either prior to mixing or during the kneading phase. This feature can prove useful on colder days or when you are using larger quantities of ingredients, such as milk, straight from the refrigerator, as you do not have to wait for them to come to room temperature before making the bread.

DELAY TIMER

This button allows you to pre-set the bread machine to switch on automatically at a specified time. So, for example, you can have freshly baked bread for breakfast or when you return from work. The timer should not be used for dough that contains perishable ingredients such as fresh dairy products or meats, which deteriorate in a warm environment.

CRUST COLOUR CONTROL

The majority of bread machines have a default medium crust setting. If, however, you prefer a paler crust or the appearance of a high-bake loaf, most machines will give you the option of a lighter or darker crust. Breads high in sugar, or that contain eggs or cheese, may colour too much on a medium setting, so a lighter option may be preferable for these.

WARMING INDICATOR

When the bread has finished baking, it is best to remove it from the machine immediately. If for any reason this is not possible, the warming facility will switch on as soon as the bread is baked, to help prevent condensation of the steam, which otherwise would result in a soggy loaf. Most machines continue in this mode for an hour, some giving an audible reminder every few minutes to remove the bread.

LEFT: French Bread can be baked in the machine on a French bread setting, or the dough can be removed to make the traditional shape by hand.

REMINDER LIGHTS

A few models are fitted with a set of lights which change colour to serve as your reminder that certain essential steps have been followed. This helps to ensure that the kneading blade is fitted, and that basic ingredients such as liquid, flour and yeast have been placed in the bread pan.

LOAF SIZE

On larger bread machines you may have the option of making up to three different sizes of loaf. The actual sizes vary between individual machines, but approximate to small, medium and large loaves of around 450g/1lb, 675g/1½lb and 900g/2lb respectively. However, this control in some machines is for visual indication only and does not alter the baking time or cycle. Check the manufacturer's instructions.

BAKING PROGRAMMES

All machines have a selection of programmes to help ensure you produce the perfect loaf of bread. The lengths of kneading, rising and baking times are varied to suit the different flours and to determine the texture of the finished loaf.

BASIC OR NORMAL

This mode is the most commonly used programme, ideal for white loaves and mixed grain loaves where white bread flour is the main ingredient.

RAPID

This cycle reduces the time to make a standard loaf of bread by about 1 hour and is handy when speed is the main criterion. The finished loaf may not rise as much as one made on the basic programme and may therefore be a little more dense.

WHOLE WHEAT

This is a longer cycle than the basic one, to allow time for the slower rising action of doughs containing a high percentage of strong wholemeal (whole-wheat) flour. Some machines also have a multigrain mode for breads made with cereals and grains such as Granary (whole-wheat) and

ABOVE: Sun-dried tomatoes can be added to the dough at the raisin beep to make deliciously flavoured bread.

rye, although it is possible to make satisfactory breads using either this or the basic mode, depending on the percentages of the flours.

FRENCH

This programme is best suited for low-fat and low-sugar breads, and it produces loaves with an open texture and crispier crust. More time within the cycle is devoted to rising, and in some bread machines the loaf is baked at a slightly higher temperature.

SWEET BREAD

A few bread machines offer this feature in addition to crust colour control. It is useful if you intend to bake breads with a high fat or sugar content which tend to colour too much.

CAKE

Again, this is a feature offered on a few machines. Some will mix a quick nonyeast teabread-type cake and then bake it; others will mix yeast-raised cakes. If you do not have this facility, teabreads and non-yeast cakes can easily be mixed in a bowl and cooked in the bread pan on a "bake only" cycle.

BAKE

This setting allows you to use the bread machine as an oven, either to bake cakes and ready-prepared dough from the supermarket or to extend the standard baking time if you prefer your bread to be particularly well done.

SANDWICH

This facility, which enables you to bake a loaf with a soft crust that is particularly suitable for sandwich slices, is available on one or two models only.

RAISIN BEEP

Additional ingredients can be added midcycle on most programmes. The machine gives an audible signal – usually a beep – and some machines pause late in the kneading phase so that ingredients such as fruit and nuts can be added. This late addition reduces the risk of them being crushed during the kneading phase.

If your machine does not have this facility, you can set a kitchen timer to ring 5 minutes before the end of the kneading cycle and add the extra ingredients then.

DOUGH PROGRAMMES

Most machines include a dough programme: some models have dough programmes with extra features.

DOUGH

This programme allows you to make dough without machine-baking it, which is essential for all hand-shaped breads. The machine mixes, kneads and proves the dough, ready for shaping, final proving and baking in a conventional oven. If you wish to make different shaped loaves or rolls, buns and pastries, you will find this facility invaluable.

OTHER DOUGH PROGRAMMES

Some machines include cycles for making different types of dough, such as a rapid dough mode for pizzas and Focaccia or a longer mode for wholemeal dough and bagel dough. Some "dough only" cycles also include the raisin beep facility.

BAKING, COOLING AND STORING

A bread machine should always bake a perfect loaf of bread, but it is important to remember that it is just a machine and cannot think for itself. It is essential that you measure the ingredients carefully and add them to the bread pan in the order specified by the manufacturer of your machine. Ingredients should be at room temperature, so take them out of the refrigerator in good time, unless your machine has a pre-heat cycle.

Check the dough during the kneading cycles; if your machine does not have a window, open the lid and look into the bread pan. The dough should be slightly tacky to the touch. If it is very soft add a little more flour; if the dough feels very firm and dry add a little more liquid. It is also worth checking the dough towards the end of the rising period. On particularly warm days your bread may rise too high. If this happens it may rise over the bread pan and begin to travel down the outside during the first few minutes of baking. If your bread looks ready for baking before the baking cycle is due to begin, you have two options. You can either override and cancel the programme, then re-programme using a "bake only" cycle, or you can try pricking the top of the loaf with a cocktail stick to deflate it slightly and let the programme continue.

Different machines will give different browning levels using the same recipe. Check when you try a new recipe and make a note to select a lighter or darker setting next time if necessary.

BELOW: Use a cocktail stick to prick dough that has risen too high.

REMOVING THE BREAD FROM THE PAN

Once the bread is baked it is best removed from the bread pan immediately. Turn the bread pan upside down, holding it with oven gloves or a thick protective cloth – it will be very hot – and shake it several times to release the bread. If removing the bread is difficult, rap the corner of the bread pan on a wooden board several times or try turning the base of the shaft underneath the base of the bread pan. Don't try to free the bread by using a knife or similar metal object, or you will scratch the non-stick coating.

If the kneading blade remains inside the loaf, you should use a heat-resistant plastic or wooden implement to prise it out. The metal blade and the bread will be too hot to use your fingers.

ABOVE: Multigrain Bread is made with honey which, like other sweeteners, acts as a preservative. The loaf should stay moist for longer.

BELOW: Use a serrated bread knife when slicing bread so that you do not damage the texture of the crumb.

COOLING
Place the bread on a wire rack to allow the steam to escape and leave it for at least 30 minutes before slicing. Always slice bread using a serrated knife to avoid damaging the crumb structure.

STORING
Cool the bread, then wrap it in foil or place it in a plastic bag and seal it, to preserve the freshness. If your bread has a crisp crust, this will soften on storage, so until it is sliced it is best left uncovered. After cutting, put the loaf in a large paper bag, but try to use it fairly quickly, as bread starts to dry out as soon as it is cut. Breads containing eggs tend to dry out even more quickly, while those made with honey or added fats stay moist for longer.

BELOW: Parker House Rolls can be frozen after baking, as soon as they are cool. They taste delicious warm, so refresh them in the oven just before serving.

ABOVE: If you are freezing bread to be used for toasting, slice the loaf first.

Ideally, freshly baked bread should be consumed within 2–3 days. Avoid storing bread in the refrigerator as this causes it to go stale more quickly.

Freeze cooked breads if you need to keep them for longer. Place the loaf or rolls in a freezer bag, seal and freeze for up to 3 months. If you intend to use the bread for toast or sandwiches, it is easier

ABOVE: Store bread with a crispy crust in a large paper bag.

to slice it before freezing, so you can remove only the number of slices you need. Thaw the bread at room temperature, still in its freezer bag.

With some loaves, however, freezing may not be a sensible option. For example, very crusty bread, such as French Couronne, tends to come apart after it has been frozen and thawed.

STORING BREAD DOUGHS
If it is not convenient to bake bread dough immediately you can store it in an oiled bowl covered with clear film (plastic wrap), or seal it in a plastic bag. Dough can be stored in the refrigerator for up to 2 days if it contains butter, milk or eggs and up to 4 days if no perishable ingredients are included.

Keep an eye on the dough and knock it back (punch it down) occasionally. When you are ready to use the dough, bring it back to room temperature, then shape, prove and bake it in the normal way.

You can make dough in your machine, shape it, then keep it in the refrigerator overnight, ready for baking conventionally next morning for breakfast. Cover with oiled clear film as usual.

Bread dough can be frozen in a freezer-proof bag for up to 1 month. When you are ready to use it, thaw the dough overnight in the refrigerator or at room temperature for 2–3 hours. Once the dough has thawed, place it in a warm place to rise, but bear in mind that it will take longer to rise than freshly made dough.

ABOVE: Store dough in the refrigerator in an oiled bowl covered in clear film or in a plastic bag.

ABOVE: Prepare rolls the night before and store in the refrigerator, ready to bake the following morning.

HAND-SHAPED LOAVES

One of the most useful features a bread machine can have is the dough setting. Use this, and the machine will automatically mix the ingredients, and will then knead and rest the dough before providing the ideal conditions for it to rise for the first time. The whole cycle, from mixing through to rising, takes around 1¾ hours, but remember it will vary slightly between machines.

KNOCKING BACK

1 At the end of the cycle, the dough will have almost doubled in bulk and will be ready for shaping. Remove the bread pan from the machine.

2 Lightly flour a work surface. Gently remove the dough from the bread pan and place it on the floured surface. Knock back (punch down) or deflate the dough to relieve the tension in the gluten and expel some of the carbon dioxide.

3 Knead the dough lightly for 1–2 minutes; shape into a tight ball. At this stage, a recipe may suggest you cover the dough with oiled clear film (plastic wrap) or an upturned bowl and leave it to rest for a few minutes. This allows the gluten to relax so dough will be easier to handle.

SHAPING

Techniques to shape dough vary, depending on the finished form of the bread you wish to make. The following steps illustrate how to form basic bread, roll and yeast pastry shapes.

BAGUETTE

1 To shape a baguette or French stick, flatten the dough into a rectangle about 2.5cm/1in thick, either using the palms of your hands or a rolling pin.

2 From one long side fold one-third of the dough down and then fold over the remaining third of dough and press gently to secure. Repeat twice more, resting the dough in between folds to avoid tearing.

3 Gently stretch the dough and roll it backwards and forwards with your hands to make a breadstick of even thickness and the required length.

4 Place the baguette dough between a folded floured dishtowel, or in a banneton, and leave in a warm place to prove. The dishtowel or banneton will help the baguette to keep the correct shape as it rises.

BLOOMER

1 Roll the dough out to a rectangle 2.5cm/1in thick. Roll up from one long side and place it, seam side up, on a floured baking sheet. Cover and leave to rest for 15 minutes.

2 Turn the loaf over and place on another floured baking sheet. Using your fingertips, tuck the sides and ends of the dough under. Cover; leave to finish rising.

TIN LOAF

Roll the dough out to a rectangle the length of the bread tin (pan) and three times as wide. Fold the dough widthways, bringing the top third down and the bottom third up. Press the dough down well, turn it over and place it in the tin.

COTTAGE LOAF

1 To shape a cottage loaf, divide the dough into two pieces, approximately one-third and two-thirds in size. Shape each piece of dough into a plump round ball and place on lightly floured baking sheets. Cover with inverted bowls and leave to rise for 30 minutes, or until 50 per cent larger.

2 Flatten the top of the large loaf. Using a sharp knife, cut a cross about 4cm/ 1½in across in the centre. Brush the area lightly with water and place the small round on top.

3 Using one or two fingers or the floured handle of a wooden spoon, press the centre of the top round, penetrating into the middle of the dough beneath.

TWIST

1 To shape bread for a twist, divide the dough into two equal pieces. Using the palms of your hands, roll each piece of dough on a lightly floured surface into a long rope, about 4–5cm/1½–2in thick. Make both ropes the same length.

2 Place the two ropes side by side. Starting from the centre, twist one rope over the other. Continue in the same way until you reach the end, then pinch the ends together and tuck the join underneath. Turn the dough around and repeat the process with the other end, twisting the dough in the same direction as the first.

BREADSTICK

To shape a breadstick, roll the dough to a rectangle about 1cm/½in thick, and cut out strips that are about 7.5cm/3in long and 2cm/¾in wide. Using the palm of your hand, gently roll each strip into a long thin rope.

It may help to lift each rope and pull it very gently to stretch it. If you are still finding it difficult to stretch the dough, leave it to rest for a few minutes and then try again.

COURONNE

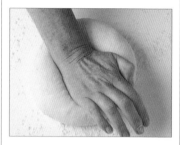

1 Shape the dough into a ball. Using the heal of your hand make a hole in the centre. Gradually enlarge the centre, turning the dough to make a circle, with a 13cm–15cm/5–6in cavity.

2 Place on a lightly oiled baking sheet. Put a small, lightly oiled bowl in the centre of the ring to prevent the dough from filling in the centre during rising.

SCROLL

Roll out the dough using the palms of your hands, until it forms a rope, about 25cm/10in long, with tapered ends. Form into a loose "S" shape, then curl the ends in to make a scroll. Leave a small space to allow for the final proving.

CROISSANT

1 To shape a croissant, roll out the dough on a lightly floured surface and then cut it into strips that are about 15cm/6in wide.

2 Cut each strip along its length into triangles with 15cm/6in bases and 18cm/7in sides.

3 Place with the pointed end towards you and the 15cm/6in base at the top; gently pull each corner of the base to stretch it slightly.

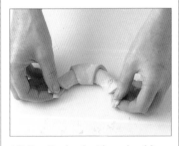

4 Roll up the dough with one hand from the base while pulling, finishing with the dough point underneath. Finally, curve the corners around in the direction of the pointed end to make the curved croissant shape.

BRAIDED ROLL

1 To shape a braided roll, place the dough on a lightly floured surface and roll out. Divide the dough into balls, the number depending on the amount of dough and how many rolls you would like to make.

2 Divide each ball of dough into three equal pieces. Using your hands, roll into long, thin ropes of equal length and place them side by side.

3 Pinch one of the ends together and plait the pieces of dough. Finally, pinch the remaining ends together and then tuck the join under.

FILLED BRAID

1 Place the dough for the braid on a lightly floured surface. Roll out and shape into a rectangle. Using a sharp knife, make diagonal cuts down each of the long sides of the dough, about 2cm/¾in wide. Place the filling in the centre of the uncut strip.

2 Fold in the end strip of dough, then fold over alternate strips of dough to form a braid over the filling. Tuck in the final end to seal the braid.

PROVING

After the dough has been shaped, it will need to be left to rise again. This is sometimes referred to as proving the dough. Most doughs are left in a warm place until they just about double in bulk. How long this takes will vary – depending on the ambient temperature and richness of the dough – but somewhere between 30 and 60 minutes is usual.

Avoid leaving dough to rise for too long (over-proving) or it may collapse in the oven or when it is slashed before baking. Equally, you need to leave it to rise sufficiently, or the finished loaf will be heavy.

To test if the dough is ready to bake, press it lightly with your fingertip; it should feel springy, not firm. The indentation made by your finger should slowly fill and spring back.

ABOVE: A dough that has been shaped and placed in a bread tin to rise. The unproved dough should reach just over halfway up the tin.

ABOVE: Leave the dough in a warm, draught-free place to rise. This should take between 30 and 60 minutes. Once risen, the dough will have almost doubled in bulk.

SLASHING

Slashing bread dough before baking serves a useful purpose as well as adding a decorative finish, as found on the tops of traditional loaf shapes such as bloomers and French sticks. When the dough goes into the oven it has one final rise, known as "oven spring", so the cuts or slashes allow the bread to expand without tearing or cracking the sides.

The earlier you slash the dough the wider the splits will be. Depth is important, too: the deeper the slashes the more the bread will open during baking. Most recipes suggest slashing just before glazing and baking. If you think a bread has slightly over-proved keep the slashes fairly shallow and gentle to avoid the possibility of the dough collapsing.

Use a sharp knife or scalpel blade to make a clean cut. Move smoothly and swiftly to avoid tearing the dough. Scissors can also be used to make an easy decorative finish to rolls or breads.

SLASHING A SPLIT TIN OR FARMHOUSE LOAF

A long slash, about 1cm/½in deep, can be made along the top of the dough just before baking. You can use this slashing procedure for both machine and hand-shaped loaves. Using a very sharp knife, plunge into one end of the dough and pull the blade smoothly along the entire length, but make sure you do not drag the dough.

If flouring the top of the loaf, sprinkle with flour before slashing.

SLASHING A BAGUETTE

To slash a baguette, cut long slashes of equal length and depth four or five times along its length. A razor-sharp blade is the best tool for slashing breads. Used with care, a scalpel is perfectly safe and has the advantage that the blades can be changed to ensure you always have a sharp edge.

USING SCISSORS TO SLASH ROLLS

Rolls can be given quick and interesting finishes using a pair of sharp-pointed scissors. You could experiment with all sorts of ideas. Try the following to start you off.

• Just before baking cut across the top of the dough first in one direction then the other to make a cross.
• Make six horizontal or vertical cuts equally spaced around the sides of the rolls. Leave for 5 minutes before baking.
• Cut through the rolls in four or five places from the edge almost to the centre, just before baking.

ABOVE: Top rolls: making a cross; middle rolls: horizontal cuts around the side; bottom rolls: cuts from the edge almost to the centre.

BAKING BREAD WITH A CRISP CRUST

For a crisper crust, it is necessary to introduce steam into the oven. The moisture initially softens the dough, so that it can rise, resulting in a crispier crust. Moisture also improves the crust colour by encouraging caramelization of the natural sugars in the dough. Standing the loaf on a baking stone or unglazed terracotta tiles also helps to produce a crisp crust, the effect being similar to when breads are cooked in a clay or brick oven. The porous tiles or stone hold heat and draw moisture from the bread base while it is baking.

1 About 30 minutes before you intend to bake, place the baking stone on the bottom shelf of the oven, then preheat the oven. Alternatively line the oven shelf with unglazed terracotta tiles, leaving air space all around to allow for the free circulation of the hot air.

2 When ready to bake, using a peel (baker's shovel), place the bread directly on the tiles or baking stone.

3 Using a water spray bottle, mist the oven walls two or three times during the first 5–10 minutes of baking. Open the oven door as little as possible, spray the oven walls and quickly close the door to avoid unnecessary heat loss. Remember not to spray the oven light, fan or heating elements.

GLAZES

Both machine-baked breads and hand-shaped loaves benefit from a glaze to give that final finishing touch. Glazes may be used before baking, or during the early stages of baking to give a more golden crust or to change the texture of the crust. This is particularly noticeable with hand-shaped breads but good results may also be obtained with machine-baked loaves. Glazes may also be applied after baking to give flavour and a glossy finish. Another important role for glazes is to act as an adhesive, to help any topping applied to the loaf stick to the surface of the dough.

For machine-baked breads, the glaze should either be brushed on to the loaf just before the baking cycle commences, or within 10 minutes of the start of the baking cycle. Apply the glaze quickly, so there is minimal heat loss while the bread machine lid is open. Avoid brushing the edges of the loaf with a sticky glaze as this might make the bread stick to the pan.

Glazes using egg, milk and salted water can also be brushed over freshly cooked loaves. Brush the glaze over as soon as the baking cycle finishes, then leave the bread inside the machine for 3–4 minutes, to allow the glaze to dry to a shine. Then remove the loaf from the machine and pan in the usual way. This method is useful if you want to sprinkle over a topping.

For hand-shaped loaves, you can brush with glaze before or after baking, and some recipes, such as Parker House Rolls will suggest that you do both.

GLAZES USED BEFORE OR DURING BAKING

For a crust with an attractive glossy shine, apply a glaze before or during baking.

MILK

Brush on loaves, such as potato breads, where a softer golden crust is desired. Milk is also used for bridge rolls, buns (such as teacakes) and flatbreads where a soft crust is desirable. It can also be used on baps and soft morning rolls before dusting with flour.

OLIVE OIL

This is mainly used with Continental-style breads, such as Focaccia, Stromboli and Fougasse. It adds flavour and a shiny finish; and the darker the oil the fuller the flavour, so use extra virgin olive oil for a really deep taste. Olive oil can be used before and/or after baking.

BELOW: French Fougasse is brushed with olive oil just before baking.

BUTTER

Rolls and buns are brushed with melted butter before baking to add colour, while also keeping the dough soft. American Parker House Rolls are brushed before and after baking, while Bubble Corn Bread is drizzled with melted butter before being baked. Butter adds a rich flavour to the breads glazed with it.

SALTED WATER

Mix 10ml/2 tsp salt with 30ml/2 tbsp water and brush over the dough immediately before baking. This gives a crisp baked crust with a slight sheen.

EGG WHITE

Use 1 egg white mixed with 15ml/1 tbsp water for a lighter golden, slightly shiny crust. This is often a better alternative to egg yolk for savoury breads.

EGG YOLK

Mix 1 egg yolk with 15ml/1 tbsp milk or water. This classic glaze, also known as egg wash, is used to give a very golden, shiny crust. For sweet buns, breads and yeast cakes add 15ml/1 tbsp caster (superfine) sugar, for extra colour and flavour.

GLAZES ADDED AFTER BAKING

Some glazes are used after baking, often on sweet breads, cakes and pastries. These glazes generally give a glossy and/or sticky finish, and also help to keep the bread or cake moist. They are suited to both machine and hand-shaped breads.

BUTTER

Breads such as Italian Panettone and stollen are brushed with melted butter after baking to soften the crust. Clarified butter is also sometimes used as a glaze to soften flatbreads such as Naan.

HONEY, MALT, MOLASSES AND GOLDEN SYRUP

Liquid sweeteners can be warmed and brushed over breads, rolls, teabreads and cakes to give a soft, sweet, sticky crust. Honey is a traditional glaze and provides a lovely flavour, for example. Both malt and molasses have quite a strong flavour, so use these sparingly, matching them to compatible breads such as fruit loaves and cakes. Or you could mix them with a milder-flavoured liquid sweetener, such as golden (light corn) syrup, to reduce their impact slightly.

SUGAR GLAZE

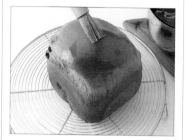

Dissolve 30–45ml/2–3 tbsp granulated sugar in the same amount of milk or water. Bring to the boil then simmer for 1–2 minutes, until syrupy. Brush over fruit loaves or buns for a glossy sheen. For extra flavour, use rose water.

SYRUPS

Yeast cakes, such as Savarin, are often drizzled with sugar syrup, flavoured with liqueurs, spirits or lemon juice. The syrup moistens the bread, while adding a decorative topping at the same time.

PRESERVES

Jam or marmalade can be melted with a little liquid. Choose water, liqueur, spirits (such as rum or brandy) or fruit juice, depending on the bread to be glazed. The liquid thins the preserve and adds flavour. It can be brushed over freshly baked warm teabreads, Danish Pastries and sweet breads to a give a glossy, sticky finish. Dried fruit and nuts can then be sprinkled on top.

Select a flavoured jam to complement your bread or teacake. If in doubt, use apricot jam.

ICING SUGAR GLAZE

Mix 30–45ml/2–3 tbsp icing (confectioners') sugar with 15ml/1 tbsp fruit juice, milk, single (light) cream (flavoured with natural vanilla essence/extract) or water and drizzle or brush over warm sweet breads, cakes and pastries. You can also add a pinch of spice to the icing sugar to bring out the flavour of the loaf.

LEFT: The glossy top to Hot Cross Buns is achieved by glazing after baking with a mixture of milk and sugar.

274

TOPPINGS

In addition to glazes, extra ingredients can be sprinkled over breads to give the finished loaf further interest. Toppings can alter the appearance, flavour and texture of the bread, so are an important part of any recipe. They also allow you to add your own individual stamp to a bread by using a topping of your own invention.

MACHINE-BAKED BREADS
A topping can be added at various stages: at the beginning of the baking cycle, about 10 minutes after baking begins, or immediately after baking while the bread is still

hot. If you choose to add the topping at the beginning of baking, only open the lid for the shortest possible time, so heat loss is limited to the minimum. Before you add a topping, brush the bread with a glaze. This will ensure that the topping sticks to the loaf. Most machine breads are brushed with an egg, milk or water glaze.

If applying a topping to a bread after baking, remove the bread pan carefully from the machine and close the lid to retain the heat. Using oven gloves, quickly loosen the bread from the pan, then put it back in the pan again (this will make the

ABOVE: Flaked almonds have been sprinkled over the top of this Raspberry and Almond Teabread, giving a broad hint of its delicious flavour and adding extra crunch.

final removal easier) then brush the loaf with the glaze and sprinkle over the chosen topping. Return the bread in the pan to the bread machine for 3–4 minutes, which allows the glaze to bake on and secure the topping. With this method, the chosen topping will not cook and brown in the same way it would were it added at the beginning of baking.

When using grain as a topping, the general rule is to match it to the grain or flour used in the bread itself; for example, a bread containing millet flakes or millet seeds is often sprinkled with millet flour.

If a flavouring has been incorporated into the dough, you may be able to top the loaf with the same ingredient, to provide a hint of what is inside. Try sprinkling a little grated Parmesan on to a cheese loaf about 10 minutes after baking begins, or, for a loaf flavoured with herbs, add an appropriate dried herb as a topping immediately after baking.

LEFT: Rolled oats and wheat grain are sprinkled on to Sweet Potato Bread just before it begins to bake to give the loaf a delightful rustic look.

FLOUR

To create a farmhouse-style finish, brush the loaf with water or milk glaze within 10 minutes of the start of baking and dust lightly with flour. Use white flour, or wholemeal (whole-wheat) or Granary (whole-wheat) for a more rustic finish.

SMALL SEEDS

Seeds can be used to add flavour and texture in addition to a decorative finish. Try sesame, poppy, aniseed, caraway or cumin seeds. If adding sesame seeds immediately after baking, lightly toast until golden before adding.

SALT

Brush the top of a white loaf with water or egg glaze and sprinkle with a coarse sea salt, to give an attractive and crunchy topping. Sea salt is best applied at the beginning of baking or 10 minutes into the baking cycle.

CORN MEAL OR POLENTA

Use corn meal, polenta, semolina or other speciality flours as a finish for breads containing these flours, such as Courgette Country Grain Bread.

LARGE SEEDS

Gently press pumpkin or sunflower seeds on to the top of a freshly glazed loaf to give an attractive finish and a bonus crunch.

WHEAT AND OAT BRAN FLAKES

These add both texture and fibre to bread as well as visual appeal. Sprinkle them over the top of the loaf after glazing at the beginning of baking.

ROLLED OATS

These make a decorative finish for white breads and breads flavoured with oatmeal. Rolled oats are best added just before or at the very beginning of baking.

PEPPER AND PAPRIKA

Freshly ground black pepper and paprika both add spiciness to savoury breads. This tasty topping can be added before, during or after baking.

ICING SUGAR

Dust cooked sweet breads, teabreads or cakes with icing (confectioners') sugar after baking for a finished look. If you like, add 2.5ml/½tsp spice before sprinkling.

HAND-SHAPED BREAD

All of the toppings used on machine-baked breads can also be added to breads that are hand-shaped and baked in an oven. There are several methods that can be used for adding a topping to hand-shaped rolls and breads.

SPRINKLING WITH FLOUR

If you are using flour, this should be sprinkled over the dough immediately after shaping and again before slashing and baking, to give a rustic finish. Match the flour to the type of bread being made. Unbleached white bread flour is ideal for giving soft rolls and breads a fine finish. Use corn meal, ground rice or rice flour for crumpets and muffins and brown, wholemeal and Granary (whole-wheat) flours on wholegrain breads.

GROUND RICE OR RICE FLOUR

Muffins are enhanced with a ground rice or rice flour topping.

WHOLEMEAL FLOUR

Wholemeal (whole-wheat) flour toppings complement wholegrain dough whether made into loaves or rolls.

ABOVE: An Easter Tea Ring is glazed with an icing made from icing sugar and orange juice, then sprinkled with pecan nuts and candied orange.

ROLLING DOUGH IN SEEDS

Sprinkle seeds, salt or any other fine topping on a work surface, then roll the shaped but unproved dough in the chosen topping until it is evenly coated. This is ideal for coating wholegrain breads with pumpkin seeds or wheat flakes. After rolling, place the dough on the sheet for its final rising.

SESAME SEEDS

Dough sticks can be rolled in small seeds for a delicious crunchy topping.

ADDING A TOPPING AFTER A GLAZE

Some toppings are sprinkled over the bread after glazing and immediately before baking. In addition to the toppings suggested for machine-baked breads, these toppings can be used:

CANDIED FRUITS

Candied fruits make an attractive topping for festive breads and buns. Add the fruits after an egg glaze. Candied fruits can also be used after baking, with a jam or icing (confectioners') sugar glaze to stick the fruits to the bread.

NUTS

Just before baking, brush sweet or savoury breads and rolls with glaze and sprinkle with chopped or flaked (sliced) almonds, chopped cashews, chopped or whole walnuts or pecan nuts.

MILLET GRAIN, BLACK ONION SEEDS AND MUSTARD SEEDS
These small grains and seeds all add texture and taste to breads. Try them as a topping for loaves and flatbreads such as Lavash and Naan.

VEGETABLES

Brush savoury breads and rolls with an egg glaze or olive oil and then sprinkle with finely chopped raw onion, raw (bell) peppers, sun-dried tomatoes or olives for an extremely tasty crust.

CHEESE

Grated cheeses, such as Parmesan, Cheddar or Pecorino, are best for sprinkling on to dough just before baking, resulting in a chewy, flavoursome crust.

FRESH HERBS

Use fresh herbs, such as rosemary, thyme, sage or basil for Italian-style flatbreads. Chopped herbs also make a good topping for rolls.

USING SUGAR AS A TOPPING

Sugar is available in many forms, so chose one appropriate for your topping.

DEMERARA SUGAR

Before baking, brush buns and cakes with butter or milk, then sprinkle with demerara (raw) sugar for a crunchy finish.

SUGAR COATING

Yeast doughs that are deep-fried, such as Doughnuts and Saffron Braids can be sprinkled or tossed in a sugar coating. Toss doughnuts in caster (superfine) sugar which has been mixed with a little ground cinnamon or grated nutmeg, or flavoured using a vanilla pod (bean).

DUSTING WITH ICING SUGAR

Use a fine sieve to sprinkle cooked buns and yeast cakes, such as Devonshire Splits and Calas, with icing sugar. Large cakes and breads such as Panettone, Kugelhopf and Strudel also benefit from a light dusting of icing sugar, as do fruit-filled Savarins. If serving a bread or cake warm, dust with icing sugar when ready to serve to avoid the topping soaking into the bread.

USING SOURDOUGHS AND STARTERS

For bread to rise, some sort of raising agent – or leaven – must be used. In most cases, this will be yeast, or perhaps bicarbonate of soda (baking soda), but it is also possible to initiate the fermentation process naturally, by the action of wild yeasts, present in the air, on a medium such as flour or potatoes. When this is done, the mixture that results is called a starter.

There are two basic starters: a natural leaven and a yeasted starter. The former uses only airborne yeast spores, which create a lactic fermentation, as when milk turns sour. A yeasted starter includes a small amount of baker's yeast to kick-start the fermentation and develop a desired strain of yeast.

Sourdoughs are made using starters which develop over several days to produce a distinctive tanginess or "soured" flavour. Depending on how starters are made, how long they are left to ferment and how they are used, different flavours as well as textures can be achieved. Many of the Continental breads owe their flavours and textures to starters, which also influence their keeping qualities.

BREADMAKING METHODS

There are three basic methods of making breads: the direct method, the sourdough method, and the sponge method.

In the direct method, the flour, water and yeast are mixed, and once the dough has risen, the bread is baked in the shortest possible time. This is the conventional way of bread making.

The sourdough method is a much lengthier process. First, a starter must be made – this takes several days – and then this must be mixed with additional flour and other ingredients, often in several stages, called "refreshments", a process that takes at least 24 hours.

The sponge method is a compromise between the previous two. The dough is made using baker's yeast. A portion of the dough is mixed and allowed to ferment before the remaining ingredients are added. The process enhances the flavour and texture of the finished bread.

THE SOURDOUGH METHOD

Sourdough breads can be made from either a natural leaven or a yeasted starter. Most natural sourdough cultures can be turned into a starter within about 5 days. Flour and water are the basic ingredients, but other ingredients may be added to encourage the fermentation, such as honey, malt extract, soured milk, ground cumin or even a little baker's yeast.

The French term for this flour and water mixture is a "chef". The chef is left to ferment for 2–3 days, which brings about a lactic acid action, giving rise to the basic sour flavour. Once this dough is aerated and slightly sour, it is mixed or "refreshed" with more flour and water, to feed the fermentation process. After another 24 hours or so it is refreshed again, and becomes a natural leavener, or levain. This is left to ferment for about 8 hours more, when it is ready for use in the final bread dough.

Bread made by this method will taste slightly sour and will have a dense moist crumb, chewy crust and extremely good keeping qualities. Sourdough starters have varying textures, so do not worry if you come across different consistencies. Often American starters tend to be less stiff.

THE FRENCH SPONGE METHOD

The French sponge or poolish is made with yeast and some of the flour and water from the bread recipe, but no salt to retard the fermentation. The poolish is usually fermented for a minimum of 2 hours, and for up to 8 hours. Usually less yeast is used than with the direct method so the dough rises more slowly, giving it time to ripen and develop a springy texture. It combines the chewiness of a sourdough with the lightness of a basic bread.

The wetter the mix, the quicker it will rise, as the flour and water will provide less resistance for the yeast.

THE ITALIAN SPONGE METHOD

The Italian sponge or biga takes at least 12 hours, often longer, to ripen, allowing time for the dough to develop and rise to three times its original bulk before collapsing. The longer it is left the more developed the flavour will be. These breads have an open, holey, slightly moist and chewy texture. Their flavour and aroma tend to be yeasty and champagne-like. Ciabatta is a perfect example.

MAKING AN ITALIAN SPONGE

1 The flour, water and yeast for the biga are added to the bread machine and mixed as usual.

2 It is allowed to rise for several hours until it has tripled in size. After 12 hours it should be starting to collapse.

3 When the dough collapses, it is ready to be combined with the remaining ingredients for the bread.

THE OLD DOUGH METHOD

A variation of the direct method, this approach is exactly what its name suggests. A small piece of dough is removed from a batch of risen dough and set aside for adding to the dough for the next loaf of bread. This is a quick and easy alternative to making a starter and will add texture and improve the taste of the bread to which it is added.

The old dough method is perfect for the bread machine. Make a batch of dough using the regular dough cycle. When the bread is ready for shaping, pull off about 115g/4oz of the dough, place it in a bowl and cover with clear film (plastic wrap). If using within 4 hours leave at room temperature; if not, put the bowl in the refrigerator, but let the dough return to room temperature before using it. It can either be kneaded into a batch of dough for shaping by hand or added with the ingredients for a machine-baked bread.

If you are adding old dough to a loaf which is to be baked in a machine, reduce the flour and liquid slightly when you make up the new batch of dough. The following recipe is suitable for a medium or large machine. If you have a smaller machine reduce the quantities by a quarter. You can increase the quantities by a quarter for a large machine if you like.

USING THE OLD DOUGH METHOD

1 Tear about 115g/4oz dough off bread that is ready for shaping. Place in a bowl and cover with clear film. Set aside at room temperature or, if not using within 4 hours, in the refrigerator. Return to room temperature before using.

ABOVE: San Francisco-style Sourdough is made from airborne spores of yeast, and has no baker's yeast added to it. The variety of yeast strains in the atmosphere will mean that the bread tastes slightly different from place to place.

2 Pour 280ml/10fl oz/1¼ cups water into the bread machine pan. Add the old dough which has been reserved. However, if the instructions for your machine specify that the dry ingredients are to be placed in the bread pan first, reverse the order in which you add the dry ingredients and the water and reserved dough.

3 Sprinkle over 450g/1lb/4 cups unbleached white bread flour. Add 7.5ml/1½ tsp salt, 15ml/1 tbsp granulated sugar and 25g/1oz butter, placing these ingredients in separate corners of the bread pan.

4 Make a small indent in the centre of the flour and add 5ml/1 tsp easy-blend (rapid-rise) dried yeast.

5 Set the bread machine to the basic/normal setting, medium crust. Press Start. At the end of the baking cycle, remove the bread from the pan and turn out on to a wire rack to cool.

MAKING A YOGURT STARTER

Variations on the basic flour and water starter can be made to add complexity and uniqueness to the flavour and texture of bread. This yogurt starter will give a flavour similar to that of San Francisco-style Sourdough because the lactose in the milk products sours in a similar way.

1 Place 75ml/5 tbsp natural (plain) yogurt in a bowl. Pour 175ml/6fl oz/¾ cup skimmed milk into a pan and heat gently.

2 Stir the milk into the yogurt. Cover with clear film and leave in a warm place for 8–24 hours, or until thickened. Stir in any clear liquid which may have separated and risen to the surface.

REPLENISHING A STARTER

After making the starter for the first time, use or replenish within 3–4 days. When half has been used, replenish with 50g/2oz/½ cup white bread flour and 45ml/3 tbsp skimmed milk and 15ml/1 tbsp natural yogurt or 60ml/4 tbsp skimmed milk. If used daily, the starter can be kept at room temperature. If not, store in the refrigerator; bring back to room temperature before use.

3 Gradually mix in 115g/4oz/1 cup organic white bread flour, stirring to incorporate evenly.

BELOW: French Couronne is made using a chef starter which becomes a levain, a natural leavener.

4 Cover and leave in a warm place for 2–3 days, until the mixture is full of bubbles and smells pleasantly sour. (Uncover to check the aroma of the starter.) Use instead of the usual starter for San Francisco-style Sourdough or incorporate into a basic bread recipe.

2 Stir the starter and use the amount required in the recipe. If your purpose in bringing the starter to room temperature is just so that you can feed it, pour half of the starter into a measuring jug (cup), note the volume, then throw it away. This is so you will know how much to replenish.

USING A STARTER IN YOUR BREAD MACHINE

You can try adding a sourdough starter to one of your favourite recipes for a more complex flavour. Add it to a basic white, wholemeal (whole-wheat), mixed grain or rye bread. Here are a few pointers:

• Always bring the starter back to room temperature before using if it has been stored in the refrigerator.

• If your starter was made from a mixture of roughly half flour and half liquid, when you add it to the recipe, reduce the liquid in the recipe by the quantity of liquid in the starter, that is by half the total volume of the starter.

• The starter can be used in two ways. Try it in doughs that are made in the bread machine but shaped by hand and baked in the oven, or use it in a dough that is made and baked in the machine. If the latter, check the dough during the rising stage to make sure it is not rising too high; you can always override the programme and set the machine to the bake only programme.

• If the dough hasn't risen as much as you would like, you will need to bake it in the oven. Remove the dough from the bread machine and shape it by hand. Leave to rise until it has almost doubled in size, then bake in the normal way.

ABOVE : Ciabatta is made using the Italian sponge method.

REFRESHING A SOURDOUGH STARTER

Each time you use a sourdough starter, it needs to be replenished. Also, if you are not likely to be using it for some time, it is important to "feed" the starter regularly, with flour and liquid, to keep it active. The amount of flour and water you add to the starter to replenish it should equate to what was removed, either to be used in dough or discarded.

Once established, a sourdough starter can be kept in the refrigerator almost indefinitely. In fact, the flavour of the sourdough starter gets better with age. If your starter begins to turn pink or develops a mould, however, discard it and start again.

3 Replenish the starter by adding a quantity of flour and water (in equal parts by volume). Use organic white or wholemeal (whole-wheat) bread flour, or a combination of both. Wholemeal flour develops a more intense sour flavour. Add a quantity that equates to the amount of starter that has been removed. Mix until smooth.

1 Remove the starter from the refrigerator. It should be at room temperature before it's added to a recipe or fed to keep it active.

4 Cover and leave in a warm place for a few hours until it starts to bubble and ferment. Place in the refrigerator until needed.

GETTING THE BEST FROM YOUR MACHINE

Even the most comprehensive bread-machine manual cannot possibly cover all the hints and tips you will need. As you gain experience and confidence you will be able to solve more and more of any little problems that crop up. Here are a few pointers to help you along the road to successful baking.

TEMPERATURE AND HUMIDITY
The bread machine is not a sealed environment, and temperature and humidity can affect the finished results. On dry days, dry ingredients contain less water and on humid days they hold more.

The temperature of the ingredients is a very important factor in determining the success of machine-baked bread. Some machines specify that all ingredients should be at room temperature; others state that ingredients can be added from the refrigerators. Some machines have preheating cycles to bring the ingredients to an optimum temperature of around 20–25°C/68–77°F, before mixing starts. It is recommended that you use ingredients at room temperature. Water can be used straight from the cold tap. Lukewarm water may be beneficial for the rapid bake cycle on cold days.

Hot weather can mean that doughs will rise faster, so on very hot days start with chilled ingredients, using milk or eggs straight from the refrigerator.

Icy winter weather and cold draughts will inhibit the action of the yeast, so either move your machine to a warmer spot, or warm liquids before adding them to the bread pan. On very cold days, let the water stand at room temperature for about half an hour before adding the other ingredients to the pan, or add a little warm water to bring it up to a temperature of around 20°C/68°F, but no hotter.

QUALITY PRODUCE
Use only really fresh, good quality ingredients. The bread machine can not improve poor quality produce. Make sure the yeast is within its use-by date. Yeast beyond its expiry date will produce poor results.

MEASURING INGREDIENTS

Measure both the liquids and the dry ingredients carefully. Most problems occur when ingredients are inaccurately measured, when one ingredient is forgotten or when the same ingredient is added twice. Do not mix imperial and metric measurements, as they are not interchangeable; stick to one set for the whole recipe.

Do not exceed the quantities of flour and liquid recommended for your machine. Mixing the extra ingredients may overload the motor and if you have too much dough it is likely to rise over the top of the pan.

FOLLOW THE INSTRUCTIONS
Always add the ingredients in the order suggested by the manufacturer. Whatever the order, keep the yeast dry and separate from any liquids added to the bread pan.

ADDING INGREDIENTS

Cut butter into pieces, especially if it is fairly firm, and/or when larger amounts than usual are required in the recipe. If a recipe requires ingredients such as cooked vegetables or fruit or toasted nuts to be added, leave them to cool to room temperature before adding them.

USING THE DELAY TIMER

Perishable ingredients such as eggs, fresh milk, cheese, meat, fruit and vegetables may deteriorate, especially in warm conditions, and could present a health risk. They should be only be used in breads that are made immediately. Only use the delay timer for bread doughs that contain non-perishable ingredients.

CLEANING YOUR MACHINE
Unplug the machine before starting to clean it. Wipe down the outside regularly using a mild washing-up liquid (detergent) and a damp, soft cloth. Avoid all abrasive cleansers and materials, even those that are designated for use on non-stick items, and do not use alcohol-based cleansers.

BREAD PAN AND KNEADING BLADE
Clean the bread pan and blade after each use. These parts should not be washed in the dishwasher as this might affect the non-stick surface and damage the packing around the shaft. Avoid immersing the bread pan in water. If you have difficulty extracting the blade from the pan, fill the base of the pan with lukewarm water and leave it to soak for a few minutes. Remove the blade and wipe it with a damp cloth. Wash the bread pan with mild washing-up liquid then rinse thoroughly. Always store the bread machine with the kneading blade removed from the shaft. The bread machine and components must be completely dry before putting away.

ABOVE: A Granary loaf should be baked on the whole wheat setting, which has a longer rising cycle.

SPECIAL CONSIDERATIONS

Breads made with whole grains and heavier flours such as wholemeal (whole-wheat), oatmeal or rye, or with added ingredients such as dried fruits and nuts, are likely to rise more slowly than basic white loaves and will be less tall. The same applies to breads with a lot of fat or egg. Breads that include cheese, eggs or a high proportion of fats and/or sugar are more susceptible to burning. To avoid over-cooked crusts, select a light bake crust setting.

WATCHING THE DOUGH

Keep a flexible rubber spatula next to the machine and, if necessary, scrape down the sides of the pan after 5–10 minutes of the initial mixing cycle. The kneading blade sometimes fails to pick up a thick or sticky dough from the corners of the pan.

COOLING THE BREAD

It is best to remove the loaf from the pan as soon as the baking cycle finishes, or it may become slightly damp, even with a "stay warm" programme.

CHECKING THE DOUGH

Check the dough within the first 5 minutes of mixing, especially when you are trying a recipe for the first time. If the dough seems too wet and, instead of forming a ball, sticks to the sides of the pan, add a little flour, a spoonful at a time. However, the bread machine requires a dough that is slightly wetter than if you were mixing it by hand. If the dough is crumbly and won't form a ball, add liquid, one spoonful at a time. You will soon get used to the sound of the motor and notice if it is labouring due to a stiff mix. It is also worth checking the dough just before baking, to make sure it isn't about to rise over the top of the bread machine pan.

ABOVE: Dough is too wet and requires more flour.

ABOVE: Dough is too dry and requires more water.

ADAPTING RECIPES FOR USE IN A BREAD MACHINE

After you have cooked a number of the recipes from this book you may wish to branch out and adapt some of your own favourites. This sample recipe is used to explain some of the factors you will need to take into consideration.

INGREDIENTS

Read the list of ingredients carefully before you start, and adjust if necessary.

MALT EXTRACT AND GOLDEN SYRUP

High sugar levels and/or dried fruit may cause the bread to over-brown. Reduce the malt extract and golden (light corn) syrup quantities by one-third and increase other liquids to compensate. Machine breads require the inclusion of sugar. Allow 5–10ml/1–2 tsp per 225g/8oz/2 cups flour.

BUTTER

High fat levels mean that the bread will take longer to rise. Reduce to 50g/2oz/¼ cup per 450g/1lb/4 cups flour. You may need to add an extra 30ml/2 tbsp liquid.

FLOUR

This recipe uses white flour, but remember that a wholemeal (whole-wheat) loaf works better if you replace half the wholemeal flour with strong white flour.

YEAST

Replace fresh yeast with easy-blend (rapid-rise) dried yeast. In a wholemeal bread, for example, start by using 5ml/1 tsp for up to 375g/13oz/3¼ cups flour or 7.5ml/1½ tsp for up to 675g/1½lb/6 cups flour.

MILK

Use skimmed milk at room temperature where possible. If you wish to use the time delay cycle you should replace with fresh milk with milk powder.

DRIED FRUIT

Additions that enrich the dough, such as dried fruits, nuts, seeds and wholegrains, make the dough heavier, and the bread will not rise as well. Limit them to about a quarter of the total flour quantity.

MALTED FRUIT LOAF

50g/2oz/scant ¼ cup malt extract
30ml/2 tbsp golden (light corn) syrup
75g/3oz/6 tbsp butter
450g/1lb/4 cups unbleached white bread flour
5ml/1 tsp mixed (apple pie)spice
20g/¾oz fresh yeast
150ml/5fl oz/⅔ cup lukewarm milk
50g/2oz/¼ cup currants
50g/2oz/⅓ cup sultanas (golden raisins)
50g/2oz/¼ cup ready-to-eat dried apricots
25g/1oz/2 tbsp mixed chopped (candied)peel
30ml/2 tbsp milk
30ml/2 tbsp caster (superfine) sugar

MAKES 2 LOAVES

1 Grease two 450g/1lb loaf tins (pans).
2 Melt the malt extract, syrup and butter in a pan. Leave to cool.
3 Sift the flour and spice into a large bowl; make a central well. Cream the yeast with a little of the milk; blend in the rest. Add the yeast mixture with the malt extract to the flour and make a dough.
4 Knead on a floured surface until smooth and elastic, about 10 minutes. Place in an oiled bowl; cover with oiled clear film (plastic wrap). Leave in a warm place for 1½–2 hours, until doubled in bulk.
5 Turn the dough out on to a lightly floured surface and knock back (punch down).
6 Gently knead in the dried fruits.
7 Divide the dough in half; shape into two loaves. Place in the tins and cover with oiled clear film. Leave to rise for 1–1½ hours or until the dough reaches the top of the tins.
8 Meanwhile, preheat the oven to 200°C/400°F/Gas 6. Bake the loaves for 35–40 minutes, or until golden. When cooked, transfer to a wire rack.
9 Gently heat the milk and sugar for the glaze in a pan. Brush the warm loaves with the glaze.

METHOD

Use a similar bread machine recipe as a guide for adapting a conventional recipe.

STEP 1

Obviously, you can only make one machine-baked loaf at a time. Make 1 large loaf or reduce the quantity of ingredients if your machine is small.

STEP 2

There is no need to melt the ingredients before you add them, but remember to chop the butter into fairly small pieces.

STEP 3

When adding ingredients to the bread pan, pour in the liquid first then sprinkle over the flour, followed by the mixed spice. (Add the liquid first unless your machine requires dry ingredients to be placed in the bread pan first.)

Add easy-blend dried yeast to a small indent in the flour, but make sure it does not touch the liquid underneath.

Place salt and butter in separate corners of the pan. If your recipe calls for egg, add this with the water or other liquid.

Use water straight from the tap and other liquids at room temperature.

STEPS 4–8

Ignore these steps, apart from step 6. The bread machine will automatically mix, rise and cook the dough. Use a light setting for the crust due to the sugar, fat and fruit content of the Malted Fruit Loaf. Ordinary breads, such as a white loaf, need a medium setting; loaves that contain wholemeal flour should be baked on the whole wheat setting.

If you are adding extra ingredients, such as dried fruit, set the bread machine on raisin setting and add the ingredients when it beeps. If you do not have this facility, add approximately 5 minutes before the end of the kneading cycle.

STEP 9

Make the glaze as usual and brush over the loaf at the end of the baking cycle.

USEFUL GUIDELINES

Here are a few guidelines that are worth following when adapting your own favourite recipes.

• Make sure the quantities will work in your machine. If you have a small bread machine it may be necessary to reduce them. Use the flour and water quantities in recipes in the book as a guide, or refer back to your manufacturer's handbook.

• It is important that you keep the flour and the liquid in the correct proportions, even if reducing the quantities means that you end up with some odd amounts. You can be more flexible with spices and flavourings such as fruit and nuts, as exact quantities are not so crucial.

• Monitor the recipe closely the first time you make it and jot down any ideas you have for improvements next time.

• Check the consistency of the dough when the machine starts mixing. You may need to add one or two extra spoonfuls of water, as breads baked in a machine

BELOW: Use a similar bread machine recipe to help you adapt a bread you usually make conventionally. For example, if you have a favourite swede bread recipe, try adapting a machine recipe for parsnip bread.

ABOVE: Some conventional recipes call for you to knead ingredients, such as fried onions, into a dough. When adapting for a bread machine, add to the dough at the raisin beep.

require a slightly softer dough, which is wet enough to relax back into the shape of the bread pan.

• If a dough mixes perfectly in your machine but then fails to bake properly, or if you want bread of a special shape, use the dough cycle on your machine, then shape by hand before baking in a conventional oven.

• Look through bread machine recipes and locate something that is similar. This will give you some idea as to quantities, and which programme you should use. Be prepared to make more adjustments after testing your recipe for the first time.

USING BREAD MIXES

Packaged bread mixes can be used in your machine. Check your handbook, as some manufacturers may recommend specific brands.

• Check that your machine can handle the amount of dough the bread mix makes. If the packet quantity is only marginally more than you usually make, use the dough cycle and then bake the bread conventionally.

• Select an appropriate setting; for instance, use the normal or rapid setting for white bread.

1 Place the recommended amount of water in the bread pan.

2 Spoon over the bread mix and place the pan in the machine.

3 Select the programme required and press Start. Check the consistency of the dough after 5 minutes, adding a little more water if the mixture seems too dry.

4 At the end of the baking cycle, remove the cooked bread from the bread pan and turn out on to a wire rack to cool.

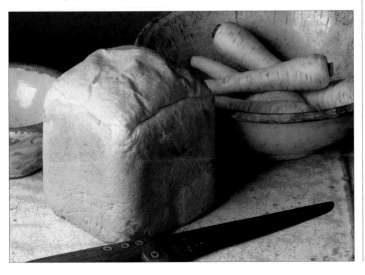

TROUBLESHOOTING

Bread machines are incredibly easy to use and, once you have become familiar with yours, you will wonder how you ever did without it. However, they are machines and they cannot think for themselves. Things can go wrong and you need to understand why. Here are a few handy troubleshooting tips.

BREAD RISES TOO MUCH

• Usually caused by too much yeast; reduce by 25 per cent.
• An excess of sugar will promote yeast action; try reducing the quantity of sugar.
• Did you leave out the salt or use less than was recommended? If so, the yeast would have been uncontrolled and a tall loaf would have been the likely result.
• Too much liquid can sometimes cause a loaf to over-rise. Try reducing by 15–30ml/ 1–2 tbsp next time.
• Other possibilities are too much dough or too hot a day.

BREAD DOES NOT RISE ENOUGH

• Insufficient yeast or yeast that is past its expiry date.
• A rapid cycle was chosen, giving the bread less time to rise.

• The yeast and salt came into contact with each other before mixing. Make sure they are placed in separate areas when added to the bread pan.
• Too much salt inhibits the action of the yeast. You may have added salt twice, or added other salty ingredients, such as ready-salted nuts or feta cheese.
• Wholegrain and wholemeal breads tend not to rise as high as white flour breads. These flours contain bran and wheat germ, which makes the flour heavier.
• You may have used a plain white flour instead of a strong bread flour, which has a higher gluten content.
• The ingredients were not at the correct temperature. If they were too hot, they may have killed the yeast; if they were too cold, they may have retarded the action of the yeast.
• Insufficient liquid. In order for dough to rise adequately, it needs to be soft and pliable. If the dough was dry and stiff, add more liquid next time.
• The lid was open during the rising stage for long enough to let warm air escape.
• No sugar was added. Yeast works better where there is at least 5ml/1 tsp sugar to feed it. Note, however, that high sugar levels may retard yeast action.

BREAD DOES NOT RISE AT ALL

• No yeast was added or it was past its expiry date.
• The yeast was not handled correctly and was probably killed by adding ingredients that were too hot.

THE DOUGH IS CRUMBLY AND DOESN'T FORM A BALL

• The dough is too dry. Add extra liquid a small amount at a time until the ingredients combine to form a pliable dough.

THE DOUGH IS VERY STICKY AND DOESN'T FORM A BALL

• The dough is too wet. Try adding a little extra flour, a spoonful at a time, waiting for it to be absorbed before adding more. You must do this while the machine in still mixing and kneading the dough.

BREAD MIXED BUT NOT BAKED

• A dough cycle was selected. Remove the dough, shape it and bake it in a conventional oven or bake it in the machine on the "bake only" cycle.

BREAD COLLAPSED AFTER RISING OR DURING BAKING

• Too much liquid was added. Reduce the amount by 15–30ml/1–2 tbsp next time, or add a little extra flour.
• The bread rose too much. Reduce the amount of yeast slightly in the future, or use a quicker cycle.
• Insufficient salt. Salt helps to prevent the dough from over-proving.
• The machine may have been placed in a draught or may have been knocked or jolted during rising.
• High humidity and warm weather may have caused the dough to rise too fast.
• Too much yeast may have been added.
• The dough may have contained a high proportion of cheese.

THERE ARE DEPOSITS OF FLOUR ON THE SIDES OF THE LOAF

• The dry ingredients, especially the flour, stuck to the sides of the pan during kneading, and then adhered to the rising dough. Next time, use a flexible rubber spatula to scrape down the sides of the pan after 5–10 minutes of the initial mixing cycle, if necessary, but take care to avoid the kneading blade.

CRUST IS SHRIVELLED OR WRINKLED

• Moisture condensed on top of the loaf while it was cooling. Remove from the bread machine as soon as it is cooled.

CRUMBLY, COARSE TEXTURE

• The bread rose too much; try reducing the quantity of yeast slightly next time.
• The dough didn't have enough liquid.
• Too many whole grains were added. These soaked up the liquid. Next time, either soak the whole grains in water first or increase the general liquid content.

BURNT CRUST

• There was too much sugar in the dough. Use less or try a light crust setting for sweet breads.
• Choose the sweet bread setting if the machine has this option.

PALE LOAF

• Add milk, either dried or fresh, to the dough. This encourages browning.
• Set the crust colour to dark.
• Increase the sugar slightly.

CRUST TOO CHEWY AND TOUGH

• Increase the butter or oil and milk.

BREAD NOT BAKED IN THE CENTRE OR ON TOP

• Too much liquid was added; next time, reduce the liquid by 15ml/1 tbsp or add a little extra flour.
• The quantities were too large and your machine could not cope with the dough.
• The dough was too rich; it contained too much fat, sugar, eggs, nuts or grains.
• The bread machine lid was not closed properly, or the machine was used in too cold a location.
• The flour may have been too heavy. This can occur when you use rye, bran and whole-meal (whole-wheat) flours. Replace some of it with white bread flour next time.

CRUST TOO SOFT OR CRISP

• For a softer crust, increase the fat and use milk instead of water. For a crisper crust, do the opposite.
• Use the French bread setting for a crisper crust.
• Keep a crisper crust by lifting the bread out of the pan and turn it out on to a wire rack as soon as the baking cycle finishes.

AIR BUBBLE UNDER THE CRUST

• The dough was not mixed well or didn't deflate properly during the knock-down cycle between risings. This is likely to be a one-off problem, but if it persists, try adding an extra spoonful of water.

ADDED INGREDIENTS WERE CHOPPED UP INSTEAD OF REMAINING WHOLE

• They were added too soon and were chopped by the kneading blade. Add on the machine's audible signal, or 5 minutes before the end of the kneading cycle.
• Leave chopped nuts and dried fruits in larger pieces.

ADDED INGREDIENTS NOT MIXED IN

• They were probably added too late in the kneading cycle. Next time, add them a couple of minutes sooner.

THE BREAD IS DRY

• The bread was left uncovered to cool too long and dried out.
• Breads low in fat dry out rapidly. Increase the fat or oil in the recipe.
• The bread was stored in the refrigerator. Next time place in a plastic bag when cool and store in a bread bin.

BREAD HAS A HOLEY TEXTURE

• The dough was too wet; use less liquid.
• Salt was omitted.
• Warm weather and/or high humidity caused the dough to rise too quickly.

A STICKY LAYERED UNRISEN MESS

• You forgot to put the kneading blade in the pan before adding the ingredients.
• The kneading blade was not correctly inserted on the shaft.
• The bread pan was incorrectly fitted.

SMOKE EMITTED FROM THE MACHINE

• Ingredients were spilt on the heating element. Remove the bread pan before adding ingredients, and add any extra ingredients carefully.

OTHER FACTORS

Creating the ideal conditions for your bread machine is largely a matter of trial and error. Take into account the time of year, the humidity and your altitude. Bread machines vary between models and manufacturers, and flour and yeast may produce slightly different results from brand to brand or country to country. Breads made in Australia, for example, often need slightly more water than those made in Britain.

You will soon get to know your machine. Watch the dough as it is mixing and check again before it begins to bake. Make a note of any tendencies (do you generally need to add more flour? does the bread often over-rise?) and adapt recipes accordingly.

FLOUR

The largest single ingredient used in bread, the right flour is the key to good bread making. Wheat is the primary grain for grinding into flour. Apart from rye, wheat is the only flour with sufficient gluten to make a well-leavened bread.

WHEAT FLOURS

Wheat consists of an outer husk or bran that encloses the wheat kernel. The kernel contains the wheat germ and the endosperm, which is full of starch and protein. It is these proteins that form gluten when flour is mixed with water. When dough is kneaded, gluten stretches like elastic to trap the bubbles of carbon dioxide, the gas released by the action of the yeast, and the dough rises.

Wheat is defined as either soft or hard, depending on its protein content, and is milled in various ways to give the wide range of flours we know today.

Wheat is processed to create many sorts of flour. White flours, for example, contain about 75 per cent of the wheat kernel. The outer bran and the wheat germ are removed to leave the endosperm, which is milled into a white flour. Unbleached flour is the best type to use, as it has not been chemically treated to make it unnaturally white. This type is gradually replacing much of the bleached flour.

RIGHT: Clockwise from top: strong, French, self-raising and plain flour

PLAIN WHITE FLOUR

Plain white (all-purpose) flour contains less protein and gluten than bread flour, typically around 9.5–10 per cent. Sometimes a small amount of this type of flour is mixed with bread flour to achieve a closer-grained texture, but the main use for plain white flour is in quick teabreads, when chemical raising agents such as baking powder are added to give a light, airy crumb.

ABOVE: Clockwise from top left: Granary, stoneground strong wholemeal, strong brown, stoneground wholemeal

STRONG WHITE FLOUR

This flour is milled from hard wheat flour, which has a higher protein level than soft wheat flour. Levels vary between millers but the typical figure is around 12 per cent. Some types of bread flour have lower levels – around 10.5–11 per cent – but these have ascorbic acid added to act as a dough enhancer.

SELF-RAISING FLOUR

Called self-rising in the USA, this is not used in traditional breads, but is ideal for quick teabreads and cakes cooked in the bread machine. Sodium bicarbonate and calcium phosphate are mixed into the flour and act as raising agents.

FINE FRENCH PLAIN FLOUR

Used principally for baking in France, this unbleached light flour is very fine and thus free-flowing. A small amount is often added to French bread recipes to reduce the gluten content slightly and achieve the texture associated with French specialities.

ORGANIC FLOURS

Organic white flour is produced using only natural fertilizers, and the wheat has not been sprayed with pesticides. Organic bread flours are recommended when developing natural yeasts for starters and sourdoughs.

WHOLEMEAL FLOURS

Because it is made from the complete wheat kernel, including the bran and wheat germ, wholemeal (whole-wheat) is coarse textured and full-flavoured with a nutty taste. For making machine breads, you should use strong wholemeal bread flour, with a protein content of around 12.5 per cent. Plain wholemeal flour can be used with baking powder or bicarbonate of soda (baking soda) for teabreads. Loaves made with 100 per cent wholemeal bread flour tend to be very dense. The bran inhibits the release of gluten, so the dough rises slower. For these reasons, many machine recipes recommend blending wholemeal bread flour with some white bread flour.

Stoneground flour results when complete wheat grain is ground between two stones. Wholemeal flours that are not stoneground have the bran and wheat germ removed during milling. They are replaced at the end of processing.

BROWN BREAD FLOUR

This flour contains about 80–90 per cent of the wheat kernel, with some of the bran removed. It is a good alternative to wholemeal flour, as it produces a loaf with a lighter finish, but with a denser texture and fuller flavour than white bread.

GRANARY FLOUR

A combination of wholemeal, white and rye flours mixed with malted wheat grains, this adds texture and contributes a flavour that is slightly sweet and nutty. Malthouse is similar to Granary flour.

ABOVE: Left to right: semolina, spelt

SPELT FLOUR

Rich in nutrients, this is made from spelt grain, an ancient precursor of modern wheat. It is best used in combination with white bread flour. Even though it contains gluten, some gluten-intolerant people can digest it, so it is included in some diets for people who are allergic to wheat.

SEMOLINA

A high gluten flour, semolina is made from the endosperm of durum or hard winter wheat before it is fully milled into a fine flour. It can be ground to a coarse granular texture or a finer flour. The finer flour is traditionally used for making pasta, but also makes a delicious bread when combined with other flours. If 100 per cent semolina is used, a heavy loaf will result.

OTHER WHEAT GRAINS

WHEAT BRAN

This is the outer husk of the wheat, which is separated from white flour during processing. It adds fibre, texture and flavour. You can add a spoonful or two to your favourite recipe or use it in place of part of the white bread flour.

WHEAT GERM

The germ is the embryo or heart of the wheat grain kernel. Use in its natural state, or lightly toasted, giving a nutty flavour. Wheat germ is a rich source of vitamin E and increases the nutritional value of bread. However, it inhibits the action of gluten, so do not use more than 30ml/2 tbsp for every 225g/8oz/2 cups flour.

CRACKED WHEAT

This is whole wheat kernel, broken into rather large pieces. It is quite hard, so you may like to soften it. Simmer in hot water for 15 minutes, then drain and cool. Add 15–30ml/1–2 tbsp to a dough 5 minutes before the end of the kneading cycle.

BELOW: Clockwise from top left: bran, bulgur wheat, wheat germ, cracked wheat

BULGUR WHEAT

This is made from the wheat grain. It is partially processed by boiling, which cracks the wheat kernel. Add to bread doughs, to give a crunchy texture. There is no need to cook it first. However you may wish to soak it in water first, to soften it further.

NON-WHEAT FLOURS
RYE FLOUR

Rye flour is used extensively in breads, partly because it grows well in climates that are cold and wet and not suitable for wheat cultivation. This is why so many of the Russian and Scandinavian breads include rye. Light and medium rye flours are produced from the endosperm while dark rye includes all the grain, resulting in a coarser flour which adds more texture to the bread. Rye contains gluten, but when used on its own produces a very heavy bread. Rye dough is very sticky and difficult to handle. For machine-made breads, rye flour must be combined with other flours. Even a small amount adds a distinctive tang.

MILLET FLOUR

Another high-protein, low-gluten grain, millet produces a light yellow flour with a distinctly sweet flavour and a slightly gritty texture. It tends to give breads a dry, crumbly texture, so you may need to add extra fat when using it. If using millet flour, boost the gluten content of the dough by using at least 75 per cent white bread flour.

BARLEY

Barley seeds are processed to remove the bran, leaving a product called pearl barley. This is ground to make barley flour, which is mild, slightly sweet and earthy. It gives breads a soft, almost cake-like texture, as it has a very low gluten content. White flour must be combined with barley flour in a ratio of at least 3:1 for machine bread.

BUCKWHEAT FLOUR

This greyish-brown flour has a distinctive, bitter, earthy flavour. Buckwheat is the seed of a plant related to the rhubarb family. It is rich in calcium and vitamins A and B, high in protein but low in gluten. Traditionally used to make pancakes, Russian blinis and French galettes, it is best used in combination with other flours, to produce full-bodied and tasty multigrain breads.

BELOW: Top to bottom: millet, buckwheat, barley

ABOVE: Left to right: polenta, corn meal, millet

OTHER GRAINS
OATMEAL

When oats are cleaned and the outer husk has been removed, what remains is the oat kernel or groat. This is then cut into pieces to make either fine, medium or coarse oatmeal, or fully ground to make flour. All of these ingredients can be used in multigrain breads, adding a rich flavour and texture. The coarser the oats, the more texture they will contribute to the

ABOVE: Top to bottom: oatmeal, rye

bread. Oatmeal contains no gluten, so it needs to be combined with wheat flour for bread making. The coarser textured oatmeal makes an attractive topping on breads and rolls.

POLENTA AND CORN MEAL

Dried corn kernels are ground to make coarse, medium and fine meal. The medium grain is known as polenta and the fine grain is known as corn meal. For bread making, this gluten-free flour has to be combined with white bread flour. It adds a sweet flavour and an attractive yellow colour to the dough. For shaping the bread by hand, use polenta, which is slightly coarser and adds a pleasant finish to the bread.

MILLET GRAIN

This tiny, golden yellow, round grain is used in breads in Europe and Russia to give added texture. Include 15–30ml/ 1–2 tbsp in a multigrain bread, or even in a simple basic white loaf, for added interest. Millet grains make an attractive topping for breads such as Lavash. Millet flakes are also used in some breads.

RICE

Rice grains can be used in a variety of ways. Cooked long grain rice can be added to doughs for bread with a moist crumb. Wild rice, although strictly an aquatic grass, will add a beautiful texture and flavour. Add it near the end of the kneading cycle to keep the grain intact and give attractive dark flecks of colour to the bread. Ground rice and rice flour are milled from rice grains. Both brown and white rice flour are used, brown flour being more nutritious. Ground rice is more granular, similar to semolina. Either can replace some white bread flour in a recipe; they will add a sweet flavour

ABOVE: Clockwise from top left: ground rice, rice flour, wild rice, long grain rice

and chewy texture to the bread. Ground rice and rice flour can also be used as toppings. They are often dusted over English muffins or crumpets.

As rice is gluten-free, use only a small percentage of it with the bread flour, otherwise your loaf of bread will be rather dense.

ROLLED OATS

The inedible husk is removed from the oat kernel and the grain is then sliced, steamed and rolled to produce rolled oats. You can get jumbo-size oat flakes as well as traditional old-fashioned rolled porridge oats. For bread making, use the old-fashioned oats rather than the "quick cook" oats. Add rolled oats to bread doughs to give a chewy texture and nutty taste, or use as a topping for an attractive finish on rolls and breads.

OAT BRAN

High in soluble fibre, this is the outer casing of the oat kernel. It acts in a similar way to wheat bran, reducing the elasticity of the gluten, so use a maximum of 15ml/1 tbsp per 115g/4oz/1 cup flour. When using oat bran, you may need to add a little extra liquid to the dough.

LEFT: Clockwise from top right: jumbo oats, rolled oats, oat bran

LEAVENS AND SALT

Yeast is a living organism which, when activated by contact with liquid, converts the added sugar or sucrose, and then the natural sugars in the flour, into gases. These gases cause the bread to rise. As yeast is live, you must treat it with respect. It works best within the temperature range 21–36°C/70–97°F. Too hot and it will die; too cold and it will not activate. Yeast must be used before its use-by date, as old yeast loses its potency and eventually dies.

In most bread machine recipes dried yeast is used. In this book, all the recipes have been tested using easy-blend (rapid-rise) dried yeast, which does not need to be dissolved in liquid first. It is also called fast-action yeast. If you can find dried yeast especially made for use in bread machines, this will produce good results. You may need to adjust the quantities in individual recipes as variations occur between different makes of yeast.

ABOVE: Yeast is available in two forms, fresh and dried. From top to bottom: fresh yeast, dried yeast.

ABOVE: Add liquid to dissolve and activate fresh yeast.

Fresh yeast is considered by some bakers to have a superior flavour. It can be used with caution when baking in a bread machine, but is best used in the "dough only" cycle. It is hard to give exact quantities for breads, which will be made using a range of machines operating in different temperatures. The difficulty lies in preventing the bread from rising over the top of the bread pan during baking; doughs made from easy-blend dried yeast are easier to control where uniform results are required.

NATURAL LEAVENS

Long before yeast was sold commercially, sourdough starters were used to make breads. These were natural leavens made by fermenting yeast spores that occurred naturally in flour, dairy products, plant matter and spices. Breads are still produced by the same method today. Breads made using natural leavens have different flavours and textures from the breads made with commercial yeast.

BELOW: Buckwheat and Walnut Bread is made using easy-blend dried yeast, which gives good, uniform results.

ABOVE: Place dried yeast in a shallow indent in the flour.

ABOVE: Fresh yeast is dissolved before placing in the bread pan.

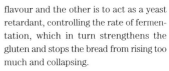

*RIGHT: Left
to right:
cream of tartar,
baking powder,
bicarbonate of soda*

CHEMICAL LEAVENS

Raising agents other than yeasts can be used for bread. When using a bread machine, other raising agents are best used for teabreads and cakes that are mixed in a bowl, then baked in the bread pan.

Bicarbonate of soda (baking soda) is an alkaline raising agent that is often used for quick breads. When moistened with liquid it gives off carbon dioxide, which makes the cake or quick bread rise. The heat from the oven cooks and sets the risen batter before it has a chance to collapse.

Cream of tartar is an acid, which is often combined with bicarbonate of soda to boost the latter's leavening qualities. It also helps to neutralize the slightly soapy taste from the bicarbonate of soda.

BELOW: Bicarbonate of soda is the raising agent used for this Apricot, Prune and Peach Teabread.

Baking powder is a ready-made mixture of acid and alkaline chemicals, usually bicarbonate of soda and cream of tartar, but sometimes bicarbonate of soda and sodium pyrophosphate. All these raising agents are fast acting. The bubbles are released the moment the powder comes into contact with a liquid, so such breads must be mixed and baked quickly.

SALT

Bread without salt tastes very "flat". While it is possible to make a saltless bread (there is, in fact, a famous saltless Tuscan bread which is eaten with salty cheese or preserved meats such as salami), salt is normally an indispensable ingredient. Salt has two roles: one is to improve the flavour and the other is to act as a yeast retardant, controlling the rate of fermentation, which in turn strengthens the gluten and stops the bread from rising too much and collapsing.

When adding salt to the bread pan, it is vital to keep it away from the yeast, as concentrated salt will severely impede the activity of the yeast.

Fine table salt and sea salt can both be used in bread that is to be baked in a machine. Coarse sea salt is best used as a topping. It can be sprinkled on top of unbaked breads and rolls to give a crunchy texture and agreeable flavour.

Salt substitutes are best avoided as few of these contain sodium.

DOUGH CONDITIONERS

These are added to breads to help stabilize the gluten strands and hold the gases formed by the yeast. Chemical conditioners are often added to commercially-produced bread, and you will also find bread improvers listed among the ingredients on fast-action yeast packets.

Two natural dough conditioners which help to ensure a higher rise, lighter texture, and stronger dough are lemon juice and malt extract. Gluten strength can vary between bags of flour, so you can add some lemon juice to the dough to help to strengthen it, particularly when making wholegrain breads. You can add 5ml/1 tsp lemon juice with every 225g/8oz/2 cups bread flour without affecting the flavour of the bread.

Malt extract helps to break down the starch in wheat into sugars for the yeast to feed on and so encourages active fermentation. If you use up to 5ml/1 tsp malt extract with every 225g/8oz/2 cups bread flour you will not effect a noticeable flavour change. If you like the flavour of malt extract, you can increase the amount used.

LIQUIDS

Some form of liquid is essential when making bread. It rehydrates and activates the yeast, and brings together the flour and any other dry ingredients to make the dough. Whatever the liquid, the temperature is important for successful machine breads. If your machine has a preheating cycle, cold liquids, straight from the refrigerator, can be used. If not, use liquids at room temperature, unless it is a very hot day. Water from the tap, providing it is merely cool, is fine. On a very cold day, measure the water and leave it to stand in the kitchen for a while so that it acclimatizes before you use it.

WATER

Water is the most frequently used liquid in bread making. Bread made with water has a crisper crust than when milk is included. Tap water is chemically treated, and if it has been heavily chlorinated and fluorinated this may well slow down the rising. Hard water can also affect the rise,

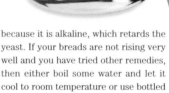

because it is alkaline, which retards the yeast. If your breads are not rising very well and you have tried other remedies, then either boil some water and let it cool to room temperature or use bottled spring water.

BELOW: Cranberry juice and orange juice may be used in teabreads.

MILK

Milk helps to enrich the dough and produces a creamy-coloured, tender crumb and golden crust. Use full-cream (whole), semi-skimmed (low-fat) or skimmed milk, according to your preference. You can also replace fresh milk with skimmed milk powder. This can be useful if you intend using the timer to delay the starting time for making bread, as, unlike fresh milk, the milk powder will not deteriorate. Sprinkle it on top of the flour in the bread pan to keep it separated from the water until mixing starts.

BUTTERMILK

Used instead of regular milk, this makes bread more moist and gives it an almost cake-like texture. Buttermilk is made from skimmed milk which is pasteurized, then cooled. After this a cultured bacteria is added which ferments it under controlled conditions to produce its slightly tangy, acidic, but pleasant flavour. This flavour is noticeable in the finished loaf.

ABOVE: Clockwise from top left: milk, buttermilk, milk powder

Yogurt and Other Dairy Products

Another alternative to milk, yogurt also has good tenderizing properties. Use natural (plain) yogurt or try flavoured ones, such as lemon or hazelnut in similarly flavoured breads.

Sour cream, cottage cheese and soft cheeses such as ricotta, fromage frais and mascarpone can all be used as part of the liquid content of the bread. They are valued more for their tenderizing properties than for their flavour.

Coconut Milk

Use 50:50 with water to add flavour to sweet breads and buns.

Fruit Juices

Fruit juices such as orange, mango, pineapple or cranberry can be added to the dough for fruit-flavoured breads to enhance their fruitiness.

Vegetable Juices and Cooking Liquids

The liquid left over from cooking vegetables will add flavour and extra nutritional value to breads and is particularly useful when making savoury breads. Potato water has several benefits. The extra starch acts as an additional food for the yeast, and produces a greater rise and also a softer, longer-lasting loaf.

Vegetables themselves contain liquid juices and when added to a bread machine will alter the liquid balance.

Soaking Juices

When dried vegetables such as mushrooms, especially wild ones, and sun-dried tomatoes are rehydrated in water, a

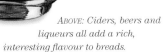

Above: Ciders, beers and liqueurs all add a rich, interesting flavour to breads.

flavoursome liquid is produced. This is much too good to waste. Rehydrate the vegetables, drain off the liquid and add it as part of the liquid in a savoury bread. In sweet breads, the liquid drained from dried fruits that have been plumped up in fruit juices, spirits and liqueurs is equally useful.

Beers, Ales, Ciders and Liqueurs

All of these can be added to bread recipes. Beers and ales, in particular, have a great affinity with dark, heavy flours. The added sugars stimulate the yeast by providing more food. Dark beers and ales impart a stronger flavour.

Eggs

If a bread recipe includes eggs, these should be considered part of the liquid content. Eggs add colour, improve the structure and give the bread a rich flavour, although they are inclined to dry out more quickly than plain bread. It is worth adding extra fat to compensate for this. All the recipes in this book use medium eggs unless stated otherwise.

Above: Use soaking and cooking liquids in savoury breads.

FATS AND SWEETENERS

FATS

Whether solid (butter, margarine) or liquid (oil), small amounts of fats are often added to breads. They enrich doughs and add flavour, and, with eggs, they give a soft, tender texture to the crumb. Fats help to extend the freshness of the loaf, and in rich doughs, help to cancel out the drying effect that eggs can cause.

In small amounts, fat contributes to the elasticity of the gluten, but use too much and the opposite effect will result. The fat coats the gluten strands and this forms a barrier between the yeast and flour. This slows down the action of the yeast, and hence increases the rising time. For this reason it is best to limit the amount of fat in a machine-baked bread, or risk a heavy, compact loaf.

When making rich, brioche-style bread, it is best to use the bread machine only for making the dough. It may be necessary to use the cycle twice. Afterwards, shape the dough by hand and leave it to rise for as long as required, before baking the bread conventionally.

SOLID FATS

Butter, margarine or lard (shortening) can all be used in small quantities (of up to 15g/½oz/1 tbsp) without adding any noticeable flavour to the dough. Where a recipe calls for a larger quantity of fat, use butter, preferably unsalted (sweet). If you only have salted butter, and you are using quite a lot of it, you may need to reduce the amount of salt added to the dough. Cut the butter into small pieces so that it will mix in better. Avoid letting the fat come into contact with the yeast as it may inhibit the dissolving of the yeast.

BELOW: Left to right: olive oil, sunflower oil, hazelnut oil and walnut oil can all be used to impart a slightly different flavour to bread.

Where butter is layered in yeast pastry for croissants and Danish pastries, it is important to soften it so it has the same consistency as the dough. Although it is possible to use low-fat spreads in bread-making, there is not much point in doing so, as they may contain up to 40 per cent water and do not have the same properties as butter.

LIQUID FATS

Sunflower oil is a good alternative to butter if you are concerned about the cholesterol level, while olive oil can be used where flavour is important. Use a fruity, full-flavoured extra virgin olive oil from the first pressing of the olives.

Nut oils, such as walnut and hazelnut, are quite expensive and have very distinctive flavours, but are wonderful when teamed with similarly flavoured breads.

Fats and oils are interchangeable in many recipes. If you wish to change a solid fat for a liquid fat or oil the amount of liquid in the dough needs to be adjusted to accommodate the change. This is only necessary for amounts over 15ml/1 tbsp.

LEFT: Left to right: margarine, butter, lard

ABOVE: Left to right:
dark brown sugar,
light muscovado (brown) sugar, light
brown soft sugar, granulated sugar,
caster sugar

SWEETENERS

Sugars and liquid sweeteners accelerate the fermentation process by providing the yeast with extra food. Modern types of yeast no longer need sugar; they are able to use the flour efficiently to provide food. Even so, it is usual to add a small amount of sweetener. This makes the dough more active than if it were left to feed slowly on the natural starches and sugars in the flour. Enriched breads and heavy wholegrain breads need the increased yeast action to help the heavier dough to rise.

Sugar helps delay the staling process in bread because it attracts moisture. It also creates a tender texture.Too much sugar can cause dough to over-rise and collapse. Sweet breads have a moderate sugar level and gain extra sweetness from dried fruits, sweet glazes and icings.

BELOW: Left to right: treacle, golden
syrup, molasses, malt extract,
maple syrup, honey

Sweeteners contribute to the colour of the bread. A small amount enhances the crust colour. Some bread machines over-brown sweet doughs, so select a light crust setting or a sweet bread setting, if available, when making sweet yeast cakes.

Any liquid sweetener can be used instead of sugar, but should be counted as part of the total liquid content of the bread. Adjustments may need to be made.

WHITE SUGARS

Granulated or caster (superfine) sugar can be used for bread making. They are almost pure sucrose and add little flavour to the finished bread. Do not use icing (confectioners') sugar as the anti-caking agent can affect the flavour. Save icing sugar for glazing and dusting.

BROWN SUGARS

Use light or dark brown, refined or unrefined brown sugar. The darker unrefined sugars will add more flavour, having a higher molasses content. Brown sugars add a touch of colour and also increase the acidity, which can be beneficial.

MALT EXTRACT

An extract from malted wheat or barley, this has a strong flavour, so use sparingly. It is best used in fruit breads.

HONEY AND MAPLE SYRUP

Clear honey can be used as a substitute for sugar, but only use two-thirds of the amount suggested for sugar, as it is sweeter. Maple syrup is the reduced sap of the maple tree; use it in place of honey or sugar. It is slightly sweeter than sugar but not as sweet as honey.

MOLASSES, GOLDEN SYRUP AND TREACLE

All these sweeteners are by-products of sugar refining. Molasses is a thick concentrated syrup with a sweet, slightly bitter flavour. It adds a golden colour to bread. Golden (light corn) syrup is light and sweet with a slight butterscotch flavour. Treacle is brownish black and more intensely flavoured, and, like molasses, adds a slight bitterness to the bread.

ADDITIONAL INGREDIENTS

MEATS

Meats can be used to flavour bread recipes. The best results often come from using cured meats, such as ham, bacon or salami, and cooked sausages such as pepperoni.

When you use a strongly flavoured meat, it is best to chop it finely and add it to the dough during its final kneading. You don't need much – 25–50g/1–2oz will be quite sufficient to add extra flavour without overpowering the bread.

Ham and bacon are best added as small pieces, late on in the kneading cycle. Dice ham small. Fry or grill (broil) bacon rashers, then crumble them or cut into pieces, or use ready-cut cubes of bacon or pancetta and sauté them first. Make sure the bacon is fully cooked before adding it to the bread dough.

Thinly sliced preserved meats, such as prosciutto, pastrami, speck, pepperoni and smoked venison can be added as thin strips towards the end of the kneading cycle or incorporated in the dough during shaping, for hand-shaped loaves. Cured and smoked venison marinated in olive oil and herbs gives a basic loaf of bread a wonderful burst of flavour, or you could try adding pastrami to a bread containing rye flour. Strongly flavoured meats will make the most impact, but remember that you need only small amounts.

LEFT: Sausages and bacon are a good addition to bread. They should be cooked before adding to a dough.

USING BACON IN THE BREAD MACHINE

1 Cut the bacon into thin strips and grill it, or dry-fry in a non-stick frying pan, until it is crisp.

2 Transfer the cooked bacon to a plate lined with kitchen paper, to blot up excess fat. Leave to cool.

3 Add the strips to the breadmaking machine towards the end of the kneading process or when the machine beeps.

USING MEATS

Some meats are best kept whole or coarsely chopped and used as a filling, as when sausage is layered through a brioche dough, or used as a topping on tray-baked breads and pizzas. There are many different types of salami, flavoured with spices such as peppercorns, coriander or paprika, as well as pepperoni and cooked spicy Continental-style sausages, all of which are suitable.

LEFT: From top to bottom: salami, pepperoni, thinly sliced smoked venison, prosciutto

RIGHT: From left to right: cottage cheese, mascarpone, fromage frais

CHEESES

Cheese can be added to a wide variety of breads, to make them more moist and to give them more taste. Some cheeses have powerful flavours that really impact on the bread, while others are much more subtle, and are indistinguishable from the other ingredients except for the richness and tenderness they impart. Soft cheeses such as cottage cheese, mascarpone, fromage frais and ricotta are added in this way as part of the liquid content of the recipe. They contribute little to the overall taste of the bread, but help to create a more tender loaf with a softer crumb.

Grated or chopped hard cheeses can be added at the beginning of kneading so they are totally incorporated in the dough, or else towards the end of kneading, meaning that small amounts can clearly be detected in the bread. Alternatively, the cheese can be sprinkled over the top just before baking, to add colour and texture to the crust, or used as a topping or filling, as in pizzas or calzones.

For maximum cheese flavour, use small amounts of strongly flavoured cheeses such as extra-mature Cheddar, Parmesan, Pecorino, or blue cheeses such as Roquefort, Gorgonzola, Danish Blue or Stilton.

RIGHT: Selection of cheeses, clockwise from top left: Cheddar, Emmenthal, feta, Gorgonzola; centre: mozzarella

If the cheese is salty, reduce the amount of added salt, or the action of the yeast will be retarded and the bread may taste unacceptably salty.

Machine-made breads incorporating hard cheeses may not rise as high as ones without, due to the increased richness in the dough, but the texture and flavour are likely to be superb.

USING CHEESE IN THE BREAD MACHINE

• Add a soft cheese to the bread pan with the liquids before adding the dry ingredients, unless the instructions for your breadmaking machine state that you should add dry ingredients first.
• Add grated cheese at the beginning of the dough cycle so that it becomes evenly incorporated throughout the cooked bread.

• Add coarsely crumbled cheeses when the machine beeps towards the end of the kneading, so that it retains some of its form and remains in small pockets in the dough.

HERBS AND SPICES

Use herbs and spices as the main flavouring ingredient in bread or to enhance other ingredients.

HERBS

Fresh herbs have the most wonderful aroma, matched only by their flavour in freshly baked breads. Use fresh herbs if possible. Dried herbs that are oily and pungent, such as sage, rosemary and thyme, also work well. Rosemary is especially pungent, so use sparingly. Dried oregano is a fine substitute for fresh. Dried herbs have a more concentrated flavour than fresh; use about a third of the quantity recommended for fresh.

A number of herbs are now available freshly chopped and preserved in oil, which is a good alternative for more delicate herbs such as basil and coriander

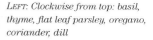

LEFT: Clockwise from top: basil, thyme, flat leaf parsley, oregano, coriander, dill

(cilantro) which do not dry well. Add fresh herbs toward the end of the kneading cycle. Dried herbs can be added with the dry ingredients. Avoid using dried parsley; substitute a different herb instead.

SPICES

Spices are the dried, intensely aromatic, seeds, pods, stems, bark, buds or roots of plants. As with herbs, the fresher they are the more aromatic they will be; the volatile oils fade with age. Use freshly grated black pepper and nutmeg. Cumin, fennel, caraway and cardamom can be bought as whole seeds, and ground in a spice mill, or a coffee mill kept for the purpose, as needed. If you buy ground spices, use them within 6 months.

Add saffron, nutmeg, cinnamon, anise, allspice and cardamom to sweet or savoury breads. Mixed spice and ginger are sweet spices, while juniper berries, cumin, coriander and black onion seeds provide aromatic flavourings for savoury breads. A number of whole spices can also be used as toppings for breads.

BELOW: From left to right: Front row: black onion seeds, saffron, fennel, nutmeg; back row: allspice, cinnamon, cumin, ginger

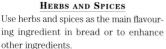

ADDING HERBS AND SPICES

• Frozen chopped herbs are a quick alternative to fresh herbs. Add them to the dough just before the end of the kneading process.
• Add ground spices after the flour, so they do not come into contact with the liquid before mixing.
• Add whole spices along with the dry ingredients if you want them to break down during kneading. If not, add them when the machine beeps, towards the end of kneading.

ABOVE: *Clockwise from top right: pistachio nuts, pecan nuts, pine nuts, walnuts, slivered almonds, macadamia nuts*

NUTS

Nuts make a wonderful addition to home-made breads. Their crunchiness combines equally well with the sweetness of both dried fruits and fresh fruits. They go well with savoury additions such as cheese, herbs and spices and they can be used on their own to make rustic-style breads.

Nuts contain natural oils which turn rancid if stored too warm or for too long. Buy in small quantities, store in an air-tight container in a cool place and use them within a few weeks.

Pecan nuts, almonds, macadamia nuts, pistachio nuts and walnuts give wonder-ful flavour and texture when added to basic breads towards the end of the kneading process. They can be added to teabreads, or used as a decoration on top of sweet breads or yeast cakes. Walnut bread is a rich brown loaf with a soft crunch, perfect with cheeses.

Lightly toast pine nuts, hazelnuts and almonds first to bring out their flavour. Spread the nuts on a baking sheet and place them in an oven preheated to 180°C/350°F/Gas 4 for 5–8 minutes, or grill (broil) until golden. Avoid scorching, and cool before adding them to the bread.

Hazelnuts, almonds and walnuts can be finely ground and used as a nutritious and flavoursome flour substitute. Replace up to 15 per cent of the flour with the ground nuts. If using hazelnuts, remove the skin first, as it is bitter. This will easily rub off if you toast the nuts in the oven.

Use coconut freshly grated or choose desiccated (dry unsweetened shredded), either plain or toasted.

CHESTNUT BREAD

These quantities are for a medium loaf. Increase all ingredients by 25 per cent for a large machine; decrease by 25 per cent for a small one.

1 Put 175g/6oz/½ cup unsweetened chestnut purée in a bowl and stir in 250ml/9fl oz/scant 1¼ cups water. Mix well. Place in the bread pan.

2 Sprinkle over 450g/1lb/4 cups white bread flour and 50g/2oz/½ cup whole-meal (whole-wheat) flour. Add 30ml/2 tbsp skimmed milk powder (non fat dry milk), 2.5ml/½tsp ground cloves and 5ml/1 tsp grated nutmeg. Place 5ml/1 tsp salt, 15ml/1 tbsp light muscovado (brown) sugar and 40g/1½oz/3 tbsp butter in corners. Make a shallow indent; add 7.5ml/1½tsp easy-blend (rapid-rise) dried yeast.

3 Set to the basic/normal setting, with raisin setting (if available), light crust. Press Start. Add 75g/3oz/¾ cup coarsely chopped walnuts at the beep or after the first kneading. Cool on a wire rack.

VEGETABLES

Raw, canned, dried and freshly cooked vegetables all make perfect additions to savoury breads. Making bread also provides a good opportunity to use up any leftover cooked vegetables. Vegetable breads are richer than basic breads, the vegetables contributing flavour and texture to the finished loaves. Many vegetable breads are subtly coloured or dotted with attractive flecks.

Fresh vegetables are relatively high in liquid, so if you add them, calculate that about half of their weight will be water

BELOW: Clockwise from top: spinach, green, red and yellow (bell) peppers, courgettes (zucchini), sweet potatoes

LEFT: Clockwise from top right: garlic, spring onions (scallions), chilli peppers, dried sliced onion, onions

and deduct the equivalent amount of liquid from the recipe. Keep an eye on the dough as it mixes and add more flour or liquid as needed.

STARCHY VEGETABLES

Potatoes, sweet potatoes, parsnips, carrots, swede and other varieties of starchy vegetables sweeten the bread and contribute a soft texture. You can use leftover mashed or even instant potato, adding 115g/4oz/1⅓ cups–225g/8oz/2⅔ cups to a basic bread recipe depending on the size of your machine. Adjust the liquid accordingly.

SPINACH

Fresh spinach leaves need to be blanched briefly in boiling water before being used. After blanching, add them whole with the liquid ingredients at the beginning

---

PREPARING PEPPERS

1 Cut each (bell) pepper into three or four flat pieces. Remove the core and seeds. Place in a grill (broiling) pan or roasting pan and brush the pieces lightly with olive oil or sunflower oil.

2 Grill (broil) until the skins blister and begin to char. Remove each piece as it is cooked and place inside a plastic bag. Seal the bag and leave to cool.

3 Peel off and discard the skin, then chop the peppers and add when the bread machine beeps, or 5 minutes before the kneading cycle ends.

LEFT: Fresh or dried mushrooms work well in breads

of the kneading process, and they will mix in and become finely chopped as the cycle progresses. Frozen chopped spinach can be substituted for fresh, but thaw it completely first and reduce the liquid in the recipe to allow for the extra water.

ONIONS, LEEKS AND CHILLIES

These vegetables are best if you sauté them first in a little butter or oil, which brings out their flavour. Caramelized onions will add richness and a light golden colour to the bread. For speed, you can add dried sliced onions instead of fresh onions, but you may need to add an extra 15ml/1 tbsp or so of liquid.

MUSHROOMS

Dried wild mushrooms can be used in the same way as sun-dried tomatoes to produce a very tasty loaf for serving with soups, casseroles and stews. Strain the soaking water, if you intend to use it in a recipe, to remove any grit.

TOMATOES

Tomatoes are very versatile and give bread a delicious flavour. They can be puréed, canned, fresh or sun-dried. Depending on when you add sun-dried tomatoes they will either remain as pieces, making a bread with interesting flecks of colour, or be fully integrated in the dough to provide flavour. To intensify the taste, choose regular sun-dried tomatoes, rather than the ones preserved in oil,

reconstitute them in water, then use the soaking water as the liquid in the recipe. Other tomato products are best added at the beginning of the breadmaking cycle, to ensure a richly coloured, full-bodied loaf with a distinct tomato flavour.

OTHER VEGETABLES

Add vegetables such as corn kernels, chopped olives or chopped spring onions (scallions) towards the end of the kneading cycle to ensure that they remain whole. All will impart flavour, colour and texture.

Frozen vegetables should be thawed completely before using in the machine. You may need to reduce the liquid quantity in the recipe if you use frozen vegetables instead of fresh. Canned vegetables should be well drained.

CHICKPEAS

The starchiness of chickpeas, like that of potatoes, produces a light bread with good keeping qualities. Add cooked drained chickpeas whole; the machine will reduce them to a pulp very effectively. Chickpeas add a pleasant, nutty flavour to breads.

ADDING VEGETABLES TO BREAD

There are several ways of preparing vegetables ready to add to the machine.

• Add grated raw vegetables such as courgettes (zucchini), carrots or beetroot (beet), when you add the water to the pan.

• Sweet potatoes, parsnips, potatoes, winter squashes and pumpkin should be cooked first. Drain, reserving the cooking liquid, and mash them. When cool, add both the cooking liquid and the mashed vegetable to the dough.

• If you want vegetables to remain identifiable in the finished bread add them when the machine beeps for adding extra ingredients or 5 minutes before the end of the kneading cycle, so they stay as slices or small pieces.

FRUIT

Whether you use them fresh, dried or as purées or juices, fruits add complementary flavours to breads and teacakes. The natural sugars help to feed the yeast and improve the leavening process, while fruits with natural pectin will improve the keeping quality of baked goods.

DRIED CAKE FRUITS

The familiar dried cake fruits such as sultanas (golden raisins), currants and raisins can easily be incorporated in basic breads, adding their own distinctive flavours. Sprinkle them in gradually, when the machine beeps or towards the end of the kneading cycle. For added flavour, plump them up in fruit juice or liqueur. You can add up to 50g/2oz/⅓ cup of dried fruit for a small bread machine, 115g/4oz/⅔ cup

BELOW: Clockwise from top left: candied citrus peel, dried pears, dried cranberries, dried prunes, dried mango, and dried figs

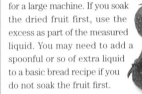

ABOVE: Pears, bananas, apples

for a large machine. If you soak the dried fruit first, use the excess as part of the measured liquid. You may need to add a spoonful or so of extra liquid to a basic bread recipe if you do not soak the fruit first.

RIGHT: Strawberries, raspberries, blueberries

DRIED, SEMI-DRIED AND READY-TO-EAT DRIED FRUITS

These are perfect for breads, because their flavours are so concentrated, and there is a vast range to choose from. Use combinations of exotic dried fruits, such as mango, papaya, melon and figs. Small dried fruits such as cranberries and cherries can be added whole, while the larger exotic fruits need to be chopped coarsely, as do apricots, pears, dates and peaches. Dried fruits such as pitted prunes can be soaked in sherry or a liqueur, as for cake fruits.

FRESH FRUITS

Some fruits such as berries can be frozen before they are added to the dough. This helps to keep them intact. Spread the fruits out in a single layer on a baking sheet and freeze them until they are solid. Add to the dough in the machine just before the end of the kneading cycle. You can also use ready-frozen fruits in this way. When adding juicy fruits, toss them with a little extra flour, to keep the consistency of the bread dough correct. Soft fruits can be added to teabread mixtures too; just fold them in at the end of mixing.

Firm fruits, such as apples or pears, can be added raw, chopped into small chunks. Plums and rhubarb can also be used raw; simply cut them into small pieces. Rhubarb can also be poached first, so that it softens slightly. You can also grate firm fruits, or mash soft ripe fruits such as bananas and pears.

PINEAPPLE AND BANANA BREAD

The quantities given here are for a medium bread machine. Increase by 25 per cent for a large machine; decrease by 25 per cent for a small.

1 Pour 60ml/4 tbsp pineapple juice and 200ml/7fl oz/⅞ cup buttermilk into the bread pan. Mash 1 large banana (about 180g/6½oz) and add. Add the dry ingredients first if your machine specifies this.

2 Sprinkle over 450g/1lb/4 cups white bread flour and 50g/2oz/½ cup wholemeal (whole-wheat) flour. Place 5ml/1 tsp salt, 45ml/3 tbsp caster (super-fine) sugar and 40g/1½oz/3 tbsp butter in separate corners. Make an indent in the flour; add 5ml/1 tsp easy-blend dried yeast.

3 Set to the basic/normal setting, with raisin setting (if available), light crust. Press Start. Add 75g/3oz/½ cup chopped pineapple chunks at the beep or towards the end of the cycle. Remove from the pan and turn out on to a wire rack.

ADDING FRUIT TO BREADS

When you add the fruit and how heavily processed it is will determine whether it remains clearly detectable as whole pieces or blends fully into the dough to impart an even flavour and moistness throughout the bread.

• Add frozen orange concentrate or fruit juice right at the beginning of the mixing process, unless the instructions for your machine state you should add the dry ingredients first.

• Add purées, such as apple, pear or mango, after the water in the recipe has been poured into the bread pan. Alternatively, blend the two together first, then add the mixture to the pan.

BELOW: Fruit juice can replace part of the water quantity in some breads. Left to right: apple juice, pineapple juice, mango juice

• If you wish to add mashed or grated fruits, such as bananas or pears, put them in after the liquids.

• Add fresh or frozen whole fruits, such as berries, when the machine beeps or about 5 minutes before the end of the kneading cycle. Chopped fruits, such as apples and plums, as well as dried fruits, should also be added towards the end of the kneading process.

EQUIPMENT

The accessories required for bread-making are quite simple, the most expensive being the bread machine, which you probably already own. The essential pieces of equipment are largely concerned with accurate measuring; the remaining items are useful for hand-shaped breads.

MEASURING

Items to measure ingredients accurately are vital for making machine-breads.

SCALES

Electronic scales give the most accurate results and are well worth investing in. You can place the bread pan directly on the scales and weigh the ingredients straight into it. The display can be set to zero after each ingredient has been added, which makes additions to the pan easy to perform and absolutely precise.

MEASURING SPOONS

Smaller quantities of dry ingredients, such as sugar, salt and, most importantly, yeast, need to be measured carefully. A set of measuring spoons from 1.5ml/¼ tsp to 15ml/1 tbsp is ideal. Always level off the ingredient in the spoon for an accurate measure.

MEASURING JUGS (CUPS)

Heatproof glass jugs that are clearly marked in metric and imperial units are very useful. Place the measuring jug on a flat surface to ensure accuracy, and check the level of the ingredients by bending down so the measurements are at eye level.

LEFT: Having a range of different-size glass bowls is useful.

LEFT: Bannetons may be used for final proving before the bread is baked.

LEFT: Use scales and measuring jugs, cups and spoons to ensure the correct quantity of ingredients. Accuracy is essential to give good results.

MIXING AND RISING

The bread machine will automatically mix dough and make it rise, but there may be some items of equipment you need for hand-shaped breads.

GLASS BOWLS

While most of the mixing will take place inside the machine, you will still need to mix glazes, add extra ingredients, transfer doughs or batters to a large bowl, or use a large bowl as a cover for hand-shaped bread during the final proving period. Glass bowls give all-round visibility and a selection of sizes will prove universally useful around the kitchen.

BELOW: A French baguette tray will give French loaves their traditional shape.

LEFT: Speciality cake tins such as a kugelhopf tin and small brioche moulds may be worth acquiring.
BELOW: Assorted cake tins (pans), fluted loose-based tart tin

dough partway through the cycle, set a kitchen timer. It is also a good idea to set a timer if the beep of your bread machine is not particularly loud and you are unlikely to be in the kitchen when the signal goes off.

BANNETON
During the final proving, breads are sometimes supported in cloth-lined baskets, called bannetons. Place baguettes in long bannetons and round loaves in round baskets. Flour the cloth well to prevent the dough from sticking. When the dough has risen you can up-turn the basket and place the bread directly on a prepared baking sheet.

DISHTOWELS AND CLEAR FILM
Use a clean dishtowel or clear film (plastic wrap) to cover the dough during proving. This prevents a dry crust from forming. Before using, lightly flour the dishtowel or oil the clear film to prevent the dough from sticking to the cover.

TIMER
If your bread machine does not have an audible signal to remind you to add extra ingredients, or you want to remember to check the

BAKING HAND-SHAPED LOAVES
A variety of tins (pans), trays and other equipment will help you bake breads of interesting shapes or with a crispier crust.

BREAD PANS AND MOULDS
Heavy gauge baking tins and moulds are best, because they are less likely to distort in the oven. A number of shapes and sizes are useful. A 1kg or a 2lb loaf tin (pan) measuring 18.5–11.5cm/ 7¼ × 4½in is a good basic size and shape, or try a longer, slightly narrower tin about 23–28cm/9–10in long. Both round and square cake tins are used for bread making, to support the dough while it rises. A 15cm/6in deep cake tin is used for baking pannetone.

RIGHT: Baking trays and loaf tins

*BELOW: A peel is useful
when making pizzas*

Springform cake tins (pans) with diameters of 20–25cm/8–10in make the removal of sweet breads and cakes much easier than when a fixed-based cake tin is used. Square and rectangular tins are perfect for both sweet-and-savoury topped breads.

Focaccia or deep-pan pizzas are best cooked in a large, shallow, round cake tin with a diameter of 25–28cm/10–11in. A fluted loose-based tart pan and shallow pizza pan are good investments if you cook those types of bread regularly.

Shaped moulds are often used for baking speciality breads. A fluted mould with sloping sides is the classic shape for both individual and large Brioche. Kugelhopf is made in a deep fluted tin with a central hole, Savarin in a shallow ring mould and Babas in shallow, individual ring moulds.

FRENCH BAGUETTE TRAY

A moulded tray, designed to hold two or three loaves, this has a perforated base to ensure an even heat while baking. The bread is given its final proving in the tray, which is then placed in the oven for baking. Loaves baked in a tray will have small dimples on the base and sides.

BAKING SHEETS

A number of free-form breads need to be transferred to a baking sheet for cooking. A selection of strong, heavy baking sheets is best. Use either totally flat baking sheets, or ones with a lip on one edge only. These make it possible to remove the cooked breads easily.

BAKING STONE

For more rustic bread, sourdoughs, pizza and focaccia, a baking stone or pizza stone helps to ensure a crisp crust.

TERRACOTTA TILES

Unglazed quarry tiles or terracotta tiles can be used instead of a baking stone. The tiles will draw out moisture and help to produce the traditional crisp crust.

PEEL

If you are regularly going to use a baking stone or tiles, a peel (baker's shovel) is a useful piece of equipment. Use it to slide pizzas and bread doughs into the oven, placing

them directly on to the preheated surface. Flour the peel generously and place the bread on it for its final proving. Give it a gentle shake just before placing it in the oven to make sure the base of the bread doesn't stick to the peel.

WATER SPRAY BOTTLE

Use a water spray bottle to mist the oven when you wish to achieve a crisp crust. A pump-action plastic bottle with a fine spray-head is ideal.

USEFUL TOOLS

This section includes tools for preparing ingredients and for finishing hand-shaped and machine breads.

CUTTERS

Plain cutters are used to cut dough for muffins and rolls. Metal cutters are best as they are not distorted when pressure is applied. A range of cutters 5–10cm/2–4in in diameter is most useful.

VEGETABLE PEELER

Use a fixed-blade vegetable peeler for peeling vegetables and fruit, or removing strips of citrus peel. A swivel-blade peeler is useful for paring very thin layers of citrus skin.

ZESTER

Many sweet breads and cakes include fresh citrus zest and this handy little tool makes light work of preparing it. The zester has a row of holes with cutting edges which shave off thin strips of zest without including the bitter pith that lies just beneath the coloured citrus peel. You may then wish to chop the strips into smaller pieces with a very sharp knife.

PASTRY BRUSHES

These are used to apply washes and glazes. Avoid nylon brushes, which will melt if used on hot breads. Brushes made from natural fibre are better.

LEFT: A baking stone, terracotta tiles and a water spray all help to produce breads with a crispier crust.

PLASTIC SCRAPER AND SPATULA

Make sure these tools are pliable. Use them to help remove dough that is stuck on the inside of the bread machine pan. The scraper also comes in handy for lifting and turning sticky dough and dividing dough into pieces for shaping into rolls.

KNIVES

You will need a sharp cook's knife for slashing doughs and a smaller paring knife for preparing fruit and vegetables. Use stainless steel for acidic fruits.

SCISSORS AND SCALPEL

Both these items can be used for slashing breads and rolls, to give decorative finishes before baking. A medium-size pair of scissors with thin, pointed blades is perfect. If you use a scalpel, replace the blade regularly, as it must be sharp.

ROLLING PINS

Some breads and buns need to be rolled out for shaping. Cylindrical wooden pins are best. Use a heavy rolling pin about 45cm/18in long for breads and a smaller one for individual rolls, buns and pastries. A child's toy rolling pin can be very useful for fiddly items.

LEFT: Selection of rolling pins

ABOVE: From left to right: spatula, cook's knife, vegetable knife, scalpel and scissors

THERMOMETERS

All ovens cook with slightly different heat intensities. An oven thermometer will enable you to establish how your oven cooks so you can make any necessary adjustments to recipes.

The time-honoured way of testing if a loaf of bread is cooked through is to tap it on the base to determine if it sounds hollow.

A much more scientific method is to insert a thermometer into the centre of a hand-shaped loaf and check the internal temperature. It should be 190–195°C (375–383°F).

SIEVES

A large sieve is essential for sifting flours together, and it will be handy to have one or two small sieves for sifting ingredients such as dried skimmed milk, icing (confectioners') sugar and ground spices. Use a plastic sieve for icing sugar, so as not to discolour it.

COOLING AND SLICING

Cooling a bread properly gives a crispier crust. The bread is then ready to eat.

OVEN GLOVES

A thick pair of oven gloves or mitts is essential for lifting the bread pan from the machine or breads from the oven, because the metal items will be very hot.

WIRE RACK

The hot cooked bread should be turned out on to a wire rack and left to cool before storing or slicing.

BREAD KNIFE AND BOARD

To preserve the delicate crumb structure, bread should be sawn with a sharp knife that has a long serrated blade. Cut the bread on a wooden board to prevent damaging the serrated knife.

ABOVE: Oven gloves, and a wire rack for cooling bread

RECIPES USING A BREAD MACHINE

With the help of your bread machine you can create a vast array of distinctive breads, both sweet and savoury. The machine-baked breads have three sets of ingredients – for small, medium and large bread machines – as the quantities are crucial for success. Other breads can be mixed in any machine, shaped by hand then baked in an oven. Fresh bread tastes delicious and fills the kitchen with a wonderful aroma; now making it has never been easier.

BASIC BREADS

These recipes are the everyday breads that you will want to make time and again. They are some of the easiest breads to make in your machine; perfect for serving toasted with lashings of butter or for use in sandwiches. The range of breads includes wholemeal, Granary and rye breads, and those flavoured and enriched with milk, buttermilk, eggs, potato or rice. If you haven't made bread in your machine before, this is the place to start.

RAPID WHITE BREAD

A delicious basic white loaf which can be cooked on the fastest setting.
It is the ideal bread if you are in a hurry.

SMALL
210ml/7½fl oz/scant 1 cup water
22ml/1½ tbsp sunflower oil
375g/13oz/3¼ cups unbleached white
bread flour
15ml/1 tbsp skimmed milk powder
(non fat dry milk)
7.5ml/1½ tsp salt
15ml/1 tbsp granulated sugar
5ml/1 tsp easy-blend (rapid-rise)
dried yeast

MEDIUM
315ml/11fl oz/1⅓ cups water
30ml/2 tbsp sunflower oil
500g/1lb 2oz/4½ cups unbleached
white bread flour
22ml/1½ tbsp skimmed milk powder
7.5ml/1½ tsp salt
22ml/1½ tbsp granulated sugar
7.5ml/1½ tsp easy-blend dried yeast

LARGE
420ml/15fl oz/generous 1¾
cups water
45ml/3 tbsp sunflower oil
675g/1½lb/6 cups unbleached white
bread flour
30ml/2 tbsp skimmed milk powder
10ml/2 tsp salt
30ml/2 tbsp granulated sugar
10ml/2 tsp easy-blend dried yeast

MAKES 1 LOAF

2 Sprinkle over the flour, covering the water. Add the milk powder. Place the salt and sugar in separate corners of the bread pan. Make a shallow indent in the centre of the flour (but not down as far as the liquid) and add the yeast.

3 Set the bread machine to the rapid/quick setting, medium crust. Press Start.

4 Remove the bread at the end of the baking cycle and turn out on to a wire rack to cool.

COOK'S TIP
On the quick setting the yeast has less time to work, and breads may not rise as high as those cooked on the basic/normal setting.
In cold weather it may be necessary to use lukewarm water, to help speed up the action of the yeast.

1 Pour the water and the sunflower oil into the bread machine pan. However, if the instructions for your particular machine specify that the yeast is to be placed in the pan first, then reverse the order in which you add the liquid and dry ingredients.

MILK LOAF

—

Adding milk results in a soft, velvety grained loaf with a beautifully browned crust. Milk also improves the keeping quality of the bread.

SMALL
180ml/6½fl oz/generous ¾ cup milk
60ml/2fl oz/¼ cup water
375g/13oz/3¼ cups unbleached white bread flour
7.5ml/1½ tsp salt
10ml/2 tsp granulated sugar
20g/¾oz/1½ tbsp butter
2.5ml/½ tsp easy-blend (rapid-rise) dried yeast

MEDIUM
200ml/7fl oz/⅞ cup milk
100ml/3½fl oz/7 tbsp water
450g/1lb/4 cups unbleached white bread flour
7.5ml/1½ tsp salt
10ml/2 tsp granulated sugar
25g/1oz/2 tbsp butter
5ml/1 tsp easy-blend dried yeast

LARGE
280ml/10fl oz/1¼ cups milk
130ml/4½fl oz/½ cup + 1 tbsp water
675g/1½lb/6 cups unbleached white bread flour
10ml/2 tsp salt
15ml/1 tbsp granulated sugar
25g/1oz/2 tbsp butter
7.5ml/1½ tsp easy-blend dried yeast

MAKES 1 LOAF

COOK'S TIP
The milk should be at room temperature, or it will retard the action of the yeast and the bread will not rise properly. Remove the milk from the refrigerator 30 minutes before use. You can use full-cream (whole) or semi-skimmed (low-fat) milk.

1 Pour the milk and water into the bread machine pan. If the instructions for your machine specify that the yeast is to be placed in the pan first, reverse the order in which you add the liquid and dry ingredients.

2 Sprinkle over the flour, ensuring that it covers the water. Add the salt, sugar and butter in separate corners of the bread pan. Make a small indent in the centre of the flour (but not down as far as the liquid) and add the yeast.

3 Set the bread machine to the basic/normal setting, medium crust. Press Start.

4 Remove the bread at the end of the baking cycle and turn out on to a wire rack to cool.

WHITE BREAD

This is a simple all-purpose white bread recipe, which makes the perfect basis for experimenting. Try using different brands of flours and be prepared to make minor alterations to quantities if necessary, to find the optimum recipe for your machine.

SMALL
210ml/7½fl oz/scant 1 cup water
375g/13oz/3¼ cups unbleached white
bread flour
7.5ml/1½ tsp salt
15ml/1 tbsp granulated sugar
25g/1oz/2 tbsp butter
5ml/1 tsp easy-blend (rapid-rise)
dried yeast
unbleached white bread flour,
for dusting

MEDIUM
320ml/11¼fl oz/generous 1⅛ cups water
500g/1lb 2oz/4½ cups unbleached
white bread flour
7.5ml/1½ tsp salt
15ml/1 tbsp granulated sugar
25g/1oz/2 tbsp butter
5ml/1 tsp easy-blend dried yeast
unbleached white bread flour,
for dusting

LARGE
420ml/15fl oz/generous 1¾ cups water
675g/1½lb/6 cups unbleached white
bread flour
10ml/2 tsp salt
22ml/1½ tbsp granulated sugar
40g/1½oz/3 tbsp butter
7.5ml/1½ tsp easy-blend dried yeast
unbleached white bread flour,
for dusting

MAKES 1 LOAF

1 Pour the water into the bread machine pan. However, if the instructions for your machine specify that the yeast is to be placed in the pan first, reverse the order in which you add the liquid and dry ingredients.

2 Sprinkle over the flour, ensuring that it covers the water. Add the salt, sugar and butter in separate corners of the bread pan. Make a small indent in the centre of the flour (but not down as far as the liquid) and add the yeast.

COOK'S TIP
To give the crust a richer golden appearance, add skimmed milk powder (non fat dry milk) to the flour. For a small loaf, you will need 15ml/1 tbsp; for a medium loaf 22ml/1½ tbsp and for a large loaf 30ml/2 tbsp.

3 Set the bread machine to the basic/normal setting, medium crust. Press Start.

4 Remove the bread at the end of the baking cycle and turn out on to a wire rack to cool.

Egg-enriched White Loaf

Adding egg to a basic white loaf gives a richer flavour and creamier crumb, as well as a golden finish to the crust.

1 Put the egg(s) in a measuring jug (cup) and add sufficient water to give 240ml/8½fl oz/generous 1 cup, 300ml/10½fl oz/1⅓ cups or 430ml/15fl oz/scant 1⅞ cups, according to the size of loaf selected.

2 Mix lightly and pour into the bread machine pan. If your instructions specify that the yeast is to be placed in the pan first, reverse the order in which you add the liquid and the dry ingredients.

SMALL
1 egg
water, see method
375g/13oz/3¼ cups unbleached white bread flour
7.5ml/1½ tsp granulated sugar
7.5ml/1½ tsp salt
20g/¾oz/1½ tbsp butter
4ml/¾ tsp easy-blend (rapid-rise) dried yeast

MEDIUM
1 egg plus 1 egg yolk
water, see method
500g/1lb 2oz/4½ cups unbleached white bread flour
10ml/2 tsp granulated sugar
7.5ml/1½ tsp salt
25g/1oz/2 tbsp butter
5ml/1 tsp easy-blend dried yeast

LARGE
2 eggs
water, see method
675g/1½lb/6 cups unbleached white bread flour
15ml/1 tbsp granulated sugar
10ml/2 tsp salt
25g/1oz/2 tbsp butter
7.5ml/1½ tsp easy-blend dried yeast

MAKES 1 LOAF

3 Sprinkle over the flour, covering the water. Add the sugar, salt and butter in separate corners of the pan. Make a small indent in the centre of the flour and add the yeast.

4 Set the machine to the basic/normal setting, medium crust. Press Start. At the end of the baking cycle, turn out on to a wire rack to cool.

BUTTERMILK BREAD

Buttermilk adds a pleasant, slightly sour note to the flavour of this bread. It also gives the bread a good light texture and a golden brown crust. Buttermilk bread tastes especially delicious when toasted and simply spread with a little good quality butter.

SMALL
230ml/8fl oz/1 cup buttermilk
30ml/2 tbsp water
15ml/1 tbsp clear honey
15ml/1 tbsp sunflower oil
250g/9oz/2¼ cups unbleached white bread flour
125g/4½oz/generous 1 cup wholemeal (whole-wheat) bread flour
7.5ml/1½ tsp salt
5ml/1 tsp easy-blend (rapid-rise) dried yeast

MEDIUM
285ml/10fl oz/1¼ cups buttermilk
65ml/4½ tbsp water
22ml/1½ tbsp clear honey
22ml/1½ tbsp sunflower oil
350g/12oz/3 cups unbleached white bread flour
150g/5½oz/1⅓ cup wholemeal bread flour
7.5ml/1½ tsp salt
7.5ml/1½ tsp easy-blend dried yeast

LARGE
370ml/13fl oz/scant 1⅝ cups buttermilk
80ml/5½ tbsp water
30ml/2 tbsp clear honey
30ml/2 tbsp sunflower oil
475g/1lb 1oz/4¼ cups unbleached white bread flour
200g/7oz/1¾ cups wholemeal bread flour
10ml/2 tsp salt
10ml/2 tsp easy-blend dried yeast

MAKES 1 LOAF

COOK'S TIP
Buttermilk is a by-product of butter making and is the fairly thin liquid left after the fat has been made into butter. It is pasteurized and mixed with a special culture which causes it to ferment, resulting in the characteristic slightly sour flavour. If you run short of buttermilk, using a low-fat natural (plain) yogurt and 5–10ml/1–2 tsp lemon juice is an acceptable alternative.

1 Pour the buttermilk, water, honey and oil into the bread machine pan. If your instructions specify that the yeast is to be placed in the pan first, reverse the order of the liquid and dry ingredients.

2 Sprinkle over both the white and wholemeal flours, ensuring that the water is completely covered. Add the salt in one corner of the bread pan. Make a small indent in the centre of the flour (but not down as far as the liquid) and add the yeast.

3 Set the bread machine to the basic/normal setting, medium crust. Press Start.

4 Remove the bread from the pan at the end of the baking cycle and turn out on to a wire rack to cool.

LIGHT WHOLEMEAL BREAD

A tasty, light wholemeal loaf which can be cooked on the quicker basic or normal setting.

SMALL
280ml/10fl oz/1¼ cups water
250g/9oz/2¼ cups wholemeal
(whole-wheat) bread flour
125g/4½oz/generous 1 cup white
bread flour
7.5ml/1½ tsp salt
7.5ml/1½ tsp granulated sugar
20g/¾oz/1½ tbsp butter
5ml/1 tsp easy-blend (rapid-rise)
dried yeast

MEDIUM
350ml/12fl oz/1½ cups water
350g/12oz/3 cups wholemeal bread flour
150g/5½oz/1⅓ cups white bread flour
10ml/2 tsp salt
10ml/2 tsp granulated sugar
25g/1oz/2 tbsp butter
7.5ml/1½ tsp easy-blend dried yeast

LARGE
450ml/16fl oz/scant 2 cups water
475g/1lb 1oz/4¼ cups wholemeal bread flour
200g/7oz/1¾ cups white bread flour
10ml/2 tsp salt
15ml/1 tbsp granulated sugar
25g/1oz/2 tbsp butter
10ml/2 tsp easy-blend dried yeast

MAKES 1 LOAF

VARIATION
This is a fairly light brown loaf as it contains a mixture of white and wholemeal bread flour.
Another option for a lighter brown bread is to replace the wholemeal bread flour with brown bread flour.
This contains less bran and wheatgerm than wholemeal flour, so produces a slightly lighter bread.

1 Pour the water into the bread machine pan. If the instructions for your bread machine specify that the yeast is to be placed in the pan first, reverse the order in which you add the liquid and dry ingredients to the pan.

2 Sprinkle over each type of flour in turn, ensuring that the water is completely covered. Add the salt, sugar and butter in separate corners of the bread pan. Make a small indent in the centre of the flour and add the yeast.

3 Set the bread machine to the basic/normal setting, medium crust. Press Start.

4 Remove the bread at the end of the baking cycle and turn out on to a wire rack to cool.

CORN MEAL BREAD

*This scrumptuous bread has a sweet flavour and crumbly texture.
Use a finely ground meal from the health-food store. The coarsely ground
meal used for polenta makes a good topping.*

COOK'S TIP
This bread is best cooked on a rapid
setting, even though the inclusion of
corn meal will result in a slightly
shallow loaf. Corn meal, also known as
maize meal, is available from most
health-food stores.

1 Pour the water, milk and corn oil into
the pan. Reverse the order in which you
add the wet and dry ingredients if the
instructions to your machine specify this.

3 Set the bread machine to the rapid/
quick setting, medium crust. Press
Start. Just before the baking cycle
commences brush the top of the loaf
with water and sprinkle with polenta.

2 Add the flour and the corn meal,
covering the water. Place the salt and
sugar in separate corners. Make a
shallow indent in the flour; add the yeast.

4 Remove the bread at the end of the
baking cycle and turn out on to a wire
rack to cool.

ANADAMA BREAD

This traditional New England bread is made with a mixture of white and wholemeal flours and polenta, which is a coarse corn meal. The molasses sweetens the bread and gives it a rich colour.

SMALL
200ml/7fl oz/⅞ cup water
45ml/3 tbsp molasses
5ml/1 tsp lemon juice
275g/10oz/2½ cups unbleached white bread flour
65g/2½oz/generous ½ cup wholemeal (whole-wheat) bread flour
40g/1½oz/⅓ cup polenta
7.5ml/1½ tsp salt
25g/1oz/2 tbsp butter
5ml/1 tsp easy-blend (rapid-rise) dried yeast

MEDIUM
240ml/8½fl oz/generous 1 cup water
60ml/4 tbsp molasses
5ml/1 tsp lemon juice
360g/12½oz/generous 3 cups unbleached white bread flour
75g/3oz/¾ cup wholemeal bread flour
65g/2½oz/generous ½ cup polenta
10ml/2 tsp salt
40g/1½oz/3 tbsp butter
5ml/1 tsp easy-blend dried yeast

LARGE
280ml/10fl oz/1¼ cups water
90ml/5 tbsp molasses
10ml/2 tsp lemon juice
500g/1lb 2oz/4¼ cups unbleached white bread flour
90g/generous 3oz/scant 1 cup wholemeal bread flour
75g/3oz/¾ cup polenta
12.5ml/2½ tsp salt
50g/2oz/¼ cup butter
10ml/2 tsp easy-blend dried yeast

MAKES 1 LOAF

3 Set the bread machine to the basic/normal setting, medium crust. Press Start.

4 Remove the bread at the end of the baking cycle and turn out on to a wire rack to cool.

1 Pour the water, molasses and lemon juice into the bread machine pan. If the instructions for your machine specify that the yeast is to be placed in the pan first, reverse the order in which you add the liquid and dry ingredients.

2 Sprinkle over both types of flour, then the polenta, so that the water is completely covered. Add the salt and butter in separate corners of the bread pan. Make a small indent in the centre of the flour and add the yeast.

210ml/7½fl oz/scant 1 cup water
350g/12oz/3 cups unbleached white
bread flour, plus extra for dusting
25g/1oz/¼ cup wholemeal
(whole-wheat) bread flour
15ml/1 tbsp skimmed milk powder
(non fat dry milk)
7.5ml/1½ tsp salt
7.5ml/1½ tsp granulated sugar
15g/½oz/1 tbsp butter
4ml/¾ tsp easy-blend (rapid-rise)
dried yeast
water, for glazing

MEDIUM

320ml/11¼fl oz/generous 1⅓ cups water
425g/15oz/3¾ cups unbleached white
bread flour, plus extra for dusting
75g/3oz/¾ cup wholemeal bread flour
22ml/1½ tbsp skimmed milk powder
7.5ml/1½ tsp salt
7.5ml/1½ tsp granulated sugar
25g/1oz/2 tbsp butter
5ml/1 tsp easy-blend dried yeast
water, for glazing

LARGE

420ml/15fl oz/generous 1¾ cups water
600g/1lb 5oz/5¼ cups unbleached white
bread flour, plus extra for dusting
75g/3oz/¾ cup wholemeal
bread flour
30ml/2 tbsp skimmed milk powder
10ml/2 tsp salt
10ml/2 tsp granulated sugar
25g/1oz/2 tbsp butter
7.5ml/1½ tsp easy-blend dried yeast
water, for glazing

MAKES 1 LOAF

1 Pour the water into the bread pan. If the instructions for your machine specify that the yeast is to be placed in the pan first, reverse the order in which you add the liquid and dry ingredients. Sprinkle over both the flours, covering the water completely. Add the milk powder. Add the salt, sugar and butter in separate corners. Make a small indent in the centre of the flour (but not down as far as the liquid) and add the yeast.

FARMHOUSE LOAF

The flour-dusted split top gives a charmingly rustic look to this tasty wholemeal-enriched white loaf.

2 Set the bread machine to the basic/normal setting, medium crust. Press Start.

3 Ten minutes before the baking time commences, brush the top of the loaf with water and dust with a little white bread flour. Slash the top of the bread with a sharp knife.

4 Remove the bread at the end of the baking cycle and turn out on to a wire rack to cool.

COOK'S TIP
Try this rustic bread using Granary (whole-wheat) instead of wholemeal bread flour for added texture.

GRANARY BREAD

Granary flour – like Malthouse flour – is a blend, and contains malted wheat grain which gives a crunchy texture to this loaf.

1 Add the water to the bread machine pan. If the instructions for your machine specify that the yeast is to be placed in the pan first, simply reverse the order in which you add the liquid and dry ingredients to the pan.

2 Sprinkle over the flour, ensuring that it covers the water. Add the salt, sugar and butter in separate corners of the bread pan. Make a small indent in the centre of the flour (but not down as far as the liquid) and add the yeast.

3 Set the bread machine to the whole wheat or multi-grain setting, medium crust. Press Start.

4 Remove the bread at the end of the baking cycle and turn out on to a wire rack to cool.

COOK'S TIP
This bread tastes just as good if you use Malthouse bread flour instead of Granary flour.

SMALL
240ml/8½fl oz/generous 1 cup water
375g/13oz/3¼ cups Granary
(whole-wheat) bread flour
5ml/1 tsp salt
10ml/2 tsp granulated sugar
20g/¾oz/1½ tbsp butter
2.5ml/½ tsp easy-blend (rapid-rise) dried yeast

MEDIUM
350ml/12fl oz/1½ cups water
500g/1lb 2oz/4½ cups Granary bread flour
7.5ml/1½ tsp salt
15ml/1 tbsp granulated sugar
25g/1oz/2 tbsp butter
7.5ml/1½ tsp easy-blend dried yeast

LARGE
400ml/14fl oz/generous 1⅔ cups water
675g/1½lb/6 cups Granary bread flour
10ml/2 tsp salt
15ml/1 tbsp granulated sugar
25g/1oz/2 tbsp butter
7.5ml/1½ tsp easy-blend dried yeast

MAKES 1 LOAF

MALTED LOAF

A malt and sultana loaf makes the perfect breakfast or tea-time treat.
Serve it sliced and generously spread with butter.

200ml/7fl oz/⅞ cup water
15ml/1 tbsp golden (light corn) syrup
22ml/1½ tbsp malt extract
350g/12oz/3 cups unbleached white bread flour
22ml/1½ tbsp skimmed milk powder (non fat dry milk)
2.5ml/½ tsp salt
40g/1½oz/3 tbsp butter
2.5ml/½ tsp easy-blend dried (rapid-rise) yeast
75g/3oz/½ cup sultanas (golden raisins)

280ml/10fl oz/1¼ cups water
22ml/1½ tbsp golden syrup
30ml/2 tbsp malt extract
500g/1lb 2oz/4½ cups unbleached white bread flour
30ml/2 tbsp skimmed milk powder
5ml/1 tsp salt
50g/2oz/¼ cup butter
5ml/1 tsp easy-blend dried yeast
100g/3½oz/generous ½ cup sultanas

360ml/scant13fl oz/1½ cups water
30ml/2 tbsp golden syrup
45ml/3 tbsp malt extract
675g/1½lb/6 cups unbleached white bread flour
30ml/2 tbsp skimmed milk powder
5ml/1 tsp salt
65g/2½oz/5 tbsp butter
7.5ml/1½ tsp easy-blend dried yeast
125g/4½oz/generous ⅔ cup sultanas

MAKES 1 LOAF

1 Pour the water, golden syrup and malt extract into the bread machine pan. If the instructions for your machine specify that the yeast is to be placed in the pan first, reverse the order in which you add the liquid and dry ingredients.

2 Sprinkle over the flour so that it covers the liquid. Add the milk powder. Add the salt and butter in separate corners. Make a shallow indent in the centre of the flour and add the yeast.

3 Set the bread machine to the basic/normal setting, with raisin setting (if available), medium crust. Press Start. Add the sultanas when the machine beeps or after the first kneading.

4 Remove at the end and turn out on to a wire rack. If you like, glaze the bread immediately. Dissolve 15ml/1 tbsp caster (superfine) sugar in 15ml/1 tbsp milk and brush over the top crust.

LIGHT RYE AND CARAWAY BREAD

Rye flour adds a distinctive slightly sour flavour to bread. Rye breads can be dense, so the flour is usually mixed with wheat flour to lighten the texture.

1 Add the water, lemon juice and oil to the bread pan. If your instructions specify that the yeast is to be placed in the pan first, reverse the order in which you add the liquid and dry ingredients.

2 Sprinkle over the rye flour and the white bread flour, ensuring they cover the water. Add the skimmed milk powder and caraway seeds. Add the salt and sugar in separate corners of the bread pan. Make a small indent in the centre of the flour, but not down as far as the liquid, and add the yeast.

3 Set the bread machine to the basic/normal setting, medium crust. Press Start.

4 Remove the bread from the pan at the end of the cycle and transfer to a wire rack to cool.

SMALL

210ml/7½fl oz/scant 1 cup water
5ml/1 tsp lemon juice
15ml/1 tbsp sunflower oil
85g/3oz/¾ cup rye flour
285g/10oz/2½ cups unbleached white bread flour
15ml/1 tbsp skimmed milk powder (non fat dry milk)
5ml/1 tsp caraway seeds
5ml/1 tsp salt
10ml/2 tsp light muscovado (brown) sugar
3.5ml/¾ tsp easy-blend (rapid-rise) dried yeast

MEDIUM

300ml/10½ fl oz/1¼ cups water
10ml/2 tsp lemon juice
22ml/1½ tbsp sunflower oil
125g/4½oz/generous 1 cup rye flour
375g/13oz/3¼ cups unbleached white bread flour
22ml/1½ tbsp skimmed milk powder
7.5ml/1½ tsp caraway seeds
7.5ml/1½ tsp salt
15ml/1 tbsp light muscovado sugar
5ml/1 tsp easy-blend dried yeast

LARGE

370ml/13fl oz/scant 1⅝ cups water
10ml/2 tsp lemon juice
30ml/2 tbsp sunflower oil
175g/generous 6oz/generous 1½ cups rye flour
500g/1lb 2oz/4½ cups unbleached white bread flour
30ml/2 tbsp skimmed milk powder
10ml/2 tsp caraway seeds
10ml/2 tsp salt
20ml/4 tsp light muscovado sugar
7.5ml/1½ tsp easy-blend dried yeast

MAKES 1 LOAF

FRENCH BREAD

French bread traditionally has a crisp crust and light, chewy crumb. Use the special French bread setting on your bread machine to help to achieve this unique texture.

SMALL
MAKES 1 LOAF
150ml/5fl oz/⅔ cup water
225g/8oz/2 cups unbleached white bread flour
5ml/1 tsp salt
7.5ml/1½ tsp easy-blend (rapid-rise) dried yeast

MEDIUM
MAKES 2–3 LOAVES
315ml/11fl oz/1⅓ cups water
450g/1lb/4 cups unbleached white bread flour
7.5ml/1½ tsp salt
7.5ml/1½ tsp easy-blend dried yeast

LARGE
MAKES 3–4 LOAVES
500ml/17½fl oz/2⅛ cups water
675g/1½lb/6 cups unbleached white bread flour
10ml/2 tsp salt
10ml/2 tsp easy-blend dried yeast

1 Add the water to the bread machine pan. If the instructions for your machine specify that the yeast is to be placed in the pan first, reverse the order in which you add the liquid and dry ingredients.

2 Sprinkle over the flour, to cover the water. Add the salt in a corner. Make an indent in the centre of the flour and add the yeast. Use the French bread dough setting (see Cook's Tip). Press Start.

3 When the dough cycle has finished, remove the dough from the machine, place it on a lightly floured surface and knock it back (punch it down). Divide it into two or three equal portions if using the medium quantities or three or four portions if using the large quantities.

4 On a floured surface shape each piece of dough into a ball, then roll out to a rectangle measuring 18–20 × 7.5cm/ 7–8 × 3in. Fold one-third up lengthways and one-third down, then press. Repeat twice more, leaving the dough to rest between foldings to avoid tearing.

5 Gently roll and stretch each piece to a 28–33cm/11–13in loaf, depending on whether you aim to make smaller or larger loaves. Place each loaf in a floured banneton or between the folds of a floured and pleated dishtowel, so that the French bread shape is maintained during rising.

6 Cover with lighly oiled clear film (plastic wrap) and leave in a warm place for 30–45 minutes. Preheat the oven to 230°C/450°F/Gas 8.

7 Roll the loaf or loaves on to a baking sheet, spaced well part. Slash the tops with a knife. Place at the top of the oven, spray the inside of the oven with water and bake for 15–20 minutes, or until golden. Transfer to a wire rack.

COOK'S TIP
Use the French bread baking setting if you do not have a French bread dough setting. Remove the dough before the final rising stage and shape as directed.

ITALIAN BREADSTICKS

These crisp breadsticks will keep for a couple of days if stored in an airtight container. If you like, you can refresh them in a hot oven for a few minutes before serving. The dough can be made in any breadmaking machine, regardless of capacity.

200ml/7fl oz/⅞ cup water
45ml/3 tbsp olive oil, plus extra
350g/12oz/3 cups unbleached white bread flour
7.5ml/1½ tsp salt
7.5ml/1½ tsp easy-blend (rapid-rise) dried yeast
poppy seeds and coarse sea salt, for coating (optional)

MAKES 30

1 Pour the water and olive oil into the bread machine pan. If the instructions for your machine specify that the yeast is to be placed in the pan first, reverse the order in which you add the liquid and dry ingredients.

2 Sprinkle over the flour, ensuring that it covers the water completely. Add the salt in one corner of the pan. Make a small indent in the centre of the flour (but not down as far as the liquid) and add the easy-blend dried yeast.

3 Set the bread machine to the dough setting; use basic dough setting (if available). Press Start.

4 Lightly oil two baking sheets. Preheat the oven to 200°C/400°F/Gas 6.

5 When the dough cycle has finished, remove the dough from the machine, place it on a lightly floured surface and knock it back (punch it down). Roll it out to a rectangle measuring 23 × 20cm/9 × 8in.

6 Cut into three 20cm/8in long strips. Cut each strip widthways into ten. Roll and stretch each piece to 30cm/12in.

7 Roll in poppy seeds or sea salt if you like. Space well apart on the baking sheets. Brush lightly with olive oil, cover with clear film (plastic wrap) and leave in a warm place for 10–15 minutes.

8 Bake for 15–20 minutes, or until golden, turning once. Transfer to a wire rack to cool.

COOK'S TIP
If you are rolling the breadsticks in sea salt, don't use too much. Crush the sea salt slightly if the crystals are large.

RICE BREAD

*Rice is an unusual ingredient, but makes delicious bread that is moist,
flavoursome and with an interesting texture. The perfect vehicle for leftover
cooked rice, it tastes so good that it's worth cooking some specially.*

1 Pour the water into the bread machine pan, then add the egg. There is no need to beat the egg before you add it as the machine will mix all of the ingredients together thoroughly. If the instructions for your bread machine specify that the yeast is to be placed in the pan first, simply reverse the order in which you add the liquid and dry ingredients.

2 Sprinkle over the flour, ensuring that it covers the water. Add the rice and milk powder. Add the salt, sugar and butter in separate corners of the bread pan. Make a small indent in the centre of the flour and add the yeast.

3 Set the bread machine to the basic/normal setting, medium crust. Press Start.

4 Remove the bread at the end of the baking cycle and turn out on to a wire rack to cool.

COOK'S TIPS

Make sure the rice is cold before using it in this bread. It is important to drain it very well, or the bread dough may become too moist. Watch the dough as it mixes and add a little more flour if necessary.

POTATO BREAD

This golden crusty loaf has a moist soft centre and is perfect for sandwiches.
Use the water in which the potatoes have been cooked to make this bread.
If you haven't got enough, make up the remainder with tap water.

1 Pour the water and sunflower oil into the bread machine pan. However, if the instructions for your machine specify that the yeast is to be placed in the pan first, reverse the order in which you add the liquid and dry ingredients.

2 Sprinkle over the flour, ensuring that it covers the water. Add the mashed potato and milk powder. Add the salt and sugar in separate corners of the bread pan. Make a small indent in the centre of the flour (but not down as far as the liquid) and add the yeast.

3 Set the bread machine to the basic/normal setting, medium crust. Press Start. To glaze the loaf, brush the top with milk either at the beginning of the cooking time or halfway through.

4 Remove the bread at the end of the baking cycle and turn out on to a wire rack to cool.

SMALL
200ml/7fl oz/⅞ cup potato cooking water, at room temperature
30ml/2 tbsp sunflower oil
375g/13oz/3¼ cups unbleached white bread flour
125g/4½oz/1½ cups cold mashed potato
15ml/1 tbsp skimmed milk powder (non fat dry milk)
5ml/1 tsp salt
7.5ml/1½ tsp granulated sugar
5ml/1 tsp easy-blend (rapid-rise) dried yeast
milk, for glazing

MEDIUM
225ml/8fl oz/scant 1 cup potato cooking water, at room temperature
45ml/3 tbsp sunflower oil
500g/1lb 2oz/4½ cups unbleached white bread flour
175g/6oz/2 cups cold mashed potato
22ml/1½ tbsp skimmed milk powder
7.5ml/1½ tsp salt
10ml/2 tsp granulated sugar
7.5ml/1½ tsp easy-blend dried yeast
milk, for glazing

LARGE
330ml/11½fl oz/scant 1½ cups potato cooking water, at room temperature
60ml/4 tbsp sunflower oil
675g/1½lb/6 cups unbleached white bread flour
225g/8oz/2⅔ cups cold cooked mashed potato
30ml/2 tbsp skimmed milk powder
10ml/2 tsp salt
15ml/1 tbsp granulated sugar
7.5ml/1½ tsp easy-blend dried yeast
milk, for glazing

MAKES 1 LOAF

COOK'S TIP

If using leftover potatoes mashed with milk and butter you may need to reduce the liquid a little. If making the mashed potato, use 175g/6oz, 200g/7oz or 275g/10oz raw potatoes, depending on machine size.

SPECIALITY GRAINS

This selection of recipes includes classic flours from around the world, producing loaves with a variety of textures and flavours. Gluten is an essential part of the structure of bread, to ensure an open, light crumb and texture. Most grains other than wheat have little or no gluten, so millet, buckwheat, barley and rye have been blended with wheat flours to provide rich, nutty flavoured loaves which can be successfully baked in your bread machine.

260ml/9fl oz/scant 1⅛ cups water
30ml/2 tbsp sunflower oil
15ml/1 tbsp clear honey
300g/10½oz/2⅔ cups unbleached
white bread flour
75g/3oz/¾ cup wholemeal
(whole-wheat) bread flour
150g/5½oz/1½ cups unsweetened fruit
and nut muesli (granola)
45ml/3 tbsp skimmed milk powder
(non fat dry milk)
7.5ml/1½ tsp salt
7.5ml/1½ tsp easy-blend (rapid-rise)
dried yeast
65g/2½oz/scant ½ cup stoned (pitted)
dates, chopped

MAKES 1 LOAF

1 Pour the water, oil and honey into the
bread pan. Reverse the order in which
you add the wet and dry ingredients if
necessary. Sprinkle over the flours,
covering the water. Add the muesli and
milk powder, then the salt, in a corner.

MUESLI AND DATE BREAD

*This makes the perfect breakfast or brunch bread. Use your own favourite
unsweetened muesli to ring the changes.*

2 Make a small indent in the flour; add
the yeast. Set to the dough setting; use
basic raisin dough setting (if available).
Press Start. Add the dates at the beep
or during the last 5 minutes of kneading.
Lightly oil a baking sheet.

3 When the dough cycle has finished,
remove from the machine and place it
on a surface dusted with wholemeal
flour. Knock back (punch down) gently.

4 Shape the dough into a plump round
and place it on the prepared baking
sheet. Using a sharp knife make three
cuts on the top about 1cm/½in deep, to
divide the bread into six sections.

5 Cover the loaf with lightly oiled clear
film (plastic wrap) and leave for 30–45
minutes, or until almost doubled in size.

6 Preheat the oven to 200°C/400°F/
Gas 6. Bake the loaf for 30–35 minutes
until it is golden and hollow sounding.
Transfer it to a wire rack to cool.

COOK'S TIP
The amount of water required may
vary with the type of muesli used.
Add another 15ml/1 tbsp water if
the dough is too firm.

BARLEY-ENRICHED FARMHOUSE LOAF

*Barley adds a very distinctive, earthy, slightly nutty flavour to this
crusty white loaf.*

260ml/9fl oz/1⅛ cups water
45ml/3 tbsp double (heavy) cream
400g/14oz/3½ cups unbleached white
bread flour
115g/4oz/1 cup barley flour
10ml/2 tsp granulated sugar
10ml/2 tsp salt
7.5ml/1½ tsp easy-blend (rapid-rise)
dried yeast
25g/1oz/2 tbsp pumpkin seeds
flour, for dusting

MAKES 1 LOAF

1 Pour the water and cream into the
pan. Reverse the order in which you add
the liquid and dry ingredients if
necessary. Sprinkle over both types of
flour, covering the water completely.
Add the sugar and salt, placing them in
separate corners of the pan. Make a
shallow indent in the centre of the flour
and add the yeast.

2 Set the bread machine to the dough
setting; use basic raisin dough setting (if
available). Press Start. Add the pumpkin
seeds when the machine beeps or
during the last 5 minutes of kneading.
Lightly oil a 900g/2lb loaf tin (pan)
measuring 18.5 × 12cm/7¼ × 4½in.

3 When the dough cycle has finished,
remove the dough from the machine and
place on a lightly floured surface. Knock
back (punch down) gently. Shape the
dough into a rectangle, making the
longer side the same length as the tin.

4 Roll the dough up lengthways, and
tuck the ends under. Place it in the
prepared tin, with the seam underneath.
Cover with oiled clear film (plastic
wrap) and leave for 30–45 minutes, or
until the dough reaches the top of the tin.

5 Dust the loaf with flour then make a
deep lengthways cut along the top.
Leave to rest for 10 minutes. Preheat
the oven to 220°C/425°F/Gas 7.

6 Bake the loaf for 15 minutes, then
reduce the oven temperature to 200°C/
400°F/Gas 6 and bake for 20–25 minutes
more, or until the bread is golden and
sounds hollow when tapped on the base.
Transfer it to a wire rack to cool.

BRAN AND YOGURT BREAD

This soft-textured yogurt bread is enriched with bran. It is high in fibre and makes wonderful toast.

SMALL

150ml/5fl oz/⅔ cup water

125ml/4½fl oz/generous ½ cup
natural (plain) yogurt

15ml/1 tbsp sunflower oil

15ml/1 tbsp molasses

200g/7oz/1¾ cups unbleached white
bread flour

150g/5½oz/1⅓ cups wholemeal
(whole-wheat) bread flour

25g/1oz/⅓ cup wheat bran

5ml/1 tsp salt

4ml/¾ tsp easy-blend (rapid-rise)
dried yeast

MEDIUM

185ml/6½fl oz/generous ¾ cup water

175ml/6fl oz/¾ cup natural yogurt

22ml/1½ tbsp sunflower oil

30ml/2 tbsp molasses

260g/generous 9oz/2⅓ cups
unbleached white bread flour

200g/7oz/1¾ cups wholemeal
bread flour

40g/1½oz/½ cup wheat bran

7.5ml/1½ tsp salt

5ml/1 tsp easy-blend dried yeast

LARGE

230ml/8fl oz/1 cup water

210ml/7½fl oz/scant 1 cup
natural yogurt

30ml/2 tbsp sunflower oil

30ml/2 tbsp molasses

375g/13oz/3¼ cups unbleached white
bread flour

250g/9oz/2¼ cups wholemeal
bread flour

50g/2oz/⅔ cup wheat bran

10ml/2 tsp salt

7.5ml/1½ tsp easy-blend dried yeast

MAKES 1 LOAF

COOK'S TIP

Molasses is added to this bread to give added flavour and colour. You can use treacle or golden (light corn) syrup instead, to intensify or lessen the flavour respectively, if desired.

1 Pour the water, yogurt, oil and molasses into the bread machine pan. If the instructions for your machine specify that the yeast is to be placed in the pan first, reverse the order in which you add the liquid and dry ingredients.

2 Sprinkle over both the white and the wholemeal flours, ensuring that the liquid mixture is completely covered. Add the wheat bran and salt, then make a small indent in the centre of the dry ingredients (but not down as far as the liquid) and add the easy-blend dried yeast.

3 Set the bread machine to the basic/normal setting, medium crust. Press Start.

4 Remove the bread from the pan at the end of the baking cycle and turn out on to a wire rack to cool. Serve when still just warm, if you like.

POLENTA AND WHOLEMEAL LOAF

Polenta adds an interesting grainy quality to the texture of this rich wholemeal bread, which is perfect for everyday use.

SMALL
220ml/scant 8fl oz/scant 1 cup water
30ml/2 tbsp clear honey
25g/1oz/2 tbsp polenta
25g/1oz/¼ cup unbleached white bread flour
325g/11½oz/scant 3 cups wholemeal (whole-wheat) bread flour
5ml/1 tsp salt
20g/¾oz/1½ tbsp butter
4ml/¾ tsp easy-blend (rapid-rise) dried yeast

MEDIUM
300ml/10½fl oz/1¼ cups water
45ml/3 tbsp clear honey
50g/2oz/scant ½ cup polenta
50g/2oz/½ cup unbleached white bread flour
400g/14oz/3½ cups wholemeal bread flour
7.5ml/1½ tsp salt
25g/1oz/2 tbsp butter
7.5ml/1½ tsp easy-blend dried yeast

LARGE
350ml/12fl oz/1½ cups water
60ml/4 tbsp clear honey
75g/3oz/scant ¾ cup polenta
75g/3oz/¾ cup unbleached white bread flour
525g/1lb 3oz/4¾ cups wholemeal bread flour
10ml/2 tsp salt
40g/1½oz/3 tbsp butter
10ml/2 tsp easy-blend dried yeast

MAKES 1 LOAF

1 Add the water and honey to the pan. If necessary, reverse the order in which you add the liquid and dry ingredients. Sprinkle over the polenta and flours, ensuring that the liquid is covered.

2 Add the salt and butter in separate corners of the pan. Make a small indent in the centre of the flour (but not down as far as the liquid) and add the yeast.

3 Set the machine to the whole wheat setting, medium crust. Press Start.

COOK'S TIP
This bread is perfect for breakfast and it may be baked using the automatic delay timer. The small quantity of butter should be fine overnight, but if you wish, substitute vegetable oil and adjust the liquid accordingly.

4 Remove the loaf from the bread pan at the end of the baking cycle and turn out on to a wire rack to cool.

TOASTED MILLET AND RYE BREAD

The dough for this delectable loaf is made in the bread machine, but it is shaped by hand before being baked in the oven.

300ml/10½fl oz/1¼ cups water
50g/2oz/½ cup rye flour
450g/1lb/4 cups unbleached white bread flour
25g/1oz/¼ cup millet flakes
15ml/1 tbsp light muscovado (brown) sugar
5ml/1 tsp salt
25g/1oz/2 tbsp butter
5ml/1 tsp easy-blend (rapid-rise) dried yeast
50g/2oz/⅓ cup millet seeds
millet flour, for dusting
MAKES 1 LOAF

COOK'S TIP
Before adding, toast the millet seeds under a preheated grill (broiler) to enhance their distinctive sweet flavour.

1 Pour the water into the bread pan. If the instructions for your bread machine specify that the yeast is to be placed in the pan first, reverse the order in which you add the liquid and dry ingredients.

2 Sprinkle over both types of flour, then add the millet flakes, ensuring that the water is completely covered. Add the sugar, salt and butter, placing them in separate corners. Make an indent in the centre of the flour (but not down as far as the liquid) and add the yeast.

3 Set the bread machine to the dough setting; use basic raisin dough setting (if available). Press Start. Add the millet seeds when the machine beeps or during the last 5 minutes of kneading. Lightly flour a baking sheet.

4 When the dough cycle has finished, knock the dough back (punch it down) gently on a lightly floured surface.

5 Shape the dough into a rectangle. Roll it up lengthways, then shape it into a thick baton with square ends. Place it on the prepared baking sheet, making sure that the seam is underneath. Cover it with lightly oiled clear film (plastic wrap) and leave in a warm place for 30–45 minutes, or until almost doubled in size.

6 Remove the clear film and dust the top of the loaf with the millet flour. Using a sharp knife, make slanting cuts in alternate directions along the top of the loaf. Leave it to stand for about 10 minutes. Meanwhile, preheat the oven to 220°C/425°F/Gas 7.

7 Bake the loaf for 25–30 minutes, or until golden and hollow-sounding. Turn out on to a wire rack to cool.

BUCKWHEAT AND WALNUT BREAD

Buckwheat flour is made from toasted buckwheat groats. It has a distinctive earthy taste, perfectly mellowed when blended with white flour and walnuts in this compact bread, flavoured with molasses.

SMALL
210ml/7½fl oz/scant 1 cup water
10ml/2 tsp molasses
22ml/1½ tbsp walnut or olive oil
315g/11oz/2¾ cups unbleached white bread flour
50g/2oz/½ cup buckwheat flour
15ml/1 tbsp skimmed milk powder (non fat dry milk)
5ml/1 tsp salt
2.5ml/½ tsp granulated sugar
5ml/1 tsp easy-blend (rapid-rise) dried yeast
40g/1½oz/⅓ cup walnut pieces

MEDIUM
15ml/3 tsp molasses
315ml/11fl oz/1⅓ cups water
30ml/2 tbsp walnut or olive oil
425g/15oz/3¾ cups unbleached white bread flour
75g/3oz/¾ cup buckwheat flour
22ml/1½ tbsp skimmed milk powder
7.5ml/1½ tsp salt
4ml/¾ tsp granulated sugar
5ml/1 tsp easy-blend dried yeast
50g/2oz/½ cup walnut pieces

LARGE
420ml/15fl oz/generous 1¾ cups water
20ml/4 tsp molasses
45ml/3 tbsp walnut or olive oil
575g/1¼lb/5 cups unbleached white bread flour
115g/4oz/1 cup buckwheat flour
30ml/2 tbsp skimmed milk powder
10ml/2 tsp salt
5ml/1 tsp granulated sugar
7.5ml/1½ tsp easy-blend dried yeast
75g/3oz/¾ cup walnut pieces

MAKES 1 LOAF

3 Set the bread machine to the basic/normal setting; use raisin setting (if available), medium crust. Press Start. Add the walnut pieces when the machine beeps or after the first kneading.

4 Remove the bread from the machine pan at the end of the baking cycle and turn out on to a wire rack.

1 Pour the water, molasses and walnut or olive oil into the bread pan. If the instructions for your machine specify that the yeast is to be placed in the pan first, reverse the order in which you add the liquid and dry ingredients.

2 Sprinkle over the flours, covering the liquid. Add the milk powder. Place the salt and sugar in separate corners. Make a small indent in the centre of the flour (but not down as far as the liquid) and add the easy-blend dried yeast.

WILD RICE, OAT AND POLENTA BREAD

*Coarse-textured polenta, rolled oats and nutty-tasting wild rice blend
perfectly to make this delightful, nourishing bread.
The dark, slender grains of wild rice add beautiful flecks of colour which
are revealed when this bread is split open.*

50g/2oz/¼ cup wild rice
300ml/10½fl oz/1¼ cups water
30ml/2 tbsp sunflower oil
325g/11½oz/scant 3 cups unbleached
white bread flour
50g/2oz/½ cup strong wholemeal
(whole-wheat) flour
50g/2oz/½ cup polenta
50g/2oz/½ cup rolled oats
30ml/2 tbsp skimmed milk powder
(non fat dry milk)
30ml/2 tbsp golden (light corn) syrup
10ml/2 tsp salt
5ml/1 tsp easy-blend (rapid-rise)
dried yeast

MAKES 1 LOAF

3 Sprinkle over the white bread flour and the strong wholemeal flour, then add the polenta, rolled oats and skimmed milk powder, ensuring that the water is completely covered.

4 Add the golden syrup and the salt, placing them in separate corners of the bread pan. Make a shallow indent in the centre of the flour mixture (but not down as far as the liquid) and add the easy-blend dried yeast.

5 Set the bread machine to the dough setting; use basic raisin dough setting (if available). Press Start.

8 Divide the dough into six equal pieces. In turn, shape each piece of dough into an oblong mini loaf, about 13cm/5in in length. Then place the six dough shapes widthways, side by side, in the prepared loaf tin.

9 Cover the dough with lightly oiled clear film (plastic wrap) and leave to rise in a warm place for about 30–45 minutes, or until the dough almost reaches the top of the tin. Meanwhile preheat the oven to 220°C/425°F/Gas 7.

10 Bake the loaf for 30–35 minutes, or until it is golden and sounds hollow when tapped on the base. Turn out on to a wire rack to cool.

1 Cook the wild rice in boiling salted water according to the instructions on the packet.

6 Add the cooked wild rice when the machine beeps or during the last 5 minutes of kneading. Lightly oil a 23 × 13cm/9 × 5in loaf tin (pan).

7 When the dough cycle has finished, remove the dough from the bread machine pan and place it on a surface that has been lightly floured. Knock the dough back (punch it down) gently.

2 Pour the water and the sunflower oil into the bread machine pan. If the instructions for your machine specify that the yeast is to be placed in the pan first, reverse the order in which you add the liquid and dry ingredients.

VARIATIONS
This bread can also be made with other varieties of rice. Long grain brown rice and white rice are both good, and they are also much faster to cook than wild rice.
If you like, use the wild or red Camargue rice. This variety takes about an hour to cook, but the vivid red colour of the rice will give unusual and very attractive flecks of colour in the bread.

FOUR SEED BREAD

280ml/10fl oz/1¼ cups water
30ml/2 tbsp extra virgin olive oil
400g/14oz/3½ cups unbleached white
bread flour
50g/2oz/½ cup millet flour
50g/2oz/½ cup wholemeal
(whole-wheat) bread flour
15ml/1 tbsp granulated sugar
10ml/2 tsp salt
5ml/1 tsp easy-blend (rapid-rise)
dried yeast
30ml/2 tbsp pumpkin seeds
30ml/2 tbsp sunflower seeds
22ml/1½ tbsp linseeds
22ml/1½ tbsp sesame seeds,
lightly toasted
15ml/1 tbsp milk
30ml/2 tbsp golden linseeds

MAKES 1 LOAF

This light wholemeal and millet bread has added bite, thanks to a variety of tasty seeds, all readily available from your local health-food store.

1 Pour the water and oil into the bread pan. Reverse the order in which you add the wet and dry ingredients if your machine specifies this.

2 Sprinkle over all three types of flour, ensuring that the water is completely covered. Add the sugar and salt in separate corners of the bread pan.

3 Make a shallow indent in the centre of the flour and add the yeast. Set the bread machine to the dough setting; use basic raisin dough setting (if available). Press Start. Add the seeds when the machine beeps to add extra ingredients or during the last 5 minutes of kneading.

4 When the dough cycle has finished, place the dough on a lightly floured surface and knock back (punch down) gently.

5 Lightly oil a baking sheet. Shape the dough into a round flat loaf. Make a hole in the centre with your finger. Gradually enlarge the cavity, turning the dough, until you have a ring. Place the ring on the baking sheet. Cover it with lightly oiled clear film (plastic wrap) and leave in a warm place for 30–45 minutes, or until the dough has doubled in size.

6 Meanwhile, preheat the oven to 200°C/400°F/Gas 6. Brush the top of the bread with milk and sprinkle it with the golden linseeds. Make slashes around the loaf, radiating outwards.

7 Bake for 30–35 minutes, or until golden and hollow-sounding. Turn out on to a wire rack to cool.

HAZELNUT AND FIG BREAD

—

This healthy, high-fibre bread is flavoured with figs and hazelnuts.

230ml/8fl oz/1 cup water
5ml/1 tsp lemon juice
280g/10oz/2½ cups unbleached white
bread flour
75g/3oz/¾ cup brown bread flour
45ml/3 tbsp toasted wheatgerm
15ml/1 tbsp skimmed milk powder
(non fat dry milk)
5ml/1 tsp salt
10ml/2 tsp granulated sugar
20g/¾oz/1½ tbsp butter
5ml/1 tsp easy-blend (rapid-rise)
dried yeast
25g/1oz/3 tbsp ready-to-eat dried figs
25g/1oz/3 tbsp skinned hazelnuts,
roasted and chopped

MEDIUM

280ml/10fl oz/1¼ cups water
7.5ml/1½ tsp lemon juice
350g/12oz/3 cups unbleached white
bread flour
100g/3½oz/scant 1 cup brown
bread flour
60ml/4 tbsp toasted wheatgerm
30ml/2 tbsp skimmed milk powder
7.5ml/1½ tsp salt
15ml/1 tbsp granulated sugar
25g/1oz/2 tbsp butter
7.5ml/1½ tsp easy-blend dried yeast
40g/1½oz/¼ cup ready-to-eat dried figs
40g/1½oz/⅓ cup skinned hazelnuts,
roasted and chopped

LARGE

450ml/16fl oz/scant 2 cups water
10ml/2 tsp lemon juice
500g/1lb 2oz/4½ cups unbleached
white bread flour
115g/4oz/1 cup brown bread flour
75ml/5 tbsp toasted wheatgerm
45ml/3 tbsp skimmed milk powder
10ml/2 tsp salt
20ml/4 tsp granulated sugar
40g/1½oz/3 tbsp butter
7.5ml/1½ tsp easy-blend dried yeast
50g/2oz/⅓ cup ready-to-eat dried figs
50g/2oz/½ cup skinned hazelnuts,
roasted and chopped

1 Pour the water and the lemon juice into the bread machine pan. If the instructions for your machine specify that the yeast is to be placed in the pan first, reverse the order in which you add the liquid and dry ingredients.

2 Sprinkle over the flours, then the wheatgerm, covering the water. Add the milk powder. Add the salt, sugar and butter in separate corners. Make an indent in the flour; add the yeast.

3 Set the bread machine to the basic/normal setting; use raisin setting (if available), medium crust. Press Start. Coarsely chop the dried figs. Add the hazelnuts and the figs to the bread pan when the machine beeps or after the first kneading has finished.

4 Remove the bread at the end of the baking cycle and turn out on to a wire rack to allow to cool.

MAKES 1 LOAF

SPELT AND BULGUR WHEAT BREAD

Two unusual grains are used here. Spelt is a variety of wheat which is not widely grown, but is ground by some specialist millers. Cracked wheat or bulgur is the cracked wheat berry which has been softened by steaming. It contributes crunch while the spelt flour adds a nutty flavour.

SMALL
110ml/scant 4fl oz/scant ½ cup water
100ml/3½fl oz/7 tbsp buttermilk
5ml/1 tsp lemon juice
250g/9oz/2¼ cups unbleached white bread flour
100g/3½oz/scant 1 cup spelt flour
30ml/2 tbsp bulgur wheat
5ml/1 tsp salt
10ml/2 tsp granulated sugar
5ml/1 tsp easy-blend (rapid-rise) dried yeast

MEDIUM
220ml/scant 8fl oz/scant 1 cup water
125ml/4½fl oz/generous ½ cup buttermilk
7.5ml/1½ tsp lemon juice
350g/12oz/3 cups unbleached white bread flour
150g/5½oz/1⅓ cups spelt flour
45ml/3 tbsp bulgur wheat
7.5ml/1½ tsp salt
15ml/1 tbsp granulated sugar
7.5ml/1½ tsp easy-blend dried yeast

LARGE
280ml/10fl oz/1¼ cups water
140ml/5fl oz/⅝ cup buttermilk
10ml/2 tsp lemon juice
425g/15oz/3¾ cups unbleached white bread flour
200g/7oz/1¾ cups spelt flour
60ml/4 tbsp bulgur wheat
10ml/2 tsp salt
20ml/4 tsp granulated sugar
10ml/2 tsp easy-blend dried yeast

MAKES 1 LOAF

VARIATION
The buttermilk adds a characteristic slightly sour note to this bread. You can replace it with low-fat natural (plain) yogurt or semi-skimmed (low-fat) milk for a less tangy flavour.

1 Pour the water, buttermilk and lemon juice into the bread machine pan. If the instructions for your machine specify that the yeast is to be placed in the pan first, reverse the order in which you add the liquid and dry ingredients.

2 Sprinkle over both types of flour, then the bulgur wheat, ensuring that the liquid is completely covered. Add the salt and sugar, placing them in separate corners of the bread pan.

3 Make a small indent in the centre of the flour (but not down as far as the liquid) and add the yeast.

4 Set the bread machine to the basic/normal setting, medium crust. Press Start.

5 Remove the bread at the end of the baking cycle and turn out on to a wire rack to allow to cool.

MULTIGRAIN BREAD

This healthy, mixed grain bread owes its wonderfully rich flavour to honey and malt extract.

1 Add the water, honey and malt extract to the pan. If your machine's instructions specify that the yeast is to be placed in the pan first, reverse the order in which you add the liquid and dry ingredients.

2 Sprinkle over all four types of flour, ensuring that the liquid is completely covered. Add the jumbo oats and skimmed milk powder.

3 Place the salt and butter in separate corners of the bread machine pan. Make a small indent in the centre of the flour (but not down as far as the liquid) and add the yeast.

4 Set the bread machine to the whole wheat setting, medium crust. Press Start. Remove the bread at the end of the baking cycle and turn out on to a wire rack to allow to cool.

SMALL

230ml/8fl oz/1 cup water
15ml/1 tbsp clear honey
7.5ml/1½ tsp malt extract
115g/4oz/1 cup Granary
(whole-wheat) flour
50g/2oz/½ cup rye flour
75g/3oz/¾ cup unbleached white
bread flour
140g/5oz/1¼ cups wholemeal
(whole-wheat) bread flour
15ml/1 tbsp jumbo oats
15ml/1 tbsp skimmed milk powder
(non fat dry milk)
5ml/1 tsp salt
20g/¾oz/1½ tbsp butter
4ml/¾ tsp easy-blend (rapid-rise)
dried yeast

MEDIUM

300ml/10½fl oz/scant 1⅓ cups water
30ml/2 tbsp clear honey
15ml/1 tbsp malt extract
150g/5½oz/1⅓ cups Granary flour
75g/3oz/¾ cup rye flour
75g/3oz/¾ cup unbleached white
bread flour
200g/7oz/1¾ cups wholemeal
bread flour
30ml/2 tbsp jumbo oats
30ml/2 tbsp skimmed milk powder
7.5ml/1½ tsp salt
25g/1oz/2 tbsp butter
5ml/1 tsp easy-blend dried yeast

LARGE

375ml/13fl oz/scant 1⅔ cups water
30ml/2 tbsp clear honey
22ml/1½ tbsp malt extract
200g/7oz/1¾cups Granary flour
115g/4oz/1 cup rye flour
115g/4oz/1 cup unbleached white
bread flour
225g/8oz/2 cups wholemeal
bread flour
45ml/3 tbsp jumbo oats
45ml/3 tbsp skimmed milk powder
10ml/2 tsp salt
40g/1½ oz/3 tbsp butter
7.5ml/1½ tsp easy-blend dried yeast

MAKES 1 LOAF

RUSSIAN BLACK BREAD

*European rye breads often include cocoa and coffee to add colour to this dark
traditionally dense, chewy bread. Slice it thinly, serve it with cold meats or
pâtés or use it as the basis of an open sandwich.*

SMALL

230ml/8fl oz/1 cup water
30ml/2 tbsp sunflower oil
30ml/2 tbsp molasses
115g/4oz/1 cup rye flour
*50g/2oz/½ cup wholemeal
(whole-wheat) bread flour*
*175g/6oz/1½ cups unbleached white
bread flour*
25g/1oz/2 tbsp oat bran
50g/2oz/½ cup dried breadcrumbs
15ml/1 tbsp cocoa powder (unsweetened)
30ml/2 tbsp instant coffee granules
7.5ml/1½ tsp caraway seeds
5ml/1 tsp salt
*5ml/1 tsp easy-blend (rapid-rise)
dried yeast*

MEDIUM

360ml/12½fl oz/generous 1½ cups water
30ml/2 tbsp sunflower oil
40ml/2½ tbsp molasses
140g/5oz/1¼ cups rye flour
85g/3oz/¾ cup wholemeal bread flour
*250g/9oz/2¼ cups unbleached white
bread flour*
40g/1½oz/3 tbsp oat bran
75g/3oz/¾ cup dried breadcrumbs
22ml/1½ tbsp cocoa powder
40ml/2½ tbsp instant coffee granules
7.5ml/1½ tsp caraway seeds
7.5ml/1½ tsp salt
7.5ml/1½ tsp easy-blend dried yeast

LARGE

430ml/15fl oz/generous 1⅔ cups water
45ml/3 tbsp sunflower oil
45ml/3 tbsp molasses
200g/7oz/1¾ cups rye flour
*100g/3½oz/scant 1 cup wholemeal
bread flour*
*300g/10½oz/generous 2½ cups
unbleached white bread flour*
50g/2oz/4 tbsp oat bran
100g/3½oz/scant 1 cup dried breadcrumbs
30ml/2 tbsp cocoa powder
45ml/3 tbsp instant coffee granules
10ml/2 tsp caraway seeds
10ml/2 tsp salt
10ml/2 tsp easy-blend dried yeast

MAKES 1 LOAF

1 Pour the water, sunflower oil and
molasses into the bread machine pan.
If the instructions for your machine
specify that the yeast is to be placed
in the bread pan first, then simply
reverse the order in which you add the
liquid and dry ingredients.

2 Sprinkle over the rye, wholemeal and
white flours, then the oat bran and
breadcrumbs, ensuring that the water
is completely covered. Add the cocoa
powder, coffee granules, caraway
seeds and salt. Make a small indent
in the centre of the flour (but not
down as far as the liquid) and add
the easy-blend dried yeast.

3 Set the bread machine to the whole
wheat setting, medium crust and then
press Start.

4 Remove the bread at the end of the
baking cycle and turn out on to a wire
rack to cool.

MAPLE AND OATMEAL LOAF

*Rolled oats and oat bran add texture to this wholesome bread, which is
suffused with the delectable flavour of maple syrup.*

1 Pour the water into the bread machine pan and then add the maple syrup. If the instructions for your machine specify that the yeast is to be placed in the pan first, reverse the order in which you add the liquid and dry ingredients.

2 Sprinkle over both the white and wholemeal flours, then the rolled oats and oat bran, ensuring that the water is completely covered.

3 Add the salt, sugar and butter, placing them in separate corners of the bread pan. Make a small indent in the centre of the flour (but not down as far as the liquid) and add the yeast.

4 Set the bread machine to the basic/normal setting, medium crust. Press Start.

5 Remove the bread at the end of the baking cycle and turn out on to a wire rack to cool.

SMALL
210ml/7½fl oz/scant 1 cup water
15ml/1 tbsp maple syrup
300g/11oz/2⅔ cups unbleached white bread flour
50g/2oz/½ cup wholemeal (whole-wheat) bread flour
20g/¾oz/¼ cup rolled oats
15ml/1 tbsp oat bran
5ml/1 tsp salt
5ml/1 tsp granulated sugar
25g/1oz/2 tbsp butter
5ml/1 tsp easy-blend (rapid-rise) dried yeast

MEDIUM
315ml/11fl oz/1⅓ cups water
30ml/2 tbsp maple syrup
375g/13oz/3¼ cups unbleached white bread flour
75g/3oz/¾ cup wholemeal bread flour
40g/1½oz/½ cup rolled oats
30ml/2 tbsp oat bran
5ml/1 tsp salt
5ml/1 tsp granulated sugar
40g/1½oz/3 tbsp butter
5ml/1 tsp easy-blend dried yeast

LARGE
410ml/14½fl oz/1¾ cups water
45ml/3 tbsp maple syrup
500g/1lb 2oz/4½ cups unbleached white bread flour
115g/4oz/1 cup wholemeal bread flour
50g/2oz/¾ cup rolled oats
45ml/3 tbsp oat bran
7.5ml/1½ tsp salt
7.5ml/1½ tsp granulated sugar
50g/2oz/¼ cup butter
7.5ml/1½ tsp easy-blend dried yeast

MAKES 1 LOAF

COOK'S TIP
Use 100 per cent pure maple syrup. Less expensive products are often blended with cane or corn syrup, which does not have the smooth rich flavour of the real thing.

PARTYBROT

FOR THE MILK ROLLS
145ml/5fl oz/scant ⅔ cup milk
225g/8oz/2 cups unbleached white
bread flour
7.5ml/1½ tsp granulated sugar
5ml/1 tsp salt
15g/½oz/1 tbsp butter
2.5ml/½ tsp easy-blend (rapid-rise)
dried yeast

FOR THE WHOLEMEAL ROLLS
175ml/6fl oz/¾ cup water
175g/6oz/1½ cups wholemeal
(whole-wheat) bread flour
75g/3oz/⅔ cup unbleached white
bread flour
7.5ml/1½ tsp granulated sugar
5ml/1 tsp salt
25g/1oz/2 tbsp butter
2.5ml/½ tsp easy-blend dried yeast

FOR THE TOPPING
1 egg yolk, mixed with 15ml/1 tbsp
cold water
15ml/1 tbsp rolled oats or cracked wheat
15ml/1 tbsp poppy seeds

MAKES 19 ROLLS

1 Pour the milk for making the milk rolls into the bread machine pan. However, if the instructions for your bread machine specify that the yeast is to be placed in the pan first, simply reverse the order in which you add the liquid and dry ingredients.

2 Sprinkle over the white bread flour, making sure that it covers the milk completely. Add the sugar, salt and butter, placing them in separate corners of the bread pan.

3 Make a small indent in the centre of the flour (but not down as far as the liquid underneath) and add the easy-blend dried yeast.

4 Set the bread machine to the dough setting; use basic dough setting (if available). Press Start.

These traditional Swiss-German rolls are baked as one, in a round tin.
As the name suggests, partybrot is perfect for entertaining.

5 Lightly oil a 25cm/10in springform or loose-based cake tin (pan), and a large mixing bowl. When the dough cycle has finished, remove the dough from the machine and place it in the mixing bowl.

6 Cover the dough with oiled clear film (plastic wrap) and put it in the refrigerator while you make the wholemeal dough. Follow the instructions for the milk roll dough, but use water instead of milk.

7 Remove the milk roll dough from the refrigerator 20 minutes before the end of the wholemeal dough cycle. When the wholemeal dough is ready, remove it from the machine and place on a lightly floured surface. Knock it back (punch down) gently. Do the same with the milk roll dough.

8 Divide the milk roll dough into nine pieces and the wholemeal dough into 10. Shape each piece of dough into a small round ball.

9 Place 12 balls, equally spaced, around the outer edge of the prepared cake tin, alternating milk dough with wholemeal.

10 Add an inner circle with six more balls and place the remaining ball of wholemeal dough in the centre.

11 Cover the tin with lightly oiled clear film and leave the rolls to rise in a warm place for 30–45 minutes, or until they have doubled in size. Meanwhile, preheat the oven to 200°C/400°F/Gas 6.

12 Brush the wholemeal rolls with the egg yolk and water glaze. Sprinkle with rolled oats or cracked wheat. Glaze the white rolls and sprinkle with poppy seeds. Bake for 35–40 minutes, until the partybrot is golden. Leave for 5 minutes to cool in the tin, then turn out on to a wire rack to cool. Serve warm or cold.

FLATBREADS AND PIZZAS

Flatbreads are fun to bake and make delicious meal accompaniments. Naan, often flavoured with coriander or black onion seeds, is typical of Indian flatbread, whilst Lavash, Pitta and Pide are traditional Middle Eastern specialities. Italy is famous for Focaccia, pizzas and Calzone, while the French version of pizza is the Pissaladière. All of these breads can be made in your machine using the "dough only" setting and then hand-shaped and oven-baked.

GARLIC AND CORIANDER NAAN

Indian restaurants the world over have introduced us to several differently flavoured examples of this leavened flatbread, and this version is particularly tasty and will become a great favourite. The bread is traditionally made in a tandoor oven, but this method has been developed to give almost identical results.

100ml/3½ fl oz/7 tbsp water
60ml/4 tbsp natural (plain) yogurt
280g/10oz/2½ cups unbleached white bread flour
1 garlic clove, finely chopped
5ml/1 tsp black onion seeds
5ml/1 tsp ground coriander
5ml/1 tsp salt
10ml/2 tsp clear honey
15ml/1 tbsp melted ghee or butter, plus 30–45ml/2–3 tbsp
5ml/1 tsp easy-blend (rapid-rise) dried yeast
15ml/1 tbsp chopped fresh coriander (cilantro)

MAKES 3

VARIATION
For a basic naan omit the coriander, garlic and black onion seeds. Include a little ground black pepper or chilli powder for a slightly piquant note.

1 Pour the water and natural yogurt into the bread machine pan. If the instructions for your bread machine specify that the easy-blend dried yeast is to be placed in the pan first, then simply reverse the order in which you add the liquid and dry ingredients.

2 Sprinkle over the flour, ensuring that it covers the liquid completely. Add the garlic, black onion seeds and ground coriander. Add the salt, honey and the 15ml/1 tbsp melted ghee or butter in separate corners of the bread pan. Make a small indent in the centre of the flour (but not down as far as the liquid) and add the easy-blend dried yeast.

3 Set the bread machine to the dough setting; use basic or pizza dough setting (if available). Press Start.

4 When the dough cycle has finished, preheat the oven to its highest setting. Place three baking sheets in the oven to heat. Remove the dough from the breadmaking machine and place it on a lightly floured surface.

5 Knock the naan dough back (punch it down) gently and then knead in the chopped fresh coriander. Divide the dough into three equal pieces.

6 Shape each piece into a ball and cover two of the pieces with oiled clear film (plastic wrap). Roll out the remaining piece of dough into a large teardrop shape, making it about 5–8mm/¼–⅓in thick. Cover with oiled clear film while you roll out the remaining two pieces of dough to make two more naan.

7 Preheat the grill (broiler) to its highest setting. Place the naan on the preheated baking sheets and then bake them for 4–5 minutes, until puffed up. Remove the baking sheets from the oven and place them under the hot grill for a few seconds, until the naan start to brown and blister.

8 Brush the naan with melted ghee or butter and serve warm.

CARTA DI MUSICA

This crunchy, crisp bread looks like sheets of music manuscript paper, which is how it came by its name. It originated in Sardinia and can be found throughout southern Italy, where it is eaten not only as a bread, but as a substitute for pasta in lasagne. It also makes a good pizza base.

280ml/10fl oz/1¼ cups water
450g/1lb/4 cups unbleached white bread flour
7.5ml/1½ tsp salt
5ml/1 tsp granulated sugar
5ml/1 tsp easy-blend (rapid-rise) dried yeast

MAKES 8

COOK'S TIP
Cutting the partially cooked breads in half is quite tricky. You may find it easier to divide the dough into six or eight pieces, and roll these as thinly as possible before baking. The cutting stage can then be avoided.

1 Pour the water into the bread machine pan. If the instructions specify that the yeast should be placed in the pan first, simply reverse the order in which you add the liquid and dry ingredients to the pan.

2 Sprinkle over the white bread flour, ensuring that it covers the water. Add the salt in one corner of the bread pan and the sugar in another corner. Make a small indent in the centre of the flour (but not down as far as the liquid) and add the easy-blend dried yeast.

3 Set the bread machine to the dough setting; use basic dough setting (if available). Press Start.

4 When the dough cycle has finished, remove the dough from the machine and place it on a lightly floured surface. Knock it back (punch it down) gently and divide it into four equal pieces. Shape each piece of dough into a ball, then roll a piece out until about 3mm/⅛in thick.

5 Now roll out the other three pieces. If the dough starts to tear, cover it with oiled clear film (plastic wrap) and leave it to rest for 2–3 minutes.

6 When all the dough has been rolled out, cover with oiled clear film and leave to rest on the floured surface for 10–15 minutes. Preheat the oven to 230°C/450°F/Gas 8. Place two baking sheets in the oven to heat.

7 Keeping the other dough rounds covered, place one round on each baking sheet. Bake for 5 minutes, or until puffed up.

8 Remove from the oven and cut each round in half horizontally to make two thinner breads. Place these cut side up on the baking sheets, return them to the oven and bake for 5–8 minutes more, until crisp. Turn out on to a wire rack and cook the remaining breads.

LAVASH

*250ml/generous 8½fl oz/generous
1 cup water
45ml/3 tbsp natural (plain) yogurt
350g/12oz/3 cups unbleached white
bread flour
115g/4oz/1 cup wholemeal
(whole-wheat) bread flour
5ml/1 tsp salt
5ml/1 tsp easy-blend (rapid-rise)
dried yeast*

*FOR THE TOPPING
30ml/2 tbsp milk
30ml/2 tbsp millet seeds*

MAKES 10

VARIATION
Instead of making individual lavash
you could divide the dough into five
or six pieces and make large lavash.
Serve these on a platter in the centre
of the table and invite guests to break
off pieces as required.

*These Middle Eastern flatbreads puff up slightly during cooking, to make a
bread which is crispy, but not as dry and crisp as a cracker. Serve warm
straight from the oven or cold, with a little butter, if wished.*

1 Pour the water and yogurt into the bread machine pan. If the instructions for your machine specify that the yeast is to be placed in the pan first, reverse the order in which you add the liquid and dry ingredients.

2 Sprinkle over both types of flour, ensuring that the liquid is completely covered. Add the salt in one corner of the bread pan. Make an indent in the centre of the flour; add the yeast.

3 Set the bread machine to the dough setting; use basic or pizza dough setting (if available). Press Start.

4 When the dough cycle has finished, place the dough on a lightly floured surface. Knock it back gently (punch it down) and divide it into 10 equal pieces.

5 Shape each piece into a ball, then flatten into a disc with your hand. Cover with oiled clear film (plastic wrap); leave to rest for 5 minutes. Preheat the oven to 230°C/450°F/Gas 8. Place three or four baking sheets in the oven.

6 Roll each ball of dough out very thinly, then stretch it over the backs of your hands, to make the lavash. If the dough starts to tear, leave it to rest for a few minutes after rolling. Stack the lavash between layers of oiled clear film and cover to keep moist.

7 Place as many lavash as will fit comfortably on each baking sheet, brush with milk and sprinkle with millet seeds. Bake for 5–8 minutes, or until puffed and starting to brown. Transfer to a wire rack and cook the remaining lavash.

PITTA BREADS

*210ml/7½fl oz/scant 1 cup water
15ml/1 tbsp olive oil
350g/12oz/3 cups unbleached white
bread flour, plus extra for sprinkling
7.5ml/1½ tsp salt
5ml/1 tsp granulated sugar
5ml/1 tsp easy-blend (rapid-rise)
dried yeast*

MAKES 6–10

1 Pour the water and oil into the bread machine pan. If your instructions specify that the yeast is to be placed in the pan first, reverse the order in which you add the liquid and dry ingredients. Add the flour, ensuring it covers the water.

2 Add the salt and sugar in separate corners. Make a shallow indent in the centre of the flour and add the yeast. Set to the dough setting; use basic or pizza dough setting (if available). Start.

*These well-known flatbreads are easy to make and extremely versatile.
Serve them warm with dips or soups, or split them in half and stuff the
pockets with your favourite vegetable, meat or cheese filling.*

3 When the dough cycle has finished, remove the dough from the machine. Place it on a lightly floured surface and knock it back (punch it down) gently.

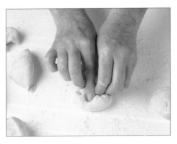

4 Divide the dough into six or ten equal-size pieces, depending on whether you want large or small pitta breads. Shape each piece into a ball.

5 Cover the balls of dough with oiled clear film (plastic wrap) and leave them to rest for about 10 minutes. Preheat the oven to 230°C/450°F/Gas 8. Place three baking sheets in the oven to heat.

6 Flatten each piece of dough slightly, and then roll out into an oval or round, about 5mm/¼in thick.

7 Lightly sprinkle each pitta with flour. Cover with oiled clear film and leave to rest for 10 minutes.

8 Place the pittas on the baking sheets and bake for 5–6 minutes, or until they are puffed up and lightly browned. Transfer the pitta breads on to wire racks to cool.

MOROCCAN KSRA

200ml/7fl oz/⅞ cup water
250g/9oz/2¼ cups unbleached white
bread flour
75g/3oz/¾ cup semolina
5ml/1 tsp aniseed
7.5ml/1½ tsp salt
2.5ml/½ tsp granulated sugar
5ml/1 tsp easy-blend (rapid-rise)
dried yeast
olive oil, for brushing
sesame seeds, for sprinkling

MAKES 2

1 Pour the water into the machine pan. Reverse the order in which you add the wet and dry ingredients if necessary. Add the flour, semolina and aniseed, covering the water. Place the salt and sugar in separate corners. Make an indent in the flour; add the yeast. Set the machine to the dough setting; use the basic dough setting if available.

This leavened flatbread is made with semolina and spiced with aniseed. It is the traditional accompaniment to tagine, a spicy Moroccan stew, but is equally good with salad, cheeses or dips. It can be served warm or cold.

2 Press Start on your bread machine, then lightly flour two baking sheets. When the cycle has finished, place the dough on a lightly floured surface.

3 Knock the dough back (punch it down) gently, shape into two balls, then flatten into 2cm/¾in thick discs. Place each dough disc on a baking sheet.

4 Cover the dough discs with oiled clear film (plastic wrap) and leave to rise for 30 minutes, or until doubled in bulk.

5 Preheat the oven to 200°C/400°F/Gas 6. Brush the top of each piece of dough with olive oil and sprinkle with sesame seeds. Prick the surface with a skewer.

6 Bake for about 20–25 minutes, or until the ksra are golden and sound hollow when tapped underneath. Turn out on to a wire rack to cool.

> **VARIATION**
> Replace up to half the white bread flour with wholemeal (whole-wheat) bread flour for a nuttier flavour.

PIDE

240ml/8½fl oz/generous 1 cup water
30ml/2 tbsp olive oil
450g/1lb/4 cups unbleached white
bread flour
5ml/1 tsp salt
5ml/1 tsp sugar
5ml/1 tsp easy-blend (rapid-rise)
dried yeast
1 egg yolk mixed with 10ml/2 tsp
water, for glazing
nigella or poppy seeds, for sprinkling

MAKES 3

1 Pour the water and oil into the machine pan. If the instructions for your machine specify that the yeast is to be added first, reverse the order in which you add the liquid and dry ingredients.

2 Sprinkle over the flour, ensuring that it covers the liquid. Add the salt in one corner of the bread pan and the sugar in another corner. Make a small indent in the centre of the flour; add the yeast.

A traditional Turkish ridged flatbread, this is often baked plain, but can also be sprinkled with aromatic black nigella seeds, which taste rather like oregano. If you can't find nigella seeds, use poppy seeds.

3 Set the bread machine to the dough setting; use basic dough setting (if available). Press Start.

4 When the dough cycle has finished, remove the pide dough from the bread machine and place it on a surface lightly dusted with flour. Knock the dough back (punch it down) gently and divide it into three equal-size pieces. Shape each piece of dough into a ball.

5 Roll each ball of dough into a round, about 15cm/6in in diameter. Cover with oiled clear film (plastic wrap) and leave for 20 minutes. Meanwhile, preheat the oven to 230°C/450°F/Gas 8.

6 Using your fingers, ridge the bread, while enlarging it until it is 5mm/¼in thick. Start from the top of the round, pressing your fingers down and away from you, into the bread. Repeat a second row beneath the first row, and continue down the bread.

7 Turn the bread by 90 degrees and repeat the pressing to give a criss-cross ridged effect. Place the pide on floured baking sheets, brush with egg glaze and sprinkle with nigella or poppy seeds. Bake for 9–10 minutes, or until puffy and golden. Serve immediately.

OLIVE FOUGASSE

A French hearth bread, fougasse is traditionally baked on the floor of the hot bread oven, just after the fire has been raked out. It can be left plain or flavoured with olives, herbs, nuts or cheese.

210ml/7½fl oz/scant 1 cup water
*15ml/1 tbsp olive oil, plus extra
for brushing*
*350g/12oz/3 cups unbleached white
bread flour*
5ml/1 tsp salt
5ml/1 tsp granulated sugar
*5ml/1 tsp easy-blend (rapid-rise)
dried yeast*
*50g/2oz/½ cup pitted black
olives, chopped*

MAKES 1 FOUGASSE

1 Pour the water and the oil into the machine pan. Reverse the order in which you add wet and dry ingredients if necessary. Sprinkle over the flour, ensuring that it covers the liquid. Add the salt in one corner of the bread pan and the sugar in another corner. Make a small indent in the centre of the flour (but not down as far as the liquid) and add the yeast.

2 Set the bread machine to the dough setting; use basic or pizza dough setting (if available). Press Start. When the cycle has finished, remove the dough from the machine and place it on a lightly floured surface.

3 Knock the dough back (punch it down) gently and flatten it slightly. Sprinkle over the olives and fold over the dough two or three times to incorporate them.

4 Flatten the dough and roll it into an oblong, about 30cm/12in long. With a sharp knife make four or five parallel cuts diagonally through the body of the dough, but leaving the edges intact. Gently stretch the fougasse dough so that it resembles a ladder.

5 Lightly oil a baking sheet, then place the shaped dough on it. Cover with oiled clear film (plastic wrap) and leave in a warm place for about 30 minutes, or until the dough has doubled in bulk.

6 Preheat the oven to 220°C/425°F/ Gas 7. Brush the top of the fougasse with olive oil, place in the oven and bake about for 20–25 minutes, or until the bread is golden. Turn out on to a wire rack to cool.

ONION FOCACCIA

Focaccia, with its characteristic texture and dimpled surface, has become hugely popular in recent years. This version has a delectable red onion and fresh sage topping.

210ml/7½fl oz/scant 1 cup water
15ml/1 tbsp olive oil
350g/12oz/3 cups unbleached white bread flour
2.5ml/½ tsp salt
5ml/1 tsp granulated sugar
5ml/1 tsp easy-blend (rapid-rise) dried yeast
15ml/1 tbsp chopped fresh sage
15ml/1 tbsp chopped red onion

FOR THE TOPPING
30ml/2 tbsp olive oil
½ red onion, thinly sliced
5 fresh sage leaves
10ml/2 tsp coarse sea salt
coarsely ground black pepper

MAKES 1 FOCACCIA

1 Pour the water and oil into the bread pan. Reverse the order in which you add the wet and dry ingredients if necessary.

2 Sprinkle over the flour, ensuring that it covers the liquid. Add the salt and sugar in separate corners. Make a small indent in the flour and add the yeast.

3 Set the bread machine to the dough setting. If your machine has a choice of settings use the basic or pizza dough setting. Press Start.

4 Lightly oil a 25–28cm/10–11in shallow round cake tin or pizza pan. When the cycle has finished, remove the dough from the pan and place it on a surface lightly dusted with flour.

5 Knock the dough back (punch it down) and flatten it slightly. Sprinkle over the sage and red onion and knead gently to incorporate. Shape the dough into a ball, flatten it, then roll it into a round of about 25–28cm/10–11in. Place in the prepared tin. Cover with oiled clear film (plastic wrap) and leave to rise in a warm place for 20 minutes.

6 Meanwhile, preheat the oven to 200°C/400°F/Gas 6. Uncover the risen focaccia, and, using your fingertips, poke the dough to make deep dimples over the surface. Cover and leave to rise for 10–15 minutes, or until the dough has doubled in bulk.

7 Drizzle over the olive oil and sprinkle with the onion, sage leaves, sea salt and black pepper. Bake for 20–25 minutes, or until golden. Turn out on to a wire rack to cool slightly. Serve warm.

TOMATO AND PROSCIUTTO PIZZA

This combination of fresh plum tomatoes, sun-dried tomatoes, garlic and prosciutto with three cheeses is truly mouthwatering. Pizzas provide the perfect opportunity for exercising your individuality, so experiment with different topping ingredients if you prefer.

SMALL AND MEDIUM
MAKES ONE 30CM/12IN PIZZA
140ml/5fl oz/⅔ cup water
15ml/1 tbsp extra virgin olive oil
225g/8oz/2 cups unbleached white bread flour
5ml/1 tsp salt
2.5ml/½ tsp granulated sugar
2.5ml/½ tsp easy-blend (rapid-rise) dried yeast

FOR THE FILLING
45ml/3 tbsp sun-dried tomato paste
150g/5½oz mozzarella cheese, sliced
4 fresh plum tomatoes, about 400g/14oz, roughly chopped
1 small yellow (bell) pepper, halved, seeded and cut into thin strips
50g/2oz prosciutto, torn into pieces
8 fresh basil leaves
4 large garlic cloves, halved
50g/2oz feta cheese, crumbled
30ml/2 tbsp extra virgin olive oil
30ml/2 tbsp freshly grated Parmesan cheese
salt and freshly ground black pepper

LARGE
MAKES TWO 30CM/12IN PIZZAS
280ml/10fl oz/1¼ cups water
30ml/2 tbsp extra virgin olive oil
450g/1lb/4 cups unbleached white bread flour
7.5ml/1½ tsp salt
2.5ml/½tsp granulated sugar
5ml/1 tsp easy-blend dried yeast

FOR THE FILLING
90ml/6 tbsp sun-dried tomato paste
300g/11oz mozzarella cheese, sliced
8 fresh plum tomatoes, about 800g/1¾lb, roughly chopped
1 large yellow (bell) pepper, halved, seeded and cut into thin strips
115g/4oz prosciutto, torn into pieces
8 fresh basil leaves
8 large garlic cloves, halved
115g/4oz feta cheese, crumbled
45ml/3 tbsp extra virgin olive oil
60ml/4 tbsp freshly grated Parmesan cheese
salt and freshly ground black pepper

1 Pour the water and olive oil into the bread machine pan. If the instructions for your machine specify that the yeast is to be placed in the pan first, reverse the order in which you add the liquid and dry ingredients.

2 Sprinkle over the flour, ensuring that it covers the liquid. Add the salt in one corner of the bread pan and the sugar in another corner. Make a small indent in the centre of the flour, then add the yeast.

3 Set the bread machine to the dough setting; use basic or pizza dough setting (if available). Press Start. Lightly oil one or two pizza pans or baking sheets.

4 When the dough cycle has finished, remove the dough from the machine and place it on a lightly floured surface. Knock it back (punch it down) gently. If making the larger quantity divide the dough into two equal pieces. Preheat the oven to 220°C/425°F/Gas 7.

5 Roll out the pizza dough into one or two 30cm/12in rounds. Place in the prepared pan(s) or on the baking sheet(s). Spread the sun-dried tomato paste over the pizza base(s) and arrange two-thirds of the mozzarella slices on top.

6 Scatter with the chopped tomatoes, pepper strips, prosciutto, whole basil leaves, garlic, remaining mozzarella and feta. Drizzle over the olive oil and sprinkle with the Parmesan. Season with salt and pepper. Bake the pizza for 15–20 minutes, or until golden and sizzling. Serve immediately.

VARIATION
This topping lends itself particularly well to the nutty flavour of a wholemeal pizza base. Replace half the unbleached white bread flour with wholemeal (whole-wheat) bread flour. You may need to add a little more water as wholemeal flour absorbs more liquid.

PISSALADIÈRE

*This French version of an Italian pizza is typical of Niçoise dishes, with
anchovies and olives providing the distinctive flavour typical of the region.*

100ml/3½fl oz/7 tbsp water
1 egg
*225g/8oz/2 cups unbleached white
bread flour*
5ml/1 tsp salt
25g/1oz/2 tbsp butter
*5ml/1 tsp easy-blend (rapid-rise)
dried yeast*

FOR THE FILLING
60ml/4 tbsp olive oil
575g/1¼lb onions, thinly sliced
15ml/1 tbsp Dijon mustard
*3–4 tomatoes, about 280g/10oz, peeled
and sliced*
10ml/2 tsp chopped fresh basil
12 drained canned anchovies
12 black olives
salt and freshly ground black pepper

SERVES 6

1 Pour the water and egg into the machine
pan. If the instructions for your machine
specify that the yeast is to be added first,
reverse the order in which you add the liquid
and the dry ingredients.

2 Sprinkle over the white bread flour,
ensuring that it completely covers the
water and the egg. Add the salt in one
corner of the pan and the butter in
another corner. Make a small indent
in the centre of the flour (but not down
as far as the liquid) and add the easy-
blend dried yeast.

3 Set the bread machine to the dough
setting; use basic or pizza dough setting
(if available). Press Start. Then lightly
oil a 27 × 20cm/11 × 8in Swiss (jelly) roll
tin (pan) that is about 1cm/½in deep.

4 Make the filling. Heat the olive oil in a
large frying pan and cook the onions
over a low heat for about 20 minutes,
until very soft. Set aside to cool.

5 When the dough cycle has finished,
remove the dough from the machine and
place it on a lightly floured surface. Knock
it back (punch it down) gently, then roll it
out to a rectangle measuring about 30 ×
23cm/12 × 9in. Place in the prepared tin,
and press outwards and upwards, so that
the dough covers the base and sides.

6 Spread the mustard over the dough.
Arrange the tomato slices on top.
Season the onions with salt, pepper
and basil and spread the mixture over
the tomatoes.

7 Arrange the anchovies in a lattice and
dot with the olives. Cover with oiled
clear film (plastic wrap) and leave to
rise for 10–15 minutes. Meanwhile
preheat the oven to 200°C/400°F/Gas 6.
Bake the pissaladière for 25–30 minutes,
or until the base is cooked and golden
around the edges. Serve hot or warm.

SICILIAN SFINCIONE

Sfincione is the Sicilian equivalent of pizza. The Sicilians insist they were making these tasty snacks long before pizzas were made in mainland Italy.

1 Pour the water and oil into the bread pan. If your instructions specify that the yeast is to be placed in the bread pan first, reverse the order in which you add the liquid and the dry ingredients.

2 Sprinkle over the flour, ensuring that it covers the liquid. Add the salt in one corner of the bread pan and the sugar in another corner. Make a small indent in the centre of the flour; add the yeast.

3 Set the bread machine to the dough setting; use basic or pizza dough setting (if available). Press Start. Then lightly oil two baking sheets.

4 Make the topping. Peel and chop the tomatoes. Put in a bowl, add the garlic and 15ml/1 tbsp of the olive oil and toss together. Heat the sunflower oil in a small pan and sauté the onions until softened. Set aside to cool.

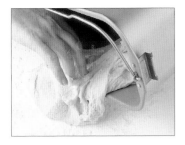

5 When the dough cycle has finished, remove the dough from the machine and place it on a lightly floured surface. Knock it back (punch it down) gently and divide it into four equal pieces.

6 Roll each piece of dough out to a round, each about 15–18cm/6–7in in diameter. Space the rounds well apart on the prepared baking sheets, then push up the dough edges on each to make a thin rim. Cover with oiled clear film (plastic wrap) and leave to rise for 10 minutes. Meanwhile, preheat the oven to 220°C/425°F/Gas 7.

7 Sprinkle the topping over the bases, ending with the Pecorino. Season, then drizzle with the remaining olive oil.

8 Bake near the top of the oven for 15–20 minutes or until the base of each sfincione is cooked. Serve immediately.

200ml/7fl oz/⅞cup water
30ml/2 tbsp extra virgin olive oil
350g/12oz/3 cups unbleached white
bread flour
7.5ml/1½ tsp salt
2.5ml/½ tsp granulated sugar
5ml/1 tsp easy-blend (rapid-rise)
dried yeast

FOR THE TOPPING
6 tomatoes
2 garlic cloves, chopped
45ml/3 tbsp olive oil
15ml/1 tbsp sunflower oil
2 onions, chopped
8 pitted black olives, chopped
10ml/2 tsp dried oregano
90ml/6 tbsp grated Pecorino cheese
salt and freshly ground black pepper

MAKES 4

CALZONE

130ml/4½fl oz/generous ½ cup water
30ml/2 tbsp extra virgin olive oil,
plus extra for brushing
225g/8oz/2 cups unbleached white
bread flour
5ml/1 tsp salt
2.5ml/½ tsp granulated sugar
5ml/1 tsp easy-blend (rapid-rise)
dried yeast

FOR THE FILLING
75g/3oz salami, in one piece
50g/2oz/½ cup drained sun-dried
tomatoes in olive oil, chopped
100g/4oz/⅔ cup mozzarella cheese,
cut into small cubes
50g/2oz/⅔ cup freshly grated
Parmesan cheese
50g/2oz Gorgonzola cheese, cubed
75g/3oz/scant ½ cup ricotta cheese
30ml/3 tbsp chopped fresh basil
2 egg yolks
salt and freshly ground black pepper

MAKES 2

1 Pour the water and olive oil into the bread pan. Reverse the order in which you add the liquid and dry ingredients if this is necessary for your machine. Sprinkle over the white bread flour, ensuring that it covers the liquid.

VARIATIONS

The ingredients for the filling can be varied, depending on what you have in the refrigerator, and to suit personal tastes. Replace the salami with ham or sautéed mushrooms. Add a freshly chopped chilli for a more piquant version. Make four individual calzones instead of two large ones.

Calzone is an enclosed pizza, with the filling inside. It originates from Naples and was originally made from a rectangular piece of pizza dough, unlike the modern version, which looks like a large Cornish pasty.

2 Add the salt and sugar in separate corners of the bread pan. Make a small indent in the centre of the flour (but not down as far as the liquid) and add the easy-blend dried yeast.

3 Set the bread machine to the dough setting; use basic or pizza dough setting (if available). Press Start.

4 To make the topping, cut the salami into 5mm/¼in dice. Put the dice in a bowl and add the sun-dried tomatoes, mozzarella, Parmesan, Gorgonzola and ricotta cheeses, basil and egg yolks. Mix well and season to taste with salt and plenty of ground black pepper. Lightly oil a large baking sheet.

5 When the cycle has finished, remove the calzone dough from the bread pan and place it on a lightly floured surface. Knock it back (punch it down) gently then divide the dough into two equal pieces. Roll out each piece of dough into a flat round, about 5mm/¼in thick. Preheat the oven to 220°C/425°F/Gas 7.

COOK'S TIP

Calzone can be made in advance, ready for baking. Make the dough, then transfer to a bowl, cover with oiled clear film and store in the refrigerator for up to 4 hours. Knock back if the dough starts to rise to the top of the bowl. Bring back to room temperature, then continue with the shaping and filling. If preferred, shape and fill up to 2 hours before baking. Place the calzone in the refrigerator until you are ready to bake them.

6 Divide the filling between the two pieces of dough, placing it on one half only, in each case. Leave a 1.5cm/½in border of the dough all round.

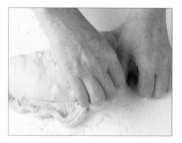

7 Dampen the edges of each dough round with water, fold the remaining dough over the filling and then crimp the edges of each calzone with your fingers to seal securely.

8 Place the calzone on the baking sheet, brush with olive oil and bake for 20 minutes, or until golden and well risen.

SOURDOUGHS AND STARTER DOUGH BREADS

Breads made with starters acquire their wonderful textures and flavours from the multiple ferments and starter doughs. The bread machine provides the perfect environment to nurture these doughs. This section also includes a recipe for bread made with fresh yeast.

FRESH YEAST BREAD

15g/½oz fresh yeast
5ml/1 tsp granulated sugar
260ml/9fl oz/1⅛ cups water
30ml/2 tbsp sunflower oil
450g/1lb/4 cups unbleached white
bread flour
30ml/2 tbsp skimmed milk powder
(non fat dry milk)
10ml/2 tsp salt
75ml/5 tbsp sunflower seeds, for coating

MAKES 1 LOAF

If you particularly like the flavour of fresh yeast, try this recipe. Bread machine manufacturers do not recommend using fresh yeast for bread baked in their appliances, but if the bread is to be baked in the oven, the machine can be used to prepare the dough.

5 Sprinkle the sunflower seeds on a clean area of work surface and roll the bread in them until evenly coated. Place on the prepared baking sheet. Cover with lightly oiled clear film (plastic wrap) or a large inverted bowl and leave to rise in a warm place for 30–45 minutes, or until doubled in size.

6 Meanwhile, preheat the oven to 230°C/450°F/Gas 8. Cut two slashes, one on each side of the loaf, then cut two slashes at right angles to the first to make a noughts and crosses grid.

7 Bake the loaf for 15 minutes, then reduce the oven temperature to 200°C/400°F/Gas 6. Bake for 20 minutes more, or until the bread sounds hollow when tapped on the base. Turn out on to a wire rack to cool.

COOK'S TIP
This makes a basic fresh yeast bread which you can shape or flavour to suit yourself. Leave out the sunflower seeds, if you like.

1 In a small bowl, cream the fresh yeast with the sugar and 30ml/2 tbsp of the water. Leave to stand for 5 minutes then scrape the mixture into the bread machine pan. Add the remaining water and the sunflower oil. However, if the instructions for your bread machine specify that the yeast is to be placed in the pan first, simply reverse the order in which you add the liquid and dry ingredients to the pan.

2 Sprinkle over the flour, ensuring that it covers the water completely. Add the skimmed milk powder and salt to the bread pan.

3 Set the bread machine to the dough setting; use basic dough setting (if available). Press Start, then lightly oil a baking sheet.

4 When the dough cycle has finished, remove the dough from the machine and place it on a lightly floured surface. Knock it back (punch it down) gently, and then knead for 2–3 minutes. Roll the dough into a ball and pat it into a plump round cushion shape.

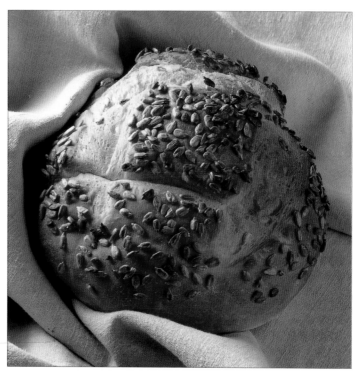

SCHIACCIATA CON UVA

*A Tuscan bread baked to celebrate the grape harvest. The fresh grapes on top
are the new crop while the raisins inside symbolize last year's gathering-in.*

FOR THE STARTER
200ml/7fl oz/⅞ cup water
*175g/6oz/1½ cups organic white
bread flour*
*1.5ml/¼ tsp easy-blend (rapid-rise)
dried yeast*

FOR THE SCHIACCIATA DOUGH
200g/7oz/generous 1 cup raisins
150ml/5fl oz/⅔ cup Italian red wine
45ml/3 tbsp extra virgin olive oil
45ml/3 tbsp water
*280g/10oz/2½ cups unbleached white
bread flour*
50g/2oz/¼ cup granulated sugar
7.5ml/1½ tsp salt
*5ml/1 tsp easy-blend (rapid-rise)
dried yeast*

FOR THE TOPPING
280g/10oz small black seedless grapes
30ml/2 tbsp demerara (raw) sugar

MAKES 1 LOAF

1 Pour the water for the starter into the bread machine pan. If the instructions for your machine specify that the yeast is to be placed in the pan first, reverse the order in which you add the liquid and dry ingredients.

2 Sprinkle over the organic flour, ensuring that it completely covers the water. Make a small indent in the centre of the flour (but not down as far as the liquid) and add the easy-blend dried yeast. Set the bread machine to the dough setting; use basic dough setting (if available). Press Start. Mix for 5 minutes, then switch off the machine and set aside.

3 Leave the starter to ferment inside the machine for 24 hours. Do not lift the lid. If you need the machine, transfer the starter to a bowl, cover it with a damp dishtowel and leave it to stand at room temperature.

4 Place the raisins for the dough in a small pan. Add the wine and heat gently until warm. Cover and set aside.

5 Remove the bread pan from the machine. Return the starter to the pan, if necessary, and pour in the oil and water. Sprinkle over the flour. Add the sugar and salt in separate corners. Make a shallow indent in the centre of the flour and add the yeast.

6 Set the bread machine to the dough setting. If your machine has a choice of settings, use the basic dough setting. Press Start. Lightly oil a baking sheet.

7 When the dough cycle has finished, remove the dough from the machine and place it on a lightly floured surface. Knock it back (punch it down) gently, then divide it in half. Roll each piece of dough out into a circle, about 1cm/½in thick. Place one circle on the prepared baking sheet.

8 Spread the raisins over the dough. Place the remaining piece of dough on top and pinch the edges together to seal. Cover with lightly oiled clear film (plastic wrap) and leave to rise in a warm place for 30–45 minutes, or until it is almost doubled in size.

9 Meanwhile, preheat the oven to 190°C/375°F/Gas 5. Cover the schiacciata with the fresh black grapes, pressing them lightly into the dough. Sprinkle with the sugar. Bake for 40 minutes, or until the bread is golden and sounds hollow when tapped on the base. Turn out on to a wire rack to cool slightly before serving.

FRENCH COURONNE

This crown-shaped loaf is made with a chef starter, which is fermented for at least 2 days and up to a week; the longer it is left the more it will develop the characteristic sourdough flavour.

FOR THE CHEF
0.6ml/⅛ tsp easy-blend (rapid-rise)
dried yeast
50g/2oz/½ cup organic white bread flour
45ml/3 tbsp water

FOR THE 1ST REFRESHMENT
65ml/4½ tbsp water
115g/4oz/1 cup organic white
bread flour

FOR THE LEVAIN
115ml/4fl oz/½ cup water
115g/4oz/1 cup unbleached white
bread flour

FOR THE COURONNE DOUGH
240ml/8½fl oz/generous 1 cup
cold water
325g/11½oz/scant 3 cups unbleached
white bread flour, plus extra for dusting
7.5ml/1½ tsp salt
5ml/1 tsp granulated sugar
2.5ml/½ tsp easy-blend (rapid-rise)
dried yeast

MAKES 1 LOAF

1 Mix the yeast and organic white bread flour for the chef in a small bowl. Add the water and gradually mix to a stiff dough with a metal spoon. Cover the bowl with oiled clear film (plastic wrap) and set aside in a warm place for 2–3 days.

2 Break open the crust on the chef – the middle should be aerated and sweet smelling. Mix in the water and flour for the first refreshment, stirring to form a fairly stiff dough. Replace the clear film cover and set aside for a further 2 days in a warm place.

3 Transfer the chef to the machine pan. If the instructions for your machine specify that the yeast is to be placed in the pan first, reverse the order in which you add the liquid and dry ingredients.

4 Add the water for the levain. Sprinkle over the flour, ensuring that it covers the water. Set the bread machine to the dough setting; use basic dough setting (if available). Press Start.

5 When the dough cycle has finished, switch the machine off, leaving the levain inside. Do not lift the lid. Leave the levain for 8 hours. If you need the machine, transfer the levain to a bowl, cover it with a damp dishtowel and leave it at room temperature.

6 Take the bread pan out of the machine. Remove about half of the levain from the pan. If the levain is in a bowl, put 200g/7oz/scant 1 cup of it back in the pan. Reserve the spare levain to replenish and use for your next loaf of bread. Meanwhile pour the water for the dough into the bread pan. Sprinkle over the flour. Add the salt and sugar, placing them in separate corners of the bread pan. Make a small indent in the centre of the flour and add the yeast.

7 Set the bread machine to the dough setting; use basic dough setting (if available). Press Start. Lightly oil a baking sheet.

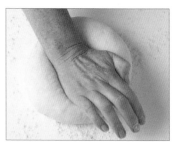

8 When the dough cycle has finished, remove the dough from the machine and place it on a lightly floured surface. Knock it back (punch it down) gently, then shape it into a ball and make a hole in the centre with the heel of your hand. Gradually enlarge this cavity, using your fingertips and turning the dough, then use both hands to stretch the dough gently into a large doughnut shape. The cavity should measure 13–15cm/5–6in across.

9 Place the shaped dough on the prepared baking sheet. Fit a small bowl into the centre to prevent the dough from filling in the hole when it rises. Cover it with lightly oiled clear film and leave it in a warm place for an hour, or until almost doubled in size.

10 Preheat the oven to 230°C/450°F/ Gas 8. Dust the loaf with flour and make four slashes at equal intervals around the couronne. Bake for 35–40 minutes, or until the bread is golden and sounds hollow when tapped on its base. Turn out on to a wire rack to cool.

HONEY AND BEER RYE BREAD

*The flavour of this rye bread is enhanced by leaving the sourdough starter to
develop over 3 days as a prelude to making the dough.*

For the Starter
175ml/6fl oz/¾ cup milk
115g/4oz/1 cup rye flour
4ml/¾ tsp easy-blend (rapid-rise)
dried yeast

For the Dough
170ml/6fl oz/scant ¾ cup flat beer
300g/10½oz/scant 2¾ cups
unbleached white bread flour
85g/3oz/¾ cup rye flour
15ml/1 tbsp clear honey
7.5ml/1½ tsp salt
2.5ml/½ tsp easy-blend dried yeast
wholemeal (whole-wheat) flour,
for dusting
Makes 1 Loaf

1 Mix the milk, flour and yeast for the
starter in a large bowl. Stir, then cover
with a damp dishtowel. Rest in a warm
place for 3 days; stir once a day.

2 Make the dough. Tip the starter into
the bread machine pan and add the
beer. If the instructions for your
machine specify that the yeast is to be
placed in the pan first, simply reverse
the order in which you add the liquid
and dry ingredients.

3 Sprinkle over both types of flour,
ensuring that the beer is completely
covered. Add the honey and salt, placing
them in separate corners of the bread
pan. Make a small indent in the centre
of the flour (but not down as far as the
liquid) and add the yeast.

4 Set the bread machine to the dough
setting; use basic dough setting (if
available). Press Start. Lightly oil a 17cm/
6½in square tin (pan) that is fairly deep.

5 When the dough cycle has finished,
remove the dough from the machine
and place it on a lightly floured surface.
Knock it back (punch it down) gently.

6 Roll the dough into a rectangle about
2cm/¾in thick. It needs to be the same
width as the tin and three times as long.
Fold the bottom third of the dough up
and the top third down, then seal the
edges with the rolling pin.

7 Place the folded dough in the prepared
tin, cover it with lightly oiled clear film
(plastic wrap) and leave in a warm place
for 45–60 minutes, or until the dough
has risen almost to the top of the tin.

8 Meanwhile, preheat the oven to 220°C/
425°F/Gas 7. Dust the top of the loaf
with a little wholemeal flour.

9 Using a sharp knife slash the loaf with
four long cuts. Repeat with five cuts in
the opposite direction to give a cross-
hatched effect.

10 Bake the bread for 30–35 minutes, or
until it sounds hollow when tapped on
the base. Turn out on to a wire rack to
cool slightly before serving.

PANE ALL'OLIO

*Italians love to use olive oil in cooking, as this bread amply proves.
The combined flavours of the olive oil and the biga starter give a rich,
earthy and yeasty flavour to the bread.*

1 Pour the water for the biga into the bread machine pan. If the instructions for your machine specify that the yeast is to be placed in the pan first, reverse the order in which you add the liquid and dry ingredients.

2 Sprinkle over the flour, covering the water. Make a shallow indent in the centre of the flour and add the yeast.

3 Set the machine to the dough setting; use basic dough setting (if available). Press Start.When the dough cycle has finished, switch the machine off, but leave the biga inside, with the lid closed, for 8 hours. If you need the machine during this time, transfer the biga to a bowl, cover it with a damp dishtowel and leave it at room temperature.

4 Remove the bread pan from the machine. Break the biga into three or four pieces. If you took it out of the bread pan, put it back.

5 Pour in the water and olive oil for the dough. Sprinkle over the flour, covering the liquid. Add the salt and sugar in separate corners of the bread pan.

6 Set the bread machine to the dough setting; use basic dough setting (if available). Press Start. Lightly flour a peel (baker's shovel) or baking sheet.

7 When the dough cycle has finished, place the dough on a lightly floured surface. Knock it back (punch it down) gently, then shape it into a plump round.

For the Biga
105ml/7 tbsp water
175g/6oz/1½ cups white bread flour
5ml/1 tsp easy-blend (rapid-rise) dried yeast

For the Dough
90ml/6 tbsp water
60ml/4 tbsp extra virgin olive oil
*225g/8oz/2 cups unbleached white
bread flour, plus extra for dusting*
10ml/2 tsp salt
5ml/1 tsp granulated sugar

Makes 1 Loaf

COOK'S TIP
If you haven't got a baking stone, you can use unglazed terracotta tiles. Place several tiles edge to edge, ensuring that the air can flow around the outside edges.

8 Using the palms of your hands, gently roll the dough backwards and forwards, concentrating on the ends, until it forms a tapered, torpedo-shaped loaf about 30cm/12in long. Place the loaf on the prepared peel or baking sheet and cover it with lightly oiled clear film (plastic wrap). Leave it to rise in a warm place for 45–60 minutes, or until the dough has almost doubled in size.

9 Meanwhile, place a baking stone on a shelf about a third of the way up from the bottom of the oven. Preheat the oven to 230°C/450°F/Gas 8. Dust the top of the bread lightly with flour and slash it along its length. Transfer the bread to the hot baking stone.

10 Mist the inside of the oven with water. Bake the loaf for 15 minutes, misting the oven again after 2 minutes and then after 4 minutes. Reduce the oven temperature to 190°C/375°F/Gas 5 and bake the loaf for 20–25 minutes more, or until it is golden all over and the bread sounds hollow when tapped on the base. Turn out on to a wire rack before serving warm or cooled.

PAIN DE CAMPAGNE

This rustic-style French bread is made using a poolish or sponge. The fermentation period is fairly short, which makes for a loaf which is not as sour as some breads of this type. It is also lighter and slightly less chewy.

For the Poolish
200ml/7fl oz/⅞ cup water
175g/6oz/1½ cups unbleached white bread flour
50g/2oz/½ cup wholemeal (whole-wheat) bread flour
1.5ml/¼ tsp easy-blend (rapid-rise) dried yeast

For the Dough
120ml/4fl oz/½ cup water
225g/8oz/2 cups unbleached white bread flour, plus extra for dusting
50g/2oz/½ cup wholemeal bread flour
25g/1oz/¼ cup rye flour
7.5ml/1½ tsp salt
2.5ml/½ tsp granulated sugar
2.5ml/½ tsp easy-blend dried yeast
Makes 1 Loaf

1 Pour the water for the poolish into the bread machine pan. If the instructions for your machine specify that the yeast is to be placed in the pan first, reverse the order in which you add the liquid and dry ingredients.

2 Sprinkle over both types of flour, ensuring that the water is completely covered. Make a small indent in the centre of the flour; add the yeast. Set the bread machine to the dough setting; use basic dough setting (if available). Press Start.

3 When the dough cycle has finished, switch the machine off, but leave the poolish inside, with the lid closed, for 2 – 8 hours, depending on how sour you like your bread to taste.

4 Remove the bread pan from the machine. Pour in the water for the dough. Sprinkle over each type of flour, then add the salt and sugar in separate corners. Make a small indent in the centre of the flour; add the yeast. Set the bread machine to the dough setting. If your machine has a choice of settings, use the basic dough setting. Press Start.

5 When the dough cycle has finished, place the dough on a lightly floured surface. Knock it back (punch it down) gently, then shape it into a plump, round ball. Place on a lightly oiled baking sheet.

6 Cover with a large glass bowl or lightly oiled clear film (plastic wrap) and leave to rise in a warm place for 30–45 minutes, or until almost doubled in bulk. Preheat the oven to 220°C/425°F/Gas 7.

7 Dust the top of the loaf with flour. Cut three parallel slashes across the loaf, then cut three more slashes at right angles to the first set.

8 Transfer the baking sheet to a rack near the bottom of the oven and bake the bread for 40 minutes, or until it is golden and sounds hollow when tapped on the base. Turn out on to a wire rack.

CIABATTA

*This popular flat loaf is irregularly shaped and typically has large air holes
in the crumb. The dough for this bread is extremely wet. Do not be tempted to
add more flour – it's meant to be that way.*

FOR THE BIGA
200ml/7fl oz/⅞ cup water
*175g/6oz/1½ cups unbleached white
bread flour*
*2.5ml/½ tsp easy-blend (rapid-rise)
dried yeast*

FOR THE CIABATTA DOUGH
200ml/7fl oz/⅞ cup water
30ml/2 tbsp milk
30ml/2 tbsp extra virgin olive oil
*325g/11½oz/scant 3 cups unbleached
white bread flour, plus extra for dusting*
7.5ml/1½ tsp salt
2.5ml/½ tsp granulated sugar
1.5ml/¼ tsp easy-blend dried yeast

MAKES 2 LOAVES

1 Pour the water for the biga into the bread pan. If necessary, reverse the order in which you add the liquid and dry ingredients. Sprinkle over the flour, covering the water. Make an indent in the centre of the flour; add the yeast.

2 Set the bread machine to the dough setting; use basic dough setting (if available). Press Start. Mix for 5 minutes, then switch off the machine.

3 Leave the biga in the machine, or place in a large mixing bowl covered with oiled clear film (plastic wrap), overnight or for at least 12 hours, until the dough has risen and is just starting to collapse.

4 Return the biga to the pan, if necessary. Add the water, milk and oil for the ciabatta dough. Sprinkle over the flour. Add the salt and sugar in separate corners. Make a small indent in the centre of the flour and add the yeast.

5 Set the bread machine to the dough setting; use the basic dough setting (if available). Press Start.

6 When the cycle has finished, transfer the dough to a bowl and cover with oiled clear film. Leave to rise for about 1 hour, until the dough has tripled in size. Sprinkle two baking sheets with flour.

7 Using a spoon or a dough scraper, divide the dough into two portions. Carefully tip one portion of the dough on to one of the prepared baking sheets, trying to avoid knocking the air out of the dough. Using well-floured hands shape the dough into a rectangular loaf about 2.5cm/1in thick, pulling and stretching as necessary. Repeat with the remaining piece of dough.

8 Sprinkle both loaves with flour. Leave them, uncovered, in a warm place for about 20–30 minutes. The dough will spread and rise. Meanwhile, preheat the oven to 220°C/425°F/Gas 7.

9 Bake the ciabatta for 25–30 minutes, or until both loaves have risen, are light golden in colour and sound hollow when tapped on the base. Transfer them to a wire rack to cool before serving with butter, or olive oil for dipping.

PAIN DE SEIGLE

*Based on a rye starter, this is typical of the breads eaten in the Pyrenees.
Serve it thickly buttered – it makes the perfect accompaniment for shellfish.*

FOR THE CHEF
200ml/7fl oz/⅞ cup water
175g/6oz/1½ cups rye flour
*1.5ml/¼ tsp easy-blend (rapid-rise)
dried yeast*

FOR THE 1ST REFRESHMENT
70ml/2½fl oz/¼ cup + 1 tbsp water
50g/2oz/½ cup plain (all-purpose) flour

FOR THE 2ND REFRESHMENT
15ml/1 tbsp water
50g/2oz/½ cup plain (all-purpose) flour

FOR THE BREAD DOUGH
15ml/1 tbsp water
*225g/8oz/2 cups unbleached white
bread flour*
10ml/2 tsp salt
5ml/1 tsp clear honey
2.5ml/½ tsp easy-blend dried yeast
*unbleached white bread flour, for
dusting*

MAKES 1 LOAF

1 Pour the water for the chef into the machine pan. If the instructions for your machine specify that the yeast is to be added first, reverse the order in which you add the liquid and dry ingredients.

2 Sprinkle over the rye flour, ensuring that it covers the water completely. Make a small indent in the centre of the flour (but not down as far as the liquid) and add the easy-blend dried yeast. Set the bread machine to the dough setting; use basic dough setting (if available). Press Start. Mix the dough for about 10 minutes, and then switch off the bread machine.

3 Leave the chef to ferment in the machine, with the lid closed, for about 24 hours. If you need the machine, transfer the chef to a bowl, cover it with a damp dishtowel and then set aside at room temperature.

4 Remove the bread pan from the machine. Return the chef to the bread pan, if necessary, and add the water and flour for the first refreshment. Set the bread machine to the dough setting, press Start and mix for 10 minutes. Switch off the machine and leave the dough inside for a further 24 hours.

5 Add the water and flour for the second refreshment. Mix as for the first refreshment, but this time leave the dough in the machine for only 8 hours.

6 Add the water for the bread dough to the mixture in the bread machine pan. Sprinkle over the flour. Place the salt and honey in separate corners of the bread pan. Make a small indent in the centre of the flour and add the yeast. Set the bread machine to the dough setting; use basic dough setting (if available). Press Start. Lightly flour a baking sheet.

COOK'S TIP
When shaping the loaf into a twist make sure that you continue to twist it in the same direction after you have turned the dough round to finish shaping the loaf.

7 When the dough cycle has finished, place the dough on a lightly floured surface. Knock it back (punch it down) gently, then divide the dough into two equal pieces. Roll each piece of dough into a rope about 45cm/18in long.

8 Place the two ropes side by side. Starting at the centre, place one piece of dough over the other. Continue twisting in this fashion until you reach the end of the rope. Turn the dough around and twist the other ends. Dampen the ends with water; tuck them under to seal.

9 Place the twist on the baking sheet, cover with oiled clear film (plastic wrap) and leave in a warm place for 45 minutes, or until almost doubled in size.

10 Preheat the oven to 220°C/425°F/ Gas 7. Dust the top of the loaf lightly with flour and bake for 40 minutes, or until the bread is golden and sounds hollow when tapped on the base. Switch off the oven, but leave the loaf inside, with the door slightly ajar, for 5 minutes. Turn out on to a wire rack to cool.

SAN FRANCISCO-STYLE SOURDOUGH

This tangy, chewy bread originated in San Francisco, but the flavour will actually be unique to wherever it is baked. The bread is made without baker's yeast, instead using airborne yeast spores to ferment a flour and water paste.

For the Starter
25g/1oz/¼ cup organic plain (all-purpose) flour
15–30ml/1–2 tbsp warm water

1st Refreshment for the Starter
30ml/2 tbsp water
15ml/1 tbsp milk
50g/2oz/½ cup organic plain flour

2nd Refreshment for the Starter
90ml/6 tbsp water
15–30ml/1–2 tbsp milk
175g/6oz/1½ cups organic white bread flour

For the Dough
100ml/3½fl oz/7 tbsp water
175g/6oz/1½ cups organic white bread flour

1st Refreshment for the Dough
100ml/3½fl oz/7 tbsp water
175g/6oz/1½ cups organic white bread flour
50g/2oz/½ cup organic wholemeal (whole-wheat) bread flour
7.5ml/1½ tsp salt
5ml/1 tsp granulated sugar
unbleached white bread flour, for dusting

Makes 1 Loaf

1 Place the flour in a bowl and stir in enough water for the starter to make a firm, moist dough. Knead for 5 minutes. Cover with a damp cloth. Leave for 2–3 days until a crust forms and the dough inflates with tiny bubbles. Remove the hardened crust and place the moist centre in a clean bowl. Add the water and milk for the 1st refreshment.

2 Gradually add the flour and mix to a firm but moist dough. Cover and leave for 1–2 days as before. Then repeat as for 1st refreshment using the ingredients for the 2nd refreshment. Leave for 8–12 hours in a warm place until well risen.

3 Pour the water for the dough into the pan. Add 200g/7oz/scant 1 cup of starter. If necessary for your machine, add the dry ingredients first. Sprinkle over the flour, covering the water. Set the machine to the dough setting; use basic dough setting (if available). Press Start.

4 Mix for 10 minutes then turn off the machine. Leave the dough in the machine for 8 hours. Add the water for the 1st dough refreshment to the pan, then sprinkle over the flours.

5 Add the salt and sugar in separate corners. Set the machine as before. Press Start. Lightly flour a baking sheet.

6 When the dough cycle ends put the dough on a floured surface. Knock it back (punch it down) gently; shape into a plump ball. Place on the baking sheet; cover with oiled clear film (plastic wrap). Leave for 2 hours, or until almost doubled in bulk.

7 Meanwhile, preheat the oven to 230°C/450°F/Gas 8. Dust the loaf with flour and slash the top in a star shape. Bake for 25 minutes, spraying the oven with water three times in the first 5 minutes. Reduce the oven temperature to 200°C/400°F/Gas 6. Bake the loaf for 10 minutes more or until golden and hollow-sounding. Cool on a wire rack.

CHALLAH

—

The flavour of this traditional Jewish festival bread is enhanced by the use of a sponge starter, which is left to develop for 8–10 hours before the final dough is made. The dough is often braided, but can also be shaped into a coil. This shape is favoured for Jewish New Year celebrations, and symbolizes continuity and eternity.

FOR THE SPONGE
200ml/7fl oz/⅞ cup water
225g/8oz/2 cups unbleached white
bread flour
15ml/1 tbsp granulated sugar
5ml/1 tsp salt
7.5ml/1½ tsp easy-blend (rapid-rise)
dried yeast

FOR THE DOUGH
2 eggs
225g/8oz/2 cups unbleached white
bread flour
15ml/1 tbsp granulated sugar
5ml/1 tsp salt
50g/2oz/¼ cup butter, melted

FOR THE TOPPING
1 egg yolk
15ml/1 tbsp water
poppy seeds

MAKES 1 LOAF

1 Pour the water for the sponge into the bread machine pan. Reverse the order in which you add the wet and dry ingredients if necessary.

2 Sprinkle over the flour ensuring that it covers the water. Add the sugar and salt in separate corners. Make an indent in the centre of the flour and add the yeast.

3 Set the bread machine to the dough setting; use basic dough setting (if available). Press Start.

4 When the dough cycle has finished, switch the machine off, leaving the sponge inside. Do not lift the lid. Leave the sponge in the machine for 8 hours. If necessary, transfer to a bowl, cover with a damp dishtowel and set aside.

5 Remove the bread pan from the machine and replace the sponge (if necessary). Add the eggs for the dough to the sponge. Sprinkle over the flour. Place the sugar, salt and melted butter in separate corners of the bread pan. Set the bread machine to the dough setting; use basic dough setting (if available). Press Start. Lightly oil a baking sheet.

6 When the dough cycle has finished, remove the dough from the machine and place it on a lightly floured surface. Knock it back (punch it down) gently, then flatten the dough until it is about 2.5cm/1in thick. Fold both sides to the centre, fold the dough over again and press to seal.

7 Using your palms, gradually roll the dough into a rope with tapered ends. It should be about 50cm/20in long. Coil the rope into a spiral shape, sealing the final end by tucking it under the loaf. Place the coil on the prepared baking sheet. Cover it with a large glass bowl or lightly oiled clear film (plastic wrap) and leave in a warm place for 45–60 minutes, or until almost doubled in size.

8 Preheat the oven to 190°C/375°F/Gas 5. In a small bowl, beat the egg yolk with the water for the topping. Brush the mixture over the challah. Sprinkle evenly with the poppy seeds and bake for 35–40 minutes, or until the bread is a deep golden brown and sounds hollow when tapped on the base. Transfer it to a wire rack to cool before slicing.

SAVOURY BREADS

Adding flavourings to a basic dough provides many new ideas. Herbs, such as rosemary, dill and sage, along with garlic and onion will fill the kitchen with delicious scents. Cottage cheese and feta give loaves a subtle flavour, while Gorgonzola, Parmesan and mascarpone are combined with chives to give a rich loaf with a wonderful aroma. Sausages, smoked venison, salami and pancetta are just a few of the meats you can add to savoury breads.

210ml/7½fl oz/scant 1 cup water
350g/12oz/3 cups unbleached white
bread flour
25g/1oz/¼ cup wholemeal
(whole-wheat) bread flour
15ml/1 tbsp skimmed milk powder
(non fat dry milk)
5ml/1 tsp salt
7.5ml/1½ tsp granulated sugar
5ml/1 tsp easy-blend (rapid-rise)
dried yeast
40g/1½oz/scant ½ cup well drained,
pitted black olives, chopped
50g/2oz feta cheese, crumbled
15ml/1 tbsp olive oil, for brushing

MAKES 1 LOAF

COOK'S TIP
Depending on the moisture content of
the olives and cheese you may need
to add a tablespoon or two of flour to
the bread dough when adding these
extra ingredients.

FETA CHEESE AND BLACK OLIVE LOAF
———

Conjuring up memories of holidays in Greece, this bread has a delicious
flavour, thanks to the Mediterranean ingredients.

1 Pour the water into the bread pan. If
necessary, reverse the order in which
you add the liquid and dry ingredients.
Sprinkle over the flours, covering the
water completely. Add the skimmed
milk powder. Place the salt and sugar in
separate corners of the bread pan. Make
an indent in the flour; add the yeast.

2 Set the bread machine to the dough
setting; use basic raisin dough setting
(if available). Press Start. Lightly oil a
18–20cm/7–8in deep round cake tin (pan).

3 Add the olives and feta cheese when
the bread machine beeps or 5 minutes
before the end of the kneading cycle.
Once the dough cycle has finished, place
the dough on a lightly floured surface
and knock back (punch it down) gently.

4 Shape into a plump ball, the same
diameter as the tin. Place in the tin,
cover with oiled clear film (plastic wrap)
and leave to rise for 30–45 minutes.
Preheat the oven to 200°C/400°F/Gas 6.

5 Remove the clear film and brush the
olive oil over the top of the loaf. Bake
for 35–40 minutes, or until golden. Turn
the bread out on to a wire rack to cool.

LEEK AND PANCETTA TRAY BREAD
———

Serve this bread sliced, with a simple salad of dressed leaves, for a tasty
supper or lunchtime snack.

90ml/6 tbsp water
1 egg
225g/8oz/2 cups unbleached white
bread flour
5ml/1 tsp salt
25g/1oz butter
5ml/1 tsp easy-blend (rapid-rise)
dried yeast

FOR THE FILLING
575g/1¼lb/4–5 leeks
30ml/2 tbsp sunflower oil
75g/3oz sliced pancetta or streaky
(fatty) bacon, cut into strips
140ml/5fl oz/⅔ cup sour cream
70ml/2½fl oz/5 tbsp milk
2 eggs, lightly beaten
15ml/1 tbsp chopped fresh basil leaves
salt and freshly ground black pepper

MAKES 1 LOAF

1 Pour the water and egg into the bread
machine pan. Reverse wet and dry
ingredients if necessary. Sprinkle over
the flour, ensuring that it covers the
liquid. Place the salt and butter in
separate corners. Make a shallow indent
in the centre of the flour (but not down
as far as the liquid) and add the yeast.

2 Set the bread machine to the dough
setting; use basic or pizza dough setting
(if available). Press Start. Then lightly
oil a 20 × 30cm/8 × 12in Swiss (jelly) roll
tin (pan) that is about 1cm/½in deep.

3 Slice the leeks thinly. Heat the
sunflower oil in a large frying pan and
cook the leeks over a low heat for about
5 minutes, until they have softened
slightly but not browned. Set them
aside to cool.

4 When the dough cycle has finished,
place the dough on a lightly floured
surface. Knock it back (punch it down)
gently, then roll it out to a rectangle
measuring about 23 × 33 cm/9 × 13in.
Place in the prepared tin and press the
edges outwards and upwards, so that the
dough covers the base and sides evenly.
Preheat the oven to 190°C/375°F/Gas 5.

5 Sprinkle the leeks over the dough.
Arrange the pancetta slices on top.
Mix the sour cream, milk and eggs
together. Add the basil and season with
salt and ground black pepper. Pour the
mixture over the leeks.

6 Bake for 30–35 minutes, or until the
filling has set and the base is golden
around the edges. Serve the bread hot
or warm.

GRAINY MUSTARD AND BEER LOAF

*For a ploughman's lunch par excellence, serve chunks of this wonderful
bread with cheese and pickles.*

SMALL

180ml/6½fl oz/generous ¾ cup flat beer
15ml/1 tbsp vegetable oil
30ml/2 tbsp wholegrain mustard
*250g/9oz/2¼ cups unbleached white
bread flour*
*125g/4½oz/generous 1 cup wholemeal
(whole-wheat) bread flour*
15ml/1 tbsp skimmed milk powder
5ml/1 tsp salt
7.5ml/1½ tsp granulated sugar
*5ml/1 tsp easy-blend (rapid-rise)
dried yeast*

MEDIUM

280ml/10fl oz/1¼ cups flat beer
15ml/1 tbsp vegetable oil
45ml/3 tbsp wholegrain mustard
*350g/12oz/3 cups unbleached white
bread flour*
*150g/5½oz/1⅓ cups wholemeal
bread flour*
22ml/1½ tbsp skimmed milk powder
7.5ml/1½ tsp salt
10ml/2 tsp granulated sugar
5ml/1 tsp easy-blend dried yeast

LARGE

*360ml/12½fl oz/generous 1½ cups
flat beer*
30ml/2 tbsp vegetable oil
60ml/4 tbsp wholegrain mustard
*475g/1lb 1oz/4¼ cups unbleached
white bread flour*
*200g/7oz/1¾ cups wholemeal
bread flour*
*30ml/2 tbsp skimmed milk powder
(non fat dry milk)*
7.5ml/1½ tsp salt
15ml/1 tbsp granulated sugar
7.5ml/1½ tsp easy-blend dried yeast

MAKES 1 LOAF

COOK'S TIP
Use pale ale for a more subtle taste or
brown ale if you prefer a stronger
flavour to your bread. Open at least
1 hour before using, to make sure
it is flat.

1 Pour the beer and oil into the bread
machine pan. Add the mustard. If the
instructions for your machine specify
that the yeast is to be placed in the pan
first, reverse the order in which you add
the liquid and dry ingredients.

2 Sprinkle over the white and
wholemeal flours, ensuring that the
liquid is completely covered. Add the
skimmed milk powder. Add the salt
and sugar, placing them in separate
corners of the bread pan. Make a small
indent in the centre of the flour (but
not down as far as the liquid) and add
the yeast.

3 Set the bread machine to the
basic/normal setting, medium crust.
Press Start.

4 Remove the bread at the end of the
baking cycle and turn out on to a wire
rack to cool.

COTTAGE CHEESE–PEPPERONI LOAF

Cottage cheese gives this bread an interesting texture. It is quite filling, and has a delicious, spicy taste, thanks to the pepperoni and oregano. Serve it with vegetable soups or salad.

SMALL
100g/3½oz/scant ½ cup cottage cheese
160ml/5½fl oz/generous ⅔ cup water
15ml/1 tbsp extra virgin olive oil
375g/13oz/3¼ cups unbleached white bread flour
5ml/1 tsp dried oregano
5ml/1 tsp salt
7.5ml/1½ tsp granulated sugar
5ml/1 tsp easy-blend (rapid-rise) dried yeast
25g/1oz pepperoni, cut into 5mm/¼in chunks
1 spring onion (scallion), chopped

MEDIUM
170g/6oz/¾ cup cottage cheese
210ml/7½fl oz/scant 1 cup water
22ml/1½ tbsp extra virgin olive oil
500g/1lb 2oz/4½ cups unbleached white bread flour
7.5ml/1½ tsp dried oregano
5ml/1 tsp salt
10ml/2 tsp granulated sugar
7.5ml/1½ tsp easy-blend dried yeast
50g/2oz pepperoni, cut into 5mm/¼in chunks
2 spring onions, chopped

LARGE
225g/8oz/1 cup cottage cheese
280ml/10fl oz/1¼ cups water
30ml/2 tbsp extra virgin olive oil
675g/1½lb/6 cups unbleached white bread flour
10ml/2 tsp dried oregano
7.5ml/1½ tsp salt
15ml/1 tbsp granulated sugar
7.5ml/1½ tsp easy-blend dried yeast
75g/3oz pepperoni, cut into 5mm/¼in chunks
3 spring onions, chopped

MAKES 1 LOAF

COOK'S TIP
Extra ingredients are usually added towards the end of the kneading cycle, and some machines will alert you to this by means of a beep or buzzing noise. Consult the handbook for your machine if necessary.

1 Place the cottage cheese in the bread machine pan and pour in the water and extra virgin olive oil. If the instructions for your machine specify that the easy-blend dried yeast is to be placed in the bread pan first, then simply reverse the order in which you add the liquid and dry ingredients.

2 Sprinkle over the flour, ensuring that it covers the water. Add the oregano. Add the salt and sugar in separate corners of the bread pan. Make a small indent in the centre of the flour (but not down as far as the liquid) and add the easy-blend dried yeast.

3 Set the bread machine to the basic/normal setting, with raisin setting (if available), medium crust. Press Start. Add the pepperoni and spring onion when the machine beeps or sprinkle them over the dough 5 minutes before the end of the kneading cycle.

4 Remove the bread at the end of the baking cycle and turn out on to a wire rack to cool.

200ml/7fl oz/⅞ cup water
350g/12oz/3 cups unbleached white
bread flour
2.5ml/½ tsp granulated sugar
5ml/1 tsp salt
5ml/1 tsp easy-blend (rapid-rise)
dried yeast

FOR THE FILLING
175g/6oz mozzarella cheese, grated or
finely chopped
75g/3oz/1 cup freshly grated
Parmesan cheese
15ml/1 tbsp chopped fresh parsley
30ml/2 tbsp fresh basil leaves
5ml/1 tsp freshly ground black pepper
1 garlic clove, finely chopped

FOR THE TOPPING
15ml/1 tbsp extra virgin olive oil
4–5 small fresh rosemary sprigs,
woody stems removed

MAKES 1 LOAF

STROMBOLI

This variation on Italian Focaccia takes its name from the volcanic island of Stromboli, near Sicily. The dough is pierced to allow the filling to "erupt" through the holes during baking. This bread can be served warm or cold.

1 Pour the water into the machine pan. Reverse the order in which you add the wet and dry ingredients if necessary. Sprinkle over the flour, ensuring that it covers the water. Add the sugar and salt in separate corners of the pan. Make a shallow indent in the centre of the flour and add the yeast.

2 Set the bread machine to the dough setting; use basic dough setting (if available). Press Start.

3 Lightly oil a baking sheet.When the dough cycle has ended, remove the dough and place on a lightly floured surface. Knock it back (punch it down) gently. Roll out into a rectangle 30 × 23cm/12 × 9in. Cover with oiled clear film (plastic wrap) and leave to rest for 5 minutes.

4 Sprinkle over the cheeses leaving a 1cm/½in clear border along each edge. Add the parsley, basil, pepper and garlic.

5 Starting from a shorter side, roll up the dough, Swiss roll fashion, tucking the side edges under to seal. Place the roll, seam down, on the baking sheet. Cover with lightly oiled clear film and leave in a warm place for 30 minutes, or until the dough roll has almost doubled in size.

6 Preheat the oven to 200°C/400°F/ Gas 6. Brush the top of the bread with olive oil, then use a skewer to prick holes in the bread, from the top right through to the base. Sprinkle the rosemary over the bread. Bake for 30–35 minutes, or until the bread is golden. Transfer it to a wire rack.

THREE CHEESES BREAD

A tempting trio of Italian cheeses – mascarpone, Gorgonzola and Parmesan – are responsible for the marvellous flavour of this round loaf.

180ml/6½fl oz/generous ¾ cup water
1 egg
100g/3½oz/5 tbsp mascarpone cheese
400g/14oz/3½ cups unbleached white
bread flour
50g/2oz/½ cup Granary
(whole-wheat) flour
10ml/2 tsp granulated sugar
5ml/1 tsp salt
7.5ml/1½ tsp easy-blend (rapid-rise)
dried yeast
75g/3oz Mountain Gorgonzola cheese,
cut into small dice
75g/3oz/1 cup freshly grated
Parmesan cheese
45ml/3 tbsp chopped fresh chives

FOR THE TOPPING
1 egg yolk
15ml/1 tbsp water
15ml/1 tbsp wheat flakes

MAKES 1 LOAF

1 Add the water, egg and mascarpone to the pan. Reverse the order in which you add the wet and dry ingredients if necessary. Sprinkle over both types of flour, covering the water completely. Add the sugar and salt in separate corners. Make a small indent in the flour; add the yeast. Set the machine to the dough setting; use basic raisin dough setting (if available). Press Start.

2 Add the Gorgonzola, Parmesan and chives as the machine beeps or during the last 5 minutes of kneading. Lightly oil a baking sheet.

3 When the dough cycle has finished, place the dough on a floured surface. Knock back (punch down) gently, then shape it into a round loaf, about 20cm/ 8in in diameter.

4 Cover with oiled clear film (plastic wrap); leave in a warm place for 30–45 minutes. Preheat the oven to 200°C/400°F/Gas 6.

5 Mix the egg yolk and water together and brush this glaze over the top of the bread. Sprinkle with wheat flakes. Score the top of the bread into eight equal segments. Bake for 30–35 minutes, or until golden and hollow-sounding. Turn out on to a wire rack to cool.

VENISON TORDU

230ml/8fl oz/1 cup water
350g/12oz/3 cups unbleached white
bread flour
5ml/1 tsp granulated sugar
5ml/1 tsp salt
5ml/1 tsp easy-blend (rapid-rise)
dried yeast
40g/1½oz smoked venison, cut into strips
5ml/1 tsp freshly ground black pepper
5ml/1 tsp juniper berries, crushed
unbleached white bread flour,
for dusting

MAKES 1 LOAF

This pretty twisted bread is punctuated with strips of smoked venison, black pepper and crushed juniper berries. It tastes delicious on its own, perhaps with a glass of red wine. Alternatively, cut the bread into thick slices and serve it with olives and nuts as a precursor to an Italian meal.

1 Pour the water into the bread machine pan. If the instructions for your bread machine specify that the yeast is to be placed in the pan first, simply reverse the order in which you add the liquid and dry ingredients to the pan.

2 Sprinkle over the white bread flour, ensuring that it completely covers the water. Add the sugar and salt, placing them in separate corners of the bread pan. Make a shallow indent in the centre of the flour (but not down as far as the liquid) and add the easy-blend dried yeast.

3 Set the bread machine to the dough setting; use basic dough setting (if available). Press Start. Meanwhile, lightly oil a baking sheet.

4 When the dough cycle has finished, remove the dough from the bread machine pan and place it on a lightly floured surface. Knock it back (punch it down) gently. Shape the dough into a ball and flatten the top slightly.

5 Roll the dough out to a round, about 2cm/¾in thick. Sprinkle the top of the dough with venison strips, black pepper and juniper berries. Leave a 1cm/½in clear border around the edge.

6 Fold one side of the dough to the centre, then repeat on the other side.

7 Press the folds gently with a rolling pin to seal them, then fold again along the centre line.

COOK'S TIP
Try using cured and smoked venison, marinated in olive oil and herbs, for this recipe. The olive oil and herbs add an extra flavour which beautifully complements this bread. Alternatively, sprinkle 5ml/1 tsp of dried herbs such as rosemary, thyme, sage or oregano over the dough in step 4.

8 Press the seam gently to seal, then roll the dough backwards and forwards to make a loaf about 65cm/26in long.

9 Using the side of your hand, press across the centre of the loaf to make an indentation. Bring both ends towards each other to make an upside down "U" shape and twist together.

10 Place the venison tordu on the prepared baking sheet. Cover the loaf with lightly oiled clear film (plastic wrap) and leave to rise in a warm place for 30 minutes, or until it has almost doubled in size. Meanwhile, preheat the oven to 220°C/425°F/Gas 7. Remove the clear film and dust the top of the twisted loaf with white bread flour.

11 Bake for 25–30 minutes, or until the bread is golden and sounds hollow when tapped on the base. Turn out on to a wire rack to cool. Serve freshly baked, while the bread is still slightly warm.

POPPY SEED LOAF

Poppy seeds are popular in Eastern European breads. They have a mild, sweet, slightly nutty flavour and make an interesting addition to this loaf.

SMALL
180ml/6½fl oz/generous ¾ cup milk
60ml/2fl oz/¼ cup water
375g/13oz/3¼ cups unbleached white bread flour
45ml/3 tbsp poppy seeds
7.5ml/1½ tsp salt
10ml/2 tsp granulated sugar
20g/¾oz/1½ tbsp butter
5ml/1 tsp easy-blend (rapid-rise) dried yeast

MEDIUM
200ml/7fl oz/⅞ cup milk
100ml/3½fl oz/7 tbsp water
450g/1lb/4 cups unbleached white bread flour
60ml/4 tbsp poppy seeds
7.5ml/1½ tsp salt
10ml/2 tsp granulated sugar
25g/1oz/2 tbsp butter
5ml/1 tsp easy-blend dried yeast

LARGE
280ml/10fl oz/1¼ cup milk
130ml/4½fl oz/generous ½ cup water
675g/1½lb/6 cups unbleached white bread flour
75ml/5 tbsp poppy seeds
10ml/2 tsp salt
15ml/1 tbsp granulated sugar
25g/1oz/2 tbsp butter
7.5ml/1½ tsp easy-blend dried yeast

FOR THE GLAZE (OPTIONAL)
½ egg white
5ml/1 tsp water

MAKES 1 LOAF

1 Pour the milk and water into the bread machine pan. If the instructions for your machine specify that the yeast is to be placed in the pan first, reverse the order in which you add the liquid and dry ingredients.

2 Sprinkle over the flour, ensuring that it covers the water. Add the poppy seeds. Add the salt, sugar and butter in separate corners of the bread pan. Make a small indent in the centre of the flour (but not down as far as the liquid) and add the yeast.

3 Set the bread machine to the basic/normal setting, medium crust. Press Start.

4 If glazing, mix the egg white and water and brush over the loaf just before the baking cycle starts.

5 Remove the bread at the end of the baking cycle and turn out on to a wire rack to cool.

COOK'S TIP
To ensure the poppy seeds stay whole, add them when the machine beeps, or during the last 5 minutes of kneading.

ROSEMARY AND RAISIN LOAF

Inspired by a classic Tuscan bread – panmarino – this bread is flavoured with rosemary and raisins and enriched with eggs and olive oil.

1 Pour the water, extra virgin olive oil and egg(s) into the bread machine pan. If the instructions for your machine specify that the yeast is to be placed in the pan first, then simply reverse the order in which you add the liquid and dry ingredients.

2 Sprinkle over the flour, ensuring that it covers the water. Add the skimmed milk powder and rosemary. Add the salt and sugar in separate corners of the bread pan. Make a small indent in the centre of the flour (but not down as far as the liquid) and add the yeast.

3 Set the bread machine to the basic/normal setting, with raisin setting (if available), medium crust. Press Start. Add the raisins when the machine beeps or 5 minutes before the kneading cycle ends.

4 Remove the bread at the end of the baking cycle and turn out on to a wire rack to cool.

SMALL
135ml/4½fl oz/scant ⅔ cup water
45ml/3 tbsp extra virgin olive oil
1 egg
375g/13oz/3¼ cups unbleached white bread flour
15ml/1 tbsp skimmed milk powder (non fat dry milk)
10ml/2 tsp fresh rosemary, chopped
5ml/1 tsp salt
10ml/2 tsp granulated sugar
5ml/1 tsp easy-blend (rapid-rise) dried yeast
75g/3oz/½cup raisins

MEDIUM
160ml/5½fl oz/generous ⅔ cup water
60ml/4 tbsp extra virgin olive oil
2 eggs
500g/1lb 2oz/4½ cups unbleached white bread flour
30ml/2 tbsp skimmed milk powder
15ml/1 tbsp fresh rosemary, chopped
7.5ml/1½ tsp salt
10ml/2 tsp granulated sugar
5ml/1 tsp easy-blend dried yeast
115g/4oz/generous ⅔ cup raisins

LARGE
200ml/7fl oz/⅞ cup water
75ml/5 tbsp extra virgin olive oil
3 eggs
675g/1½lb/6 cups unbleached white bread flour
45ml/3 tbsp skimmed milk powder
20ml/4 tsp fresh rosemary, chopped
7.5ml/1½ tsp salt
15ml/1 tbsp granulated sugar
7.5ml/1½ tsp easy-blend dried yeast
150g/5oz/1 cup raisins

MAKES 1 LOAF

VARIATION
This savoury bread can be made with chopped almonds and sultanas (golden raisins) or dried figs, instead of raisins. All are delicious flavours for serving with soft cheese.

CAJUN SPICED BRAID

The traditional Deep South flavours of tomatoes, garlic, spices and hot seasonings make this piquant, spicy loaf irresistible.

300ml/10½fl oz/1¼ cups water
30ml/2 tbsp vegetable oil
15ml/1 tbsp tomato purée (paste)
500g/1lb 2oz/4½ cups unbleached white bread flour
7.5ml/1½ tsp paprika
5ml/1 tsp cayenne pepper
5ml/1 tsp dried oregano
2.5ml/½ tsp freshly ground black pepper
1 garlic clove, crushed
7.5ml/1½ tsp salt
2.5ml/½ tsp sugar
7.5ml/1½ tsp easy-blend (rapid-rise) dried yeast

FOR THE GLAZE
1 egg yolk
15ml/1 tbsp water

MAKES 1 LOAF

1 Pour the water and vegetable oil into the bread machine pan, then add the tomato purée. If the instructions for your machine specify that the yeast is to be placed in the pan first, reverse the order in which you add the liquid and dry ingredients.

2 Sprinkle over the flour, ensuring that it covers the liquid. Add the paprika, cayenne, oregano, black pepper and crushed garlic. Place the salt and sugar in separate corners of the bread pan. Make a small indent in the centre of the flour (but not down as far as the liquid) and add the yeast.

3 Set the bread machine to the dough setting; use basic dough setting (if available). Press Start. Lightly oil a baking sheet.

4 Once the dough cycle has finished, place the dough on a floured surface. Knock it back (punch it down) and divide into three.

5 Roll the pieces into equal ropes. Put next to each other. From the centre, braid from left to right, working towards you. Press the ends together and tuck under.

6 Turn the dough around and braid the remaining ropes. Place on the prepared baking sheet, cover with oiled clear film (plastic wrap) and leave in a warm place to rise for 30–45 minutes. Meanwhile, preheat the oven to 200°C/400°F/Gas 6.

7 Mix the egg yolk and water for the glaze together. Remove the clear film and brush the glaze over the braid. Bake for 30–35 minutes, or until golden.

SALAMI AND PEPPERCORN BREAD

This loaf marbled with salami and black pepper makes a great accompaniment to hot soup. For a quick snack, try it toasted with a cheese topping.

210ml/7½fl oz/scant 1 cup water
15ml/1 tbsp olive oil
350g/12oz/3 cups unbleached white flour
50g/2oz/½ cup grated mature (sharp) Cheddar cheese
2.5ml/½ tsp salt
5ml/1 tsp granulated sugar
5ml/1 tsp easy-blend (rapid-rise) dried yeast
5ml/1 tsp black peppercorns, coarsely crushed
50g/2oz salami, chopped
milk, for brushing

MAKES 1 LOAF

1 Pour the water and oil into the bread machine pan. If the instructions for your bread machine specify that the yeast is to be placed in the pan first, then simply reverse the order in which you add the liquid and dry ingredients.

2 Sprinkle over the flour, ensuring that it covers the liquid. Add half the cheese. Add the salt in one corner of the bread pan and the sugar in another corner. Make a small indent in the centre of the flour (but not down as far as the liquid) and add the yeast.

3 Set the bread machine to the dough setting; use basic or pizza dough setting (if available). Press Start. Then lightly oil a baking sheet.

4 Once the dough cycle has finished, remove the dough from the machine and place it on a lightly floured surface. Knock it back (punch it down) gently and flatten it slightly. Sprinkle over the peppercorns and salami and knead gently until both are evenly incorporated.

5 Shape into a round loaf; place on the baking sheet. Cover with an oiled bowl and leave in a warm place for 30 minutes. Preheat the oven to 200°C/400°F/Gas 6.

6 Uncover the bread, brush it with milk and sprinkle with the remaining cheese. Bake for about 30–35 minutes, or until golden. Turn out on to a wire rack to cool.

MARBLED PESTO BREAD

140ml/5fl oz/⅝ cup milk
150ml/5fl oz/scant ⅔ cup water
30ml/2 tbsp extra virgin olive oil
450g/1lb/4 cups unbleached white
bread flour
7.5ml/1½ tsp granulated sugar
7.5ml/1½ tsp salt
7.5ml/1½ tsp easy-blend (rapid-rise)
dried yeast
100g/3½oz/7 tbsp ready-made
pesto sauce

FOR THE TOPPING
15ml/1 tbsp extra virgin olive oil
10ml/2 tsp coarse sea salt

MAKES 1 LOAF

Using ready-made pesto sauce means that this scrumptuous bread is very easy to make. Use a good quality sauce – or, if you have the time, make your own – so that the flavours of garlic, basil, pine nuts and Parmesan cheese can be clearly discerned.

3 Make a small indent in the centre of the flour (but do not go down as far as the liquid) and pour the dried yeast into the hollow.

4 Set the bread machine to the dough setting. If your machine has a choice of settings use the basic dough setting. Press Start. Lightly oil a 25 × 10cm/ 10 × 4in loaf tin (pan).

5 When the dough cycle has finished, remove the dough from the machine and place it on a lightly floured surface. Knock it back (punch it down) gently, then roll it out to a rectangle about 2cm/ ¾in thick and 25cm/10in long. Cover with oiled clear film (plastic wrap) and leave to relax for a few minutes, if the dough proves difficult to roll out.

7 Cover with oiled clear film and set aside in a warm place to rise for 45 minutes or until the dough has more than doubled in size and reaches the top of the loaf tin. Meanwhile, preheat the oven to 220°C/425°F/Gas 7.

8 Remove the clear film and brush the olive oil over the top of the loaf. Use a sharp knife to score the top with four diagonal cuts. Repeat the cuts in the opposite direction to make a criss-cross pattern. Sprinkle with the sea salt.

9 Bake for 25–30 minutes, or until the bread is golden and sounds hollow when tapped on the base. Turn out on to a wire rack to cool.

1 Remove the milk from the refrigerator 30 minutes before using, to bring it to room temperature. Pour the water, milk and extra virgin olive oil into the bread machine pan. If the instructions for your bread machine specify that the yeast is to be placed in the pan first, then simply reverse the order in which you add the liquid and dry ingredients.

2 Sprinkle over the flour, ensuring that it covers the liquid mixture completely. Add the sugar and salt, placing them in separate corners of the bread pan.

6 Spread the pesto sauce over the dough. Leave a clear border of 1cm/½in along one long edge. Roll up the dough lengthways, Swiss (jelly) roll fashion, tuck the ends under and place seam down in the prepared tin.

COOK'S TIP
For a really luxurious twist to this bread, make your own pesto filling. Put 75g/3oz basil leaves, 1 clove garlic, 30ml/2 tbsp pine nuts, salt and pepper, and 90ml/3fl oz olive oil in a mortar and crush to a paste with a pestle, or alternatively, place in a blender and blend until creamy. Work in 50g/2oz freshly grated Parmesan cheese.
Any leftover pesto can be kept for up to 2 weeks in the refrigerator.

SUN-DRIED TOMATO BREAD

The dense texture and highly concentrated flavour of sun-dried tomatoes makes them perfect for flavouring bread dough, and when Parmesan cheese is added, the result is an exceptionally tasty loaf.

SMALL

15g/½oz/¼ cup sun-dried tomatoes
130ml/4½fl oz/½ cup + 1 tbsp water
70ml/2½fl oz/¼ cup + 1 tbsp milk
15ml/1 tbsp extra virgin olive oil
325g/11½oz/scant 3 cups unbleached white bread flour
50g/2oz/½ cup wholemeal (whole-wheat) bread flour
40g/1½oz/½ cup freshly grated Parmesan cheese
5ml/1 tsp salt
5ml/1 tsp granulated sugar
4ml/¾ tsp easy-blend (rapid-rise) dried yeast

MEDIUM

25g/1oz/½ cup sun-dried tomatoes
190ml/6¾fl oz/scant ⅞ cup water
115ml/4fl oz/½ cup milk
30ml/2 tbsp extra virgin olive oil
425g/15oz/3¾ cups unbleached white bread flour
75g/3oz/¾ cup wholemeal bread flour
50g/2oz/⅔ cup freshly grated Parmesan cheese
7.5ml/1½ tsp salt
10ml/2 tsp granulated sugar
5ml/1 tsp easy-blend dried yeast

LARGE

40g/1½oz/¾ cup sun-dried tomatoes
240ml/8½fl oz/generous 1 cup water
140ml/5fl oz/⅝ cup milk
45ml/3 tbsp extra virgin olive oil
575g/1¼lb/5 cups unbleached white bread flour
100g/4oz/1 cup wholemeal bread flour
75g/3oz/1 cup freshly grated Parmesan cheese
10ml/2 tsp salt
10ml/2 tsp granulated sugar
7.5ml/1½ tsp easy-blend dried yeast

MAKES 1 LOAF

1 Place the sun-dried tomatoes in a small bowl and pour over enough warm water to cover them. Leave to soak for 15 minutes, then tip into a sieve placed over a bowl. Allow to drain thoroughly, then chop finely.

2 Check the quantity of tomato water against the amount of water required for the loaf, and add more water if this is necessary. Pour it into the bread machine pan, then add the milk and olive oil. If the instructions for your machine specify that the yeast is to be placed in the pan first, then simply reverse the order in which you add the liquid and dry ingredients.

3 Sprinkle over both types of flour, ensuring that the liquid is completely covered. Sprinkle over the Parmesan, then add the salt and sugar, placing them in separate corners of the bread pan. Make a small indent in the centre of the flour (but not down as far as the liquid) and add the yeast.

4 Set the bread machine to the basic/normal setting; use raisin setting (if available), medium crust. Press Start. Add the tomatoes at the beep or during the last 5 minutes of kneading. Remove the bread at the end of the baking cycle and turn out on to a wire rack to cool.

GARLIC AND HERB WALNUT BREAD

Walnut bread is very popular in France. This variation includes both garlic and basil for additional flavour.

SMALL
150ml/5fl oz/⅔ cup milk
60ml/2fl oz/4 tbsp water
30ml/2 tbsp extra virgin olive oil
325g/11½oz/scant 3 cups unbleached white bread flour
40g/1½oz/scant ⅓ cup rolled oats
40g/1½oz/⅓ cup chopped walnuts
1 garlic clove, finely chopped
5ml/1 tsp dried oregano
5ml/1 tsp drained fresh basil in sunflower oil
5ml/1 tsp salt
7.5ml/1½ tsp granulated sugar
2.5ml/½ tsp easy-blend (rapid-rise) dried yeast

MEDIUM
185ml/6½fl oz/generous ¾ cup milk
105ml/7 tbsp water
45ml/3 tbsp extra virgin olive oil
450g/1lb/4 cups unbleached white bread flour
50g/2oz/½ cup rolled oats
50g/2oz/½ cup chopped walnuts
1½ garlic cloves, finely chopped
7.5ml/1½ tsp dried oregano
7.5ml/1½ tsp drained fresh basil in sunflower oil
7.5ml/1½ tsp salt
10ml/2 tsp granulated sugar
5ml/1 tsp easy-blend dried yeast

LARGE
200ml/7fl oz/scant 1 cup milk
140ml/5fl oz/⅔ cup water
60ml/4 tbsp extra virgin olive oil
600g/1lb 5oz/generous 5¼ cups unbleached white bread flour
65g/2½oz/scant ⅔ cup rolled oats
65g/2½oz/generous ½ cup chopped walnuts
2 garlic cloves, finely chopped
7.5ml/1½ tsp dried oregano
7.5ml/1½ tsp drained fresh basil in sunflower oil
10ml/2 tsp salt
10ml/2 tsp granulated sugar
7.5ml/1½ tsp easy-blend dried yeast

MAKES 1 LOAF

2 Sprinkle over the flour and rolled oats, ensuring that they completely cover the liquid mixture. Add the chopped walnuts, garlic, oregano and basil. Place the salt and sugar in separate corners of the bread machine pan. Make a small indent in the centre of the flour (but do not go down as far as the liquid) and add the easy-blend dried yeast.

3 Set the bread machine to the basic/normal setting, medium crust. Press Start.

4 Remove the bread at the end of the baking cycle and turn out on to a wire rack to cool.

1 Pour the milk, water and olive oil into the bread machine pan. If the instructions for your machine specify that the yeast is to be placed in the pan first, reverse the order in which you add the liquid and dry ingredients.

280ml/10fl oz/1¼ cups water
30ml/2 tbsp extra virgin olive oil
100g/3½oz/scant 1 cup rye flour
350g/12½oz/generous 3 cups
unbleached white bread flour, plus
extra for dusting
30ml/2 tbsp skimmed milk powder
(non fat dry milk)
10ml/2 tsp light muscovado
(brown) sugar
5ml/1 tsp salt
5ml/1 tsp easy-blend (rapid-rise)
dried yeast
15ml/1 tbsp dried dill
15ml/1 tbsp dill seeds
30ml/2 tbsp dried onion slices

MAKES 2 LOAVES

1 Pour the water and oil into the bread pan. Reverse the order in which you add the wet and dry ingredients if necessary. Sprinkle both types of flour over the water. Add the milk powder. Place the sugar and salt in separate corners.

DILL, ONION AND RYE BREAD

These crusty loaves are perfect partners for your favourite sandwich filling, or can be served solo with pasta, salads and soups.

2 Make a shallow indent in the centre of the flour; add the yeast. Set the machine to the dough setting; use basic raisin dough setting (if available). Press Start.

3 Add the dried dill, dill seeds and dried onion as the machine beeps or during the last 5 minutes of kneading. Lightly oil a baking sheet.

4 When the dough cycle has finished, remove the dough from the machine and place it on a lightly floured surface. Knock it back (punch it down) gently.

5 Divide the dough into two equal pieces. Roll out each piece to a disc, about 2.5cm/1in thick. Fold one side to the centre and press gently with the rolling pin to seal. Repeat with the other side, then fold again along the centre line.

6 Press gently along the seam to seal it, then roll backwards and forwards to make a loaf about 30cm/12in in length. Make a second loaf with the remaining dough.

7 Place the loaves on the baking sheet, leaving plenty of room for rising. Cover with lightly oiled clear film (plastic wrap) and leave in a warm place for 30–45 minutes, or until almost doubled in size.

8 Remove the clear film and dust the tops of the loaves with flour. Using a sharp knife, make slashes along the top of both of them. Leave to stand for 10 minutes. Meanwhile, preheat the oven to 220°C/425°F/Gas 7.

9 Bake the loaves for 20 minutes, or until they sound hollow when tapped on the base. Transfer to a wire rack to cool.

SAGE AND SAUSAGE LOAF

15ml/1 tbsp sunflower oil
200g/7oz spicy Mediterranean sausages
3 eggs
30ml/2 tbsp water
350g/12½oz/generous 3 cups
unbleached white bread flour
30ml/2 tbsp skimmed milk powder
(non fat dry milk)
10ml/2 tsp granulated sugar
7.5ml/1½ tsp salt
50g/2oz/¼ cup butter, melted
5ml/1 tsp easy-blend (rapid-rise)
dried yeast
5ml/1 tsp dried sage
1 egg yolk, to glaze
15ml/1 tbsp water, to glaze

MAKES 1 LOAF

1 Heat the oil in a heavy frying pan. Add the sausages. Fry them over a medium heat for 7–10 minutes or until cooked, turning frequently. Cool.

When this tasty loaf is sliced, the sausage filling is revealed. It is perfect for picnics, parties or as a lunchtime meal with salad.

2 Add the eggs and water to the bread pan. Reverse the order in which you add the wet and dry ingredients if necessary.

3 Sprinkle over the flour, covering the liquid. Add the milk powder. Place the sugar, salt and butter in separate corners of the pan. Make a small indent in the centre of the flour; add the yeast.

4 Set the bread machine to the dough setting; use basic raisin dough setting (if available). Press Start. Add the sage when the machine beeps or during the last 5 minutes of kneading. Lightly oil a 23 × 13cm/9 × 5in loaf tin (pan).

5 When the dough cycle has finished, place the dough on a floured surface. Knock back (punch down) gently. Roll into a rectangle 2.5cm/1in × 23cm/9in.

6 Place the sausages down the centre and roll the dough tightly around them. Place in the tin. Cover with lightly oiled clear film (plastic wrap) and leave to rise in a warm place for 30–45 minutes.

7 Preheat the oven to 190°C/375°F/Gas 5. To glaze, mix the yolk and water; brush over the bread and bake for 30–35 minutes, or until golden. Turn out on to a wire rack to cool.

MIXED HERB COTTAGE LOAF

300ml/10½fl oz/1¼ cups water
450g/1lb/4 cups unbleached white
bread flour, plus extra for dusting
7.5ml/1½ tsp granulated sugar
7.5ml/1½ tsp salt
7.5ml/1½ tsp easy-blend (rapid-rise)
dried yeast
15ml/1 tbsp chopped fresh chives
10ml/2 tsp chopped fresh thyme
15ml/1 tbsp chopped fresh tarragon
30ml/2 tbsp chopped fresh parsley
5ml/1 tsp salt, to glaze
15ml/1 tbsp water, to glaze

MAKES 1 LOAF

There's something very satisfying about the shape of a cottage loaf, and the flavour of fresh herbs – chives, thyme, tarragon and parsley – adds to the appeal. This loaf makes the perfect centrepiece for the table, for guests to help themselves.

3 Set the bread machine to the dough setting; use basic raisin dough setting (if available). Press Start.

4 Add the chives, thyme, tarragon and parsley when the machine beeps to add extra ingredients, or during the final 5 minutes of kneading. Lightly flour two baking sheets.

5 When the dough cycle has finished, remove the dough from the machine. Place it on a surface that has been lightly floured. Knock the dough back (punch it down) gently and then divide it into two pieces, making one piece twice as large as the other.

6 Take each piece of dough in turn and shape it into a plump ball. Place the balls of dough on the prepared baking sheets and cover each with a lightly oiled mixing bowl.

7 Leave in a warm place for about 20–30 minutes, or until the dough has almost doubled in size.

8 Cut a cross, about 4cm/1½in across, in the top of the larger piece of dough. Brush the surface with water and place the smaller round on top.

9 Carefully press the handle of a wooden spoon through the centre of both pieces of dough. Cover the loaf with oiled clear film (plastic wrap) and leave it to rise for 10 minutes.

10 Meanwhile, preheat the oven to 220°C/425°F/Gas 7. Mix the salt and water for the glaze in a bowl, then brush the mixture over the top of the bread.

11 Using a sharp knife, make eight long slashes around the top of the bread and 12 small slashes around the base. Dust the top of the bread lightly with white bread flour.

12 Bake for 30–35 minutes, or until the bread is golden and sounds hollow when tapped on the base. Turn the loaf out on to a wire rack to cool.

1 Pour the water into the bread machine pan. If the operating instructions for your bread machine specify that the yeast is to be placed in the pan first, then simply reverse the order in which you add the water and dry ingredients.

2 Sprinkle over the flour, ensuring that it covers the water completely. Add the granulated sugar and the salt, placing them in separate corners of the bread machine pan. Make a small indent in the centre of the flour (but do not go down as far as the water) and add the easy-blend dried yeast.

VARIATION
Vary the combination of fresh herbs you use, according to availability and taste. You should aim for just under 75ml/5 tbsp in all, but use more pungent herbs sparingly, so they do not become too overpowering.

VEGETABLE BREADS

The subtle orange hue from pumpkin or carrot, the orangey-red crumb from tomatoes and the amazing colours of spinach or beetroot bread are only part of the story. Vegetables – grated, puréed, mashed or chopped – can be incorporated into bread doughs to provide wonderfully flavoured and coloured loaves. Almost any vegetable can be used, often in conjunction with spices, as in Carrot and Fennel Bread, or fresh herbs, as in Fresh Tomato and Basil Loaf.

SPINACH AND PARMESAN BLOOMER

This pretty pale green loaf is flavoured with spinach, onion and Parmesan cheese. Whole pine nut kernels are dispersed through the dough of this perfect summertime bread.

15ml/1 tbsp olive oil
1 onion, chopped
115g/4oz fresh young spinach leaves
120ml/generous 4fl oz/½ cup water
1 egg
450g/1lb/4 cups unbleached white bread flour
2.5ml/½ tsp freshly grated nutmeg
50g/2oz/⅔ cup freshly grated Parmesan cheese
7.5ml/1½ tsp salt
5ml/1 tsp granulated sugar
7.5ml/1½ tsp easy-blend (rapid-rise) dried yeast
30ml/2 tbsp pine nuts

MAKES 1 LOAF

1 Heat the olive oil in a frying pan, add the chopped onion and sauté until a light golden colour. Add the spinach, stir well to combine and cover the pan very tightly. Remove from the heat and leave to stand for 5 minutes. Then stir again and leave the pan uncovered, to cool.

2 Tip the spinach mixture into the bread machine pan. Add the water and egg. If the instructions for your machine specify that the yeast is to be placed in the pan first, then simply reverse the order in which you add the liquid mixture and dry ingredients.

3 Sprinkle over the white bread flour, ensuring that it completely covers the liquid mixture in the bread pan. Sprinkle the grated nutmeg and the Parmesan cheese over the flour.

4 Place the salt and sugar in separate corners of the bread pan. Make a small indent in the centre of the flour (but not down as far as the liquid) and add the easy-blend dried yeast.

5 Set the bread machine to the dough setting; use basic raisin dough setting (if available). Press Start. Lightly flour two baking sheets.

6 Add the pine nuts to the dough when the machine beeps or during the last 5 minutes of the kneading process.

7 When the dough cycle has finished, remove the dough from the machine and place it on a surface that has been lightly floured. Gently knock the dough back (punch it down), then carefully roll it out to a rectangle about 2.5cm/1in thick.

8 Roll up the rectangle of dough from one long side to form a thick baton shape, with a square end.

9 Place the baton on the prepared baking sheet, seam side up, cover it with lightly oiled clear film (plastic wrap) and leave to rest for 15 minutes.

10 Turn the bread over and place on the second baking sheet. Plump up the dough by tucking the ends and sides under. Cover it with lightly oiled clear film again and leave it to rise in a warm place for 30 minutes. Meanwhile preheat the oven to 220°C/425°F/Gas 7.

11 Using a sharp knife, slash the top of the bloomer with five diagonal slashes. Bake it for 30–35 minutes, or until it is golden and the bottom sounds hollow when tapped. Turn the bread out on to a wire rack to cool.

VARIATION
Use Swiss chard instead of spinach, if you prefer. Choose young leaves, stripping them off the ribs. If fresh spinach is unavailable you could replace it with defrosted frozen spinach. Make sure any excess water has been squeezed out first, before placing in the bread machine. It may be worth holding a little of the water back and checking the dough as it starts to mix in step 5.

CHICKPEA AND PEPPERCORN BREAD

Bread may be a basic food, but it certainly isn't boring, as this exciting combination proves. Chickpeas help to keep the dough light, while pink and green peppercorns add colour and "explosions" of flavour.

SMALL
200ml/7fl oz/⅞ cup water
15ml/1 tbsp extra virgin olive oil
125g/4½oz/generous ⅔ cup canned chickpeas
375g/13oz/3¼ cups unbleached white bread flour
7.5ml/1½ tsp drained fresh pink peppercorns in brine
7.5ml/1½ tsp drained fresh green peppercorns in brine
15ml/1 tbsp skimmed milk powder (non fat dry milk)
5ml/1 tsp salt
7.5ml/1½ tsp granulated sugar
5ml/1 tsp easy-blend (rapid-rise) dried yeast
milk, for brushing (optional)

MEDIUM
250ml/9fl oz/generous 1 cup water
30ml/2 tbsp extra virgin olive oil
175g/6oz/1 cup canned chickpeas
500g/1lb 2oz/4½ cups unbleached white bread flour
10ml/2 tsp drained fresh pink peppercorns in brine
10ml/2 tsp drained fresh green peppercorns in brine
22ml/1½ tbsp skimmed milk powder
7.5ml/1½ tsp salt
10ml/2 tsp granulated sugar
7.5ml/1½ tsp easy-blend dried yeast
milk, for brushing (optional)

LARGE
330ml/11½fl oz/1⅜ cups water
45ml/3 tbsp extra virgin olive oil
225g/8oz/1⅓ cups canned chickpeas
675g/1½lb/6 cups unbleached white bread flour
15ml/1 tbsp drained fresh pink peppercorns in brine
15ml/1 tbsp drained fresh green peppercorns in brine
30ml/2 tbsp skimmed milk powder
10ml/2 tsp salt
15ml/1 tbsp granulated sugar
7.5ml/1½ tsp easy-blend dried yeast
milk, for brushing (optional)

MAKES 1 LOAF

1 Pour the water and extra virgin olive oil into the bread machine pan. Add the well-drained chickpeas. If the instructions for your bread machine specify that the yeast is to be placed in the pan first, then simply reverse the order in which you add the liquid and dry ingredients to the bread pan.

2 Sprinkle over the flour, ensuring that it covers the ingredients already placed in the pan. Add the pink and green peppercorns and milk powder.

3 Place the salt and sugar in separate corners of the pan. Make a small indent in the centre of the flour (but not down as far as the liquid) and add the yeast.

4 Set the bread machine to the basic/normal setting, medium crust. Press Start. If you like, brush the top of the loaf with milk just before the bread starts to bake.

5 Remove the bread at the end of the baking cycle and turn out on to a wire rack to cool.

CARROT AND FENNEL BREAD

The distinctive flavour of fennel is the perfect foil for the more subtle carrot taste in this unusual bread. It looks pretty when sliced, thanks to the attractive orange flecks of carrot.

1 Pour the water, oil and honey into the bread machine pan. Sprinkle over the grated carrot. If the instructions for your machine specify that the yeast is to be placed in the pan first, reverse the order in which you add the liquid and dry ingredients.

2 Sprinkle over the flour, ensuring that it covers the water. Add the milk powder and fennel seeds. Add the salt in one corner of the bread pan. Make a small indent in the centre of the flour (but not down as far as the liquid) and add the yeast.

SMALL
180ml/6½fl oz/generous ¾ cup water
15ml/1 tbsp sunflower oil
5ml/1 tsp clear honey
140g/5oz/1 cup grated carrot
375g/13oz/3¼ cups unbleached white bread flour
15ml/1 tbsp skimmed milk powder (non fat dry milk)
5ml/1 tsp fennel seeds
5ml/1 tsp salt
5ml/1 tsp easy-blend (rapid-rise) dried yeast

MEDIUM
210ml/7½fl oz/scant 1 cup water
30ml/2 tbsp sunflower oil
10ml/2 tsp clear honey
200g/7oz/scant 1½ cups grated carrot
500g/1lb 2oz/4½ cups unbleached white bread flour
30ml/2 tbsp skimmed milk powder
7.5ml/1½ tsp fennel seeds
7.5ml/1½ tsp salt
5ml/1 tsp easy-blend dried yeast

LARGE
285ml/10fl oz/1¼ cups water
45ml/3 tbsp sunflower oil
15ml/1 tbsp clear honey
250g/9oz/scant 2 cups grated carrot
675g/1½lb/6 cups unbleached white bread flour
45ml/3 tbsp skimmed milk powder
10ml/2 tsp fennel seeds
10ml/2 tsp salt
7.5ml/1½ tsp easy-blend dried yeast

MAKES 1 LOAF

3 Set the machine to the basic/normal setting, medium crust. Press Start.

4 Remove at the end of the baking cycle and turn out on to a wire rack to cool.

COOK'S TIP

When adding the grated carrot, sprinkle it over lightly and evenly. This avoids clumps, which would not mix evenly through the dough.

FRESH TOMATO AND BASIL LOAF

15ml/1 tbsp extra virgin olive oil
1 small onion, chopped
3 plum tomatoes, about 200g/7oz,
peeled, seeded and chopped
500g/1lb 2oz/4½ cups unbleached
white bread flour
2.5ml/½ tsp freshly ground black pepper
7.5ml/1½ tsp salt
10ml/2 tsp granulated sugar
5ml/1 tsp easy-blend (rapid-rise)
dried yeast
15ml/1 tbsp chopped fresh basil

For the Glaze
1 egg yolk
15ml/1 tbsp water

MAKES 1 LOAF

Here are some classic Mediterranean flavours incorporated into a bread. Sweet plum tomatoes, onions and fresh basil complement each other in this attractively shaped loaf. Serve to accompany lunch either with butter or with individual bowls of best quality extra virgin olive oil for dipping.

1 Heat the extra virgin olive oil in a small frying pan or pan. Add the chopped onion and fry over a moderate heat for 3–4 minutes, until the onion is light golden in colour.

2 Add the plum tomatoes and cook for 2–3 minutes, until slightly softened. Drain through a sieve placed over a measuring jug (cup) or bowl, pressing the mixture gently with the back of a spoon to extract the juices.

3 Set the tomato and onion mixture aside. Make the cooking juices up to 280ml/10fl oz/1¼ cups with water (but see Variation). Set aside. When the liquid is cold, pour it into the bread machine pan. If the instructions for your machine specify that the yeast is to be placed in the pan first, reverse the order in which you add the liquid and dry ingredients.

4 Sprinkle over the flour, ensuring that it covers the tomato and onion liquid. Add the ground black pepper, then place the salt and sugar in separate corners of the bread machine pan.

5 Make a small indent in the centre of the flour (but not down as far as the liquid) and add the yeast.

6 Set the bread machine to the dough setting; use basic dough setting (if available). Press Start. Then lightly oil a 23 × 13cm/9 × 5in bread tin (pan).

7 When the dough cycle has finished, remove the dough from the bread machine and place it on a lightly floured surface. Knock it back (punch it down) gently.

8 Knead in the reserved tomato and onion mixture and the chopped fresh basil. You may need to add a little extra flour if the dough becomes too moist when you have incorporated the vegetable mixture.

9 Flatten the dough and shape it into a 2.5cm/1in thick rectangle. Fold the sides to the middle and press down the edge to seal. Make a hollow along the centre and fold in half again. Gently roll it into a loaf about 40cm/16in long.

10 Shape into an "S" shape and place in the prepared tin. Cover with oiled clear film (plastic wrap) and leave in a warm place for 30–45 minutes. Meanwhile preheat the oven to 200°C/400°F/Gas 6.

11 Make the glaze by mixing the egg yolk and water together. Remove the clear film and brush the glaze over the bread. Bake in the preheated oven for 35–40 minutes, or until golden.

VARIATION
To intensify the tomato flavour of the loaf, substitute 15ml/1 tbsp sun-dried tomato purée (paste) for 15ml/1 tbsp of water when you are topping up the cooking juices in step 3.

CHILLI BREAD

There's a warm surprise waiting for anyone who bites into this tasty wholemeal bread. Fresh chillies are speckled throughout the crumb. Use Kenyan chillies for a milder flavour or Scotch Bonnets for a fiery taste.

SMALL
15ml/1 tbsp sunflower oil
1–2 fresh chillies, chopped
210ml/7½fl oz/scant 1 cup water
250g/9oz/2¼ cups unbleached white bread flour
125g/4½oz/generous 1 cup wholemeal (whole-wheat) bread flour
7.5ml/1½ tsp salt
7.5ml/1½ tsp granulated sugar
25g/1oz/2 tbsp butter
5ml/1 tsp easy-blend (rapid-rise) dried yeast

MEDIUM
15ml/1 tbsp sunflower oil
2–3 fresh chillies, chopped
320ml/11fl oz/generous 1⅓ cups water
350g/12oz/3 cups unbleached white bread flour
150g/5½oz/1⅓ cups wholemeal bread flour
10ml/2 tsp salt
10ml/2 tsp granulated sugar
25g/1oz/2 tbsp butter
5ml/1 tsp easy-blend dried yeast

LARGE
30ml/2 tbsp sunflower oil
3–4 fresh chillies, chopped
420ml/15fl oz/generous 1¾ cups water
475g/1lb 1oz/4¼ cups unbleached white bread flour
200g/7oz/1¾ cups wholemeal bread flour
10ml/2 tsp salt
15ml/1 tbsp granulated sugar
40g/1½oz/3 tbsp butter
7.5ml/1½ tsp easy-blend dried yeast

MAKES 1 LOAF

VARIATION
Use chilli flakes instead of fresh chillies, if you prefer. You will need 10–20 ml/2–4 tsp, depending on the size of the loaf and how hot you wish to make the bread.

1 Heat the oil in a small frying pan. Add the chillies and sauté them over a moderate heat for 3–4 minutes until softened. Set aside to cool.

2 Tip the chillies and their oil into the bread machine pan. Pour in the water. Reverse the order in which you add the wet and dry ingredients if necessary.

3 Sprinkle over both types of flour, ensuring that the liquid is covered. Place the salt, sugar and butter in separate corners of the bread machine pan. Make an indent in the flour (but not down as far as the liquid) and add the yeast.

4 Set the bread machine to the basic/normal setting, medium crust. Press Start.

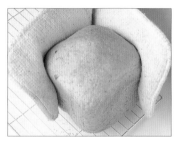

5 Remove the bread at the end of the baking cycle and turn out on to a wire rack to cool.

COURGETTE COUNTRY GRAIN BREAD

The grated courgette combines with the flour during the kneading process to make a succulent bread, while the seeds add both texture and flavour.

1 Pour the buttermilk and water into the bread machine pan. Sprinkle over the grated courgette. If the instructions for your machine specify that the yeast is to be placed in the pan first, reverse the order in which you add the liquid and dry ingredients.

2 Sprinkle over both types of flour, ensuring the liquids are completely covered. Add the sunflower seeds, pumpkin seeds and millet seeds. Place the salt, sugar and butter in separate corners of the bread pan. Make a small indent in the flour (but not down as far as the liquid) and add the yeast.

3 Set the bread machine to the basic/normal setting, medium crust. Press Start. Just before the baking cycle, brush the top with water and sprinkle with corn meal.

4 Remove the bread at the end of the baking cycle and turn out on to a wire rack to cool.

SMALL
55ml/2fl oz/¼ cup buttermilk
70ml/2½fl oz/5 tbsp water
115g/4oz/⅔ cup grated
courgette (zucchini)
280g/10oz/2½ cups unbleached white
bread flour
50g/2oz/½ cup wholemeal
(whole-wheat) bread flour
15ml/1 tbsp sunflower seeds
15ml/1 tbsp pumpkin seeds
5ml/1 tsp millet seeds
5ml/1 tsp salt
5ml/1 tsp granulated sugar
25g/1oz/2 tbsp butter
5ml/1 tsp easy-blend (rapid-rise)
dried yeast
corn meal, for sprinkling

MEDIUM
75ml/5 tbsp buttermilk
55ml/2fl oz/¼ cup water
175g/6oz/1 cup grated courgette
375g/13oz/3¼ cups unbleached white
bread flour
75g/3oz/¾ cup wholemeal bread flour
22ml/1½ tbsp sunflower seeds
22ml/1½ tbsp pumpkin seeds
10ml/2 tsp millet seeds
7.5ml/1½ tsp salt
7.5ml/1½ tsp granulated sugar
40g/1½oz/3 tbsp butter
7.5ml/1½ tsp easy-blend dried yeast
corn meal, for sprinkling

LARGE
100ml/3½fl oz/7 tbsp buttermilk
130ml/4½fl oz/generous ½ cup water
225g/8oz/1⅓ cups grated courgette
500g/1lb 2oz/4½ cups unbleached
white bread flour
115g/4oz/1 cup wholemeal bread flour
30ml/2 tbsp sunflower seeds
30ml/2 tbsp pumpkin seeds
15ml/1 tbsp millet seeds
10ml/2 tsp salt
10ml/2 tsp granulated sugar
50g/2oz/¼ cup butter
7.5ml/1½ tsp easy-blend dried yeast
corn meal, for sprinkling

MAKES 1 LOAF

SMALL

175g/6oz sweet potatoes, peeled
190ml/6¾fl oz/scant ⅞ cup water
350g/12oz/3 cups unbleached white
bread flour
30ml/2 tbsp rolled oats
22ml/1½ tbsp skimmed milk powder
(non fat dry milk)
5ml/1 tsp salt
15ml/1 tbsp muscovado
(molasses) sugar
25g/1oz/2 tbsp butter
5ml/1 tsp easy-blend (rapid-rise)
dried yeast
FOR THE TOPPING
10ml/2 tsp water
5ml/1 tsp rolled oats
5ml/1 tsp wheat grain

MEDIUM

225g/8oz sweet potatoes, peeled
210ml/7½fl oz/scant 1 cup water
500g/1lb 2oz/4½ cups unbleached
white bread flour
45ml/3 tbsp rolled oats
30ml/2 tbsp skimmed milk powder
7.5ml/1½ tsp salt
22ml/1½ tbsp muscovado sugar
40g/1½oz/3 tbsp butter
7.5ml/1½ tsp easy-blend dried yeast
FOR THE TOPPING
15ml/1 tbsp water
10ml/2 tsp rolled oats
10ml/2 tsp wheat grain

LARGE

350g/12oz sweet potatoes, peeled
320ml/11¼fl oz/scant 1⅜ cups water
675g/1½lb/6 cups unbleached white
bread flour
60ml/4 tbsp rolled oats
30ml/2 tbsp skimmed milk powder
7.5ml/1½ tsp salt
22ml/1½ tbsp muscovado sugar
50g/2oz/¼ cup butter
7.5ml/1½ tsp easy-blend dried yeast
FOR THE TOPPING
15ml/1 tbsp water
15ml/1 tbsp rolled oats
15ml/1 tbsp wheat grain

MAKES 1 LOAF

SWEET POTATO BREAD

Adding sweet potato to the dough creates a loaf with a rich golden crust
and the crumb is beautifully moist. Make sure you use the deep yellow
sweet potatoes, in preference to the white variety of sweet potatoes,
to give the bread a lovely colour.

1 Cook the sweet potato in plenty of boiling water for 40 minutes or until very tender. Drain, and when cool enough to handle, peel off the skin. Place the sweet potato in a large bowl and mash well, but do not add any butter or milk.

2 Pour the water into the bread machine pan. However, if the instructions for your bread machine specify that the yeast is to be placed in the bread pan first, simply reverse the order in which you add the liquid and dry ingredients.

VARIATION
This bread is a good opportunity to use up any leftover sweet potato. If the potato has been mashed with milk and butter you may need to reduce the quantity of liquid a little. Use the following quantities of cooked, mashed sweet potatoes:
small machine: 125g/4½oz/1½ cups
medium machine: 175g/6oz/2 cups
large machine: 225g/8oz/2⅔ cups

COOK'S TIP
Rolled oats add a chewy texture and nutty taste to this loaf of bread. Make sure you use the traditional old-fashioned rolled oats, rather than "quick cook" oats.

3 Sprinkle the white bread flour, rolled oats and skimmed milk powder over the water, covering it completely. Weigh or measure the cooked sweet potatoes to ensure the quantity matches the amount given in the variation. Then add the potatoes to the bread pan.

4 Place the salt, sugar and butter in three separate corners of the bread machine pan. Make a shallow indent in the flour (but not down as far as the liquid underneath) and add the easy-blend dried yeast.

5 Set the bread machine to the basic/normal setting, medium crust. Press Start.

6 When the rising cycle is almost complete, just before the bread begins to bake, add the topping: brush the top of the loaf with the water and sprinkle the rolled oats and wheat grain over the top of the bread.

7 Remove the bread at the end of the baking cycle and turn out on to a wire rack to cool.

Parsnip and Nutmeg Bread

The moment you cut into this loaf, the irresistible aroma of nutmeg and parsnips fills the air. Stopping at a single slice is the tricky part.

SMALL
225ml/7fl oz/scant 1 cup water
125g/4½oz/1½ cups mashed
cooked parsnips
375g/13oz/3¼ cups unbleached white
bread flour
15ml/1 tbsp skimmed milk powder
(non fat dry milk)
2.5ml/½ tsp freshly grated nutmeg
25g/1oz/2 tbsp butter
5ml/1 tsp salt
5ml/1 tsp granulated sugar
5ml/1 tsp easy-blend (rapid-rise)
dried yeast

MEDIUM
225ml/8fl oz/scant 1 cup water
175g/6oz/2 cups mashed
cooked parsnips
500g/1lb 2oz/4½ cups unbleached
white bread flour
30ml/2 tbsp skimmed milk powder
5ml/1 tsp freshly grated nutmeg
40g/1½oz/3 tbsp butter
7.5ml/1½ tsp salt
7.5ml/1½ tsp granulated sugar
7.5ml/1½ tsp easy-blend dried yeast

LARGE
320ml/11½fl oz/scant 1½ cups water
225g/8oz/2⅔ cups mashed
cooked parsnips
675g/1½lb/6 cups unbleached white
bread flour
45ml/3 tbsp skimmed milk powder
5ml/1 tsp freshly grated nutmeg
50g/2oz/¼ cup butter
10ml/2 tsp salt
10ml/2 tsp granulated sugar
7.5ml/1½ tsp easy-blend dried yeast

MAKES 1 LOAF

COOK'S TIP
Drain the parsnips thoroughly before mashing so that the dough does not become too wet. Leave the mashed parsnips to cool completely before adding them to the bread.

1 Pour the water into the bread machine pan and add the mashed parsnips. If the instructions for your machine specify that the yeast is to be placed in the pan first, reverse the order in which you add the liquid mixture and dry ingredients.

2 Sprinkle over the flour, ensuring it covers the ingredients already placed in the pan. Add the milk powder and freshly grated nutmeg. Place the butter, salt and sugar in separate corners of the bread machine pan. Make a small indent in the centre of the flour (but do not go down as far as the liquid) and add the easy-blend dried yeast.

3 Set the bread machine to the basic/normal setting, medium crust. Press Start.

4 Remove the bread at the end of the baking cycle and turn out on to a wire rack to cool.

BEETROOT BREAD

This spectacular bread takes on the colour of the beetroot juice. It is also flecked with beetroot flesh, which gives the finished loaf a slightly sweet flavour and delightful consistency.

SMALL
150ml/5fl oz/⅔ cup water
140g/5oz/1 cup grated raw
beetroot (beets)
2 spring onions (scallions), chopped
375g/13oz/3¼ cups unbleached white
bread flour
15g/½oz/1 tbsp butter
7.5ml/1½ tsp salt
5ml/1 tsp granulated sugar
5ml/1 tsp easy-blend (rapid-rise)
dried yeast

MEDIUM
170ml/6fl oz/¾ cup water
225g/8oz/1½ cups grated raw beetroot
3 spring onions, chopped
500g/1lb 2oz/4½ cups unbleached
white bread flour
25g/1oz/2 tbsp butter
10ml/2 tsp salt
5ml/1 tsp granulated sugar
5ml/1 tsp easy-blend dried yeast

LARGE
280ml/10fl oz/1¼ cups water
280g/10oz/2 cups grated raw beetroot
4 spring onions, chopped
675g/1½lb/6 cups unbleached white
bread flour
40g/1½oz/3 tbsp butter
10ml/2 tsp salt
7.5ml/1½ tsp granulated sugar
7.5ml/1½ tsp easy-blend dried yeast

MAKES 1 LOAF

3 Sprinkle the flour over the beetroot and water, ensuring it covers them both. Add the butter, salt and sugar in separate corners. Make a small indent in the centre of the flour (but not down as far as the liquid) and add the yeast.

4 Set the bread machine to the basic/normal setting, medium crust. Press Start. If you like, slash the top of the loaf with diagonal slashes just before the baking cycle starts.

5 Remove at the end of the baking cycle and turn out on to a wire rack.

1 Pour the water into the bread pan. Sprinkle over the grated beetroot. If the instructions for your machine specify that the yeast is to be placed in the pan first, reverse the order in which you add the liquid mixture and dry ingredients.

2 Add the chopped spring onions. However, if your bread machine offers you the option of adding any extra ingredients during the kneading cycle, set the spring onions aside so that you may add them later on.

BUBBLE CORN BREAD

85ml/3fl oz/⅜ cup milk
120ml/4fl oz/½ cup water
1 egg
400g/14oz/3½ cups unbleached white bread flour
100g/3½oz/scant 1 cup yellow corn meal
5ml/1 tsp granulated sugar
5ml/1 tsp salt
7.5ml/1½ tsp easy-blend (rapid-rise) dried yeast
15ml/1 tbsp chopped fresh green chilli
115g/4oz/⅔ cup drained canned corn kernels
25g/1oz/2 tbsp butter

MAKES 1 LOAF

This recipe brings together two traditional American breads – corn bread and bubble loaf. It has the flavour of corn and is spiked with hot chilli. Chunks or "bubbles" of bread can easily be pulled from the bread for easy eating.

1 Pour the milk and water into the bread pan. Add the egg. Reverse the order in which you add the liquid and dry ingredients, if necessary. Sprinkle over the flour and corn meal, covering the liquid. Add the sugar and salt in separate corners. Make a small indent in the flour; add the yeast.

2 Set the bread machine to the dough setting; use basic raisin dough setting (if available). Press Start. Add the chilli and corn when the machine beeps or during the last 5 minutes of kneading. Lightly oil a baking sheet.

3 When the dough cycle has finished, remove the dough and gently knock it back (punch it down), then cut it into 20 equal pieces. Shape into balls.

4 Arrange half of the dough balls in the base of a 22cm/8½in non-stick springform cake tin (pan), spacing them slightly apart. Place the remaining balls of dough on top so that they cover the spaces.

5 Cover the tin with oiled clear film (plastic wrap) and leave to rise in a warm place for about 30–45 minutes, or until the dough has almost doubled in bulk. Meanwhile preheat the oven to 200°C/400°F/Gas 6.

6 Melt the butter in a small pan. Drizzle it over the top of the risen loaf. Bake the bread for 30–35 minutes, or until golden and well risen. Turn the bread out on to a wire rack to cool. Serve warm or cold.

MIXED PEPPER BREAD

½ red (bell) pepper, cored and seeded
½ green (bell) pepper, cored and seeded
½ yellow (bell) pepper, cored and seeded
200ml/7fl oz/⅞ cup milk
120ml/generous 4fl oz/½ cup water
500g/1lb 2oz/4½ cups unbleached white bread flour
10ml/2 tsp granulated sugar
7.5ml/1½ tsp salt
7.5ml/1½ tsp easy-blend (rapid-rise) dried yeast
milk, for brushing
5ml/1 tsp cumin seeds

MAKES 1 LOAF

Colourful and full of flavour, this bread looks good when sliced, as the pretty pepper studs can be seen to advantage. Add orange pepper too, if you like.

1 Cut the peppers into fine dice. Pour the milk and water into the bread pan. Reverse the order in which you add the wet and dry ingredients if necessary. Sprinkle over the flour, ensuring that it covers the liquid. Add the sugar and salt in separate corners of the pan.

2 Make a small indent in the centre of the flour and add the yeast. Set the bread machine to the dough setting; use basic raisin dough setting (if available). Press Start. Lightly oil a baking sheet.

3 Add the mixed peppers when the machine beeps or during the last 5 minutes of kneading.

4 When the dough cycle has finished, remove the dough from the machine and place it on a lightly floured surface. Gently knock it back (punch it down) and shape it into a plump ball. Roll gently into an oval. Place on the prepared baking sheet, cover with oiled clear film (plastic wrap) and leave for 30–45 minutes, or until doubled in bulk.

5 Preheat the oven to 200°C/400°F/Gas 6. Brush the loaf top with the milk and sprinkle with the cumin seeds. Use a sharp knife to cut a lengthways slash.

6 Bake for 35–40 minutes, or until the bread is golden and the bottom sounds hollow when tapped. Turn the bread out on to a wire rack to cool.

SUN-DRIED TOMATO AND CEP LOAF

The powerful concentrated flavours of cep mushrooms and sun-dried tomatoes exude from this Mediterranean-style bread.

SMALL

10g/½oz dried cep mushrooms
200ml/7fl oz/⅞ cup warm water
375g/13oz/3¼ cups unbleached white bread flour
7.5ml/1½ tsp salt
15ml/1 tbsp granulated sugar
25g/1oz/2 tbsp butter
5ml/1 tsp easy-blend (rapid-rise) dried yeast
25g/1oz/¼ cup well-drained sun-dried tomatoes in olive oil

MEDIUM

15g/½oz dried cep mushrooms
200ml/7fl oz/⅞ cup warm water
500g/1lb 2oz/4½ cups unbleached white bread flour
7.5ml/1½ tsp salt
15ml/1 tbsp granulated sugar
25g/1oz/2 tbsp butter
5ml/1 tsp easy-blend dried yeast
40g/1½oz/⅓ cup well-drained sun-dried tomatoes in olive oil

LARGE

25g/1oz dried cep mushrooms
200ml/7fl oz/⅞ cup warm water
675g/1½lb/6 cups unbleached white bread flour
10ml/2 tsp salt
22ml/1½ tbsp granulated sugar
40g/1½oz/3 tbsp butter
7.5ml/1½ tsp easy-blend dried yeast
50g/2oz/⅓ cup well-drained sun-dried tomatoes in olive oil

MAKES 1 LOAF

1 Place the dried mushrooms in a small bowl and pour over the warm water. Leave to soak for about 30 minutes. Pour the mushrooms into a sieve placed over a bowl. Drain thoroughly, reserving the soaking liquid. Set the mushrooms aside. Make up the soaking liquid to 210ml/7½fl oz/scant 1 cup, 320ml/11fl oz/generous 1⅓ cups or 420ml/15fl oz/generous 1¾ cups, depending on the size of loaf you are making.

2 Pour the liquid into the bread pan. If necessary, reverse the order in which you add the liquid and dry ingredients.

3 Sprinkle over the flour, covering the water. Add the salt, sugar and butter, placing them in separate corners.

COOK'S TIP
Add a tablespoon or two of extra flour if the dough is too soft after adding the mushrooms and tomatoes.

4 Make a small indent in the flour; add the yeast. Set the bread machine to the basic/normal setting; use raisin setting (if available), medium crust. Press Start.

5 Chop the reserved mushrooms and the tomatoes. Add them to the dough when the machine beeps, or during the last 5 minutes of the kneading cycle.

6 Remove the bread at the end of the baking cycle and turn out on to a wire rack to cool.

GOLDEN PUMPKIN BREAD

*The pumpkin purée gives this loaf a rich golden crumb, a soft crust and a
beautifully moist light texture, as well as a delightfully sweet-savoury flavour.
It is perfect for serving with soups and casseroles.*

1 Mash the pumpkin and put it in the
bread machine pan. Add the buttermilk,
water and oil. If the instructions for your
machine specify that the easy-blend
dried yeast is to be placed in the pan
first, reverse the order in which you add
the liquid mixture and dry ingredients.

2 Sprinkle over the flour and corn meal,
ensuring that the liquid is completely
covered. Add the golden syrup and salt
in separate corners of the bread
machine pan. Make an indent in the
centre of the flour (but not down as far
as the liquid) and add the yeast.

SMALL

150g/5½oz cooked pumpkin, cooled
90ml/6 tbsp buttermilk
60ml/4 tbsp water
15ml/1 tbsp extra virgin olive oil
325g/11½oz/scant 3 cups unbleached
white bread flour
50g/2oz/½ cup corn meal
15ml/1 tbsp golden (light corn) syrup
5ml/1 tsp salt
4ml/¾ tsp easy-blend (rapid-rise)
dried yeast
15ml/1 tbsp pumpkin seeds

MEDIUM

200g/7oz cooked pumpkin, cooled
110ml/scant 4fl oz/scant ½ cup
buttermilk
45ml/3 tbsp water
30ml/2 tbsp extra virgin olive oil
425g/15oz/3¾ cups unbleached white
bread flour
75g/3oz/¾ cup corn meal
22ml/1½ tbsp golden syrup
7.5ml/1½ tsp salt
5ml/1 tsp easy-blend dried yeast
22ml/1½ tbsp pumpkin seeds

LARGE

250g/9oz cooked pumpkin, cooled
150ml/5fl oz/⅔ cup buttermilk
80ml/scant 3fl oz/⅓ cup water
45ml/3 tbsp extra virgin olive oil
575g/1¼lb/5 cups unbleached white
bread flour
100g/3½oz/scant 1 cup corn meal
30ml/2 tbsp golden (light corn) syrup
10ml/2 tsp salt
7.5ml/1½ tsp easy-blend dried yeast
30ml/2 tbsp pumpkin seeds

MAKES 1 LOAF

3 Set the bread machine to the basic/
normal setting; use raisin setting (if
available), medium crust. Press Start.
Add the pumpkin seeds when the
machine beeps, or during the last
5 minutes of kneading.

4 Remove at the end of the baking cycle.
Turn out on to a wire rack to cool.

POTATO AND SAFFRON BREAD

A dough that includes potato produces a moist loaf with a springy texture and good keeping qualities. Saffron adds an aromatic flavour and rich golden colour to this bread.

1 large potato, about 225g/8oz, peeled
5ml/1 tsp saffron threads
1 egg
450g/1lb/4 cups unbleached white bread flour
30ml/2 tbsp skimmed milk powder (non fat dry milk)
25g/1oz/2 tbsp butter
15ml/1 tbsp clear honey
7.5ml/1½ tsp salt
7.5ml/1½ tsp easy-blend (rapid-rise) dried yeast
MAKES 1 LOAF

COOK'S TIP
If you have time, soak the saffron for 3–4 hours. The longer it soaks, the better the colour and flavour will be.

1 Place the potato in a pan of boiling water, reduce the heat and simmer until tender. Drain the potato, reserving 200ml/7fl oz/⅞ cup of the cooking water. Add the saffron to the hot water; leave to stand for 30 minutes. Mash the potato (without adding butter or milk) and leave to cool.

2 Add the saffron water to the bread pan. Add the mashed potato and the egg. Reverse the order in which you add the wet and dry ingredients if necessary.

3 Sprinkle over the flour, ensuring that it covers the ingredients already placed in the pan. Spoon over the milk powder. Add the butter, honey and salt in separate corners of the bread pan. Make a small indent in the centre of the flour (but not down as far as the liquid) and add the yeast.

4 Set the bread machine to the dough setting; use basic dough setting (if available). Press Start. Lightly flour a baking sheet.

5 When the dough cycle has finished, remove the dough from the machine and place on a lightly floured surface. Gently knock it back (punch it down).

6 Shape the dough into a plump ball. Place on the baking sheet, cover with oiled clear film (plastic wrap) and leave to rise for 30–45 minutes. Meanwhile preheat the oven to 200°C/400°F/Gas 6.

7 Slash the top of the loaf with three or four diagonal cuts, then rotate and repeat to make a criss-cross effect.

8 Bake the bread for 35–40 minutes, or until the bottom sounds hollow when tapped. Turn out on to a wire rack.

CARAMELIZED ONION BREAD

The unmistakable, mouthwatering flavour of golden fried onions is captured in this coburg-shaped bread. Serve with soup, cheeses or salad.

50g/2oz/¼ cup butter
2 onions, chopped
280ml/10fl oz/1¼ cups water
15ml/1 tbsp clear honey
450g/1lb/4 cups unbleached white bread flour
7.5ml/1½ tsp salt
2.5ml/½ tsp freshly ground black pepper
7.5ml/1½ tsp easy-blend (rapid-rise) dried yeast

MAKES 1 LOAF

1 Melt the butter in a frying pan and sauté the onions over a low heat until golden. Remove the pan from the heat and let the onions cool slightly. Place a sieve over the bread machine pan, then tip the contents of the frying pan into it, so that the juices fall into the pan. Set the onions aside to cool completely.

2 Add the water and honey to the bread pan. Reverse the order in which you add the wet and dry ingredients if necessary. Sprinkle over the flour, covering the liquid. Place the salt and pepper in separate corners. Make a shallow indent in the centre of the flour; add the yeast.

3 Set the bread machine to the dough setting; use basic raisin dough setting (if available). Press Start. Add the onions when the machine beeps or in the last 5 minutes of kneading. Lightly flour a baking sheet.

4 When the cycle has finished, remove the dough from the bread pan and place on a lightly floured surface.

5 Knock back (punch down) gently; shape into a ball. Place on the baking sheet and cover with oiled clear film (plastic wrap). Leave to rise for about 45 minutes. Preheat the oven to 200°C/400°F/Gas 6. Slash a 1cm/½in deep cross in the top of the loaf. Bake for 35–40 minutes. Cool on a wire rack.

ROLLS, BUNS AND PASTRIES

These hand-shaped delights include French Ham and Cheese Croissants, Swedish Saffron Braids and fruit-filled Danish Pastries. Chelsea Buns, Yorkshire Teacakes and Pikelets are British classics, while Parker House Rolls and Doughnuts are traditional American offerings. Savoury rolls using mixed grains and onions, herb and ricotta-flavoured knots or Cashew and Olive Scrolls are just a few of the characterful small breads in this section to enjoy.

CALAS

50g/2oz/generous ⅓ cup pudding rice
280ml/10fl oz/1¼ cups milk
140ml/5fl oz/⅝ cup water
2 eggs
125g/4½oz/generous 1 cup
unbleached white bread flour
5ml/1 tsp grated lemon rind
2.5ml/½ tsp ground ginger
2.5ml/½ tsp freshly grated nutmeg
50g/2oz/¼ cup caster (superfine) sugar
1.5ml/¼ tsp salt
5ml/1 tsp easy-blend (rapid-rise)
dried yeast
oil, for deep-frying
icing (confectioners') sugar, for dusting

MAKES ABOUT 25

These tasty morsels are a Creole speciality, made from a rice-based yeast dough which is then deep-fried. They are delicious served warm with coffee or as a breakfast treat.

1 Place the rice, milk and water in a pan and slowly bring to the boil. Lower the heat, cover and simmer for 20 minutes, stirring occasionally, until the rice is soft and the liquid absorbed. Leave to cool.

2 Add the eggs to the bread machine pan. Reverse the order in which you add the wet and dry ingredients if necessary.

3 Add the rice. Sprinkle over the flour, then the lemon rind, ginger and nutmeg. Add the sugar and salt, placing them in separate corners of the bread pan. Make a small indent in the centre of the flour (but not down as far as the liquid) and add the yeast.

4 Set the bread machine to the dough setting; use basic dough setting (if available). Press Start. When the dough cycle has finished, lift out the pan containing the batter from the machine.

5 Preheat the oven to 140°C/275°F/ Gas 1. Heat the oil for deep-frying to 180°C/350°F or until a cube of dried bread, added to the oil, turns golden in 45 seconds. Add tablespoons of batter a few at a time and fry for 3–4 minutes, turning occasionally, until golden.

6 Use a slotted spoon to remove the calas from the oil and drain on kitchen paper. Keep them warm in the oven while you cook the remainder. When all the calas have been cooked, dust them with icing sugar and serve warm.

> **COOK'S TIP**
> If you are using a large bread machine it is a good idea to make double the quantity of dough. If you use the quantities listed here, it is important to check that all the flour is thoroughly mixed with the liquid.

AMERICAN BREAKFAST PANCAKES

2 eggs
280ml/10fl oz/1¼ cups milk
225g/8oz/2 cups unbleached white
bread flour
5ml/1 tsp salt
15ml/1 tbsp caster (superfine) sugar
15g/½oz/1 tbsp butter, melted
5ml/1 tsp easy-blend (rapid-rise)
dried yeast
maple syrup or wild cranberry sauce,
to serve

MAKES ABOUT 15

These thick, succulent breakfast pancakes are often served with a sauce made from wild cranberries, also known as ligonberries. They are equally delicious served with maple syrup and with strips of crispy bacon.

1 Separate 1 egg and set the white aside. Place the yolk in the machine pan and add the whole egg and the milk. If the instructions for your machine specify that the yeast is to be placed in the pan first, reverse the order in which you add the liquid and dry ingredients.

2 Sprinkle over the flour, ensuring that it covers the liquid. Add the salt, sugar and butter, placing them in separate corners of the bread pan. Make a small indent in the centre of the flour (but not down as far as the liquid) and add the easy-blend dried yeast.

3 Set the bread machine to the dough setting; use basic dough setting (if available). Press Start.

4 When the dough cycle has finished pour the batter into a large measuring jug. Whisk the reserved egg white; fold it into the batter. Preheat the oven to 140°C/275°F/Gas 1.

5 Lightly oil a large heavy frying pan or griddle and place over a medium heat. Add about 45ml/3 tbsp batter, letting it spread out to form a pancake about 10cm/4in wide. If room, make a second pancake alongside the first.

6 Cook each pancake until the surface begins to dry out, then turn over using a fish slice or spatula and cook the other side for about 1 minute, or until golden.

7 Stack the pancakes between sheets of baking parchment on a warm plate and keep them warm in the oven while you cook the rest of the batter. Serve the pancakes with the syrup or sauce.

WHOLEMEAL ENGLISH MUFFINS

—

350ml/12fl oz/1½ cups milk
225g/8oz/2 cups unbleached white
bread flour
225g/8oz/2 cups stoneground
wholemeal (whole-wheat) bread flour
5ml/1 tsp caster (superfine) sugar
7.5ml/1½ tsp salt
15g/½oz/1 tbsp butter
7.5ml/1½ tsp easy-blend (rapid-rise)
dried yeast
rice flour or fine semolina, for dusting

MAKES 9

COOK'S TIP

If you don't have a griddle, cook the muffins in a heavy frying pan. It is important that they cook slowly.

After a long walk on a wintry afternoon, come home to warm muffins,
carefully torn apart and spread thickly with butter.

1 Pour the milk into the bread machine pan. If the instructions for your bread machine specify that the yeast is to be placed in the pan first, then reverse the order in which you add the liquid and dry ingredients.

2 Sprinkle over each type of flour in turn, making sure that the milk is completely covered. Add the caster sugar, salt and butter, placing each of them in separate corners of the bread pan. Then make a small indent in the centre of the flour (but do not go down as far as the liquid underneath) and add the easy-blend dried yeast.

3 Set the machine to the dough setting; use basic dough setting (if available). Press Start. Sprinkle a baking sheet with rice flour or semolina.

4 When the dough cycle has finished, place the dough on a floured surface. Knock it back (punch it down) gently. Roll out the dough until it is about 1cm/½in thick.

5 Using a floured 7.5cm/3in plain cutter, cut out nine muffins. If you like, you can re-roll the trimmings, knead them together and let the dough rest for a few minutes before rolling it out again and cutting out an extra muffin or two.

6 Place the muffins on the baking sheet. Dust with rice flour or semolina. Cover with oiled clear film (plastic wrap) and leave in a warm place for 20 minutes, or until almost doubled in size.

7 Heat a griddle over a medium heat. You should not need any oil if the griddle is well seasoned; if not, add the merest trace of oil. Cook the muffins slowly, three at a time, for about 7 minutes on each side. Serve warm.

PIKELETS

Pikelets are similar to crumpets, and have the same distinctive holey tops, but crumpets are thicker and are cooked inside a ring, which supports them while they set. Serve pikelets warm with preserves and butter. They are also excellent with soft cheese and smoked salmon.

140ml/5fl oz/⅝ cup water
140ml/5fl oz/⅝ cup milk
15ml/1 tbsp sunflower oil
225g/8oz/2 cups unbleached white bread flour
5ml/1 tsp salt
5ml/1 tsp caster (superfine) sugar
7.5ml/1½ tsp easy-blend (rapid-rise) dried yeast
1.5ml/¼ tsp bicarbonate of soda (baking soda)
60ml/4 tbsp water
1 egg white
MAKES ABOUT 20

5 Dissolve the bicarbonate of soda in the remaining water and stir it into the batter. Whisk the egg white in a grease-free bowl until it forms soft peaks, then fold it into the batter.

6 Cover the batter mixture with oiled clear film (plastic wrap) and leave the mixture to rise for 30 minutes. Preheat the oven to 140°C/275°F/Gas 1.

7 Lightly grease a griddle and heat it gently. When it is hot, pour generous tablespoonfuls of batter on to the hot surface, spacing them well apart to allow for spreading, and cook until the tops no longer appear wet and have acquired lots of tiny holes.

8 When the base of each pikelet is golden, turn it over, using a spatula or palette knife, and cook until pale golden.

9 Remove the cooked pikelets and layer them in a folded dishtowel. Place in the oven to keep them warm while you cook the remaining batter. Serve the pikelets immediately.

2 Sprinkle over the white bread flour, ensuring that it covers the liquid completely. Add the salt and caster sugar, placing them in separate corners of the bread pan. Make a shallow indent in the centre of the flour (but not down as far as the liquid) and add the easy-blend dried yeast.

3 Set the breadmaking machine to the dough setting; use basic dough setting (if available). Press Start. Then lightly oil two baking sheets.

4 When the dough cycle has finished, carefully lift the bread pan out of the machine and pour the batter for the pikelets into a large mixing bowl.

1 Pour the water into the bread machine pan, then add the milk and sunflower oil. If the instructions for your bread machine specify that the yeast is to be placed in the pan first, reverse the order in which you add the liquid and dry ingredients to the pan.

PETITS PAINS AU CHOCOLAT

A freshly baked petit pain au chocolat is almost impossible to resist, with its buttery, flaky yet crisp pastry concealing a delectable chocolate filling. For a special finish, drizzle melted chocolate over the tops of the freshly baked and cooked pastries.

125ml/4½fl oz/generous ½ cup water
250g/9oz/2¼ cups unbleached white bread flour
30ml/2 tbsp skimmed milk powder (non fat dry milk)
15ml/1 tbsp caster (superfine) sugar
2.5ml/½ tsp salt
140g/5oz/⅔ cup butter, softened
7.5ml/1½ tsp easy-blend (rapid-rise) dried yeast
225g/8oz plain (semisweet) chocolate, broken into pieces

For the Glaze
1 egg yolk
15ml/1 tbsp milk

Makes 9

1 Pour the water into the machine pan. If the instructions for your machine specify that the yeast is to be placed in the pan first, then reverse the order in which you add liquid and dry ingredients.

2 Sprinkle over the flour, then the skimmed milk powder, ensuring that the water is completely covered.

3 Add the caster sugar, salt and 25g/1oz/2 tbsp of the softened butter, placing them in separate corners of the bread pan. Make a small indent in the centre of the flour (but not down as far as the liquid) and add the yeast.

4 Set the breadmaking machine to the dough setting; use basic dough setting (if available). Press Start. Meanwhile shape the remaining softened butter into an oblong-shaped block, about 2cm/¾in thick.

5 Lightly grease two baking sheets. When the dough cycle has finished, place the dough on a floured surface. Knock back (punch down) and shape into a ball. Cut a cross halfway through the top of the dough.

6 Roll out around the cross, leaving a risen centre. Place the butter in the centre. Fold the rolled dough over the butter to enclose; seal the edges.

7 Roll to a rectangle 2cm/¾in thick, twice as long as wide. Fold the bottom third up and the top down; seal the edges with a rolling pin. Wrap in lightly oiled clear film (plastic wrap). Place in the refrigerator and chill for 20 minutes.

8 Do the same again twice more, giving a quarter turn and chilling each time. Chill again for 30 minutes.

9 Roll out the dough to a rectangle measuring 52 × 30cm/21 × 12in. Using a sharp knife, cut the dough into three strips lengthways and widthways to make nine 18 × 10cm/7 × 4in rectangles.

10 Divide the chocolate among the nine dough rectangles, placing the pieces lengthways at one short end.

11 Mix the egg yolk and milk for the glaze together. Brush the mixture over the edges of the dough.

12 Roll up each piece of dough to completely enclose the chocolate, then press the edges together to seal.

13 Place the pastries seam side down on the prepared baking sheets. Cover with oiled clear film and leave to rise in a warm place for about 30 minutes or until doubled in size.

14 Meanwhile, preheat the oven to 200°C/400°F/Gas 6. Brush the pastries with the remaining glaze and bake for about 15 minutes, or until golden. Turn out on to a wire rack to cool just slightly and serve warm.

VARIATION
Fill this flaky yeast pastry with a variety of sweet and savoury fillings. Try chopped nuts, tossed with a little brown sugar and cinnamon or, for a savoury filling, thin strips of cheese, wrapped in ham or mixed with chopped cooked bacon.

50g/2oz/¼ cup butter
1 large onion, finely chopped
280ml/10fl oz/1¼ cups water
280g/10oz/2½ cups unbleached white
bread flour
115g/4oz/1 cup Granary
(whole-wheat) bread flour
25g/1oz/¼ cup oat bran
10ml/2 tsp salt
10ml/2 tsp clear honey
7.5ml/1½ tsp easy-blend (rapid-rise)
dried yeast
corn meal, for dusting
30ml/2 tbsp millet grain
15ml/1 tbsp coarse oatmeal
15ml/1 tbsp sunflower seeds
MAKES 12

MIXED GRAIN ONION ROLLS

These crunchy rolls, flavoured with golden onions, are perfect for snacks,
sandwiches or to serve with soup.

1 Melt half the butter in a frying pan. Add the chopped onions and sauté for 8–10 minutes, or until softened and lightly browned. Set aside to cool.

2 Pour the water into the machine pan. If the instructions for your machine state the yeast is to be placed in the pan first, reverse the order in which you add the wet and dry ingredients.

3 Sprinkle over the white bread flour, Granary flour and oat bran, ensuring that the water is completely covered. Add the salt, honey and remaining butter, placing them in separate corners of the bread pan. Make a small indent in the centre of the flour (but not down as far as the liquid) and add the yeast.

4 Set the bread machine to the dough setting; use basic raisin dough setting (if available). Press Start. Lightly oil two baking sheets and sprinkle them with corn meal.

5 Add the millet grain, coarse oatmeal, sunflower seeds and cooked onion when the machine beeps. If your machine does not have this facility add these ingredients 5 minutes before the end of the kneading cycle.

6 When the dough cycle has finished, remove the dough from the bread machine and place it on a surface that has been lightly floured. Knock the dough back (punch it down) gently, then divide it into 12 equal pieces.

VARIATION
If time is short you can omit the cutting in step 9 and cook as round shaped rolls.

7 Shape each piece into a ball, making sure that the tops are smooth. Flatten them slightly with the palm of your hand or a small rolling pin. Place the rolls on the prepared baking sheets and dust them with more corn meal.

8 Cover the rolls with oiled clear film (plastic wrap) and leave them in a warm place for 30–45 minutes, or until doubled in size. Meanwhile, preheat the oven to 200°C/400°F/Gas 6.

9 Using a pair of lightly floured sharp scissors snip each roll in five places, cutting inwards from the edge, almost to the centre. Bake for 18–20 minutes, or until the rolls are golden. Turn them out on to a wire rack to cool.

PARKER HOUSE ROLLS

—

These stylish rolls were first made in a hotel in Boston, after which they are named. They are delicious served warm.

1 Pour the milk and egg into the bread machine pan. If the instructions for your bread machine specify that the yeast is to be placed in the pan first, reverse the order in which you add the liquid and dry ingredients.

2 Sprinkle over the flour, ensuring that it covers the liquid. Add the sugar, salt and 25g/1oz/2 tbsp of the melted butter, placing them in separate corners of the bread pan. Make a small indent in the centre of the flour (but do not go down as far as the liquid underneath) and add the easy-blend dried yeast.

3 Set the machine to the dough setting; use basic dough setting (if available). Press Start. Lightly oil two baking sheets.

4 When the dough cycle has finished, remove the dough from the machine, place it on a lightly floured surface and knock it back (punch it down) gently.

180ml/6½fl oz/generous ¾ cup milk
1 egg
450g/1lb/4 cups unbleached white bread flour
10ml/2 tsp caster (superfine) sugar
7.5ml/1½ tsp salt
75g/3oz/6 tbsp butter, melted
5ml/1 tsp easy-blend (rapid-rise) dried yeast

MAKES 10 ROLLS

COOK'S TIP
If you do not have a small rolling pin – and can't borrow one from a child's cooking set – use a small clean bottle or the rounded handle of a knife to shape the rolls.

5 Roll out to a 1cm/½in thickness. Use a 7.5cm/3in cutter to make ten rounds, then use a small rolling pin to roll or flatten each across the centre in one direction, to create a valley about 5mm/¼in thick.

6 Brush with a little remaining melted butter to within 1cm/½in of the edge. Fold over, ensuring the top piece of dough overlaps the bottom. Press down lightly on the folded edge.

7 Place the rolls on the prepared baking sheets, just overlapping, brush them with more melted butter and cover with oiled clear film (plastic wrap). Leave in a warm place for 30 minutes, or until doubled in size.

8 Preheat the oven to 200°C/400°F/ Gas 6. Bake the rolls for 15–18 minutes, or until they are golden. Brush the hot rolls with the last of the melted butter and transfer them to a wire rack to cool.

BRIDGE ROLLS

Milk and egg flavour these small, soft-textured finger rolls. Use them for canapés or serve them with soup.

1 egg
100ml/3½ fl oz/7 tbsp milk
225g/8oz/2 cups unbleached white
bread flour
5ml/1 tsp salt
2.5ml/½ tsp caster (superfine) sugar
50g/2oz/¼ cup butter
5ml/1 tsp easy-blend (rapid-rise)
dried yeast
30ml/2 tbsp milk, for glazing (optional)

MAKES 12

COOK'S TIP
Make double the quantity and freeze the surplus. You will only need the same amount of yeast.

1 Pour the egg and milk into the bread pan. If necessary for your machine, place the dry ingredients in the pan before the liquid.

2 Sprinkle over the flour, ensuring that it covers the liquid. Add the salt, sugar and butter, placing them in separate corners of the bread machine pan. Then make a small indent in the centre of the flour (but do not go down as far as the liquid) and add the easy-blend dried yeast.

3 Set the bread machine to the dough setting; use basic dough setting (if available). Press Start. Lightly oil two baking sheets.

4 When the dough cycle has finished, remove the dough from the machine and place it on a lightly floured surface. Knock it back (punch it down) gently, then divide it into 12 pieces and cover with a piece of oiled clear film (plastic wrap).

5 Take one piece of dough, leaving the rest covered, and shape it on the floured surface into a tapered long roll. Repeat with the remaining dough until you have 12 evenly shaped rolls.

6 Place six rolls in a row, keeping them fairly close to each other, on each baking sheet. Cover with oiled clear film and leave in a warm place for about 30 minutes, or until the rolls have doubled in size and are touching each other. Meanwhile, preheat the oven to 220°C/425°F/Gas 7.

7 Brush the bridge rolls with milk, if you like, and bake them for 15–18 minutes, or until lightly browned. Transfer the batch to a wire rack to cool, then separate into rolls.

WHOLEMEAL BAPS

There's nothing nicer than waking up to the aroma of fresh baked bread. The wholemeal flour adds extra flavour to these soft breakfast rolls.

140ml/5fl oz/scant ⅔ cup milk
140ml/5fl oz/scant ⅔ cup water
225g/8oz/2 cups stoneground
wholemeal (whole-wheat) bread
flour, plus extra for dusting
225g/8oz/2 cups unbleached white
bread flour
7.5ml/1½ tsp salt
10ml/2 tsp caster (superfine) sugar
5ml/1 tsp easy-blend (rapid-rise)
dried yeast
milk, for glazing

MAKES 10

1 Pour the milk and water into the pan. Reverse the order in which you add the wet and dry ingredients if necessary. Sprinkle over the flours, covering the liquid. Add the salt and sugar in separate corners. Make a shallow indent in the centre of the flour and add the yeast. Set the bread machine to the dough setting; use basic dough setting (if available). Press Start.

2 When the dough cycle has finished, remove the dough and place it on a lightly floured surface. Knock it back (punch it down) gently, then divide it into ten pieces and cover with lightly oiled clear film (plastic wrap).

3 Take one piece of dough, leaving the rest covered, and cup your hands around it to shape it into a ball. Place it on the lightly floured surface and roll it into a flat oval measuring 10 × 7.5cm/4 × 3in.

4 Repeat with the remaining dough so that you have ten flat oval dough pieces. Lightly oil two baking sheets.

5 Place the baps on the prepared baking sheets. Cover with oiled clear film and leave to rise in a warm place for about 30 minutes, or until the baps are almost doubled in size. Meanwhile, preheat the oven to 200°C/400°F/Gas 6.

6 Using three middle fingers, press each bap in the centre to help disperse any large air bubbles. Brush with milk and dust lightly with wholemeal flour.

7 Bake for 15–20 minutes, or until the baps are lightly browned. Turn out on to a wire rack and serve warm.

RICOTTA AND OREGANO KNOTS

60ml/4 tbsp ricotta cheese
225ml/8fl oz/scant 1 cup water
450g/1lb/4 cups unbleached white
bread flour
45ml/3 tbsp skimmed milk powder
(non fat dry milk)
10ml/2 tsp dried oregano
5ml/1 tsp salt
10ml/2 tsp caster (superfine) sugar
25g/1oz/ 2 tbsp butter
5ml/1 tsp easy-blend (rapid-rise)
dried yeast

FOR THE TOPPING
1 egg yolk
freshly ground black pepper

MAKES 12

The ricotta cheese adds a wonderful moistness to these beautifully shaped rolls. Serve them slightly warm to appreciate fully the flavour of the oregano as your butter melts into the crumb.

1 Spoon the cheese into the bread machine pan and add the water. Reverse the order in which you add the liquid and dry ingredients if necessary.

2 Sprinkle over the flour, ensuring that it covers the cheese and water. Add the skimmed milk powder and oregano. Place the salt, sugar and butter in separate corners of the bread pan. Make a small indent in the centre of the flour (but not down as far as the liquid) and add the yeast.

3 Set the bread machine to the dough setting; use basic dough setting (if available). Press Start. Lightly oil two baking sheets.

4 When the dough cycle has finished, remove the dough from the machine and place it on a lightly floured surface.

5 Knock the dough back (punch it down) gently, then divide it into 12 pieces and cover with oiled clear film (plastic wrap).

6 Take one piece of dough, leaving the rest covered, and roll it on the floured surface into a rope about 25cm/10in long. Lift one end of the dough over the other to make a loop. Push the end through the hole in the loop to make a neat knot.

7 Repeat with the remaining dough. Place the knots on the prepared baking sheets, cover them with oiled clear film and leave to rise in a warm place for about 30 minutes, or until doubled in size. Meanwhile, preheat the oven to 220°C/425°F/Gas 7.

8 Mix the egg yolk and 15ml/1tbsp water for the topping in a small bowl. Brush the mixture over the rolls. Sprinkle some with freshly ground black pepper and leave the rest plain.

9 Bake for about 15–18 minutes, or until the rolls are golden brown. Turn out on to a wire rack to cool.

WHOLEMEAL AND RYE PISTOLETS

A wholemeal and rye version of this French and Belgian speciality. Unless your bread machine has a programme for wholewheat dough, it is worth the extra effort of the double rising, because this gives a lighter roll with a more developed flavour.

290ml/10¼fl oz/1¼ cups water
280g/10oz/2½ cups stoneground wholemeal (whole-wheat) bread flour
50g/2oz/½ cup unbleached white bread flour, plus extra for dusting
115g/4oz/1 cup rye flour
30ml/2 tbsp skimmed milk powder (non fat dry milk)
10ml/2 tsp salt + 5ml/1tsp to glaze
10ml/2 tsp caster (superfine) sugar
25g/1oz/2 tbsp butter
7.5ml/1½ tsp easy-blend (rapid-rise) dried yeast

MAKES 12

1 Pour the water into the bread pan. If the instructions for your machine specify that the yeast is to be placed in the pan first, reverse the order in which you add the liquid and dry ingredients.

2 Sprinkle over all three types of flour, ensuring that the water is completely covered. Add the skimmed milk powder. Then add the salt, sugar and butter, placing them in separate corners of the bread pan. Make a small indent in the centre of the flour (but do not go down as far as the water underneath) and add the easy-blend dried yeast.

3 Set the bread machine to the dough setting; use wholewheat dough setting (if available). If you have only one basic dough setting you may need to repeat the programme to allow sufficient time for this heavier dough to rise. Press Start. Lightly oil two baking sheets.

4 When the dough cycle has finished, remove the dough from the bread machine pan and place it on a surface that has been lightly floured. Knock the dough back (punch it down) gently, then divide it into 12 pieces. Cover with oiled clear film (plastic wrap).

5 Leaving the rest of the dough covered, shape one piece into a ball. Roll on the floured surface into an oval. Repeat with the remaining dough.

6 Place the rolls on the prepared baking sheets. Cover them with oiled clear film and leave them in a warm place for about 30–45 minutes, or until almost doubled in size. Meanwhile preheat the oven to 220°C/425°F/Gas 7.

7 Mix the salt with 15ml/1tbsp water for the glaze and brush over the rolls. Dust the tops of the rolls with flour.

8 Using the oiled handle of a wooden spoon held horizontally, split each roll almost in half, along its length. Replace the clear film and leave for 10 minutes.

9 Bake the rolls for 15–20 minutes, until the bases sound hollow when tapped. Turn out on to a wire rack to cool.

HAM AND CHEESE CROISSANTS

The crispy layers of yeast pastry melt in your mouth to reveal a cheese and ham filling. Serve the croissants freshly baked and still warm.

115ml/4fl oz/½ cup milk
30ml/2 tbsp water
1 egg
280g/10oz/2½ cups unbleached white bread flour
50g/2oz/½ cup fine French plain (all-purpose) flour
5ml/1 tsp salt
15ml/1 tbsp caster (superfine) sugar
25g/1oz/2 tbsp butter, plus
175g/6oz/¾ cup butter, softened
7.5ml/1½ tsp easy-blend (rapid-rise) dried yeast
1 egg yolk, to glaze
15ml/1 tbsp milk, to glaze

FOR THE FILLING
175g/6oz Emmenthal or Gruyère cheese, cut into thin batons
70g/2½oz thinly sliced dry cured smoked ham, torn into small pieces
5ml/1 tsp paprika

MAKES 12

1 Pour the milk, water and egg into the pan. Reverse the order in which you add the wet and dry ingredients, if necessary.

2 Sprinkle over the flours. Place the salt, sugar and 25g/1oz/2 tbsp butter in separate corners. Add the yeast in an indent in the flour. Set to the dough setting; use basic dough setting (if available). Press Start. Shape the softened butter into an oblong block 2cm/¾in thick.

3 When the dough cycle has finished, place the dough on a floured surface and knock back (punch down) gently. Roll out to a rectangle slightly wider than the butter block, and just over twice as long. Place the butter on one half of the pastry, fold it over and seal the edges, using a rolling pin.

4 Roll out again into a rectangle 2cm/¾in thick, twice as long as it is wide. Fold the top third down, the bottom third up, seal, wrap in clear film (plastic wrap) and chill for 15 minutes. Repeat the rolling, folding and chilling twice more, giving the pastry a quarter turn each time. Wrap in clear film and chill for 30 minutes.

5 Lightly oil two baking sheets. Roll out the pastry into a rectangle measuring 52 × 30cm/21 × 12in. Cut into two 15cm/6in strips. Using one strip, measure 15cm/6in along one long edge and 7.5cm/3in along the opposite long edge. Using the 15cm/6in length as the base of your first triangle, cut two diagonal lines to the 7.5cm/3in mark opposite, using a sharp knife. Continue along the strip, cutting six triangles in all. You will end up with two scraps of waste pastry, at either end of the strip. Repeat with the remaining strip.

6 Place a pastry triangle on the work surface in front of you, with the pointed end facing you. Divide the cheese and ham into 12 portions and put one portion on the wide end of the triangle. Hold and gently pull each side point to stretch the pastry a little, then roll up the triangle from the filled end with one hand while pulling the remaining point gently towards you with the other hand.

7 Curve the ends of the rolled triangle away from you to make a crescent. Place this on one of the baking sheets, with the point underneath. Fill and shape the remaining croissants. Cover with oiled clear film and leave to rise for 30 minutes, until almost doubled in size. Preheat the oven to 200°C/400°F/Gas 6.

8 Mix the egg yolk and milk for the glaze and brush over the croissants. Bake for 15–20 minutes, until golden. Turn out on to a wire rack. Serve warm.

SAFFRON BRAIDS

Delicately scented and coloured with saffron, these deep-fried braids are favourite coffee-time treats in Scandinavia.

1 Heat the milk until hot but not boiling. Pour over the saffron in a bowl. Leave for 45 minutes or until cold.

2 Pour the saffron milk into the bread machine pan, then add the eggs. If the instructions for your machine specify that the yeast is to be placed in the pan first, reverse the order in which you add the liquid and dry ingredients.

3 Sprinkle over the flour, ensuring that it covers the saffron milk completely. Add the salt, sugar and butter, placing them in separate corners of the bread machine pan. Make a small indent in the centre of the flour (but do not go down as far as the liquid) and add the easy-blend dried yeast.

4 Set the bread machine to the dough setting; use basic dough setting (if available). Press Start. Lightly oil two baking sheets.

5 When the dough cycle has finished, remove the dough for the saffron braids from the bread machine and place it on a lightly floured surface. Knock it back (punch it down) gently, then divide the dough into eight pieces. Cover with a piece of oiled clear film (plastic wrap).

200ml/7fl oz/⅞ cup milk
3.5ml/¾ tsp saffron threads
2 eggs
450g/1lb/4 cups unbleached white bread flour
2.5ml/½ tsp salt
50g/2oz/¼ cup caster (superfine) sugar
50g/2oz/¼ cup butter
5ml/1 tsp easy-blend (rapid-rise) dried yeast
sunflower oil, for deep-frying
caster (superfine) sugar, for sprinkling

MAKES 8

6 Take one piece of dough (leaving the rest covered). Divide into three. Roll out each small piece into a 20cm/8in rope.

7 Place the ropes next to each other, pinch the ends together and braid them from left to right. When you reach the other end, press the ends together and tuck them under.

8 Repeat with the remaining portions of dough. Place the braid on the baking sheets. Cover with oiled clear film and leave in a warm place for 30–45 minutes or until almost doubled in size.

9 Preheat the oil for deep-frying to 180°C/360°F or until a cube of dried bread, added to the oil, turns golden brown in 30–60 seconds.

10 Fry the saffron braids two at a time for 4–5 minutes, until they are risen and golden. Drain on kitchen paper and sprinkle with caster sugar. Serve warm.

CHINESE-STYLE CHICKEN BUNS

These delectable sesame seeded buns, filled with chicken flavoured with ginger and soy sauce, are perfect for picnics.

140ml/5fl oz/⅝ cup semi-skimmed (low-fat) milk
225g/8oz/2 cups unbleached white bread flour
2.5ml/½ tsp salt
2.5ml/½ tsp granulated sugar
15g/½oz/1 tbsp butter
5ml/1 tsp easy-blend (rapid-rise) dried yeast

FOR THE FILLING
30ml/2 tbsp sunflower oil
5cm/2in piece of fresh root ginger, grated
30ml/2 tbsp soy sauce
15ml/1 tbsp clear honey
225g/8oz chicken breast fillets, chopped
3 spring onions (scallions), chopped
15ml/1 tbsp chopped fresh coriander (cilantro)
salt and freshly ground black pepper

FOR THE TOPPING
1 egg yolk
15ml/1 tbsp water
sesame seeds

MAKES 8

1 Pour the milk into the bread machine pan. If the instructions for your bread machine specify that the yeast is to be placed in the pan first, simply reverse the order in which you add the liquid and dry ingredients.

2 Sprinkle over the flour, ensuring that the milk is completely covered. Add the salt, sugar and butter, placing them in separate corners of the bread pan. Make a small indent in the centre of the flour (but not down as far as the liquid) and add the easy-blend dried yeast.

3 Set the bread machine to the dough setting; use basic dough setting (if available). Press Start. Lightly grease a baking sheet.

4 Make the filling. Mix half the oil with the grated ginger, soy sauce and honey. Add the chicken and toss to coat. Cover and set aside for 30 minutes.

5 Heat a non-stick wok or frying pan and add the remaining oil. When it is hot, add the chicken mixture and stir-fry over medium heat for 5–6 minutes. Add the spring onions and cook for 2 minutes more, or until the chicken is cooked. Stir in the coriander and seasoning. Set aside to cool.

6 When the dough cycle has finished, remove the dough from the machine and place it on a lightly floured surface. Knock it back gently, then divide it into eight pieces.

7 Roll out each piece of dough to a 13cm/5in round. Divide the chicken filling among the rounds of dough, placing in the centre of each.

8 Beat the egg yolk and water for the topping in a small bowl. Brush a little of the mixture around the edge of each dough round.

9 Bring up the sides of the dough to cover the filling and pinch the edges together to seal. Place the buns seam-side down on the baking sheet.

10 Cover the buns with oiled clear film (plastic wrap) and leave to rise in a warm place for about 30 minutes or until almost doubled in size. Meanwhile, preheat the oven to 200°C/400°F/Gas 6.

11 Brush the tops of the buns with the remaining egg glaze and sprinkle with the sesame seeds. Bake for about 18–20 minutes, or until the buns are golden brown. Turn out on to a wire rack to cool slightly. If you like, serve immediately, while the buns are hot.

VARIATION
If you have any leftover stir-fried vegetables, use as a filling in place of the chicken filling. To make another vegetarian version of these buns, cut 225g/8oz mixed vegetables into small pieces or strips and marinade as for the chicken in step 4. Use vegetables such as carrots, broccoli, leeks, bean-sprouts and (bell) peppers.

SPANISH PICOS

200ml/7fl oz/⅞ cup water
45ml/3 tbsp extra virgin olive oil
350g/12½oz/3 cups unbleached white bread flour
5ml/1 tsp salt
2.5ml/½ tsp granulated sugar
5ml/1 tsp easy-blend (rapid-rise) dried yeast
30ml/2 tbsp water
15ml/1 tbsp sea salt
15ml/1 tbsp sesame seeds

MAKES ABOUT 70

COOK'S TIP
Make these tasty nibbles up to a day in advance. Re-heat in a moderate oven for a few minutes, to refresh.

1 Pour the water and oil into the pan. If necessary, reverse the order in which you add the liquid and dry ingredients.

These small bread shapes, dusted with salt and sesame seeds, are often eaten in Spain with pre-dinner drinks, but can also be served as an accompaniment to an appetizer or soup.

2 Sprinkle over the flour, ensuring that it covers the liquid. Add the salt and sugar, placing them in separate corners of the bread pan. Make a small indent in the centre of the flour (but not down as far as the liquid) and add the yeast.

3 Set the machine to the dough setting; use basic dough setting (if available). Press Start. Then lightly oil two baking sheets.

4 When the dough cycle has finished, remove the dough from the machine and place it on a lightly floured surface. Knock it back (punch it down) gently, then roll it out to a rectangle measuring 30 × 23cm/12 × 9in. Cut lengthways into three strips, then cut each strip of dough into 2.5cm/1in wide ribbons.

5 Preheat the oven to 200°C/400°F/ Gas 6. Tie each ribbon into a loose knot and place on the baking sheets, spacing them well apart. Cover with oiled clear film (plastic wrap) and leave to rise in a warm place for 10–15 minutes. Leave the picos plain or brush with water and sprinkle with salt or sesame seeds. Bake for 10–15 minutes, or until golden.

CASHEW AND OLIVE SCROLLS

140ml/5fl oz/⅝ cup milk
120ml/4fl oz/½ cup water
30ml/2 tbsp extra virgin olive oil
450g/1lb/4 cups unbleached white bread flour
5ml/1 tsp salt
2.5ml/½ tsp caster (superfine) sugar
7.5ml/1½ tsp easy-blend (rapid-rise) dried yeast
5ml/1 tsp finely chopped fresh rosemary or thyme
50g/2oz/½ cup salted cashew nuts, finely chopped
50g/2oz/½ cup pitted green olives, finely chopped
45ml/3 tbsp freshly grated Parmesan cheese, for sprinkling

MAKES 12

1 Pour the milk, water and oil into the pan. If necessary, reverse the order in which you add the wet and dry ingredients.

These attractively shaped rolls have a crunchy texture and ooze with the flavours of olives and fresh herbs.

2 Sprinkle over the flour, ensuring that it covers the liquid. Add the salt and sugar, placing them in separate corners of the bread pan. Make a small indent in the centre of the flour (but not down as far as the liquid) and add the yeast.

3 Set the machine to the dough setting; use basic raisin dough setting (if available). Press Start. Add the herbs, cashew nuts and olives when the machine beeps. If your machine does not have this facility, then add these ingredients about 5 minutes before the end of the kneading period. Lightly oil two baking sheets.

4 When the dough cycle has finished, remove the dough from the machine and place it on a lightly floured surface. Knock it back (punch it down) gently.

5 Divide the dough into 12 pieces of equal size and cover with oiled clear film (plastic wrap). Take one piece of dough, leaving the rest covered. Roll it into a rope about 23cm/9in long, tapering the ends. Starting from the middle, shape the rope into an "S" shape, curling the ends in to form a neat spiral.

6 Transfer the spiral – or scroll – to a prepared baking sheet. Make 11 more scrolls in the same way. Cover with oiled clear film and leave to rise in a warm place for 30 minutes, or until doubled in size.

7 Meanwhile, preheat the oven to 200°C/ 400°F/Gas 6. Sprinkle the rolls with Parmesan cheese and bake them for 18–20 minutes, or until risen and golden. Turn out on to a wire rack to cool.

HOT CROSS BUNS

The traditional cross on these Easter buns originates from early civilization and probably symbolized the four seasons; it was only later used to mark Good Friday and the Crucifixion.

210ml/7½fl oz/scant 1 cup milk
1 egg
450g/1lb/4 cups unbleached white bread flour
7.5ml/1½ tsp mixed (apple pie) spice
2.5ml/½ tsp ground cinnamon
2.5ml/½ tsp salt
50g/2oz/¼ cup caster (superfine) sugar
50g/2oz/¼ cup butter
7.5ml/1½ tsp easy-blend (rapid-rise) dried yeast
75g/3oz/scant ½ cup currants
25g/1oz/3 tbsp sultanas (golden raisins)
25g/1oz/3 tbsp cut mixed (candied) peel

FOR THE PASTRY CROSSES
50g/2oz/½ cup plain (all-purpose) flour
25g/1oz/2 tbsp margarine

FOR THE GLAZE
30ml/2 tbsp milk
25g/1oz/2 tbsp caster sugar

MAKES 12

1 Pour the milk and egg into the bread pan. Reverse the order in which you add the liquid and dry ingredients if your machine requires this.

2 Sprinkle over the flour, ensuring that it covers the liquid. Add the mixed spice and cinnamon. Place the salt, sugar and butter in separate corners of the pan. Make a shallow indent in the centre of the flour and add the yeast.

COOK'S TIP
If preferred, to make the crosses roll out 50g/2oz shortcrust (unsweetened) pastry, and cut into narrow strips. Brush the buns with water to attach the crosses.

3 Set the bread machine to the dough setting; use basic raisin dough setting (if available). Press Start. Lightly grease two baking sheets.

4 Add the dried fruit and peel when the machine beeps or 5 minutes before the end of the kneading period.

5 When the dough cycle has finished, remove the dough from the machine and place it on a lightly floured surface. Knock it back (punch it down) gently, then divide it into 12 pieces. Cup each piece between your hands and shape it into a ball. Place on the prepared baking sheets, cover with oiled clear film (plastic wrap) and leave for 30–45 minutes or until almost doubled in size.

6 Meanwhile, preheat the oven to 200°C/ 400°F/Gas 6. Make the pastry for the crosses. In a bowl, rub the flour and margarine together until the mixture resembles fine breadcrumbs. Bind with enough water to make a soft pastry which can be piped.

7 Spoon the pastry into a piping bag fitted with a plain nozzle and pipe a cross on each bun. Bake the buns for 15–18 minutes, or until golden.

8 Meanwhile, heat the milk and sugar for the glaze in a small pan. Stir thoroughly until the sugar dissolves. Brush the glaze over the top of the hot buns. Turn out on to a wire rack. Serve warm or cool.

HAMAN POCKETS

These delicate tricorn-shaped pastries are properly known as Hamantaschel and are traditionally eaten at the Jewish festival of Esther. They can be filled with dried fruits or poppy seeds.

1 Pour the milk and egg into the bread machine pan. However, if the instructions for your machine specify that the easy-blend dried yeast is to be placed in the bread machine pan first, simply reverse the order in which you add the liquid and dry ingredients to the pan.

2 Sprinkle over the flour, ensuring that it covers the milk and egg mixture. Add the sugar, salt and butter, placing them in separate corners of the bread pan. Make a small indent in the centre of the flour (but not down as far as the liquid) and add the yeast.

3 Set the bread machine to the dough setting; use basic dough setting (if available). Press Start. Lightly grease two baking sheets.

4 Make the filling. Put the poppy seeds in a heatproof bowl, pour over boiling water to cover and leave to cool. Drain thoroughly through a fine sieve. Melt 15g/½oz/1 tbsp of the butter in a small pan, add the poppy seeds and cook, stirring, for 1–2 minutes. Remove from the heat and stir in the ground almonds, honey, mixed peel and sultanas. Cool.

5 When the dough cycle has finished, place the dough on a lightly floured surface. Knock it back (punch it down) gently and then shape it into a ball.

6 Roll out the pastry to a thickness of about 5mm/¼in. Cut out 10cm/4in circles using a plain cutter, re-rolling the trimmings as necessary. Then melt the remaining butter.

100ml/3½fl oz/7 tbsp milk
1 egg
250g/9oz/2¼ cups unbleached white bread flour
25g/1oz/2 tbsp caster (superfine) sugar
2.5ml/½ tsp salt
25g/1oz/2 tbsp butter, melted
5ml/1 tsp easy-blend (rapid-rise) dried yeast
50g/2oz/4 tbsp poppy seeds
40g/1½oz/3 tbsp butter
25g/1oz/¼ cup ground almonds
15ml/1 tbsp clear honey
15ml/1 tbsp chopped mixed (candied) peel
15ml/1 tbsp sultanas (golden raisins), chopped
beaten egg, to glaze

MAKES 10–12

7 Brush each circle of dough with the melted butter and place a spoonful of filling in the centre. Bring up the edges over the filling to make tricorn shapes, leaving a little of the filling showing. Transfer the shaped pastries to the prepared baking sheets, cover them with oiled clear film (plastic wrap) and leave for 30 minutes or until the haman pockets are doubled in size.

8 Preheat the oven to 190°C/375°F/Gas 5. Brush the pastries with the beaten egg and bake for 15 minutes, or until golden. Turn out on to a wire rack.

VARIATION
For the filling, chopped ready-to-eat prunes can be used instead of poppy seeds, or use a mixture of chopped raisins and sultanas.

CHELSEA BUNS

225ml/8fl oz/scant 1 cup milk
1 egg
500g/1lb 2oz/4½ cups unbleached white bread flour
2.5ml/½ tsp salt
75g/3oz/6 tbsp caster (superfine) sugar
50g/2oz/¼ cup butter, softened
5ml/1 tsp easy-blend (rapid-rise) dried yeast
50g/2oz/¼ cup caster (superfine) sugar, to glaze
5ml/1 tsp orange flower water, to glaze

FOR THE FILLING
25g/1oz/2 tbsp butter, melted
115g/4oz/⅔ cup sultanas (golden raisins)
25g/1oz/3 tbsp mixed chopped (candied) peel
25g/1oz/2 tbsp currants
25g/1oz/2 tbsp soft light brown sugar
5ml/1 tsp mixed (apple pie) spice

MAKES 12 BUNS

Chelsea buns are said to have been invented by the owner of the Chelsea Bun House in London at the end of the 17th century. They make the perfect accompaniment to a cup of coffee or tea. They are so delicious, it is difficult to resist going back for more!

1 Pour the milk into the bread machine pan. Add the egg. If the instructions for your machine specify that the yeast is to be placed in the pan first, reverse the order in which you add the liquid and dry ingredients.

2 Sprinkle over the flour, ensuring that it completely covers the liquid. Add the salt, sugar and butter in three separate corners of the bread machine pan. Make a small indent in the centre of the flour (but not down as far as the liquid) and add the yeast.

3 Set the bread machine to the dough setting; use basic dough setting (if available). Press Start.

4 Lightly grease a 23cm/9in square cake tin (pan). When the dough cycle has finished, remove the dough from the machine and place it on a lightly floured surface.

5 Knock the dough back (punch it down) gently, then roll it out to form a square that is approximately 30cm/12in.

6 Brush the dough with the melted butter for the filling and sprinkle it with the sultanas, candied peel, currants, brown sugar and mixed spice, leaving a 1cm/½in border along one edge.

7 Starting at a covered edge, roll the dough up, Swiss (jelly) roll fashion. Press the edges together to seal. Cut the roll into 12 slices and then place these cut side uppermost in the prepared tin.

COOK'S TIP

Use icing (confectioners') sugar instead of caster sugar and make a thin glaze icing to brush over the freshly baked buns.

---

8 Cover with oiled clear film (plastic wrap). Leave to rise in a warm place for 30–45 minutes, or until the dough slices have doubled in size. Meanwhile preheat the oven to 200°C/400°F/Gas 6.

9 Bake the buns for 15–20 minutes, or until they have risen well and are evenly golden all over. Once they are baked, leave them to cool slightly in the tin before turning them out on to a wire rack to cool further.

10 Make the glaze. Mix the caster sugar with 60ml/4tbsp water in a small pan. Heat, stirring occasionally, until the sugar is completely dissolved. Then boil the mixture rapidly for 1–2 minutes without stirring, until syrupy.

11 Stir the orange flower water into the glaze and brush the mixture over the warm buns. Serve slightly warm.

YORKSHIRE TEACAKES

280ml/10fl oz/scant 1¼ cups milk
450g/1lb/4 cups unbleached white
bread flour
5ml/1 tsp salt
40g/1½oz/3 tbsp caster
(superfine) sugar
40g/1½oz/3 tbsp lard (shortening)
or butter
5ml/1 tsp easy-blend (rapid-rise)
dried yeast
50g/2oz/¼ cup currants
50g/2oz/⅓ cup sultanas
(golden raisins)
milk, for glazing

MAKES 8–10

These fruit-filled tea-time treats are thought to be a refinement of the original medieval manchet or "handbread" – a hand-shaped loaf made without a tin. Serve them split and buttered, either warm from the oven or toasted.

1 Pour the milk into the bread machine pan. If the instructions for your machine specify that the yeast is to be placed in the pan first, then simply reverse the order in which you add the liquid and dry ingredients to the pan.

2 Sprinkle over the flour, ensuring that it covers the milk completely. Add the salt, sugar and lard or butter, placing them in separate corners of the bread machine pan. Make a small indent in the centre of the flour (but do not go down as far as the liquid underneath) and pour the easy-blend dried yeast into the hollow.

3 Set the bread machine to the dough setting; use basic raisin dough setting (if available). Press Start. Add the currants and sultanas when the machine beeps. If your machine does not have this facility, simply add the dried fruits 5 minutes before the end of the kneading period.

4 Lightly grease two baking sheets. When the dough cycle has finished, remove the dough from the machine and place it on a lightly floured surface. Knock it back (punch it down) gently.

5 Divide the dough into eight or ten portions, depending on how large you like your Yorkshire teacakes, and shape into balls. Flatten out each ball into a disc about 1cm/½in thick.

6 Place the discs on the prepared baking sheets, about 2.5cm/1in apart. Cover them with oiled clear film (plastic wrap) and leave in a warm place for 30–45 minutes, or until they are almost doubled in size. Meanwhile, preheat the oven to 200°C/400°F/Gas 6.

7 Brush the top of each teacake with milk, then bake for 15–18 minutes, or until golden. Turn out on to a wire rack to cool slightly.

8 To serve, split open while still warm and spread with lashings of butter, or let the buns cool, then split and toast them before adding butter.

DEVONSHIRE SPLITS

A summer afternoon, a scrumptious cream tea; Devonshire splits are an essential part of this British tradition.

140ml/5fl oz/⅔ cup milk
225g/8oz/2 cups unbleached white bread flour
25g/1oz/2 tbsp caster (superfine) sugar
2.5ml/½ tsp salt
5ml/1 tsp easy-blend (rapid-rise) dried yeast
icing (confectioners') sugar, for dusting

FOR THE FILLING
clotted cream or whipped double (heavy) cream
raspberry or strawberry jam

MAKES 8

5 When the dough cycle has finished, remove the dough and place it on a floured surface. Knock back (punch down) gently, then divide into eight portions.

6 Shape each portion of dough into a ball, using cupped hands. Place on the prepared baking sheets, and flatten the top of each ball slightly. Cover with oiled clear film (plastic wrap). Leave to rise for 30–45 minutes or until doubled in size.

7 Meanwhile, preheat the oven to 220°C/425°F/Gas 7. Bake the buns for 15–18 minutes, or until they are light golden in colour. Turn out on to a wire rack to cool.

8 Split the buns open and fill them with cream and jam. Dust them with icing sugar just before serving.

1 Pour the milk into the bread pan. If your machine instructions specify it, reverse the order in which you add the liquid and dry ingredients.

2 Sprinkle over the flour, ensuring that it covers the liquid completely. Add the caster sugar and salt, placing them in separate corners of the bread machine pan.

3 Make a small indent in the centre of the flour (do not go down as far as the milk underneath) and pour the easy-blend dried yeast into the hollow.

4 Set the bread machine to the dough setting; use basic dough setting (if available). Press Start. Lightly grease two baking sheets.

DOUGHNUTS

90ml/6 tbsp water
140ml/5fl oz/scant ⅔ cup milk
1 egg
*450g/1lb/4 cups unbleached white
bread flour*
50g/2oz/¼ cup caster (superfine) sugar
5ml/1 tsp salt
50g/2oz/¼ cup butter
*7.5ml/1½ tsp easy-blend (rapid-rise)
dried yeast*
oil for deep-frying
caster (superfine) sugar, for sprinkling
ground cinnamon, for sprinkling

FOR THE FILLING
45ml/3 tbsp red jam
5ml/1 tsp lemon juice

MAKES ABOUT 16

*The main thing to remember about doughnuts is the speed with which they
disappear, so make plenty of both the cinnamon-coated rings and the round
ones filled with jam.*

1 Pour the water and milk into the bread machine pan. Break in the egg. If the instructions for your bread machine specify that the yeast is to be placed in the pan first, simply reverse the order in which you add the liquid and dry ingredients.

2 Sprinkle over the flour, ensuring that it covers the liquid. Add the sugar, salt and butter, placing them in separate corners of the bread pan. Make a small indent in the centre of the flour (but not down as far as the liquid) and add the easy-blend dried yeast.

3 Set the bread machine to the dough setting; use basic dough setting (if available). Press Start.

4 When the dough cycle has finished, remove the dough from the machine and place it on a lightly floured surface.

5 Knock the dough back (punch it down) gently and divide it in half. Cover one half with lightly oiled clear film (plastic wrap). Divide the remaining piece into eight equal portions.

6 Take each portion in turn and use your hands to roll it into a smooth ball. Lightly oil two baking sheets.

7 Place the eight dough balls on one of the prepared baking sheets. Cover them with oiled clear film and leave in a warm place to rise for about 30 minutes, or until doubled in size.

8 Roll the remaining dough out to a thickness of 1cm/½in. Cut into circles using a 7.5cm/3in plain cutter. Then make the dough circles into rings using a 4cm/1½in plain cutter.

9 Place the rings on the remaining baking sheet, cover them with oiled clear film and leave them in a warm place for about 30 minutes, or until doubled in size.

10 Heat the oil for deep-frying to 180°C/350°F, or until a cube of dried bread, added to the oil, turns golden brown in 30–60 seconds. Add the doughnuts, three or four at a time.

11 Cook the doughnuts for about 4–5 minutes, or until they are golden. Remove from the oil using a slotted spoon and drain on kitchen paper.

VARIATION

Make oblong shaped doughnuts and split almost in half lengthways once cold. Fill with whipped cream and your favourite jam.

12 Toss the round doughnuts in caster sugar and the ring doughnuts in a mixture of caster sugar and ground cinnamon. Set aside to cool.

13 Heat the jam and lemon juice in a small pan until warm, stirring to combine. Leave to cool, then spoon the mixture into a piping (pastry) bag fitted with a small plain nozzle.

14 When the round doughnuts have cooled, use a skewer to make a small hole in each. Insert the piping nozzle and squeeze a little of the jam mixture into each doughnut.

MARZIPAN AND ALMOND TWISTS

If you like almonds, you'll love these. Amaretto liqueur, marzipan and flaked almonds make up a triple whammy.

90ml/6 tbsp water
1 egg
60ml/4 tbsp Amaretto liqueur
350g/12oz/3 cups unbleached white
bread flour
30ml/2 tbsp skimmed milk powder
(non fat dry milk)
40g/1½oz/3 tbsp caster (superfine) sugar
2.5ml/½ tsp salt
50g/2oz/¼ cup butter, melted
7.5ml/1½ tsp easy-blend (rapid-rise)
dried yeast
115g/4oz/1 cup ground almonds
50g/2oz/½ cup icing
(confectioners') sugar
2–3 drops of almond essence (extract)
1 egg, separated
10ml/2 tsp milk
flaked (sliced) almonds, for sprinkling

MAKES 9

1 Pour the water, egg and Amaretto into the bread machine pan. If the instructions for your machine specify that the yeast is to be placed in the pan first, reverse the order in which you add the liquid and dry ingredients.

2 Sprinkle over the flour, ensuring that it covers the liquid. Add the skimmed milk powder. Place the sugar, salt and butter in separate corners of the bread pan. Make a small indent in the centre of the flour (but not down as far as the liquid) and pour the easy-blend dried yeast into the hollow.

3 Set the bread machine to the dough setting; use basic dough setting (if available). Press Start. Lightly grease two baking sheets and set aside.

4 Make the marzipan filling. Mix the ground almonds, icing sugar, almond essence, egg white and 15ml/3 tsp water in a bowl and set aside. In a separate bowl, beat the egg yolk with 10ml/2 tsp water.

5 When the dough cycle has finished, remove the dough from the machine and place it on a lightly floured surface. Knock it back (punch it down) gently and then roll it out into a 45 × 23cm/18 × 9in rectangle. Cut this in half lengthways to make two 23cm/9in squares.

6 Spread the filling over one of the squares to cover it completely. Brush some beaten egg yolk mixture over the remaining square and place it egg side down on top of the marzipan filling.

7 Cut nine strips, each 2.5cm/1in wide. Cut a lengthways slit near the end of one of the strips. Twist the strip, starting from the uncut end, then pass the end through the slit and seal the ends together, with egg mixture. Repeat with the remaining strips.

8 Place the twists on the baking sheets and cover with oiled clear film (plastic wrap). Leave in a warm place to rise for 30 minutes or until doubled in size.

9 Meanwhile, preheat the oven to 200°C/400°F/Gas 6. Mix the remaining egg yolk mixture with the milk and brush the mixture over the twists to glaze. Sprinkle with a few flaked almonds and bake for 12–15 minutes, or until golden. Turn out on to a wire rack to cool.

COCONUT MILK SUGAR BUNS

A hint of coconut flavours these spiral-shaped rolls. Serve them warm or cold with butter and preserves.

1 Pour the coconut milk, milk, egg and vanilla essence into the bread machine pan. If the instructions for your bread machine specify that the yeast is to be placed in the pan first, reverse the order in which you add the liquid and dry ingredients to the pan.

2 Sprinkle over the flour, then the coconut, ensuring that the liquid is completely covered. Add the salt, caster sugar and butter, placing them in separate corners of the bread pan. Make a small indent in the centre of the flour (but not down as far as the liquid) and add the yeast.

3 Set the bread machine to the dough setting; use basic dough setting (if available). Press Start. Then lightly oil two baking sheets.

4 When the dough cycle has finished, remove the dough and place it on a lightly floured surface. Knock it back (punch it down) gently. Divide the dough into 12 equal pieces and cover these with oiled clear film (plastic wrap).

5 Take one piece of dough, leaving the rest covered; roll it into a rope about 38cm/15in long.

115ml/4fl oz/½ cup canned coconut milk
115ml/4fl oz/½ cup milk
1 egg
2.5ml/½ tsp natural vanilla essence (extract)
450g/1lb/4 cups unbleached white bread flour
25g/1oz/⅓ cup desiccated (dry unsweetened shredded) coconut
2.5ml/½ tsp salt
50g/2oz/¼ cup caster (superfine) sugar
40g/1½oz/3 tbsp butter
5ml/1 tsp easy-blend (rapid-rise) dried yeast
50g/2oz/¼ cup butter, melted
30ml/2 tbsp demerara (raw) sugar

MAKES 12

6 Curl the rope into a loose spiral on one of the prepared baking sheets. Tuck the end under to seal. Repeat with the remaining pieces of dough, spacing the spirals well apart.

7 Cover with oiled clear film and leave to rise in a warm place for 30 minutes, or until doubled in size. Preheat the oven to 220°C/425°F/Gas 7.

8 Brush the buns with the melted butter and sprinkle them with the demerara sugar. Bake for 12–15 minutes, or until the buns are golden. Turn out on to a wire rack to cool.

APPLE AND SULTANA DANISH PASTRIES

These Danish pastries are filled with fruit and are beautifully light and flaky.

For the Danish Pastry
1 egg
75ml/5 tbsp milk
225g/8oz/2 cups unbleached white bread flour
15g/½oz/1 tbsp caster (superfine) sugar
2.5ml/½ tsp salt
140g/5oz/⅔ cup butter, softened
7.5ml/1½ tsp easy-blend (rapid-rise) dried yeast

For the Filling
25g/1oz/2 tbsp butter
350g/12oz cooking apples, diced
15ml/1 tbsp cornflour (cornstarch)
25g/1oz/2 tbsp caster (superfine) sugar
30ml/2 tbsp water
5ml/1 tsp lemon juice
25g/1oz/3 tbsp sultanas (golden raisins)

To Finish
1 egg, separated
flaked (sliced) almonds, for sprinkling

MAKES 12

1 Place the egg and milk in the bread pan. Reverse the order in which you add the liquid and dry ingredients if necessary. Sprinkle over the flour, covering the liquid. Add the sugar, salt and 25g/1oz/2 tbsp of the butter in separate corners.

2 Make a shallow indent in the centre of the flour; add the yeast. Set the bread machine to the dough setting; use basic dough setting (if available). Press Start. Lightly oil two baking sheets.

3 Shape the remaining butter into a block 2cm/¾in thick. When the dough cycle has finished, remove the prepared dough and place it on a lightly floured surface. Knock it back (punch it down) gently and then roll it out into a rectangle that is slightly wider than the butter block, and just over twice as long.

4 Place the butter on one half, fold the pastry over it, then seal the edges, using a rolling pin. Roll the butter-filled pastry into a rectangle 2cm/¾in thick, making it twice as long as it is wide. Fold the top third down and the bottom third up, seal the edges, wrap in clear film (plastic wrap) and chill for 15 minutes. Repeat the folding and rolling process twice, giving the pastry a quarter turn each time. Wrap in clear film; chill for 20 minutes.

5 Make the filling. Melt the butter in a pan. Toss the apples, cornflour and sugar in a bowl. Add to the pan and toss.

6 Add the water and lemon juice. Cook over a medium heat for 3–4 minutes, stirring. Stir in the sultanas.

7 Leave the filling to cool. Meanwhile, roll out the pastry into a rectangle measuring 40 × 30cm/16 × 12in. Cut into 10cm/4in squares. Divide the filling among the squares, spreading it over half of each piece of pastry so that when they are folded, they will make rectangles.

8 Brush the pastry edges on each square with the lightly beaten egg white, then fold the pastry over the filling to make a rectangle measuring 10 × 5cm/4 × 2in and press the edges together firmly. Make a few cuts along the long joined edge of each pastry.

9 Place the pastries on the baking sheets, cover them with oiled clear film (plastic wrap) and leave to rise for 30 minutes.

10 Preheat the oven to 200°C/400°F/ Gas 6. Mix the egg yolk with 15ml/1 tbsp water and brush over the pastries. Sprinkle with a few flaked almonds and bake for 15 minutes, or until golden. Transfer to a wire rack to cool.

APRICOT STARS

When in season these light pastries can be decorated with fresh apricots.

1 quantity Danish pastry – see Apple and Sultana Danish Pastries

For the Filling
50g/2oz/½ cup ground almonds
50g/2oz/½ cup icing (confectioners') sugar
1 egg, lightly beaten
12 drained canned apricot halves

For the Glaze
1 egg yolk
30ml/2 tbsp water
60ml/4 tbsp apricot jam

MAKES 12

1 Roll out the pastry into a rectangle measuring 40 × 30cm/16 × 12in. Cut into 10cm/4in squares. On each square, make a 2.5cm/1in diagonal cut from each corner towards the centre. Mix the ground almonds, icing sugar and egg together. Divide the filling among the pastry squares, placing it in the centre.

2 Beat the egg yolk for the glaze with half the water. On each square, fold one corner of each cut section to the centre. Secure with the glaze. Place an apricot half, round side up on top in the centre.

3 Lightly oil two baking sheets. Place the pastries on them and cover with oiled clear film (plastic wrap). Leave them to rise for 30 minutes or until doubled in size. Preheat the oven to 200°C/400°F/Gas 6.

4 Brush the pastries with the remaining egg glaze and bake them for 15 minutes, until golden. While the stars are cooking, heat the apricot jam in a small pan with the remaining water. Transfer the cooked pastries on to a wire rack, brush them with the warm apricot glaze and leave to cool.

CHERRY FOLDOVERS

Danish pastries are filled with a sweet cherry filling spiked with Kirsch.

FOR THE DANISH PASTRY DOUGH
1 egg
75ml/2½fl oz/⅓ cup water
225g/8oz/2 cups unbleached white
bread flour
2.5ml/½ tsp ground cinnamon
15ml/1 tbsp caster (superfine) sugar
2.5ml/½ tsp salt
125g/4½oz/generous ½ cup
butter, softened
7.5ml/1½ tsp easy-blend
(rapid-rise) dried yeast

FOR THE FILLING AND TOPPING
225g/8oz drained pitted morello
cherries in syrup, plus 15ml/1 tbsp
syrup from the jar or can
25g/1oz/2 tbsp caster (superfine) sugar
15ml/1 tbsp cornflour (cornstarch)
30ml/2 tbsp Kirsch
1 egg, separated
30ml/2 tbsp water
30ml/2 tbsp apricot jam

MAKES 12

1 Pour the egg and water into the pan. Reverse the order in which you add the liquid and dry ingredients if necessary.

2 Sprinkle over the flour and cinnamon, covering the liquid. Add the sugar, salt and 25g/1oz/2 tbsp of the butter, placing them in separate corners. Make a shallow indent in the flour; add the yeast. Set the bread machine to the dough setting; use basic or pizza dough setting (if available). Press Start. When the cycle has finished, remove the dough and place on a lightly floured surface. Knock back (punch down) gently, then roll out to a rectangle about 1cm/½in thick.

3 Divide the remaining butter into three and dot one portion over the top two-thirds of the dough, leaving the edges clear. Fold the unbuttered portion of dough over half the buttered area and fold the remaining portion on top. Seal the edges with a rolling pin. Give the dough a quarter turn and repeat the buttering and folding. Wrap in clear film (plastic wrap) and chill for 30 minutes. Repeat the folding and chilling with the remaining butter, then repeat again, this time without any butter. Wrap and chill the dough for 30 minutes.

4 Make the filling. Put the cherries, cherry syrup, caster sugar, cornflour and Kirsch in a pan and toss. Cook over a medium heat for 3–4 minutes, stirring until thickened. Leave to cool.

5 Roll out the dough to a rectangle measuring 40 × 30cm/16 × 12in. Cut into 10cm/4in squares. Place a tablespoon of filling in the middle of each square. Brush one corner of each pastry square with lightly beaten egg white, then bring the opposite corner over to meet it, setting it back slightly to leave some of the cherry filling exposed. Press down to seal.

6 Place the foldovers on lightly greased baking sheets. Cover with oiled clear film and leave to rise for 30 minutes. Preheat the oven to 200°C/400°F/Gas 6.

7 Mix the egg yolk with half the water and brush over the dough. Bake for 15 minutes, or until golden. Mix the jam and remaining water in a pan; heat until warm. Brush over the pastries and turn out on to a wire rack to cool.

GINGER AND RAISIN WHIRLS

Tasty spirals of buttery pastry, studded with dried fruit and crystallized ginger.

1 quantity Danish pastry dough –
see Cherry Foldovers

FOR THE FILLING
40g/1½oz/3 tbsp butter, softened
40g/1½oz/3 tbsp caster (superfine) sugar
2.5ml/½ tsp grated nutmeg
25g/1oz/2 tbsp crystallized
(candied) ginger
25g/1oz/2 tbsp candied orange peel
75g/3oz/½ cup raisins

FOR THE GLAZE AND ICING
1 egg yolk, beaten with 15ml/1 tbsp water
30ml/2 tbsp icing (confectioners')
sugar, sifted
15ml/1 tbsp orange juice

MAKES 12

1 Roll the pastry into a 30 × 23cm/12 × 9in rectangle. Cream the butter, sugar and nutmeg together and spread over the dough. Finely chop the ginger and peel. Sprinkle over the dough with the raisins. Lightly oil two baking sheets.

2 Tightly roll up the dough from one long side, as far as the centre. Repeat with the remaining long side, so the two meet at the centre. Brush the edges where the rolls meet with egg glaze.

3 Cut into 12 slices and place, spaced well apart, on the baking sheets. Cover with oiled clear film (plastic wrap) and leave to rise for 30 minutes.

4 Preheat the oven to 200°C/400°F/Gas 6. Brush the whirls with the egg glaze and bake for 12–15 minutes, or until golden. Turn out on to a wire rack to cool. Mix the icing sugar and orange juice together and use to ice the pastries.

SWEET BREADS AND YEAST CAKES

Fresh fruit-flavoured loaves and rich yeast cakes filled with nuts, dried fruits or chocolate are all part of this diverse range of breads. A bread machine is the perfect tool for mixing and proving the rich doughs of Continental specialities, which are often prepared for special occasions.

BLUEBERRY AND OATMEAL BREAD

*The blueberries add a subtle fruitiness to this loaf, while the oatmeal
contributes texture and a nutty flavour. This is best eaten on the day it is
baked, which shouldn't be a problem.*

SMALL
75ml/5 tbsp water
75ml/5 tbsp milk
1 egg
*325g/11½oz/scant 3 cups unbleached
white bread flour, plus 30ml/2 tbsp for
coating the blueberries*
25g/1oz/¼ cup coarse oatmeal
5ml/1 tsp mixed (apple pie) spice
40g/1½oz/3 tbsp caster (superfine) sugar
2.5ml/½ tsp salt
25g/1oz/2 tbsp butter
5ml/1 tsp easy-blend (rapid-rise) dried yeast
50g/2oz/½ cup blueberries

MEDIUM
110ml/scant 4 fl oz/scant ½ cup water
120ml/4fl oz/½ cup milk
1 egg
*450g/1lb/4 cups unbleached white
bread flour, plus 30ml/2 tbsp for
coating the blueberries*
50g/2oz/½ cup coarse oatmeal
7.5ml/1½ tsp mixed spice
50g/2oz/¼ cup caster sugar
3.5ml/¾ tsp salt
40g/1½oz/3 tbsp butter
7.5ml/1½ tsp easy-blend dried yeast
75g/3oz/¾ cup blueberries

LARGE
140ml/5fl oz/scant ⅔ cup water
150ml/5fl oz/⅔ cup milk
2 eggs
*625g/1lb 6oz/5½ cups unbleached
white bread flour, plus 30ml/2 tbsp for
coating the blueberries*
50g/2oz/½ cup coarse oatmeal
10ml/2 tsp mixed spice
65g/2½oz/5 tbsp caster sugar
3.5ml/¾ tsp salt
50g/2oz/¼ cup butter
10ml/2 tsp easy-blend dried yeast
100g/3½oz/scant 1 cup blueberries

MAKES 1 LOAF

COOK'S TIP
Use the light crust setting if your
bread machine produces a rich, fairly
dark crust in a sweet loaf.

1 Pour the water, milk and egg(s) into
the bread machine pan. If the
instructions for your machine specify
that the yeast is to be placed in the pan
first, reverse the order in which you add
the liquid and dry ingredients.

2 Sprinkle over the flour, ensuring it
covers the liquid. Add the oatmeal and
spice. Add the sugar, salt and butter in
separate corners. Make a small indent in
the centre of the flour (but not down as
far as the liquid) and add the yeast.

3 Set the bread machine to the basic/
normal setting, with raisin setting (if
available), medium crust. Press Start.
Toss the berries with the extra flour to
coat. Add to the dough when the
machine beeps, or after the first kneading.

4 Remove the bread from the pan at the
end of the baking cycle and turn out on
to a wire rack to cool.

CRANBERRY AND ORANGE BREAD

The distinctive tart flavour of cranberries is intensified when these American fruits are dried. They combine well here with orange rind and pecan nuts.

1 Pour the water, orange juice and egg(s) into the bread machine pan. If the instructions for your machine specify that the yeast is to be placed in the pan first, reverse the order in which you add the liquid and dry ingredients.

2 Sprinkle over the flour, ensuring that it covers the water. Add the skimmed milk powder. Place the sugar, salt and butter in separate corners of the bread pan. Make a small indent in the centre of the flour (but not down as far as the liquid) and add the yeast.

3 Set the bread machine to the basic/normal setting, with raisin setting (if available), medium crust. Press Start. Add the orange rind, cranberries and pecan nuts when the machine beeps, or after the first kneading.

4 Remove the bread from the pan at the end of the baking cycle and turn out on to a wire rack. Mix the orange juice and caster sugar in a small pan. Heat, stirring, until the sugar dissolves, then boil until syrupy. Brush the syrup over the loaf and leave to cool.

SMALL
70ml/2½ fl oz/scant 5 tbsp water
80ml/scant 3 fl oz/⅓ cup orange juice
1 egg
375g/13oz/3¼ cups unbleached white bread flour
15ml/1 tbsp skimmed milk powder (non fat dry milk)
40g/1½oz/3 tbsp caster (superfine) sugar
2.5ml/½ tsp salt
25g/1oz/2 tbsp butter
5ml/1 tsp easy-blend (rapid-rise) dried yeast
10ml/2 tsp grated orange rind
40g/1½oz/⅓ cup dried cranberries
25g/1oz/¼ cup pecan nuts, chopped

MEDIUM
120ml/4fl oz/½ cup water
120ml/4fl oz/½ cup orange juice
1 egg
500g/1lb 2oz/4½ cups unbleached white bread flour
30ml/2 tbsp skimmed milk powder
50g/2oz/¼ cup caster sugar
3.5ml/¾ tsp salt
40g/1½oz/3 tbsp butter
7.5ml/1½ tsp easy-blend dried yeast
15ml/1 tbsp grated orange rind
50g/2oz/scant ½ cup dried cranberries
40g/1½oz/3 tbsp pecan nuts, chopped

LARGE
140ml/5fl oz/scant ⅔ cup water
150ml/5fl oz/⅔ cup orange juice
2 eggs
675g/1½lb/6 cups unbleached white bread flour
45ml/3 tbsp skimmed milk powder
65g/2½oz/5 tbsp caster sugar
5ml/1 tsp salt
50g/2oz/¼ cup butter
7.5ml/1½ tsp easy-blend dried yeast
20ml/4 tsp grated orange rind
75g/3oz/¾ cup dried cranberries
50g/2oz/½ cup pecan nuts, chopped

FOR GLAZING
30ml/2 tbsp each fresh orange juice and caster sugar

MAKES 1 LOAF

THREE CHOCOLATE BREAD

If you like chocolate, you'll adore this bread. The recipe suggests three specific types of chocolate, but you can combine your own favourites.

COOK'S TIP

Gradually add the chocolate to the bread machine pan, making sure that it is mixing into the dough before adding more.

1 Pour the water into the bread pan and add the egg(s). If necessary for your machine, reverse the order in which you add the liquid and dry ingredients.

2 Sprinkle over the flour, ensuring that it covers the water. Add the sugar, salt and butter, placing them in separate corners of the bread pan. Make a small indent in the centre of the flour; add the easy-blend dried yeast.

3 Set the bread machine to the basic/normal setting, with raisin setting (if available), medium crust. Press Start. Coarsely chop all the chocolate (it is not necessary to keep them separate). Add when the machine beeps, or after the first kneading (see Cook's Tip).

4 Remove the bread at the end of the baking cycle and turn out on to a wire rack to cool.

LEMON AND MACADAMIA BREAD

—

Originally from Australia, macadamia nuts were introduced into California and Hawaii about 50 years ago and are now very popular. Their buttery taste combines well with the tangy flavour of the lemon rind and yogurt in this delicious bread.

1 Pour the egg(s), yogurt and milk into the pan. If necessary, reverse the order of adding the wet and dry ingredients.

2 Sprinkle over the flour, ensuring that it covers the water. Add the sugar, salt and butter, placing them in separate corners of the bread pan. Make a small indent in the flour (but not down as far as the liquid) and add the yeast.

3 Set the bread machine to the basic/normal setting, with raisin setting (if available), medium crust. Press Start. Add the nuts and lemon rind when the machine beeps, or after the first kneading finishes.

4 Remove the lemon and macadamia bread from the bread pan at the end of the baking cycle and turn out on to a wire rack to cool.

SMALL
1 egg
125ml/4½fl oz/generous ½ cup
lemon yogurt
60ml/4 tbsp milk
375g/13oz/3¼ cups unbleached white
bread flour
40g/1½oz/3 tbsp caster (superfine) sugar
2.5ml/½ tsp salt
25g/1oz/2 tbsp butter
5ml/1 tsp easy-blend (rapid-rise)
dried yeast
25g/1oz/¼ cup macadamia
nuts, chopped
10ml/2 tsp grated lemon rind

MEDIUM
1 egg
175ml/6fl oz/¾ cup lemon yogurt
115ml/4fl oz/½ cup milk
500g/1lb 2oz/4½ cups unbleached
white bread flour
50g/2oz/¼ cup caster sugar
3.5ml/¾tsp salt
40g/1½oz/3 tbsp butter
7.5ml/1½ tsp easy-blend dried yeast
40g/1½oz/⅓ cup macadamia
nuts, chopped
15ml/1 tbsp grated lemon rind

LARGE
2 eggs
200ml/7fl oz/⅞ cup lemon yogurt
115ml/4fl oz/½ cup milk
675g/1½lb/6 cups unbleached white
bread flour
65g/2½oz/5 tbsp caster sugar
5ml/1 tsp salt
50g/2oz/¼ cup butter
7.5ml/1½ tsp easy-blend dried yeast
50g/2oz/½ cup macadamia
nuts, chopped
20ml/4 tsp grated lemon rind

MAKES 1 LOAF

COOK'S TIP
Select light crust setting if your bread machine tends to produce a rich crust when you make a sweet bread.

RUM AND RAISIN LOAF

*Juicy raisins, plumped up with dark rum, flavour this tea-time loaf.
It's more than good enough to serve just as it is, but slices can also be
lightly toasted and buttered to ring the changes.*

SMALL
75g/3oz/generous ½ cup raisins
22ml/1½ tbsp dark rum
1 egg
140ml/5fl oz/⅝ cup milk
350g/12oz/3 cups unbleached white
bread flour
1.5ml/¼ tsp ground ginger
25g/1oz/2 tbsp caster (superfine) sugar
2.5ml/½ tsp salt
40g/1½oz/3 tbsp butter
5ml/1 tsp easy-blend (rapid-rise)
dried yeast
10ml/2 tsp clear honey, warmed

MEDIUM
90g/3¼oz/⅔ cup raisins
30ml/2 tbsp dark rum
1 egg
240ml/8½fl oz/generous 1 cup milk
500g/1lb 2oz/4½ cups unbleached
white bread flour
2.5ml/½ tsp ground ginger
40g/1½oz/3 tbsp caster sugar
3.5ml/¾ tsp salt
50g/2oz/¼ cup butter
7.5ml/1½ tsp easy-blend dried yeast
15ml/1 tbsp clear honey, warmed

LARGE
115g/4oz/⅔ cup raisins
45ml/3 tbsp dark rum
2 eggs, lightly beaten
290ml/½pint/1¼ cups milk
675g/1½lb/6 cups unbleached white
bread flour
5ml/1 tsp ground ginger
50g/2oz/¼ cup caster sugar
5ml/1 tsp salt
65g/2½oz/5 tbsp butter
7.5ml/1½ tsp easy-blend dried yeast
15ml/1 tbsp clear honey, warmed

MAKES 1 LOAF

1 Place the raisins and rum in a small bowl and leave to soak for 2 hours, or longer if you can. Add the egg(s) and milk to the bread machine pan. If necessary for your machine, reverse the order in which you add the liquid and dry ingredients.

2 Sprinkle over the flour, ensuring that it covers the liquid completely. Add the ground ginger. Add the caster sugar, salt and butter, placing them in separate corners of the bread machine pan. Make a small indent in the centre of the flour (but not down as far as the liquid) and pour in the dried yeast.

3 Set the bread machine to the basic/normal setting, with raisin setting (if available), medium crust. Press Start. Add the raisins when the machine beeps to add extra ingredients, or after the first kneading.

4 Remove the bread at the end of the baking cycle and turn out on to a wire rack. Brush the top with honey and leave the loaf to cool.

MANGO AND BANANA BREAD

*Tropical fruit juice, fresh banana and dried mango give this light-textured
loaf its Caribbean flavour.*

1 Pour the fruit juice and buttermilk
into the bread machine pan. Add the
mashed banana(s) to the bread pan,
with the honey. If necessary for your
machine, reverse the order in which you
add the liquid and dry ingredients.

2 Sprinkle over the flour, ensuring that
it covers the liquid. Place the salt and
butter in separate corners of the bread
pan. Make a shallow indent in the centre
of the flour and add the yeast.

3 Set the bread machine to the basic/
normal setting, with raisin setting (if
available), medium crust. Press Start.

4 Add the chopped mango pieces when
the machine beeps to add extra
ingredients, or 5 minutes before the
end of the kneading cycle.

5 Remove the bread from the pan at the
end of the baking cycle and turn out on
to a wire rack to cool.

SMALL
30ml/2 tbsp orange and mango juice
*150ml/generous 5fl oz/scant ⅔ cup
buttermilk*
*150g/5oz/1 medium banana, peeled
and mashed*
30ml/2 tbsp clear honey
*350g/12oz/3 cups unbleached white
bread flour*
5ml/1 tsp salt
25g/1oz/2 tbsp butter
*5ml/1 tsp easy-blend (rapid-rise)
dried yeast*
25g/1oz/¼ cup dried mango, chopped

MEDIUM
*60ml/2fl oz/¼ cup orange and
mango juice*
200ml/7fl oz/⅞ cup buttermilk
*175g/6oz/1 large banana, peeled
and mashed*
45ml/3 tbsp clear honey
*500g/1lb 2oz/4½ cups unbleached
white bread flour*
5ml/1 tsp salt
40g/1½oz/3 tbsp butter
5ml/1 tsp easy-blend dried yeast
40g/1½oz/⅓ cup dried mango, chopped

LARGE
*60ml/2fl oz/¼ cup orange and
mango juice*
260ml/9fl oz/1⅛ cups buttermilk
*300g/10½oz/2 medium bananas,
peeled and mashed*
60ml/4 tbsp clear honey
*675g/1½lb/6 cups unbleached white
bread flour*
7.5ml/1½ tsp salt
50g/2oz/¼ cup butter
7.5ml/1½ tsp easy-blend dried yeast
50g/2oz/½ cup dried mango, chopped

MAKES 1 LOAF

COOK'S TIP
Select ripe bananas if you can for
this recipe, as they are softer
and easier to mash.

150ml/5fl oz/⅔ cup water
1 egg
75g/3oz/¾ cup grated tart green
eating apple
450g/1lb/4 cups unbleached white
bread flour
30ml/2 tbsp skimmed milk powder
(non fat dry milk)
50g/2oz/¼ cup caster (superfine) sugar
40g/1½oz/3 tbsp butter, melted
7.5ml/1½ tsp easy-blend (rapid-rise)
dried yeast
225g/8oz cherries, pitted
225g/8oz white almond paste, grated
5ml/1 tsp ground cinnamon

For the Topping
beaten egg white
15ml/1 tbsp demerara (raw) sugar
30ml/2 tbsp flaked (sliced) almonds

MAKES 1 CAKE

1 Pour the water and egg into the bread machine pan. Sprinkle over the grated apple. If the instructions for your machine specify that the yeast is to be placed in the pan first, simply reverse the order in which you add the liquid and dry ingredients.

2 Sprinkle over the flour, ensuring that it covers the water, egg and apple completely. Add the skimmed milk powder then add the sugar and butter, placing them in separate corners of the bread pan.

3 Make a small indent in the centre of the flour (but not down as far as the liquid underneath) and pour the easy-blend dried yeast into the hollow.

AUSTRIAN COFFEE CAKE

This attractive cake is layered with marzipan and fresh cherries and has just a hint of cinnamon and apple. It is a rich cake, perfect with freshly made coffee, or try it warm as a tasty dessert, served with cream, crème fraîche or yogurt.

4 Set the bread machine to the dough setting; use basic dough setting (if available). Press Start.

5 When the dough cycle has finished, remove the dough from the machine and place it on a lightly floured surface. Knock it back (punch it down) gently, then roll it out to form a 40cm/16in square.

6 Arrange the cherries on top and then sprinkle the grated almond paste and ground cinnamon over the fruit.

7 Carefully roll the dough up, as you would when making a Swiss (jelly) roll, then gently roll and stretch the sausage shape until it is 55cm/22in long. Twist the roll into a loose coil and place in a 23cm/9in non-stick springform cake tin (pan).

COOK'S TIP
Try this cake layered with thick slices of fresh apricots or plums when cherries are out of season.

8 Cover the tin with lightly oiled clear film (plastic wrap) and leave in a warm place for about 30–45 minutes, to allow the dough to rise. Meanwhile, preheat the oven to 190°C/375°F/Gas 5.

9 Brush the top of the risen dough with egg white and sprinkle with demerara sugar and flaked almonds.

10 Bake for 30–35 minutes, or until the cake is golden and well risen. Let it cool for a few minutes in the tin, then transfer the cake to a wire rack to cool. Serve warm or cold, cut into wedges.

85ml/3fl oz/⅓ cup milk
1 egg
*225g/8oz/2 cups unbleached white
bread flour*
2.5ml/½ tsp salt
25g/1oz/2 tbsp caster (superfine) sugar
25g/1oz/2 tbsp butter, melted
*5ml/1 tsp easy-blend (rapid-rise)
dried yeast*
icing (confectioners') sugar, to dust

FOR THE FILLING
120ml/4fl oz/½ cup single (light) cream
2 eggs
25g/1oz/2 tbsp caster (superfine) sugar
2.5ml/½ tsp freshly grated nutmeg
3 pears, peeled, halved and cored
50g/2oz/½ cup redcurrants

SERVES 6–8

SWISS PEAR AND REDCURRANT TART

*Juicy pears and redcurrants in a nutmeg cream custard provide an
unforgettable filling for this Swiss tart.*

1 Pour the milk and egg into the bread machine pan. If the instructions for your bread machine specify it, reverse the order in which you add the liquid and dry ingredients.

2 Sprinkle over the flour, ensuring that it covers the liquid completely. Add the salt, sugar and butter, placing them in separate corners of the bread pan. Make a small indent in the centre of the flour (but not down as far as the liquid) and add the yeast.

3 Set the bread machine to the dough setting; use basic dough setting (if available). Press Start. Lightly oil a 25cm/10in pizza pan, shallow pie pan or flan tin.

4 When the dough cycle has finished, remove the dough from the machine and place it on a lightly floured surface. Knock it back (punch it down) gently.

5 Roll out the dough to a 28cm/11in round. Place it in the oiled pizza pan or pie or flan tin. With your fingers, press the dough outwards and upwards so that it covers the base and sides of the tin evenly. Then preheat the oven to 190°C/375°F/Gas 5.

6 Make the filling by beating the cream with the eggs, sugar and nutmeg in a bowl. Pour it into the dough-lined tin, then arrange the pears on top, placing them cut side down. Sprinkle the redcurrants in the centre.

7 Bake the tart for 35–40 minutes, or until the filling has set and the crust is golden. Let it cool for a few minutes in the tin, then sprinkle it with sugar. Cut it into wedges and serve immediately.

APRICOT AND VANILLA SLICES

Fresh apricots are perfect for these fruit slices, but there's no need to deny yourself when they are out of season. Just use well-drained canned ones.

115ml/4fl oz/½ cup water
225g/8oz/2 cups unbleached white
bread flour
2.5ml/½ tsp salt
25g/1oz/2 tbsp caster
(superfine) sugar
25g/1oz/2 tbsp butter, melted
5ml/1 tsp easy-blend (rapid-rise)
dried yeast

FOR THE FILLING
40g/1½oz/3 tbsp caster
(superfine) sugar
15ml/1 tbsp cornflour (cornstarch)
140g/5oz/⅔ cup mascarpone cheese
175g/6oz/¾ cup curd
(farmer's) cheese
2 eggs, lightly beaten
2.5ml/½ tsp vanilla essence (extract)
30ml/2 tbsp apricot conserve
9 apricots, halved and stoned (pitted)

MAKES ABOUT 14

1 Pour the water into the bread machine pan. If the instructions for your bread machine specify that the yeast is to be placed in the pan first, simply reverse the order in which you add the liquid and dry ingredients.

2 Sprinkle over the flour, ensuring that it covers the water. Add the salt, sugar and butter, placing them in separate corners of the bread pan.

3 Make a small indent in the centre of the flour (but not down as far as the liquid underneath) and add the yeast.

4 Set the bread machine to the dough setting; use basic dough setting (if available). Press Start. Then lightly oil a 33 × 20cm/13 × 8in Swiss (jelly) roll tin (pan).

5 When the dough cycle has finished, remove the dough from the machine and place it on a lightly floured surface.

6 Knock the dough back (punch it down) gently, then roll out to a rectangle, measuring 35 × 23cm/14 × 9in. Lift it on to the Swiss roll tin. Using your fingers, press the dough outwards and upwards so that it covers the base and sides of the tin evenly. Cover with oiled clear film (plastic wrap). Set aside.

7 Preheat the oven to 200°C/400°F/ Gas 6. Make the filling. Mix the sugar and cornflour in a cup or small bowl. Put the mascarpone and curd cheese into a large mixing bowl and beat in the sugar mixture, followed by the eggs and vanilla essence.

8 Spread the apricot conserve evenly over the base of the dough, then spread the vanilla mixture on top. Arrange the apricots over the filling, placing them cut-side down.

9 Bake for 25–30 minutes, or until the filling is set and the dough has risen and is golden. Leave to cool slightly before cutting into slices. Serve warm.

PEACH STREUSELKUCHEN

This peach-filled German yeast cake is finished with a crunchy almond and cinnamon topping which is quite irresistible.

100ml/3½fl oz/7 tbsp milk
1 egg
250g/9oz/2¼ cups unbleached white bread flour
2.5ml/½ tsp salt
40g/1½oz/3 tbsp caster (superfine) sugar
25g/1oz/2 tbsp butter, melted
5ml/1 tsp easy-blend (rapid-rise) dried yeast
4 peaches, halved and stoned (pitted)

For the Topping
75g/3oz/¾ cup plain (all-purpose) flour
40g/1½oz/⅓ cup ground almonds
50g/2oz/¼ cup butter, diced and softened
40g/1½oz/4 tbsp caster sugar
5ml/1 tsp ground cinnamon

Serves 8

1 Pour the milk and egg into the bread pan. If the instructions for your bread machine specify that the yeast should go in first, reverse the order of wet and dry ingredients.

2 Sprinkle over the flour, ensuring that it covers the milk and egg completely. Then add the salt, sugar and butter, placing them in three separate corners of the bread pan. Make a small indent in the centre of the flour (but not down as far as the liquid) and add the easy-blend dried yeast.

3 Set the bread machine to the dough setting; use basic dough setting (if available). Press Start. Lightly oil a 25cm/10in springform cake tin (pan).

4 When the dough cycle has finished, remove the dough from the pan and place it on a lightly floured surface. Knock it back (punch it down) gently, then roll it out to fit the tin. Ease it into position.

5 Slice the peaches thickly and arrange them on top of the dough. Next, make the topping. Rub the flour, ground almonds and butter together until the mixture resembles coarse breadcrumbs. Stir in the caster sugar and cinnamon. Sprinkle the topping over the peaches.

6 Cover the dough with lightly oiled clear film (plastic wrap) and leave in a warm place for about 20–25 minutes, to rise slightly. Meanwhile, preheat the oven to 190°C/375°F/Gas 5.

7 Bake the cake for 25–30 minutes, or until evenly golden. Leave it to cool in the tin for a few minutes and serve warm, or turn out on to a wire rack to allow to cool completely.

BAVARIAN PLUM CAKE

As this bakes, the juices from the plums trickle through to the base, making a deliciously succulent, fruity cake. Serve it with coffee or as a dessert with crème fraîche or ice cream.

1 Pour the milk into the bread machine pan and add the egg. If the instructions for your machine specify that the yeast is to be placed in the pan first, simply reverse the order in which you add the liquid and dry ingredients.

VARIATION
Replace the plums with apple wedges or nectarine slices. Use dessert apples as cooking apples will be too tart. Allow four to five depending on their size. Sprinkle the top with demerara (raw) sugar 5 minutes before the end of baking, and return to the oven.

2 Sprinkle over the flour, ensuring that it covers the milk and egg completely. Add the ground cinnamon. Place the salt, sugar and butter in separate corners of the bread pan.

90ml/6 tbsp milk
1 egg
225g/8oz/2 cups unbleached white bread flour
5ml/1 tsp ground cinnamon
2.5ml/½ tsp salt
40g/1½oz/3 tbsp caster (superfine) sugar
25g/1oz/2 tbsp butter, melted
5ml/1 tsp easy-blend (rapid-rise) dried yeast
675g/1½lb plums
icing (confectioners') sugar, for dusting

SERVES 8

3 Make a small indent in the centre of the flour (but not down as far as the liquid) and add the yeast.

4 Set the bread machine to the dough setting; use basic dough setting (if available). Press Start. Lightly oil a 27 × 18cm/10½ × 7in rectangular baking tin (pan) that is about 4cm/1½in deep.

5 When the dough cycle has finished, remove the dough and place it on a lightly floured surface. Knock it back (punch it down) gently, then roll it out to fit the tin. Ease it into position.

6 Cut the plums into quarters and remove the stones (pits). Arrange on the dough, so that they overlap slightly. Cover with lightly oiled clear film (plastic wrap) and leave in a warm place for 30–45 minutes, to rise. Meanwhile, preheat the oven to 190°C/375°F/Gas 5.

7 Bake the cake for 30–35 minutes, or until golden and well risen. Dust with icing sugar and serve warm.

FINNISH FESTIVE WREATH

This traditional sweet bread, enriched with egg and delicately scented with
saffron and cardamom, is called pulla in its native Finland.
For festive occasions, elaborately shaped versions of the bread, like this
pretty wreath, are prepared.

5ml/1 tsp saffron threads
200ml/7fl oz/⅞ cup milk
2 eggs
500g/1lb 2oz/4½ cups unbleached
white bread flour
5ml/1 tsp ground cardamom seeds
2.5ml/½ tsp salt
50g/2oz/¼ cup caster (superfine) sugar
55g/2oz/¼ cup butter, melted
5ml/1 tsp easy-blend (rapid-rise)
dried yeast
1 egg yolk, to glaze
15ml/1 tbsp water, to glaze

FOR THE TOPPING
45ml/3 tbsp flaked (sliced) almonds
40g/1½oz/3 tbsp granulated sugar
15ml/1 tbsp rum
15ml/1 tbsp candied lime peel,
chopped (optional)

SERVES 8–10

VARIATION
Instead of candied lime peel, other
ingredients can be used for the
topping, if preferred. Try angelica or
candied orange peel instead. Glacé
fruits such as cherries or peaches are
also good, or you could use dried
mango or dried pear.

1 Place the saffron threads in a small
mixing bowl. Heat half of the milk in a
small pan, pour it over the saffron and
leave to infuse (steep) until the milk is
at room temperature.

2 Pour the saffron milk into the bread
machine pan, then add the remaining
milk and the eggs. However, if the
instructions for your bread machine
specify that the yeast is to be placed in
the bread pan first, simply reverse the
order in which you add the liquid and
dry ingredients.

3 Sprinkle over the flour, ensuring that
it covers the liquid completely, then add
the cardamom seeds.

4 Add the salt, caster sugar and butter,
placing them in separate corners of the
bread pan. Make a shallow indent in the
centre of the flour (but not down as far
as the milk and eggs) and add the easy-
blend dried yeast.

5 Set the bread machine to the dough
setting; use basic dough setting (if
available). Press Start. Lightly oil a
baking sheet.

6 When the dough cycle has finished,
remove the dough from the bread
machine pan and place it on a surface
that has been lightly floured. Knock the
dough back gently, then divide it into
three equal (punch it down) pieces.

7 Roll each piece of dough into a rope,
about 65cm/26in long. Place the ropes
lengthways, next to each other, to begin
the braid.

8 Starting from the centre, braid the
pieces together, working towards
yourself and from left to right. Turn the
dough around and repeat the braiding
process. Bring the ends of the plait
together to form a circular wreath and
pinch to seal.

9 Place the wreath on the baking sheet.
Cover with lightly oiled clear film
(plastic wrap) and leave for 45–60
minutes, or until almost doubled in size.

10 Meanwhile, preheat the oven to
190°C/375°F/Gas 5. Make the glaze by
mixing the egg yolk and water in a bowl.
In a separate bowl, mix the almonds,
sugar, rum and peel for the topping.
Brush the glaze over the loaf and
sprinkle the almond mixture on top.

11 Bake for 20 minutes, then reduce the
oven temperature to 180°C/350°F/Gas 4
and bake for 10–15 minutes more, or
until the wreath is golden and well risen.
Turn out on to a wire rack to cool.

30ml/2 tbsp instant coffee powder
140ml/5fl oz/scant ⅔ cup milk
1 egg, plus 2 egg yolks
*400g/14oz/3½ cups unbleached white
bread flour*
15ml/1 tbsp cocoa powder (unsweetened)
5ml/1 tsp ground cinnamon
2.5ml/½ tsp salt
75g/3oz/6 tbsp caster (superfine) sugar
75g/3oz/6 tbsp butter, softened
*7.5ml/1½ tsp easy-blend (rapid-rise)
dried yeast*
*115g/4oz plain Continental chocolate,
coarsely chopped*
*45ml/3 tbsp pine nuts, lightly toasted
melted butter, for glazing*

SERVES 8–10

COOK'S TIP
The dough for this bread is quite
rich and may require a longer rising
time than that provided for by your
bread machine. Check the dough at
the end of the dough cycle. If it does
not appear to have risen very much
in the bread pan, leave the dough in
the machine, with the machine
switched off and the lid closed, for a
further 30 minutes to allow it to rise
to the required degree.

1 In a small bowl, dissolve the coffee in
30ml/2tbsp hot water. Pour the mixture
into the bread machine pan and then
add the milk, egg and egg yolks. If the
instructions for your bread machine
specify that the yeast is to be placed in
the pan first, simply reverse the order in
which you add the liquid and dry
ingredients.

MOCHA PANETTONE

*Panettone is the traditional Italian Christmas bread from Milan. This tall
domed loaf is usually filled with dried fruits; for a change try this coffee-
flavoured bread studded with chocolate and pine nuts.*

2 Sift the flour and cocoa powder
together. Sprinkle the mixture over the
liquid, ensuring that it is completely
covered. Add the ground cinnamon.
Place the salt, sugar and butter in
separate corners of the bread pan. Make
a small indent in the centre of the flour
(but not down as far as the liquid) and
add the yeast.

3 Set the bread machine to the dough
setting; use basic dough setting (if
available). Press Start. Lightly oil a
15cm/6in deep cake tin (pan) or soufflé
dish. Using a double sheet of baking
parchment that is 7.5cm/3in wider than
the depth of the tin or dish, line the
container so that the excess paper
creates a collar.

4 When the dough cycle has finished,
remove the dough from the machine and
place it on a lightly floured surface. Knock
it back (punch it down) gently. Gently
knead in the chocolate and pine nuts
and shape the dough into a ball. Cover it
with lightly oiled clear film (plastic
wrap) and leave it to rest for 5 minutes.

5 Shape the dough into a plump round
loaf which has the same diameter as the
cake tin or soufflé dish, and place in the
base of the container. Cover with oiled
clear film and leave the dough to rise in
a slightly warm place for 45–60 minutes,
or until the dough has almost reached
the top of the greaseproof paper collar.

6 Meanwhile, preheat the oven to 200°C/
400°F/Gas 6. Brush the top of the loaf
with the melted butter and cut a deep
cross in the top. Bake the bread for
about 10 minutes.

7 Reduce the oven temperature to
180°C/350°F/Gas 4 and continue to bake
the panettone for 30–35 minutes more,
or until it is evenly golden all over and
a metal skewer inserted in the centre
comes out clean without any crumb
sticking to it.

8 Leave the panettone in the tin or dish
for 5–10 minutes, then turn out on to a
wire rack and leave it until it is quite
cold before slicing.

STRAWBERRY CHOCOLATE SAVARIN

This light spongy cake is soaked in a wine and brandy syrup before being filled with succulent fresh strawberries to make an exquisite dessert.

100ml/3½fl oz/7 tbsp milk
4 eggs
225g/8oz/2 cups unbleached white bread flour
40g/1½oz/3 tbsp cocoa powder (unsweetened)
2.5ml/½ tsp salt
25g/1oz/2 tbsp caster (superfine) sugar
100g/3½oz/7 tbsp butter, melted
5ml/1 tsp easy-blend (rapid-rise) dried yeast
115g/4oz/½ cup granulated sugar
75ml/2½fl oz/scant ⅓ cup white wine
45ml/3 tbsp brandy
physalis and strawberry leaves, to decorate

FOR THE FILLING
150ml/5fl oz/⅔ cup double (heavy) cream, whipped, or crème fraîche
225g/8oz/2 cups strawberries, halved
115g/4oz/1 cup raspberries

SERVES 6–8

VARIATION
The savarin can be filled with other fruits, such as grapes, raspberries, currants, peaches or blackberries. Alternatively, fill with chantilly cream, (slightly sweetened, vanilla flavoured whipped cream) and sprinkle chopped nuts over the top.

1 Pour the milk and eggs into the bread pan. If your machine specifies that the yeast is to be placed in the pan first, reverse the order in which you add the liquid and dry ingredients.

2 Sift the flour and cocoa powder together. Sprinkle the mixture over the liquid in the pan, covering it completely. Place the salt, sugar and butter in separate corners. Make a shallow indent in the centre of the flour; add the yeast.

3 Set the machine to the dough setting; use basic dough setting (if available). Press Start. Lightly oil a 1.5 litre/2½ pint/6¼ cup savarin or ring mould.

4 When the machine has finished mixing the ingredients, leave it on the dough setting for 20 minutes then stop the machine. Pour the dough mixture into the mould, cover with oiled clear film (plastic wrap) and leave in a warm place for 45–60 minutes, or until the dough almost reaches the top of the tin.

5 Meanwhile, preheat the oven to 200°C/400°F/Gas 6. Bake for 25–30 minutes, or until the savarin is golden and well risen. Turn out on to a wire rack to cool, with a plate beneath the rack.

6 Make the syrup. Place the sugar, wine and 75ml/2½fl oz/⅓ cup water in a pan. Heat gently, stirring until the sugar dissolves. Bring to the boil then lower the heat and simmer for 2 minutes. Remove from the heat and stir in the brandy.

7 Spoon the syrup over the savarin. Repeat with any syrup which has collected on the plate. Transfer to a serving plate and leave to cool. To serve, fill the centre with the cream or crème fraîche and top with the strawberries and raspberries. Decorate with physalis and strawberry leaves.

PEACH BRANDY BABAS

These light, delicate sponges are moistened with a syrup flavoured with peach brandy before being filled with whipped cream and fruit. You can vary the flavour of the syrup by using orange or coconut liqueur or dark rum.

1 Pour the milk and eggs into the bread pan. If the instructions for your machine specify that the yeast is to be placed in the pan first, reverse the order in which you add the liquid and dry ingredients to the pan.

2 Sprinkle over the flour, ensuring that it covers the liquid. Add the cinnamon, then place the salt and sugar in separate corners. Make a small indent in the centre of the flour (but not down as far as the liquid) and add the yeast.

3 Set the bread machine to the dough setting; use basic dough setting (if available). Press Start. Lightly oil eight small savarin tins, each with a diameter of 10cm/4in.

4 When the machine has finished mixing the dough, let the dough cycle continue for a further 15 minutes, then stop the machine and scrape the dough into a large measuring jug (cup). Gradually beat in the melted butter.

5 Pour the batter into the prepared tins, half filling them. Cover with oiled clear film (plastic wrap) and leave in a warm place until the batter reaches the tin tops.

6 Meanwhile, preheat the oven to 190°C/375°F/Gas 5. Bake for 20 minutes, or until golden and well risen. Turn out on to a wire rack to cool. Slide a large tray under the rack.

7 To make the syrup for the babas, place the granulated sugar and water in a small pan and heat gently, stirring occasionally, until the sugar has dissolved. Bring to the boil and boil hard for 2 minutes without stirring. Remove the syrup from the heat and stir in the peach brandy. Spoon the syrup over the babas. Then scrape up any syrup which has dripped on to the tray with a spatula and repeat the process until all the syrup is absorbed.

8 When the babas are cold, whip the cream, sugar and vanilla essence in a bowl until the cream just forms soft peaks. Fill the babas with the flavoured cream and decorate them with the fresh fruits of your choice.

100ml/3½fl oz/7 tbsp milk
4 eggs
225g/8oz/2 cups unbleached white bread flour
5ml/1 tsp ground cinnamon
2.5ml/½ tsp salt
25g/1oz/2 tbsp caster (superfine) sugar
5ml/1 tsp easy-blend (rapid-rise) dried yeast
100g/3½oz/7 tbsp butter, melted
115g/4oz/½ cup granulated sugar
150ml/5fl oz/⅔ cup water
90ml/6 tbsp peach brandy

FOR THE DECORATION
150ml/5fl oz/⅔ cup double (heavy) cream
15ml/1 tbsp caster (superfine) sugar
3–4 drops natural vanilla essence (extract)
fresh fruits, to decorate

MAKES 8

MIXED PEEL BRAID

A succulent citrus filling with a hint of ginger provides the pleasant surprise in this attractively braided coffee-time cake.

90ml/6 tbsp milk
1 egg
280g/10oz/2½ cups unbleached white bread flour
5ml/1 tsp mixed (apple pie) spice
2.5ml/½ tsp salt
25g/1oz/2 tbsp caster (superfine) sugar
50g/2oz/¼ cup butter, melted
5ml/1 tsp easy-blend (rapid-rise) dried yeast
115g/4oz/⅔ cup mixed (candied) peel
50g/2oz/⅓ cup sultanas (golden raisins)
25g/1oz/¼ cup walnut pieces, chopped
25g/1oz/2 tbsp chopped glacé (candied) ginger
45ml/3 tbsp three fruit marmalade

FOR THE GLAZE
1 egg yolk
15ml/1 tbsp caster (superfine) sugar
15ml/1 tbsp milk

SERVES 8

1 Pour the milk and egg into the bread machine pan. If necessary for your bread machine, reverse the order of adding the wet and dry ingredients.

2 Sprinkle over the flour to cover the liquid. Add the mixed spice. Put the salt, sugar and butter in separate corners. Make a small indent in the centre of the flour and add the yeast.

3 Set the bread machine to the dough setting; use basic dough setting (if available). Press Start. Lightly oil a baking sheet.

4 When the dough cycle has finished, remove the dough from the machine and place it on a lightly floured surface. Knock it back (punch it down) gently, then roll it out to a 28 × 40cm/11 × 16in rectangle.

5 Make the filling by combining the mixed peel, sultanas, walnuts, ginger and marmalade in a bowl. Spread the mixture lengthways over the middle third of the rolled-out dough, leaving a 2.5cm/1in border at either end. Using a sharp knife, cut the two strips of dough either side of the filling into diagonal strips angled towards you, 2cm/¾in wide.

6 Working from the far end, fold in the end piece of dough, then braid the dough strips over the filling. Tuck in the end to seal. Place the braid on the baking sheet. Cover it with lightly oiled clear film (plastic wrap) and leave in a warm place for 30–45 minutes to rise.

7 Meanwhile, preheat the oven to 200°C/400°F/Gas 6. Make the glaze by mixing the egg yolk, sugar and milk in a bowl. Brush the mixture over the braid. Bake for 10 minutes, then reduce the oven temperature to 190°C/375°F/Gas 5 and bake for 10–15 minutes more, or until the braid is golden and well risen. Turn out on to a wire rack to cool.

HAZELNUT TWIST CAKE

Easy to make yet impressive, this sweet bread consists of layers of ground nuts, twisted through a rich dough, topped with a maple-flavoured icing.

230ml/8fl oz/1 cup water
1 egg
450g/1lb/4 cups unbleached white
bread flour
45ml/3 tbsp skimmed milk powder
(non fat dry milk)
grated rind of 1 orange
2.5ml/½ tsp salt
50g/2oz/¼ cup caster (superfine) sugar
75g/3oz/6 tbsp butter, melted
7.5ml/1½ tsp easy-blend (rapid-rise)
dried yeast
flaked (sliced) almonds or slivered
hazelnuts, to decorate

FOR THE FILLING
115g/4oz/1 cup ground hazelnuts
100g/3½oz/1 cup ground almonds
100g/3½oz/scant ½ cup light
muscovado (brown) sugar
2.5ml/½ tsp freshly grated nutmeg
2 egg whites
15ml/1 tbsp brandy

FOR THE TOPPING
60ml/4 tbsp icing
(confectioners') sugar
15ml/1 tbsp hot water
30ml/2 tbsp natural maple syrup

SERVES 6–8

1 Pour the water and egg into the bread pan. Reverse the order in which you add the wet and dry ingredients if necessary. Sprinkle over the flour, covering the liquid. Add the milk powder and orange rind. Place the salt, sugar and butter in separate corners. Make a shallow indent in the centre of the flour; add the yeast.

2 Set the bread machine to the dough setting; use basic dough setting (if available). Press Start. Lightly oil a 23cm/9in springform ring cake tin (pan).

3 When the dough cycle has finished, place the dough on a lightly floured surface. Knock it back (punch it down) gently, then roll it out to a 65 × 45cm/ 26 × 18in rectangle. Cut the dough in half lengthways.

4 Make the filling by mixing all of the ingredients in a bowl. Divide the filling in half. Spread one portion over each piece of dough, leaving a 1cm/½in clear border along one long edge of each piece.

5 Starting from the other long edge, roll up each piece of dough, Swiss (jelly) roll fashion. Place the two pieces next to each other and twist them together.

6 Brush the ends of the dough rope with a little water. Loop the rope in the prepared springform tin and gently press the ends together to seal.

7 Cover the tin with lightly oiled clear film (plastic wrap) and then leave the dough in a warm place for 30–45 minutes, or until it has risen and is puffy. Preheat the oven to 200°C/400°F/Gas 6.

8 Bake for 30–35 minutes, or until golden and well risen. Leave to cool slightly, then turn out on to a wire rack.

9 Make the icing by mixing the icing sugar, hot water and maple syrup in a bowl. Drizzle over the warm cake. Sprinkle with a few flaked almonds or slivered hazelnuts and leave to cool completely before serving.

MINI BRIOCHE

*Rich yet light, these buttery breads, with their characteristic fluted shape,
can be eaten with both sweet and savoury foods.*

30ml/2 tbsp milk
2 eggs
225g/8oz/2 cups unbleached white
bread flour
2.5ml/½ tsp salt
15ml/1 tbsp caster (superfine) sugar
50g/2oz butter, melted
7.5ml/1½ tsp easy-blend (rapid-rise)
dried yeast
1 egg yolk, to glaze
15ml/1 tbsp milk, to glaze

MAKES 12

COOK'S TIP
This is a rich dough and may need
more than the standard proving time.
If it has not risen very much by the
time the dough programme ends,
leave the dough in the machine for
another 30 minutes, turning off the
machine and leaving the lid shut.

1 Pour the milk and eggs into the bread
machine pan. If the instructions for your
bread machine specify that the yeast is
to be placed in the pan first, simply
reverse the order in which you add the
liquid and dry ingredients.

2 Sprinkle over the flour, ensuring that
it covers the liquid. Add the salt, sugar
and butter, placing them in separate
corners of the bread pan. Make a small
indent in the centre of the flour (but not
down as far as the liquid) and add the
easy-blend dried yeast.

3 Set the bread machine to the dough
setting; use basic dough setting (if
available). Press Start. Lightly oil
12 small brioche moulds.

4 When the dough cycle has finished,
remove from the machine and place on a
floured surface. Knock it back (punch it
down) gently. Slice off a quarter of the
dough, cover with oiled clear film
(plastic wrap) and set aside. Divide the
remaining dough into 12 pieces.

5 Knead each piece of dough into a
small round. Place each round in an
oiled mould. Divide the reserved piece
of dough into 12 and shape into small
pear shapes.

6 To shape each mini brioche, make a
small hole or cut a cross in the top of
each large piece of dough. Place the
pear-shaped pieces of dough on top,
narrow end down. Cover with lightly
oiled clear film and leave in a warm
place for 30–45 minutes, or until well
risen. Meanwhile preheat the oven to
220°C/425°F/Gas 7.

7 Make the glaze by mixing the egg yolk
and milk together. Brush the mixture
over each brioche. Bake for 15 minutes,
or until the brioche are golden and have
risen well. Transfer them to a wire rack
to cool. Serve warm or cold.

LEMON AND PISTACHIO STRUDEL

For a special occasion serve this superb strudel, which is made up of thin layers of dough interleaved with a tasty curd and goat's cheese filling.

1 Pour the milk and egg into the bread machine pan. If the instructions for your bread machine specify that the yeast is to be placed in the pan first, simply reverse the order in which you add the liquid and dry ingredients.

2 Sprinkle over the flour, ensuring that it covers the liquid. Add the salt, sugar and butter, placing them in separate corners of the bread pan. Make a small indent in the centre of the flour (but not down as far as the liquid) and add the easy-blend dried yeast.

3 Set the bread machine to the dough setting; use basic dough setting (if available). Press Start. Then lightly oil a baking sheet.

4 Make the filling. Put both types of cheese, the egg yolks, sugar, lemon rind and vanilla in a bowl. Mix well. Stir in the raisins, pistachios and apricots.

5 When the dough cycle has finished, place the dough on a lightly floured surface. Knock back (punch it down) gently. Roll out to a rectangle 35 × 25cm/14 × 10in.

90ml/6 tbsp milk
1 egg
225g/8oz/2 cups unbleached white bread flour
2.5ml/½ tsp salt
15ml/1 tbsp caster (superfine) sugar
50g/2oz/¼ cup butter
5ml/1 tsp easy-blend (rapid-rise) dried yeast
icing (confectioners') sugar, for dusting

FOR THE FILLING
115g/4oz/½ cup montrachet or soft goat's cheese
115g/4oz/½ cup curd cheese, sieved
2 egg yolks
50g/2oz/¼ cup caster sugar
grated rind of 1 lemon
2.5ml/½ tsp vanilla essence (extract)
50g/2oz/¼ cup raisins
50g/2oz/¼ cup pistachio nuts, peeled
50g/2oz/¼ cup ready-to-eat dried apricots, chopped
50g/2oz/¼ cup butter, melted
50g/2oz/½ cup ground almonds

SERVES 6–8

6 Brush the dough with melted butter and sprinkle with the ground almonds. Spread the cheese filling over, leaving a narrow border around the edges. Fold in the edges along both long sides.

7 Starting from a short side roll up like a Swiss (jelly) roll. Place on the baking sheet, seam side down. Cover with oiled clear film (plastic wrap). Leave to rise for 30 minutes. Preheat the oven to 190°C/375°F/Gas 5.

8 Bake for 25–30 minutes, until golden. Turn out on to a wire rack to cool. Dust with icing sugar and serve warm.

EASTER TEA RING

90ml/6 tbsp milk
1 egg
225g/8oz/2 cups unbleached white
bread flour
2.5ml/½ tsp salt
25g/1oz/2 tbsp caster (superfine) sugar
25g/1oz/2 tbsp butter
5ml/1 tsp easy-blend (rapid-rise)
dried yeast
50g/2oz/½ cup ready-to-eat
dried apricots
15g/½oz/1 tbsp butter
50g/2oz/¼ cup light muscovado
(brown) sugar
7.5ml/1½ tsp ground cinnamon
2.5ml/½ tsp allspice
50g/2oz/⅓ cup sultanas (golden raisins)
milk, for brushing

FOR THE DECORATION
45ml/3 tbsp icing (confectioners')
sugar
15–30ml/1–2 tbsp orange liqueur or
orange juice
pecan nuts and candied fruits

SERVES 8–10

This Easter tea ring is too good to serve just once a year. Bake it as a family weekend treat whenever you feel self-indulgent. Perfect for a mid-morning coffee break or for tea time.

3 Set the bread machine to the dough setting; use basic dough setting (if available). Press Start. Then lightly oil a baking sheet.

4 When the dough cycle has finished, remove the dough from the bread pan. Place it on a surface that has been lightly floured. Knock the dough back (punch it down) gently, then roll it out into a 30 × 45cm/12 × 18in rectangle.

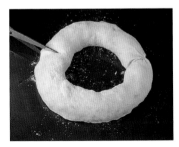

1 Pour the milk and egg into the bread machine pan. If the instructions for your bread machine specify that the yeast is to be placed in the pan first, simply reverse the order in which you add the liquid and dry ingredients.

2 Sprinkle over the flour, ensuring that it covers the liquid. Add the salt, sugar and butter, placing them in separate corners of the bread pan. Make a small indent in the centre of the flour (but not down as far as the liquid) and add the easy-blend dried yeast.

5 Chop the dried apricots into small pieces. Melt the butter for the filling and brush it over the dough. Then sprinkle the dough with the muscovado sugar, ground cinnamon, allspice, sultanas and chopped apricots.

6 Starting from one long edge, roll up the rectangle of dough, as when making a Swiss (jelly) roll. Turn the dough so that the seam is underneath.

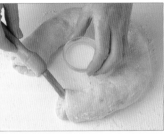

7 Curl the dough into a circle, brush the ends with a little milk and seal. Place on the prepared baking sheet.

8 Using a pair of scissors, snip through the circle at 4cm/1½in intervals, each time cutting two-thirds of the way through the dough. Twist the sections so they start to fall sideways.

9 Cover the ring with lightly oiled clear film (plastic wrap) and leave in a warm place for about 30 minutes, or until the dough is well risen and puffy.

10 Preheat the oven to 200°C/400°F/ Gas 6. Bake the ring for 20–25 minutes, or until golden. Turn out on to a wire rack to cool.

11 While the tea ring is still warm, make the decoration by mixing together the icing sugar and liqueur or orange juice. Drizzle the mixture over the ring, then arrange pecan nuts and candied fruit on top. Cool completely before serving.

VARIATION
There is a vast range of dried fruits available in the supermarkets. Vary the sultanas and apricots; try dried peaches, mango, melon, cherries and raisins, to name a few. Just make sure that the total quantity stays the same as in the recipe.

POLISH BABKA

Vodka is the surprise ingredient in this classic Polish cake, made at Eastertime. The dough is enriched with eggs and flavoured with citrus peel and raisins.

60ml/4 tbsp vodka
2.5ml/½ tsp saffron threads
15ml/1 tbsp grated orange rind
15ml/1 tbsp grated lemon rind
115g/4oz/½ cup butter, softened
75g/3oz/6 tbsp caster (superfine) sugar
3 eggs
30ml/2 tbsp water
400g/14oz/3½ cups unbleached white bread flour
2.5ml/½ tsp salt
10ml/2 tsp easy-blend (rapid-rise) dried yeast
75g/3oz/½ cup raisins
75g/3oz/½ cup dried sour cherries
115g/4oz/1 cup icing (confectioners') sugar
15ml/1 tbsp lemon juice

FOR THE DECORATION
toasted flaked almonds
pared orange rind or candied orange peel

SERVES 8–10

1 Steep the vodka, saffron and citrus rinds together for 30 minutes. Beat the butter and sugar in a bowl until pale and creamy. Tip the saffron mixture into the bread pan, then add the eggs and water. If necessary, reverse the order in which you add the liquid and dry ingredients.

2 Add the flour, covering the liquid. Add the salt in a corner. Make an indent in the flour; add the yeast. Set to the dough setting; use basic raisin dough setting (if available). Press Start.

3 Mix for 5 minutes, then add the creamed butter and sugar mixture.

4 Tip in the raisins and dried sour cherries when the machine beeps, or 5 minutes before the end of the kneading cycle. Lightly oil a brioche tin. When the cycle has finished, remove the dough from the pan and place on a floured surface.

5 Knock back (punch down) gently, and shape into a plump round ball. Place in the prepared tin, cover with lightly oiled clear film (plastic wrap) and leave in a warm place for about 2 hours, or until it has risen almost to the top of the tin.

6 Preheat the oven to 200°C/400°F/Gas 6. Bake the babka for 20 minutes. Reduce the oven temperature to 190°C/375°F/Gas 5 and continue to bake for 15–20 minutes more, until golden.

7 Turn the babka out on to a wire rack to cool. Meanwhile, make the icing. Place the icing sugar in a small bowl and add the lemon juice and 15ml/1 tbsp hot water. Mix well, then drizzle the icing over the cake. Sprinkle over the almonds and pared orange rind or candied orange peel to decorate.

SPICED FRUIT KUGELHOPF

Sultanas steeped in spiced rum flavour this brioche-style bread, which is baked in a special fluted mould with a central funnel.

1 Mix the rum, ginger, cloves, cinnamon stick and nutmeg in a small pan and place over a medium heat until hot, but not bubbling. Remove from the heat, add the sultanas and set aside in the pan for 30 minutes.

2 Pour the milk into the machine pan. Add three of the eggs, then separate the remaining eggs, setting the whites aside, and add the egg yolks to the pan.

3 Remove the cloves and cinnamon from the pan and discard (although the cinnamon stick can be dried for re-use later). Place a sieve over the bread pan and drain the sultanas in it so that the juices fall through into the pan. Set the sultanas aside. If the instructions for your bread machine specify that the yeast is to be placed in the machine pan first, then simply reverse the order in which you add the liquid and dry ingredients to the pan.

4 Sprinkle over the flour, ensuring that it covers the liquid mixture completely. Add the salt and sugar in separate corners of the bread pan. Make a small indent in the centre of the flour (but not down as far as the liquid) and add the easy-blend dried yeast.

5 Set the bread machine to the dough setting; use basic dough setting (if available). Press Start. Mix for 5 minutes, then gradually add the melted butter. Lightly oil a non-stick kugelhopf tin.

6 When the dough cycle has finished, put the dough in a large mixing bowl. In a separate, grease-free bowl, whisk the egg whites to soft peaks. Add the reserved sultanas and cut mixed peel to the dough and fold in, using your hands. Gradually fold in the egg whites to form a soft dough.

7 Spoon the dough into the kugelhopf tin in three or four batches, making sure it is evenly distributed. Cover with lightly oiled clear film (plastic wrap) and leave in a slightly warm place for 1–1½ hours, or until the dough has risen and is almost at the top of the tin.

8 Preheat the oven to 190°C/375°F/Gas 5. Bake the kugelhopf for 50–60 minutes or until it has browned and is firm to the touch. You can cover the surface with baking parchment if it starts to brown too quickly. Turn out on to a wire rack to cool. Dust with icing sugar.

100ml/3½fl oz/7 tbsp dark rum
5ml/1 tsp ground ginger
3 whole cloves
1 cinnamon stick
5ml/1 tsp freshly grated nutmeg
115g/4oz/⅔ cup sultanas
(golden raisins)
30ml/2 tbsp milk
5 eggs
500g/1lb 2oz/4½ cups unbleached
white bread flour
2.5ml/½ tsp salt
75g/3oz/6 tbsp caster
(superfine) sugar
10ml/2 tsp easy-blend (rapid-rise)
dried yeast
75g/3oz/6 tbsp butter, melted
75g/3oz/½ cup cut mixed
(candied) peel
icing (confectioners') sugar,
for dusting

MAKES 1 LOAF

TEABREADS AND CAKES

Traditional teabreads and cakes use baking powder rather than yeast as a raising agent,
giving them a light texture and a good flavour. Classic cakes, such as Madeira Cake, Marble
Cake and Gingerbread can easily be baked in a bread machine. For more exotic combinations,
there are recipes for Tropical Fruit Loaf, flavoured with pineapple, papaya, mango and melon;
fresh Raspberry and Almond Teabread or sugar-topped Crunchy Pear and Cherry Cake.

MADEIRA CAKE

Delicately flavoured with vanilla, this classic plain cake has a firm yet light texture. Serve the traditional way with a glass of its namesake.

SMALL
115g/4oz/½ cup butter, cut into pieces
115g/4oz/generous ½ cup caster
(superfine) sugar
a few drops vanilla essence (extract)
125g/4½oz/1 cup self-raising
(self-rising) flour
40g/1½oz/6 tbsp plain
(all-purpose) flour
2 eggs, lightly beaten
15–30ml/1–2 tbsp milk

MEDIUM
140g/5oz/⅔ cup butter, cut into pieces
140g/5oz/¾ cup caster sugar
1.5ml/¼ tsp vanilla essence
165g/5½oz/generous 1¼ cups self-
raising flour
40g/1½oz/6 tbsp plain flour
3 eggs, lightly beaten
15–30ml/1–2 tbsp milk

LARGE
175g/6oz/¾ cup butter, cut into pieces
175g/6oz/⅞ cup caster sugar
1.5ml/¼ tsp vanilla essence
175g/6oz/1½ cups self-raising flour
50g/2oz/½ cup plain
(all-purpose) flour
3 eggs, lightly beaten
15–30ml/1–2 tbsp milk

MAKES 1 CAKE

1 Prepare the machine. Remove the kneading blade from the bread pan and line the base with baking parchment.

2 Cream the butter and sugar together until the mixture is very light and fluffy, then beat in the vanilla essence.

3 Sift the flours together. Gradually beat the eggs into the creamed mixture, beating well after each addition, and adding a little flour if the mixture starts to curdle.

COOK'S TIP
Cakes cooked in a bread pan tend to have browner sides than when cooked conventionally, in an oven, as the cooking element is around the sides of the bread pan. Cakes such as this, which have a high proportion of fat and sugar, need to be watched closely, as the edges will easily overcook.

4 Fold in the remaining flour mixture, using a metal spoon, then add enough of the milk to give a dropping consistency.

5 Spoon the mixture into the prepared bread pan and set the bread machine on the "bake only" setting. Set the timer, if possible, for the recommended time. If, on your bread machine, the minimum time on the "bake only" setting is for longer than the time suggested here, set the timer and check the cake after the shortest recommended time. Bake the small madeira cake for 40–45 minutes, the medium for 45–50 minutes and the large cake for 55–60 minutes.

6 The cake should be well risen and firm to the touch. Test by inserting a skewer into the centre of the cake. It should come out clean. If necessary, bake for a few minutes more.

7 Remove the bread pan from the machine. Leave it to stand for about 2–3 minutes, then turn the madeira cake out on to a wire rack to cool.

CRUNCHY PEAR AND CHERRY CAKE

Made from quick all-in-one cake mixture and filled with juicy pears and cherries, this cake has a crunchy demerara topping which contrasts beautifully with the soft crumb.

1 Remove the kneading blade from the bread pan and line the base of the pan with non-stick baking paper or greased greaseproof (waxed) paper.

2 Mix the margarine and caster sugar in a large bowl. Add the eggs, milk, flour and baking powder. Beat together for 1–2 minutes. Fold in the pears, cherries and ginger, using a metal spoon.

3 Spoon the mixture into the prepared pan and sprinkle half the demerara sugar over the top. Set the machine to the "bake only" setting. Set the timer, if possible, for the recommended time. If not, set the timer and check the cake after the shortest recommended time. Bake the small cake for 45–50 minutes, the medium cake for 50–55 minutes and the large cake for 65–70 minutes.

4 Sprinkle the remaining sugar over after 25 minutes if baking the small cake, after 30 minutes if baking the medium cake, and after 35 minutes if baking the large cake.

5 Remove the bread pan from the machine. Leave the cake to stand for 2–3 minutes, then turn out on to a wire rack to cool.

SMALL

75g/3oz/6 tbsp soft margarine
75g/3oz/scant ½ cup caster (superfine) sugar
2 eggs
30ml/2 tbsp milk
170g/6oz/1½ cups plain (all-purpose) flour
7.5ml/1½ tsp baking powder
50g/2oz/½ cup ready-to-eat dried pears, chopped
40g/1½oz/2 tbsp glacé (candied) cherries, quartered
25g/1oz/2 tbsp crystallized (candied) ginger, chopped
22ml/1½ tbsp demerara (raw) sugar

MEDIUM

100g/3½oz/7 tbsp soft margarine
100g/3½oz/½ cup caster sugar
2 eggs
60ml/4 tbsp milk
225g/8oz/2 cups plain flour
10ml/2 tsp baking powder
65g/2½oz/generous ½ cup ready-to-eat dried pears, chopped
65g/2½oz/generous ¼ cup glacé cherries, quartered
40g/1½oz/3 tbsp crystallized ginger, chopped
30ml/2 tbsp demerara sugar

LARGE

140g/5oz/⅔ cup soft margarine
140g/5oz/⅔ cup caster sugar
3 eggs
60ml/4 tbsp milk
280g/10oz/2½ cups plain flour
12.5ml/2½ tsp baking powder
75g/3oz/⅔ cup ready-to-eat dried pears, chopped
75g/3oz/scant ½ cup glacé cherries, quartered
50g/2oz/4 tbsp crystallized ginger, chopped
30ml/2 tbsp demerara sugar

MAKES 1 CAKE

HONEY CAKE

If you like the taste of honey, you are sure to love this cake. Serve it with tea or coffee or as a dessert with fresh fruit and crème fraîche.

SMALL
40g/1½oz/3 tbsp butter
100ml/3½fl oz/7 tbsp clear honey
75g/3oz/¾ cup plain
(all-purpose) flour
pinch of salt
5ml/1 tsp baking powder
2.5ml/½ tsp bicarbonate of soda
(baking soda)
2.5ml/½ tsp mixed (apple pie) spice
75g/3oz/¾ cup wholemeal
(whole-wheat) flour
15ml/1 tbsp milk
1 egg, lightly beaten
30ml/2 tbsp thick-cut marmalade

MEDIUM
50g/2oz/¼ cup butter
150ml/5fl oz/⅔ cup clear honey
115g/4oz/1 cup plain flour
pinch of salt
7.5ml/1½ tsp baking powder
2.5ml/½ tsp bicarbonate of soda
5ml/1 tsp mixed spice
115g/4oz/1 cup wholemeal flour
2 eggs, lightly beaten
45ml/3 tbsp thick-cut marmalade

LARGE
65g/2½oz/5 tbsp butter
180ml/6½fl oz/generous ¾ cup
clear honey
140g/5oz/1¼ cups plain flour
pinch of salt
10ml/2 tsp baking powder
3.5ml/¾ tsp bicarbonate of soda
5ml/1 tsp mixed spice
140g/5oz/1¼ cups wholemeal flour
15ml/1 tbsp milk
2 eggs, lightly beaten
60ml/4 tbsp thick-cut marmalade

MAKES 1 CAKE

1 Remove the kneading blade from the bread pan and line the base of the pan with baking parchment or greased greaseproof (waxed) paper.

2 Place the butter and honey in a small pan and heat gently, stirring all the time until the butter has melted.

3 Sift the plain flour, salt, baking powder, bicarbonate of soda and mixed spice into a mixing bowl. Stir in the wholemeal flour.

4 Stir the milk, if using, into the beaten egg, if making the small or large cake. Gradually pour on to the flour mixture, alternately with the honey and butter mixture, beating well after each addition of liquid.

5 Spoon the mixture into the prepared bread pan. Set the bread machine to the "bake only" setting. Set the timer, if possible, for the recommended time. If not, set the timer and check the cake after the shortest recommended time. Bake the small cake for 35–40 minutes, the medium cake for 40–45 minutes and the large cake for 50–55 minutes, or until well risen and firm to the touch.

6 Test by inserting a skewer into the centre of the cake. It should come out clean. If necessary, bake the cake for a few minutes more.

7 Remove the pan from the machine. Leave it to stand for 2–3 minutes, then turn the cake out on to a wire rack.

8 Melt the marmalade in a small pan and brush it over the warm cake, to glaze.

GINGERBREAD

This tea-time favourite can be baked easily in your bread machine. Store it in an airtight tin for a couple of days to allow the characteristic moist sticky texture to develop fully.

1 Remove the blade from the bread pan and line the base with baking parchment or greased greaseproof (waxed) paper. Sift the flour, ginger, baking powder, bicarbonate of soda and mixed spice together into a large bowl.

2 Melt the sugar, butter, syrup and treacle in a pan over a low heat.

3 Make a well in the centre of the dry ingredients and pour in the melted mixture. Add the milk, egg and stem ginger and mix thoroughly.

4 Pour the mixture into the bread pan and set the machine to the "bake only" setting. Set the timer, if possible, for the recommended time. If not, set the timer and check the gingerbread after the shortest recommended time. Bake the small gingerbread for 45–50 minutes, the medium for 50–55 minutes and the large for 65–70 minutes, or until well risen.

5 Remove the bread pan from the machine. Let stand for 2–3 minutes, then turn the gingerbread out on to a wire rack to cool.

SMALL

175g/6oz/1½ cups plain
(all-purpose) flour
3.5ml/¾ tsp ground ginger
5ml/1 tsp baking powder
1.5ml/¼ tsp bicarbonate of soda
(baking soda)
2.5ml/½ tsp mixed (apple pie) spice
75g/3oz/6 tbsp light muscovado
(brown) sugar
50g/2oz/¼ cup butter, cut into pieces
75g/3oz/scant ⅓ cup golden
(light corn) syrup
40g/1½oz black treacle (molasses)
105ml/7 tbsp milk
1 egg, lightly beaten
40g/1½oz/¼ cup drained preserved
stem ginger, thinly sliced

MEDIUM

225g/8oz/2 cups plain flour
5ml/1 tsp ground ginger
7.5ml/1½ tsp baking powder
2.5ml/½ tsp bicarbonate of soda
2.5ml/½ tsp mixed spice
115g/4oz/½ cup light muscovado sugar
75g/3oz/6 tbsp butter, cut into pieces
100g/3½oz/generous ⅓ cup
golden syrup
50g/2oz black treacle
150ml/5fl oz/⅔ cup milk
1 egg, lightly beaten
50g/2oz/⅓ cup drained preserved
stem ginger, thinly sliced

LARGE

280g/10oz/2½ cups plain flour
7.5ml/1½ tsp ground ginger
10ml/2 tsp baking powder
3.5ml/¾ tsp bicarbonate of soda
3.5ml/¾ tsp mixed spice
125g/4½oz/generous ½ cup light
muscovado sugar
115g/4oz/½ cup butter, cut into pieces
125g/4½oz/scant ½ cup golden syrup
50g/2oz black treacle
200ml/7fl oz/⅞ cup milk
1 egg, lightly beaten
50g/2oz/⅓ cup drained preserved
stem ginger, thinly sliced

MAKES 1 LOAF

SMALL

75g/3oz/6 tbsp butter or
margarine, softened
115g/4oz/generous ½ cup caster
(superfine) sugar
2 eggs, lightly beaten
115g/4oz/1⅓ cups desiccated (dry
unsweetened shredded) coconut
85g/3oz/¾ cup self-raising
(self-rising) flour
55ml/2fl oz/¼ cup sour cream
5ml/1 tsp grated lemon rind

MEDIUM

100g/3½oz/7 tbsp butter or
margarine, softened
140g/5oz/¾ cup caster sugar
2 large eggs, lightly beaten
140g/5oz/1⅔ cups desiccated coconut
100g/3½oz/scant 1 cup self-raising flour
70ml/2½fl oz/scant ⅓ cup sour cream
7.5ml/1½ tsp grated lemon rind

LARGE

115g/4oz/½ cup butter or
margarine, softened
175g/6oz/scant 1 cup caster sugar
3 eggs, lightly beaten
175g/6oz/2 cups desiccated coconut
115g/4oz/1 cup self-raising flour
85ml/3fl oz/⅜ cup sour cream
10ml/2 tsp grated lemon rind

MAKES 1 CAKE

1 Remove the kneading blade from the bread pan and line the base of the pan with baking parchment.

2 Cream the butter or margarine and sugar together until pale and fluffy, then add the eggs a little at a time, beating well after each addition.

COCONUT CAKE

Desiccated coconut gives this simple, speedy cake a wonderful
moist texture and delectable aroma.

3 Add the desiccated coconut, flour, sour cream and lemon rind. Gradually mix together, using a non-metallic spoon.

4 Spoon into the pan. Set the machine to the "bake only" setting. Set the timer, if possible, for the recommended time. If not, set the timer and check after the shortest recommended time. Bake the small or medium cake for 45–50 minutes and the large cake for 65–70 minutes.

5 Test by inserting a skewer into the centre of the cake. It should come out clean. If necessary, bake for a few minutes more.

6 Remove the bread pan from the machine. Let stand for 2–3 minutes, then turn the cake out on to a wire rack to cool.

COOK'S TIP

This is delicious with a lemon syrup drizzled over the cooked cake. Heat 30ml/2 tbsp lemon juice with 100g/3½oz/scant ½ cup granulated sugar and 85ml/3fl oz/6 tbsp water in a pan, stirring until the sugar has dissolved. Bring to the boil, then simmer for 2–3 minutes before drizzling the syrup over the warm coconut cake.

RASPBERRY AND ALMOND TEABREAD

*Fresh raspberries and almonds combine perfectly to flavour this
mouthwatering cake. Toasted flaked almonds make a crunchy topping.*

1 Remove the kneading blade from the
bread pan and line the base of the pan
with baking parchment or greased
greaseproof (waxed) paper.

2 Sift the self-raising flour into a large
bowl. Add the butter and rub in with
your fingertips until the mixture
resembles fine breadcrumbs.

3 Stir in the caster sugar and ground
almonds. Gradually beat in the egg(s).
If making the small or large teabread,
beat in the milk.

4 Fold in the raspberries, then spoon
the mixture into the prepared tin.
Sprinkle over the flaked almonds.

SMALL
*140g/5oz/1¼ cups self-raising
(self-rising) flour*
70g/2½oz/5 tbsp butter, cut into pieces
*70g/2½oz/generous ⅓ cup caster
(superfine) sugar*
25g/1oz/¼ cup ground almonds
1 egg, lightly beaten
30ml/2 tbsp milk
115g/4oz/1 cup raspberries
*22ml/1½ tbsp toasted flaked
(sliced) almonds*

MEDIUM
175g/6oz/1½ cups self-raising flour
90g/3½oz/7 tbsp butter, cut into pieces
90g/3½oz/½ cup caster sugar
40g/1½oz/⅓ cup ground almonds
2 eggs, lightly beaten
140g/5oz/1¼ cups raspberries
30ml/2 tbsp toasted flaked almonds

LARGE
225g/8oz/2 cups self-raising flour
115g/4oz/½ cup butter, cut into pieces
115g/4oz/generous ½ cup caster sugar
50g/2oz/½ cup ground almonds
2 eggs, lightly beaten
45ml/3 tbsp milk
175g/6oz/1½ cups raspberries
30ml/2 tbsp toasted flaked almonds

MAKES 1 TEABREAD

5 Set the bread machine to the "bake
only" setting. Set the timer, if possible,
for the recommended time. If not, set
the timer and check after the shortest
recommended time. Bake the small
teabread for 35–40 minutes, the medium
for 45–50 minutes and the large cake for
65–70 minutes or until well risen.

6 Test by inserting a skewer into the
centre of the teabread. It should come
out clean. If necessary, bake for a few
minutes more. Then remove the pan
from the machine. Turn out on to a wire
rack to cool after 2–3 minutes.

PASSION CAKE

Don't be misled into assuming this cake contains passion fruit. It is actually a carrot and walnut cake and a very good one, too. Topped with a tangy lemon cheese icing, it makes the perfect tea-time treat.

SMALL
115g/4oz/½ cup butter
115g/4oz/½ cup soft light brown sugar
2 eggs, separated
5ml/1 tsp lemon juice, plus 5ml/1 tsp for the topping
115g/4oz/1 cup self-raising flour
2.5ml/½ tsp baking powder
25g/1oz/¼ cup ground almonds
65g/2½oz/generous ½ cup walnut pieces, chopped
175g/6oz/scant 1¼ cups grated carrot
115g/4oz/½ cup mascarpone cheese
25g/1oz/2 tbsp icing (confectioners') sugar
22ml/1½ tbsp walnut pieces, to decorate

MEDIUM
140g/5oz/scant ⅔ cup butter
140g/5oz/scant ⅔ cup soft light brown sugar
2 eggs, separated
10ml/2 tsp lemon juice, plus 5ml/1 tsp for the topping
15ml/1 tbsp milk
140g/5oz/1¼ cups self-raising flour
3.5ml/¾ tsp baking powder
40g/1½oz/⅓ cup ground almonds
75g/3oz/¾ cup walnut pieces, chopped
200g/7oz/scant 1½ cups grated carrot
140g/5oz/⅔ cup mascarpone cheese
40g/1½oz/3 tbsp icing sugar
30ml/2 tbsp walnut pieces, to decorate

LARGE
175g/6oz/¾ cup butter
175g/6oz/¾ cup soft light brown sugar
3 eggs, separated
15ml/1 tbsp lemon juice, plus 7.5ml/1½ tsp for the topping
175g/6oz/1½ cups self-raising flour
5ml/1 tsp baking powder
50g/2oz/½ cup ground almonds
115g/4oz/1 cup walnut pieces, chopped
225g/8oz/1½ cups grated carrot
175g/6oz/¾ cup mascarpone cheese
40g/1½oz/3 tbsp icing sugar
45ml/3 tbsp walnut pieces, to decorate

MAKES 1 CAKE

1 Remove the kneading blade from the bread pan and line the base of the pan with baking parchment or greased greaseproof (waxed) paper.

2 Place the butter and sugar together in a large mixing bowl and cream until light and fluffy. Beat in the egg yolks, one at a time, then beat in the lemon juice. If making the medium cake, beat in the milk.

3 Sieve the flour and baking powder together and fold in. Add the ground almonds and chopped walnut pieces.

4 Meanwhile, whisk the egg whites in a grease-free bowl until stiff.

5 Fold the egg whites into the creamed cake mixture, together with the grated carrot and mix.

6 Spoon the mixture into the prepared bread pan and set the machine to the "bake only" setting. Set the timer, if possible, for the recommended time. If, on your bread machine, the minimum time on the "bake only" setting is for longer than the time suggested here, set the timer and check after the shortest recommended time. Bake the small and the medium cake for 45–50 minutes and the large cake for 65–70 minutes.

7 The passion cake should be well risen and firm to the touch. Test by inserting a skewer into the centre of the cake. It should come out clean. If necessary, bake for a few minutes more.

8 Remove the pan from the machine. Leave the cake to stand for 2–3 minutes, then turn out on to a wire rack to cool.

9 To finish the passion cake, beat the mascarpone cheese with the icing sugar and lemon juice. Spread the topping mixture over the top of the cake and sprinkle with the walnut pieces.

COOK'S TIP
If you can't locate mascarpone cheese, use cream cheese instead. It doesn't matter whether it is full-fat or a light cheese.

MIXED FRUIT TEABREAD

When mixed dried fruits are plumped up by being soaked in orange juice before baking, the result is a succulent teabread which keeps well.

SMALL
*75g/3oz/½ cup sultanas
(golden raisins)
50g/2oz/⅓ cup raisins
25g/1oz/2 tbsp currants
15g/½oz/1 tbsp cut mixed (candied)
peel
75g/3oz/6 tbsp soft light brown sugar
150ml/5fl oz/⅔ cup orange juice
1 egg, lightly beaten
65g/2½oz/generous ½ cup plain
(all-purpose) white flour
65g/2½oz/generous ½ cup plain
wholemeal (whole-wheat) flour
5ml/1 tsp baking powder
1.5ml/¼ tsp ground cinnamon
1.5ml/¼ tsp freshly grated nutmeg*

MEDIUM
*115g/4oz/⅔ cup sultanas
75g/3oz/½ cup raisins
40g/1½oz/3 tbsp currants
25g/1oz/2 tbsp cut mixed peel
115g/4oz/½ cup soft light brown sugar
200ml/7fl oz/⅞ cup orange juice
1 egg, lightly beaten
90g/3¼oz/generous ¾ cup plain
white flour
90g/3¼oz/generous ¾ cup plain
wholemeal flour
7.5ml/1½ tsp baking powder
2.5ml/½ tsp ground cinnamon
2.5ml/½ tsp freshly grated nutmeg*

LARGE
*175g/6oz/1 cup sultanas
125g/4½oz/¾ cup raisins
50g/2oz/¼ cup currants
25g/1oz/2 tbsp cut mixed peel
175g/6oz/¾ cup soft light brown sugar
300ml/10½fl oz/generous 1¼ cups
orange juice
1 egg, lightly beaten
115g/4oz/1 cup plain white flour
115g/4oz/1 cup plain wholemeal flour
7.5ml/1½ tsp baking powder
2.5ml/½ tsp ground cinnamon
2.5ml/½ tsp freshly grated nutmeg*

MAKES 1 TEABREAD

1 Place the dried fruit, peel and sugar in a bowl. Pour over the orange juice and leave to soak for 8 hours or overnight.

2 Remove the kneading blade from the bread pan and line the base of the pan with baking parchment or greased greaseproof (waxed) paper.

3 Add the egg, both types of flour, the baking powder, and spices to the fruit mixture and beat thoroughly to combine. Spoon the mixture into the prepared bread pan.

4 Set the machine to the "bake only" setting. Set the timer, if possible, for the recommended time. If not, set the timer and check the cake after the recommended time. Bake the small cake for 40–45 minutes, the medium for 55–60 minutes and the large cake for 75–80 minutes. Check after the shortest recommended time. It should be well risen and firm to the touch.

5 Remove the bread pan from the machine. Turn the cake out on to a wire rack after 2–3 minutes.

VANILLA-CHOCOLATE MARBLE CAKE

White and dark chocolate, marbled together, make a cake that tastes as good as it looks. Serve it for tea, or cut it into chunks, mix it with fresh peach slices and add a sprinkling of orange or peach liqueur for an impressive dessert.

1 Remove the blade from the bread pan and line the base with baking parchment or greased greaseproof (waxed) paper. Cream the margarine or butter and sugar together until light and fluffy. Slowly add the eggs, beating thoroughly. Place half the mixture in another bowl.

2 Place the white chocolate in a heatproof bowl over a pan of simmering water. Stir until the chocolate is melted.

3 Melt the plain chocolate in a separate bowl, in the same way. Stir the white chocolate and the vanilla essence into one bowl of creamed mixture and the plain chocolate into the other. Divide the flour equally between the two bowls and lightly fold it in with a metal spoon.

4 Put alternate spoonfuls of the two mixtures into the prepared bread pan. Use a round-bladed knife to swirl the mixtures together to marble them.

5 Set the bread machine to the "bake only" setting. Set the timer, if possible, for the recommended time. If not, set the timer and check the cake after the shortest recommended time. Bake the small cake for 45–50 minutes, the medium for 50–55 minutes and the large for 65–70 minutes, until well risen.

SMALL
115g/4oz/½ cup margarine or butter
115g/4oz/generous ½ cup caster (superfine) sugar
2 eggs, lightly beaten
40g/1½oz white chocolate, in pieces
40g/1½oz plain (semisweet) chocolate, in pieces
1.5ml/¼ tsp vanilla essence (extract)
175g/6oz/1½ cups self-raising (self-rising) flour
icing (confectioners') sugar and cocoa powder (unsweetened), for dusting

MEDIUM
125g/4½oz/generous ½ cup margarine or butter
125g/4½oz/scant ¾ cup caster sugar
2 eggs, lightly beaten
50g/2oz white chocolate, in pieces
50g/2oz plain chocolate, in pieces
2.5ml/½ tsp vanilla essence
200g/7oz/1¾ cups self-raising flour
icing sugar and cocoa powder, for dusting

LARGE
200g/7oz/scant 1 cup margarine or butter
200g/7oz/1 cup caster sugar
3 eggs, lightly beaten
75g/3oz white chocolate, in pieces
75g/3oz plain chocolate, in pieces
2.5ml/½ tsp vanilla essence (extract)
280g/10oz/2½ cups self-raising flour
icing sugar and cocoa powder, for dusting

MAKES 1 CAKE

6 The cake should be just firm to the touch. Test by inserting a skewer into the centre of the cake. It should come out clean. If necessary, bake for a few minutes more. Remove the pan from the machine. Stand for 2–3 minutes, then turn the cake out on to a wire rack. Dust with icing sugar and cocoa powder and serve in slices or chunks.

75g/3oz/6 tbsp butter, softened
150g/5½oz/generous ¾ cup caster
(superfine) sugar
2 eggs, lightly beaten
175g/6oz/1½ cups self-raising
(self-rising) flour, sifted
150g/5½oz peeled ripe bananas
70ml/2½fl oz/5 tbsp buttermilk
1.5ml/¼ tsp baking powder
2.5ml/½ tsp freshly grated nutmeg
100g/3½oz/generous ½ cup sultanas
(golden raisins)
65g/2½oz/generous ½ cup pecan
nuts, chopped
15ml/1 tbsp banana or apricot
jam, melted
15ml/1 tbsp banana chips

MEDIUM

100g/3½oz/7 tbsp butter, softened
175g/6oz/⅞ cup caster sugar
2 large eggs, lightly beaten
200g/7oz/1¾ cups self-raising
flour, sifted
200g/7oz peeled ripe bananas
85ml/3fl oz/6 tbsp buttermilk
2.5ml/½ tsp baking powder
5ml/1 tsp freshly grated nutmeg
125g/4½oz/⅔ cup sultanas
75g/3oz/¾ cup pecan nuts, chopped
30ml/2 tbsp banana or apricot
jam, melted
30ml/2 tbsp banana chips

LARGE

115g/4oz/½ cup butter, softened
200g/7oz/1 cup caster sugar
3 eggs, lightly beaten
225g/8oz/2 cups self-raising
flour, sifted
225g/8oz peeled ripe bananas
100ml/3½fl oz/7 tbsp buttermilk
2.5ml/½ tsp baking powder
5ml/1 tsp freshly grated nutmeg
140g/5oz/scant 1 cup sultanas
90g/3½oz/scant 1 cup pecan
nuts, chopped
30ml/2 tbsp banana or apricot
jam, melted
30ml/2 tbsp banana chips

MAKES 1 TEABREAD

BANANA AND PECAN TEABREAD

This moist, light teabread is flavoured with banana, lightly spiced with nutmeg and studded with sultanas and pecan nuts. Weigh the bananas after peeling them – it is important to use the precise quantities given.

1 Remove the kneading blade from the bread pan and line the base of the pan with baking parchment or greased greaseproof (waxed) paper.

2 Cream the butter and caster sugar in a mixing bowl until pale and fluffy. Gradually beat in the eggs, beating well after each addition, and adding a little of the flour if the mixture starts to curdle.

3 Mash the bananas until completely smooth. Beat into the creamed mixture with the buttermilk.

4 Sift the remaining flour and the baking powder into the bowl. Add the nutmeg, sultanas and pecans; beat until smooth.

5 Spoon into the prepared bread pan. Set the machine to the "bake only" setting. Set the timer, if possible, for the recommended time. If not, set the timer and check the cake after the shortest recommended time. Bake the small or medium cake for 55–60 minutes and the large cake for 65–70 minutes. Test by inserting a skewer in the centre of the teabread. It should come out clean. If necessary, bake for a few minutes more.

6 Remove the pan from the machine. Leave it to stand for about 5 minutes, then turn the cake out on to a wire rack.

7 While the cake is still warm, brush the top with the melted jam and sprinkle over the banana chips. Leave to cool completely before serving.

APRICOT, PRUNE AND PEACH TEABREAD

The succulent dried fruits complement the crunchy texture of the hazelnuts and Granary flour. Serve this unusual fruit bread in slices, either plain or spread thinly with butter.

1 Remove the kneading blade from the bread pan and line the base of the pan with baking parchment or greased greaseproof (waxed) paper.

2 Chop the apricots, prunes and the peaches. Sift the flour, mixed spice and baking powder together into a large bowl. Add the butter and rub in with your fingers until the mixture resembles fine breadcrumbs.

3 Stir in the sugar, apricots, prunes, peaches and hazelnuts. Gradually beat in the milk and egg.

4 Spoon the mixture into the prepared bread pan. Set the machine to the "bake only" setting. Set the timer, if possible, for the recommended time. If not, set the timer and check the cake after the shortest recommended time. Bake the small cake for 40–45 minutes, the medium cake for 45–50 minutes and the large cake for 60–65 minutes, or until well risen and firm to the touch.

5 Test by inserting a skewer in the centre of the teabread. It should come out clean. If necessary, bake for a few minutes more. Then remove the bread pan from the machine. Leave it to stand for 2–3 minutes, then turn the teabread out on to a wire rack to cool.

SMALL
65g/2½oz/generous ¼ cup ready-to-eat
dried apricots
65g/2½oz/generous ¼ cup ready-to-eat
prunes, pitted
50g/2oz/¼ cup ready-to-eat
dried peaches
175g/6oz/1½ cups Granary
(whole-wheat) flour
5ml/1 tsp mixed (apple pie) spice
7.5ml/1½ tsp baking powder
50g/2oz/¼ cup butter, diced
50g/2oz/4 tbsp light muscovado
(brown) sugar
40g/1½oz/⅓ cup hazelnuts, halved
100ml/3½fl oz/7 tbsp milk
1 egg, lightly beaten

MEDIUM
75g/3oz/generous ⅓ cup ready-to-eat
dried apricots
75g/3oz/generous ⅓ cup ready-to-eat
prunes, pitted
65g/2½oz/generous ¼ cup ready-to-eat
dried peaches
225g/8oz/2 cups Granary flour
7.5ml/1½ tsp mixed spice
10ml/2 tsp baking powder
65g/2½oz/5 tbsp butter, diced
65g/2½oz/5 tbsp light muscovado sugar
50g/2oz/½ cup hazelnuts, halved
150ml/5fl oz/⅔ cup milk
1 egg, lightly beaten

LARGE
100g/3½oz/scant ½ cup ready-to-eat
dried apricots
100g/3½oz/scant ½ cup ready-to-eat
prunes, pitted
75g/3oz/scant ⅓ cup ready-to-eat
dried peaches
280g/10oz/2½ cups Granary flour
7.5ml/1½ tsp ground mixed spice
12.5ml/2½ tsp baking powder
75g/3oz/6 tbsp butter, diced
75g/3oz/6 tbsp light muscovado sugar
75g/3oz/½ cup hazelnuts, halved
200ml/7fl oz/⅞ cup milk
1 egg, lightly beaten

MAKES 1 TEABREAD

TROPICAL FRUIT LOAF

*There's a tempting tropical taste in every slice of this wonderfully moist loaf.
Speckled with delicious little chunks of papaya, mango, melon and
pineapple, it is topped with a tangy lime soft cheese icing and finished
with fresh toasted coconut.*

SMALL

125g/4½oz/1 cup plain (all-purpose) flour
5ml/1 tsp baking powder
40g/1½oz/½ cup desiccated (dry
unsweetened shredded) coconut
65g/2½oz/5 tbsp butter, diced
65g/2½oz/5 tbsp caster (superfine) sugar
100g/3½oz/generous ½ cup ready-to-eat
dried tropical fruits, chopped
100ml/3½ fl oz/7 tbsp milk
1 egg, lightly beaten
grated rind and juice of ½ lime
FOR THE ICING AND THE DECORATION
75g/3oz/scant ½ cup full-fat soft white
(farmer's) cheese
45ml/3 tbsp icing (confectioners') sugar
juice of ½ lime
pared lime rind and fresh coconut
shavings or shreds, to decorate

MEDIUM

175g/6oz/1½ cup plain flour
5ml/1 tsp baking powder
50g/2oz/⅔ cup desiccated coconut
100g/3½oz/7 tbsp butter, diced
100g/3½oz/7 tbsp caster sugar
140g/5oz/scant 1 cup ready-to-eat dried
tropical fruits, chopped
130ml/4½fl oz/½ cup + 1 tbsp milk
1 egg, lightly beaten
grated rind and juice of ½ lime
ICING AND DECORATION (FOR MEDIUM AND
LARGE LOAVES)
125g/4½oz/½ cup full-fat soft white cheese
60ml/4 tbsp icing sugar
juice of ½ lime
pared lime rind and fresh coconut
shavings or shreds, to decorate

LARGE

225g/8oz/2 cups plain flour
7.5ml/1½ tsp baking powder
75g/3oz/1 cup desiccated coconut
115g/4oz/½ cup butter, diced
125g/4½oz/⅔ cup caster sugar
175g/6oz/1 cup ready-to-eat dried
tropical fruits, chopped
200ml/7fl oz/⅞ cup milk
1 large egg, lightly beaten
grated rind and juice of ½ lime

MAKES 1 LOAF

1 Remove the kneading blade from the
bread pan and line the base of the pan
with baking parchment or greased
greaseproof (waxed) paper.

2 Sift the flour and baking powder into a
large bowl. Then mix in the desiccated
coconut. Add the butter and rub in with
your fingers until the mixture resembles
fine breadcrumbs.

3 Stir in the sugar and dried tropical
fruits. Gradually add the milk, egg,
grated lime rind and juice, beating well
after each addition.

4 Spoon the mixture into the prepared
bread pan and set the bread machine on
the "bake only" setting. Set the timer, if
possible, for the recommended time.
If, on your bread machine, the minimum
time on the "bake only" setting is for
longer than the time suggested here, set
the timer and check the cake after the
recommended time. Bake the small cake
or medium cake for 45–50 minutes and
the large cake for 65–70 minutes.

5 The fruit loaf should be well risen and
firm to the touch. Test by inserting a
skewer into the centre of the loaf. It
should come out perfectly clean.

6 Remove the bread pan from the bread
machine. Leave the loaf to stand for
about 5 minutes, then turn it out on to a
wire rack to cool.

7 Meanwhile, make the icing. Cream the
soft cheese, icing sugar and lime juice
together in a bowl. Spread the mixture
over the top of the loaf.

8 Lightly toast the coconut shavings or
shreds. Leave to cool for 2–3 minutes,
then use them to decorate the top of the
loaf, with the pared lime rind.

COOK'S TIP
When testing the cake with a skewer,
try to avoid piercing a piece of dried
fruit, or the skewer will come out
sticky and might therefore give you
a misleading result.

AMERICAN COFFEE BREAD

This quick and easy sweet bread keeps well and so makes a useful standby.

SMALL

*175g/6oz/1½ cups plain
(all-purpose) flour
7.5ml/1½ tsp baking powder
pinch of salt
75g/3oz/6 tbsp light muscovado
(brown) sugar
50g/2oz/½ cup pecan nuts, chopped
7.5ml/1½ tsp instant coffee
20g/¾oz/1½ tbsp butter, melted
75ml/5 tbsp milk
1 egg, lightly beaten*

MEDIUM

*200g/7oz/1¾ cups plain flour
10ml/2 tsp baking powder
pinch of salt
100g/3½oz/scant ½ cup light
muscovado sugar
75g/3oz/¾ cup pecan nuts, chopped
10ml/2 tsp instant coffee
25g/1oz/2 tbsp butter, melted
100ml/3½fl oz/7 tbsp milk
2 eggs, lightly beaten*

LARGE

*280g/10oz/2½ cups plain flour
15ml/1 tbsp baking powder
pinch of salt
150g/5½oz/⅔ cup light muscovado sugar
115g/4oz/1 cup pecan nuts, chopped
15ml/1 tbsp instant coffee
40g/1½oz/3 tbsp butter, melted
160ml/5½fl oz/⅔ cup milk
2 eggs, lightly beaten*

MAKES 1 LOAF

COOK'S TIP
For a special tea-time treat, drizzle
the loaf with coffee glacé icing and
decorate with pecan nut halves.

1 Remove the kneading blade from the
bread pan and line the base of the pan
with baking parchment or greased
greaseproof (waxed) paper.

2 Sift the flour, baking powder and salt into
a large bowl. Stir in the sugar and pecan
nuts. Dissolve the coffee granules or powder
with 15ml/1 tbsp hot water in a cup.

3 Add the coffee, the melted butter,
milk and egg(s), to the dry ingredients.
Beat thoroughly to mix. Spoon the
mixture into the prepared bread pan
and set the bread machine to the "bake
only" setting.

4 Set the timer, if possible, for the
recommended time. If not, set
the timer and check after the shortest
recommended time. Bake the small
cake for 40–45 minutes, the medium
for 45–50 minutes and the large for
55–60 minutes.

5 Test by inserting a skewer into the centre
of the loaf. It should come out clean. If
necessary, bake for a few minutes more.

6 Remove the bread pan from the
machine. Let stand for 2–3 minutes,
then turn the bread out on to a wire
rack to cool.

PEANUT BUTTER TEABREAD

*Peanut butter is used instead of butter or margarine in this tasty
teabread, giving it a distinctive flavour and an interesting texture, thanks
to the peanut pieces.*

SMALL
75g/3oz/¼ cup crunchy peanut butter
65g/2½oz/⅓ cup caster
(superfine) sugar
1 egg, lightly beaten
105ml/7 tbsp milk
200g/7oz/1¾ cups self-raising
(self-rising) flour

MEDIUM
115g/4oz/⅓ cup crunchy
peanut butter
75g/3oz/scant ½ cup caster sugar
1 egg, lightly beaten
175ml/6fl oz/¾ cup milk
300g/10½oz/generous 2½ cups self-
raising flour

LARGE
150g/5½oz/scant ½ cup crunchy
peanut butter
125g/4½oz/scant ¾ cup caster sugar
2 eggs, lightly beaten
200ml/7fl oz/⅞ cup milk
400g/14oz/3½ cups self-raising flour

MAKES 1 TEABREAD

1 Remove the kneading blade from the
bread pan and line the base of the pan
with baking parchment or greased
greaseproof (waxed) paper.

2 Cream the peanut butter and sugar in
a bowl together until light and fluffy,
then gradually beat in the egg(s).

3 Add the milk and flour and mix with a
wooden spoon.

COOK'S TIP
Leave a rough finish on the top of the
cake before baking to add character.

4 Spoon the mixture into the prepared
bread pan and set the machine to the
"bake only" setting.

5 Set the timer for the recommended
time. If the minimum time on the "bake
only" setting on your machine is longer
than the time suggested here, then set
the timer and check the teabread after
the shortest recommended time. Bake
the small or medium teabread for 45–50
minutes, and the large teabread for
60–65 minutes.

6 The teabread should be well risen and
just firm to the touch. Test by inserting
a skewer in the centre of the teabread.
It should come out clean. If necessary,
bake for a few minutes more.

7 Remove the bread pan from the bread
machine. Leave it to stand in the pan for
2–3 minutes, then transfer on to a wire
rack to cool.

TREACLE, DATE AND WALNUT CAKE

Layered with date purée and finished with a crunchy sugar and walnut topping, this cake is absolutely irresistible.

SMALL
115g/4oz/⅔ cup pitted dates
grated rind and juice of ½ lemon
115g/4oz/1 cup self-raising
(self-rising) flour
2.5ml/½ tsp each ground cinnamon,
ginger and grated nutmeg
50g/2oz/¼ cup butter
50g/2oz/¼ cup light muscovado
(brown) sugar
15ml/1 tbsp treacle (molasses)
30ml/2 tbsp golden (light corn) syrup
40ml/2½ tbsp milk
1 egg
40g/1½oz/⅓ cup chopped walnuts

MEDIUM
140g/5oz/scant 1 cup pitted dates
grated rind and juice of 1 lemon
170g/6oz/1½ cups self-raising flour
3.5ml/¾ tsp each ground cinnamon,
ginger and grated nutmeg
75g/3oz/6 tbsp butter
75g/3oz/6 tbsp light muscovado sugar
22ml/1½ tbsp treacle
45ml/3 tbsp golden syrup
60ml/4 tbsp milk
1 large egg
50g/2oz/½ cup chopped walnuts

LARGE
170g/6oz/1 cup pitted dates
grated rind and juice of 1 lemon
225g/8oz/2 cups self-raising flour
5ml/1 tsp each ground cinnamon,
ginger and grated nutmeg
115g/4oz/½ cup butter
115g/4oz/½ cup light muscovado sugar
30ml/2 tbsp treacle
60ml/4 tbsp golden syrup
80ml/3fl oz/⅓ cup milk
1 large egg
75g/3oz/¾ cup chopped walnuts

TOPPING FOR ALL SIZES OF LOAF
25g/1oz/2 tbsp butter
50g/2oz/¼ cup light muscovado sugar
22ml/1½ tbsp plain (all-purpose) flour
3.5ml/¾ tsp ground cinnamon
40g/1½oz/⅓ cup chopped walnuts

MAKES 1 CAKE

1 Remove the kneading blade from the bread pan and line the base with baking parchment or greased greaseproof (waxed) paper. Mix the dates, lemon rind and lemon juice in a pan. Add 60ml/4 tbsp of water and bring to the boil, then simmer until soft. Purée in a blender or food processor until smooth.

2 Sift the flour and spices together. Cream the butter and sugar until pale and fluffy. Warm the treacle, golden syrup and milk in a pan, until just melted then beat into the creamed butter mixture. Add the egg and beat in the flour mixture. Stir in the walnuts.

COOK'S TIP

Try increasing the quantities of the toppings by 25 per cent if you are making a large cake, or decrease by 25 per cent if you are making a small cake.

3 Place half the mixture in the bread pan. Spread over the date purée, leaving a narrow border of cake mix all round. Top with the remaining cake mixture, spreading it evenly over the date purée.

4 Set the machine to the "bake only" setting. Set the timer, if possible, for the recommended time. If not, set the timer and check after the recommended time. Bake the small cake for 35 minutes, the medium cake for 40 minutes and the large cake for 45 minutes.

5 Mix all of the topping ingredients together. When the cake has baked for the recommended time, sprinkle the topping over and cook for 10–15 minutes more, until the topping starts to bubble and the cake is cooked. Remove the bread pan from the machine. Leave to stand for 10 minutes, then turn out on to a wire rack to cool.

Strawberry Teabread

—

*Perfect for a summertime treat, this hazelnut-flavoured teabread
is laced with luscious fresh strawberries.*

Small
115g/4oz/1 cup strawberries
115g/4oz/½ cup butter, softened
*115g/4oz/generous ½ cup caster
(superfine) sugar*
2 eggs, beaten
*140g/5oz/1¼ cups self-raising
(self-rising) flour, sifted*
25g/1oz/¼ cup ground hazelnuts

Medium
170g/6oz/1½ cups strawberries
140g/5oz/⅔ cup butter, softened
140g/5oz/¾ cup caster sugar
2 eggs, beaten
15ml/1 tbsp milk
*155g/5½oz/1⅓ cups self-raising
flour, sifted*
40g/1½oz/⅓ cup ground hazelnuts

Large
200g/7oz/1¾ cups strawberries
175g/6oz/¾ cup butter, softened
175g/6oz/⅞ cup caster sugar
3 eggs, beaten
*175g/6oz/1½ cups self-raising
flour, sifted*
50g/2oz/½ cup ground hazelnuts

Makes 1 Teabread

1 Remove the kneading blade from the
bread pan and line the base of the pan
with baking parchment or greased
greaseproof (waxed) paper.

2 Hull the strawberries and chop them
roughly. Set them aside. Cream the
butter and sugar in a mixing bowl until
pale and fluffy.

3 Gradually beat in the eggs and milk
(if you are making the medium cake),
beating well after each addition to
combine quickly without curdling.

4 Mix the self-raising flour and the
ground hazelnuts together and gradually
fold into the creamed mixture, using a
metal spoon.

5 Fold in the strawberries and spoon the
mixture into the prepared bread pan.
Set the machine to the "bake only"
setting. Set the timer, if possible, for the
recommended time. If, on your bread
machine, the minimum time on the
"bake only" setting is longer than the
time suggested here, set the timer and
check after the shortest recommended
time. Bake the small or medium
teabread for 45–50 minutes and the
large teabread for 55–60 minutes.

6 Test by inserting a skewer in the
centre of the teabread. It should come
out clean. If necessary, bake for a few
minutes more.

7 Remove the bread pan. Leave the
teabread to stand for 2–3 minutes, then
turn out on to a wire rack to cool.

SUPPLIERS

The following flour mills, bakeries and foodhalls are worth visiting. Most mills sell flour direct, but it is best to telephone before visiting.

AUSTRALIA
Bowan Island Bakery
202 Lyons Road
Drummoyne NSW 2047
Tel: (02) 9181 3524

Brown's Bakeries
PO Box 1298
Windsor VIC 3181
Tel: (03) 9510 9520

Dallas Bread
28 Cross Street
Brookvale NSW 2100
Tel: (02) 9905 6021

David Jones Food Hall
Cnr. Market and
    Castlereagh Streets
Sydney NSW 2000
Tel: (02) 9266 6065

Haberfield Bakery
153 Ramsay Road
Haberfield
Sydney NSW
Tel: (02) 9797 7715

Il Gianfornaio
414 Victoria Avenue
Chatswood
Sydney NSW
Tel: (02) 413 4833

Infinity Sourdough Bakery
225 Victoria Street
Darlinghurst NSW 2031
Tel: (02) 9380 4320

La Gerbe d'Or
257 Glenmore Road
Paddington
Sydney NSW
Tel: (02) 9331 1070

New Norcia Bakeries
163A Scarborough
    Beach Road
Mt Hawthorn WA 6016
Tel: (08) 9443 9437

Quinton's Sourdough and
    Danish Shop
179 The Mall
Leura NSW 2780
Tel: (02) 9266 6065

Simon Johnson Purveyor of
    Quality Foods
181 Harris Street
Pyrmont
Sydney NSW 2009
Tel: (02) 9552 2522
and
12–14 Saint David Street
Fitzroy VIC 3065
Tel: (03) 9486 9456

Victoire
285 Darling Street
Balmain
Sydney NSW
Tel: (02) 9818 5529

ENGLAND
& Clarke's
122 Kensington Church Street
Notting Hill Gate
London W8 4BH
Tel: 020 7229 2190

Baker & Spice
46 Walton Street
London SW3 1RB
Tel: 020 7589 4734

Country Market
139–146 Golders Green Road
London NW11 8HB
Tel: 020 8455 3289

Crowdy Mill
Bow Road, Harbertonford
Totnes, Devon TQ9 7HU
Tel: 01803 732 340

Euphorium Bakery
203 Upper Street
London N1 1RQ
Tel: 020 7359 7146

The Flour Bag
Burford Street
Lechlade
Gloucestershire
GL7 3AP
Tel: 01367 252 322

Funchal Patisserie
141 Stockwell Road
London SW9 9TN
Tel: 020 7733 3134

Harrods Food Hall
Knightsbridge
London SW1X 7XL
Tel: 020 7730 1234

Harvey Nichols
Food Hall
109–125 Knightsbridge
London SW1X 7RJ
Tel: 020 7235 5000

Hobb's House Bakery
39 High Street
Chipping Sodbury
Bristol BS37 6BA
Tel: 01454 321 629
and
2 North Parade
Yate
South Gloucestershire
BS37 4AN
Tel: 01454 320 890

Konditor & Cook
22 Cornwall Street
London SE1 8TW
Tel: 020 7261 0456
and
10 Stoney Street
London SE1 9AD
Tel: 020 7407 5100

Letheringsett Watermill
Riverside Road, Letheringsett
Norfolk NR25 7YD
Tel: 01263 713 153

Maison Blanc
102 Holland Park Avenue
London W11 4UA
Tel: 020 7221 2494

Mortimer & Bennett
33 Turnham Green Terrace
London W4 1RG
Tel: 020 8995 4145

Neal's Yard Bakery
6 Neal's Yard
London WC2H 9DP
Tel: 020 7836 5199

The Old Farmhouse Bakery
Steventon
Nr Abingdon
Oxon OX13 6RP
Tel: 01235 831 230

Panadam Delicatessen
2 Marius Road
London SW17 7QQ
Tel: 020 8673 4062

Pimhill Organic Centre and
    Farm Shop
Lea Hall
Harmer Hill
Nr Shrewsbury SY4 3DY
Tel: 01939 290 075

Rushall Mill
Rushall, Pewsey
Wiltshire SN9 6EB
Tel: 01980 630 335

Sally Lunn's
4 North Parade Passage
Bath BA1 1NX
Tel: 01225 461 634

Selfridges Food Hall
400 Oxford Street
London W1A 1AB
Tel: 020 7629 1234

Shipton Mill Limited
Long Newton
Nr Tetbury
Gloucestershire GL8 8RP
Tel: 01666 505 050

The Village Bakery
Melmerby Road
Melberby, Penrith
Cumbria CA10 1HE
Tel: 01768 881 515

Villandry Foodstore Restaurant
170 Great Portland Street
London W1N 5TB
Tel: 020 7631 3131

SCOTLAND
Aberfeldy Water Mill
Mill Street
Aberfeldy
Tayside PH15 2BG
Tel: 01887 820 803

Fisher and Donaldson
21 Crossgate
Cupar
Fife KY15 5HA
Tel: 01334 652 551
and
3 Church Street
St Andrews
Fife KY16 9NW
Tel: 01334 472 201

Ian Mellis
30A Victoria Street
Edinburgh EH1 2JW
Tel: 0131 226 6215
and
205 Bruntsfield Place
Edinburgh EH10 4DH
Tel: 0131 447 8889
and
492 Great Western Road
Glasgow G12 8EW
Tel: 0141 339 8998

Star Continental Bakery
158 Fore Street
Scottoun
Glasgow G14 0AE
Tel: 0141 959 7307

Taylor's of Waterside Bakery
Waterside Street
Strathaven ML10 6AW
Tel: 01357 521 260

Valvona & Crolla
19 Elm Row
Edinburgh EH7 4AA
Tel: 0131 556 6066

Victor Hugo
26–7 Melville Terrace
Edinburgh
EH9 2PR
Tel: 0131 667 1827

WALES
Derwen Bakehouse
Museum of Welsh Life
St Fagans
Cardiff
Glamorgan CF5 6XB
Tel: 01222 573 500

UNITED STATES

Arrowhead Mills
P.O. Box 866
Hereford, TX 79045
Tel: (806) 364-0730

Bob's Red Mill
5209 S.E. International Way
Milwaukie, OR 97222
Tel: (503) 654-3215
Fax: (503) 653 1339

Bread Baker's Guild of America
P.O. Box 22254
Pittsburgh, PA 15222
Tel: (412) 322-8275

The Chef's Catalogue
3215 Commercial Avenue
Northbrook
IL 60062-1900
Tel: (800) 338-3232

Commodities
117 Hudson Street
New York, NY 10013
Tel: (212) 334-8330

Community Mill and Bean
267 Route 89 South
Savannah, NY 13146
Tel: (800) 755-0554

Dean & Deluca
110 Greene Street
Suite 304
New York, NY 10012
Tel: (800) 221-7714

FBM (French Baking
    Machines)
2666 Route 130
Cranbury, NJ 08512
Tel: (609) 860-0577

Kenyon Cornmeal Company
Osquepough
RI 02836
Tel: (401) 783-4054

King Arthur Flour
P.O. Box 876
Norwich
VT 05055-0876
Tel: (800) 827-6836

New Hope Mills, Inc.
RR2, Box 269A
Moravia, NY 13119
Tel: (315) 497-0783

N.Y. Cake & Bake Distributor
56 West 22nd Street
New York, NY 10010
Tel: (800) 94-CAKE-9
Fax: (212) 675-7099

Poulsbo Bakery
P.O. Box 2778
18924 Front Street NE
Poulsbo, WA 98370
Tel: (360) 779-2798
Fax: (360) 677-3581

San Francisco French
    Bread Co.
580 Julie Ann Way
Oakland, CA 94629
Tel: (888) 661-7687
or (510) 568-7697

Walnut Acres Organic Farms
Penns Creek, PA 17862
Tel: (800) 433-3998

Williams-Sonoma
P.O. Box 7456
San Francisco
CA 94120-7456
Tel: (800) 541-2233

Von Snedaker's Magic
    Baking Sheet
12021 Wilshire Boulevard
Suite 231
Los Angeles, CA 90025
Tel: (310) 395-6365

INDEX

A

Aberdeen buttery rowies, 34
acid breads, 117
acorns, 14
adapting recipes, 284–5
air bubbles, 286
aiysh, 12, 78
aiysh shami, 78
ale, 14, 113, 295
ale barm, 117
alentejano, 54
all-purpose flour, American, 108
    see also plain flour
Allinson, Dr, 102
almond paste
    Austrian coffee cake, 462
    marzipan and almond
        twists, 448
almonds
    apricot stars, 450
    Finnish festive wreath, 468
    hazelnut twist cake, 475
    lemon and pistachio strudel, 477
    peach streuselkuchen, 466
    raspberry and almond
        teabread, 489
American breads, 84–95, 226–37
American breakfast pancakes, 422
American coffee bread, 498
Amish, 91
anadama bread, 91, 231, 321
anchovies: pissaladière, 360
apfelnussbrot, 62
apples
    apple and sultana Danish
        pastries, 450
    Austrian coffee cake, 462
apricots: apricot and vanilla
        slices, 465
    apricot, prune and peach
        teabread, 495
    apricot stars, 450
    Easter tea ring, 478
    lemon and pistachio strudel, 477
Assizes of Bread, 14
atta flour, 111
Australian breads, 100–2
Austrian breads, 60
Austrian coffee cake, 462

B

babas, peach brandy, 473
babka, 88
babka, Polish, 480

bacon, 298
    leek and pancetta tray
        bread, 380
bagels, 81–2, 233
baguettes, 38–9, 158, 268, 271
    Japanese French bread, 104
    shaping, 121
    slashing, 122
bailys, 82
bajra flour, 111
baked brown bread, 91
bakehouses, 14, 15
bakers and bakeries, 7
    Australia, 100
    Tudor times, 14
baking
    methods, 15
    preparation for, 122
    times, 124
baking powder, 112, 293
baking sheets, 128
baking stones, 129
balabusky, 72
bananas
    banana and pecan teabread, 494
    banana bread, 88–90
    mango and banana bread, 461
    pineapple and banana bread, 305
bangeli, 62
bannetons, 121, 129
bannocks
    barley, 34, 152
    Selkirk, 34
baps, wholemeal, 430
    see also morning rolls
bara brith, 32, 154
barbari, 78, 253
barley, 13, 14, 16, 110
barley bannock, 34, 152
barley bread, 70, 110, 220
barley flour, 290
    barley-enriched farmhouse
        loaf, 332
barley meal, 12, 110
barm brack, 36
basic breads, 313–29
basil

fresh tomato and basil
    loaf, 406
garlic and herb walnut
    bread, 395
marbled pesto bread, 392
bâtard, 38
batch-baked breads, 7
batched bread
    British, 20
    Goan batch bread, 99
batons, Vienna, 24
bauerruch, 62
baumbrot, 60
Bavarian plum cake, 467
beans, 14
beer, 295
    beer barm, 13, 113, 117
    beer bread, 86–7
    grainy mustard and beer
        loaf, 382
    honey and beer rye bread, 370
beetroot bread, 413
Belgian breads, 45
Berkeley sourdough, 94
besan, 111
bhakris, 98, 111
bhaturas, 242
Biblical times, 13
bicarbonate of soda, 36,
    112–13, 293
biga starter, 112, 117
biova, 46
black bread
    Polish, 71
    Russian, 71–2
blinis, 70, 214
bloomers, 20–1, 268
    poppy-seeded, 268
    spinach and Parmesan
        bloomer, 402
blueberry and oatmeal bread, 456
bollo, 52
bolo do caco, 55
bolo-rei *see* Twelfth Night bread
Borodinsky loaf, 72
Boston brown bread, 91, 230
boule de meule, 44
boulkas, 81
bowls, 126
box breads, 56–7
braided loaves, 23, 64
    Cajun spiced braid, 390
    challah, 80, 232
    filled braid, 270
    mixed peel braid, 474
    rolls, 270

    Russian, 71
    saffron braids, 435
    shaping, 121
    Swedish cardamom, 68
    Swiss, 102
    tresse, 66
    tsoureki, 75, 197
bran, 16, 108, 289, 291
    bran and yogurt bread, 334
brandy
    peach brandy babas, 473
    strawberry chocolate savarin, 472
bread knives, 127
bread mixes, 285
bread of the dead, 97, 238
bread ovens, 15
bread tins, 121, 127
breadsticks, 269
    Greek and Turkish, 74
    Italian, 48, 184, 327
breakfast pancakes, American, 422
brewer's yeast, 113
brick loaves, 20
bridge rolls, 430
brioche, 39–40, 171
    mini, 476
British breads, 20–37, 134–55
    history, 13–15
broa de milo, 54
brown bread flour, 289
brown breads, 14
    American, 85
    baked, 91
    Boston, 91, 230
brown flour, 109
bubble corn bread, 414
bubble loaf, 94, 228
buchty, 208
buckwheat, 16, 70
buckwheat flour, 110, 290
    buckwheat and walnut
        bread, 337
Bulgarian kolach, 72, 214

bulgur wheat, 290
   spelt and bulgur wheat
      bread, 342
bulla buns, 96
buns
   bulla, 96
   burger, 84
   Caribbean, 96
   Chelsea buns, 442
   chicken, 103
   Chinese-style chicken buns, 436
   coconut milk sugar buns, 449
   Devonshire splits, 445
   ensaimadas, 53, 194
   fasterlavnsboiller, 66
   Georgian khachapuri, 211
   hot cross, 27–8, 440
   Majorcan potato, 53
   man to, 103
   peony, 103
   sweet, 103
   see also rolls
burger bun, 84
butter, 114, 115, 296
   adapting recipes, 284
   glazes, 272, 273
buttermilk, 36, 294
   buttermilk bread, 318
   New England buttermilk
      rolls, 91
   spelt and bulgar wheat
      bread, 342

C

Cajun spiced braid, 390
cake flour, American, 108
cakes, 483
   coconut cake, 488
   crunchy pear and cherry
      cake, 485
   gingerbread, 487
   honey cake, 486
   Madeira cake, 484
   passion cake, 490
   treacle, date and walnut
      cake, 500
   vanilla-chocolate marble
      cake, 493
   see also yeast cakes, teabreads
calas, 422
calzone, 362
candied fruit toppings, 277
   Finnish festive wreath, 468
cantelo, 55
caracas, 55
caramelized onion bread, 418
carasaù, 46

caraway seeds
   balabusky, 72
   German bread with, 60
   light rye and caraway bread, 325
   Polish caraway bread, 71
   Russian potato bread with,
      72, 213
   Swedish caraway bread, 68
carbon dioxide, 112
cardamom braid, Swedish, 68
Caribbean breads, 96, 239
carnival buns, 66
carrots
   carrot and fennel bread, 405
   passion cake, 490
carta di musica, 46, 351
cashew and olive scrolls, 438
ceps: sun-dried tomato and cep
   loaf, 416
cereale, 45
challah, 64, 80, 232, 377
chapati flour, 111
chapatis, 98, 248
cheese, 299
   apricot and vanilla slices, 465
   calzone, 362
   Cheddar cheese bread, 90
   cheese and onion loaf, 139
   cottage cheese-pepperoni
      loaf, 383
   feta cheese and black olive
      loaf, 380
   Georgian khachapuri, 211
   ham and cheese croissants, 434
   lemon and pistachio strudel, 477
   pain battu au fromage, 43
   passion cake, 490
   ricotta and oregano knots, 432
   savoury Danish crown, 217
   spinach and Parmesan
      bloomer, 402
   spoon bread, 236
   Stromboli, 384
   three cheeses bread, 384
   tomato and prosciutto
      pizza, 358

   toppings, 277
chef starter, 41, 113, 117
Chelsea buns, 442
chemical leavens, 293
chenyi khilb, 72
chequerboard, 21
cherries
   Austrian coffee cake, 462
   cherry foldovers, 452
   crunchy pear and cherry
      cake, 485
   Polish babka, 480
chestnuts: savoury nut bread, 301
chica, 52
chicken buns, 103
   Chinese-style, 436
chickpeas, 111
   chickpea and peppercorn
      bread, 404
chillies, 303
   bubble corn bread, 414
   chilli bread, 408
Chinese breads, 103
Chinese-style chicken buns, 436
chocolate
   American chocolate
      breads, 87–8
   filled croissants, 160
   melon and milk chocolate
      rolls, 104
   mocha panettone, 470
   pane al cioccolata, 49, 187
   petit pain au chocolat, 426
   strawberry chocolate
      savarin, 472
   three chocolate bread, 458
   vanilla-chocolate marble
      cake, 493
Christianity and bread, 13, 59
Christmas breads
   christopsomo, 75, 196
   cranberry nut bread, 95
   Hungarian, 72, 212
   julekage, 66, 218
   kolach, 72, 214
   panettone, 50, 186
   stollen, 59, 206
christopsomo, 75, 196

chung yau beng, 103
ciabatta, 46–7, 175
cider, 295
cilician bread, 76, 272
cleaning bread machines, 283
cob loaves
   British, 21
   British granary, 134
   shaping, 121
   slashing, 122
   Welsh, 32
coburg, 21, 122
coconut cake, 488
coconut milk, 295
   coconut milk sugar buns, 449
coffee
   American coffee bread, 498
   Austrian coffee cake, 462
   mocha panettone, 470
conditioners, 293
cook's knives, 126
cooling bread, 267
coriander: garlic and coriander
   naan, 350
corn, 16–17, 52, 54, 110
corn breads, 110
   British cornmeal, 21–2
   broa de milo, 54
   bubble, 414
   double corn bread, 234
   jalapeño, 94
   pane di mais, 50
   Portuguese, 189
   southern, 95
   Yankee, 92
Corn Laws, 15
corn meal, 21, 52, 97, 110, 291
   corn meal bread, 320
   corn meal loaf, 21–2
   toppings, 275
   see also polenta
Cornell bread, 85
Cornish saffron cake, 26, 147
cottage cheese-pepperoni loaf, 383
cottage loaves, 269
   English, 26, 138
   mixed herb cottage loaf, 398
   Welsh, 32
courgette country grain bread, 409
   see also zucchini
couronnes, 121, 129, 269, 368
cracked wheat, 289
cracked wheat bread, 85
cramique, 45
cranberry and orange bread, 457
cranberry nut bread, 95
cream bread, Japanese, 104
cream fairy-tale rolls, Japanese, 105
cream of tartar, 113, 293

crispbreads
    Dutch, 61
    Scandinavian, 68, 220
croissants, 40, 160, 270
    ham and cheese croissants, 434
crown, savoury Danish, 217
crumpets, 27, 148
crunchy pear and cherry cake, 485
crust
    crispness, 271
    problems with, 124, 287
currants
    Chelsea buns, 442
    hot cross buns, 440
    malted currant bread, 151
    Yorkshire teacakes, 444
    see also dried fruit
curry bread, Japanese, 105
customs, 6
Czechoslovakian hoska, 73

D
daktyla, 75–6
damper bread, 101–2
dairy products, 295
dana rotis, 98
Danish, 22
Danish breads, 65–6, 217–18
Danish pastries
    apple and sultana, 450
    apricot stars, 450
    cherry foldovers, 452
    ginger and raisin whirls, 452
dates
    muesli and date bread, 332
    treacle, date and walnut cake, 500
dead, bread of the, 97, 238
Devonshire splits, 445
dill bread, 87
dill, onion and rye bread, 396
dimpled rolls, French, 168
dinner rolls, shaped, 145
direct method, 278

dosas, red lentil, 246
double corn bread, 234
double soft white, 104
dough
    checking, 283
    conditioners, 293
    knives/scrapers, 126
    proving, 270
    shaping, 268–20
    slashing, 271
    storing, 267
doughnuts, 446
Dr Allinson bread, 102
dried fruit
    adapting recipes, 284
    malted fruit loaf, 284
    mixed fruit teabread, 492
    see also currants; raisins; sultanas
Dutch breads, 61
Dutch oven bread, 91
Dutch ovens, 15, 53

E
Easter breads
    Finnish, 69
    hornazo, 52
    hot cross buns, 27–8
    kulich, 72–3
    tea ring, 478
    tsoureki, 75, 197
Eastern European breads,
    70–3, 208–14
easy-blend yeast, 112, 116
egg harbour bread, 91
eggs, 114, 295
    egg-enriched white loaf, 317
    glazes, 272
Egyptians, 12, 78
eiweckerl, 59
ekmek, 76
elioti (olive bread), 75, 198
English breads, 26–31, 138,
    142, 147–50, 155
English muffins, 424
ensaimadas, 53, 194
épi, 40, 163
equipment, 125–129, 306–9
Estonian rye, 71

F
fantans, New England, 237
farine fluide, 108
farls
    Irish soda, 37
    Yorkshire, 31

farmhouse loaves, 322
    barley-enriched farmhouse
        loaf, 332
    British, 22–3
    Hungarian split, 210
    pagnotta, 49
    slashing, 271
fast-action yeast, 112, 116
fasterlavnsboiller, 66
fats, 114, 115, 296
fennel seeds: carrot and fennel
    bread, 405
fermentation, 13, 112, 113, 119, 120
    sourdough, 278
feta cheese and black olive
    loaf, 380
ficelle, 38
figs: hazelnut and fig bread, 341
fine French plain flour, 108
Finnish breads, 69, 70, 220
Finnish festive wreath, 468
flatbrauo, 69
flatbreads, 15, 78, 349–57
    barley bannock, 34, 152
    carta di musica, 351
    cilician bread, 76
    focaccia, 47–8, 178
    fougasse, 40–1, 166
    garlic and coriander naan, 350
    hornazo, 52
    Indian, 98–9, 111, 242–50
    johnny cakes, 96
    lavash, 352
    matzo, 83
    Middle Eastern, 78–9, 251–3
    Moroccan ksra, 354
    Native American fry-bread, 95
    Norwegian, 67
    olive fougasse, 356
    onion focaccia, 357
    piadine, 184
    pide, 354
    pitta breads, 76, 195, 352
    polar, 69
    rotis, 97, 98, 239, 243, 250

    schiacciata, 188
    stottie, 31
    tortillas, 96–7, 234
flours, 12, 108–11, 288–91
    adapting recipes, 284
    toppings, 275, 276
flower pots, 128
flute, 38
focaccette, 47–8
focaccia, 47–8, 178
    onion, 357
food mixers, 119, 125
food processors, 119
fouacés see fougasse
fougasse, 40–1, 166
    olive, 356
four cereal bread, 59
four seed bread, 340
francescine, 48
French bread, 326
    Japanese, 104
    New Orléans, 95
French breads, 38–45, 117, 158–71
French couronne, 269, 368
French plain flour, 288
    fine, 108
French sponge method, 278
Frisian sugar loaf, 61
fruit, 115, 304–5
fruit breads, 115
    British, 26, 27, 28, 29, 32, 34,
        36, 147, 150, 151, 154
    Dutch, 61
    Finnish, 69
    German, 59, 60, 206
    hobo bread, 94
    Japanese, 105
    julekage, 66, 218
    kulich, 72–3
    pain allemand aux fruits, 43–4
    panettone, 50, 186
    Portuguese, 97
    Swedish cardamom, 68
    tropical fruit loaf, 496
    see also teabreads

fruit juices, 295
fry-bread, Native American, 95
funerals, 6

G

gâche, Guernsey, 27
garlic
    garlic and coriander naan, 350
    garlic and herb walnut
        bread, 395
gâteau de Gannat, 44
gebildbrote, 59
gee bao, 103
Georgian khachapuri, 211
German breads, 56–60, 203–8
ginger
    ginger and raisin whirls, 452
    gingerbread, 487
gipfelteig, 64
glazes, 272–3
glazing, 122, 124
gluten, 26, 108, 110, 111, 118
    dough conditioners, 293
Goan batch bread, 99
gofio, 53
golden pumpkin bread, 417
golden raisins *see* sultanas
golden syrup, 273, 297
goldgrain, 60
Graham bread, 84–5
Graham flour, 109
Grahamsbrot, 57
grains, 16–17
grainy mustard and beer loaf, 382
gram flour, 111
Granary flour, 109, 289
    apricot, prune and peach
        teabread, 495
    Granary bread, 323
    Granary cob, 134
    mixed grain onion rolls, 428
    multigrain bread, 343
Grant loaves, 135

grapes: schiacciata con uva, 367
Greek breads, 74–6, 196–8
Greeks, 12
griddles, 129
grissini, 48, 184
grist, 17
ground rice toppings, 276
Guernsey gâche, 27

H

halkaka, 69
ham and cheese croissants, 434
haman pockets, 441
hand-shaped loaves, 268–71
    equipment, 307–8
    toppings, 276–7
hard-dough bread, 96
harvest loaves
    carta da musica, 46
    English, 27, 142
    épi, 40, 163
Hawaiian breads, 97
hazelnuts
    hazelnut and fig bread, 341
    hazelnut twist cake, 475
heavy sour rye bread, 93
herbs, 115, 300
    garlic and herb walnut
        bread, 395
    mixed herb cottage loaf, 398
    toppings, 277
    see also basil; oregano etc
history of bread, 6–7, 12–15
hobo bread, 94
hoe cakes, 92
holiday bread, Moroccan, 79, 199
holy bread, 74
honey, 297
    glazes, 273
    honey and beer rye bread, 370
    honey cake, 486
hornazo, 52
horse bread, 14
hoska, 73
hot cross buns, 27–8, 440
Hovis, 23
humidity, 282
Hungarian breads, 72, 210, 212
hwa jwen, 103

I

Icelandic breads, 69
icing sugar
    glazes, 273
    toppings, 275, 277

Indian breads, 98–9, 242–50
Indian flours, 111
ingredients, 288–305
    adding, 282
    additional, 114–15
    flours, 108–11
    leavens, 112–13
Innes Original, 23
Iranian barbari, 78, 253
Irish breads, 36–7, 146
Italian breads, 46–51, 117, 174–88
Italian breadsticks, 327
Italian sponge method, 278

J

jalapeño corn bread, 94
Japanese breads, 104–5
Jewish breads, 13, 80–3, 91, 232–3
johnny cakes, 96
jowar flour, 98, 111
julekage, 66, 218

K

kalach *see* kolach
kastenbrots, 56–7
kernebrod, 66
kesret, 79
khachapuri, Georgian, 211
khobz, 78
khoubiz, 78
knackebrod, Finnish, 69
knackerbröd, Swedish, 68, 220
kneading dough, 118–19, 120
knives, 126–7
knocking back, 120, 268
knots, ricotta and oregano, 432
kolach, 72, 214
kolindet, 73
kornkracker, 61
koulouria, 74
krendel, 73

krisprolls, 68
krustenbrots, 56, 57–60
ksra, Moroccan, 354
kubaneh, 82–3
kugelhopf, 60, 176
    spiced fruit, 481
kulich, 72–3

L

lagana, 75
landbrot, 58
lard, 296
lardy cake, 28, 150
latkes, 83
lavash, 79, 251, 352
leavens, 12–13, 112–13, 292–3
leeks, 303
    leek and pancetta tray
        bread, 380
lemon
    dough conditioners, 293
    lemon bread, 90
    lemon and macadamia
        bread, 459
    lemon and pistachio
        strudel, 477
levadura de masa starter, 52
levain method, 43, 44, 113
light rye and caraway bread, 325
light wholemeal bread, 319
limpa, 67
Lincolnshire plum bread, 29
liqueurs, 295
liquids, 294–5
loaf tins, 121, 127
longuets, 129
Lunn, Sally, 30
lusse bröd, 222

M

macadamia nuts: lemon and
    macadamia bread, 459
Madeira cake, 484
maia bread, 55
maize, 16–17, 110
maize breads, 15
maizemeal *see* corn meal
Majorcan potato buns, 53
makos es dios kalacs, 72
Mallorcan ensaimadas, 53, 194
malt extract, 297
    dough conditioners, 293
    glazes, 273
    malted currant bread, 151
    malted fruit loaf, 284

malted loaf, 324
malthouse flour, 109
man to, 103
manchets, 14
mandel bread, 83
mandelbrot, 83
mango and banana bread, 461
mankoush, 97–9
mannaeesh, 78–9
manoucher, 115
maple syrup, 297
    maple and oatmeal loaf, 345
marble cake, vanilla-chocolate, 493
marbled pesto bread, 392
margarine, 296
Marrakesh spiced bread, 79
marzipan and almond twists, 448
masa harina, 97
maslin, 14
matzo, 13, 83
measuring jugs, 125
measuring spoons, 125
meat, 298
Mediterranean breads, 174–99
mehrkorn, 60
mella, 79
melon bread, 104
Melrose loaf, 34
Mexican breads, 96–7, 234, 238
mezza luna, 48
michetta, 48
Middle Eastern breads, 78–9, 251–3
milk, 114, 294
    adapting recipes, 284
    bridge rolls, 430
    glazes, 272
    milk loaf, 315
    partybrot, 346
millet, 14, 17
millet flakes: toasted millet and
    rye bread, 336
millet flour, 110, 290
millet grain, 277, 291
    courgette country grain
        bread, 409

mixed grain onion rolls, 428
mills and milling, 13–14, 17
mini brioche, 476
missi rotis, 111, 250
mixed fruit teabread, 492
mixed grain onion rolls, 428
mixed herb cottage loaf, 398
mixed peel
    mixed peel braid, 474
    spiced fruit kugelhopf, 481
mixed pepper bread, 414
mixing dough, 118
mocha panettone, 470
molasses, 297
    glazes, 273
monkey bread, 94, 228
moon bread, 62
morning rolls
    Spanish, 52
    Scottish, 35, 144
Moroccan breads, 79, 199, 354
moulds, 127–8
muesli and date bread, 332
mueslibrot, 57
muffin sheets, 128
muffins
    English, 29, 148
    wholemeal English, 424
multigrain bread, 60, 343
mushrooms, 303
    sun-dried tomato and cep
        loaf, 416
mustard
    grainy mustard and beer loaf, 382
    toppings, 277

N
naan, 98–9, 244
    garlic and coriander, 350
nane lavash, 79
Native American fry-bread, 95
New England buttermilk
    rolls, 91

New England fantans, 237
New Norica bakery, Australia, 100
New Orléans bread, 95
nigella seeds, 75–6
North African breads, 78–9
North European breads, 202–15
Norwegian breads, 65, 67
nut oils, 296
nutmeg: parsnip and nutmeg
        bread, 412
nuts, 115, 301
    cranberry nut bread, 95
    pane con noci, 49–50
    toppings, 277
    see also almonds; walnuts etc

O
oat bran, 291
    toppings, 275
oatcakes
    Scottish, 152
    Staffordshire, 31
oatmeal, 26, 110
oatmeal breads
    American, 88
    English, 26
    oatmeal soda bread, 36
oats, 13, 14, 17, 26, 110, 291
    blueberry and oatmeal
        bread, 456
    maple and oatmeal loaf, 345
    toppings, 275
    wild rice, oat and polenta
        bread, 338
oils, 296
old dough method, 279
olive breads
    cashew and olive scrolls, 438
    feta cheese and black olive
        loaf, 380
    Greek, 75, 198
    Italian, 51, 177
    olive fougasse, 356
    olive Toscano, 101
    pissaladière, 360
olive oil, 46, 52, 296
    glazes, 272
    pane all'olio, 371
olive oil breads
    pan aceite, 53
    panini all'olio, 176
onions, 303
    caramelized onion bread, 418
    cheese and onion loaf, 139
    dill, onion and rye bread, 396
    mixed grain onion rolls, 428
    onion focaccia, 357

pissaladière, 360
savoury Danish crown, 217
Syrian onion bread, 252
orange: cranberry and orange
    bread, 457
oregano
    garlic and herb walnut
        bread, 395
    ricotta and oregano knots, 432
organic flours, 108, 289
oven-bottom loaves, 7
ovens, 15
    adding moisture to, 124
    temperatures, 122, 124

P
paesana, 48–9
pagnotta, 49
pain, 38
pain allemand aux fruits, 43–4
pain au levain, 44
pain au seigle, 42
pain aux noix, 42, 167
pain battu au fromage, 43
pain bouillie, 162
pain de campagne, 41, 372
pain de campagne rustique,
        41, 164
pain de fantaisie, 38
pain de mie, 42
pain de Provence, 44–5
pain de seigle, 42, 374
pain ménage, 41
pain poilâne, 42
pain polka, 43, 159
pan aceite, 53
pan bread, 74
pan cateto, 52
pan coburg, 21
pan de cebada, 191
pan de muerto see bread of
        the dead
pan gallego, 52, 190
pan quemado, 53
panada, 105
pancakes, American breakfast, 422
pancakes, blinis, 70, 214

pancetta: leek and pancetta
    tray bread, 380
Pandemain, 14
pane al cioccolata, 49, 187
pane all'olio, 371
pane con noci, 49–50
pane di mais, 50
pane Toscano (pane sciapo
    Toscano, pane sciocco),
    50, 181
panettone, 50, 186
panettone, mocha, 470
panini all'olio, 176
panis lunatis, 62
papo secos, 55
parathas, 98, 247
Parker House rolls, 429
parsnip and nutmeg bread, 412
partybrot, 346
passion cake, 490
Passover, 13, 83
Passover rolls, 83
pastries
    apple and sultana Danish
pastries, 450
    apricot stars, 450
    cherry foldovers, 452
    ginger and raisin whirls, 452
    ham and cheese croissants, 434
    haman pockets, 441
    petit pain au chocolat, 426
pastry brushes, 127
patty tins, 128
peach brandy babas, 473
peaches
    apricot, prune and peach
        teabread, 495
    peach streuselkuchen, 466
peanut butter teabread, 499
pears
    crunchy pear and cherry
        cake, 485
    Swiss pear and redcurrant
        tart, 464
peas, 14
peasant loaf, Swiss, 63
pecan nuts
    American coffee bread, 498
    banana and pecan teabread, 494
peony buns, 103
peppercorns
    chickpea and peppercorn
        bread, 404
    cottage cheese-pepperoni
        loaf, 383
    salami and peppercorn
        bread, 390
    toppings, 275
peppers, 302

mixed pepper bread, 414
pesto bread, marbled, 392
petit pain au chocolat, 426
petits pains, 38
petits pains au lait, 39, 168
piadine, 184
picos, Spanish, 438
picture bread, 59
pide, 354
    see also pitta
pideh, 79
pikelets, 30, 425
pineapple and banana bread, 305
pio, 99
pissaladière, 360
pistachio nuts
    lemon and pistachio strudel, 477
pistolet, 45
pistolets, wholemeal and rye, 433
pitta breads, 76, 195, 352
pizza genovese see focaccia
pizza rustica see focaccia
pizzas
    calzone, 362
    pissaladière, 360
    Sicilian sfincione, 361
    tomato and prosciutto
        pizza, 358
plain flour, 108, 288
plaited loaves see braided loaves
plum breads, 29
plum cake, Bavarian, 467
Poilâne bakery, Paris, 42
polar flat breads, 69
polenta, 291
    anadama bread, 321
    pane di mais, 50
    polenta and wholemeal
        loaf, 335
    polenta bread, 180
    toppings, 275
    wild rice, oat and polenta
        bread, 338
Polish breads, 70–1, 208–9, 212, 480
pooris, 98, 248
poppadoms, 99
poppy seeds
    bubble loaf, 94, 228
    challah, 377
    haman pockets, 441
    kolach, 72, 214
    poppy seed loaf, 388

poppy seed roll, 212
poppy-seeded bloomer, 136
porcupine, 21, 122
Portuguese breads, 53, 54–5,
    97, 189
pot bread, Welsh, 33, 141
potatoes, 15
    Irish potato bread, 37
    latkes, 83
    Majorcan potato buns, 53
    potato and saffron bread, 418
    potato bread, 329
    Russian potato bread with
        caraway seeds, 72, 213
pottage, 14
preserves, glazes, 273
pretzels, 59, 203
problems, 286–7
prosciutto loaf, 183
prosciutto: tomato and
    prosciutto pizza, 358
prosforo, 74
protein, 108, 110
Provence, pain de, 44–5
proving, 119
proving baskets, 121
proving dough, 270
prunes
    apricot, prune and
        peach teabread, 495
pugliese, 50–1, 174
Pullman loaf, 86
pulses, 303
pumpernickel
    Dutch, 61
    German, 56–7, 204
    sweet, 71
pumpkin and walnut bread, 229
pumpkin bread, golden, 417
pumpkin seeds
    courgette country grain
        bread, 409
punching down see knocking back
puris see pooris

R
ragayig, 79
ragbröd, 68
raisin bread, Japanese, 105
raising agents, 293
raisins
    ginger and raisin whirls, 452
    Polish babka, 480
    rosemary and raisin loaf, 389
    rum and raisin loaf, 460
    schiacciata con uva, 367
rapid-rise yeast see easy-
        blend yeast
rapid white bread, 314
raspberry and almond teabread, 489
red bean rolls, 105
red lentil dosas, 246
redcurrants: Swiss pear and
        redcurrant tart, 464
rice, 17, 105, 110, 291
    calas, 422
    rice bread, 328
    rice cakes, 105
    rice flour, 110
    rice flour toppings, 276
ricotta and oregano knots, 432
rieska, 69
rising of dough, 119, 121, 124
rising, problems, 286
rituals, 6
rogbröd, 67
roggebrood, Dutch, 61
roggenbrot
    kastenbrot, 57
    krustenbrots, 57–8
rolling pins, 126
rolls
    Aberdeen buttery rowies, 34
    bagels, 81–2, 233
    bailys, 82
    balabusky, 72
    bridge rolls, 430
    buchty, 208
    caracas, 55

cashew and olive scrolls, 438
focaccette, 47–8
French dimpled, 168
German-style, 59
Japanese cream, 104, 105
melon and milk chocolate, 104
michetta, 48
mixed grain onion rolls, 428
New England buttermilk, 91
New England fantans, 237
panada, 105
panini all'olio, 176
papo secos, 55
Parker House rolls, 429
partybrot, 346
Passover, 83
petit pains au lait, 39, 168
red bean, 105
ricotta and oregano knots, 432
St Lucia, 68, 222
Scottish morning, 35, 144
shaped dinner, 145
slashing, 271
Spanish morning, 52
sumsums, 82
Vienna, 39
wegglitag, 64
wholemeal and rye pistolets, 433
wholemeal baps, 430
see also buns; croissants
Romans, 13
roscon de reyes see Twelfth
    night bread
rosemary and raisin loaf, 389
rosetta, 48
rosquilha, 54
rossisky, 72
roti tawar, 105
rotis, 98
    missi, 111, 250
    tandoori, 243
    West Indian, 97, 239
rotlas, 98, 111
rowies, Aberdeen buttery, 34
rum
    rum and raisin loaf, 460
    spiced fruit kugelhopf, 481
rumpy loaf, 21
Russian black bread, 344
Russian breads, 70, 71–2, 72–3,
    213, 214
rye, 13, 14, 17, 58, 110, 111
rye breads, 117
    American, 93
    Australian, 102
    Danish, 65–6
    Dutch, 61
    Estonian, 71
    German, 56–7, 57–9, 204

halkaka, 69
Jewish, 83

pain bouillie, 162
pain de seigle, 42
Polish, 70, 71, 209
Russian, 71–2
sunshine loaf, 216
Swedish, 67–8, 223
Ukranian, 72, 73
rye flour, 56, 111, 290
    dill, onion and rye bread, 396
    honey and beer rye bread, 370
    light rye and caraway
        bread, 325
    multigrain bread, 343
    pain de seigle, 374
    Russian black bread, 344
    toasted millet and rye
        bread, 336
    wholemeal and rye
        pistolets, 433

S
sacramental bread, 13, 14, 74
safety, 261, 283
saffron
    Cornish saffron cake, 26, 147
    Finnish festive wreath, 468
    potato and saffron bread, 418
    saffron braids, 435
sage and sausage loaf, 396
St Lucia rolls, 68, 222
sako, 62–3
salami
    calzone, 362
    salami and peppercorn
        bread, 390
Sally Lunn
    American, 95
    English, 30, 155
salt, 114, 293
    salt-rising bread, 93
    toppings, 272, 275
salted water, glazes, 272
saltless bread, Tuscan, 50, 181

saluf, 78
San Franciscan sourdough,
    94, 226
San Francisco-style sour-
    dough, 376
sandwich loaves
    British, 24
    pain de mie, 42
sandwiches, 6
    Danish open, 66
sausages: sage and sausage
    loaf, 396
savarin, strawberry chocolate, 472
savoury breads, 379–99
    Cajun spiced plait, 390
    cottage cheese-pepperoni
        loaf, 383
    dill, onion and rye bread, 396
    feta cheese and black olive
        loaf, 380
    garlic and herb walnut
        bread, 395
    grainy mustard and beer
        loaf, 382
    leek and pancetta tray
        bread, 380
    marbled pesto bread, 392
    mixed herb cottage loaf, 398
    poppy seed loaf, 388
    rosemary and raisin loaf, 389
    sage and sausage loaf, 396
    salami and peppercorn
        bread, 390
    Stromboli, 384
    sun-dried tomato bread, 394
    three cheeses bread, 384
    venison tordu, 386
scales, 125
Scandinavian breads, 65–8, 216–23
schiacciata, 188
schiacciata con uva, 367
schwarzbrot, 57

scissors, slashing rolls, 271
Scottish breads, 34–5, 144, 152
scrolls, 269
    cashew and olive scrolls, 438
seeded rye bread, 93
seeds
    four seed bread, 340
    toppings, 275, 276, 277
    see also caraway; pumpkin etc
self-raising (self-rising) flour,
    108, 288
Selkirk bannock, 34
semmel, 59
semolina, 51, 109, 289
    Moroccan ksra, 354
sesame seeds
    Spanish picos, 438
    toppings, 276
seven-grain bread, 86
sfilatino, 51
sfinicione, Sicilian, 361
Shabbat breakfast bread, 82–3
shaping dough, 120–1
shaping loaves, 268–70
shrak, 78
Sicilian scroll, 51, 182
Sicilian sfinicione, 361
sieves, 125
simits, 77
sin-eating, 6
slashing dough, 271
slashing loaves, 122
smoked venison tordu, 386
smorrebrod, 66
soaking juices, 295
soda, bicarbonate of, 112–13
soda breads
    Irish, 36, 37, 146
    Melrose loaf, 34
    Yorkshire farl, 31
soft flour, 108
sonnenblumenbrot, 57

sopaipillas, 94
sourdough breads, 7, 13, 117
    American, 93, 94, 226
    Australian, 101
    baumbrot, 60
    British, 23, 30
    French, 41, 42, 44, 164
    German, 205
    Innes Original, 23
    pagnotta, 49
    pan cateto, 52
    pan de cebada, 191
    Polish, 71
    see also rye breads
sourdough starter, 278, 279,
    281, 292
    San Francisco-style
        sourdough, 376
sourdoughs, 113, 117
South-east Asian breads, 105
southern corn bread, 95
Spanish breads, 52–3, 190–94
Spanish picos, 438
spelt, 17, 109
spelt flour, 289
    spelt and bulgur wheat
        bread, 342
spiced bread, Marrakesh, 79
spiced fruit kugelhopf, 481
spices, 115, 300
spinach, 302–3
    spinach and Parmesan
        bloomer, 402
spiral, 23
split farmhouse loaf, Hungarian, 210
split tin loaf, 24, 122, 140
split tins, slashing, 271
sponge method, 60, 112, 117, 278
spoon bread, 95, 236
spring onion bread, 103
Staffordshire oatcakes, 31
star, Scandinavian, 68
starters, 113, 117, 278–81
stollen, 59, 206
stoneground wholemeal flour, 108
storing bread, 267
stottie, 31
strawberries

strawberry chocolate savarin, 472
strawberry teabread, 501
streuselkuchen, peach, 466
Stromboli, 384
strong white flour, 108, 288
strong wholemeal flour, 108
strudel, lemon and pistachio, 477
sugar, 114, 297
    Frisian sugar loaf, 61
    glazes, 273
    toppings, 277
sultanas
    apple and sultana Danish
        pastries, 450
    banana and pecan teabread, 494
    Chelsea buns, 442
    Easter tea ring, 478
    hot cross buns, 440
    malted loaf, 324
    mixed peel braid, 474
    spiced fruit kugelhopf, 481
    Yorkshire teacakes, 444
sumsums, 82
sun-dried tomato and cep
    loaf, 416
sun-dried tomato bread, 87, 394
sunflower oil, 296
sunflower seeds
    courgette country grain
        bread, 409
sunshine loaf, 216
supermarkets, 7
Swansea loaf, 33
Swedish breads, 67–8, 220, 222–23
sweet breads, 455–61
    American coffee bread, 498
    blueberry and oatmeal
        bread, 456
    cranberry and orange
        bread, 457
    Easter tea ring, 478
    Finnish festive wreath, 468
    lemon and macadamia
        bread, 459
    mango and banana bread, 461
    mini brioche, 476
    mixed peel braid, 474
    mocha panettone, 470
    rum and raisin loaf, 460
    three chocolate bread, 458
sweet potato bread, 410
sweetcorn: bubble corn bread, 414
sweeteners, 297
swirl bread, 86
Swiss breads, 62–4, 202
Swiss pear and redcurrant
    tart, 464
Syrian onion bread, 252
syrups, glazes, 273

T
tandoori rotis, 243
tart, Swiss pear and redcurrant, 464
teabreads, 483
    American, 88–90
    apricot, prune and peach, 495
    banana and pecan, 494
    Caribbean bun, 96
    cramique, 45
    lemon bread, 90
    malted fruit loaf, 284
    mixed fruit, 492
    mueslibrot, 57
    peanut butter, 499
    raspberry and almond, 489
    rum and raisin loaf, 460
    strawberry, 501
    tropical fruit loaf, 496
    Twelfth Night bread, 53, 192
    see also fruit breads
teacakes, Yorkshire, 444
techniques
    knocking back, shaping and
        final rising, 120–1
    mixing, kneading and
        rising, 118–19
    topping and baking, 122–4
    using yeast, 112, 113, 116–17
    what went wrong, 124
temperature, 282
texture, problems, 287
thessalonikis, 74
three cheeses bread, 384
three chocolate bread, 458
tiganópsoma, 74
tin loaves, 268
    American, 85
    British, 24
    Welsh, 33
tins, loaf, 121, 127
toasted millet and rye bread, 336
tomatoes, 303
    fresh tomato and basil loaf, 406
    pissaladière, 360
    Sicilian sfincione, 361
    sun-dried tomato and cep
        loaf, 416
    sun-dried tomato bread, 87, 394
    tomato bread, 87
    tomato and prosciutto
        pizza, 358
    toppings, 274–7
tordu, venison, 386
tortillas, 96–7, 234
tortino, 51
traditions, 6
treacle, 297
    treacle, date and walnut
        cake, 500

trenchers, 14–15
tresse, 66
triticale bread, 88
tropical fruit loaf, 496
tsoureki, 75, 197
Tunisian breads, 79
Turkestan bread, 77
Turkish breads, 74, 75–7,
        102, 195
Tuscan saltless bread, 50, 181
Twelfth Night bread, 53, 192
twists, 269

U
Ukrainian breads, 72, 73
unbleached white flour, 108
unleavened breads, 12, 13

V
vanilla
    apricot and vanilla slices, 465
    vanilla-chocolate marble
        cake, 493
vegetable breads, 302–3, 401–19
    beetroot bread, 413
    bubble corn bread, 414
    caramelized onion bread, 418
    carrot and fennel bread, 405
    chickpea and peppercorn
        bread, 404
    chilli bread, 408
    courgette country grain
        bread, 409
    fresh tomato and basil loaf, 406
    golden pumpkin bread, 417
    mixed pepper bread, 414
    parsnip and nutmeg bread, 412
    potato and saffron bread, 418
    spinach and Parmesan
        bloomer, 402
    sun-dried tomato and cep
        loaf, 416
    sweet potato bread, 410
vegetable juices, 295
vegetable toppings, 277
venison tordu, 386

Vienna batons, 24
Vienna rolls, 39
Virginia spoon bread, 95, 236
VitBe, 24
Vogel loaf, 63–4
vollkornbrot, 57
vört limpa, 67, 223

W
walnuts
    British walnut bread, 24
    buckwheat and walnut
        bread, 337
    garlic and herb walnut
        bread, 395
    pain aux noix, 42, 167
    passion cake, 490
    pumpkin and walnut bread, 229
    savoury nut bread, 301
    treacle, date and walnut
        cake, 500
    see also nuts
water, 114, 294
watermills, 13–14
wedding breads
    boulkas, 81
    cantelo, 55
wegglitag, 64
weights, 125
weisenkeimbrot, 57

Welsh breads, 32–3, 141, 154
West Indian rotis, 97, 239
wheat, 13, 14, 15, 16, 78
wheat bran, 289
wheat flake toppings, 275
wheat flours, 12, 108–9, 288
wheat germ, 16, 108, 109, 289
wheat germ breads
    Cornell bread, 85
    Hovis, 23
    weisenkeimbrot, 57
wheat germ flour, 109
wheat grains, 16
wheat kernels, 16, 109
wheaten loaf, 37
white bread flour, 108
white breads, 14, 316
    American, 85
    Japanese double soft, 104
white flours, 108, 288
white loaf, egg-enriched, 317
wholemeal breads
    American, 85–6
    baps, 430
    Graham bread, 84–5
    light wholemeal bread, 319
    Norwegian, 67
    wholemeal and rye
        pistolets, 433
wholemeal English muffins, 424
wholemeal flours, 108, 289
wholemeal grains, 16

whole-wheat breads; flours;
    grains see wholemeal
wiborgs kringla, 69
wild rice, oat and polenta
    bread, 338
windmills, 13–14, 17
wine
    schiacciata con uva, 367
    strawberry chocolate savarin, 472
wreath, Finnish festive, 468

Y
Yankee corn bread, 92
yeast, 12–13, 112, 120, 122, 292
    adapting recipes, 284
    fresh yeast bread, 366

    starter, 278
    techniques, 112, 113, 116–17, 124
yeast cakes, 455
    apricot and vanilla slices, 465
    Austrian coffee cake, 462
    Bavarian plum cake, 467
    hazelnut twist cake, 475
    lemon and pistachio
        strudel, 477
    peach brandy babas, 473
    peach streuselkuchen, 466
    Polish babka, 480
    spiced fruit kugelhopf, 481
    strawberry chocolate
        savarin, 472
    Swiss pear and redcurrant
        tart, 464
yogurt, 295
    bran and yogurt bread, 334
    lemon and macadamia
        bread, 459
    starters, 280
Yorkshire farl, 31
Yorkshire teacakes, 444

Z
zopf, 64
zucchini bread, 95
    see also courgette
zupfe, 64, 202

ACKNOWLEDGEMENTS

PHOTOGRAPHY ACKNOWLEDGEMENTS

All recipe pictures and chapter openers by Nicki Dowey. The pictures on pages 6–129 by Amanda Heywood, except for the following, reproduced with the kind permission of those listed: p. 6t, p. 7t, p. 108b and p. 510 Maison Blanc Ltd; p. 7b Jan Suttle/Life File; p. 13t and 17b Emma Lee/Life File; p. 16t Lionel Moss/Life File; p. 16b Jeff Griffin/Life File; p. 12t and b e.t. archive; p. 13b English Heritage Photographic Library; p. 14t e.t. archive; p. 14b Biblioteca Estense, Modena/e.t. archive; p. 15t Andreas von Einsiedel/National Trust

Photographic Library; p. 15b Eric Crichton/National Trust Photographic Library; p. 17 Food Features.

PUBLISHER'S ACKNOWLEDGEMENTS

The publishers would like to thank Jo Lethaby and Jenni Fleetwood for their skilful editing; Jill Jones, who tracked down almost all the breads for the *Breads of the World* section; Jenny Blair for sourcing the Scottish breads; Amy Willenski, who tracked down or specially baked all the US breads; Angus Henderson and Jacky Lannel at Villandry Foodstore Restaurant, who specially baked the fougasse, épi and pane au cioccolato loaves; Christine Gough, the baker at the Museum of Welsh Life, for baking and supplying

traditional Welsh breads; and Giacomo and Nuala Farruggia at Il Forno for baking and supplying many of the Italian breads, as well as the harvest loaf and hot cross buns. The publishers would also like to thank the following companies who lent equipment and ingredients for photography: Dove Farm Foods Ltd; Hinari; Jim Wilkinson Promotions Ltd; Magimix; Panasonic; PIFCO; Prima International; Pulse Home Products Ltd; Spillers Consumer Foods; Tefal UK Ltd and West Mill Foods Ltd.